T0238587

Communications
in Computer and Information Science   400

Editorial Board

Simone Diniz Junqueira Barbosa
  Pontifical Catholic University of Rio de Janeiro (PUC-Rio),
  Rio de Janeiro, Brazil
Phoebe Chen
  La Trobe University, Melbourne, Australia
Alfredo Cuzzocrea
  ICAR-CNR and University of Calabria, Italy
Xiaoyong Du
  Renmin University of China, Beijing, China
Joaquim Filipe
  Polytechnic Institute of Setúbal, Portugal
Orhun Kara
  TÜBİTAK BİLGEM and Middle East Technical University, Turkey
Igor Kotenko
  St. Petersburg Institute for Informatics and Automation
  of the Russian Academy of Sciences, Russia
Krishna M. Sivalingam
  Indian Institute of Technology Madras, India
Dominik Ślęzak
  University of Warsaw and Infobright, Poland
Takashi Washio
  Osaka University, Japan
Xiaokang Yang
  Shanghai Jiao Tong University, China

Guodong Zhou   Juanzi Li   Dongyan Zhao
Yansong Feng (Eds.)

Natural Language Processing and Chinese Computing

Second CCF Conference, NLPCC 2013
Chongqing, China, November 15-19, 2013
Proceedings

 Springer

Volume Editors

Guodong Zhou
Soochow University
Suzhou, China
E-mail: gdzhou@suda.edu.cn

Juanzi Li
Tsinghua University
Beijing, China
E-mail: lijuanzi@tsinghua.edu.cn

Dongyan Zhao
Peking University
Beijing, China
E-mail: zhaody@pku.edu.cn

Yansong Feng
Peking University
Beijing, China
E-mail: fengyansong@pku.edu.cn

ISSN 1865-0929   e-ISSN 1865-0937
ISBN 978-3-642-41643-9   e-ISBN 978-3-642-41644-6
DOI 10.1007/978-3-642-41644-6
Springer Heidelberg New York Dordrecht London

Library of Congress Control Number: 2013951162

CR Subject Classification (1998): I.2.7, H.3.1, H.1.2, H.3.3, H.3.5, H.5.2, I.2.1

© Springer-Verlag Berlin Heidelberg 2013
This work is subject to copyright. All rights are reserved by the Publisher, whether the whole or part of the material is concerned, specifically the rights of translation, reprinting, reuse of illustrations, recitation, broadcasting, reproduction on microfilms or in any other physical way, and transmission or information storage and retrieval, electronic adaptation, computer software, or by similar or dissimilar methodology now known or hereafter developed. Exempted from this legal reservation are brief excerpts in connection with reviews or scholarly analysis or material supplied specifically for the purpose of being entered and executed on a computer system, for exclusive use by the purchaser of the work. Duplication of this publication or parts thereof is permitted only under the provisions of the Copyright Law of the Publisher's location, in ist current version, and permission for use must always be obtained from Springer. Permissions for use may be obtained through RightsLink at the Copyright Clearance Center. Violations are liable to prosecution under the respective Copyright Law.
The use of general descriptive names, registered names, trademarks, service marks, etc. in this publication does not imply, even in the absence of a specific statement, that such names are exempt from the relevant protective laws and regulations and therefore free for general use.
While the advice and information in this book are believed to be true and accurate at the date of publication, neither the authors nor the editors nor the publisher can accept any legal responsibility for any errors or omissions that may be made. The publisher makes no warranty, express or implied, with respect to the material contained herein.

Typesetting: Camera-ready by author, data conversion by Scientific Publishing Services, Chennai, India

Printed on acid-free paper

Springer is part of Springer Science+Business Media (www.springer.com)

Preface

NLPCC (CCF Conference on Natural Language Processing and Chinese Computing) is the annual conference of CCF TCCI (Technical Committee of Chinese Information). As a leading conference in the field of NLP and Chinese Computing of CCF, NLPCC is the premier forum for NLP researchers and practitioners from academia, industry, and government in China and Pacific Asia to share their ideas, research results and experiences, which will highly promote the research and technical innovation in these fields domestically and internationally. The papers contained in these proceedings address challenging issues in Web mining and big data, knowledge acquisition, search and ads, social networks, machine translation and multi-lingual information access, question answering and user interface, machine learning for NLP, as well as the fundamentals and applications of Chinese computing.

This year, NLPCC received 203 submissions. After a thorough reviewing process, 31 English papers and 14 Chinese papers were selected for presentation as full papers, with an acceptance rate of 22.17%. Furthermore, this year's NLPCC also included 11 English papers and 14 Chinese papers as posters, with an acceptance rate of 12.32%. Additionally, five industrial/demo papers were selected. The Chinese full papers together with posters are published by ACTA Scientiarum Naturalium Universitatis Pekinensis, and are not included in these proceedings. This volume contains the 31 English full papers presented at NLPCC 2013 and 13 short papers including the 11 English posters and two industrial/demo papers.

The high-quality program would not have been possible without the authors who chose NLPCC 2013 as a venue for their publications. We are also very grateful to the Program Committee members and Organizing Committee members, who put a tremendous amount of effort into soliciting and selecting research papers with a balance of high quality and new ideas and new applications.

We hope that you enjoy reading and benefit from the proceedings of NLPCC 2013.

November 2013
Guodong Zhou
Juanzi Li

Organization

NLPCC 2013 was organized by the Technical Committee of the Chinese Information of CCF, Peking University, and Microsoft Research Asia.

Organizing Committee

Conference Co-chairs

Ming Zhou   Microsoft Research Asia, China
Dan Yang   Chongqing University, China

Program Co-chairs

Guodong Zhou   Soochow University, China
Juanzi Li   Tsinghua University, China

Area Chairs

Fundamentals on CIT

Qiang Zhou   Tsinghua University, China
Tuergen   Xinjiang University, China

Applications on CIT

Donghong Ji   Wuhan University, China
Chenglin Liu   Chinese Academy of Sciences

Machine Translation

Yajuan Lv   Chinese Academy of Sciences
Muyun Yang   Harbin Institute of Technology, China

Web Ming and Big Data

Shiqi Zhao   Baidu, China
Zhongyang Xiong   Chongqing University, China

Machine Learning for NLP

Liwei Wang   Peking University, China
Xiaofei He   Zhejiang University, China

Knowledge Acquisition

Juanzi Li   Tsinghua University, China
Kuo Zhang   Sogou, China

NLP for Social Networks

Jie Tang   Tsinghua University, China
Shoushan Li   Soochow University, China

NLP for Search and Ads

Jun Ma   Shandong University, China
Bin Wang   Chinese Academy of Sciences, China

QA and User Interaction

Zhengtao Yu   Kunming University of Science and Technology,
                                     China
Furu Wei   Microsoft Research Asia, China

Panel Chair

Chengqing Zong   Chinese Academy of Sciences

Demo Co-chairs

Qingsheng Li   Anyang Normal University, China
Xiaojun Wan   Peking University, China

ADL/Tutorial Chair

Min Zhang   Soochow University, China
Mu Li   Microsoft Research Asia, China

Organizing Chair

Dongyan Zhao   Peking University, China

Local Arrangements Chair

Zhongyang Xiong   Chongqing University, China

Publication Chair

Yansong Feng   Peking University, China

Evaluation Chair

Xiaojun Wan   Peking University, China

Financial Chair

Zhengyu Zhu   China Computer Federation, China

Sponsor Chair

Tang Zhi   Peking University, China

Website Chair

Aixia Jia   Peking University, China

Program Committee

Jiajun Chen	Nanjing University
Hsin-Hsi Chen	National Taiwan University
Zhumin Chen	Shandong University
Xiaoqing Ding	Tsinghua University
Xinghua Fan	Chongqing University of Posts and Telecommunications
Yang Feng	Sheffield University, UK
Guanglai Gao	Inner Mongolia University
Zhiqiang Gao	Southeast University
Tingting He	Huazhong Normal University
Yulan He	Open University, UK
Yu Hong	Soochow University
Hongxu Hou	Inner Mongolia University
Degen Huang	Dalian University of Technology
Heming Huang	Qinghai Normal University
Xiaojun Huang	Founder Apabi
Xuanjing Huang	Fudan University
Wenbin Jiang	Institute of Computing Technology, CAS
Jing Jiang	Singapore Management University
Long Jiang	Alibaba Corp.
Shengyi Jiang	Guangdong University of Foreign Studies
Peng Jin	Leshan Normal University
Fang Kong	Soochow University
Baoli Li	Henan University of Technology
Fenghua Li	Institute of Information Engineering, CAS
Ning Li	Beijing Information Science and Technology University
Wenjie Li	Hong Kong Polytechnic University
Zhenxing Li	Agile Century
Henry Li	Microsoft Research Asia
Qingsheng Li	Anyang Normal University
Zhouhui Lian	Peking University

Bangyong Liang	STCA, Microsoft
Hongfei Lin	Dalian University of Technology
Wai Lam	Chinese University of Hong Kong
Bingquan Liu	Harbin Institute of Technology
Dexi Liu	Jiangxi University of Finance and Economics
Pengyuan Liu	Beijing Language and Culture University
Xiaohua Liu	Microsoft Research Asia
Yang Liu	Shandong University
Yang Liu	Tsinghua University
Changqing Liu	Ningxia University
Xueqiang Lyu	TRS Inc., China
Jie Ma	Nankai University
Qing Ma	RyuKoku University, Japan
Shaoping Ma	Tsinghua University
Yanjun Ma	Baidu Inc.
Jian-Yun Nie	University of Montreal, Canada
Zhendong Niu	Beijing Institute of Technology
Ngodrup	Tibet University
Longhua Qian	Soochow University
Bing Qin	Harbin Institute of Technology
Tao Qin	Microsoft Research Asia
Weiguang Qu	Nanjing Normal University
Liyun Ru	Sohu Inc., China
Junichi Tsujii	Microsoft Research Asia
Xiaodong Shi	Xiamen University
Jinsong Su	Xiamen University
Chengjie Sun	Harbin Institute of Technology
Weiwei Sun	Peking University
Bo Wang	Tianjin University
Haifeng Wang	Baidu Inc.
Houfeng Wang	Peking University
Mingwen Wang	Jiangxi Normal University
Shuaiqiang Wang	Shandong University of Finance and Economics
Xiaojie Wang	Beijing University of Posts and Telecommunications
Gang Wu	Northeastern University
Yunqing Xia	Tsinghua University
Deyi Xiong	Singapore I2R, Singapore
Jinan Xu	Beijing Jiaotong University
Jun Xu	Huawei

Endong Xun	Beijing Language and Culture University
Wenchuan Yang	Beijing University of Posts and Telecommunications
Tianfang Yao	Shanghai Jiao Tong University
Jianmin Yin	Huaguang Inc.
Masaaki Nagata	NTT, Japan
Hongzhi Yu	Northwest University for Nationalities
Yusufu	Xinjiang Normal University
Dongdong Zhang	Microsoft Research Asia
Jiajun Zhang	Automation Institute, CAS
Jianguo Zhang	Founder Electronics
Jianpei Zhang	Harbin Engineering University
Junsong Zhang	Xiamen University
Min Zhang	Tsinghua University
Qi Zhang	Fudan University
Ruiqiang Zhang	Yahoo!, USA
Yangsen Zhang	Beijing Information Science Technology University
Yujie Zhang	Beijing Jiaotong University
Hai Zhao	Shanghai Jiao Tong University
Jun Zhao	Institute of Automation, CAS
Tiejun Zhao	Harbin Institute of Technology
Yanyan Zhao	Harbin Institute of Technology
Deyu Zhou	Southeast University
Guomin Zhou	Agricultural Information Institute, CAAS
Junsheng Zhou	Nanjing Normal University
Wen Zhou	Shanghai University
Xueguang Zhou	Navy Engineering University
Jingbo Zhu	Northeastern University
Qiaoming Zhu	Soochow University
Qing Zhu	Renmin University of China
Tse ring rgyal	Qinghai Normal University

Organizers

Organized by

China Computer Federation, China

Hosted by

Chongqing University   State Key Laboratory of Digital Publishing

In Cooperation with:

Tsinghua University   ACTA Scientiarum Naturalium   Springer
                       Universitatis Pekinensis

Sponsoring Institutions

Microsoft Research Asia   Sogou Inc.   Sina Weibo

Tencent Weibo   Sichuan Institute   Mingbo
                     of Computer Science   Education Technology

Keynote Talks

Knowledge Mining and Semantic Search

Wei-Ying Ma

Microsoft Research Asia, Beijing, China
wyma@microsoft.com

Abstract. Today's search engines are primarily operated based on terms and string matching. While this term-based paradigm has been pretty successful in the past 15 years, it has started to show many limitations given the rapid evolution of the Web. The Web today contains not only static documents but also dynamic information about real world entities. It is becoming a digital copy of the world, capturing data from people, products, services, locations, and even objects. This new Web requires a new paradigm that can directly fulfill people's information needs and empower them with knowledge. In this talk, I will introduce a new entity-based search paradigm and various knowledge mining techniques to construct knowledge graphs from different types of data. I will show how we can use the knowledge to understand queries, enable semantic matching, and provide direct answers to natural language queries.

Bio: Dr. Wei-Ying Ma is an Assistant Managing Director at Microsoft Research Asia, where he oversees multiple research groups including Web Search and Mining, Natural Language Computing, Data Management and Analytics, and Internet Economics and Computational Advertising. He and his team of researchers have developed many key technologies that have been transferred to Microsoft's Online Services Division, including Bing Search Engine and Microsoft Advertising. He has published more than 250 papers at international conferences and journals. He is a Fellow of the IEEE and a Distinguished Scientist of the ACM. He currently serves on the editorial boards of ACM Transactions on Information System (TOIS) and is a member of the International World Wide Web (WWW) Conferences Steering Committee. In recent years, he has served as program co-chair of WWW 2008 and as general co-chair of ACM SIGIR 2011. He received a Bachelor of Science in electrical engineering from the National Tsing Hua University in Taiwan in 1990. He earned both a Master of Science and a doctorate in electrical and computer engineering from the University of California at Santa Barbara in 1994 and 1997, respectively. More information about him can be found at http://research.microsoft.com/en-us/people/wyma/

Domestic Chinese Treebanks Need to Strengthen the Predicate-Argument Structure Description

Changning Huang

Department of Computer Science and Technology, Tsinghua University
Beijing, 100084, China
cnhuang0908@126.com

Abstract. Base on Penn English Treebank (PTB-II), 1998–2000 the University of Pennsylvania built the Penn Chinese Treebank (CTB) with the news corpus of Xinhua News Agency. CTB not only sets the predicate-argument structure description as its important goal in the very beginning, but also defines a standard hierarchy structure of phrases based on the X-bar Theory. According to this hierarchy structure CTB strives to make each bracket pair or sub-tree dominated by a phrase node to represent only one abstract grammatical relation. A comparative review has been made on domestic and oversea Chinese treebanks. Although domestic treebanks generally annotates the phrasal notes, such as NP, VP, PP, etc., with internal structures information, such as subject-predicate, verb-object, and modifier-head, etc., and in order to indicate the head of the phrase an integer or other symbol is attached to the phrase note. Apparently they did not set the predicate-argument structure description as an important goal of treebank construction. Starting from the X-bar Theory about the representation of general phrase structure, the article illustrates the terms of complement, adjunct and specifier in Contemporary Syntax, explains the applications of empty category and co-indexing in the syntactic structure. Then, by the CTB specific examples the article describes the predicate-argument structure on the syntactic trees.

Above is the first part of my speech, in the following part I'll briefly reviews the research of Chinese information processing in the past three decades and looking to the near future. I will be happy to discuss with my colleagues and graduate students on my teaching and research experience.

Bio: Professor Chang-Ning Huang graduated from Department of Automatic Control, Tsinghua University, Beijing, China, on 1961. He joined Microsoft Research Asia (MSRA) as a senior researcher and the research manager of the NLC group on April 1999. Before that he was the professor of the Department of Computer Science and Technology, Tsinghua University, and the founder and Director of the NLP research group in Tsinghua from 1982 to 1999. He was retired from Microsoft on August 2012. His research interest includes Chinese word segmentation, POS tagging, named entity recognition, word sense disambiguation, coreference resolution, syntactic parsing and mechine translation, etc.

Some Mathematical Models to Turn Social Media into Knowledge

Xiaojin Zhu

Department of Computer Sciences,
University of Wisconsin-Madison, WI, USA
`jerryzhu@cs.wisc.edu`

Abstract. Social media data-mining opens up many interesting research questions, whose answers correspond to elegant mathematical models that go beyond traditional NLP techniques. In this talk we present two examples, namely estimating intensity from counts and identifying the most chatty users. In both examples, naive heuristic methods do not take full advantage of the data. In contrast, there are mathematical models, in the first case inhomogeneous Poisson process and in the second case multi-arm bandit, with provable properties that better extract knowledge from social media.

Bio: Xiaojin Zhu is an Associate Professor in the Department of Computer Sciences at the University of Wisconsin-Madison, with affiliate appointments in the Departments of Electrical and Computer Engineering and Psychology. Dr. Zhu received his B.S. and M.S. degrees in Computer Science from Shanghai Jiao Tong University in 1993 and 1996, respectively, and a Ph.D. degree in Language Technologies from Carnegie Mellon University in 2005. He was a research staff member at IBM China Research Laboratory from 1996 to 1998. Dr. Zhu received the National Science Foundation CAREER Award in 2010. His research interest is in machine learning, with applications in natural language processing, cognitive science, and social media. `http://pages.cs.wisc.edu/jerryzhu/`

Table of Contents

Fundamentals on Language Computing

Applications on Language Computing

Machine Learning for NLP

Machine Translation and Multi-Lingual Information Access

NLP for Social Media and Web Mining

Knowledge Acquisition

NLP for Search Technology and Ads

Short Papers I: NLP Fundamentals

Short Papers II: NLP Applications

Short Papers III: NLP for Social Media (Industrial Paper Included)

Text Window Denoising Autoencoder: Building Deep Architecture for Chinese Word Segmentation

Ke Wu, Zhiqiang Gao, Cheng Peng, and Xiao Wen

School of Computer Science & Engineering, Southeast University,
Nanjing 210096, China

Abstract. Deep learning is the new frontier of machine learning research, which has led to many recent breakthroughs in English natural language processing. However, there are inherent differences between Chinese and English, and little work has been done to apply deep learning techniques to Chinese natural language processing. In this paper, we propose a deep neural network model: *text window denoising autoencoder*, as well as a complete pre-training solution as a new way to solve classical Chinese natural language processing problems. This method does not require any linguistic knowledge or manual feature design, and can be applied to various Chinese natural language processing tasks, such as Chinese word segmentation. On the PKU dataset of Chinese word segmentation bakeoff 2005, applying this method decreases the F1 error rate by 11.9% for deep neural network based models. We are the first to apply deep learning methods to Chinese word segmentation to our best knowledge.

Keywords: Deep Learning, Word Segmentation, Denoising Autoencoder, Chinese Natural Language Processing.

1 Introduction

Researchers have applied deep learning methods to sequence tagging problems in natural language processing (NLP) of *English*, such as chucking, named entity recognition, etc, and great results have been achieved [4]. The basic idea is to firstly construct a real-valued vector for common English words (these vectors are called word embeddings [1]), and then use a multi-layer neural network to process these vectors.

However, there are inherent differences between *Chinese* and *English*, therefore one cannot simply apply deep learning methods for English NLP to Chinese. There are two major differences: 1) The Chinese language is composed of characters, while English of words. According to our statistical experiments on Chinese and English Wikipedia corpus, it only takes a Chinese dictionary of roughly 5,000 characters to cover more than 99% of all characters used in the entire Chinese Wikipedia, compared to an English dictionary of more than 120,000 words to cover the same portion of words in English Wikipedia. This shows that there

G. Zhou et al. (Eds.): NLPCC 2013, CCIS 400, pp. 1–12, 2013.
© Springer-Verlag Berlin Heidelberg 2013

are far less commonly used Chinese characters than English words. 2) Meanings in Chinese are conveyed by complex relationships between characters. Although Chinese characters have meanings themselves, they can still form words that have completely different meanings from the meanings represented by the characters alone. By using deep architectures, these kinds of complex relationships between Chinese characters can be represented and extracted as highly abstract features, therefore deep architectures are even more important in Chinese NLP.

Because of these differences, a complete pre-training is more beneficial for deep models for Chinese NLP. The current deep learning approaches for English NLP lack a complete pre-training solution for building deep architectures both theoretically and practically. For example, in [4], they only pre-trained the word embeddings, and the weights of the hidden layers were simply initialized randomly. Part of the reason is that due to the very large vocabulary of commonly used English words, most parameters in deep models for English NLP are in the word embeddings. That's not the case in deep models for Chinese NLP, so a proper pre-training of the hidden layers is even more necessary. Another issue is, although methods for pre-training English word embeddings by training a neural language model have been proposed, there is no explanation on why training a neural language model is a good way to pre-train the word embeddings, or its relationship with other commonly used pre-training methods.

In this paper, we follow the fundamental architectures used in deep learning methods for English NLP and apply them to Chinese. On top of that, we propose a *complete pre-training solution*. Note that our method can be used on any sequence tagging tasks in Chinese NLP, and in this paper we focus on Chinese word segmentation. Our major contributions are: 1) We use a different criterion to build Chinese neural language model, and get better convergence than the criterions commonly used in training English neural language model. 2) We explain that the training process of our neural language model is essentially the same as training a special denoising autoencoder on text window, which we call *text window denoising autoencoder (TINA)*. 3) We describe the method to stack text window denoising autoencoders as a way to pre-train deep neural networks for Chinese word segmentation.

This paper is organized as follows. Section 2 describes the neural network framework we used for Chinese word segmentation. In section 3 we propose our Chinese neural language model training criterion. In Section 4 we propose text window denoising autoencoder, and we also describe how to stack TINA and build pre-trained deep neural network models for Chinese word segmentation. Section 5 gives our experiments showing the effectiveness of the TINA model. Section 6 introduces related work briefly. We conclude our work in section 7.

2   Deep Neural Network Framework for Chinese Word Segmentation

We view Chinese word segmentation as a sequence tagging problem, which means to assign a tag to each Chinese character (we use the "BIU" tag schema [9]).

The input of the neural network model is a fixed size text window (a window of Chinese characters in a sentence), and the output is a probability distribution of tags for the character in the center of the text window. The neural network architecture [4] is shown in Figure 1. The *embedding layer* performs a matrix lookup operation, and finds the corresponding real-valued vector in Chinese character embeddings (a real-valued matrix) for each character in the input text window. These real-valued vectors will then be concatenated and input to the *hidden layers*, which are classical neural network layers. The *output layer* is a softmax layer, which ensures all of the output values are between 0 and 1, and that their sum is 1. It is a generalization of the logistic function to multiple variables, which is called softmax function. Each output node corresponds to a specific tag.

More formally, for each character $c \in \mathcal{D}$ ($\mathcal{D}$ is a Chinese character dictionary), there is a corresponding d-dimensional real-valued vector in the matrix $\mathbf{W} \in \mathfrak{R}^{d \times |\mathcal{D}|}$. This matrix is the Chinese character embeddings. The first layer of the neural network is a table lookup and concatenate operation: $L_{input}(\mathbf{c_1}, \ldots, \mathbf{c_s}) = (\mathbf{W} \cdot \mathbf{c_1}, \ldots, \mathbf{W} \cdot \mathbf{c_s})$, in which $\mathbf{c}$ is the one-hot representation of the character. The hidden layers take the form of classical neural network, and we choose tanh as the activation function: $L_{hidden} = \tanh(\mathbf{w} \cdot \mathbf{x} + \mathbf{b})$. The output layer is a softmax layer, in which the output of node i is:

$$L_{output_i} = \frac{\exp(\mathbf{w_i} \cdot \mathbf{x} + b_i)}{\sum\limits_{j=1}^{n} \exp(\mathbf{w_j} \cdot \mathbf{x} + b_j)}. \tag{1}$$

We could train this neural network using standard backpropagation (without pre-training), but that will only lead to poor results even with very few hidden layers. According to recent researches in deep learning, pre-training can significantly improve the performance of deep neural networks. In the following sections, we introduce a complete pre-training solution, which pre-trains both the embedding layer and the hidden layers.

3   Pre-train Chinese Character Embeddings

Following the work in English deep NLP [4], we can pre-train the Chinese character embeddings by training a (slightly unconventional) Chinese neural language model. We want to build a neural network to predict the center character in a text window given its context (the characters in the text window except the one in the center), or more formally, $P(w|w_{-s/2}^{-1}, w_1^{s/2})$, where s denote the size of the text window, and w_a^b denotes characters from position a to b in the text window (position of the center character is 0). The basic structure of the neural network is the same as the one described in previous section, but with a different output layer. One way to do it is to use a softmax output layer that has one output node per character for all the characters in the dictionary, thus ask the model to predict $P(w|w_{-s/2}^{-1}, w_1^{s/2})$ directly [1]. The problem with this method is that the whole model will get very large (the output layer has the same size as the dictionary), and therefore very hard to train.

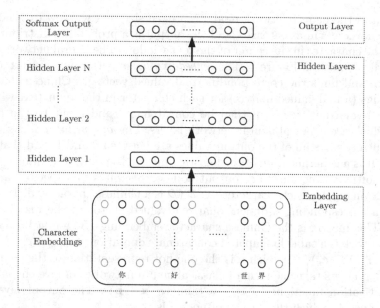

Fig. 1. The architecture of deep neural networks for Chinese NLP. The *embedding layer* maps the input text window into real-valued vectors by performing matrix lookup operation. The *hidden layers* are classical neural network layers. The *output layer* is a softmax layer, with each node corresponding to a specific tag ("BIU" for word segmentation).

Instead of predicting the probability of all the characters directly, we put forward a different training criterion. The model is given the context as well as a (random) character, and can estimate the probability that the given character is the correct one with the context. Or more formally, we try to model $P_c(c_0 = w_0|w_{-s/2}^{-1}, w_1^{s/2}, c_0)$. This is essentially the same as training a model to predict $P(w|w_{-s/2}^{-1}, w_1^{s/2})$ directly, because we can define that

$$P(w|w_{-s/2}^{-1}, w_1^{s/2}) = \frac{P_c(w = w_0|w_{-s/2}^{-1}, w_1^{s/2}, w)}{\sum_{c_i \in \mathcal{D}} P_c(c_i = w_0|w_{-s/2}^{-1}, w_1^{s/2}, c_i)}, \tag{2}$$

which means one can simply assign a fixed context to every character in the dictionary and let the model predict the probability that the character is the correct one, and then generate a joint probability on top of all the outputs.

The input of our neural language model is the context of the text window, as well as another character c_0. The output layer has only one sigmoid node, which outputs the probability $P_c(c_0 = w_0|w_{-s/2}^{-1}, w_1^{s/2}, c_0)$. The remaining layers are the same as the neural network framework introduced in the last section. This model is much smaller in terms of parameters, so it's much easier to train. The training only requires unsupervised data. Text windows are extracted directly from a given Chinese corpus as positive examples, and for every positive example, a corresponding negative example is generated by replacing the center character in the text window with a random character. We then train the model by maximizing the following log-likelihood criterion for probability $P_c(c_0 = w_0 | w_{-s/2}^{-1}, w_1^{s/2}, c_0)$:

$$\ell(\theta : \mathcal{T}) = \sum_{\forall c_0 = w_0} \log P_c(c_0 = w_0 | \theta, w_{-s/2}^{-1}, w_1^{s/2}, c_0)$$
$$- \sum_{\forall c_0' \neq w_0} \log P_c(c_0' = w_0 | \theta, w_{-s/2}^{-1}, w_1^{s/2}, c_0), \tag{3}$$

where θ denote parameters in the model, and $\mathcal{T}$ denote all the text windows.

Note that optimizing the likelihood of $P_c(c_0 = w_0 | w_{-s/2}^{-1}, w_1^{s/2}, c_0)$ is equivalent to optimizing the likelihood of $P(w | w_{-s/2}^{-1}, w_1^{s/2})$ according to our definition.

4 Pre-train Hidden Layers: (Stacked) Text Window Denoising Autoencoder

In this section, we describe our method for pre-training the hidden layers. First, we introduce text windows denoising autoencoder, then we describe how to stack TINA and build a deep neural network with both embedding layer and hidden layers pre-trained.

4.1 Neural Language Model as Text Window Denoising Autoencoder

The neural language model that we introduced in the last section is essentially a special denoising autoencoder, which we call *text window denoising autoencoder (TINA)*. A denoising autoencoder is consisted of two parts, namely encoder and decoder. The encoder processes noised data and produces real-valued vector as an "encode" (features) of the data. The decoder then processes the "encode" and try to reconstruct the clean data. Denoising autoencoders are trained by a reconstruction error criterion, which measures the error between the reconstructed clean data and the original data. Denoising autoencoders have already been shown very useful at building deep architectures [12].

The neural language model training process can be evaluated from a denoiser perspective. The data that we're trying to model is text window. We omit the center character as a way to introduce noise, and we ask the model to try to guess (reconstruct) the center character given its context as a denoise process. For example, consider a text window "你好吗世界", we give TINA the context of this text window (你好世界), and then ask the model to guess (reconstruct) the center character (吗). TINA does this by assigning each character a probability of being "the one" given the context. These probability can then be seen as a

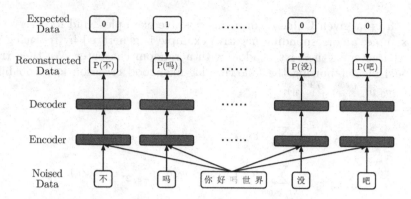

Fig. 2. An example of TINA. The text window is ”你好吗世界”. We give TINA the context of this text window (你好世界), and ask the model to guess (reconstruct) the center character (吗). TINA does this by assigning each character a probability of being ”the one” given the context. These probability can then be regarded as a reconstruction of the one-hot representation of the original center character (吗).

reconstruction of the one-hot representation of the original center character (吗). This example is illustrated in Figure 2.

Formally, given an example of our neural language model with a single hidden layer:

$$
\begin{aligned}
L_1(\mathbf{c_1}, \ldots, \mathbf{c_s}) &= L_{hidden}(L_{input}(\mathbf{c_1}, \ldots, \mathbf{c_s})) \\
&= \tanh(\mathbf{w} \cdot (\mathbf{W} \cdot \mathbf{c_1}, \ldots, \mathbf{W} \cdot \mathbf{c_s}) + \mathbf{b}) \\
L_2(\mathbf{c_1}, \ldots, \mathbf{c_s}) &= L_{output}(L_1(\mathbf{c_1}, \ldots, \mathbf{c_s})) \\
&= \mathrm{sigmoid}(\mathbf{w} \cdot (L_1(\mathbf{c_1}, \ldots, \mathbf{c_s})) + \mathbf{b}),
\end{aligned}
\tag{4}
$$

the encoder of the *text window denoising autoencoder* has the form:

$$
encoder(\mathbf{x}) = (L_1(\mathbf{x}, \mathbf{c_1}), \ldots, L_1(\mathbf{x}, \mathbf{c_s})),
\tag{5}
$$

where $\mathbf{x} = (w_{-s/2}^{-1}, w_1^{s/2})$, which is a text window with the center character omitted, and the features are:

$$
feature(\mathbf{x}) = (\mathbf{y_1}, \ldots, \mathbf{y_n}),
\tag{6}
$$

where $\mathbf{y_i} = L_1(\mathbf{x}, \mathbf{c_i})$. The decoder is:

$$
decoder(\mathbf{y}) = (L_2(\mathbf{y_1}), \ldots, L_2(\mathbf{y_n})).
\tag{7}
$$

The (square) reconstruction error that this text window denoising autoencoder is minimizing against is:

$$
E(\theta, w_{-s/2}^{-1}, w_0, w_1^{s/2}) = \sum_{\forall c_i \in \mathcal{D}} (r_i - 1_{\{c_i = w_0\}})^2,
\tag{8}
$$

Note that since:

$$r_i = L_2(\mathbf{y_i}) = P_c(c_i = w_0 | \theta, w_{-s/2}^{-1}, c_i, w_1^{s/2}), \tag{9}$$

minimizing the reconstruction loss function of the text window denoising autoencoder is exactly the same as maximizing the log-likelihood criterion we proposed for the neural language model.

4.2 Building Deep Architecture

We have already explained that our neural language model can be seen as a text window denoising autoencoder, and it becomes natural to simply follow the stacking strategy of standard denoising autoencoders [12] and build a deep neural network for Chinese word segmentation with both embedding layer and hidden layers pre-trained.

Specifically, the stacking process goes as follows: 1) Train a TINA with a single hidden layer by training a neural language model with a single hidden layer using the method we described in the last section. 2) Remove the softmax output layer, which is the decoder, and add another hidden layer as well as a new softmax output layer. 3) Train this TINA with two hidden layers the same way as step 1, and after that the model becomes one layer deeper.

This stacking process can be repeated several times until a stacked TINA model with sufficient depth (hidden layers) has been built. Then one could simply throw away the last softmax layer, and add a new softmax layer according to the specific task (which in our case is word segmentation), and lastly use back-propagation to fine-tune this pre-trained deep neural network with supervised data.

It's worth mentioning that one could also train a neural language model with a single hidden layer, then fix the word embeddings and train a standard denoising autoencoder on top of it [11]. However, this method under performs our method, which is shown in section 5.

5 Experiments and Analysis

In this section, we demonstrate[1]: 1) The performance of text window denoising autoencoder as a language model. 2) The reconstruction performance of stacked TINAs. 3) The performance of the deep neural network pre-trained by stacked TINAs on Chinese word segmentation.

We use the dataset of Chinese word segmentation bakeoff 2005. There are four different annotated corpus in this dataset, and we use the two in simplified Chinese, namely PKU and MSR dataset. All corpus have already been split into training data and test data [5].

---

[1] Our source code is available at: https://github.com/eirikrwu/tinybrain

Table 1. Comparison of log rank score of different language models. Classical 3-gram, 5-gram models (with Katz backoff), and a neural language model trained with a margin-based loss are compared to a TINA model with 1 hidden layer. The TINA model has the best performance in terms of the log rank score.

Language Model	Log Rank Score
3-Gram (Katz backoff)	2.54
5-Gram (Katz backoff)	2.53
NLM with Margin Loss	2.48
TINA with 1 Hidden Layer	**2.44**

5.1   Text Window Denoising Autoencoder as a Language Model

In the first experiment, we demonstrate the performance of text window denoising autoencoder as a language model. It can also be seen as the reconstruction performance of TINA. The TINA model we trained for this experiment uses a 100-dimensional character embeddings, and only one hidden layer of 300 units. The text window size is 11, which means that we're training the model to predict the character given 5 characters before and 5 after. The corpus that we use in this experiment is the PKU dataset of Chinese word segmentation bakeoff 2005.

We measure the error of the model by log of the rank of the predicted word [4]. We ask our model to output a probability for every character in the dictionary given a text window context, and then we compute the rank of the probability of the correct character. We average the log of the rank over all the text windows in test data as the final log rank score.

We compare our TINA model with the classical 3-gram and 5-gram models, which are trained using Katz backoff [8]. We also trained a neural language model which has the same configuration as our TINA model, except using a margin-based loss function, which is a commonly used loss function in English deep NLP [4]. The results are shown in Table 1. Our TINA model has the best performance in terms of the log rank score.

5.2   Stacking

In the second experiment, we build a deep architecture by stacking TINA models. We use the PKU corpus as in the above experiment. The TINA models we trained in this experiment use a 50-dimensional character embeddings. The text window size is 5. We first train a TINA model with a single hidden layer that has 300 units. Then we gradually add more hidden layers that have the same size and activation function as the first hidden layer, and train them along the way. The log rank score of all the TINA models with different depth is shown in Table 2.

The results show that the performance in terms of log rank score keeps getting better as more hidden layers are added. These deep TINA models can be seen as

Table 2. Comparison of stacked TINA models with different number of hidden layers. The performance in terms of log rank score keeps getting better as the model getting deeper.

Number of Hidden Layers	Log Rank Score
1 Hidden Layers	2.61
2 Hidden Layers	2.52
3 Hidden Layers	**2.45**

pre-trained deep neural networks that can extract highly representational features (that's why the log rank keeps getting lower as the model getting deeper). In the next experiment, we'll use them to build deep neural networks for specific tasks to show that these features are indeed useful.

5.3   Chinese Word Segmentation

In the third experiment, we demonstrate the performance of stacking TINA models as a pre-training method for deep neural networks for Chinese word segmentation task. We use both PKU and MSR dataset of Chinese word segmentation bakeoff 2005.

We use character embeddings of size 50. When pre-trained character embeddings are needed, we use the ones trained in the first experiment. We use a Viterbi-like decoding algorithm to retrieve the most likely valid tag sequence after the per character tag probability has been estimated [9]. We compare various model configurations, as well as different training methods.

Final results are shown in Table 3. We first train a neural network with a single hidden layer of size 300, and with all parameters initialized randomly. This basic model achieves F1 score of 92.6% on the PKU dataset. We then train neural networks with three hidden layers of size 300, with random hidden layer initialization and TINA pre-training respectively. Additionally, we pre-train the hidden layers by fixing character embeddings and using a normal denoising autoencoder with 25% masking noise [12]. The results show that compared to random initialization, TINA pre-training decreases the F1 error rate by 11.9% on the PKU dataset. Compared to the fixing character embeddings and pre-training with standard denoising autoencoder method, the F1 error rate is decreased by 7.8% on the PKU dataset. We further add one more hidden layer of size 300 with TINA pre-training, and the F1 error rate further drops 3.4%. We get similar results on the MSR dataset. TINA pre-training decreases the F1 error rate of the three-hidden-layer model by 5.3% compared to random initialization, 4.2% compared to standard denoising autoencoder. However, on the MSR dataset no further improvement is observed after adding one more TINA pre-trained hidden layer. We believe that this is because the MSR dataset is "simpler" than PKU dataset (notice the higher baseline performance).

Table 3. Word segmentation performance of different model configurations and training methods. "50CE" denote 50-dimensional character embeddings. "xL * yU" denote neural networks with x hidden layers of size y. "r" denote random initialization. "p" denote pre-trained character embeddings. "f" denote pre-trained with normal denoising autoencoders on top of fixed character embeddings. "TINA" denote pre-trained with TINA. Deep neural networks pre-trained by TINA have the best performance.

Dataset	Model	Precision	Recall$_{OOV}$	Recall$_{IV}$	F1
PKU	Baseline	83.6%	5.9%	95.6%	86.9%
	50CE(r) + 1L * 300U(r)	93.5%	75.0%	92.7%	92.6%
	50CE(p) + 1L * 300U(r)	93.7%	75.9%	93.7%	93.2%
	50CE(p) + 3L * 300U(r)	93.7%	76.0%	93.9%	93.3%
	50CE(p) + 3L * 300U(f)	93.7%	76.3%	94.6%	93.6%
	50CE(p) + 3L * 300U(TINA)	94.4%	77.9%	94.8%	94.1%
	50CE(p) + 4L * 300U(TINA)	94.6%	76.6%	95.0%	**94.3%**
MSR	Baseline	91.2%	0%	98.1%	93.3%
	50CE(r) + 1L * 300U(r)	94.5%	64.0%	95.1%	94.4%
	50CE(p) + 1L * 300U(r)	95.1%	63.6%	96.1%	95.2%
	50CE(p) + 3L * 300U(r)	95.0%	63.9%	96.0%	95.1%
	50CE(p) + 3L * 300U(f)	95.2%	64.4%	96.0%	95.2%
	50CE(p) + 3L * 300U(TINA)	95.7%	65.0%	96.4%	95.6%
	50CE(p) + 4L * 300U(TINA)	95.6%	64.9%	96.4%	**95.6%**

6   Related Works

Existing approaches for basic Chinese NLP tasks are almost all based on linear classifiers like hidden markov model or conditional random fields on simple binary word observation features [13][18]. These methods often rely on task specific manual feature design, therefore poses the risk of over-engineering. More recently, semi-supervised methods that can leverage unlabelled corpus, as well as joint training methods that integrate multiple sequence tagging tasks into one system have been proposed [7][14][16][17].

Due to the feature-oriented pre-training process, deep learning methods do not require any manual feature design. One can think of a deep neural network as two parts: all the hidden layers is a feature extractor whose sole purpose is to extract high lever features from data, and the output layer is a simple (even liner) classifier that leverages the high level features extracted from the bottom layers to complete the task. Researchers have found that it helps a lot in a non-convex optimization problem if the model has already been put to a position near the optimal before the gradient based searching starts [3]. So with a proper pre-training that concentrates on feature extraction, it puts our model near the optimal position. Denoising autoencoder [12] and restricted boltzmann machine [10] are two commonly used methods for feature-oriented pre-training.

In the pursuit of a word representation that's more suitable for deep neural network than simple one-hot vectors, Bengio et al. firstly invented the English word embeddings and neural language model [2]. Like most English deep learning NLP methods, our Chinese NLP architecture is also a follow up work on Bengio's work, so it's very similar to English deep learning NLP methods. Basically, we simply change the model input from window of the English words to Chinese characters. However, we use a different method to train the Chinese character embeddings. In addition, we proposed a method that relates to denoising autoencoder to pre-train deep neural networks for Chinese NLP tasks.

Collobert et al.'s training method for English word embeddings [4] is similar to our training method for Chinese character embeddings. However, they use a margin-based loss to train their model. Since there are too many words in English, a margin-based loss criterion will be a lot easier to optimize. We have less characters in Chinese, so we're able to use a better criterion. We choose the likelihood loss instead. Also, they did not explain why training a neural language model is a good way of pre-training the word embeddings.

Recently, researchers have done some work to apply deep learning methods to Chinese NLP. Yang et al. proposed a bilingual English-Chinese word alignment approach based on deep neural network [15]. To our best knowledge, we are the first to apply deep learning methods to Chinese word segmentation.

7   Conclusion and Future Works

We have proposed a deep neural network model: text window denoising autoencoder, as the building block to build deep architectures for Chinese word segmentation. This is a fundamentally different approach, which does not require any linguistic knowledge or manual feature design. We demonstrated that deep neural networks for Chinese word segmentation can be effectively trained with this model. We built a Chinese word segmentation system with TINA, and achieved good performance.

Although we've achieved improvements with a TINA pre-trained deep architecture, for now our best model still under perform the state of the art models on both dataset [13]. However, We think our method shows great potential. We've only tested a few possible model configurations due to time and resource limit, and it's very likely that better performance could be achieved by simply tweaking our model configuration (larger character embedding dimension, more hidden units, etc). We leave that as a future work. There also exists many tricks that can significantly boost the performance of deep neural network, among which a particular method called dropout training [6] shows the best promise. We will try to apply these methods to our model in the future.

References

1. Arisoy, E., Sainath, T.N., Kingsbury, B., Ramabhadran, B.: Deep neural network language models. In: Proceedings of the NAACL-HLT 2012 Workshop: Will We Ever Really Replace the N-gram Model? On the Future of Language Modeling for HLT, pp. 20–28. Association for Computational Linguistics (2012)

2. Bengio, Y., Ducharme, R., Vincent, P.: A neural probabilistic language model. Advances in Neural Information Processing Systems, 932–938 (2001)
3. Bengio, Y.: Learning deep architectures for AI. Foundations and Trends® in Machine Learning 2(1), 1–127 (2009)
4. Collobert, R., Weston, J., Bottou, L., Karlen, M., Kavukcuoglu, K., Kuksa, P.: Natural language processing (almost) from scratch. The Journal of Machine Learning Research 12, 2493–2537 (2011)
5. Emerson, T.: The second international chinese word segmentation bakeoff. In: Proceedings of the Fourth SIGHAN Workshop on Chinese Language Processing, vol. 133 (2005)
6. Hinton, G.E., Srivastava, N., Krizhevsky, A., Sutskever, I., Salakhutdinov, R.R.: Improving neural networks by preventing co-adaptation of feature detectors. arXiv preprint arXiv:1207.0580 (2012)
7. Jiang, W.B., Sun, M., Lv, Y.J., Yang, Y.T., Liu, Q.: Discriminative Learning with Natural Annotations: Word Segmentation as a Case Study. In: 51st Annual Meeting of the Association for Computational Linguistics (2013)
8. Katz, S.M.: Estimation of probabilities from sparse data for the language model component of a speech recogniser. IEEE Transactions on Acoustics, Speech, and Signal Processing 35(3), 400–401 (1987)
9. Low, J.K., Ng, H.T., Guo, W.: A maximum entropy approach to Chinese word segmentation. In: Proceedings of the Fourth SIGHAN Workshop on Chinese Language Processing, vol. 1612164 (2005)
10. Salakhutdinov, R., Hinton, G.E.: Deep boltzmann machines. In: Proceedings of the International Conference on Artificial Intelligence and Statistics, vol. 5(2), pp. 448–455. MIT Press, Cambridge (2009)
11. Socher, R., Pennington, J., Huang, E.H., Ng, A.Y., Manning, C.D.: Semi-supervised recursive autoencoders for predicting sentiment distributions. In: Proceedings of the Conference on Empirical Methods in Natural Language Processing, pp. 151–161. Association for Computational Linguistics (2011)
12. Vincent, P., Larochelle, H., Lajoie, I., Bengio, Y., Manzagol, P.A.: Stacked denoising autoencoders: Learning useful representations in a deep network with a local denoising criterion. The Journal of Machine Learning Research 11, 3371–3408 (2010)
13. Wang, K., Zong, C., Su, K.Y.: Integrating Generative and Discriminative Character-Based Models for Chinese Word Segmentation. ACM Transactions on Asian Language Information Processing 11(2), 7 (2012)
14. Wang, Z.G., Zong, C.Q., Xue, N.W.: A Lattice-based Framework for Joint Chinese Word Segmentation, POS Tagging and Parsing. In: 51st Annual Meeting of the Association for Computational Linguistics (2013)
15. Yang, N., Liu, S.J., Li, M., Zhou, M., Yu, N.H.: Word Alignment Modeling with Context Dependent Deep Neural Network. In: 51st Annual Meeting of the Association for Computational Linguistics (2013)
16. Zeng, X.D., Wong, F.D., Chao, S.L., Trancoso, I.: Co-regularizing character-based and word-based models for semi-supervised Chinese word segmentation. In: 51st Annual Meeting of the Association for Computational Linguistics (2013)
17. Zhang, M., Zhang, Y., Che, W.X., Liu, T.: Chinese Parsing Exploiting Characters. In: 51st Annual Meeting of the Association for Computational Linguistics (2013)
18. Zhao, H., Huang, C.N., Li, M.: An improved Chinese word segmentation system with conditional random field. In: Proceedings of the Fifth SIGHAN Workshop on Chinese Language Processing, vol. 1082117, Sydney (2006)

Language Model for Cyrillic Mongolian to Traditional Mongolian Conversion

Feilong Bao, Guanglai Gao, Xueliang Yan, and Hongwei Wang

College of Computer Science, Inner Mongolia University,
Hohhot 010021, China
{csfeilong,csggl,csyxl}@imu.edu.cn, wanghongwei6136@163.com

Abstract. Traditional Mongolian and Cyrillic Mongolian are both Mongolian languages that are respectively used in china and Mongolia. With similar oral pronunciation, their writing forms are totally different. A large part of Cyrillic Mongolian words have more than one corresponds in Traditional Mongolian. This makes the conversion from Cyrillic Mongolian to Traditional Mongolian a hard problem. To overcome this difficulty, this paper proposed a Language model based approach, which takes the advantage of context information. Experimental results show that, for Cyrillic Mongolian words that have multiple correspondence in Traditional Mongolian, the correct rate of this approach reaches 87.66%, thereby greatly improve the overall system performance.

Keywords: Cyrillic Mongolian, Traditional Mongolian, Language Model.

1 Introduction

Mongolia, as a widely used language over different countries and multiple regions, has a significant impact on the world. Its main users are distributed over China, Mongolia and Russia. A major difference between the Mongolian used in China (called Traditional Mongolian) and that used in Mongolia (called Cyrillic Mongolian or Modern Mongolian) is that they have same pronunciation but different written forms.

As a derivative language, Cyrillic Mongolian has both similar grammar and vocabulary to Traditional Mongolian. This means that the conversion of the two languages does not need to follow the traditional machine translation framework. We can just convert the two languages word by word according to their correspondence relationship. A serial of research that focus on the conversion from Cyrillic Mongolian to Traditional Mongolian has been carried out by Bao Sarina, Wuriliga and Hao Li [1-4] et al with either dictionary based approaches or rule based ones and achieved acceptable results. However, none of them have considered the multiple correspondence problems.

Observed that the correct converted word has a strong relationship to its context, we proposed a language model based approach to overcome the multiple correspondence problem. The rest of the paper is organized as follows: section 2 introduces the characteristic of Traditional Mongolian and Cyrillic Mongolian; section 3 depicts in

G. Zhou et al. (Eds.): NLPCC 2013, CCIS 400, pp. 13–18, 2013.
© Springer-Verlag Berlin Heidelberg 2013

detail the language model based conversion approach; in section 3, experiments and the corresponding results are discussed; at last, we conclude the paper in section 4.

2   Comparison between Traditional Mongolian and Cyrillic Mongolian

Although having a strong relationship to each other, the Traditional Mongolian and Cyrillic Mongolian, as two different languages, still have some significant difference as follows:

1. Tradition Mongolian is composed of 35 characters, in which 8 are vowels and 27 are consonants[5]; Cyrillic Mongolian, on the other hand, has also 35 characters. But 13 of them are vowels and 20 are consonants. Besides, it also includes a harden-character and soften-character[6]. The complete alphabets for the two languages are listed in Tab. 1 for comparison.
2. Cyrillic Mongolian is a case-sensitive language while Traditional Mongolian is not. In Cyrillic Mongolian, the usage of case is similar to English. For the Traditional Mongolian, although it's not sensitive to the case, its form will be different according to the position (top, middle or bottom) in a word [7].

Table 1. Comparison of the characters of Cyrillic Mongolian and Traditional Mongolian

Cyril	Traditional	Cyril	Traditional	Cyril	Traditional	Cyril	Traditional
Аа	᠊	Ии	᠊	Рр	᠊	Шш	᠊
Бб	᠊	Йй		Сс	᠊	Щщ	
Вв	᠊	Кк	᠊	Тт	᠊	Ъъ	
Гг	᠊	Лл	᠊	Уу	᠊	Ыы	
Дд	᠊	Мм	᠊	Үү	᠊	Ьь	
Ее	᠊	Нн	᠊	Фф	᠊	Ээ	᠊
Ёё	᠊	Оо	᠊	Хх	᠊	Юю	᠊
Жж	᠊	Өө	᠊	Цц	᠊	Яя	᠊
Зз	᠊	Пп	᠊	Чч	᠊		

3. The written direction is different for Cyrillic Mongolian and Traditional Mongolian. For Cyrillic Mongolian, the words are written from left to right and the lines are changed top-down; for Traditional Mongolian, the words are written top-down and the lines are changed from left to right.

4. The degrees of unification between the written form and oral pronunciation are different for Cyrillic Mongolian and Traditional Mongolian. Cyrillic Mongolian is a well-unified language. It has a consistent correspondence between the written form and the pronunciation; on the other hand, however, that for the Traditional Mongolian is not 1-to-1 mapping. Sometimes the vowel or consonant will be dropped, added or transformed when converting the written form to the pronunciation.

In some cases, a Cyrillic Mongolian word would have more than one Traditional Mongolian word corresponded, as shown in Fig. 1, where the three Traditional Mongolian words are different but all correspond to the Cyril word "*acap*".

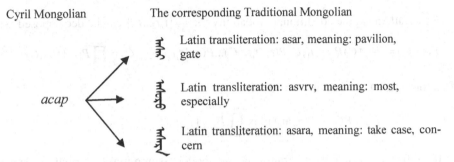

Fig. 1. An example of multiple correspondence for Cyrillic Mongolian to Traditional Mongolian

3   Language Model Based Conversion Approach

Generally speaking, Cyrillic Mongolian and Traditional Mongolian words, when converting, are one-to-one correspondence. However, a large part of Cyrillic Mongolian words have more than one corresponds in Traditional Mongolian. Take the Cyrillic Mongolian sentence "*Танай амар төвшинийг хамгаалхаар явсан юм.*" for example. The words "*амар*" and "*юм*" have more than one correspondences in Traditional Mongolian as shown in Fig. 2, where the corresponding Traditional Mongolian is represented in Latin-transliteration form. More specifically, the Cyril word "*амар*" has four correspondences in Mongolian: "*amara*", "*amar*", "*amar_a*" and "*amvr*"; the Cyril word "*юм*" has two correspondences in Traditional Mongolian: "*yagam_a*" and "*yvm*". The correct conversion for the whole sentence is denoted by the path with the line in bolder, i.e., "*tan-v amvr tobsin-I hamagalahv-bar yabvgsan yvm*" ("ᠲᠠᠨ ᠤ ᠠᠮᠤᠷ ᠲᠥᠪᠰᠢᠨ ᠢ ᠬᠠᠮᠠᠭᠠᠯᠬᠤ ᠪᠠᠷ ᠶᠠᠪᠤᠭᠰᠠᠨ ᠶᠤᠮ ").

If we consider the conversion as a stochastic process and make the final decision according to the probability of the Traditional Mongolian word sequence T conditioned on the Cyrillic Mongolian word sequence C, then the conversion problem can be represented as finding the words sequence that satisfies (1):

$$T' = \arg\max_{T \in Q} P(T \mid C) \tag{1}$$

where $T = \{t_1 t_2 ... t_m\}$ denotes the possible path and C denotes the Cyrillic Mongolian sentence to be converted.

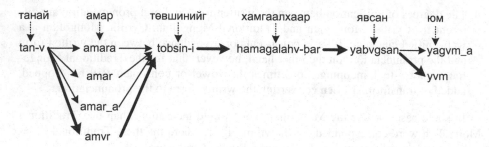

Fig. 2. A conversion example for Cyrillic Mongolian to Traditional Mongolian

As we all know, the conditional probability for $T=\{t_1t_2...t_m\}$ can be decomposed as:

$$P(T \mid C) = P(t_1 \mid C)P(t_2 \mid t_1,C)P(t_3 \mid t_1t_2,C)...P(t_m \mid t_1t_2...t_{m-1},C) = \prod_{j=1}^{m} P(t_j \mid t_1^{j-1},C) \quad (2)$$

then formula (1) can be represented as:

$$P(T \mid C) = \arg\max_{T=t_1t_2...t_m \in Q} \prod_{j=1}^{m} P(t_j \mid t_1^{j-1},C) \quad (3)$$

If we further assume the N-gram language model assumption[8], formulate (3) can then be further simplified as:

$$P(T \mid C) = \arg\max_{T=t_1t_2...t_m \in Q} \prod_{j=1}^{m} P(t_j \mid t_{j-N+1}^{j-1},C) \quad (4)$$

We use the Maximum Likelihood Estimation to estimate the parameters in (4) and adopt Kneser-ney technique[8] to overcome the sample sparseness problem.

4   Experiment

We take the Conversion Accurate Rate (CAR) as the evaluation metric, which is defined as:

$$CAR = \frac{N_{correct}}{N_{total}} \quad (5)$$

Where $N_{correct}$ denotes the total number of words that are correctly converted and N_{total} denotes the number of all the words need to be converted.

The SRILM is adopted for training the language model[9]. A dictionary that contains the Cyrillic Mongolian word to its multiple correspondences in Traditional Mongolian words is constructed for our experiment. This dictionary has 4679 Cyrillic Mongolian words in total. A Traditional Mongolian text corpus, which contains 154MB text in international standard coding, is adopted for n-gram language model training. We use a Cyrillic Mongolian corpus which contains 10000 sentences to test our approach. This corpus is composed of 87941 words, among which 14663 have more than one Traditional Mongolian words corresponded. Our conversion progress can be divided into two steps: in the first step, we convert all the Cyrillic Mongolian words to their corresponding Traditional Mongolian words according to the rule-based approach; and then, for each word, we check whether there is only one Traditional Mongolian word generated. If not, we further determine the best one according to the Language Model based approach proposed in section 3. The data set for the rule-based approach is composed of three parts: a mapping dictionary for Cyrillic Mongolian stem to Traditional Mongolian stem, which contains 52830 entries; a dictionary for Cyrillic Mongolian static inflectional suffix to Traditional Mongolian static inflectional suffix, which contains 336 suffixes; and a dictionary for Cyrillic Mongolian verb suffix to Traditional Mongolian verb suffix, which contains 498 inflectional suffixes. Based on the word formation rule of Traditional Mongolian and Cyrillic Mongolian, together with the above mentioned stem mapping dictionary and suffix mapping dictionary, we constructed a rule-based conversion system.

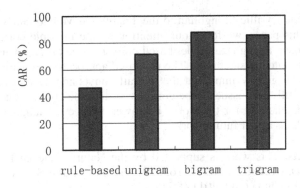

Fig. 3. Performance comparison between the LM based approaches

For the words that have more than one Traditional Mongolian correspondence, we compare the Language Model based approach with different grams (unigram, bigram and trigram) to the rule-based approach. The experiment results are illustrated in Fig 3, from where we can see that all the Language Model based approaches significantly outperform the rule-based approach, among which the bigram achieved the best performance (CAR: 87.66%). Affected by the sample sparseness problem, the trigram approach is slightly worse than the bigram approach, but still much better than the unigram one which has considered only the occurrence frequency, but no context information. This again reconfirm the fact that if the context information is not considered, the performance would be badly decreased.

We also test the overall system performance of rule-based approach and the improved one on all the Mongolian words (both 1-to-1 and 1-to-N). The experimental results are illustrated in Fig 4. In Fig 4, we can see that the conversion correctness for the rule-based approach is 81.66%. When it's integrated with the LM-based approach, the overall system correctness is greatly improved, which reaches 88.14%.

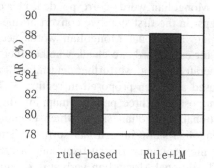

Fig. 4. Overall system performance comparision

5   Conclusions

When converting the Cyrillic Mongolian to the Traditional Mongolian, a lot of problem emerged. In this paper, we focus our attention on the multiple correspondences problem and proposed a language model based conversion approach which takes the context information into consideration. The proposed approach effectively settled this problem and thereby greatly improved the overall conversion system performance. However, there is still some issues to be considered, like the conversion problem for newly-added words and that for the words borrowed from other languages. We will take all these problems as our future work.

Acknowledgements. This work is supported by the Natural Science Foundation of China (NSFC) (NO. 61263037, NO. 71163029) and the Natural Science Foundation of Inner Mongolia of China (NO. 2011ZD11).

References

1. Sarina, B.: The Research on Conversion of Noun and Its Case from Classic Mongolian into Cyrillic Mongolian. Inner Mongolia University, Hohhot (2009)
2. Wuriliga: The Electronic Dictionary Construction of the Traditional Mongolian-Chinese and Cyrillic Mongolian-Chinese. Inner Mongolia University, Hohhot (2009)
3. Li, H., Sarina, B.: The Study of Comparison and Conversion about Traditional Mongolian and Cyrillic Mongolian. In: 2011 4th International Conference on Intelligent Networks and Intelligent Systems, pp. 199–202 (2011)
4. Gao, H., Ma, X.: Research on text-transform of Cyrillic Mongolian to Traditional Mongolian conversion system. Journal of Inner Mongolia University for Nationalities 18(5), 17–18 (2012)
5. Quejingzhabu: Mongolian code. Inner Mongolia University press, Hohhot (2000)
6. Galsenpengseg. Study Reader of Cyrillic Mongolian. Inner Mongolia education press, Hohhot (2006)
7. Qinggeertai. Mongolian Grammar. Inner Mongolia People's Publishing Press, Hohhot (1992)
8. Zong, C.: Statistical Natural Language Processing. Tsinghua University Press, Beijing (2008)
9. Stolcke, A.: SRILM - An Extensible Language Modeling Toolkit. In: Proc. Intl. Conf. Spoken Language Processing, Denver, Colorado (2002)

Sentence Compression Based on ILP Decoding Method

Hongling Wang, Yonglei Zhang, and Guodong Zhou

Natural Language Processing Lab, Soochow University, Suzhou, Jiangsu, 215006
School of Computer Science & Technology, Soochow University, Suzhou, Jiangsu, 215006
{hlwang,20104227009,gdzhou}@suda.edu.cn

Abstract. With the tremendous increasing of information, the demands of information from people advanced the development of Nature Language Processing (NLP). As a consequent, Sentence compression, which is an important part of automatic summarization, draws much more attention. Sentence compression has been widely used in automatic title generation, Searching Engine, Topic detection and Summarization. Under the framework of discriminative model, this paper presents a decoding method based on Integer Linear Programming (ILP), which considers sentence compression as the selection of the optimal compressed target sentence. Experiment results show that the ILP-based system maintains a good compression ratio while remaining the main information of source sentence. Compared to other decoding method, this method has the advantage of speed and using fewer features in the case of similar results obtained.

Keywords: Sentence Compression, Integer Linear Programming, Structured Learning.

1 Introduction

Recent years have witnessed increasing interest in text-to-text generation methods for many natural language processing applications, ranging from text summarization to question answering and machine translation. At the heart of these methods lies the ability to perform rewriting operations. Sentence compression is perhaps one of the most popular text-to-text rewriting methods. The aim is to produce a summary of a single sentence that retains the most important information while remaining grammatical.

The appeal of sentence compression lies in its potential for summarization and more generally for document compression, e.g., for displaying text on small screens such as mobile phones or PDAs (Corston-Oliver, 2001). Vandeghinste & Pan (2004) generated a title for a dialogue by deleting redundant and non-critical information while retaining the main idea. Another earlier sentence compression application is the use of voice reading devices for the blind (Grefenstette 1998). Text is compressed for voice machine to accelerate reading speed, which enables the blind way of reading similar to a normal way of speed reading. Thus, the research on sentence compression for obtaining useful information has important significance.

G. Zhou et al. (Eds.): NLPCC 2013, CCIS 400, pp. 19–29, 2013.
© Springer-Verlag Berlin Heidelberg 2013

We define the sentence compression task as follows: given an input sentence, to produce a sentence which is shorter and retains the important information from the original, and also it is grammatical. In our paper, sentence compression aims to shorten a sentence $x=l_1,l_2,......,l_n$ into a substring $y^*=c_1,c_2,......c_m$, where $c_i \in \{ l_1,l_2,......,l_n \}$. We define the function $F(c_i) \in \{1, . . . , n\}$ that maps word c_i in the compression to the index of the word in the original sentence. Then, we include the constraint $F(c_i) < F(c_{i+1})$, which forces each word in x to occur at most once in the compression y^*, so in the compression process we don't change the word's order and only delete words or phrases. This paper implements a Chinese sentence compression system by learning a sub-tree from the source parsing tree of a sentence (See Figure 1).

Example:

Original Sentence: 据 法新社 报道 ， 有 目击者 称 ， 以军 23日 空袭 加沙 地带 中部 ， 目前 尚 无 伤亡 报告 。

Pinyin: ju faxinshe baodao , you mujizhe cheng , yijun 23ri kongxi jiasha didai zhongbu , muqian shang wu shangwang baogao .

Target   Sentence: 目击者 称 以军 空袭 加沙 地带 中部

Pinyin: mujizhe cheng yijun kongxi jiasha didai zhongbu

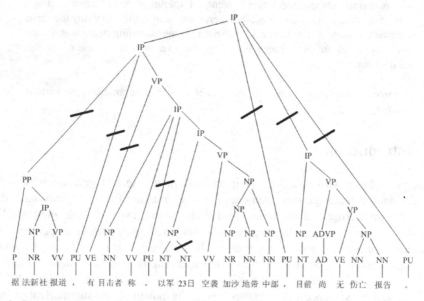

Fig. 1. Compression example, the coarse slashes means in the compressed target sentence the edges are deleted

The rest of this paper is organized as follows: Section 2 briefly reviews the related work on sentence compression and the applications of integer linear programming in the field of NLP. Section 3 describes our sentence compression system, including how to formulate sentence compression problem as an ILP problem, features, loss function and evaluations. Section 4 presents the experimental results. Finally, Sections 5 draws the conclusion.

2   Related Work

2.1   Sentence Compression

Currently, the mainstream solutions to sentence compression problem have been cast mostly in corpus-driven supervised learning models which can be divided into categories: generative model and discriminative model.

Generative model selects the optimal target sentence by estimating the joint probability $P(x, y)$ of original sentence x having the target sentence y. The main advantage of this method is the model training process is simple. And also its parameters can be easily got by counting different context transferring grammars in a parallel corpus. Knight & Marcu (2002) firstly apply the noisy-channel model (one of generative models) for sentence compression. Though the performance of the noisy-channel model is quite well, they do have their shortcomings, such as the source model which represent the probability of compressed sentences, but it is trained on uncompressed sentences, and the channel model requires aligned parse trees for both compressed and uncompressed sentences in the training set in order to calculate probability estimates. These parse trees with many mistakes for both the original and compressed versions will make alignment difficult and the channel probability estimates unreliable as a result.

Discriminative model can be used the rich features to help identify special language phenomenon during the training process. These features may be interrelated and do not meet the independent condition which must meet in the generative model-based method. Discriminative model has been widely used and achieved good performance in many natural language processing tasks, such as the tasks of dependency parsing (McDonald et al., 2005b), entity extraction (Sang & Meulder, 2003), and relation extraction (Zelenko et al. 2003).

Currently, sentence compression is often modeled in a discriminative framework, including the decision tree model, the compression model based on online learning[9], and the model based on SVM.

Knight & Marcu (2002) use the decision tree model to implement the compression by learning a decision tree to incrementally convert between original parse trees and compressed parse trees. There are four operations defined during the process: SHIFT (transfer the first word from the input list into the stack), REDUCE (pop the k syntactic trees located at the top of the stack; combine them into a new tree; and push the new tree on the top of the stack), DROP (delete from the input list subsequences of words that correspond to syntactic constituents), ASSIGNTYPE (change the label of trees at the top of the stack). This model avoid the unreliable of the tree alignment, but their model features encode properties related to including or dropping constituents from the tree with no encoding of bigram or trigram surface features to promote grammaticality. As a result, the model will generate some short and ungrammatical targets.

McDonald(2006) used max-margin leaning algorithm (MIRA, margin-infused relaxed algorithm) to study the feature weight, then rank the subtrees, and finally select the tree with the highest score as the optimal target sentence. McDonald's work had achieved a well performance by using the manual evaluations. But manual evaluations have some disadvantages, such as heavy workload, strength subjectivity, and so on. In addition, the reliability of the learning algorithm of MIRA is not better than Structured SVM (Tsochantaridis et al., 2005).

Cohn & Lapata (2007, 2008, and 2009) formulated the compression problem as tree-to-tree rewriting using a synchronous grammar. Each grammar rule is assigned a weight which is learned discriminatively within a large margin model. A specialized algorithm is used to learn the model weights and find the best scoring compression under the model. This method achieves comparable performance with McDonald's model. The main reason for limiting the performance of the model is that the model needs to do alignment between noisy syntactic trees. Zhang et al. (2013) compressed sentences based on Structured SVM model which treats the compression problem as a structured learning problem, i.e., to learn an optimal sub-tree as its compressed sentence on original sentence parse tree. The experimental results showed that it can generate target sentence which is grammatical and contains the center information of the original sentence in the case of ensuring a better compression rate.

2.2   Integer Linear Programming in NLP

ILPs are constrained optimization problems where both the objective function and the constraints are linear equations with integer variables. Integer linear programming has been applied to many natural language processing tasks, such as relation extraction (Roth & Yih, 2004), semantic role labeling (Punyakanok, 2004), syntactic parsing (Riedel & Clarke, 2006) and so on. Most of these approaches combine a local classifier with an inference procedure based on ILP. The classifier proposes possible answers which are assessed in the presence of global constraints. ILP is used to make a final decision that is consistent with the constraints and likely according to the classifier. For example, the argument for a predicate is the role of non-repetition in semantic role labeling, which can be implemented by adding global non-repeating linear constrains.

Gillick et al. (2009) and Berg-Kirpatrick et al. (2011) applied ILP to multi-document summarization task. They constructed linear constrains for the feature space corresponding to the decoding space, then used ILP to select the optimal predication target according to the feature weight.

Clarke & Lapata (2008) viewed sentence compression as an optimization problem and uses integer linear programming to infer globally optimal compressions in the presence of linguistically motivated constraints. Experimental results on written and spoken texts demonstrate improvements over state-of-the-art models. Woodsend & Lapata (2011) proposed an integer linear programming model for selecting the most appropriate simplification from the space of possible rewrites generated by the grammar. Experimental results showed that the method creates simplifications that significantly reduce the reading difficulty of the input, while maintaining grammaticality and preserving its meaning. Those studies show that ILP could be used for sentence compression or simplification in English. We will use the method in Chinese sentence compression in this paper.

3   Sentence Compression Based on ILP

In this paper, we treat the sentence compression problem as a structured learning problem, i.e. a subtree which learned from the original sentence parse tree is as its compressed sentence. Thus sentence compression task is converted to the task of how to choose the optimal subtree on original sentence syntactic tree. Here we formulate the problem of finding optimal subtree to an ILP decoding problem, that is, to find the target optimal subtree by using ILP decoding method.

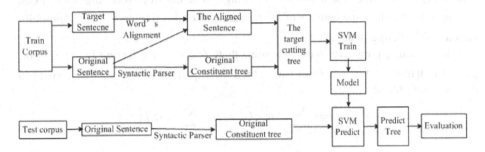

Fig. 2. The Framework of Chinese Sentence Compression

This paper uses the structured learning framework in Zhang et al. (2013) (See Figure 2). After preprocessing for the corpus, the system extracts the features which generated during the original constituent tree transformed into the target tree, and then uses the SVM to train feature weights, finally selects the tree with the highest score as the best target tree.

3.1   Linear Objective Function

Assuming the original sentence x has n words, and then the target set has 2^n elements. With the increasing number of the word the original sentence has, decoding set exponential growth. Finding an optimal target sentence in such a large decoding space, time complexity is very large. Zhang (2012) used McDonald's simplify method to decode. In this paper, we formulate the problem of finding the optimal sentence as an ILP decoding problem. Each subtree is ranked according to the trimming features and lexical features; the subtree with the highest score is the optimal target one.

Suppose x is the original sentence syntactic tree, y is the target subtree corresponding to x. Here we define two vectors: $R(y)$ represents the word set of y, $P(y)$ represents the operation set from x to y. The problem of finding the optimal subtree is transformed to solve the maximum value of following objective function.

$$score(y, x) = \arg\max_{y \in Y(x)} \sum_{r \in R(y)} v_r + \sum_{p \in P(y)} v_p \qquad (1)$$

where $Y(x)$ is the target subtree set, v_r is the weight of word r, v_p is the weight of operation p.

Before the weights are learned by machine learning, the word r and the operation p in Equation (1) need be parameterized. Suppose: w is the vector of feature weight, $g(r, y)$ and $h(p, y)$ represent the feature functions of words and operations to target sentence respectively, then:

$$v_r = <w, g(r, y)>$$
$$v_p = <w, h(p, y)> \tag{2}$$

where $g(r, y)$ includes the features of POS tags, is or not stop word, bigram of POS, etc; $h(p, y)$ includes the features of the parent node of deleting node, the parent-child structure of deleting node, etc.

After v_r and v_p parameterized, we assume that $f(y,x)$ is the feature function of bigram and trimming features from x to y, then the Equation (1) can be transformed to the following form:

$$score(y, x) = \arg\max_{y \in Y(x)} \sum_{r \in R(y)} <w, g(r, y)> + \sum_{p \in P(y)} <w, h(p, y)> \tag{3}$$

$$score(y, x) = \arg\max_{y \in Y(x)} <w, f(y, x)> \tag{4}$$

3.2   Linear Constrain

According to the previous section, to find the optimal subtree is to get the optimal solution for Equation (4). In this paper, we define a bigram indicator variable n_i (if $n_i=1$, the ith node is remained; $n_i=0$, the node is dropped) for each non-terminal node of the original constituent tree. In order to maintain the tree structure, its children nodes are all deleted when the ith node is deleted, which can be implemented by adding the following linear constrain: $n_i - n_j \geq 0$ 、 $n_i \leq \sum n_j$, where n_i is the parent node of n_j.

Similarly, we also define a bigram indicator variable w_i (if $w_i=1$, the ith node is remained; $w_i=0$, the node is dropped) for each terminal node of the original constituent tree. And a linear constrain is added: $w_i = n_j$, where n_j is the POS node of word w_i. At last, a bigram indicator variable f_i (if $f_i=1$, the ith feature appears; or, the feature doesn't appear) is defined for the ith feature. According to the restrictions of feature value, the corresponding linear constrains are added.

3.3   Features

In this paper, we mainly adopt the features which are used in Zhang (2012). There are two kinds of features: Word/POS Features and syntax features. Here in order to avoid too slow to decode the ILP problem, we redefine and extract some features under the framework of structure learning.

Due to the small size of our corpora, which will lead to sparseness and over-fitting, we mainly extract the feature of the word's POS and rarely include the word itself. In this paper, following features are used: the remaining word's bigram POS (PosBigram

(目击者 称) = NN&VV[1]), whether the dropped word is a stop word (IsStop (据) = 1), whether the dropped word is the headword of the original sentence, the number of remaining words. The features of word's bigram POS used in this paper refer to the features in original sentence instead of the ones in target sentence.

In our experiments, two following syntax features are included: the parent-children relationship of the cutting edge (del-Edge (PP) = IP-PP) and the number of the cutting edge. In addition, following dependency features are included: the dependant relation between the dropped word and its dependence word (dep_type(有)=DEP), the relation chain of the dropped word's POS with its dependence word's POS (dep_link (,) = PU-VMOD-VV), whether the dependence tree's root is deleted (del_ROOT (无) = 1), and whether each dropped word is a leaf of the dependence tree (del_Leaf (法新社) = 1).

3.4   Linear Constrains to Features

Due to different limitations of different feature values, linear constrains need to be separately defined for different types of features. For example, for the word "据", since the word is a stop word, the value of its feature indicator variable f_i depends on the value of word indicator variable w_i. When w_i=1, the word will be remained in target sentence, then f_i =0 ; Or, f_i =1. Therefore, the linear constrain can be defined as f_i=1-w_i.

In our experiments, we find that the solving time of the ILP problem is getting longer with the increasing of constrains. Especially for those bigram features of the words, there are (n-1)*n/2 constrains (n is the number of words) which lead to much longer solving time. So we use the remaining word's bigram POS as a feature of word to the original sentence.

3.5   Loss Function

In our work, loss function means the difference between the predict sentence and the gold target sentence. The selection of the loss function has great influence on system performance. In our earlier experiments, we used loss ratio of the remaining word's bigram as the loss function which lead to a decrease of decoding speed because of its large constrains. In this paper, two loss functions are tested. One is the loss ratio of bigram of the remaining word in original sentence. The other is the sum of the number of the words deleted by mistake and the number of the words remained by mistake between the predict sentence and the gold target sentence, which called word loss-based function. Since we found the latter better in our experiments, the word loss-based function is used in the follow-up experiments.

3.6   Evaluation

Currently, manual evaluation is commonly used for sentence compression. Importance and Grammaticality proposed by Knight & Marcu (2002) are mainly used in

---

[1] In Figure 1, for example (the same below).

many works. They are ranked a sentence in a scale from 1 to 5. Importance means how well the systems did with respect to selecting the most important words in the original sentence, while Grammaticality means how grammatical the target sentences were. Although manual evaluations have some disadvantages, such as heavy work-load, strength subjectivity, and so on, they still have the advantage of high accuracy compared to automatic evaluation, which makes them to be used widely.

In this paper, we also use the two evaluations to evaluate our system. In addition, we use sentence similarity and compression ratio (CR) as automatic evaluation me-tric. Here BLEU score which usually used in machine translation task is introduced as similarity evaluation to compare the n-gram difference between the predict sentence and the gold target sentence. Since sentence compression can be seen as translating the original sentence into shorter sentence with same language, the BLEU score can be also used to evaluate the compression performance. To better adapt to sentence compression we redefine the parameters of BLUE.

$$Bleu = BP * \exp(\sum_{n=1}^{N} w_n \log p_n) \tag{5}$$

where p_n is the ratio of the number of n consecutive words in candidate compressed sentence occupies the number of n consecutive words in gold target sentence. $w_n=1/N$, N is the largest n-gram order. The penalty factor BP is redefined as follows:

$$BP = \begin{cases} 1 & if\ c > r \\ e^{(1-r/c)} & if\ c \leq r \end{cases} \tag{6}$$

where c is the number of words of candidate compressed sentence, and r is the num-ber of gold target sentence.

4   Experiments

In our experiments, we use the same parallel corpus extracted from news documents and also extend the corpus using same expansion mode in Zhang (2012), i.e. 2400 pair sentences as training set, and 100 pair sentences as test set. At first, the original sentences in the corpus are parsed using the open-source tool Stanford Parser[2]. Then the words in sentence pair are aligned by the tool developed by our own. Although other open-source kits, such as Giza++, Berkeley Aligner etc, can also be used, we don't use them for their poor performance in the same language. And we use Struc-tured SVM (Tsochantaridis etc. 2005) to learn feature weights. The tool we used is an open-source tool SVM[struct3]. The convergence ε is set to 10^{-4} in the training process.

---

[2] http://nlp.stanford.edu/software/lex-parser.shtml
[3] http://download.joachims.org/svm_struct/
current/svm_struct.tar.gz

4.1   Selection of Upper and Lower Bound to Compression Ratio

Since we use an ILP decoding method to find the optimal sub-tree, it has a large decoding space. We can narrow the feasible space by adding the following linear constrain.

$$CR_{lower} * n \leq \sum_{i=1}^{n} w_i \leq CR_{up} * n \tag{7}$$

where, CR_{lower} is the lower bound of compression ratio, CR_{up} is the upper bound of compression ratio, n is the number of words in the original sentence. To select the appropriate lower and upper bound of compression ratio has a greater influence on the system performance.

Since the target compressed sentences in the corpus come from documents' title, they have a relatively uniform length. Moreover, due to the higher compression ratio and using the feature of the remaining word's bigram POS, the system will tend to generate shorter and not well grammatical compressed target. So we set the values of lower bound and upper bound at the same time. In the experiments, lower bound is set to 0.7, and upper bound is set to 10.

4.2   Experimental Results and Discussion

Table 1 shows the manual and automatic results of our Chinese sentence compression system. In the Table 1, the McDonald row shows the result of Zhang et al. (2003) which used McDonald's decoding model and the ILP row shows the result of our system used ILP decoding model.

Table 1. Results of various experiments

Model	Manual Evaluations		Automatic Evaluations	
	Importance	Grammaticality	CR	BLEU
Gold	4.335±0.265	4.977±0.077	0.291	
McDonald	4.200±0.562	4.444±0.776	0.401	0.686±0.160
ILP	4.190±0.578	4.390±0.827	0.3783	0.688±0.166

From the table 1, we can see that:

1. Compared to McDonald's model, the evaluation of CR improved 2.2% shows that using the ILP decoding method can find an optimal target sentence with better compression ratio.
2. Compared to McDonald's model, the manual evaluations (Importance and Grammaticality) are decreased slightly for two reasons. One is that our system uses simple features because many features into linear constrains is more complex. The other is the more features mean the slower decoding speed, so the number of features is less than the one in McDonald's model.
3. The BLUE scores are similar whether using McDonald's decoding method or ILP method.

In summary, compared to the McDonald's decoding method, the system based ILP decoding method achieves a comparable performance using simpler and less features. We can also be expected that the system performance will gradually improve with the number of features increases. In addition, from the operating efficiency perspective, the overall system's running time is less than before. Here are some data may illustrate the problem: for the same test set, the running time is 8.6 seconds using ILP decoding while 18.4 seconds using McDonald's decoding method.

5   Conclusions

In this paper, under the framework of structured learning, the problem of sentence compression is formulated as a problem of finding an optimal sub-tree using ILP decoding method. Compared to the previous work using McDonald's decoding method, the system which only uses simpler and fewer features achieves a comparable performance on same conditions. And this method has the advantage of speed and using fewer features in the case of similar results obtained. In the future, we will explore more efficient features and linear constrains to use in the ILP decoding method.

Acknowledgements. This research is supported by Project 10KJB520016 under the High Educational Natural Science Foundation of Jiangsu, China.

References

1. Corston-Oliver, S.: Text Compaction for Display on Very Small Screens. In: Proceedings of the NAACL Workshop on Automatic Summarization, Pittsburgh, PA, pp. 89–98 (2001)
2. Clarke, J., Lapata, M.: Global Inference for Sentence Compression An Integer Linear Programming Approach. Journal of Artificial Intelligence 31, 399–429 (2008)
3. Vandeghinste, V., Pan, Y.: Sentence compression for automated subtitling: A hybrid approach. In: Marie-Francine Moens, S.S. (ed.) Text Summarization Branches Out: Proceedings of the ACL 2004 Workshop, Barcelona, Spain, pp. 89–95 (2004)
4. Grefenstette, G.: Producing Intelligent Telegraphic Text Reduction to Provide an Audio Scanning Service for the Blind. In: Hovy, E., Radev, D.R. (eds.) Proceedings of the AAAI Symposium on Intelligent Text Summarization, Stanford, CA, USA, pp. 111–117 (1998)
5. Knight, K., Marcu, D.: Summarization beyond sentence extraction: a probabilistic approach to sentence compression. Artificial Intelligence 139(1), 91–107 (2002)
6. McDonald, R., Crammer, K., Pereira, F.: Online large-margin training of dependency parsers. In: 43rd Annual Meeting of the Association for Computational Linguistics, Ann Arbor, MI, USA, pp. 91–98 (2005b)
7. Sang, E.F.T.K., Meulder, F.: Introduction to the conll-2003 shared task: language-independent named entity recognition. In: Proceedings of the Seventh Conference on Natural Learning at HLT-NAACL 2003, pp. 142–147. Association for Computational Linguistics, Morristown (2003)
8. Zelenko, D., Aone, C., Richardella, A.: Kernel methods for relation extraction. J. Mach. Learn. Res. 3, 1083–1106 (2003)

9. McDonald, R.: Discriminative sentence compression with soft syntactic constraints. In: Proceedings of the 11th Conference of the European Chapter of the Association for Computational Linguistics, Trento, Italy, pp. 297–309 (2006)

10. Tsochantaridis, I., Joachims, T., Hofmann, T., Altun, Y.: Large margin methods for structured and interdependent output variables. Journal of Machine Learning Research 6, 1453–1484 (2005)

11. Cohn, T., Lapata, M.: Large margin synchronous generation and its application to sentence compression. In: Proceedings of the EMNLP/CoNLL 2007, Prague, Czech Republic, pp. 73–82 (2007)

12. Cohn, T., Lapata, M.: Sentence compression beyond word deletion. In: Proceedings of the 22nd International Conference on Computational Linguistics (Coling 2008), Manchester, UK, pp. 137–144 (2008)

13. Cohn, T., Lapata, M.: Sentence Compression as Tree Transduction. Journal of Artificial Intelligence Research 34, 637–674 (2009)

14. Roth, D., Yih, W.: A linear programming formulation for global inference in natural language tasks. In: Proceedings of the Annual Conference on Computational Natural Language Learning, Boston, MA, USA, pp. 1–8 (2004)

15. Punyakanok, V., Roth, D., Yih, W., Zimak, D.: Semantic role labeling via integer linear programming inference. In: Proceedings of the International Conference on Computational Linguistics, Geneva, Switzerland, pp. 1346–1352 (2004)

16. Riedel, S., Clarke, J.: Incremental integer linear programming for non-projective dependency parsing. In: Proceedings of the 2006 Conference on Empirical Methods in Natural Language Processing, Sydney, Australia, pp. 129–137 (2006)

17. Gillick, D., Favre, B.: A scalable global model for summarization. In: Proc. of ACL Workshop on Integer Linear Programming for Natural Language Processing, Boulder, Colorado, pp. 10–18 (2009)

18. Berg-Kirkpatrick, T., Gillick, D., Klein, D.: Jointly Learning to Extract and Compress. In: Proceedings of the 49th Annual Meeting of the Association for Computational Linguistics, Portland, Oregon, pp. 481–490 (2011)

19. Woodsend, K., Lapata, M.: Learning to Simplify Sentences with Quasi-Synchronous Grammar and Integer Programming. In: EMNLP 2011, pp. 409–420 (2011)

20. Zhang, Y.L., Wang, H.L., Zhou, G.D.: Sentence Compression Based on Structured Learning. Journal of Chinese Information Processing 27(2), 10–16 (2013)

21. Zhang, Y., Peng, C., Wang, H.: Research on Chinese Sentence Compression for the Title Generation. In: Ji, D., Xiao, G. (eds.) CLSW 2012. LNCS, vol. 7717, pp. 22–31. Springer, Heidelberg (2013)

Chinese Negation and Speculation Detection
with Conditional Random Fields

Zhancheng Chen, Bowei Zou, Qiaoming Zhu, and Peifeng Li

Natural Language Processing Lab, Soochow University, Suzhou, Jiangsu, 215006
School of Computer Science & Technology, Soochow University, Suzhou, Jiangsu, 215006
{whezex,zoubowei}@gmail.com, {qmzhu,pfli}@suda.edu.cn

Abstract. Negative and speculative expressions are popular in natural language. Recently, negation and speculation detection has become an important task in computational linguistics community. However, there are few related research on Chinese negation and speculation detection. In this paper, a supervised machine learning method with conditional random fields (CRFs) is proposed to detect negative and speculative information in scientific literature. This paper also evaluates the effectiveness of each feature under the character-based and word-based framework, as well as the combination of features. Experimental results show that the single-word feature and the part of speech feature are effective, and the combined features improve the performance furthest. Our Chinese negation and speculation detection system in sentence level achieves 94.70% and 87.10% of accuracy, respectively.

Keywords: negation, speculation, conditional random fields.

1 Introduction

Recent years we have witnessed an increasing interest in negation and speculation detection in natural language, especially in information extraction (IE), which supposed that information displayed in the text are factual. In order to guarantee the truth of information extracted from text, negative and speculative information should either be discarded or presented separately from factual information.

Chinese linguists defined negative and speculative information as follows. Negative information was the information which denied the existence of phenomenon or the occurrence of event [1]. Speculative information was the information which implied that some attribution of thing, such as property and state, were unreliable or uncertain, which reflected vague recognition to object [2]. Speculative information is also regarded as one of the essential attributions in natural language understanding. Take following two sentences as examples:

(1)Chinese: *巴塞罗那主席罗塞尔表示不会在今年夏天之前签下内马尔。*
Pinyin: *bā sài luó nà zhǔ xí luó sài ěr biǎo shì bú huì zài jīn nián xià tiān zhī qián qiān xià nèi mǎ ěr.*
English: *Barcelona President Russell said that he would not sign Neymar before summer.*

G. Zhou et al. (Eds.): NLPCC 2013, CCIS 400, pp. 30–40, 2013.
© Springer-Verlag Berlin Heidelberg 2013

(2)Chinese: 国际金价持续下跌的原因可能是周五塞浦路斯央行卖出黄金储备。
Pinyin: *guó jì jīn jià chí xù xià diē de yuán yīn kě néng shì zhōu wǔ sài pǔ lù sī yāng hang mài chū huáng jīn.*
English: *International gold prices continued to decline. The reason may be that Central bank of Cyprus sold gold reserves on Friday.*

Example (1) reveals that "在今年夏天之前签下内马尔"[zài jīn nián xià tiān zhī qián qiān xià nèi mǎ ěr](he would sign Neymar before summer) would not happen. In example (2), the report guesses that the reason why "国际金价持续下跌" [guó jì jīn jià chí xù xià diē](international gold prices continued to decline) was that "周五塞浦路斯央行卖出黄金储备"[zhōu wǔ sài pǔ lù sī yāng hang mài chū huáng jīn](Central bank of Cyprus sold gold reserves on Friday), but the fact was uncertain.

Negation and speculation detection aims to identify whether there is negative or speculative information in a given sentence and to detect the word or phrase indicating negative or speculative meaning. The CoNLL'2010 [3] introduced the task of speculation detection, and pointed out that if there was a word or phrase implying speculation in a sentence, then this sentence was deemed to contain unreliable or speculative information. This word or phrase can be called speculation cue. "不会" [bú huì](not) in example (1) is a negation cue and "可能"[kě néng](may) in example (2) is a speculation cue, respectively.

Negative and speculative information exist in the scientific domains, where various linguistic forms are used extensively to describe unproved proposition and express impressions, hypothesized explanations of experimental results or negative findings. Vincez et al. [4] reported that there are 13.76% and 22.29% of the negative and speculative sentences in the full paper sub-corpus of the BioScope corpus, respectively. Chen et al. [5] annotated 19 full papers from *Chinese Journal of Computers,* and reported that 15.78% and 13.88% of the sentences in corpus contained negative and speculative information, respectively.

In this paper, we propose a CRFs based classifier to identify the negative and speculative sentences in scientific literature, and then to detect the negation and speculation cues. Experimental results show that those features such as word itself and part of speech (POS) make more contributions to the system performance, and the combined features can improve the performance furthest.

The rest of this paper is organized as follows. Section 2 reviews related work. Section 3 introduces CRF model, tagging sets, feature sets and the setting of feature templates. Section 4 describes our experiments including the corpus on which our approach is evaluated, evaluation metrics, and the analysis of the results in the experiment. Finally, Section 5 concludes our work, and predicts some possible future work.

2   Related Work

Most of the initial research in this study focused on identifying negative and speculative sentences by using heuristic rules (Chapman et al. [6], Goldin et al. [7]). Machine learning methods (Morante et al. [8], Øvrelid [9], Su et al. [10]) have been largely applied after the release of the BioScope corpus [4]. These methods handled the negation and speculation detection task as a classification task which consists of classifying the tokens of a sentence as being at the beginning of the cue, inside or outside. Agarwal et al. [11] created several CRF-based models that automatically detected the speculation cues in biomedical literature, and we selected it as our baseline system.

Most research on Chinese negation and speculation detection focus on the perspective of Chinese language and literature. Sun [12] divided negative words into verbs and adverbs, and explored the usage of negative words. Xu [13] presented a definition of negative sentences, and defined the types of negative sentences and their syntactic structures. Zhang [1] studied the speculative meaning in negative sentences on semantic level. Cui et al. [14] analyzed and explored the formal meaning representation of Chinese fuzzy words. However, there were few researches on identifying Chinese negative and speculative information automatically. Ji et al. [15] annotated news documents, and proposed an automatic approach to identify speculative sentences in Chinese, in which commonly existing cue words were employed to define the score of the whole sentence.

Inspired by Maximum Entropy (ME), Conditional Random Fields (CRFs) was first introduced by Lafferty et al. [16]. It is always considered as an arbitrary undirected graphical model or Markov Random Field and can be used to label and segment sequence data. CRFs are widely applied in natural language processing tasks such as Words Segmentation, Identification of Chinese Unknown Words, Named Entity Recognition, and have achieved good performance. We regard negation and speculation detection as a classification task whether each token is inside cue or not.

3   Conditional Random Fields

In this section, we introduce the theory of CRFs, tagging sets, feature sets and the setting of feature template in detail.

3.1   Theory of CRFs

Conditional Random Fields, combining the advantages of Hidden Markov Model (HMM) and Maximum Entropy Markov Model (MEMM), is often used for sequence labeling and segmenting and has found applications in Named Entity Recognition and other tasks. It is a type of discriminative undirected probabilistic graphical model, in which each vertex represents random variables and each edge represents the probability relation between two vertexes. Following Lafferty et al. [16], the conditional probability of a sequence of tags y given a sequence of token X is:

$$P(y \mid x) = \frac{1}{Z(x)} exp(\sum_{i,k} \lambda_k f_k(y_{i-1}, y_i, x) + \sum_{i,k} u_k g_k(y_i, x)) \qquad (1)$$

Where $f_k(y_{i-1}, x)$ and $g_k(y_i, x)$ can be regarded as feature function for each edge and each vertex, and $Z(x)$ is the normalization factor over all the state sequences for the sequence. The model parameters are a set of real-valued feature weights denoted by $\lambda = \{\lambda_i, u_i\}$, which can be estimated from training data. $P(Y_i = y \mid X)$ is the marginal probability of label $Y_i = y$ given that the observation sequence is X. Marginal probability of a label can be regarded as the confident score of this label. We calculate the marginal probability by using forward-backward algorithm. In our experiments, the observation sequence is sequence of tokens or POS.

3.2 Tagging Set, Features and Feature Templates

In this paper, the negation and speculation cue detection task is regarded as a classification one. We define three tagging set used to train CRF model. If a token is the beginning of a cue, we mark it as 'BCue'. The remaining tokens in cue are marked with 'ICue' to indicate that they are inside the cue. The tokens not a part of the cue are marked with 'OCue' to indicate that they are outside the cue.

The feature set is crucial to CRFs-based systems and its quality directly affects the system performance. In Chinese annotation, character-based framework and word-based framework are deemed as two kinds of methods of text segmentation. Huang et al. [17] compared the performance of Words Segmentation by selecting the same features under the two conditions. It provided reference thoughts for us to detect negation and speculation in this paper.

- Features based on character

  Features based on character included character itself and word boundary. In Chinese, a word consists of one or more characters. In order to locate each character in one specific word, we mark each character's position by MBES method. In this method, word consisting only single character is marked with 'S'; character which is the beginning of the word consisting of multi-characters is marked with 'B'; character which is the end of the word consisting of multi-characters is marked with 'E'; other characters are marked with 'M'. For instance, "查询时间基本不受M值的影响"[chá xún shí jiān jī běn bù shòu zhí M de yǐng xiǎng](Query time mainly has nothing to do with M value), first we segment it to word sequences "查询时间 基本 不 受 M 值 的 影响"[cháxúnshíjiān jīběn bù shòu zhí M de yǐngxiǎng](Query time mainly has nothing to do with M value), then we mark each character in sentence by using MBES method and the word boundary feature sequence is "B M M E B E S S S S B E".

- Features based on word

  Features based on word included word itself and POS. In grammar, POS is a linguistic category of words, which is generally defined by the syntactic or morphological behavior of the lexical item in question. The introduction of annotation guidelines [4] was arranged with different POS of cue. All the above indicate the importance of POS feature in cue detection. In word-based framework, we assign the POS of word including one or more characters to the feature of characters. For example, the POS of "可能"[kě néng](may) is "V", so the POS feature sequence of character of "可能"[kě néng](may) is "V V".

Table 1. Feature Template

Word feature	Note	POS feature	Note
U00:%x[0,0]	Local word	U10:%x[0,1]	Local POS
U01:%x[-1,0]	Previous word	U11:%x[-1,1]	Previous POS
U02:%x[1,0]	Following word	U12:%x[1,1]	Following POS
U03:%x[-1,0]%x[0,0]	The conjunction of previous and local word	U13:%x[-1,1]%x[0,1]	The conjunction of previous and local POS
U04:%x[0,0]%x[1,0]	The conjunction of local and following word	U14:%x[0,1]%x[1,1]	The conjunction of local and following POS
U05:%x[-1,0]%x[0,0]%x[1,0]	The conjunction of previous, local and following word	U15:%x[-1,1]%x[0,1]%x[1,1]	The conjunction of previous, local and following POS

The setting of feature template affects the training of CRF model. In this paper, we combine character, word, word boundary and POS to build feature template. Besides, the window size of feature template consisting of the offset words can also affect the performance. The window size of 3 consisted of C-1,C0,C1,C-1C0,C0C1, C-1C0C1(C represents feature and number including -1,0,1 represents the offset to local word), and the feature template was showed in Table 1 presenting " U00:%x[0,0], U01:%x[-1,0], U02:%x[1,0], U03:%x[-1,0]%x[0,0], U04:%x[0,0]%x[1,0], U05:%x[-1,0]%x[0,0]%x[1,0] ". For example, when given the sentence of "候选集占比没有出现快速增长"[hòu xuǎn jí zhàn bǐ méi yǒu chū xiàn kuài sù zēng zhǎng](the proportion of candidates does not increase rapidly), we suppose that the local character is "没"[méi](not), feature of C-1C0, C0C1, C-1C0C1 will be filled with "比没"[bǐ méi], "没有"[méi yǒu](not), "比没有"[bǐ méi yǒu], respectively. CRFs first generates discrimination function responding these features, and assign each token to different labeling set by computing the maximum likelihood probability.

4   Experiments and Results

In this section, we introduce the annotated corpus and evaluation metrics. Then, we present experimental results and analyze the performance with different features.

4.1   Corpus

We adopt the Chinese Journal of Computers corpus [5] for training and testing. Firstly, authors downloaded full papers from Websites, preprocessed texts and formed raw corpus. Secondly, annotators annotated negation and speculation cues through the annotation tool to build corpus. Thirdly, they transformed the format of corpus into XML. Statistics on the corpus is showed in Table 2. The corpus consisting of 4842 sentences was chosen from 19 full papers, and 15.78% and 13.88% of the sentences in corpus contained negative and speculative information respectively. The corpus marked negation and speculation cues and the kappa value (89.82% and 88.13% respectively) indicated that annotators can distinguish cues accurately and that it was suitable to the negation and speculation detection. In our experiments, we divide the corpus into two groups with equal number of sentences, one being the training set and the other being the testing set.

Table 2. Statistics of the corpus

	Negation	Speculation
cues	941	812
cue set	42	59
sentences	15.78%	13.88%

4.2   Performance Evaluation

Four evaluation metrics, that is, Precision (P), Recall (R), F1-measure (F), are used for performance evaluation for cues detection, and Accuracy (Acc) is used for performance evaluation for sentences identification including negative and speculative information.

$$P = \frac{correct\ recognized\ cues}{all\ recognized\ cues} \times 100\%, \tag{2}$$

$$R = \frac{correct\ recognized\ cues}{all\ cues\ in\ testing\ corpus} \times 100\%, \tag{3}$$

$$F = \frac{2 \times P \times R}{P + R} \times 100\%, \tag{4}$$

$$Acc = \frac{correct\ sentences}{all\ sentences\ in\ testing\ corpus} \times 100\%, \tag{5}$$

Negative and speculative sentences contain at least one negation or speculation cue annotation. *Correct sentences* in formula (5) consist of two parts: one is negative and speculative sentence appearing both in result and test corpus, the other is sentence in which there is not one cue both in result and test corpus.

4.3   Results

In our experiments, ICTCLAS[1] implementation is employed to segment words and to tag POS, and CRF++0.58[2] implementation is employed to train model.

The experiments mainly include three parts. Firstly, we compare system performance by using variety features introduced in section 2.2 with the feature template window size of 1, 3 and 5, respectively. Secondly, we select the optimal system and compare with the baseline system implemented in [11]. Finally, we explore the influence of imbalance of data sets due to the proportion of the sentences including negative and speculative information in the corpus.

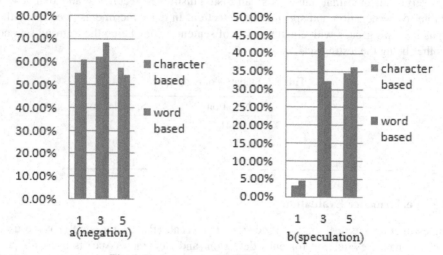

Fig. 1. Performance with different window size

We employ different feature combination for our experiments, which includes character itself, word itself, word boundary, POS and context information based character and based word. (a) and (b) in Fig 1 show the results of negation and speculation cues detection, respectively. These results indicate that the best performance is achieved when the window size is 3. When the window size increases from 1 to 3, system performance increases due to the utilization of context information. However, the performance decreases when the window size increases from 3 to 5. It is due to data sparseness while adding extra context information.

In our experiment, the best window size of feature template is 3. With this window size, the performances with different features are shown in Table 3. Origin features represent word itself based on the word or character itself based on the character. In word-based experiment, there is no word boundary feature, therefore the table cell is filled with 'N/A'. In Table 3, the best performance of negative information detection achieves 68.03% based on word. The performance of speculation detection achieves 43.20% based on character. The performance of negation cue detection system is

---

[1] http://ictclas.nlpir.org/

[2] http://crfpp.googlecode.com/svn/trunk/doc/index.html

better than the speculation. It is due to the different distribution of their cues. In Fig 2, the distribution of negation cues is on the above of the distribution of speculation cues. It shows that the distribution of negation cues is more intensive and stable, so the features are more similar. All in all, there is difference between negation detection and speculation detection, and it is more difficult to detect speculation than negation.

Table 3. Performanceofnegative and speculatve information detection

features	negation		speculation	
	character-based	word-based	character-based	word-based
origin	58.06%	42.17%	**43.20%**	32.42%
origin + word boundary	57.96%	N/A	35.27%	N/A
origin+ POS	61.63%	68.03%	37.94%	34.46%
all features	62.18%	**68.03%**	33.88%	34.46%

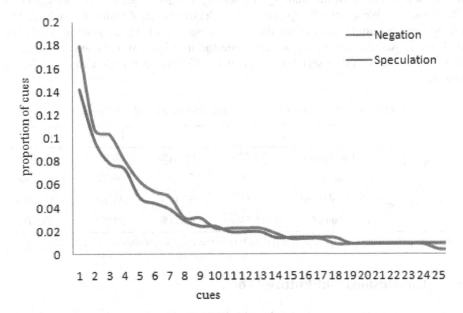

Fig. 2. Distribution of cues

Table 4 shows the comparative results between the optimal system and baseline system. The low performance of baseline system is due to the window size of feature template [11] didn't give, and we adopt the default is 1. There is great difference between optimal system and baseline system, and the results indicate that it is not enough only to use features [11] given. Besides, character feature and word boundary feature which have no equivalent in English make contributions to increase of system performance.

Table 4. Compared the best performance with baseline system

		P	R	F	ACC
Negation	Baseline	1.93%	60.00%	3.74%	24.74%
	Best system	77.72%	60.61%	68.03%	94.70%
Speculation	Baseline	2.33%	43.70%	4.43%	30.19%
	Best system	51.55%	37.17%	43.20%	87.10%

In this paper, we explore the influence of imbalance of data sets. As same as baseline system, such as negative information detection, we first select all negative sentences including at least one negation cue annotation. We count the number of negative sentences and randomly select an equal number of non-negation sentences from all non-negation sentences in corpus. Thus we obtain 1528 sentences with 764 negative sentences and 764 non-negation sentences. We pool these sentences and randomly divide them into two sets, one being the training set and the other being the testing set. Hence, both the training and testing sets for negative sentences contain 764 sentences. We carry out experiment by selecting a set of features which lead to the best performance and compare the performance with baseline system. As shown in Table 5, Acc decreases after we eliminate the imbalance of data sets. It indicates that the imbalance of data sets have no positive effective on negation and speculation detection.

Table 5. Results of performance with imbalanced and balanced data sets

		P	R	F	Acc
Negation	Imbalanced	77.72%	60.61%	68.03%	94.70%
	Balanced	78.00%	57.645	66.29%	86.60%
Speculation	Imbalanced	51.55%	37.17%	43.20%	87.10%
	Balanced	75.54%	43.21%	54.97%	75.61%

Note: The performance with imbalanced data sets is the best performances above.

5 Conclusions and Future Work

In this paper we have presented a machine-learning approach to determine whether there exist negative or speculative information and to detect negation or speculation cues in scientific literature. The experiment results show that the system performance have been raised significantly by adding context information, compared with the performance only using features of character and word. Besides, results indicate that our approach is suited for negation and speculation detection. The best performance of negation and speculation cues detection reaches to 68.03% and 43.20% when the window size is 3, respectively. In this paper, we find that there exists obvious difference for negation and speculation detection between Chinese and English. In particular, the performance decreases when training model with balanced data sets for negative information detection. Further research is in several directions. In the first place, syntactic parse features could be integrated in the system in order to optimize performance. Then, the system should be tested in different types of corpus to check its robustness.

Acknowledgement. This research was supported by National Natural Science Foundation of China (No.61070123, 61272260), the Natural Science Foundation of Jiangsu Province (No.BK2011282), the Major Project of College Natural Science Foundation of Jiangsu Province (No.11KJA520003), the Graduates Project of Science and Innovation (No.CXZZ12_0818).

References

1. Zhang, H.: Analysis of uncertainty of Chinese negative sentences in semantics level(现代汉语否定句的语义不确定倾向分析). Sichuan teachers' college, Sichuan (2006)
2. Li, Q.: Explanation of uncertainty(模糊语言及相关术语界说). Journal of Pingdingshan-college 23(6) (2008)
3. Farkas, R., Vincze, V., Mora, G., Csirik, J., Szarvas, G.: The CoNLL-2010 Shared Task: Learning to Detect Hedges and their Scope in Natural Language Text. In: Proceedings of the Fourteenth Conference on Computational Natural Language Learning(CoNLL), Shared Task, July 1-12 (2010)
4. Vincze, V., Szarvas, G., Farkas, R., et al.: The BioScope corpus: biomedical texts annotated for uncertainty, negation and their scopes. In: BioNLP 2008: Current Trends in Biomedical Natural Language Processing, Columbus, Ohio, USA, pp. 38–45 (June 2008)
5. Chen, Z., Zou, B., Zhu, Q., Li, P.: The Construction of Chinese Negation and Uncertainty Identification Corpus(汉语否定与模糊识别语料库的构建). In: Chinese Lexical Semantic Workshop, pp. 226–231 (2013)
6. Chapman, W.W., Bridewell, W., Hanbury, P., Cooper, G.F., Buchanan, B.G.: A Simple Algorithm for Identifying Negated Findings and Diseases in Discharge Summaries. Journal of Biomedical Informatics 34, 301–310 (2001)
7. Goldin, I.M., Chapman, W.W.: Learning to Detect Negation with 'Not' in Medical Texts. In: Workshop at the 26th ACM SIGIR Conference (2003)
8. Morante, R., Daelemans, W.: A metalearning approach to processing the scope of negation. In: Proceedings of the Thirteenth Conference on Computational Natural Language Learning, pp. 21–29 (2009)
9. Øvrelid, L., Velldal, E., Oepen, S.: Syntactic Scope Resolution in Uncertainty Analysis. In: Proceedings of the 23rd International Conference on Computational Linguistics (Coling 2010), pp. 1379–1387 (2010)
10. Su, Q., Huang, J., Lou, H., Liu, P.: Hedge Detection with Latent Features. In: Chinese Lexical Semantic Workshop, pp. 448–451 (2013)
11. Agarwal, S., Yu, H.: Detecting hedge cues and their scope in biomedical text with conditional random fields. Journal of Biomedical Informatics (43), 953–961 (2010)
12. Sun, Y.: Shallow Analysis of Negation cue in Chinese(现代汉语否定词初探). Journal of Anqing Teachers' college (Philosophy and Social Science Edition) (5) (1978)
13. Xu, L.: Discuss negative sentence in Chinese(试论现代汉语否定句). Journal of AnQing Teachers College (Social Science Edition) (3), 108–118 (1986)

14. Cui, X., Yi, M., Liu, W.: On the Meaning Representation of Fuzzy Words(模糊词语的意义表征研究). In: Chinese Lexical Semantic Workshop, pp. 551–554 (2013)
15. Ji, F., Qiu, X., Huang, X.: Exploring uncertainty sentences in Chinese(中文不确定性句子的识别研究). In: The 16th China Conference on Information Retreval, pp. 594–601 (2010)
16. Lafferty, J., McCallum, A., Pereira, F.: Conditional random fields: Probabilistic models for segmenting and labeling sequence data. In: Proceedings of the 18th International Conference on Machine Learning, San Francisco, pp. 282–289 (2001)
17. Huang, C., Zhao, H.: Which Is Essential for Chinese Word Segmentation: Character versus Word(Invited paper). In: The 20th Pacific Asia Conference on Language, Information and Computation (PACLIC-20), Wuhan, China, November 1-3, pp. 1–12 (2006)

Chinese Argument Extraction
Based on Trigger Mapping

Yuan Huang, Peifeng Li, and Qiaoming Zhu

Natural Language Processing Lab, Soochow University, Suzhou, Jiangsu, 215006
School of Computer Science & Technology, Soochow University, Suzhou, Jiangsu, 215006
{20114227027,pfli,qmzhu}@suda.edu.cn

Abstract. Unlike English, Chinese sentences do not have a strict syntactic structure and ellipsis is a common phenomenon, which weaken the effectiveness of syntactic structure in argument extraction. In Chinese event extraction, lots of arguments cannot be extracted from the sentence successfully, because of the loose connection between the nominal trigger and its arguments. This paper brings forward a novel argument extraction approach based on trigger mapping. It maps the nominal trigger to its predicate and uses it as a key to extract syntactic features for classification. Experimental results on the ACE 2005 Chinese Corpus show that, in terms of F1-measure in argument identification and role determination, our approach achieves an obvious improvement.

Keywords: argument identification, trigger mapping, nominal trigger.

1   Introduction

As a hot research topic in the field of information extraction, event extraction mainly aims at transferring free texts into semi-structured ones and then extracting the information the users are interested in. The process of event extraction is divided into two subtasks: event trigger (anchor) extraction and argument extraction. The former is to recognize the event trigger mentions and their types and the latter is to identify the arguments of a specific event mention and determine their roles. This paper focuses on the argument extraction on the ACE 2005 Chinese Corpus. In accordance with the definition of ACE evaluation, these terms are supposed to be defined:

- Entity: an object or a set of objects in one of the semantic categories of interest.
- Entity Mention: a reference to an entity (typically, a noun phrase).
- Event mention: a phrase or sentence within which an event is described, including a trigger and its arguments.
- Trigger (anchor): the main word which most clearly expresses the occurrence of an event, so recognizing an event can be recast as identifying a corresponding trigger.
- Argument: the entity mentions involved in an event.
- Argument role: the relation of an argument to an event where it participates.

G. Zhou et al. (Eds.): NLPCC 2013, CCIS 400, pp. 41–49, 2013.
© Springer-Verlag Berlin Heidelberg 2013

The effectiveness of syntactic features is weakened because of the looseness of Chinese syntactic structure, which is caused by the impreciseness and ubiquitous ellipsis. Meanwhile, it is difficult to extract arguments from event mentions that are triggered by nominal triggers, for nominal triggers and arguments are not closely related in syntactic structures.

Statistics on the ACE 2005 Chinese Corpus show that the number of the arguments in the event sentences with the nominal triggers (~2070) accounts for 26.6% of the total, and its performance (F1-measure) is 10% lower than that of verb triggers (refer to Table 2). Therefore, improving the performance of argument extraction on nominal triggers is helpful to improve that of the whole system.

With reference to the syntactic structure of the event sentences triggered by nominal triggers, this paper proposes an approach based on trigger mapping which maps nominal trigger to its predicate and then improves the performance of argument extraction.

2   Related Work

The study of event extraction started early abroad and has made great achievements. Nowadays, the mainstream method, known as machine learning, regards event extraction as a classification issue and most of them focused on English event extraction. For example, Chieu and Ng [7] regarded it as a classification issue and used Maximum Entropy Classifier to extract the arguments of specific roles, such as Lecturer, Time, Place and so on. Ahn [1] used a pipeline model and divided the task of event extraction into a series of sub-tasks and then took advantage of MegaM and Timble to extract the event on the ACE English Corpus. In such method, each word is used as an example to train the machine learning model and a lot of negative examples cause serious imbalance between the positive and negative examples. Hardy [8] proposed an approach based on data driven and used it to detect the event and to classify the candidate events. Ji [9] adopted an inductive learning framework which improved the performance of event extraction by taking advantage of the derived predicate cluster. Their framework was based on both parallel corpus (English and Chinese) and cross-language information extraction. Based on the consistency of the event type in the same document, Liao and Grishman [10] proposed a single document cross-event inference method. While Hong et al. [3] made use of the consistency between cross-entity to extract the event argument.

In Chinese, Zhao et al. [2] conducted a study on the Chinese event extraction. She applied a method combined auto expanding and binary classification in event identification stage. These two approaches solved the imbalance between the positive and negative samples in the training set as well as data sparsity in event extraction. Referred to Ahn's pipeline model, Chen and Ji [4] realized Chinese event extraction system, and calculated the contributions of lexical, syntactic, semantic features and so on. Tan [6] put forward a feature selection strategy based on the combination of local feature selection and plus-minus features, thus ensuring the detection effect of classifier in every event type. Hou et al. [5] proposed a trigger word detection method based on character and used CRFs model in view of the inconsistency between Chinese word segmentation and trigger word boundary to identify event mentions. Chen ret al. [11] employed a joint modeling approach to event extraction to solve the error propagation problem inherent in Li et al.'s [13] pipeline system architecture, and then investigated a variety of rich knowledge sources for Chinese event extraction that encode knowledge ranging from the character level to the discourse level. Li et al. [12] proposed a novel global argument inference model to explore specific relationships among relevant event mentions to recover those inter-sentence arguments in the sentence, discourse and document layers.

3   Mapping Based on Trigger

3.1   Basic Thoughts

In an event sentence, nominal trigger and its arguments are not closely related with regard to syntax, but their relationship can be established via the predicate if nominal triggers are mapped to the predicate. Take the following two event sentences as examples:

(E1)：巴勒斯坦的一个部队（Attacker）袭击（EM1：Attack）了以色列村庄（Target）。
(An army of Palestine attacked a village of Israel)
(E2)：巴勒斯坦（Attacker；Target）和以色列（Attacker；Target）发生冲突（EM2：Attack）
(Palestine has a conflict with Israel)

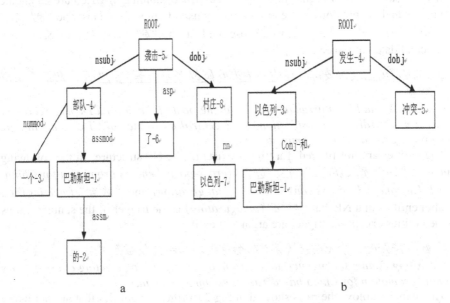

Fig. 1. Dependency parsing trees of event sentences

The two triggers (EM1 and EM2) in example (E1) and example (E2) have the different POS tag, and they play different roles in the examples, too. The verb trigger *"袭击"(attack)* in example(E1) is a predicate while the nominal trigger *"冲突" (conflict)* acts as an object in the example (E2). Fig 1 shows the dependency analysis result of the two examples. In the example (E1), with a subject-predicate relationship with *"部队"(army)* , the verbal trigger *"袭击"(attack)* shares a predicate-object relationship with *"村庄"(village)*, making it easy to identify *"部队"(army)* and *"村庄" (village)* as arguments. In the example (E2), the nominal trigger *"冲突"(conflict)* has no direct relationship with *"巴勒斯坦"(Palestine)* and *"以色列"(Israel)*. Only through the predicate *"发生"(has)* they can build the connection with each other, making it difficult to identify them as arguments.

As is shown in Fig 1, *"发生"(has)* in example (E2) functions similarly with *"袭击" (attack)* in example (E1). Therefore if we can map the nominal trigger *"冲突"(conflict)* to the predicate *"发生"(has)*, it can improve the structure similarity between the example (E1) and (E2), then it will be easy to identify *"以色列"* *(Israel)* and *"巴勒斯坦" (Palestine)* as arguments.

3.2   Filter Pseudo Instances Based on Rules

Besides, this paper observes that: only the last entities in an NP whose structure is parallel or modification can be identified as an argument in most cases. In the following instance, *"中共"* (CPC), *"中央"* (the central committee), *"直属机关"* (directly subordinated organization), *"党委"* (Party committee) and *"副书记"* (Deputy Secretary) in the NP *"中共中央直属机关党委第二副书记"* (the Second Deputy Secretary of directly subordinated organization of the central committee of CPC) are candidate arguments and the previous four entities are only used to modify the last one *"副书记"* (Deputy Secretary). In this case, we choose the last one *"副书记"* (Deputy Secretary) as the candidate's argument.

武绍祖月前已经被安排出任<u>中共中央直属机关党委第二副书记</u>，仍然享受部级的待遇。

(Shaozu Wu had been arranged to take up the post of the Second Deputy Secretary of directly subordinated organization of the central committee of CPC a month ago, still enjoying the treatment of ministers.)

The entities are not filtered if a trigger exists in the NP structure. In the following sentence, *"跨党派大陆台商权益促进会"* (cross-party benefits promotion for China-based Taiwanese businessman), *"成立"* (inaugurating) and *"大会"* (meeting) are parallel entities in a NP, but *"成立"* (inaugurating) is the trigger of the sentence, thus all the entities except the trigger are argument entities.

行政院长张俊雄今天在立法院参加跨党派大陆台商权益促进会成立大会。

(Junxiong Zhang, the premier, took part in the inaugurating meeting of cross-party benefits promotion for China-based Taiwanese businessman.)

This paper employs the rules showed in Fig 2 to filter the entities that are not likely to be arguments.

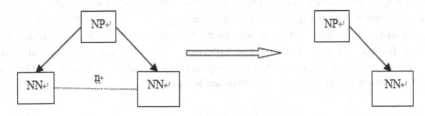

Fig. 2. Syntactic transformation

3.3 Extended Features

The goal of this paper is mapping nominal trigger to the predicate of the event sentence. Since those verb triggers do not need mapping, we only focus on those event sentences with nominal triggers.

Table 1. Feature selection of the sentence with a nominal anchor

Feature type	Feature description	Illustration
Basic features	<1>: Full word; POS tag	trigger: "冲突"; POS tag: noun
	<2>: Event type	Event type: Attack
	<3>: Entity type; Entity headword	Entity type: GPE; headword: "以色列"
Adjacent word features	<4>: Left one word of entity; POS tag	Left one word of entity: "和"; POS tag: conjunction
	<5>: Right one word of entity; POS tag	Right one word of entity: "发生"; POS tag: verb
	<6>: Left one word of trigger; POS tag	Left one word of trigger: "发生"; POS tag: verb
	<7>: Right one word of trigger; POS tag	Right one word of trigger: null; POS tag ： null
Dependency features	<8>: Dependency path from trigger to entity	dobj(发生-4, 冲突-5) nsubj(发生-4, 以色列-3)
Syntactic features	<9>: Shortest path from entity to trigger	NR↑NP↑IP↓VP↓NP↓NN
Relative position features	<10>: Relative position of entity and trigger: before or after	Relative position ： 前
New features	<11>: Predicate of the sentence with an nominal trigger	Predicate word in the sentence: "发生"
	<12>: Dependency of the predicate and trigger	dobj(发生-4, 冲突-5)

This paper uses Hou's system [5] as our baseline and adds new features to event sentences with nominal triggers. We take the entity "以色列" (Israel) in the example (E2) for instance to analyze feature selection. As is shown in Table 1, the last two are the new features. In the process of the experiment, the first three features are called basic features, while adjacent features, dependency features, syntactic features and relative position features are called expanded features.

4   Experiments

4.1   Experiments Settings

This paper adopts ACE 2005 Chinese Corpus as our experiment corpus which contains 633 Chinese documents and most of them are related to news. We randomly chose 33 documents as the development set, 534 documents as the train set and the last 66 documents as the test set. In the test set, according to the .apf.xml standard labeling document, there are 854 arguments, among which the triggers of 665 arguments are verbs, that of 185 arguments are nouns, the others (4 arguments) triggered by a preposition and a pronoun.

This experiment takes the usual Precision (P), Recall (R) and F1-measure as our evaluation standard. Stanford's Maximum Entropy Classifier with default parameters is also used. We divide the event argument extraction task into two steps: argument identification and role determination.

For evaluation, we follow the standards:

- A trigger is correctly identified if its position in the document matches a reference trigger;
- A trigger type is correctly determined if its event type and position in the document match a reference trigger;
- An argument is correctly identified if its involved event type and position in the document match any of the reference argument mentions;
- An argument role is correctly determined if its involved event type, position in the document, and role match any of the reference argument mentions.

4.2   Experimental Results

Table 2 shows the results of argument identification and role determination. We use Hou's system [5] as our baseline and verb_noun refers to the method that we divide all arguments in the training set and the candidate arguments in the test set into two sets by the POS tags of the trigger mentions and two classifiers, noun-based and verb-based classifiers, are trained with the same features as the baseline. The new features refers to features (11) and (12) in Table 1. In Table 2, our approach improves the F1-measure of argument identification and role determination by 2.8% and 3.8% respectively, largely due to the gains in those arguments whose trigger mentions are nouns (NN).

Compared with the baseline, verb_noun achieves the improvement of F1-measure by 5.7% in argument identification. The reason is that the sentences with nominal triggers and verb triggers shave great difference in syntactic structure. Besides, the number of candidate argument with verb triggers is several times than that with nominal triggers. They will affect each other if we extract argument together without distinguishing the sentential form which will lead to the decrease of system performance.

Table 2. Performance comparison of argument identification and role determination

| | Argument identification (%) | | | | | |
| | NN | | | All | | |
	P	R	F1	P	R	F1
baseline	32.4	44.9	37.6	41.4	52.8	46.4
verb_noun	36.3	53.5	43.3	43.0	55.6	48.5
+new features	39.2	55.1	45.8	43.8	56.0	49.2
	Argument role determination(%)					
	NN			All		
	P	R	F1	P	R	F1
baseline	28.2	39.5	32.9	36.8	47.9	41.6
verb_noun	31.9	47.0	38.0	39.4	48.9	43.6
+new features	34.6	48.6	40.4	40.5	51.7	45.4

The new features make the F1-measure increase by 2.5% in argument identification, compared with the verb_noun method. The reason is that those nominal triggers arc mapped to the predicates via the new features. For example, in event sentence "一名常向女儿伸手要钱的男子在一次讨钱不遂后, 竟恐吓女儿说, 要是女儿不给他钱, 他就要杀死全家人, 结果被控恐吓罪。"(A man who always asks money from his daughter but once failed. He should treat his daughter that if she did not give him the money, he would kill all the family members. As a result, he was accused of extortion), the argument is "他" (he), the nominal trigger is "死" (die) and we find that "杀" (kill) connects the two words. If we regard "杀" (kill) as the new trigger, "他" (he) will be identified as an argument. These new arguments mainly come from the sentences whose verbs share a verb-object relationship with triggers and a subject-predicate relationship with arguments.

4.3   Experimental Results Analysis

The contributions of the features in Table 1 are shown in Table 3. Since this paper mainly focuses on the argument identification where the triggers are nouns, so only the contributions of nouns are listed. We can see that the combined feature is more effective than the two simple features used in the argument extraction. The F1-measure increases by 2.5% due to a huge increase in precision.

After filtering, the ratio between negative and positive instances decreases from 3.3:1 (6390:1916) to 3:1 (5520:1817). Table 4 shows the comparison of argument extraction with filtering and without filtering.

Table 3. Feature contributions for the result of the experiment

feature	P(%)	R(%)	F1-measure(%)
Basic feature+ f (4,5,6,7)+f(8)+ f(9)+f(10)	36.3	53.5	43.3
+f(11)	+0.9	+1.1	+1.0
+f(12)	+0.1	-1.1	-0.3
+f(11)+f(12)	+2.9	+1.6	+2.5

Table 4. The results of argument extraction without filtering

	P(%)	R(%)	F1-measure(%)
Argument identification w/o filtering (%)	37.6(-1.6)	55.7(+0.6)	44.9(-0.9)
Argument role determination w/o filtering (%)	32.1(-2.5)	47.6(-1.0)	38.3(-2.1)

5   Summary

This paper brings forward a novel argument extraction approach based on trigger mapping. It maps the nominal trigger to its predicate and uses it as a key to extract syntactic features for classification. Experimental results on the ACE 2005 Chinese Corpus show that, in terms of F1-measure in argument identification and role determination, our approach achieves an obvious improvement. The next stage of our work aims at nominal triggers, considering more effective feature extraction and how to make use of global features to make inference and reach better performance.

Acknowledgement. This research was supported by National Natural Science Foundation of China (No.61070123, 61272260), the Natural Science Foundation of Jiangsu Province (No.BK2011282), the Major Project of College Natural Science Foundation of Jiangsu Province (No.11KJA520003).

References

1. Ahn, D.: The Stages of Event Extraction. In: Proceedings of the Workshop on Annotations and Reasoning about Time and Events, pp. 1–8 (2006)
2. Zhao, Y., Qin, B., Che, W., et al.: Research on Chinese Event Extraction(中文事件抽取技术研究). Journal of Chinese Information Processing 22(1), 3–8 (2008)
3. Hong, Y., Zhang, J., Ma, B., et al.: Using Cross-Entity Inference to Improve Event Extraction. In: Proceedings of the 49th Annual Meeting of the Association for Computational Linguistics, Stroudsburg, PA, USA, pp. 1127–1136 (2011)
4. Chen, Z., Ji, H.: Language specific issue and feature exploration in Chinese event extraction. In: Proceeding of the 2009 Annual Conference of the North American Chapter of the Association for Computational Linguistics Boulder, Colorado, USA, pp. 209–212 (2009)

5. Hou, L., Li, P., Zhu, Q.: Study of Event Recognition Based on CRFs and Cross-event (基于CRFs和跨事件的事件识别研究). Computer Engineering 38(24) (2012)
6. Tan, H.: Research on Chinese Event Extraction(中文事件抽取关键技术研究). Harbin Institute of Technology, Harbin (2008)
7. Chieu, H.L., Ng, H.T.: A Maximum Entropy Approach to Information Extraction from Semi-Structured and Free Text. In: Proceedings of the 18th National Conference on Artificial Intelligence, pp. 786–791 (2002)
8. Hardy, H., Kanchakouskaya, V., Stzalkowski, T.: Automatic Event Classification Using Surface Text Features. In: Proceeding of AAAI 2006 Workshop on Event Extraction and Synthesis, Boston, MA (2006)
9. Ji, H.: Unsupervised Cross-lingual Predicate Cluster Acquisition to Improve Bilingual Event Extraction. In: Proceedings of HLT-NAACL Workshop on Unsupervised and Minimally Supervised Learning of Lexical Semantics, Boulder, Colorado, pp. 27–35 (June 2009)
10. Liao, S., Grishman, R.: Using Document Level Cross-Event Inference to Improve Event Extraction. In: Proceedings of ACL-2010, Uppsala, Sweden, pp. 789–797 (July 2010)
11. Chen, C., Ng, V.: Joint Modeling of Chinese Event Extraction with Rich Linguistic Features. In: Proceedings of COLING 2012, pp. 529–544 (2012)
12. Li, P., Zhu, Q., Zhou, G.: Argument Inference from Relevant Event Mentions in Chinese Argument Extraction. In: Proceedings of ACL 2013, pp. 1477–1487 (2013)
13. Li, P., Zhu, Q., Zhou, G.: Employing compositional semantics and discourse consistency in chinese event extraction. In: Proceedings of the 2012 Joint Conference on Empirical Methods in Natural Language Processing and Computational Natural Language Learning, pp. 1006–1016 (2012)

Exploring Multiple Chinese Word Segmentation Results Based on Linear Model

Chen Su, Yujie Zhang, Zhen Guo, and Jinan Xu

School of Computer and Information Technology,
Beijing Jiaotong University, Beijing 100044, China
{12120447,yjzhang,12120416,jaxu}@bjtu.edu.cn

Abstract. In the process of developing a domain-specific Chinese-English machine translation system, the accuracy of Chinese word segmentation on large amounts of training text often decreases because of unknown words. The lack of domain-specific annotated corpus makes supervised learning approaches unable to adapt to a target domain. This problem results in many errors in translation knowledge extraction and therefore seriously lowers translation quality. To solve the domain adaptation problem, we implement Chinese word segmentation by exploring n-gram statistical features in large Chinese raw corpus and bilingually motivated Chinese word segmentation, respectively. Moreover, we propose a method of combining multiple Chinese word segmentation results based on linear model to augment domain adaptation. For evaluation, we conduct experiments of Chinese word segmentation and Chinese-English machine translation using the data of NTCIR-10 Chinese-English patent task. The experimental results showed that the proposed method achieves improvements in both F-measure of the Chinese word segmentation and BLEU score of the Chinese-English statistical machine translation system.

Keywords: Chinese Word Segmentation, Domain Adaptation, Bilingual Motivation, Linear Model, Machine Translation.

1   Introduction

In the process of developing domain-specific Chinese-English machine translation (MT) system, the accuracy of Chinese word segmentation on large amount of training text often decreases because of unknown words. The lack of domain-specific annotated corpus makes supervised learning approaches unable to adapt to a target domain. When extracting translation knowledge from large-scale Chinese-English parallel corpus, the poor accuracy of Chinese word segmentation results in many errors in extracted translation knowledge and therefore seriously lowers translation quality.

To solve this problem, a few approaches have been applied to domain adaptation of Chinese word segmentation. (Zhang et al., 2012) indicates that adding domain-specific dictionary to CRF-based Chinese word segmentation is effective for domain adaptation. In cases where no domain-specific dictionaries are available, n-gram statistical features are explored from large Chinese raw corpus to replace dictionary

G. Zhou et al. (Eds.): NLPCC 2013, CCIS 400, pp. 50–59, 2013.
© Springer-Verlag Berlin Heidelberg 2013

(Wang et al., 2011) (Guo et al., 2012). When Chinese-English parallel corpus is given for developing MT system, words in English sentences may guide Chinese word segmentation of the corresponding Chinese sentences (Ma et al., 2009) (Xi et al., 2012). (Ma et al., 2010) shows that combining different Chinese word segmentation results can improve the performance of statistical machine translation system.

In this paper, we make improvements and extensions to the above approaches and implement two Chinese word segmenters, one based on n-gram features of Chinese raw corpus and the other one based on bilingually motivated features. Furthermore, we propose a method, by which the multiple Chinese word segmentation results of the two segmenters are combined based on linear model to augment domain adaptation. In this way, we obtain an adapted Chinese word segmenter for a large scale domain-specific Chinese text.

The rest of this paper is organized as follows. In Section 2, we introduce the implementation of the two Chinese word segmenters and then describe the method of combining multiple Chinese word segmentation results in detail. The evaluation experiments conducted in patent domain are reported in Section 3. Section 4 concludes and gives avenues for future work.

2   Combining Multiple Segmentation Results with Linear Model

In the process of developing domain-specific Chinese-English machine translation system, a large-scale parallel Chinese-English corpus needs to be processed for translation knowledge extraction. There also exists a large-scale Chinese raw corpus of the same domain that needs to be translated by the MT system. For exploring these resources to improve the accuracy of Chinese word segmentation, we attempt to take n-gram features of the Chinese raw corpus and bilingually motivated features of the parallel corpus into account. The idea will be explained in more detail as follows. N-gram statistical features of the domain-specific Chinese raw corpus are to be explored for adapting a Chinese word segmenter to a specific domain. And bilingually motivated features of the parallel corpus are to be utilized as guidance for segmenting domain-specific Chinese words. In order to integrate the two kinds of features from different types of corpora, we implement two Chinese word segmenters based on n-gram features and bilingually motivated features respectively and then adopt a linear model to combine the results of the two segmenters. The framework of the idea is shown in Fig. 1.

In this paper, we implement a Chinese word segmenter based on CRF model, in which n-gram statistical features of Chinese raw corpus are integrated, called as CRF segmenter in this paper. Moreover, for using bilingually motivated features, we implement a Chinese word segmentation system based on word alignment techniques, called as bilingually motivated segmenter in this paper. We will describe the two segmenters in the following two subsections respectively, and give a detailed description about how to combine their results in the third subsection.

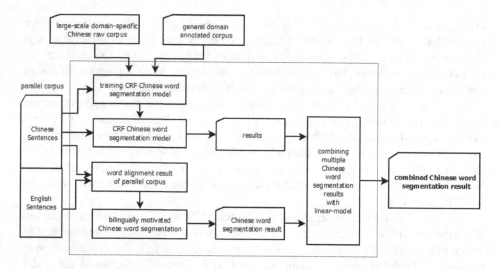

Fig. 1. Framework of combining multiple Chinese word segmentation results

2.1   Domain-Adapted Chinese Word Segmentation Based on N-gram Features

Following the work of (Guo et al., 2012), we realize a domain-adapted Chinese seg-mentation system by exploring Chinese raw corpus of target domain.

In additional to the UPENN Chinese annotated data[1], statistical features of large-scale domain-specific Chinese raw corpus are added for training segmentation model. The overview of the domain adaptation for Chinese Word Segmentation is shown in Fig. 2. We use CRF++ (version 0.55)[2] to train segmentation model. In this paper, n-gram refers to a sequence of n consecutive Chinese characters. The statistical features of n-gram include n-gram frequency feature and AV (Accessor Variety) feature (Feng et al., 2004), defined as the count of occurrences of n-gram in a corpus and the count of different context in which n-gram occurs, respectively. The feature template adopts 5-characters sliding window: two preceding characters, a current character and two subsequent characters (Jin et al., 2005).

For a sentence, CRF segmentation model produces an N-best list of alternative segmentation results with corresponding probability scores. In previous work, only 1-best result is adopted generally. By analyzing the results within N-best, however, we find that some erroneous segmentation in 1-best result may be segmented correctly in the low-ranking results, such as the example shown in Fig. 3. In this example, the character sequence "甘氨酸"(Glycine) is wrongly segmented into two words in 1-best result, whereas it is correctly segmented into one word in the 3-best result. Based on the observation, we intend to select correctly segmented parts from the N-best list. In this paper we use a 10-best list and denote the corresponding probability scores as $Conf_{CRF1}$, $Conf_{CRF2}$, ..., $Conf_{CRF10}$, which will be used to measure the confidence of words in the k-best result ($1 \le k \le 10$) (see Section 2.3).

---

[1] http://www.ldc.upenn.edu/Catalog/
[2] https://code.google.com/p/crfpp/

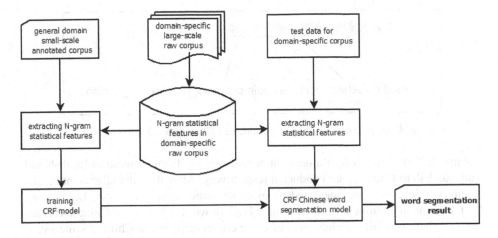

Fig. 2. Framework of domain adaptation for a Chinese word segmentation system

Fig. 3. An example of a correct segmentation occurring in 3-best result

2.2   Bilingually Motivated Chinese Word Segmentation

In Chinese-English parallel corpus, word boundaries in English sentences are ortho-graphically marked. According to alignment between words of an English sentence and Chinese characters of the corresponding Chinese sentence, the boundaries of Chinese word are inferable. This can be illustrated by the example shown in Fig. 4. In Fig. 4, a part of alignment results displayed as lines between the English sentence and the Chinese sentence is shown. English words, "sebacic", "acid-derived" and "mono-mer" are aligned with Chinese character sequence, "癸二", "酸衍生" and "单体", respectively. The alignment results imply that the Chinese characters sequence "癸二酸衍生单体" is likely to be segmented into "癸二", "酸衍生" and "单体". So the aligner between English words and Chinese characters may guide Chinese word seg-mentation, especially for domain-specific words. Based on the above consideration, we implement a bilingually motivated Chinese word segmentation using word align-ment results.

Given a Chinese-English sentence pair, $C_1^J = c_1 c_2 \ldots c_J$ and $E_1^I = e_1 e_2 \ldots e_I$, in which $c_j (1 \leq j \leq J)$ is the jth character in the Chinese sentence, and $e_i (1 \leq i \leq I)$ is the ith word in the English sentence. We use GIZA++ toolkit[3] for word alignment. It should be noted that Chinese characters in Chinese side are used as units for

---

[3] https://code.google.com/p/giza-pp/

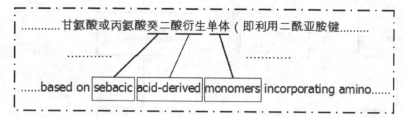

Fig. 4. An example of bilingually motivated Chinese word segmentation

alignment. Two directions of alignment processing, i.e. from Chinese to English and from English to Chinese, are conducted respectively. After that, the alignment results of the two directions are integrated by using heuristic grow-diag-final[4]. Let $a_i=< e_i, C>$ represent an alignment from one single English word e_i to a set of Chinese characters C. When the Chinese characters of C are consecutive in the Chinese sentence, C is regarded as a Chinese word.

Let $Count (a_i)$ represents the number of the alignment a_i occurring in the alignment results and $Count (e_i, C)$ represents the co-occurrence frequency, i.e. the number of times C and e_i co-occur in the parallel corpus. Let $Conf (a_i)$ represents the confidence score of a_i, by which we measure the possibility of e_i being aligned with C when they co-occur in one sentence pair. The value of $Conf(a_i)$ is therefore estimated as in (1).

$$Conf(a_i) = \frac{Count(a_i)}{Count(e_i, C)} \tag{1}$$

The algorithm of the bilingually motivated Chinese word segmentation is defined as follows.

(a) Conduct word alignments in two directions by using GIZA++ and integrate the alignment results. In using GIZA++, each character of Chinese sentence is regarded as one word.

(b) Calculate confidence scores of alignment results according to (1).

(c) For each alignment $a_i=< e_i, C>$, take C as a word segmentation and the confidence score of the word as $Conf(a_i)$, if the characters in C are consecutive in the sentence.

2.3   Combining Multiple Segmentations with Linear Model

We will describe the method of combining the multiple segmentation results of the two segmenters, which have been presented above.

The n-gram features are extracted from Chinese monolingual corpus, while the bilingually motivated features are extracted from bilingual corpus. The two types of features belong to different kinds of language resources. In order to integrate the different kinds of features in Chinese word segmentation, we instead integrate the results from the different segmenters which are implemented using different type of features

---

[4] http://www.statmt.org/moses/?n=FactoredTraining.AlignWords

respectively. For this purpose, we design a linear model to combine the multiple segmentation results for selecting the best Chinese word segmentation.

We label boundaries between Chinese characters in a sentence with sequential numbers. Such an example is shown in Figure 5, in which the numbered boundaries are displayed as nodes. B_i^j denotes the Chinese character sequence between the ith and the jth boundaries in the sentence.

From the CRF segmenter, we adopt the segmentation results in a 10-best list and take the probability score $Conf_{CRFk}$ as the confidence score of corresponding words in the k-best result ($1 \leq k \leq 10$). We then adopt the segmentation result of the bilingually motivated segmenter as the eleventh segmentation result and the confidence score of alignment $Conf(a_i)$ is taken as the confidence score of corresponding words in the result. We designed a linear model as in (2) to combine the 11 segmentation results.

$$F_{i,j} = \lambda_1 \cdot Conf_{CRF1} \cdot seg_1(i,j) + \cdots + \lambda_{10} \cdot Conf_{CRF10} \cdot seg_{10}(i,j) + \lambda_{11} \cdot Conf_{i,j} \cdot seg_{11}(i,j) \quad (2)$$

Where $F_{i,j}$ denotes the possibility score of B_i^j being a word; $seg_l(i,j)$ ($1 \leq l \leq 11$) is a two-valued function, $seg_l(i,j)=1$ when B_i^j being a word in the lth segmentation result; otherwise, $seg_l(i,j)=0$; $Conf_{CRFk}$ ($1 \leq k \leq 10$) is the confidence score of the kth segmentation result from the CRF segmenter; $Conf_{i,j}$ is the confidence score of the segmentation result from the bilingually motivated segmenter; λ_l ($1 \leq l \leq 11$) are weights of 11 segmentation results.

$$w_{i,j} = \frac{F_{i,j}}{\sum_j F_{i,j}} \quad (3)$$

$F_{i,j}$ is normalized into $w_{i,j}$ as in (3). $w_{i,j}$ is the normalized score of a word. We then represent the multiple candidate words in a lattice, as shown in Fig. 5. The nodes marked with numbers represent boundaries between characters and the directed edge $<i, j>$, from nodes i to node j, represents that B_i^j is a word with a normalized score $w_{i,j}$. The best segmentation result should be a sequence of words with a maximum product of their scores. Such a sequence can be found by a dynamic programming, also called decoding for lattice.

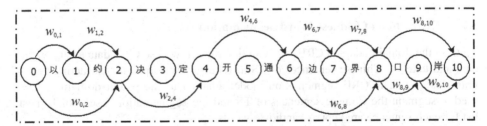

Fig. 5. An example of Chinese word segmentation lattice

To train the parameters λ_l ($1 \leq l \leq 11$), we use Powells algorithm combined with a grid-based linear optimization method as follows (William et al., 2002). First, a point in 11-dimensional parameter space is randomly selected as a initial point and then the parameters λ_l are optimized through iterative process. In each step, only one parameter is optimized w.r.t. F-measure of word segmentation, while keeping all other parameters fixed. To avoid local optimum, we select different starting points for parameter estimation.

In this way, we obtain a linear model, by which the best word segmentation is selected from the results of the two domain-adapted segmenters and therefore domain-adaptation of Chinese word segmentation is effectively augmented.

3   Experimental Result

For verifying the contribution of the proposed method, we consider a practical case of machine translation system development. For this aim, the experiments are designed on the NTCIR-10[5] Chinese-English parallel patent description sentences. We carry out word segmentation on the Chinese part of the data by using the proposed method and conduct evaluations from two aspects, accuracy of Chinese word segmentation and translation quality of MT system.

3.1   Experimental Data

The data of NTCIR-10 provides 1,000,000 sentence pairs for training, 2,000 sentence pairs for development and 2,000 sentence pairs for testing. From the training set, 300 sentence pairs are randomly selected as annotation set, denoted as AS. The remaining sentences are used as training set, denoted as TS. The purpose of this work is to increase the accuracy of Chinese word segmentation on the Chinese part of TS and bring about improvement on translation quality of MT system. We annotate the Chinese sentences of AS according to the word segmentation specification of the Penn Chinese Treebank (Xia et al., 2000). The annotated 300 sentences are then randomly divided into two parts, denoted as AS1 and AS2, used for training the parameters of the linear model and evaluating Chinese word segmentation accuracy, respectively.

The Penn Chinese Treebank (CTB 5.0), including chapter 1-270, chapter 400-931 and chapter 1001-1151, are used as annotated corpus to train the CRF segmentation model.

3.2   Evaluation of Chinese Word Segmentation

To train the domain-adapted CRF segmentation model, we use CTB data as annotated data and take the Chinese sentences of TS as a large raw corpus for extracting the n-gram features. The CRF segmentation model adapted to the patent domain is then used to segment the Chinese sentences of TS and the segmentation results of 10-best list for each sentence are kept as candidate words.

We also conduct word alignment on the Chinese-English parallel sentence pairs of TS and obtain bilingually motivated Chinese word segmentation results on the Chinese sentences of TS according to the algorithm described in Section 2.2.

---

[5] http://research.nii.ac.jp/ntcir/ntcir-10/

The parameters λ_l ($1 \leq l \leq 11$) of the linear model are trained by the 150 annotated sentences of AS1. At last, we use the linear model to combine the 11 Chinese segmentation results and obtain the best word segmentation results on the Chinese sentences of TS.

To evaluate the accuracy of the Chinese word segmentation, we segment the 150 sentences of AS2 in the same way and show the evaluation results in Table 1. We can see that the linear model outperforms the other two methods. Compared with the 1-best of CRF segmenter, the accuracy of the linear model is increased by 1% both on precision and on recall rate, and F-measure is therefore increased by 1.257%. It proves that the proposed method of combining multiple word segmentation results yields higher performance in adapting the Chinese word segmentation to the patent domain. We investigate the segmented sentences of TS and find that there are totally 37,109,126 Chinese words. This implies that the slight variation in the accuracy of Chinese word segmentation is of practical value. Furthermore, an improvement in translation quality of MT system is expected to be achieved by the improvement of Chinese word segmentation.

Table 1. Comparison of the evaluation results of three domain-adapted Chinese word segmentation methods

Chinese word segmentation method	Precision[%]	recall[%]	F-measure[%]
Bilingually motivated segmenter	73.1312	61.4480	66.7825
1-best of CRF segmenter	90.2439	90.7710	90.5067
Our method(Combining multiple segmentation results)	91.6650	91.8614	91.7631

3.3   Evaluation of Machine Translation System

We then develop a phrase-based statistical machine translation system on the Chinese-English parallel sentences of TS with Moses[6]. The Chinese sentences of TS, which have been segmented in Section 3.1, are used here. The 2,000 sentence pairs of the development set are used in the minimum error rate training (Och et al., 2003) for optimizing the MT system. At last, the MT system is evaluated on the 2,000 sentences pairs of the test set in BLEU score (Papineni et al., 2002). The evaluation results are shown in Table 2.

Table 2. Evaluation results of the MT systems using different Chinese word segmentation methods

MT systems using different segmentation methods	BLEU[%]
1-best of CRF segmenter	30.53
Our method (Combining multiple segmentation results)	31.15
Stanford Chinese segmenter	30.98
NLPIR Chinese segmenter	30.56

---

[6] http://www.statmt.org/moses/

For comparison, we also use Stanford Chinese segmenter[7] and NLPIR Chinese segmenter (ICTCLAS 2013)[8] for Chinese word segmentation of the same data and develop MT systems using the segmented data, respectively. The evaluation results on the same testing data are also shown in Table 2.

In this evaluation, we take the MT system using the result of 1-best of CRF segmenter as baseline system, whose BLEU score is 30.53%. Compared with the baseline system, the BLEU score of the MT system using the results of our method is improved by 0.62%. It proves that the proposed method not only increases the accuracy of Chinese word segmentation, but also achieves improvement in the translation quality. The BLEU scores of the MT systems using Stanford Chinese segmenter and NLPIR Chinese segmenter are 30.98% and 30.56%, respectively. So the performance of the proposed method is better than those of the two popular segmenters.

4   Conclusion

In this paper, we implement two domain-adapted Chinese word segmenters, one based on n-gram statistical feature of large Chinese raw corpus and the other one based on bilingually motivated features of parallel corpus. To augment domain adaptation, we propose a method of combining multiple Chinese segmentation results of the two segmenters based on linear model. The proposed method also provides a solution to the problem of poor performance of Chinese word segmentation in development of Chinese-English machine translation system. The experimental results on the NTCIR-10 show that both F-measure of Chinese word segmentation result and the BLEU score of the machine translation system are improved.

However, the proposed method has its limitation. The proposed method cannot be used in the application of the Chinese-English MT system for segmenting input Chinese sentences, because the corresponding English sentences are required by the bilingually motivated segmenter. In the future, we attempt to train the CRF-based segmentation model using the result of the bilingually motivated segmenter too and accordingly to achieve a word segmentation model integrated with the bilingual motivated features for application of MT system.

References

1. Zhang, M., Deng, Z., Che, W., et al.: Combining Statistical Model and Dictionary for Domain Adaption of Chinese Word Segmentation. Journal of Chinese Information Processing 26(2), 8–12 (2012)
2. Wang, Y., Kazama, J., Tsuruoka, Y., et al.: Improving Chinese word segmentation and pos tagging with semi-supervised methods using large auto-analyzed data. In: Proceedings of 5th International Joint Conference on Natural Language Processing, pp. 309–317 (2011)

---

[7] http://nlp.stanford.edu/software/segmenter.shtml
[8] http://ictclas.nlpir.org/

 3. Guo, Z., Zhang, Y., Su, C., Xu, J.: Exploration of N-gram Features for the Domain Adaptation of Chinese Word Segmentation. In: Zhou, M., Zhou, G., Zhao, D., Liu, Q., Zou, L. (eds.) NLPCC 2012. CCIS, vol. 333, pp. 121–131. Springer, Heidelberg (2012)
 4. Ma, Y., Way, A.: Bilingually motivated domain-adapted word segmentation for statistical machine translation. In: Proceedings of the 12th Conference of the European Chapter of the Association for Computational Linguistics, pp. 549–557. Association for Computational Linguistics (2009)
 5. Xi, N., Li, B., et al.: A Chinese Word Segmentation for Statistical Machine translation. Journal of Chinese Information Processing 26(3), 54–58 (2012)
 6. Ma, Y., Zhao, T.: Combining Multiple Chinese Word Segmentation Results for Statistical Machine Translation. Journal of Chinese Information Processing 1, 104–109 (2010)
 7. Feng, H., Chen, K., Deng, X., et al.: Accessor variety criteria for Chinese word extraction. Computational Linguistics 30(1), 75–93 (2004)
 8. Low, J.K., Ng, H.T., Guo, W.: A Maximum Entropy Approach to Chinese Word Segmentation. In: Proceedings of the 4th SIGHAN Workshop on Chinese Language Processing (SIGHAN 2005), pp. 161–164 (2005)
 9. Press, W.H., Teukolsky, S.A., Vetterling, W.T., Flannery, B.P.: Numerical Recipes in C++. Cambridge University Press, Cambridge (2002)
10. Xia, F.: The segmentation guidelines for the Penn Chinese Treebank (3.0). Technical report, University of Pennsylvania (2000)
11. Och, F.J.: Minimum error rate training in statistical machine translation. In: Proceedings of the 41st Annual Meeting on Association for Computational Linguistics, vol. 1, pp. 160–167. Association for Computational Linguistics (2003)
12. Papineni, K., Roukos, S., Ward, T., et al.: BLEU: a method for automatic evaluation of machine translation. In: Proceedings of the 40th Annual Meeting on Association for Computational linguistics, pp. 311–318 (2002)

A Unified Framework for Emotional Elements Extraction Based on Finite State Matching Machine[*]

Yunzhi Tan, Yongfeng Zhang, Min Zhang, Yiqun Liu, and Shaoping Ma

State Key Laboratory of Intelligent Technology and Systems,
Tsinghua National Laboratory for Information Science and Technology,
Department of Computer Science and Technology, Tsinghua University, Beijing 100084, China
cloudcompute09@gmail.com

Abstract. Traditional methods for sentiment analysis mainly focus on the construction of emotional resources based on the review corpus of specific areas, and use phrase matching technologies to build a list of product feature words and opinion words. These methods bring about the disadvantages of inadequate model scalability, low matching precision, and high redundancy. Besides, it is particularly difficult to deal with negative words. In this work, we designed a unified framework based on finite state matching machine to deal with the problems of emotional element extraction. The max-matching principal and negative words processing can be integrated into the framework naturally. In addition, the framework leverages rule-based methods to filter out illegitimate feature-opinion pairs. Compared with traditional methods, the framework achieves high accuracy and scalability in emotional element extraction. Experimental results show that the extracting accuracy is up to 84%, which has increased by 20% comparing with traditional phrase matching techniques.

Keywords: sentiment analysis, e-commerce, emotional elements extraction, finite state matching machine.

1 Introduction

With the rapid development of the Internet, E-commerce is becoming an increasingly popular network application. According to the 31th statistic report of China Internet Network Development State [1] from CNNIC (China Internet Network Information Center) in Jun 2013, there are 242 million internet users with online shopping experience up to the end of 2012. This is 20% of the total internet users. Compared with the year of 2011, the number has increased by 48.07 million with an increasing rate of 24.8%. At the same time, more and more internet users write reviews about product features and using experience. Sentiment analysis for customer reviews can help understand users' feedback about customers' attitude to each feature of a product timely and effectively. As a result, sentiment analysis for customer reviews is becoming a core technic that e-commerce websites are scrambling to develop.

---

[*] This work was supported by Natural Science Foundation (60903107, 61073071) and National High Technology Research and Development (863) Program (2011AA01A205) of China.

G. Zhou et al. (Eds.): NLPCC 2013, CCIS 400, pp. 60–71, 2013.
© Springer-Verlag Berlin Heidelberg 2013

A practical review sentiment analysis system has two very important parts: one is to build emotional resources based on user comments (e.g. sentiment lexicon); the other is to analyze customer reviews and extract emotional elements based on the constructed emotional resource. There has been a lot of work [2-11] studying the issue of building a high-quality emotional resource, however there is little work focusing on how to use the constructed emotional resources to analyze user comments, extract emotional elements and summarize emotional tendencies of customers to product features. Traditional methods for emotional elements extraction are usually based on simple string matching techniques, which bring about the disadvantages of inadequate model scalability, low matching precision, and high redundancy. Besides, it is particularly difficult to deal with negative words. Our work is an attempt to fill this gap and improve the performance of emotional elements extraction using the emotional resource constructed.

In this work, we proposed a unified framework based on finite state matching machine for emotional elements extraction. We integrated max-matching principle and negative adverbs processing into the framework. Furthermore, the framework leverages rule-based methods to filter out illegitimate feature-opinion pairs. In our framework, emotional elements extraction is divided into three steps: emotional elements matching, extracting and filtering. Experimental results show that the accuracy of emotional elements extracted is up to 84%, which is an increase of more than 20% compared with traditional phrase matching techniques. On the other hand, the redundancy of emotional elements extraction is reduced a lot. In addition, the framework we proposed has a good scalability in that one can easily integrate new rules to deal with more complex customer reviews. Sophisticated evaluation and experiments verified both the effect and efficiency of our framework.

The main contribution of this work is that, we propose a unified framework based on finite state matching machine, which extracts emotional elements from customer reviews based on an emotional resource constructed. With this framework, the practicality of sentiment analysis is improved a lot.

2   Related Work

Automatic sentiment analysis for customer reviews is an important domain in web data mining. Some previous work [2-4] discussed how to calculate sentiment score for a whole sentence for the purpose of review information retrieving and classifying. Generally speaking, a sentence may contain more than one features and more than one sentiment polarities (e.g. "电视画面清晰但是价格太高了", translated as "The picture is clear but the price is too high", contains two different sentiment polarities for the two product features "Picture" and "Price"). Sentence-level sentiment analysis can only determine whether a whole sentence is positive, negative or neutral. It cannot reveal the customer attitude towards specific product features exactly. Kim et al. [5] proposed that sentiment can be represented within four aspects, which are topic, opinion-holder, sentiment-descriptor and sentiment-polarity. That is to say, the opinion-holder uses some descriptors containing sentiment polarity to express his or her opinion about a topic. As a result, various work attempts to construct emotional resources constituting the four aspects for further sentiment analysis. Liu et al. [6] manually annotated features of products based on part-of-speech tagging. Then they used association rules to mine the association of feature words and opinion words. Li et al. [7] proposed a method using semantic relations of feature and opinion words to mine the relationship between them, which achieved good performance. There is much similar work [8-11] discussing emotional resource construction based on customer reviews, which also achieved good results. It is noteworthy that there is little work focusing on systematic research about how to use the constructed emotional resource to analyze reviews, extract emotional elements and summarize customer attitudes to the features of products.

Based on the constructed emotional resource, traditional emotional elements extraction methods use string-matching techniques. They extract emotional elements directly if an element exists in the emotional resource (e.g. Sentiment Lexicon), which face the disadvantages of low accuracy, poor scalability, redundancy and the difficulty to deal with negative words, because customer reviews are usually very colloquial and flexible. These shortages lower the practicality of the traditional methods. In this work, we designed a unified framework for emotional elements extraction based on finite state matching machine to meet these challenges. We integrate the max-matching principal and negative words processing into the unified framework. In addition, we built a set of rules to determine whether a feature-opinion pair is reasonable and filter it out if not. With our framework, the precision of emotional elements extraction has been improved a lot, with a much lower extraction redundancy. Furthermore, the unified framework is flexible enough to add new rules to deal with more complex customer reviews, such as reviews containing comparative forms or adverbs of degree. In this work, we also evaluate the performance of our framework in detail over various aspects.

3   Emotional Resource Construction

In this work, we use the method proposed in [7] to construct emotional resources. Then with the constructed emotional resource, we implement our unified framework for emotional elements extraction and evaluate its performance.

In the method proposed in [7], the emotional resource constitutes of various feature-opinion pairs attached with the corresponding sentiment polarity. The method mainly consists of three steps: feature words extraction, opinion words extraction and sentiment polarity labeling of feature-opinion pairs. In the step of feature words extraction, the method extracts a set of feature word candidates based on part of speech rules. In this step, the method also takes the words out of vocabulary into consideration. It then filters noise feature words from the candidate set based on their co-occurrence with adjective words and their frequencies in background corpus. In the second step, the method extracts opinion words based on part of speech, statistics information and word dependencies. In the last step, namely the sentiment polarity labeling of feature-opinion pairs, the method takes context and the distance between tagged feature-opinion pairs with untagged feature-opinion words into consideration.

In addition, it also uses global information to calculate the sentiment score of each feature-opinion pair iteratively.

In this work, our main consideration is not the process of emotional resource construction. In fact, we used the method in [7] to construct an emotional resource directly, and further use it to implement our unified framework for emotional elements extraction. Our framework for emotional elements extraction is introduced in the following section.

4   The Unified Framework Based on Finite State Matching Machine

In our framework, the process of emotional elements extraction is divided into 3 steps: Matching, Extracting and Filtering. In the first step, emotional elements matching, each review is mapped into a list of feature words, opinion words and negative adverbs, which are sorted by the order in which they occur in the original review. In the second step, the list will be the input of the finite state machine. We will find out the feature-opinion pairs according to the context and the sentiment lexicon. In addition the sentiment polarity of each pair is also determined in this step. Then in the last step, our framework judges the legality of each feature-opinion pair.

4.1   Emotional Elements Matching

Using traditional methods based on string matching for emotional elements extraction, there is much extracting redundancy in the results. For example, for the customer review "电视画面非常清楚(The TV picture is very clear)", there are four feature-opinion pairs matched in the sentiment lexicon, which are "画面|清楚(picture | clear)", "画面|清(picture | clear)", "电视画面|清楚(TV picture | clear)" and "电视画面|清(TV picture | clear)". Traditional methods based on string matching would extract all of the four feature-opinion pairs as emotional elements, which would bring about redundancy in feature-opinion pair extraction.

In order to solve the problem of extracting redundancy, we use the max-matching principle, which requires that the emotional elements would choose the max-length feature words and max-length opinion words if multiple feature or opinion words can be extracted. However, by taking advantage of the max-matching principle, we just extract "电视画面|清楚(TV picture | clear)" as the only emotional element.

Dealing with negative adverbs plays an important role in emotional elements extraction. A negative adverb could invert the sentiment of a review. In our framework, we build a list of words, which contains many popular negative adverbs, such as "不是(not)", "没有(without)", "不够(not enough)" and "不(no)", etc. At the same time, we notice that there exist words that are not negative as a whole, but part of them may be negative adverbs. For example, "不是一般(not a little)" does not represent a negative sentiment, but "不是(not)", which is a part of it, is exactly a negative adverb. As a result, we build a whitelist of words, which are not regarded as negative adverbs, such as "不是一般(not a little)", "差不多(almost)" and so on.

By now, we have built three resources, which are sentiment lexicon, the list of negative adverbs and the negative adverbs whitelist. In the following parts, we will introduce the process of extracting emotional elements using these resources. In order to guarantee the precision of emotional elements extraction, we deal with these three resources in the order of negative adverbs whitelist, sentiment lexicon and the list of negative adverbs. For each customer review, the process of extracting emotion elements from it is like this:

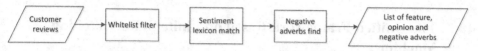

Fig. 1. Matching Process of Emotional elements

Each step in the figure above follows the max-matching principle. After the matching process of emotional elements, a review will be mapped into a list of feature words, opinion words and negative adverbs sorted by the order in the original review. For example, the review "画质不是一般的不清晰(The picture quality is not a little lack of clarity)" will be mapped into the list of words "画质(picture quality, feature word)", "不(not, negative adverb)" and "清晰(clarity, opinion word)", which is the input of the finite state machine in the next section.

4.2   Emotional Elements Extraction

For the purpose of judging whether a feature word and an opinion word is a pair according to the context, we design a finite state matching machine, which uses the resulting list of words in the previous step as input. The finite state matching machine is showed as follows:

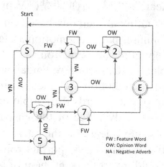

Fig. 2. The Finite State Matching Machine

When we design the finite state machine, we made two assumptions: 1) negative adverbs only occur in the front of opinion words or other correct negative adverbs; 2) when a user makes a review about more than one feature, he or she will put all the opinion words either in the front or in the back of the feature words. For example, a user may say "价格实惠画面也很清楚 (the price is reasonable and the picture is clear)", instead of "价格实惠且有清晰的画面 (The price is reasonable and the TV has a clear picture)". The two assumptions are in line with most of the user habits.

Our machine can deal with various complex conditions, such as the cases where one review contains more than one feature words, opinion words and negative adverbs. Using the list from step 1, the machine begins from state S and transforms its state according to the nature of words (feature, opinion or negative adverbs) in the list. When reaching the final state E, we get one or more than one feature-opinion pair(s). In the third step, we will further judge the legality of these feature-opinion pairs. We use the following three examples to make the process clearer:

1. The review "颜色鲜艳但是音效不是很好 (The color is bright but the sound effect is not very good)" contains feature words "颜色 (color)" and "音效 (sound effect)", opinion words "鲜艳 (bright)" and "好 (good)" and negative adverb "不是 (not)"; the process for this is S→1→ 2→E→1→3→2→E.

2. The review "不合理的价格 (It is not a reasonable price)" contains feature word "价格 (price)", opinion word "合理 (reasonable)" and negative adverb "不 (not)"; the process is S→5→6→7→E.

3. The review "时尚大方的外观 (Stylish and elegant appearance)" contains feature word "外观 (appearance)" and opinion words "时尚 (stylish)" and "大方 (elegant)"; the process is S→6→6→7→E.

4.3 Emotional Elements Filtering Based on Rules

There are still some errors in emotional elements extraction after the two steps introduced before, due to the fact that customer reviews are usually very colloquial and flexible. For example, "京东的售后服务真的很棒 (The service of JingDong is really great)" will be extracted into two feature-opinion pairs, which are "服务|真 (service | really)" and "服务|棒 (service | good)", where "服务|真 (services | really)" is not a correct pair. As a result, we build a set of rules to judge whether a feature-opinion pair is legal or not. We take four factors into consideration, which are the following:

1. The order of feature word and opinion word. There are some opinion words which could occur both in the front and in the back of a feature word, for example, "画面清楚 (the picture is clear)" an "清楚的画面 (clear picture)" are both legal. However, some opinion words can only occur either in the front or in the back, for example, people say "使用复杂 (complex usability)", and seldom do they say "复杂使用 (usability complex)".

2. The length of opinion words. The shorter an opinion word is, the more likely it's a part of another phrase. For example, "大 (big)" is a part of "强大(powerful)".

3. The distance between feature words and opinion words. Generally speaking, people tend to put opinion words close to feature words when writing a review. For example, people prefer saying "价格实惠 (The price is reasonable)" directly to inserting many other words between "价格 (price)" and "实惠 (reasonable)".

4. The probability that a feature word and an opinion word is a pair. We use the frequency of co-occurrence of a feature word and an opinion word to measure this probability, which is counted when constructing the sentiment lexicon.

Taking the four factors into consideration, the process of judging whether a feature-opinion pair is legal or not is shown in the following pseudo code:

```
Boolean Accept (FeatureWord, OpinionWord)
IF FeatureWord Occurs Before OpinionWord:
    IF (BeforeTime == 0) OR (Distance > ReviewLength/2 AND BeforeTime < β AND
    OpinionLength==1):
        RETURN False
ELSE:
    IF AfterTime==0 AND OpinionLength <3 AND (BeforeTime < γ OR Distance >
    ReviewLength/2):
        RETURN False
RETURN True
```

In the pseudo code, "BeforeTime" and "AfterTime" represent the times when the feature word occurs before and after the opinion word, correspondingly. "Distance" represents the distance between the feature and the opinion word. "ReviewLength" and "OpinionLength" indicate the length of the whole review and the opinion word. "β" and "γ" are two thresholds, which should be adjusted according to the size of the corpus used to construct the sentiment lexicon. We set $\beta=10$, $\gamma=5$ in our framework.

Now we give the whole procedure of our framework below (F-O: feature-opinion):

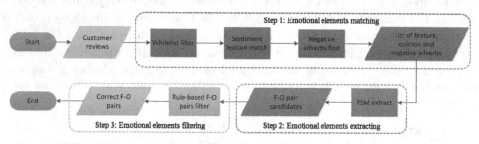

Fig. 3. Diagram of the whole framework for emotional elements extraction

We will process each customer review following the three steps above strictly. A feature-opinion pair is extracted if and only if the function "Accept" in the third step returns "True". If the function "Accept" returns "False" or the finite state machine fails to transform from one state to another, we regard these as wrong feature-opinion pairs and ignore them.

Compared with the traditional method based on string matching, our framework not only achieves a high precision, but also lowers the redundancy a lot in emotional elements extraction. In the next section, we will evaluate the effect in detail.

5   Evaluation for the Unified Framework

5.1   Data Preparation

We crawled 65549 customer reviews of 340 television products from TaoBao and JingDong. These reviews are mainly about five TV brands, which are Samsung, LG, Hisense, TCL and Skyworth. There are 263 smart television products and 77 non-smart television products. We randomly selected 80% of these reviews and used them to construct our emotional resource, resulting in a sentiment lexicon with 3800 entries in smart television domain. Each entry contains a feature-opinion pair and a the corresponding sentiment polarity, for example, "{1} 画面|细腻({1} Picture | smooth)" indicating that feature word "画面(Picture)" has a positive sentiment when described by the opinion word "细腻(smooth)". The remaining 20% of the user reviews is used to test the performance of our framework for emotional element extraction.

5.2   Accuracy of Emotional Elements Extraction

Based on the sentiment lexicon and the remaining 20% of customer reviews, we evaluated the performance of emotional elements extraction of our framework. In this section, we make a comparison among the following three methods:

1. **TSM (Traditional String Matching)**: this is the traditional method for emotional element extraction, which extracts all the feature-opinion pairs that occur in both the sentiment lexicon and the reviews.
2. **FSMM (Finite State Matching Machine)**: this method is our framework without the third step of rule-based feature-opinion pair filtering. A feature-opinion pair is extracted as long as the finite state matching machine reaches the final state.
3. **TUF (The Unified Framework)**: this method is our final unified framework. Compared with the method of FSMM, rule-based feature-opinion pairs judging and filtering technic is added into the method of TUF.

We run the experiment three times independently for the purpose of more accurate evaluation. In each experiment, we randomly selected 10% of customer reviews from the remaining 20% user reviews. Then we use the three methods above to extract emotional elements. At last, we manually annotated each emotional element into three categories, which are explained below (M=1 means the feature-opinion pair is matched correctly and P=1 means the polarity labeling is conducted correctly):

— **M=1, P=1**: Both feature-opinion pair matching and polarity labeling is correct. For example, "价格|实惠 (price | reasonable)" is extracted from "电视价格实惠 (Price of the TV is reasonable)", and the polarity is labeled as positive.
— **M=1, P=0**: The feature-opinion pair matching is correct, but the polarity is labeled incorrectly. For example, "使用|满意 (usability | satisfactory)" is extracted form "电视使用满意 (usability of the TV is satisfactory)", which is a correct feature-opinion pair, but the sentiment polarity is labeled as negative.

— **M=0:** The feature-opinion pair matching is incorrect, no matter whether the polarity is correct or incorrect. For example, "服务|真 (service | really)" is extracted from "服务真不错 (the service is really good)".

We annotated 14932 emotional elements in total, and calculated the proportion of each category in each run. The results are shown below:

Table 1. Accuracy of emotional elements extraction

Run No.	Method	M=1, P=1	M=1, P=0	M=0
1	TSM	0.5880	0.0619	0.3501
	FSMM	0.8088	0.0416	0.1496
	TUF	**0.8392**	**0.0407**	**0.1201**
2	TSM	0.6080	0.0654	0.3266
	FSMM	0.8238	**0.0421**	0.1341
	TUF	**0.8404**	0.0436	**0.1160**
3	TSM	0.6062	0.0629	0.3309
	FSMM	0.8241	**0.0453**	0.1306
	TUF	**0.8405**	0.0465	**0.1130**

In our experiments, we regard the category of M=1, P=1 as correct extractions. We can see that FSMM and TUF can achieve much higher accuracies in this category compared with TSM. Compared with TSM, FSMM increases the extracting accuracy by 23.4% at most and lowers the proportion of incorrect matching by about 20%. Compared with FSMM, we see that in the unified framework (TUF), the rule-based feature-opinion pairs filtering technique can further reduce the matching error rate, which contributes to the improvement of accuracy.

In addition, the unified framework we proposed reduces the emotional elements extraction redundancy, and has a good performance in negative adverbs processing. We evaluate the performance in these two aspects respectively next.

5.3   Reduce the Redundancy of Emotional Element Extraction

Many redundant emotional elements may be extracted using traditional methods based on string matching. The unified framework we proposed has a good effect in reducing redundancy, some typical examples are shown as follows:

1. **Example 1:** If we use traditional methods, the customer review "功能强大 (the function is powerful)" will be extracted as "功能|强大 (function | powerful)", "功能|强 (function | strong)" and "功能|大 (function | big)"; but in our framework, only "功能|强大 (function | powerful)" will be extracted because it meets the max-matching principle.
2. **Example 2:** For the review "亮度好价格也很低 (brightness is good and price is low too)", four feature-opinion pairs are extracted using traditional method, which are "亮度|好 (brightness |good)", "价格|低 (price | low)", "亮度|低 (brightness |

low)" and "价格|好 (price | good)", which contains two redundant pairs. However, only "亮度|好 (brightness | good)" and "价格|低 (price | low)" are extracted using our unified framework, because in our finite state matching machine, a feature-opinion pair will not be re-extracted as long as it reaches the final state.

As a result, the unified framework for emotional elements extraction based on finite state matching machine can not only reduce redundancy (Example 1), but also reduce the number of incorrect extractions (Example 2).

Furthermore, we counted the number of emotional elements extracted using different methods in each experiment. To compare with the traditional method TSM, we calculated the *Redundancy Reduction Rate* for method FSMM and TUF. The *Redundancy Reduction Rate* is defined as $R = (\#\mathrm{E} - \#\mathrm{E}') / \#E$, where #E represents the number of emotional elements extracted using TSM, and #E' represents the number of emotional elements using FSMM or TUF. The result is shown in Table 2 below:

Table 2. Redundancy Reduction Rate using different methods

	Experiment 1			Experiment 2			Experiment 3		
	TSM	FSMM	TUF	TSM	FSMM	TUF	TSM	FSMM	TUF
#E/#E'	2211	1517	1449	2033	1447	1397	2034	1455	1389
R	--	31.4%	34.5%	--	28.8%	31.3%	--	28.5%	31.3%

From the result above, we see that redundant emotional elements extracted can be reduced a lot using the unified framework we proposed. Compared with TSM, FSMM reduced the redundancy by 31.4% at most and TUF reduced by 34.5% at most. The underlying reason is that the max-matching principle made it possible to extract only the feature-opinion pairs of maximum length, which are most likely to be correct.

5.4   Evaluation of Negative Adverbs Processing

The traditional methods for emotional elements extraction based on string matching cannot deal with negative adverbs well, as they usually cannot take advantage of the rich context information of negative adverbs in customer reviews. In our framework, negative adverbs processing can be easily integrated into the finite state matching machine. With the context information provided by the finite state machine, we achieved good performance in negative adverbs processing. For example, "功能确实不少 (The functions are not few indeed)" can be relabeled as positive from negative by considering the negative adverb "不(not)".

In addition, the number of feature-opinion pairs whose polarities are changed by taking negative adverbs into consideration in our unified framework is 2290; and the accuracy of these changes is 88.6%.

Furthermore, we noticed that the polarities of some entries in the sentiment lexicon are labeled incorrectly, although the feature-opinion pairs extracted are correct. In order to evaluate the pure performance of negative adverbs processing, we made an evaluation under the hypothesis that the polarities are always correct, although it is not true for some entries. Following this hypothesis, if the negative adverbs processing gives a correct sentiment invert, we annotate it as M=1 and P=1, regardless of whether the polarity itself is correct or not. We randomly selected 10% of the reviews containing negative adverbs at each time and conducted three times of evaluation independently, the results are shown in the table below:

Table 3. Evaluation results of negative adverbs processing

Experiment No.	Use the hypothesis?	M=1,P=1	M=1,P=0	M=0
No.1 (394 reviews)	No	0.8219	0.0585	0.1196
	Yes	0.8626	0.0178	0.1196
No.2 (351 reviews)	No	0.8429	0.0429	0.1142
	Yes	0.8629	0.0229	0.1142
No.3 (347 reviews)	No	0.8353	0.0434	0.1213
	Yes	0.8671	0.0116	0.1213

The performance of negative adverbs processing without the hypothesis is satisfactory, which is similar to the overall performance in Table 1. This indicates that our framework performs well in terms of stability. On the other hand, under the hypothesis that the sentiment polarities are always correct in the sentiment lexicon, the precision of negative adverbs processing is more than 86%, which is about a 2% increase from that without the hypothesis. It indicates that if the quality of the sentiment lexicon were better, our unified framework would also achieve better performance, which is in good consistency with sentiment lexicon construction techniques used.

Note that, although we used many methods to improve the performance of emotional elements extraction, the proportion of emotional elements extracted where M=0, namely the incorrect extractions, is still about 10%. After analyzing the bad cases, we find that most of them are in need of leveraging semantic and knowledge information to 'understand' the meaning of a user review correctly, such as "价格当当最便宜 (The price of DangDang is the lowest)". As a result, future attempt would be devoted to the use of semantic and knowledge information in our framework to further enhance the performance of emotional elements extraction.

6   Conclusion

In this work, we proposed a unified framework based on finite state matching machine for emotional elements extraction. We integrated max-matching principle and negative adverbs processing into the framework. Furthermore, the framework leverages rule-based methods to filter out illegitimate feature-opinion pairs. Compared with traditional methods, the framework achieves high accuracy and scalability in emotional elements extraction. In addition, the framework has a good scalability in which one can easily integrate new rules to deal with more complex customer reviews. Sophisticated evaluation and experiments verified both the effect and efficiency of our framework.

In the future work, we would add more rules to our emotional elements extraction framework in order to deal with more complex reviews, such as reviews containing comparative forms or adverbs of degree. Furthermore, we would introduce semantic and knowledge information into our framework to further enhance the performance of our framework.

References

1. 中国互联网络信息中心(CNNIC). 第31次中国互联网络发展状况统计报告 1 (2013), http://www.cnnic.cn/hlwfzyj/hlwxzbg/hlwtjbg/201301/P020130122600399530412.pdf
2. Yu, H., Hatzivassiloglou, V.: Towards answering opinion questions: Separating facts from opinions and identifying the polarity of opinion sentences. In: Proceedings of the 2003 Conference on Empirical Methods in Natural Language Processing, pp. 129–136. Association for Computational Linguistics (2003)
3. Ku, L.W., Liang, Y.T., Chen, H.H.: Opinion extraction, summarization and tracking in news and blog corpora. In: Proceedings of AAAI-2006 Spring Symposium on Computational Approaches to Analyzing Weblogs (2001, 2006)
4. Dave, K., Lawrence, S., Pennock, D.M.: Mining the peanut gallery: Opinion extraction and semantic classification of product reviews. In: Proceedings of the 12th International Conference on World Wide Web, pp. 519–528. ACM (2003)
5. Kim, S.M., Hovy, E.: Determining the sentiment of opinions. In: Proceedings of the 20th International Conference on Computational Linguistics, p. 1367. Association for Computational Linguistics (2004)
6. Liu, B., Hu, M., Cheng, J.: Opinion observer: analyzing and comparing opinions on the Web. In: Proceedings of the 14th International Conference on World Wide Web, pp. 342–351. ACM (2005)
7. 李智超，面向互联网评论的情感资源构建及应用研究. 北京：清华大学计算机科学与技术系， 4 (2011)
8. Hu, M., Liu, B.: Mining opinion features in customer reviews. In: Proceedings of the National Conference on Artificial Intelligence, pp. 755–760. AAAI Press, MIT Press, Menlo Park, Cambridge (1999, 2004)
9. Hu, M., Liu, B.: Mining and summarizing customer reviews. In: Proceedings of the Tenth ACM SIGKDD International Conference on Knowledge Discovery and Data Mining, pp. 168–177. ACM (2004)
10. Popescu, A.M., Etzioni, O.: Extracting product features and opinions from reviews. In: Natural Language Processing and Text Mining, pp. 9–28. Springer, Heidelberg (2007)
11. Hiroshi, K., Tetsuya, N., Hideo, W.: Deeper sentiment analysis using machine translation technology. In: Proceedings of the 20th International Conference on Computational Linguistics, p. 494. Association for Computational Linguistics (2004)

Structure-Based Web Access Method for Ancient Chinese Characters

Xiaoqing Lu[1], Yingmin Tang[1], Zhi Tang[1], Yujun Gao[2,3], and Jianguo Zhang[2,4]

[1] Institute of Computer Science and Technology, Peking University, Beijing, 100871, China
[2] Beijing Founder Electronics Co., Ltd., Beijing, 100085, China
[3] Center for Chinese Font Design and Research, Beijing, 100871, China
[4] State Key Laboratory of Digital Publishing Technology
(Peking University Founder Group Co., Ltd.), 100871, Beijing, China
{lvxiaoqing,tangyingmin,tangzhi}@pku.edu.cn,
{gao_yujun,zjg}@founder.com

Abstract. How to preserve and make use of ancient Chinese characters is not only a mission to contemporary scientists but is also a technical challenge. This paper proposes a feasible solution to enable character collection, management, and access on the Internet. Its advantage lies in a unified representation for encoded and uncoded characters that provide a visual convenient and efficient retrieval method that does not require new users to have any prior knowledge about ancient Chinese characters. We also design a system suitable for describing the relationships between ancient Chinese characters and contemporary ones. As the implementation result, a website is established for public access to ancient Chinese characters.

Keywords: Ancient Characters, Digital Heritage, Web Access.

1   Background

Ancient Chinese Characters (ACCs) represent an important heritage of Chinese history, which contains rich cultural information and serves as a basis for contemporary research tracing the evolution of modern characters. However, the origin and development of Chinese characters (also referred to as Han characters, Han ideographs, or Hanzis) are not one-dimensional. We see increasing numbers of score marks left on cultural relics of the New Stone Age, as they are unearthed one after another (Fig.1). We come to understand that it has taken a long and complicated process to arrive at the Chinese characters in use today.

The ancient characters studied here date back to at least 3300 year-old oracle-bone inscriptions that have some correlation to modern characters. Researchers have collected more than 4500 different characters from oracle-bone inscriptions, many that are variations of the same character. Other characters such as those of ancient seals are confined in a limited space and lack context for systematic study. The largest number of relics is the newly unearthed Qin and Chu collection of bamboo slips that contain very large quantities of texts related to the Warring States Period.

G. Zhou et al. (Eds.): NLPCC 2013, CCIS 400, pp. 72–82, 2013.
© Springer-Verlag Berlin Heidelberg 2013

Fig. 1. Types of ACC: oracle-bone inscriptions, bronze inscription, ancient seal, bamboo slip

Despite the abundance of modern computer fonts, input methods, and word processing software, these tools do not suffice to duplicate the ancient characters. There are three principal reasons why it is difficult to decode ancient characters.

First, the research of ACCs involves very large quantities of modern characters. Although the number of ancient characters we have collected to date is limited, most of them represent sources for modern characters. Their relationships are complicated, including one-to-many, many-to-one, and many-to-many modes. To understand the exact meanings of ancient characters and their relationships with modern characters, we necessarily resort to a set of sufficient modern characters. However, the management of modern Chinese characters itself is a great challenge, as most of them are rarely-used. In 2012, Unicode 6.2 had totally encoded 75,215 Han characters [20], including seven main blocks of the Unicode Standard, as shown in Table 1. The term "CJK"—Chinese, Japanese, and Korean—is used in Unicode scripts to describe the languages that currently use Han ideographic characters.

Table 1. Han character encoded in Unicode 6.2

Block	Range	Comment
CJK Unified Ideographs	4E00–9FFF	common
Extension A	3400–4DBF	Rare
Extension B	20000–2A6DF	Rare, historic
Extension C	2A700–2B73F	Rare, historic
Extension D	2B740–2B81F	Uncommon, some in current use
Compatibility	F900–FAFF	Duplicates, unifiable variants, corporate characters
Compatibility Supplement	2F800–2FA1F	Unifiable variants

Lack of software code is a second problem in the research of ACCs. Today's information technology primarily focuses on modern characters, and provides little or no support for ancient characters. Software such as the GB code for China's mainland, the BIG5 code for Hong Kong and Taiwan, or Unicode for international practices, assigns a digital identity to each modern Chinese character so that each character is easily distinguished from another during processing of data streams. Because any coding system is limited by space requirements, none of the above systems is very useful in describing the entire character set of ACCs. The deep-rooted reason causing encoding difficulty is that the glyphs of ACCs vary in structure and stroke styles due to a lack of established rules, so that early ACCs have no fixed form, and one character generally has more than one shape. For instance, each of the characters of the oracle-bone inscriptions, in particular, proves to be precious due to their rarity. To further complicate matters, a single character has various forms (Fig 2). Preservation of the multiple styles used to depict characters adds to the difficulty in digitalizing Ancient Characters.

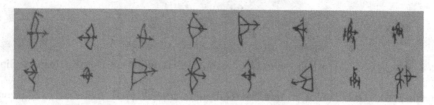

Fig. 2. An oracle-bone character "she (射)" represented by several different glyphs

Without reasonable codes, it is almost impossible to input ACCs directly into a computer, let alone support management and research requiring advanced IT technology. In fact, most contemporary research on ancient characters relies on ambiguous codes corresponding to modern characters.

Last, but not least, traditional IMEs (input method editors) do not have the capability to reproduce ACCs. These IMEs emphasize a high precision rate of character lookup by a short symbol sequence. Most of them require users to have some knowledge regarding a wanted character, such as its pronunciation, shape, or meaning. Most users will not be able to input an ACC using these IMEs, because users are not familiar with ACCs, or encoding schemes cannot guarantee the right relationship between an ACC and its counterparts in many cases. In contrast to IMEs, a practical ACC lookup service should provide users with a higher recall even for rarely used ACCs present in a very large list of candidates.

In recent years, computer technology has shown progress in applications for the study of ancient characters. In 1993, Xusheng Ji completed the electronic version "Index for Individual Characters of Bronze Inscription". In 1994, Ning Li[1] comprehensively presented some general principles for computational research of Chinese writing system. In 1996, Fangzheng Chen of the Institute of Chinese Studies, the Chinese University of Hong Kong, began the set up of a computer database for oracle-bone inscriptions, and carried out adjustment, classification, numbering, and merging of oracle bone inscriptions. Peirong Huang researched into and applied an ancient character font database. The "Statistics and analysis system for structures of Chinese characters" was established by Zaixing Zhang et al.[2], Che Wah Ho's ancient text database in Hong Kong and Derming Juang's Digital Library in Taiwan are all applicable for ancient characters classification. Zhiji Liu[3,4] conducted an investigation of the collation of glyphs of ancient writings. Minghu Jiang[5] presented a constructive method for word-base construction through syntax analysis of oracle-bone inscriptions. Derming Juang et al. [6] proposed an approach consisting of a glyph expression model, a glyph structure database, and supporting tools to resolve uncoded characters. Yi Zhuang et al. [7] proposed an interactive partial-distance map (PDM) - based high-dimensional indexing scheme to speed up the retrieval performance of large Chinese calligraphic character databases. James S. Kirk et al. [8] used self-organizing map methods to address the problem of identifying an unknown Chinese character by its visual features. Furthermore, to input ACCs by handwriting recognition is also feasible. Dan Chen et al. [9] proposed a method for on-line character recognition based on the analysis of ancient character features.

However, there is yet to be a management and search system for ancient characters open for public use in a network environment. Hence the ancient characters system proposed in this article intends to meet the requirements as follows: Design a digital resource pool of ancient characters for network applications; Search for an ancient character form corresponding to a modern character; Search for rare characters such as those beyond the scope of GBK code or even those without a correlative modern character; Search through multiple channels, by font, Unicode, phonetic, or other information.

On the above basis, we can build an academic exchange platform on the Internet that overcomes retrieval time and limited space issues and provides more extensive network services to high-profile designers, scholars studying Chinese heritage, philology research fellows, and amateurs.

2   Formalization of Relationships between ACCs and Modern Characters

To systematically manage ancient characters and provide a network service, we must clearly define and reasonably describe character classification. The latest computer technology can be employed to achieve the above-mentioned objective.

Ancient characters are divided into three categories:

Z1: Recognized characters
This refers to characters that have been studied and interpreted, and are recognized by the academic community. We can find the corresponding relationships of most of these characters with their contemporary Chinese characters. Therefore, contemporary Chinese characters can be used as an index to retrieve the glyphs of corresponding ancient characters.

It must be pointed out that quite a number of recognized glyphs are polysemous characters. In other words, the character pattern, structure, stroke, and shape of the characters are not completely the same, so they might represent different meanings that generally reflect variations of time and location such as different eras and countries.

Z2: Ambiguous characters
This refers to the characters that are provided with multi-conclusions from textual research and are not recognized unanimously by the academic community.

The index of ambiguous characters should be strongly compatible, that is, these characters should be searchable based on different information obtained from textual research. Therefore, when choosing the representative words for ambiguous characters, we must identify and distinguish them in terms of character pattern, usage, and context.

Z3: Unrecognized characters

This refers to characters that have not been defined through textual research. Such ancient characters are numerous, and have no identified correlation with contemporary Chinese characters. Therefore, special codes or symbols are necessary for indexing purposes.

As a result, we briefly state the following definitions:

$$A = \{a_1, a_2, \ldots a_n\} \tag{1}$$

A refers to the collection of existing encoded Chinese characters, a_i refers to a certain Chinese character, and i is the total number of encoded records, $i = 1, 2, \ldots n$.

$$B = \{b_1, b_2, \ldots b_m\} \tag{2}$$

B refers to the collection of marks for uncoded Chinese characters, b_j refers to a certain mark, and j is the total number of uncoded records, $j = 1, 2, \ldots m$.

The ACCs can be divided into two parts X and Y.

$$X = X_1 \cup X_2 \ldots \cup X_n \tag{3}$$

X refers to the collection of ACCs bearing corresponding relationships with contemporary encoded characters, where,

$$X_i = \{x_1, x_2, \ldots x_p\}. \tag{4}$$

X_i refers to an ACC set corresponding to a certain contemporary character. $x_k, k = 1, 2, \ldots p$ refers to a certain ACC that mainly belongs to recognized characters or ambiguous characters $\langle x_k \in Z_1 | x_k \in Z_2 \rangle$

$$Y = Y_1 \cup Y_2 \ldots \cup Y_m \tag{5}$$

Y refers to the collection of ACCs bearing no corresponding relationships with the contemporary encoded characters, where,

$$Y_j = \{y_1, y_2, \ldots y_q\}. \tag{6}$$

y_l, $l = 1, 2, \ldots q$ refers to a certain ACC that mainly belongs to one unrecognized character($y_l \in Z_3$). Y_j refers to the collection of unrecognized characters.

All ACCs that can be collected and sorted out are expressed by $Z = X \cup Y$.

The primary information expected to be used in the ancient character system is the collection of existing encoded Chinese characters and their corresponding ACCs, expressed by,

$$U = \left\{ (a_1, X_1), (a_2, X_2), \ldots (a_n, X_n) \right\}. \tag{7}$$

As for the uncoded ACCs, the corresponding relationships can be fulfilled by borrowing uncoded Chinese character marks or self-defined codes, so they can be processed together with encoded Chinese characters. This relation can be described as follows:

$$V = \left\{ (b_1, Y_1), (b_2, Y_2), \ldots (b_m, Y_m) \right\}. \tag{8}$$

Based on this model, the key to the follow-up processing of ACCs is to establish the information base that can store the U and V collections, and simultaneously provide the correct search method based on contemporary Chinese characters a_i or mark b_j.

3   Establishment of Super Large Font

As accessing ACCs relies heavily on sufficient modern characters, we need to establish a super large font to depict modern characters. However, the traditional process of font design is time-consuming and costly, including but not limited to creating basic strokes with the new style, composing radicals, and constructing characters. To speed up font creation, various innovative technologies have been developed to allow creation of new characters based on sample characters [21-26].

We have also focused on the automatic generation of Chinese characters for many years and proposed several methods [27-30]. Take the problem of deformation of stroke thickness and serif for example, as shown in Fig. 3; we adopt a distortionless resizing method for composing Chinese characters based on their components. By using a transformation sequence generating algorithm and a stroke operation algorithm, this method can generate the target glyph by an optimized scaling transformation.

(a)   (b)

Fig. 3. Typical problems in recomposing Chinese characters. (a) Adjustment of radicals; (b) Resizing of strokes.

To establish reasonable relationships between ACCs and modern characters, an intensive analysis of their structures is necessary. First, a set of rules regarding glyph structure decomposition is defined. Next, the hierarchical relationship of strokes and radicals is represented by a framework. Generally speaking, most radicals are basic components that will not be decomposed. However, some radicals are compound components, and contain multiple basic components and possibly additional strokes. Consequently, the structural decomposition of a glyph may not be limited to only one possible decomposition. To provide users with more convenience, the redundant expressions of glyph structures are permitted in our system. Furthermore, an algorithm is designed to classify the characters by their multi-level radicals and to calculate the number of corresponding strokes.

4   ACC Database

Based on the in-depth and comprehensive organization of Chinese characters, particularly by considering the varied information on ancient characters, the ACC database is effectively designed.

4.1   Relation Schema

Management of ACCs should integrate the code and related information, so we define the main relation schema in Table 2.

Table 2. Relation schema of ACC database (ACC_RS)

Item	Meaning
Unicode	Contemporary Chinese character Unicode for this ancient character.
Dynasty	Dynasty when this ancient character was used.
Type	Type of this ancient character (e.g. pictographic characters, ideograph, and phonogram)
Classification	Class type of this ancient character (e.g. inscriptions on bones or tortoise shells of the Shang Dynasty, inscriptions on bronze, seal character, etc.)
Place	Contemporary place where this ancient character was unearthed.
Carrier	Carrier of this ancient character (e.g. the name or the number of a certain bronze implement)
Country	Ancient country where this ancient character was used.
SubbaseID	Number of the font database storing this ancient character.
SubID	Code of the ancient character, used in sub-font database.
Filename	File name for the picture of this ancient character.
ID	The unique ID of this ancient character in the font database.

Other relation schemas we used include: Dynasty and Country (DC_RS), Ancient C_Character Classification (ACCC_RS), ACC Type (ACCT_RS), Unicode and Glyph (UG_RS), Radical and Component (RC_RS), Ancient Image (AI_RS), Contemporary Image (CI_RS).

To edit, sort, and manage the information of the ancient characters effectively, all tables are organized properly, and their relationships are shown in Fig. 4.

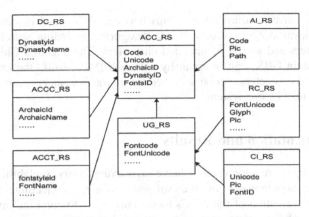

Fig. 4. Relationships of the data tables

4.2 Query and Browse Method

As Fig. 5 shows, a special engine, glyph tree is used to show characters not present in GBK code.

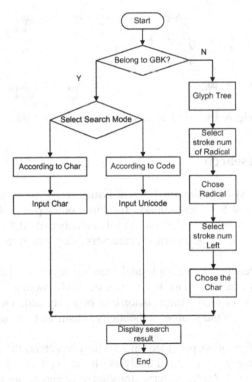

Fig. 5. Flow chart of the search process

Based on the corresponding relationships between ACCs and contemporary characters, the retrieval system consists of two categories, including search of encoded
Chinese characters and search of uncoded characters. The encoded Chinese characters, such as within GBK, can be input by common IMEs, while the rare characters
and unrecognized characters can be searched by interactive query methods with special glyphs provided by our system.

5   Implementation and Results

Several technologies are adopted to achieve high extensibility, scalability, and main-
tainability. The development of the software system, collecting, editing, and
processing the information of the ACCs took many years to combine into a comprehensive system. The search function is now available, and users can look up the
glyphs of old Chinese characters from our website (http://efont.foundertype.com/
AgentModel/FontOldQ.aspx). Fig. 6 shows the search results for the Chinese character Ma (马), yielding a number of possible ACCs related to it.

Fig. 6. The search results for the character Ma (马).

6   Further Research

In terms of the ACC system, the most urgent issues so far are how to present the information of ACCs that have lost connection with contemporary Chinese characters
(the V collection previously mentioned). As this category of ACCs cannot be backed
up by the corresponding contemporary characters, they are rarely displayed in the
computer system.

Furthermore, to benefit more people and increase academic interaction, the platform needs to be accessed by more users, experts, and scholars. Any newly discovered ancient characters or useful information can be easily added to the platform, and
we can exchange ideas on the source, authenticity, identification, and interpretation of
these characters.

With the basic information provided on ancient characters, the public can use the
system to make an in-depth study and analysis on the evolution of ancient characters
and their connection to character patterns, thus actively enhancing the cognation analysis of ACCs, radical classification and arrangement, as well as automatic analysis of
the commonly confused words.

Acknowledgment. This work is supported by Beijing Natural Science Foundation (No. 4132033).

References

1. Li, N.: Computational Research of Chinese Writing System Han4-Zi4. Literary and Linguistic Computing 9(3), 225–234 (1994)
2. Zhang, Z.-X.: On Some Issues of the Establishment of Ancient Chinese Font. Journal of Chinese Information Processing 17(6), 60–66 (2003)
3. Liu, Z.-J.: Investigation into the Collation of Glyphs of Ancient Writings for Computer Processing. Applied Linguistics No 4, 120–123 (2004)
4. Liu, Z.-J.: Encoding Ancient Chinese Characters with Unicode and the Construction of Standard Digital Platform. Journal of Hangzhou Teachers College 29(6), 37–40 (2007)
5. Jiang, M.-H.: Construction on Word-base of Oracle-Bone Inscriptions and its Intelligent Repository. Computer Engineering and Applications 40(4), 45–48 (2004)
6. Juang, D., Wang, J.H., Lai, C.Y., Hsieh, C.C., Chien, L.H., Ho, J.M.: Resolving the Unencoded Character Problem for Chinese Digital Libraries. In: Proceedings of the 5th ACM/IEEE-CS Joint Conference on Digital Libraries, JCDL 2005, pp. 311–319. ACM, Denver (2005)
7. Zhuang, Y., Zhuang, Y.-T., Li, Q., Chen, L.: Interactive High-Dimensional Index for Large Chinese Calligraphic Character Databases. ACM Transactions on Asian Language Information Processing 6(2), 8-es (2007)
8. Kirk, J.S.: Chinese Character Identification by Visual Features Using Self-Organizing Map Sets and Relevance Feedback. In: IEEE International Joint Conference on Neural Networks, pp. 3216–3221 (2008)
9. Chen, D., Li, N., Li, L.: Online recognition of ancient characters. Journal of Beijing Institute of Machinery 23(4), 32–37 (2008)
10. Allen, J.D., Becker, J., et al.: The Unicode Consortium. The Unicode Standard, Version 5.0. Addison-Wesley, Boston (2006)
11. Zhuang, Y.-T., Zhang, X.-F., Wu, J.-Q., Lu, X.-Q.: Retrieval of Chinese Calligraphic Character Image. In: Aizawa, K., Nakamura, Y., Satoh, S. (eds.) PCM 2004. LNCS, vol. 3331, pp. 17–24. Springer, Heidelberg (2004)
12. Bishop, T., Cook, R.: A Specification for CDL Character Description Language. In: Glyph and Typesetting Workshop, Kyoto, Japan (2003)
13. Lu, Q.: The Ideographic Composition Scheme and Its Applications in Chinese Text Processing. In: Proc. of the 18th International Unicode Conference, IUC-18 (2001)
14. Juang, D., Hsieh, C.-C., Lin, S.: On Resolving the Missing Character Problem for Full-text Database for Chinese Ancient Texts in Academia Sinica. In: The Second Cross-Strait Symposium on the Rectification of Ancient Texts, pp. 1–8, Beijing (1998)
15. Hsieh, C.-C.: On the Formalization and Search of Glyphs in Chinese Ancient Texts. In: Conference on Rare Book and Information Technology, pp. 1–6, Taipei (1997)
16. Hsieh, C.-C.: A Descriptive Method for Re-engineering Hanzi Information Interchange Codes-On Redesigning Hanzi Interchange Code Part 2. In: International Conference on Hanzi Character Code and Database, pp. 1–9, Kyoto (1996)
17. Hsieh, C.-C.: The Missing Character Problem in Electronic Ancient Texts. In: The First Conference on Chinese Etymology, Tianjin, pp. 1–8. Tianjin (1996)

18. Beckmann, N., Kriegel, H.P., Schneider, R., Seeger, B.: The R*-tree: An Efficient and Robust Access Method for Characters and Rectangles. In: Proceedings of ACM SIGMOD International Conference on Management of Data, ACM SIGMOD 1990, pp. 322–331. ACM, New York (1990)

19. Lin, J.-W., Lin, F.-S.: An Auxiliary Unicode Han Character Lookup Service Based on Glyph Shape Similarity. In: IEEE The 11th International Symposium on Communications & Information Technologies (ISCIT 2011), pp. 489–492 (2011)

20. The Unicode Standard The Unicode Consortium, version 6.2 (2012), http://www.unicode.org/versions/Unicode6.2.0/

21. Xu, S.-H., Jiang, H., Jin, T., Lau, F.C.M., Pan, Y.: Automatic Facsimile of Chinese Calligraphic Writings. Computer Graphics Forum 27(7), 1879–1886 (2008)

22. Xu, S.-H., Jiang, H., Jin, T., Lau, F.C.M., Pan, Y.: Automatic Generation of Chinese Calligraphic Writings with Style Imitation. IEEE Intelligent Systems 24(2), 44–53 (2009)

23. Lai, P.-K., Pong, M.-C., Yeung, D.-Y.: Chinese Glyph Generation Using Character Composition and Beauty Evaluation Metrics. In: International Conference on Computer Processing of Oriental Languages, ICCPOL 1995, Honolulu, Hawaii, pp. 92–99 (1995)

24. Lai, P.-K., Yeung, D.-Y., Pong, M.-C.: A Heuristic Search Approach to Chinese Glyph Generation Using Hierarchical Character Composition. Computer Processing of Oriental Languages 10(3), 307–323 (1996)

25. Wang, P.Y.C., Siu, C.H.: Designing Chinese Typeface using Components. In: Computer Software and Applications Conference, pp. 412–421 (1995)

26. Feng, W.-R., Jin, L.-W.: Hierarchical Chinese character database based on radical reuse. Computer Applications 26(3), 714–716 (2006)

27. Lu, X.-Q.: R&D of Super Font and Related Technologies. In: The Twenty-second International Unicode Conference, IUC22, San Jose, California, September 9–13 (2002), http://www.unicode.org/iuc/iuc22/a310.html

28. Tang, Y.-M., Zhang, Y.-X., Lu, X.-Q.: A TrueType Font Compression Method Based on the Structure of Chinese Characters. Microelectronics & Computer 24(06), 52–55 (2007)

29. Sun, H., Tang, Y.-M., Lian, Z.-H., Xiao, J.-G.: Research on Distortionless Resizing Method for Components of Chinese Characters. Application Research of Computers 30 (2013), http://www.cnki.net/kcms/detail/ 51.1196.TP.20130603.1459.008.html

30. Shi, C., Xiao, J., Jia, W., Xu, C.: Automatic Generation of Chinese Character Based on Human Vision and Prior Knowledge of Calligraphy. In: Zhou, M., Zhou, G., Zhao, D., Liu, Q., Zou, L. (eds.) NLPCC 2012. CCIS, vol. 333, pp. 23–33. Springer, Heidelberg (2012)

Simulated Spoken Dialogue System Based on IOHMM with User History

Changliang Li[*], Bo Xu, XiuYing Wang, WenDong Ge, and HongWei Hao

Interactive Digital Media Technology Research Center (IDMTech),
Institute of Automation, Chinese Academy of Sciences, Beijing, China
{Changliang.li,boxu,xiuying.wang,wendong.ge,
hongwei.hao}@ia.ac.cn

Abstract. Expanding corpora is very important in designing a spoken dialogue system (SDS). In this big data era, data is expensive to collect and there are rare annotations. Some researchers make much work to expand corpora, most of which is based on rule. This paper presents a probabilistic method to simulate dialogues between human and machine so as to expand a small corpus with more varied simulated dialogue acts. The method employs Input/output HMM with user history (UH-IOHMM) to learn system and user dialogue behavior. In addition, this paper compares with simulation system based on standard IOHMM. We perform experiments using the WDC-ICA corpus, weather domain corpus with annotation. And the experiment result shows that the method we present in this paper can produce high quality dialogue acts which are similar to real dialogue acts.

Keywords: SDS, Corpora, UH-IOHMM, dialogue acts.

1   Introduction

Recently, SDSs have been developing rapidly. For example, Apple introduced "Siri", an intelligent personal assistant and knowledge navigator which works as an application for Apple Inc.'s iOS. In addition, Android phones have employed speech-activated "Voice Actions", which can be used to call your contacts, get directions, send messages, and perform a number of other common tasks and so on[1]. Cambridge designed CamInfo system, which offers service of travel information to people, based on partially observed Markov decision process (POMDP) [2] [3].

In spite of its fast developing, SDS still remains challenging. Among the changing, insufficient available data with annotation is the biggest bottleneck. There are no corpora big enough to sufficiently explore the vast space of possible dialogue states and strategies [3]. In addition, Data is expensive to collect and annotate. So, it is vital to expand corpora in designing a SDS.

---

[*] Corresponding author.

G. Zhou et al. (Eds.): NLPCC 2013, CCIS 400, pp. 83–92, 2013.
© Springer-Verlag Berlin Heidelberg 2013

Many research efforts have been undertaken in expanding corpora, including rule-based and data-driven approaches.

The point of rule-based intention simulation approach is that the developer can create many kinds of rules, which can generate variant dialogue acts given some certain information (Chung, 2004, López-Cózar et al., 2006 and López-Cózar et al., 2003) [4] [5]. In addition, Schatzmann et al. proposed an agenda-based user simulation technique for bootstrapping a statistical dialog manager, the main feature of which is that it is without access to training data (Schatzmann et al., 2007a). It generates user dialogue acts based on a full representation of the user goal and a stack-like user agenda[6].

The main feature of data-driven approach is to use statistical methods to simulate users' dialogue acts given corpora. The "bigram" model of dialog is employed in earlier studies. Its distinguish feature is the simulated user input is decided only by the previous system utterance (Eckert et al., 1997) [7]. One of the main advantages of the approach is that it is simple and another advantage is that it is independent on domain and language. There also remains improvement, for example, Levin et al. modified the bigram model to make a more realistic degree of conventional structure in dialog (Levin et al., 2000). In order to solve the problem of lack of the goal consistency in the model proposed by Levin, Scheffler and Young introduced the use of a graph-based model (Scheffler and Young, 2000 and Scheffler and Young, 2001). The model is goal directed. The main characteristic of this model is that it defined a goal as a specification of the dialog transaction that the user wants to accomplish[8] [9] [10] [11]. Cuayahuitl, Renals, Lemon, and Shimodaira (Cuayahuitl et al., 2005) presents a method for dialogue simulation based on Hidden Markov Models (HMMs). Their method generates system and user actions [2] [12]. It expands a small corpus of dialogue data with more varied simulated conversations.

Previous works expand the corpora based on rule or probability [2]. However, they mostly focus on the system turns and neglect the user history information. This brings the problem that the expanded dialogues acts are not as similar as real dialogues acts. The simulated user often repeat dialogue acts. This paper presents a probabilistic method to simulate dialogues between human and machine based on UH-IOHMM so as to expand corpora with more varied simulated dialogue acts. The dialogues acts generated through the method presented in this article are more close to real dialogues and in task-orient domain, such as weather information inquiry domain, less turns are needed before the task is satisfied[2] [13].

The rest of this article proceeds as follows. In section 2 we present some related knowledge and technology including SDS structure and typical simulation structure. In Section 3 we present simulation system based on UH-IOHMM. In section 4 we design the experiment on WDC-ICA corpora, which consists 100 dialogue sections with annotation in the domain of weather information, and analyze the experiment result. Finally, we summarize our conclusions and point future work.

2   Related Knowledge and Technology

2.1   SDS Structure

Typically, SDSs are composed of five components: automatic speech recognition (ASR); Natural language understanding (NLU); Dialogue manager (DM), Natural Language generation (NLG); Speech generation, such as text-to-speech (TTS) [1]. Among these units, the central module of any SDS is DM, which is in charge of the course of the interaction with user: it receives the semantically parsed representation of the user input and generates an appropriate high-level representation of the next system action [1]. DM mainly includes three parts: a dialogue model representing state information such as the user's goal, the user's last dialogue act and the dialogue history; a policy which selects the system's responses based on the inferred dialogue state; and a cumulative reward function which specifies the desired behavior of the system[1] [2] [3]. Figure 1 shows the structure of spoken dialogue system.

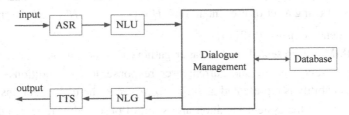

Fig. 1. The structure of spoken dialogue system

2.2   Typical Simulation Structure

A typical probabilistic dialogue simulation model often consist two main modules: system module and user module. The former's role is to control the flow of the conversation; the latter's role is to generate user's dialogue acts based on conditional probabilities. However, a training corpus with annotation is required, which is used to acquire knowledge and train system and user models [2]. The simulation model is shown in figure 2.

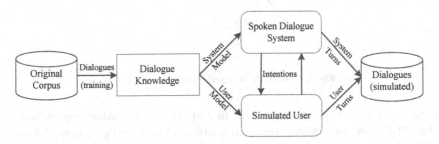

Fig. 2. The structure of simulation system

3   Simulation System

3.1   UH-IOHMM Based Simulation System

Our work in this article is to improve IOHMM based simulation system proposed by Cuayahuitl, Renals, Lemon, and Shimodaira. The proposed model is based on the assumption that a user's action depends on not only the previous system response, but also users' history information [13] [14].

A dialogue simulation system based on UH-IOHMM is shown in Figure 3, where empty circles represent visible states; the lightly shaded circles represent observations; the dark shaded circles represented user responses; A represents transfer matrix; B represents confusion matrix; U represents user action transfer matrix[2] [15]. The model is characterized by a set of visible states $S = \{S_1, S_2, ..., S_N\}$ which correspond to system turns, and a set of observations $V = \{v_1, v_2, ..., v_M\}$ which represent system action set [3] [16]. We employ q_t to represent the state at time t. The user responses are represented using a set of user intentions $H = \{H_1, H_2, ..., H_L\}$ and the user action at time t is denoted using u_t [2] [3].

UH-IOHMM we presented in this paper gathers together the next state transition q_{t+1} on the current state q_t and current user response u_t as conditions. The state transition probability is represented as $P(q_{t+1} | q_t, u_t)$, and the user intentions is conditioned not only on the system intention and symbol observed at time t, but also on the user's history acts represented as $P(u_t | q_t, c_t, u_{t-1}, u_{t-2}...u_{t-m})$, where m represents the steps we trace back the user's history acts. Apparently, the bigger m is, the more history information can be considered. But at the same time the computation complexity becomes bigger too. In this paper, in order to balance the history information and computation complexity, we select m as 1. Figure 3 illustrates the structure of dialogue simulation system based on UH-IOHMM.

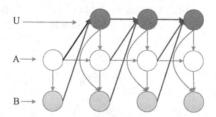

Fig. 3. UH-IOHMM based simulation system

Because there are many dialogue turns in corpora, some of which may repeat, we cut the WDC-ICA corpora into some sub goals. And each sub goal is modeled as a UH-IOHMM. We train each separate model for each sub goal. So we don't need to train a single giant IOHMM for simulating complete dialogues. The full corpora are not viewed as a whole set, but as a bag of sub goals [2] [3]. The next goal is decided by the conditional probability $P(g_n \mid g_{n-1})$ [2] [17]. Figure 4 shows the language model about sub goals [2].

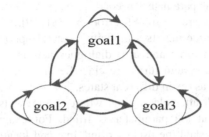

Fig. 4. Language model of sub goals

The dialogue simulation algorithm using UH-IOHMM is shown in figure 5. Simulate UH-IOHMM function generates a sequence of system intentions and user intentions.

```
1. function Simulate UH-IOHMM
2. t ← 0
3. qₜ ←random system turn from π
4. cₜ ←random system intention from
P(cₜ|qₜ)
5.    loop
6.       print cₜ
7.       uₜ←random user intention from
P(uₜ|qₜ,cₜ,uₜ₋₁)
8.       print uₜ
9.       qₜ←random system turn from
P(qₜ₊₁|qₜ,uₜ)
10.       if qₜ = qₙ then return
11.       else t ← t +1
12.       cₜ←random system intention from
P(cₜ|qₜ,uₜ)
13.    end
14. end
```

Fig. 5. Simulation algorithm

4   Experimental Design and Result

We employ WDC-ICA corpus, which consists 100 dialogue sections with annotation in the domain of weather information. The annotation consists of the system action and user intention as well as parameters needed in the domain like location and time and so on. We assume that there is no ASR error [2] [18] [19]. We use affinity propagation algorithm [20], considering its simplicity, general applicability, and performance, to classifier system turns and user dialogues acts into states used in UH-IOHMM. For example, the system turns are classified four different states and the user intention are classified as seven different states.

Table 1 shows the result after classifying, where 0 represents that the parameter lacks, and 1 represents that the parameter is filled. For example, the state "s1" represents that the system asked the user to offer time and location information, because both parameters lack.

Table 1. States and action in weather domain corpora

s1	Inquiry (time=0, location=0)
s2	Inquiry (time=0, location=1)
s3	Inquiry (time=1,location=0)
s4	Inquiry weather(time=1, location=1)
s5	Response (time=0, location=0)
s6	Response (time=0, location=1)
s7	Response (time=1,location=0)

a1	Inquiry (time, location)
a2	Inquiry (time)
a3	Inquiry (location)
a4	inquiry weather

Due to the limitation of corpora size, there may be some intentions that can't appear in the corpora. So considering unseen entries, we use Good-Turing algorithm, which provide a simple estimate of the total probability of the objects not seen, to smooth the probability distributions.

It is hard to evaluate the simulated dialogues due to the fact the flexibility of dialogues acts. The quality of the simulated dialogues has been assessed using a variety of different direct or indirect evaluation methods. We use dialogue length to evaluate the result, which computers the average number of turn per dialogue, giving a rough indication of agreement between two sets of dialogues. We train the corpora and generate 10^5 dialogues based on IOHMM and UH-IOHMM proposed in this paper. Fragments of a simulated dialogue generated by IOHMM and UH-IOHMM are shown in figure 6 at left and right side respectively. We can see that the dialogue generated based on UH-IOHMM is more efficient than that based on IOHMM.

```
dialogue 1: sentence Number = 2
请问昌平十七点天气是不是很好啊？ (s1)
调用APP。 (a4)


dialogue 2: sentence Number = 4
请问林芝天气温度怎么样？ (s3)
请问你问的是什么时候的天气？ (a2)
星期四夜间的天气。 (s6)
调用APP。 (a4)


dialogue 3: sentence Number = 4
请问天气是哪样的？ (s4)
请问你问的是什么时候哪里的天气？ (a1)
江门星期天的天气。 (s5)
调用APP。 (a4)


dialogue 4: sentence Number = 4
请问中午十一点天气温度是多少？ (s2)
请问你问的是哪里的天气？ (a3)
淮安的天气。 (s7)
调用APP。 (a4)
```

```
dialogue 5: sentence Number = 10
请问十九点天气冷不冷？ (s2)
请问你问的是哪里的天气？ (a3)
十九点的天气。 (s6)
请问你问的是什么时候哪里的天气？ (a1)
十九点的天气。 (s6)
请问你问的是什么时候的天气？ (a2)
日照的天气。 (s7)
请问你问的是什么时候的天气？ (a2)
日照十九点的天气。 (s5)
调用APP。 (a4)


dialogue 6: sentence Number = 12
请问天气怎么样？ (s4)
请问你问的是什么时候哪里的天气？ (a1)
巴中晚上九点的天气。 (s5)
请问你问的是什么时候的天气？ (a2)
巴中的天气。 (s7)
请问你问的是哪里的天气？ (a3)
巴中晚上九点的天气。 (s5)
请问你问的是什么时候哪里的天气？ (a1)
巴中的天气。 (s7)
请问你问的是什么时候的天气？ (a2)
晚上九点的天气。 (s6)
调用APP。 (a4)
```

Fig. 6. Fragments of a simulated dialogue generated by IOHMM (left) and UH-IOHMM (right)

We select 10000 dialogue sections and add up the dialogue turns in each dialogue sections. From figure 7, where horizontal axis represents the number of dialogue turns in each dialogue section while vertical axis represents the number of dialogue sections, we can make a safe conclusion that: based on WDC-ICA corpus, the method proposed in this paper can satisfy users' need in less turns than the state of the art method which is based on IOHMM.

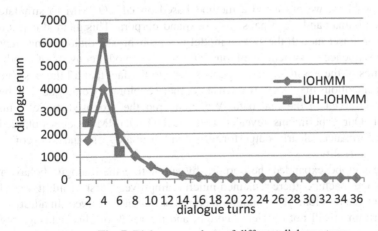

Fig. 7. Dialogue numbers of different dialogue turns

From figure 8, where the vertical axis represents the average turns of dialogues generated through both simulations systems, we can see that the simulated dialogues based on IOHMM take an average of 5.5 turns to complete the weather information inquiry task, while the simulated dialogues based on UH-IOHMM we proposed in this article takes an average of 3.7 turns to complete the task. Apparently, the dialogues generated by simulate dialogue system based on UH-IOHMM is both efficient and more similar to human's real dialogue behavior.

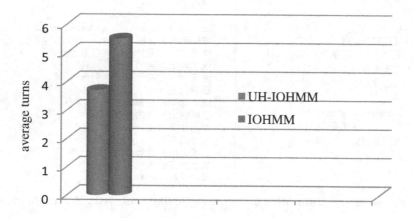

Fig. 8. Average turns of IOHMM and UH-IOHMM

5   Conclusion and Future Work

This paper focused on the problem of limitation of data scale while building SDS. To cope with this problem, we presented a method based on UH-IOHMM to simulate dialogue between human and machine, so as to expand corpora. This method learnt a system model and a user model: the system model is a probabilistic dialogue manager that models the sequence of system intentions, and the user model consists of conditional probabilities of the possible user responses. Due to the fact that all the possible system and user intentions may occur in each state, more exploratory dialogues can be generated than observed in the real data. We compared the proposed model with IOHMM model. Our experiments revealed that the UH-IOHMM models obtained very similar performance, clearly outperforming random dialogues, and are considered to be close to reality.

Although the method expanded the corpora by simulating the dialogue behavior between human and machine, there remained much to improve. First of all, it would be more efficient the problem of computation complexity can be solved. In addition, the cluster algorithm is still not efficient enough, and the result of cluster brings big influence to the simulation result. If we can find a more accurate cluster algorithm to replace the AP algorithm employed in this paper, the simulation will be trained as a more effective way. These issues will be addressed in future work.

Acknowledgement. This work is partly supported by National Program on Key Basic Research Project (973 Program) under Grant 2013CB329302. The work described in this paper represents the combined efforts of many people.

References

1. Lemon, O., Pietquin, O.: Data-Driven Methods for Adaptive Spoken Dialogue System. Springer (2012)
2. Cuayahuitl, H., Renals, S., Lemon, O., Shimodaira, H.: Human-computer dialogue simulation using hidden markov models. In: Proceedings of the IEEE Workshop on Automatic Speech Recognition and Understanding (2005); Chung, G.: Developing a Flexible Spoken Dialog System Using Simulation. In: Proc. ACL, pp. 63–70 (2004)
3. Schatzmann, J., Weilhammer, K., Stuttle, M., Young, S.: A survey of statistical user simulation techniques for reinforcement-learning of dialogue management strategies. The Knowledge Engineering Review 21, 97–126 (2006)
4. López-Cózar, R., De la Torre, A., Segura, J.C., Ru-bio., A.J.: Assessment of dialogue systems by means of a new simulation technique. Speech Communication 40(3), 387–407 (2003)
5. Ramón, L.-C., Callejas, Z., Mctear, M.: Testing the performance of spoken dialogue systems by means of an artificially simulated user. Artif. Intell. Rev. 26(4), 291–323 (2006)
6. Schatzmann, J., Thomson, B., Young, S.: Error simulation for training statistical dialogue systems. In: IEEE Workshop on Automatic Speech Recognition & Understanding, ASRU 2007, pp. 526–531 (2007a)
7. Eckert, W., Levin, E., Pieraccini, R.: User modeling for spoken dialogue system evaluation. In: Proceedings of the 1997 IEEE Workshop on Automatic Speech Recognition and Understanding, pp. 80–87 (1997)
8. Scheffler, K., Young, S.: Probabilistic simulation of human-machine dialogues. In: Proc. of ICASSP, vol. 2, pp. 1217–1220 (2000)
9. Scheffler, K., Young, S.: Corpus-based dialogue simulation for automatic strategy learning and evaluation. In: Proc. NAACL Workshop on Adaptation in Dialogue Systems, pp. 64–70 (2001)
10. Levin, E., Pieraccini, R., Eckert, W.: A stochastic model of human-machine interaction for learning dialog strategies. IEEE Trans. on Speech and Audio Processing 8(1), 11–23 (2000)
11. Schatzmann, J., Weilhammer, K., Stuttle, M., Young, S.: A survey of statistical user simulation techniques for reinforcement-learning of dialogue management strategies. The Knowledge Engineering Review 21, 97–126 (2006)
12. Fan, L., Yu, D., Peng, X., Lu, S., Xu, B.: A Spoken Dialogue System Based on FST and DBN. In: Zhou, M., Zhou, G., Zhao, D., Liu, Q., Zou, L. (eds.) NLPCC 2012. CCIS, vol. 333, pp. 34–45. Springer, Heidelberg (2012)
13. Kearns, M., Mansour, Y., Ng, A.Y.: Sparse sampling algorithm for near optimal planning in large markov decision processes. In: Proceedings of the Sixteenth International Joint Conference on Articial Intel ligence Stockholm (1999) (to appear)
14. Chen, K.: Boosting input/output hidden Markov models for sequence classification. In: Wang, L., Chen, K., S. Ong, Y. (eds.) ICNC 2005. LNCS, vol. 3611, pp. 656–665. Springer, Heidelberg (2005)
15. Litman, D.J., Pan, S.: Designing and Evaluating an Adaptive Spoken Dialogue System. User Modeling and User-Adapted Interaction 12, 111–137 (2002)

16. Chiappa, S., Bengio, S.: HMM and IOHMM Modeling of EEG Rhythms for Asynchronous BCI Systems. In: ESANN 2004 Proceedings-European Symposium on Artificial Neural Networks Bruges, Belgium, April 28-30 (2004)
17. Bengio, Y., Frasconi, P.: Input-Output HM:M' s for Sequence Processing. IEEE Transactions on Neural Networks 7(5) (September 1996)
18. Cuayahuitl, H., Renals, S., Lemon, O., Shimodaira, H.: Human-computer Dialogue Simulation using Hidden Markov Models. In: ASRU (2005)
19. Bengio, Y., Frasconi, P.: An Input Output HMM Architecture. In: Tesauro, G., Touretzky, D., Leen, T. (eds.) Advances in Neural Information Processing Systems, vol. 7, pp. 427–434. MIT Press, Cambridge (1995)
20. Young, S., Gasic, M., Thomson, B., Williams, J.D.: POMDP-based Statistical Spoken Dialogue Systems: A Review. In: Proc. IEEE, vol. X(X) (January 2012)
21. Kumaravelan, G., Sivakumar, R.: Simulation of Dialogue Management for Learning Dialogue Strategy Using Learning Automata. IEEE (2009)
22. Polifroni, J., Chung, G., Seneff, S.: Towards the Automatic Generation of Mixed-Initiative Dialogue Systems fromWeb Content. EUROSPEECH (2003)
23. Frey, B.J., Dueck, D.: Clustering by passing messages between data points. Science 315, 972–976 (2007)

A Mixed Model for Cross Lingual Opinion Analysis[*]

Lin Gui[1], Ruifeng Xu[1,**], Jun Xu[1], Li Yuan[1], Yuanlin Yao[1], Jiyun Zhou[1],
Qiaoyun Qiu[1], Shuwei Wang[1], Kam-Fai Wong[2], and Ricky Cheung[3]

[1] Key Laboratory of Network Oriented Intelligent Computation,
Shenzhen Graduate School, Harbin Institute of Technology, Shenzhen, China
{Guilin.nlp,xuruifeng.hitsz,hit.xujun,yuanlisail}@gmail.com,
{541523621,262061485,1028440296}@qq.com,
wangshuweino1@vip.qq.com
[2] Department of System Engineering and Engineering Management,
The Chinese University of Hong Kong, Hong Kong
kfwong@se.cuhk.edu.hk
[3] Social Analytics (Hong Kong) Co. Ltd., Hong Kong
ricky.cheung@hkmci.com

Abstract. The performances of machine learning based opinion analysis systems are always puzzled by the insufficient training opinion corpus. Such problem becomes more serious for the resource-poor languages. Thus, the cross-lingual opinion analysis (CLOA) technique, which leverages opinion resources on one (source) language to another (target) language for improving the opinion analysis on target language, attracts more research interests. Currently, the transfer learning based CLOA approach sometimes falls to over fitting on single language resource, while the performance of the co-training based CLOA approach always achieves limited improvement during bi-lingual decision. Target to these problems, in this study, we propose a mixed CLOA model, which estimates the confidence of each monolingual opinion analysis system by using their training errors through bilingual transfer self-training and co-training, respectively. By using the weighted average distances between samples and classification hyper-planes as the confidence, the opinion polarity of testing samples are classified. The evaluations on NLP&CC 2013 CLOA bakeoff dataset show that this approach achieves the best performance, which outperforms transfer learning and co-training based approaches.

Keywords: Cross lingual Opinion Analysis, Transfer Self-Training, Co-Training, Mixed Model.

[*] This research is supported by Open Projects Program of National Laboratory of Pattern Recognition, National Natural Science Foundation of China No. 61203378, 61370165, MOE Specialized Research Fund for the Doctoral Program of Higher Education 20122302120070, Shenzhen Foundational Research Funding JCYJ20120613152557576 and Shenzhen International Cooperation Research Funding GJHZ2012 0613110641217.
[**] Corresponding author.

G. Zhou et al. (Eds.): NLPCC 2013, CCIS 400, pp. 93–104, 2013.
© Springer-Verlag Berlin Heidelberg 2013

1   Introduction

With the rapid development of Internet, mass texts are published on self-media, such as micro-blogging, news reviews, product reviews, etc. These texts contain many valuable subjective opinions. Thus, the opinion analysis technique, which identifies and analyzes the opinions in these text become a focus topic in natural language processing research. Generally speaking, current opinion analysis techniques are camped into rule-based or machine learning based approaches. Rule-based opinion analysis approach achieves good performances in some specific tasks, but it requires manually compile of rules and patterns. The machine learning based, especially supervised learning based opinion analysis approach is the majority of existing techniques. However, their performances are always influenced by the insufficient training corpus. Such problem becomes more serious for some resource-poor languages. Thus, the cross-lingual opinion analysis (CLOA) techniques are investigated. The main idea of CLOA is to translate and project the opinion resources from one language (named as source language) to another language (named as target language) for enriching target language resources, and thereby improving the performance of opinion analysis on target language.

Normally, there are much noises occurred during mapping and projecting the source language resources to target language, which affects the classifier training. Therefore, one of the core problems in CLOA is to investigate effective mechanism for selecting high quality transferred samples for classifier training. Most existing CLOA techniques in general can be divided into two categories: 1. Transfer learning based approach, which transfers the source language resources to target language, including dictionary and opinion corpus, for improving the classifier on target language; and 2.Co-training based approach, which adopts co-training strategy to improve the opinion analysis performance on both languages. A typical transfer learning based CLOA works is conducted by J. Wiebe [1], which utilized English and Romanian aligned corpus to generate a Romanian subjectivity dictionary and then developed a dictionary/ruled based Romanian opinion analysis system. Yao [2] used Chinese and English cross-lingual dictionary to determine the polarity of Chinese text. Xu et al.[3] proposed Transfer Ada-boost and Transfer Self-training algorithms for improving the CLOA performance through selectively using the high quality transferred samples and filtering the low quality transferred samples, respectively. Furthermore, Dai [4] adopted Boosting technology to improve the system performance on target language through enhancing the weights of target language samples and reducing the weight of low quality transferred source language samples, iteratively. A typical co-training based CLOA works is conducted by Wan [5, 6], which used straight push co-training learning method for improving the opinion analysis on both languages using bilingual corpora. J. Wiebe [7] extended the bilingual learning to multi-lingual (Arabic, German, French, etc.) for improving multiple monolingual opinion analysis following co-training strategy.

Current CLOA research has yielded obvious progress, but there are still many problems left. Attribute to the small annotated opinion corpus on target language, the transfer learning based CLOA sometimes falls into an over-fitting to the transferred source language samples. Meanwhile, the co-training based CLOA, which estimates the bilingual model similarity to the samples, always leads to a relatively limited performance improvement. Target to these problems, this paper proposes a mixed CLOA model, which incorporates bilingual transfer self-training and co-training method to improve the monolingual opinion classifier, respectively. The outputs of these two models are weighted to generate the final classification results based on their training error rates. This approach is evaluated on NLP&CC2013 CLOA bakeoff data set. The experimental results show that our proposed approach outperforms transfer learning and co-training based approach. It achieves the best performance on this data set based on our knowledge.

The rest of this paper is organized as follows. Section 2 presents our mixed cross-lingual opinion analysis model. Section 3 gives the evaluation results and discussions. Finally, Section 4 concludes this paper.

2   A Mixed Cross-Lingual Opinion Analysis Model

In this section, a mixed CLOA model is proposed which adopts a weighting strategy for combining the classification output of transfer learning CLOA method and co-training CLOA method.   This mixed model aims to unite the advantages of these two CLOA methods for further improving the opinion analysis performance.

2.1   Cross-Lingual Self-training Model

Cross-lingual transfer self-training model is based on cross lingual resource transfer learning. Its main idea is to transfer opinion samples from source language to target language through translation and projection. During this process, the transfer self-training method conducts confidence estimation for choosing high confidence samples into target language training corpus, iteratively. Different from Xu's work [3] which only transfers source language resources to target language, in this work, we investigate bi-directional transfer, i.e. both transfer from source language to target language and transfer from target language to source language are considered.

In general, though the target language is lack of labeled data, there is large number of unlabeled data, which is called raw corpus. Based on the available raw corpus on target language and annotated corpus on source language, we may transfer raw corpus on target language to source and transfer annotated corpus on source language to target language, respectively, through machine translation. Now, we have annotated corpus and raw corpus on both languages. The self-training algorithm is then applied to source language and target language, respectively. It is an iterative training process. In each pass, the classifier (which is trained by using annotated corpus) is applied to classify the raw samples and estimate the classification confidence. The raw samples with high confidence are moved the annotated corpus with their classification labels. The classifier is then re-trained by using the expanded annotated corpus. Such iteration terminates until the predefined condition is satisfied. The description of bilingual cross-lingual self-training is given in Algorithm 1.

More detail, for the annotated corpus on source language D_{sa}, its translation to target language is D_{ta}; for the raw corpus on target language D_{tr}, its translation to source language is D_{sr}. We train the support vector machines (SVMs) classifier on source language and target language by using D_{sa} and D_{sr}, D_{ta} and D_{tr}, respectively.

Algorithm 1. Cross-lingual transfer self-training model

Source language side:

Input: training sample D_{sa}, training examples to be transferred D_{sr}. Iterations K, updated training set after i iterations T_i, number of appended samples after every iteration k.

  $T_0 = D_{sa}$

  For each $i \in [1, K]$
   1) Train SVMs classifier C^{i-1} on T_{i-1}
   2) Classify D_{sr} using C^{i-1}
   3) Add k classified positive and negative samples with the highest confidence to T_{i-1}, respectively
   4) $T_i = T_{i-1}$
   5) Delete the k added data from D_{sr}
  End for

Target language side:

Input: training sample D_{ta}, training examples to be transferred D_{tr}. Iterations K, updated training set after i iterations T_i, number of appended samples after every iteration k.

  $T_0 = D_{ta}$

  For each $i \in [1, K]$
   1) Train SVMs classifier C^{i-1} on T_{i-1}
   2) Classify D_{tr} using C^{i-1}
   3) Add k classified positive and negative samples with the highest confidence to T_{i-1}, respectively
   4) $T_i = T_{i-1}$
   5) Delete the k added samples from D_{tr}
  End for

Output: classifier C_s which has the minimum training error among all the iteration result of source language, classifier C_t which has the minimum training error among all the iteration result of target language

---

On the target language side, classifier C_{ta}^0 is trained on D_{ta}. This classifier is then used to classify the samples in the raw corpus D_{tr}. Suppose that the support vectors in C_{ta}^0 are $v_1, v_2 \dots v_n$, for a sample in raw corpus $d_j(d_j \in D_{tr})$:

$$W_t(d_j) = \sum_{i=1}^n \alpha_i Kernel(v_i, d_j) \tag{1}$$

Where, α_i is parameter in SVMs, *Kernel* is the kernel function of SVMs. The physical meaning of formula (1) is the distance between input samples and hyper-plane constructed by SVMs under this model. In this study, we regard this distance as the confidence to describe the probability that input samples are correctly classified. A value greater than 0 indicates the corresponding sample is a positive sample, otherwise, negative. The larger absolute value of confidence means the greater probability that they are correctly classified.

All of the classified samples in D_{tr} are sorted according to their confidence values. k samples with the maximum and minimum results are selected as high quality positive and negative examples, respectively. They are moved from D_{tr} to D_{ta}. In the next iteration, the classifier is re-trained on D_{ta} and C_{ta}^1 is obtained. C_{ta}^1 is then applied to classify the samples in D_{tr} and then move top k positive and negative samples D_{ta}. Such procedure repeats while the termination condition satisfied. Finally, the classifier C_t is obtained which has the smallest training error rate on the target language.

In the source language side, the same strategy is adopted to obtain the final classifier C_s which has the smallest training error rate on source language.

For a given target language sample x_t, we first generate its machine translation results x_s on source language. Based on the PAC learning theory [8], the actual error rate of the classifier has a high probability to converge to training error rate together with increasing training data. Thus, x_t is classification by,

$$y = \sum_{j=source\ \&\ target}(1 - E_j)W_j(x_j) \tag{2}$$

where, $E_j (j = source\ \&\ target)$ are the training errors on source language and target language, respectively. When y is greater than zero, x_t is classified as a positive example, otherwise, negative. The physical meaning of this weighting formula is that for two classifiers, the one with lower training error rate should have a higher weight in the final decision.

2.2   Cross-Lingual Co-training Model

The main procedure of cross-lingual co-training model is similar to cross-lingual transfer self-training model. The major difference is that transfer self-training regards the classifier training in both languages as two independent iterative processing, while in the co-training model, the classification results for a sample in one language and its translation in another language are incorporated for classification in each iteration. The model is described as Algorithm 2.

More detail, for the annotated corpus on source language D_{sa}, its translation to target language is D_{ta}; for the raw corpus on target language D_{tr}, its translation to source language is D_{sr}. The support vector machines (SVMs) classifiers, C_{sa}^0 and C_{ta}^0, are trained on annotated date in source language and target language, respectively.

For a sample in raw corpus on target language, $d_j(d_j \in D_{tr})$ and its corresponding translated samples in source language $d'_j(d'_j \in D_{sr})$, their classification may be determined by following formula:

$$y = W_s(d'_j) + W_t(d_j) \tag{3}$$

Where, W_s and W_t are the weights corresponding to source language side and target language side, respectively. The outputs for each d_j are sorted according to their values of y. The top k samples with the maximum and minimum y values and their corresponding translated samples are moved from raw corpus to annotated corpus on both languages, respectively. The classifier on target language is retrained on the annotated corpus and C_{ta}^1 is obtained. Similarly, the classifier on source language is trained and C_{sm}^1 is obtained. Such training process is repeated until the terminate condition satisfies. Finally, the classifiers, C_t and C_s, for target language and source language are obtained, respectively.

Algorithm 2. Cross-lingual co-training

Input: Source language training samples D_{sa}, training examples to be transferred D_{sr}, target language training sample D_{ta}, training examples to be transferred D_{tr}. Iterations K, updated source language training set after i iterations T_i^s, updated target language training set after i iterations T_i^t, number of appended samples after every iteration k.

$T_0^s = D_{sa}$, $T_0^t = D_{ta}$

For each $i \in [1, K]$

    1) Train SVMs classifier C_{i-1}^s on T_{i-1}^s

    2) Train SVMs classifier C_{i-1}^t on T_{i-1}^t

    3) Classify D_{sr} using C_{i-1}^s

    4) Classify D_{tr} using C_{i-1}^t

    6) Add k classified positive and negative samples with the highest
        confidence to T_{i-1}^t and T_{i-1}^s, respectively

    5) $T_i^s = T_{i-1}^s$, $T_i^t = T_{i-1}^t$

    6) Delete the k added data from D_{sr} and D_{tr}

End for

Output: classifier C_s which has the minimum training error among all the iteration result of source language, classifier C_t which has the minimum training error among all the iteration result of target language

---

For the target language samples to be classified x_t, its translation to source language x_t' is generated. Its classification is then determined by following formula (2).

2.3   Weighting Strategy in Mixed Model

Considering that the transfer self-training based model regards target language and source language as two separated languages, sometimes it falls to over fitting the training error in single language side. On the other hand, co-training based model obtained the improvements on both source and target languages. However, the achieved classification performance improvement by following formula (2) is always lower than transfer training model. Therefore, we propose a mixed model with weighing strategy in order to incorporate the classification results by transfer self-training based model and co-training based model.

The weighting strategy is similar to formula (2). Based on the PAC learning theory [8], we know that, with the increasing training samples, the actual classifier error rate will converge to the training error rate with a high probability:

$$Pr\left(|error_{train} - error_{test}| < \sqrt{\frac{ln\left(\frac{1}{\delta}\right)}{2m}}\right) \geq 1 - \delta \tag{4}$$

Where m is the number of training samples, δ is any positive number.

In this study, transfer self-learning model and co-training model have the same sample amounts, thus the actual error rates of the two models will have the same probability to converge to their own training error rates. Therefore, the error rates are used as weighting parameters for classifications results of two models. The model which has lower training error rate is assigned a higher weight in the voting.

Assume that after k iterations of transfer self-training, the trained classifier with the minimum training error in k trained classifiers on source language is labeled as $C_{st:s}^k$ and the trained classifiers with the minimum training error in k trained classifiers on target language is labeled as $C_{ct:t}^k$. Similarly, after k iterations of co-training, the trained classifiers with the minimum training error in k trained classifiers on source language is labeled as $C_{ct:s}^k$ and the trained classifiers the minimum training error in k trained classifiers on target language is labeled as $C_{ct:t}^k$. For a target language sample to be classified, x_t and its translations x_s in source language, the results of function W corresponding to the above four classifiers are calculated by following formula (1). The final classification is determined by weighting the classification results of the four classifiers as given in formula (5):

$$y = \sum_{j=s\&t} \sum_{i=st\&ct} (1 - E_{i:j}) W_{i:j}^k(x_j) \tag{5}$$

Similar to formula (2), when y is greater than zero, the sample sentence will be classified as positive, otherwise negative. In formula (5), the classifier with a lower error rate is assigned a higher weight in the final voting because it leads to higher probability to classification with lower error rate. This mixed method takes the confidence and training error rate into account is expected to combine multiple classifier outputs for a better performance.

3   Experiment Results and Analysis

3.1   Experiment Settings

The proposed mixed CLOA model is evaluated on NLP&CC 2013 CLOA bakeoff dataset. This dataset consists of the reviews on DVD, Book and Music category. The training data of each category contains 4,000 English annotated documents (ratio of positive and negative samples is 1:1) and Chinese raw corpus contains 17,814 DVD documents, 47,071 Book documents and 29,677 Music documents. In the testing dataset, each category contains 4,000 Chinese documents. The performance is evaluated by the correct classification accuracy for each category, and the average accuracy of the three categories, respectively.

The category accuracy is defined as:

$$Accuracy_c = \frac{\#correctly\ classified\ samples\ in\ category\ c}{4000} \tag{6}$$

Where c represent one of the DVD, Book and Music categories, respectively. The overall average accuracy is defined as:

$$Accuracy = \frac{1}{3}\sum_c Accuracy_c \tag{7}$$

In this experiment, ICTCLAS is used as the word segmentation tool. The monolingual opinion classifiers are developed based on SVMs (using SVM[light1]) while word unigram and word bigram features are employed.

Firstly, we directly use the translated source language annotated data as the training examples. The achieved baseline performances listed in Table 1:

Table 1. Baseline performance (directly using translation results)

Category	Accuracy
Accuracy$_{DVD}$	0.7373
Accuracy$_{Book}$	0.7215
Accuracy$_{Music}$	0.7423
Accuracy	0.7337

The performances of transfer self-training model, co-training model and mixed model are then evaluated and discussed in the following subsections, respectively. In the experiment, the maximum number of iterations is set to 200. The numbers of added positive and negative samples in each iteration is set to 10.

3.2   Evaluation on Transfer Self-training Model

In Experiment 1, the performance of transfer self-training model is evaluated. The achieved performances corresponding to iteratively trained classifiers are shown in Figure 1.

It is observed that the performances of transfer self-training model improved with the increasing of training iterations on both Chinese and English classifiers, but the overall performance grows slowly. Since the two classifiers on different languages

---

[1] http://svmlight.joachims.org/

are regarded independent in transfer self-training model, the weighted voting results by these two monolingual classifiers may obtain better result. In DVD category, the weighted classifier voting achieves the 2.4% and 4.6% further accuracy improvements on Chinese and English classifier, respectively. In Book category, the classifier voting obtained 5% and 3.4% further improvements, respectively. In Music category, the classifier voting obtained a lower advantage that only 0.2% higher than the Chinese classifier, but 6.3% higher than English classifier.

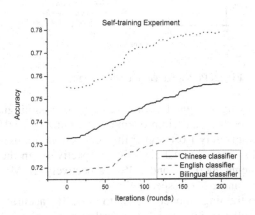

Fig. 1. Performance of transfer self-training model

Overall, the final performance of transfer self-training model achieves 2-4.7% improvement on monolingual classifier.

3.3   Evaluation of Co-training Model

Experiment 2 evaluates the co-training model. The achieved performances corresponding to iteratively trained classifiers are shown in Figure 2. In DVD category, the accuracy of Chinese classifier increased by 4.6% and the accuracy of English classifier increased by 4.7%. In Book category, the accuracy improvement for Chinese and English are 5.8% and 3.3%, respectively. In Music category, the accuracy improvements are 3.4% and 6.3%, respectively. In general, co-training model leads to obvious classifier performance improvement. The average accuracy increased by 4.7%, which is much higher than transfer self-training model. The main reason is that, during the co-training process of the two classifiers on the two languages, the selected transfer samples are more reliable by considering the confidence from both classifiers. Thus, the performance improvement of the final model is obvious.

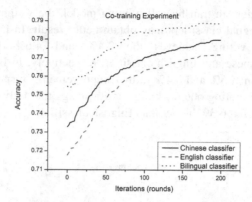

Fig. 2. Performance of co-training model

However, when applying weighted voting strategy to monolingual classifiers on the two languages, the performance improvement is limited. In DVD category, the result by weighted voting is only 1.6% higher than Chinese monolingual classifier and 1.8% higher than English monolingual classifier, respectively. In the Book category, the accuracy improvements are 1.2% and 1.3%, respectively. In Music category, the accuracy improves 0.1% and 2.5%, respectively.

In general, the co-training model leads to 1-1.7% accuracy improvement. Compared to transfer self-training model, the further performance improvement by co-training model is limited.

3.4   Evaluation on Mixed CLOA Model

Experiment 3 evaluates the mixed CLOA model which incorporates transfer self-training model and co-training model. The achieved performances corresponding to iteratively trained models are shown in Figure 3.

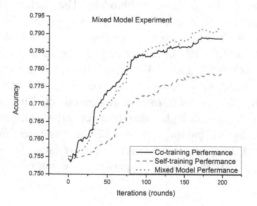

Fig. 3. Performance of the mixed CLOA model

It is observed that generally the mixed model further improve the classifier performances. In DVD category and Music category, the mixed model performance improves about 0.2% compared to the best single model classifier. In the book category, the mixed model achieved 0.6% further improvement. The reason for these different performance improvements results is as follows. In the weighted voting framework, the model which performs a better performance is assigned a higher weight. Thus, for general samples classification, the better single model plays a major role in voting. When the better single model outputs a low confidence and another model has a higher confidence, the second model plays the major role. Hence, the mixed voting strategy is shown effective to avoid the risks caused by low performance of single model.

3.5   Compared with Other Results on NLP&CC 2013 CLOA Dataset

Six teams participate the NLP&CC 2013 cross lingual opinion analysis bakeoff. The achieved performance of each team are listed in Table 2 and compared with our proposed CLOA model.

In NLP&CC 2013 CLOA bakeoff, HLT-Hitsz achieved the best accuracy performance. This system is developed by our team in the bakeoff. Meanwhile, it is shown that our proposed mixed CLOA model further improves the performance. The achieved accuracies are higher than the listed system in all of the three categories. Up to now, the final overall performance is the best result on this dataset base on our knowledge.

Table 2. Performance comparision on NLP&CC2013 CLOA dataset

Team	DVD	Music	Book	Accuracy
BISTU	0.6473	0.6605	0.5980	0.6353
HLT-Hitsz	0.7773	0.7513	0.7850	0.7712
THUIR-SENTI	0.7390	0.7325	0.7423	0.7379
SJTUGSLIU	0.7720	0.7453	0.7240	0.7471
LEO_WHU	0.7833	0.7595	0.7700	0.7709
Our Approach	**0.7965**	**0.7830**	**0.7870**	**0.7889**

4   Conclusion

This paper proposes a mixed cross-lingual opinion analysis model which weighted incorporates transfer self-training model and co-training model. This mixed model achieves the best performance on NLP&CC 2013 CLOA bakeoff dataset which shows the effectiveness of our proposed mixed CLOA model.

Since the transfer learning process does not satisfy the independent identical distribution hypothesis of training samples and test samples, actually our proposed weighted strategy based on training error rate is a kind of estimation of theory weighting. Meanwhile, the further performance improvement by following this weighting strategy is limited which is shown in the experiments. Therefore, the strategy for accurately filtering samples and estimating classifier error rate are the important problems to be solved in our future study.

References

1. Mihalcea, R., Banea, C., Wiebe, J.: Learning Multilingual Subjective Language via Cross-lingual Projections. In: Proceedings of the Association for Computational Linguistics 2007, pp. 976–983 (2007)
2. Yao, J.X., Wu, G.F., Liu, J., et al.: Using Bilingual Lexicon to Judge Sentiment Orientation of Chinese Words. In: Proceedings of the 6th International Conference on Computer and Information Technology, pp. 38–43 (2006)
3. Xu, J., Xu, R.F., Ding, Y.X., et al.: Cross Lingual Opinion Analysis via Transfer Learning. Australian Journal of Intelligent Information Processing Systems 11(2), 28–34 (2010)
4. Dai, W.Y., Yang, Q., Xue, G.R., et al.: Boosting for Transfer Learning. In: Proceedings of the 24th International Conference on Machine Learning, pp. 193–200 (2007)
5. Zhou, X.J., Wan, X.J., Xiao, J.G.: Cross-Language Opinion Target Extraction in Review Texts. In: Proceedings of IEEE 12th International Conference on Data Mining, pp. 1200–1205 (2012)
6. Wan, X.J.: A Comparative Study of Cross-Lingual Sentiment Classification. In: Proceedings of Web Intelligence, pp. 24–31 (2012)
7. Mihalcea, R., Banea, C., Wiebe, J., et al.: Multilingual Subjectivity Analysis Using Machine Translation. In: Proceedings of the 18th ACM Conference on Information and Knowledge management, pp. 127–136 (2009)
8. Valiant, L.: A Theory of the Learnable. Communications of the ACM 27(11), 1134–1142 (1984)

Semi-supervised Text Categorization
by Considering Sufficiency and Diversity

Shoushan Li[1,2], Sophia Yat Mei Lee[2], Wei Gao[1], and Chu-Ren Huang[2]

[1] Natural Language Processing Lab, School of Computer Science and Technology,
Soochow University, China
[2] CBS, The Hong Kong Polytechnic University, Hong Kong
{shoushan.li,sophiaym,wei.gao512,churenhuang}@gmail.com

Abstract. In text categorization (TC), labeled data is often limited while unlabeled data is ample. This motivates semi-supervised learning for TC to improve the performance by exploring the knowledge in both labeled and unlabeled data. In this paper, we propose a novel bootstrapping approach to semi-supervised TC. First of all, we give two basic preferences, i.e., *sufficiency* and *diversity* for a possibly successful bootstrapping. After carefully considering the *diversity* preference, we modify the traditional bootstrapping algorithm by training the involved classifiers with random feature subspaces instead of the whole feature space. Moreover, we further improve the random feature subspace-based bootstrapping with some constraints on the subspace generation to better satisfy the *diversity* preference. Experimental evaluation shows the effectiveness of our modified bootstrapping approach in both topic and sentiment-based TC tasks.

Keywords: Sentiment Classification, Semi-supervised Learning, Bootstrapping.

1 Introduction

Text categorization (TC) aims to automatically assign category labels to natural language text (Sebastiani, 2002) and this task can be grouped into two major categories: topic-based text classification (Yang and Liu, 1997) (referred to as topic classification in the following) and sentiment classification (Pang et al., 2002). While the former classifies a document according to some objective topics, such as *education, finance,* and *politics,* the latter classifies a document according to some subjective semantic orientations, such as *positive* and *negative.* Nowadays, the most popular approach to both categories of TC tasks is based on supervised learning methods which employ large amounts of labeled data to train a classifier for automatic classification. However, it is often expensive and time-consuming to obtain labeled data. To overcome this difficulty, various semi-supervised learning methods have been proposed to improve the performance by exploiting unlabeled data that are readily available for most TC tasks (Blum and Mitchell, 1998).

In principle, an unlabeled document could be helpful for classification. Consider the following review from a corpus for sentiment classification:

G. Zhou et al. (Eds.): NLPCC 2013, CCIS 400, pp. 105–115, 2013.
© Springer-Verlag Berlin Heidelberg 2013

Example 1: *This brand is the worst quality that I have purchased. I would avoid this brand.*

Each sentence in this review provides a strong indicator, i.e., *"worst quality"* and *"avoid this brand"*, for predicting the review as a *negative* one. Assume that a trained classifier has already possessed the classification knowledge for predicting *"worst quality"* but got no idea about *"avoid this brand"*. Once the review is correctly predicted and added into the labeled data for further learning, the classifier is then likely to contain the classification knowledge for predicting *"avoid this brand"*. Therefore, when we iteratively label the unlabeled documents and use them to retrain the classifier, it is possible to introduce helpful knowledge in the unlabeled documents. This process is exactly a typical implementation of the semi-supervised learning approach named bootstrapping. Intuitively, this approach should be effective for semi-supervised TC since the information of many documents are often redundant for predicting categories, that is, there are usually more than one indicator for predicting the category label. Unfortunately, bootstrapping has been reported to be a poorly-performed approach for semi-supervised TC in previous studies. For example, as reported by Li et al. (2010), bootstrapping (called self-training therein) is one of the worst approaches for semi-supervised sentiment classification and fails to improve the performance across almost all the eight domains.

In this paper, we will change the awkward situation of bootstrapping. First of all, we give two basic preferences for a possibly successful bootstrapping, namely *sufficiency* and *diversity*. While *sufficiency* indicates the ability of the classifier for correctly predicting the class to enable a successful bootstrapping, *diversity* indicates the preference of adding unlabeled samples which better represent the natural data distribution. Specifically, to better satisfy the *diversity* preference, we use several feature subspace classifiers to automatically label and select samples instead of using a single classifier over the whole feature space. In this way, selected samples tend to be more different from the existing labeled data in terms of the whole feature space. Empirical studies demonstrate a great success of our novel bootstrapping approach by using feature subspace classifiers.

The rest of this paper is organized as follows. Section 2 reviews related work on semi-supervised TC. Section 3 describes the two preferences for a successful bootstrapping. Section 4 proposes some novel alternatives of bootstrapping with a focus on the *diversity* preference. Section 5 presents experimental results on both topic and sentiment classification. Finally, Section 6 gives the conclusion and future work.

2   Related Work

2.1   Topic Classification

Generally, two major groups of methods are exploited in topic classification: the first is Expectation Maximization (EM) which estimates maximum posteriori parameters of a generative model (Dempster et al., 1977; McCallum and Nigam, 1998; Nigam et al., 2000; Cong et al., 2004) and the second one is Co-training which employs two or multiple disjoint views to train a committee of classifiers to collectively select automatically labeled data (Blum and Mitchell, 1998; Braga et al., 2009). Both of them have achieved great success on topic classification. To compare EM and Co-training, Nigam and Ghani (2000) present an extensive empirical study on two benchmark corpus: WebKB and 20News. The results show that EM performs slightly better than Co-training on WebKB while Co-training significantly outperforms EM on 20News. The general better performance of Co-training is due to its more robustness to the violated assumptions.

Except the two main groups, some studies propose other semi-supervised learning approaches for topic classification, such as transductive learning (Joachims, 1999) and SemiBoost (Mallapragada et al., 2009). All these studies confirm that using unlabeled data can significantly decrease classification error in topic classification.

2.2   Sentiment Classification

While supervised learning methods for sentiment classification have been extensively studied since the pioneer work by Pang et al. (2002), the studies on semi-supervised sentiment classification are relatively rare.

Dasgupta and Ng (2009) integrate several technologies, such as spectral clustering, active learning, transductive learning, and ensemble learning, to conduct semi-supervised sentiment classification. However, the obtained performance remains very low (the accuracies on Book and DVD domains are about 60% when using 100 labeled samples).

More recently, Li et al. (2010) propose a Co-training algorithm with personal/impersonal views for semi-supervised sentiment classification. Their experiments show that both self-training and tranductive learning completely fail and even in their co-training approach, incorporating unlabeled data is rather harmful on DVD domain.

Unlike both studies mentioned above, our bootstrapping approach is much more successful for semi-supervised sentiment classification and impressively improves the performance on Book and DVD domains when using 100 labeled samples.

3   Two Basic Preferences for Successful Bootstrapping

Bootstrapping is a commonly used approach for semi-supervised learning (Yarowsky, 1995; Abney, 2002). In bootstrapping, a classifier is first trained with a small amount of labeled data and then iteratively retained by adding most confident unlabeled samples as new labeled data.

To guarantee successful bootstrapping, two basic preferences should be reinforced. On one side, the classifier C in bootstrapping should be good enough to correctly predict the newly-added samples in each iteration as many as possible. Otherwise, many wrongly predicted samples would make bootstrapping fail completely. For clarity, we refer to this preference as *sufficiency*.

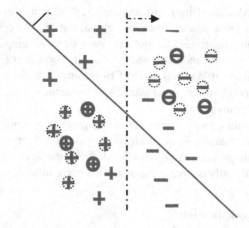

Fig. 1. Possible hyperplane (the solid red line) when the labeled samples are more concentrated

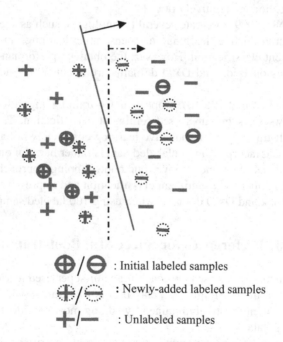

$\oplus/\ominus$: Initial labeled samples

$\oplus/\ominus$: Newly-added labeled samples

$+/-$: Unlabeled samples

Fig. 2. Possible hyperplane (the solid red line) when the labeled samples are less concentrated

On the other side, traditional bootstrapping is prone to label the samples very similar to the initial labeled data in the initial several iterations because these samples could be predicted with much more confidence due to the small scale of the labeled data. However, labeling similar samples might be dangerous because the labeled data including the initial and the newly-added ones would violate the data distribution and fail to obtain a good classification hyperplane. Figure 1 shows the trained hyperplane (the solid line) under the situation when the labeled data are concentrated. We can see that when the newly-added data is too close to the initial labeled data, the trained hyperplane might be far away from the optimal one (the dotted line). One possible way to overcome the concentration drawback is to make the added data more different from the initial data and better reflect the natural data distribution. Figure 2 shows the situation when the labeled data are less concentrated. In this case, the trained hyperlane would be much better. For clarity, we refer to this preference of letting newly-labeled data more different from existing labeled data as *diversity*.

4   Subspace-Based Bootstrapping for Semi-supervised TC

4.1   Feature Subspace in TC

A document is represented as a set of features $F = \{f_1, ..., f_m\}$ in a machine learning-based method for TC. Assume $X = (X_1, X_2, ..., X_n)$ the training data containing n documents and a document X_i is denoted as $X_i = (x_{i1}, x_{i2}, ..., x_{im})$ where x_{ij} is some statistic information of the feature f_j, e.g., tf, $tf \cdot idf$.

When a feature subset, i.e., $F^S = \{f_1^S, ..., f_r^S\}$ ($r < m$), is used to generate the feature vectors of the documents, the original m-dimensional feature space becomes an r-dimensional feature subspace. In this way, the modified training data $X^S = (X_1^S, X_2^S, ..., X_n^S)$, denoted as subspace data, consists of r-dimensional samples $X^S = (x_{i1}^S, x_{i2}^S, ..., x_{ir}^S)$ ($i = 1, ..., n$). A classifier trained with the subspace training data is called a subspace classifier.

4.2   Bootstrapping with Random Subspace

In bootstrapping, the classifier for choosing the samples with high confidences is usually trained over the whole feature space. This type of classifier tends to choose the samples much similar to the initial labeled data in terms of the whole feature space. As pointed in Section 3, this might cause the labeled data too concentrated to form a reasonable classification hyperplane. Instead, when a subspace classifier is applied, the added data is only similar to the existing labeled data in terms of the feature subspace and thus could be possibly more different in terms of the whole feature space. Generally, the extent of the differences between each two subspace classifiers largely depends on the differences of the features they used. One straight way to obtain different subspace classifiers is to randomly select r features from the whole feature set in each iteration in bootstrapping. Figure 3 illustrates the bootstrapping algorithm with random subspace classifiers.

Input:
  Labeled data L
  Unlabeled data U
Output:
  New classifier C
Procedure:
  For k=1 to N
  (1). Randomly select a feature subset F_k^S of size r from F
  (2). Generate a subspace data L_k^S with F_k^S and L
  (3). Learn a subspace classifier C_k^S with L_k^S
  (4). Use C_k^S to predict samples from U_{k-1}
  (5). Choose n most confidently predicted samples A_k
  (6). Add them into L_k, i.e., $L_k = L_k \bigcup A_k$
  (7). Remove A_k from U_k, i.e., $U_k = U_{k-1} - A_k$
  Use the updated data L_N to train a classifier C

Fig. 3. Bootstrapping algorithm with random subspace classifiers

The size of the feature subset r is an important parameter in this algorithm. The smaller r, the more different subspace classifiers are from each other. However, the value of r should not be too small because a classifier trained with too few features is not capable of correctly predicting samples.

4.3   Bootstrapping with Excluded Subspace

Although random feature selection is able to make the subspaces in different bootstrapping iterations differ from each other to some extent, the degree is still limited. To better satisfy the *diversity* preference, we improve the random subspace generation strategy with an constraint which restricts that every two adjacent subspace classifiers do not share any feature, i.e., $F_k^S \bigcap F_{k-1}^S = \varnothing$ where F_k^S represents the feature subset used in k-th iteration. This can be done by selecting a feature subset F_k^S from $F - F_{k-1}^S$ instead of F. We refer to this feature generation strategy as subspace excluding strategy. Figure 4 illustrates the bootstrapping algorithm with excluded subspace classifiers.

Input:
    Labeled data L
    Unlabeled data U

Output:
    New classifier C

Procedure:
For k=1 to N

    (1). Select a feature subset F_k^S of size r from $F - F_{k-1}^S$

    (2). Generate a subspace data L_k^S with F_k^S and L

    (3). Learn a subspace classifier C_k^S with L_k^S

    (4). Use C_k^S to predict samples from U_{k-1}

    (5). Choose n most confidently predicted samples A_k

    (6). Add them into L_k, i.e., $L_k = L_k \cup A_k$

    (7). Remove A_k from U_k, i.e., $U_k = U_{k-1} - A_k$

Use the updated data L_N to train a classifier C

Fig. 4. Bootstrapping algorithm with excluded subspace classifiers

4.4 Diversity Consideration among Different Types of Features

TC tasks, especially sentiment classification, often involve many types of features, such as word anagrams, word diagrams, or even syntactic features from dependency parsing (Xia et al., 2011). Although different types of the features may differ in morphology, some are sharing similar knowledge. Take *excellent* and *is_excellent* as examples of word unigram and bigram features respectively. Obviously, these two features share similar classification ability and are very likely to select similar samples. Therefore, it is necessary to consider the diversity among different types of features for real diversity between each two adjacent subspaces F_{k-1}^S and F_k^S.

Therefore, we introduce another constraint which restricts that every two adjacent subspace classifiers do not share any similar features. Here, two features are considered similar when they contain the same informative unigram. For example, *is_excellent* and *very_excellent* are considered similar because they both contain the informative unigram 'excellent'. In this study, we perform a standard feature selection method, mutual information (MI), on the labeled data to select top-N unigrams as the informative unigrams (Yang and Pedersen, 1997).

To satisfy this constraint, we first select a set of unigram features, denoted as F^{S-Uni}, from $F - F_{k-1}^S$; Then, we collect all the other-type features that contain any informative feature in F^{S-Uni} and put them into the feature subset. For example, assume that *excellent* is an informative feature. Once it is selected in F^{S-Uni}, we collect all bigrams like *is_excellent*, *very_excellent*, *not_excellent*, etc., and put them into the feature subset. It is important to note that the total number of the features for generating subspace is not guaranteed to a fixed value such as r. Instead, we make that size of the unigram feature set fixed, which equals $\left|F^{Uni}\right| \cdot \theta$ where F^{Uni} is the feature set of word unigrams and θ ($\theta = r / m$) is the proportion of the selected features and all features.

5   Experimentation

5.1   Experimental Setting

In topic classification, we use two common benchmark corpora: 20News and WebKB, where the former consists of 20017 articles divided almost evenly into twenty different categories (Joachims, 1999) and the latter contains 4199 web pages from four popular categories (Craven et al., 1998). In sentiment classification, we use the product reviews from four domains: book, DVD, electronic, and kitchen appliances (Blitzer et al., 2007). Each of the four domains contains 1000 positive and 1000 negative reviews. In the experiments, 200 documents in each category are served as testing data and the remaining data are served as initial labeled data and unlabeled data.

Maximum Entropy (ME) is adopted as the classification algorithm with the help of Mallet[1] tool. All parameters are set to their default values. In particular, we employ both word unigrams and bigrams as the features. Our experimental results show that combining both word unigram and bigram features achieves similar results to only using unigrams in topic classification but apparently more preferable in sentiment classification. Nevertheless, our feature subspace-based bootstrapping approach is effective in both cases. To highlight the importance of diversity consideration of bigram features, we focus on the results of using both unigram and bigram features.

5.2   Experimental Results on Bootstrapping

In this section, we systematically evaluate the performance of our feature subspace-based bootstrapping and compare it with the supervised baseline:

1) Baseline: training a classifier with the initial labeled data (no unlabeled data is employed);
2) Bootstrapping-T: the traditional bootstrapping algorithm as shown in Figure 1;
3) Bootstrapping-RS: the bootstrapping algorithm with random subspace classifiers as shown in Figure 3;
4) Bootstrapping-ES: the bootstrapping algorithm with excluded subspace classifiers as shown in Figure 4;
5) Bootstrapping-ES+: the Bootstrapping-ES implementation with a feature excluding strategy as described in Section 4.4 to guarantee the difference between different types of features, i.e., word unigrams and bigrams in this study.

Performance of Different Bootstrapping Approaches

Figure 5 illustrates the results of the baseline and different bootstrapping approaches in topic classification and sentiment classification. For those approaches involving random selection of features, we run 5 times for them and report the average results.

---

[1] http://mallet.cs.umass.edu/

Figure 5 shows that:

➢ Semi-supervised learning in sentiment classification is much more difficult than that in topic classification. While the traditional bootstrapping, i.e., Bootstrapping-T could dramatically outperforms the baseline in both datasets of topic classification, it performs much worse than baseline in all four domains of sentiment classification.

➢ Bootstrapping-RS significantly outperforms Bootstrapping-T (p-value<0.001) except in the dataset of WebKB. This may be due to the fact that topic classification on WebKB has reached its performance ceiling via traditional bootstrapping and thus become difficult to make further improvement.

➢ Bootstrapping-ES is more effective than Bootstrapping-RS across four datasets but fails to improve Bootstrapping-RS in two datasets: Book and Electronic. This failure is due to the fact that using bigrams makes each two adjacent subspaces similar to each other to some extent. In fact, if only unigrams is used, Bootstrapping-ES always outperforms Bootstrapping-RS, increasing the accuracy from 0.62 to 0.67 in Book and from 0.71 to 0.73 in Electronic.

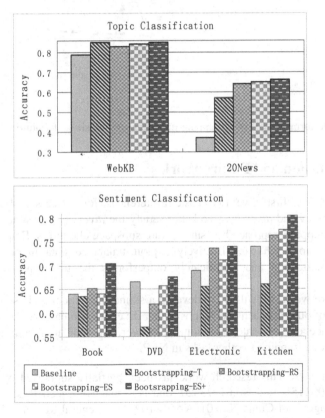

Fig. 5. Comparison of different bootstrapping approaches in topic classification (10 labeled samples per category) and sentiment classification (50 labeled samples per category)

➢ Bootstrapping-ES+ performs best among the four types of bootstrapping approaches and it almost outperforms both Bootstrapping-ES and Bootstrapping-RS in all datasets. Especially, it performs much better than Bootstrapping-ES in Book and Electronic, which verifies the importance of considering the diversity among different types of features.

Sensitiveness of the Parameter θ (r/m)

The size of the feature subspace is an important parameter in our approach. Figure 6 shows the performance of Bootstrapping-ES+ with varying sizes of the feature subspace. From Figure 6, we can see that a choice of the proportion between 1/3 and 1/6 is recommended. The size of the feature subspace should not be too small because a small amount of features would prevent a subspace well representing the samples and violate the *sufficiency* preference.

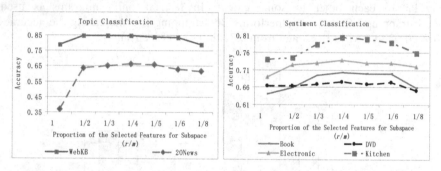

Fig. 6. Performances of Bootstrapping-ES+ over varying sizes of feature subspace

6   Conclusion and Future Work

In this paper, we first give two basic preferences for successful bootstrapping, namely *sufficiency* and *diversity*. To better satisfy the *diversity* preference, we present a novel bootstrapping approach by using feature subspace classifiers. Empirical studies show that our approach can effectively exploit unlabeled data in both topic and sentiment classification and significantly outperforms the traditional bootstrapping approach.

In our future work, we will try to develop a sound theoretical understanding to the effectiveness of our approach and propose other diversity strategies to further improve the performance on text categorization. Moreover, we will apply our feature subspace-based bootstrapping to other tasks in NLP.

Acknowledgments. This research work has been partially supported by two NSFC grants, No.61003155, and No.61273320, one National High-tech Research and Development Program of China No.2012AA011102, one General Research Fund (GRF) sponsored by the Research Grants Council of Hong Kong No.543810.

References

1. Abney, S.: Bootstrapping. In: Proceedings of ACL 2002, pp. 360–367 (2002)
2. Blitzer, J., Dredze, M., Pereira, F.: Biographies, Bollywood, Boom-boxes and Blenders: Domain Adaptation for Sentiment Classification. In: Proceedings of ACL 2007, pp. 440–447 (2007)
3. Blum, A., Mitchell, T.: Combining Labeled and Unlabeled Data with Co-training. In: Proceedings of COLT 1998, pp. 92–100 (1998)
4. Braga, I., Monard, M., Matsubara, E.: Combining Unigrams and Bigrams in Semi-supervised Text Classification. In: Proceedings of EPIA 2009: The 14th Portuguese Conference on Artificial Intelligence, pp. 489–500 (2009)
5. Cong, G., Lee, W.S., Wu, H., Liu, B.: Semi-supervised text classification using partitioned EM. In: Lee, Y., Li, J., Whang, K.-Y., Lee, D. (eds.) DASFAA 2004. LNCS, vol. 2973, pp. 482–493. Springer, Heidelberg (2004)
6. Craven, M., DiPasquo, D., Freitag, D., McCallum, A., Mitchell, T., Nigam, K., Slattery, S.: Learning to Extract Symbolic Knowledge from the World Wide Web. In: Proceedings of AAAI 1998, pp. 509–516 (1998)
7. Dasgupta, S., Ng, V.: Mine the Easy, Classify the Hard: A Semi-Supervised Approach to Automatic Sentiment Classification. In: Proceedings of ACL-IJCNLP 2009, pp. 701–709 (2009)
8. Dempster, A., Laird, N., Rubin, D.: Maximum Likelihood from Incomplete Data via the EM Algorithm. Journal of the Royal Statistical Society: Series B 39(1), 1–38 (1977)
9. Joachims, T.: Transductive Inference for Text Classification Using Support Vector Machines. In: Proceedings of ICML 1999, pp. 200–209 (1999)
10. Kullback, S., Leibler, R.: On Information and Sufficiency. Annals of Mathematical Statistics 22(1), 79–86 (1951)
11. Li, S., Huang, C., Zhou, G., Lee, S.: Employing Personal/Impersonal Views in Supervised and Semi-supervised Sentiment Classification. In: Proceedings of ACL 2010, pp. 414–423 (2010)
12. Mallapragada, P., Jin, R., Jain, A., Liu, Y.: SemiBoost: Boosting for Semi-Supervised Learning. IEEE Transaction on Pattern Analysis and Machine Intelligence 31(11), 2000–2014 (2009)
13. McCallum, A., Nigam, K.: Employing EM and Pool-Based Active Learning for Text Classification. In: Proceedings of ICML 1998, pp. 350–358 (1998)
14. Nigam, K., McCallum, A., Thrun, S., Mitchell, T.: Text Classification from Labeled and Unlabeled Documents using EM. Machine Learning 39(2/3), 103–134 (2000)
15. Nigam, K., Ghani, R.: Analyzing the Effectiveness and Applicability of Co-training. In: Proceedings of CIKM 2000, pp. 86–93 (2000)
16. Pang, B., Lee, L., Vaithyanathan, S.: Thumbs up? Sentiment Classification using Machine Learning Techniques. In: Proceedings of EMNLP 2002, pp. 79–86 (2002)
17. Sebastiani, F.: Machine Learning in Automated Text Categorization. ACM Computing Surveys 34(1), 1–47 (2002)
18. Xia, R., Zong, C., Li, S.: Ensemble of Feature Sets and Classification Algorithms for Sentiment Classification. Information Sciences 181, 1138–1152 (2011)
19. Yang, Y., Pedersen, J.: A Comparative Study on Feature Selection in Text Categorization. In: Proceedings of the 14th International Conference on Machine Learning, ICML 1997, pp. 412–420 (1997)
20. Yarowsky, D.: Unsupervised Word Sense Disambiguation Rivaling Supervised Methods. In: Proceedings of ACL 2005, pp. 189–196 (1995)

Pseudo In-Domain Data Selection from Large-Scale Web Corpus for Spoken Language Translation

Shixiang Lu, Xingyuan Peng, Zhenbiao Chen, and Bo Xu

Interactive Digital Media Technology Research Center (IDMTech),
Institute of Automation, Chinese Academy of Sciences, Beijing, China
{shixiang.lu,xingyuan.peng,zhenbiao.chen,xubo}@ia.ac.cn

Abstract. This paper is concerned with exploring efficient domain adaptation for the task of statistical machine translation, which is based on extracting sentence pairs (*pseudo in-domain subcorpora*, that are most relevant to the in domain corpora) from a large-scale general-domain web bilingual corpus. These sentences are selected by our proposed unsupervised phrase-based data selection model. Compared with the traditional bag-of-words models, our phrase-based data selection model is more effective because it captures contextual information in modeling the selection of phrase as a whole, rather than selection of single words in isolation. These pseudo in-domain subcorpora can then be used to train small domain-adapted spoken language translation system which outperforms the system trained on the entire corpus, with an increase of 1.6 BLEU points. Performance is further improved when we use these pseudo in-domain corpus/models in combination with the true in-domain corpus/model, with increases of 4.5 and 3.9 BLEU points over single in- and general-domain baseline system, respectively.

Keywords: domain adaptation, phrase-based data selection, pseudo in-domain subcorpora, spoken language translation.

1 Introduction

Statistical machine translation (SMT) system performance is dependent on the quantity and quality of available training data. It seems to be a universal truth that translation performance can always be improved by using more training data, but only if the training data is reasonably well-matched with the current translation task [14]. It is also obvious that among the large training data the topics or domains of discussion will change [3], which causes the mismatch problems with the translation task. For these reasons, one would prefer to use more in-domain data for training, and this would empirically better target the translation task at hand [12,11]. However, parallel in-domain data is usually hard to find, and so performance is assumed to be limited by the quantity of domain-specific training data used to build the model. Additional bilingual data can be

G. Zhou et al. (Eds.): NLPCC 2013, CCIS 400, pp. 116–126, 2013.
© Springer-Verlag Berlin Heidelberg 2013

readily acquired, but at the cost of specificity: either the data is entirely unrelated to the task at hand, or the data is from a broad enough pool of topics and styles, such as the web, that any use this corpus may provide is due to its size, and not its relevance [1].

Domain adaptation task in SMT is to translate a text in a particular (target) domain for which only a small amount of training data is available, using a SMT system trained on a larger set of data that is not restricted to the target domain. We call this larger set of data a *general-domain* corpus, which allows a large uncurated corpus to include some text that may be relevant to the target domain.

Many existing domain adaptation methods fall into two broad categories. First, adaptation can be done at the corpus level, by selecting or weighting the data sets upon which the models are trained [1,5,13]. Second, it can be also achieved at the model level by mixing multiple translation models together [1,4,7], often in a weighted manner. In this paper, we explore both of the two above categories.

Firstly, we propose two types (monolingual and bilingual) phrase-based data selection models, and assume that data selection should be performed at the phrase level. Compared with the traditional bag-of-words models that account for data selection of single words in isolation [5,13], our two phrase-based data selection model are potentially more effective because they captures some contextual information in modeling the selection of phrase as a whole. More precise selection can be determined for phrases than for words, as we will show in the experiments.

Nextly, we use the phrase-based data selection models for ranking the sentence pairs in a large-scale general-domain web bilingual corpus with respect to an in-domain corpus. A cutoff can then be applied to produce a very small but useful subcorpus, which in turn can be used to train a domain-adapted SMT system. We show it is possible to use our data selection models to subselect less than 18% of a large general training corpus and still increase translation performance by nearly 1.6 BLEU points on the IWSLT task.

Finally, we explore how best to use these selected subcorpora. We test their combination with the in-domain corpora, followed by examining the subcorpora to see whether they are actually in-domain, out-of-domain, or something in between. Based on this, we compare translation model combination methods. We show that these tiny translation models for model combination can improve system performance even further over the current standard way of producing a domain-adapted SMT system. The resulting process is lightweight, simple, and effective. Performance is further improved when we use these domain-adapted corpus/models in combination with the true in-domain corpus/model, with increases of 4.5 and 3.9 BLEU points over single in- and general-domain baseline system, respectively.

The remainder of this paper is organized as follows. Section 2 describes our proposed monolingual and bilingual phrase-based data selection methods. Section 3 presents the large-scale general-domain web corpus, domain adaptation results and experimental analysis, and followed by conclusions and future work in section 4.

2   Phrase-Based Data Selection

For the phrase-based translation model [6], the basic translate unit is phrase, that is to say, a continuous word sequence. It is a natural idea to use the phrase to measure the similarity between the sentence pairs in in- and general-domain corpus. If the sentence pair in general-domain corpus which are selected contain more phrases in in-domain corpus, the sentence pair is more similar to the in-domain corpus. Then we try to select the bilingual sentence pairs from the general-domain corpus which can cover more phrases of the in-domain corpus as the similar sentence pair for domain adaptation. Next, we will first describe the monolingual phrase-based data selection, and then extend it to bilingual data selection.

2.1   Monolingual Phrase-Based Data Selection

In our monolingual phrase-based data selection model, the phrases play a vital role. Inspired by the work of [9,10], we assume the following generative process. Firstly, we extract all the phrases from the source-side sentences in the in-domain bilingual corpus and assign them different weights. We take two aspects into account to estimate the weight of phrase: the information it contains and the length of the phrase.

In information theory, the information contained in a statement is measured by the negative logarithm of the probability of the statement [2,8]. Therefore, we should estimate the probability of each phrase firstly. We class the phrases with their lengths and only use the phrases whose length is not longer than five[1] in order to avoid the sparse data problem. We calculate the probabilities of the phrases based on their lengths. For a phrase p, $|p|$ represents its length, and the probability $P(p)$ is estimated by the following formula:

$$P(p) = \frac{count(p)}{\sum_{|p_i|=|p|} count(p_i)} \tag{1}$$

where the numerator $count(p)$ is the total number of phrase p appearing in the source-side sentences of the in-domain bilingual corpus, and the denominator is the total number of the phrases whose length is equal to $|p|$. It is worth to notice that letting the phrase length be one reduces the model from phrase to word, and we get word frequency. Though this is somewhat similar to TF-IDF, our approach is based on information theory, they are different in essence and get different performances.

Then, the information contained in phrase p is calculated as follows,

$$I(p) = -\log P(p) \tag{2}$$

In this way, we get the information contained in each phrase. Because the translation model is based on phrase, the longer phrase will lead to better translation. Therefore, we take $|p|$, the length of phrase, into account. We use the

---

[1] In our experiments, when the phrase length is large than five, the phrase become sparse sharply, and the performance of selected sentences decreases consistently.

square root of length, but not the length directly because of the data smoothing problem. The formula used to calculate the weight of each phrase is shown as follows,

$$W(p) = \sqrt{|p|} \cdot I(p) \qquad (3)$$

Next, we get the weight for each phrase in the source-side sentences of the in-domain bilingual corpus based on the length of the phrase and the information it contains. Then we can estimate the average weight of a source-side sentence in the sentence pair of general-domain bilingual corpus by the weights of all the phrases it contains. For a source-side sentence s_{src} in the bilingual sentence pair, if more phrases it contains appear in the source-side sentences of the in-domain bilingual corpus, we assign it a larger score. Thus, the score of the source-side sentence s_{src} can be calculated by the following formula:

$$Score_1^{mono} = \frac{\sum_{p \in P_{src}^I} W(p)}{|s_{src}|} \qquad (4)$$

where $|s_{src}|$ represents its length, and P_{src}^I is the set of all the phrases contained in the source-side sentences of the in-domain bilingual corpus.

We extract all the phrases whose length is not longer than five in sentence s_{src}, and add all the weights of phrases together. If a phrase does not appear in the source-side sentences of the in-domain corpus, the weight of the phrase is set to zero. Then, the sentence pairs are sorted by their source-side sentence's score $Score_1^{mono}$ in a descending order, and we select the sentence pair whose $Score_1^{mono}$ higher as the similar sentence pairs and add into pseudo in-domain corpus.

To further improve the performance, we also define another formula to estimate the weight of sentence s_{src}, as follows,

$$Score_2^{mono} = \frac{\sum_{p \in P_{src}^I} W(p) - \sum_{p \in (P_{src}^G - P_{src}^I)} W(p)}{|s_{src}|} \qquad (5)$$

where, P_{src}^G is the set of all the phrases contained in the source-side sentences of the general-domain bilingual corpus.

Compared with $Score_1^{mono}$, in this formula, we consider the phrases which have occurred in P_{src}^G but not occurred in P_{src}^I as the unseen phrases, assume these unseen phrases have negative information to similarity measure, and assign lower score to the source-side sentence s_{src} which has more unseen phrases. This means the sentence pair in the general-domain bilingual corpus whose source-side sentence contains more unseen phrases, would not like to be selected as the similar sentence pair. The weights of the unseen phrase are calculated as Equation (1) to Equation (3) on the source-side sentences of a random subset[2] from the general-domain bilingual corpus.

---

[2] In our experiments, the size of the random subset is equal to the size of in-domain corpus.

2.2 Bilingual Phrase-Based Data Selection

To further use the above monolingual criteria for data selection, we propose another new model that takes into account the bilingual nature of the problem. To this end, we sum monolingual phrase-based similarity score over each side of the bilingual sentence pair, both source- and target-side,

$$Score_1^{bi} = \frac{\sum_{p \in P_{src}^I} W(p)}{|s_{src}|} + \frac{\sum_{p \in P_{tgt}^I} W(p)}{|s_{tgt}|} \tag{6}$$

$$Score_2^{bi} = \frac{\sum_{p \in P_{src}^I} W(p) - \sum_{p \in (P_{src}^G - P_{src}^I)} W(p)}{|s_{src}|}$$
$$+ \frac{\sum_{p \in P_{tgt}^I} W(p) - \sum_{p \in (P_{tgt}^G - P_{tgt}^I)} W(p)}{|s_{tgt}|} \tag{7}$$

Again, the sentence pair in the general-domain bilingual corpus which has higher sum scores are presumed to be better. These two models reuse the two extract phrase sets from the source-side sentences in in- and general-domain bilingual corpus, respectively, but requires the corresponding similarly-trained twos over the English side.

3 Experiments and Results

3.1 Corpora

We conduct our experiments on the International Workshop on Spoken Language Translation (IWSLT) Chinese-to-English task. Two corpora are needed for the domain adaptation task. Our in-domain bilingual corpus consists of the Basic Traveling Expression corpus and China-Japan-Korea corpus, which contains 0.38M parallel sentence pairs with 3.5/3.82M words of Chinese/English. Our general-domain bilingual corpus are collected from web data (Baidu[3], Youdao[4], Huajian[5] and Shooter[6]), which contains 11M parallel sentences pairs with 123/135M words of Chinese/English, and they are most relevant to the spoken language domain. The test set is IWSLT 2007 test set which consists of 489 sentences with 4 English reference translations each, and the development set is IWSLT 2005 test set which consists of 506 sentences with 4 English reference translations each.

---

[3] The example bilingual sentence pairs in http://dict.baidu.com/
[4] The example bilingual sentence pairs in http://dict.youdao.com/
[5] The example bilingual sentence pairs in http://www.hjtrans.com/
[6] The bilingual subtitles in http://www.shooter.cn/xml/list/sub

3.2 System Description

We use an out-of-the-box Moses[7] *(2010-8-13 version)* framework to implement the phrase-based machine translation system. GIZA++ [17] is used to get word alignments from the bilingual corpus with *grow-diag-final-and* option. Using the English side of the corresponding bilingual corpus, we estimate the 4-gram language models (LM) by the SRILM toolkit [19] with interpolated modified Kneser-Ney discounting. We perform minimum error rate training [16] to tune the feature weights on the development set. The translation quality is evaluated by case-insensitive BLEU-4 metric [18] using the script *mteval-v13a.pl.*

3.3 Baseline System

Using the corresponding corpus, the baseline translation models (in- and general-domain) are generated by Moses with default parameter settings. The BLEU scores of the baseline single-corpus systems are in Table 3. The results show that a translation system trained on the general-domain corpus outperforms a system trained on the in-domain corpus by over 0.5 BLEU points.

Table 1. Baseline translation results for in- and general-domain corpus

Corpus	BLEU	
	Development	Test
In	51.94	40.62
General	48.32	41.15

3.4 Selecting Subset from the General-Domain Corpus

The baseline results show that a translation system trained on the general-domain corpus outperforms a system trained on the in-domain corpus by over 0.5 BLEU points. However, this can be further improved. In our experiments, we consider the following methods for extracting domain targeted sentence pairs from the general-domain bilingual corpus:

TF-IDF is the foundation of our experiment since it has gained significant performance for data selection based translation model adaptation [5,13]. We use it as the source-side monolingual formula for data selection.

Bilingual Cross-Entropy Difference (BCED) [1] is chosen to be compared with our approach, because it also captures contextual information when selecting similar data, and it is used to select data from large-scale general-domain corpus for SMT. It sum cross-entropy difference over each side of the sentence pair in general-domain bilingual corpus, both source- and target-side:

$$[H_{I-src}(s_{src}) - H_{G-src}(s_{src})] + [H_{I-tgt}(s_{tgt}) - H_{G-tgt}(s_{tgt})] \qquad (8)$$

---

[7] http://www.statmt.org/moses/index.php?n=Main.HomePage

where, in our implementation, the in-domain source- and target-side LM are estimated by the corresponding side of in-domain bilingual corpus, the general-domain source- and target-side LM are estimated on the corresponding side of a random subset of 0.38M sentences pairs[8] from the general-domain corpus, respectively.

Score$_1^{mono}$ and **Score**$_2^{mono}$ are our proposed source-side monolingual phrase-based data selection model, and **Score**$_1^{bi}$ and **Score**$_2^{bi}$ are our proposed bilingual phrase-based data selection model, respectively.

Regardless of method, the overall procedure is the same. Using the scoring method, we rank the individual sentence pairs of the general-domain corpus. The net effect is that of domain adaptation via threshhold filtering. New SMT systems are then trained solely on these small subcorpora, and compared against the baseline model trained on the entire 11M sentence pairs of the general-domain corpus.

We select the top N sentence pairs using each scoring method, varying N from 0.5M to 6M, and then train the corresponding translation models on these subcorpora. These translation models are then used to test the performance on the development set, as shown in Fig. 1. These subcorpora outperforms the entire general-domain corpus, and yet, no of them are anywhere near the performance of the in-domain corpus. From this, it can be deduced that data selection methods are not finding data that is strictly in-domain. Rather they are selecting *pseudo in-domain data* which is relevant, but with a different distribution than the original in-domain corpus. The results show that the top 2M pseudo in-domain sentence pairs works best. From now, we use this top 2M sentence pairs out of the 11M general-domain corpus for the next experiments.

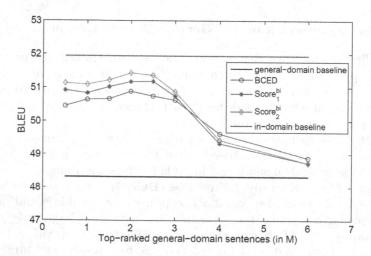

Fig. 1. The translation results of pseudo in-domain sentence pairs selection from the large-scale general-domain corpus on the development set

---

[8] Which is equal to the size of in-domain corpus.

Table 2. Translation results of using only a subset of the general-domain corpus

Method	Sentence Pairs	BLEU	
		Development	Test
General	11M	48.32	41.15
TF-IDF	2M	50.15	41.92
BCED	2M	50.68	42.43
$Score_1^{mono}$	2M	50.42	42.21
$Score_1^{mono}$	2M	50.56	42.13
$Score_1^{bi}$	2M	50.97	42.51
$Score_2^{bi}$	2M	51.23	42.77

Table 2 contains BLEU scores of the systems trained on subsets (pseudo in-domain sentence pairs) of the general-domain corpus. Using only the source-side monolingual phrase-based score ($Score_1^{mono}$ and $Score_1^{mono}$) are able to outperform the general-domain model when selecting 2M out of the entire 11M sentence pairs. The previous BCED (bilingual cross-entropy difference) works better. The bilingual phrase-based method ($Score_1^{bi}$ and $Score_2^{bi}$) proposed in this paper work best, especially $Score_2^{bi}$ consistently boosting performance by +1.6 BLEU points while using less than 18% of the available training data (2M sentence pairs). Consider the unseen phrases can further improve the performance of the phrase-based data selection model ($Score_2^{bi}$ vs. $Score_1^{bi}$; $Score_2^{mono}$ vs. $Score_1^{mono}$).

3.5   Mixing Corpus

As further evidence, consider the results of mixing the in-domain corpus with the best extracted sub pseudo in-domain corpus to train a single translation system in Table 3.

Table 3. Translation results of mixing the in-domain and pseudo in-domain data to train a single model

Method	Sentence Pairs	BLEU	
		Development	Test
In	0.38M	51.94	40.62
General	11M	48.32	41.15
BCED	2M	50.68	42.43
$Score_1^{bi}$	2M	50.97	42.51
$Score_2^{bi}$	2M	51.23	42.77
In+BCED	2.38M	53.51	44.24
In+$Score_1^{bi}$	2.38M	53.83	44.46
In+$Score_2^{bi}$	2.38M	54.16	44.52

The change in both the development and test scores appears to reflect dissimilarity in the underlying data. Were the two data sets more alike, one would expect the models to reinforce each other rather than cancel out. Mixing the pseudo in-domain data with in-domain data outperforms the in- and general-domain data, and with increases of 3.9 ("In+$Score_2^{bi}$" vs. "In") and 3.4 ("In+$Score_2^{bi}$" vs. "General") BLEU points, respectively.

3.6   Mixing Models

Finally, we test the approach in [4,7], passing the two phrase tables directly to the decoder and tuning a system using both phrase tables in parallel. Each phrase table receives a separate set of weights during tuning, thus this mixed translation model has more parameters than a normal single-table system. Unlike the previous work [15], we explicitly did not attempt to resolve any overlap between the two phrase tables, as there is no need to do so with the multiple decoding paths. Any phrase pairs appearing in both models will be treated separately by the decoder. However, the exact overlap between the phrase tables was tiny, minimizing this effect.

It is well to use the in-domain data to select pseudo in-domain data from the general-domain corpus, but given that this requires access to an in-domain corpus, one might as well use it. As such, we used the in-domain translation model alongside the pseudo in-domain translation models. The detail translation results are in Table 4.

Table 4. Translation results from mixing in-domain and pseudo in-domain translation models together

Method	BLEU	
	Development	Test
In	51.94	40.62
General	48.32	41.15
In,General	53.61	43.57
In,BCED 2M	54.77	44.82
In,$Score_1^{bi}$ 2M	55.03	44.99
In,$Score_2^{bi}$ 2M	55.17	45.16

A translation system trained on the pseudo in-domain subset of the general-domain corpus, can be further improved by combining with an in-domain model. Furthermore, this system combination works better than the conventional mixing multi-model approach by up to 0.6 BLEU points ("In,$Score_2^{bi}$ 2M" vs. "In+$Score_2^{bi}$") on the test set. Thus a domain-adapted system mixing two phrase tables trained on a total of 2.38M sentences outperforms the standard multi-model system which is trained on 11M sentences. This model-combined system is also 4 BLEU points better than the general-domain system by itself, and 4.5 BLEU points ("In,$Score_2^{bi}$ 2M" vs. "In") better than the in-domain system alone.

4 Conclusions and Future Work

To improve the performance of spoken language translation, we have collected large-scale general-domain web parallel corpus, such as example bilingual sentence pairs and bilingual subtitles. However, sentence pairs from these general-domain web bilingual corpus that seem similar to an in-domain corpus may not actually represent the same distribution of language. Nonetheless, we have shown that relatively tiny amounts of the pseudo in-domain data can prove more useful than the entire general-domain corpus for the purposes of domain-targeted translation tasks. A translation model trained on any of these subcorpora can be comparable or substantially better than a translation system trained on the entire corpus.

We have also proposed two types phrase-based data selection methods to extract these pseudo in-domain sentence pairs from the general-domain corpus. Compared with the traditional bag-of-words models, our proposed methods are more effective in that they can capture contextual information instead of selecting single words in isolation, and are shown to be more efficient and stable for SMT domain adaptation. Translation models trained on data selected in this way consistently outperform the general-domain baseline while using as few as 18% (2M out of the entire 11M sentence pairs) and result in an increase of 1.6 BLEU points. Next, we have shown that mixing pseudo in-domain corpus/model with the true in-domain corpus/model significantly outperforms the two state-of-the-art translation systems trained on in- and general-domain corpus, with increases of 4.5 and 3.9 BLEU points, respectively.

In the future, it will be instructive to explore other approaches for bilingual data selection, such word-based translation model [12], bilingual topic model [11]. Besides improving translation performance, this work also provides a way to mine very large corpora in a computationally-limited environment in the future, such as on a mobile terminal. The maximum size of a useful general-domain corpus is now limited only by the availability of data, rather than by how large a translation model can be fit into memory at once.

Acknowledgments. This work was supported by 863 program in China (No. 2011AA01A207). We thank the anonymous reviewers for their insightful and helpful comments.

References

1. Axelrod, A., He, X., Gao, J.: Domain adaptation via pseudo in-domain data selection. In: Proceedings of EMNLP, pp. 355–362 (2011)
2. Cover, T.M., Thomas, J.A.: Elements of information theory. Wiley, New York (1991)
3. Eck, M., Vogel, S., Waibel, A.: Language model adaptation for statistical machine translation based on information retrieval. In: Proceedings of LREC, pp. 327–330 (2004)

4. Foster, G., Kuhn, R.: Mixture-model adaptation for SMT. In: Proceedings of ACL, pp. 128–135 (2007)
5. Hildebrand, A.S.: Adaptation of the translation model for statistical machine translation based on information retrieval. In: Proceedings of EAMT, pp. 133–142 (2005)
6. Koehn, P., Och, F.J., Marcu, D.: Statistical phrase-based translation. In: Proceedings of NAACL, pp. 48–54 (2003)
7. Koehn, P., Schroeder, J.: Experiments in domain adaptation for statistical machine translation. In: Proceedings of WMT (2007)
8. Lin, D.: An information-theoretic definition of similarity. In: Proceedings of ICML, pp. 296–304 (1998)
9. Liu, P., Zhou, Y., Zong, C.: Approach to selecting best development set for phrase-base statistical machine translation. In: Proceedings of PACLIC, pp. 325–334 (2009)
10. Liu, P., Zhou, Y., Zong, C.: Data selection for statistical machine translation. In: Proceedings of NLP-KE, pp. 232–236 (2010)
11. Lu, S., Fu, X., Wei, W., Peng, X., Xu, B.: Joint and coupled bilingual topic model based sentence representations for language model adpataiton. In: Proceedings of IJCAI, pp. 2141–2147 (2013)
12. Lu, S., Wei, W., Fu, X., Xu, B.: Translation model based cross-lingual language model adaptation: from word models to phrase models. In: Proceedings of EMNLP-CoNLL, pp. 512–522 (2012)
13. Lv, Y., Huang, J., Liu, Q.: Improving statistical machine translation peformance by training data selection and optimization. In: Proceedings of EMNLP, pp. 343–350 (2007)
14. Moore, R., Lewis, W.: Intelligent selection for language model training data. In: Proceedings of ACL, pp. 220–224 (2010)
15. Nakov, P.: Improving English-Spanish statistical machine translation: experiments in domain adaptation, sentence paraphrasing, tokenization, and recasing. In: Proceedings of WMT (2008)
16. Och, F.J.: Minimum error rate training in statistical machine translation. In: Proceedings of ACL, pp. 160–167 (2003)
17. Och, F.J., Ney, H.: Improved statistical alignment models. In: Proceedings of ACL, pp. 440–447 (2000)
18. Papineni, K., Roukos, S., Ward, T., Zhu, W.: BLEU: A method for automatic evaluation of machine translation. In: Proceedings of ACL, pp. 311–318 (2002)
19. Stolcke, A.: SRILM - An extensible language modeling toolkit. In: Proceedings of ICSLP, pp. 901–904 (2002)

Discriminative Latent Variable Based Classifier for Translation Error Detection

Jinhua Du[1], Junbo Guo[2], and Fei Zhao[1]

[1] Faculty of Automation and Information Engineering
jhdu@xaut.edu.cn
[2] Faculty of High Vocational Education,
Xi'an University of Technology, Xi'an, 710048 China

Abstract. This paper presents a discriminative latent variable model (DPLVM) based classifier for improving the translation error detection performance for statistical machine translation (SMT). It uses latent variables to carry additional information which may not be expressed by those original labels and capture more complicated dependencies between translation errors and their corresponding features to improve the classification performance. Specifically, we firstly detail the mathematical representation of the proposed DPLVM method, and then introduce features, namely word posterior probabilities (WPP), linguistic features, syntactic features. Finally, we compare the proposed method with MaxEnt and SVM classifiers to verify its effectiveness. Experimental results show that the proposed DPLVM-based classifier reduce classification error rate (CER) by relative 1.75%, 1.69%, 2.61% compared to the MaxEnt classifier, and relative 0.17%, 0.91%, 2.12% compared to the SVM classifier over three different feature combinations.

Keywords: Translation Error Detection, Binary Classification, MaxEnt Classifier, SVM Classifier, DPLVM Classifier.

1 Introduction

In recent years, a number of different types of SMT methods have been proposed, such as the phrase-based, hierarchical phrased-based, and syntax-based models etc., which significantly improve the translation quality, and a lot of effort has been put to apply SMT systems to practical use. However, the translation quality cannot fully satisfy the actual demand of industry yet. For example, the ungrammatical errors and disordered words in the translation often increase human cost. Therefore, high-quality automatic translation error detection or word-level confidence estimation is necessary to further improve the working efficiency of the post-editors or translators.

Typically, most translation error detection methods utilize system-based features (e.g. WPP) combining with extra knowledge such as linguistic features to decrease the classification error rate (CER) [1–9]. As to the system-based features, a number of different algorithms to calculate the WPP were proposed

G. Zhou et al. (Eds.): NLPCC 2013, CCIS 400, pp. 127–138, 2013.
© Springer-Verlag Berlin Heidelberg 2013

based on the N-best list or word lattice, and had been applied to SMT translation quality estimation. Afterwards, some researchers try to introduce more
useful knowledge sources such as syntactic and semantic features to further improve the error detection capability. However, these features are not that easy to
extract due to their complexity, low generalization capability, and dependency
on specific languages etc. Hence, currently the system-based features such as
WPP and lexicalized features (e.g. word and part-of-speech (POS)) still play
the main role in the error detection task or the confidence estimation task.

Generally, translation error detection can be regarded as a binary classification
task. Thus, the accuracy of the classifier also plays an important role in terms
of improving the prediction capability besides adding new features and extra
knowledge. This paper presents a more effective classifier – discriminative probabilistic latent variable model based classifier that uses latent variables to carry
additional information which may not be expressed by those original labels and
capture more complicated dependencies between errors and their corresponding
features to improve the classification performance [10–12].

The rest of the paper is organized as follows: Section 2 briefs the related
work. Section 3 describes the DPLVM-based classifier as well as the feature
representation. In Section 4, three typical WPP and three linguistic features are
described. Experimental settings, implementation and analysis are reported in
Section 5. Some observations from the results are also given in this section. The
final section concludes and gives avenues for future work.

2   Related Work

The question of translation confidence estimation has attracted a number of researcher due to its importance in promoting SMT application. In 2004, Blatz et
al. improved the basic confidence estimation method by combining the neural
network and a naive Bayes classifier to predict the word-level and the sentence-
level translation errors [2]. The features they used include WPP calculated from
the N-best list, translation model-based features, semantic feature extracted
from the WordNet, as well as simple syntactic features. Experimental results
show that all among these features, WPP is more effective with strong generalization capability than linguistic features.

Ueffing and Ney exhaustively explore various kinds of WPP features to perform confidence measures, and proposed different WPP algorithms to verify the
effectiveness in confidence estimation task [1, 3]. In their task, the words in the
generated target sentence can be tagged as *correct* or *false* to facilitate post-
editing or work in an interactive translation environment. Their experiments
conducted on different data sets show that different WPP algorithms perform
differently, but basically each can reduce the CER. Furthermore, the combination of different features can perform better than any individual features.

Specia et al. have done a lot of work with regard to the confidence estimation in the computer-aided translation field [13, 14]. They categorize translations
into "bad" or "good" classes based on sentence-level binary scores of the post-
edition MT fragments. The features used are called "black-box" features, which

can be extracted from any MT systems only if the information from the input (source) and translation (target) sentences are given, such as source and target sentence lengths and their ratios, the edit distance between the source sentence and sentences in the corpus used to train the SMT system. Recently, Specia et al. (2011) have started exploiting linguistic information for sentence-level quality estimation, for instance, used POS tagging, chunking, dependency relations and named entities for English-Arabic quality estimation [6, 7]. Hardmeier explored the use of constituency and dependency trees for English-Swedish/Spanish quality estimation [8].

Xiong et al. proposed an MaxEnt classifier based error detection method to predict translation errors (each word is tagged as *correct* or *incorrect*) by integrating a WPP feature, a syntactic feature extracted from LG parser and some lexical features [4]. The experimental results show that linguistic features can reduce CER when used alone, and it outperforms WPP. Moreover, linguistic features can further provide complementary information when combined with WPP, which collectively reduce the classification error rate.

On the basis of Xiong's work, Du and Wang carried out a systematic comparison between the MaxEnt and SVM classifiers in order to show the influence of different classifiers on the error detection capability. Under the conditions of same data sets and same feature sets, their experiments indicated that the SVM-based classifier performed better than the MaxEnt-based classifier in terms of the CER [9].

On the basis of previous work, this paper mainly focuses on introducing a new classifier to significantly improve the classification performance. Specifically, this paper

- verifies the performance of various classifiers, namely the MaxEnt classifier and the SVM classifier on the translation error detection task;
- presents a new classifier – DPLVM-based classifier – to obtain better results.

3 Discriminative Probabilistic Latent Variable Model Based Classifier

In this section, we come up with a new classifier – DPLVM-based classifier – to perform our translation error detection task.

In natural language processing (NLP) such as sequential labeling [11], DPLVM demonstrated excellent capability of learning latent dependencies of the specific problems, and have outperformed several commonly-used conventional models, such as support vector machines, conditional random fields and hidden Markov models. In this section, we theoretically introduce the definition and mathematical description of the DPLVM algorithm in our task and compare the classification performance with two other classifiers in later sections.

Given a sequence of observations $\mathbf{x} = \{x_1, x_2, \ldots, x_m\}$ and a sequence of labels $\mathbf{y} = \{y_1, y_2, \ldots, y_m\}$, the task is to learn a mapping between $\mathbf{x}$ and $\mathbf{y}$. y_i is a class label and is a member of a set $\mathbf{Y}$ of possible class labels. DPLVM also assumes a sequence of latent variables $\mathbf{h} = \{h_1, h_2, \ldots, h_m\}$, which is hidden in the training examples.

The DPLVM is defined as in (1)(Morency et al., [10]; Sun and Tsujii, [11]):

$$P(\mathbf{y}|\mathbf{x}, \Theta) = \sum_{\mathbf{h}} P(\mathbf{y}|\mathbf{h}, \mathbf{x}, \Theta)P(\mathbf{h}|\mathbf{x}, \Theta) \qquad (1)$$

where Θ are the parameters of the model. It can be seen that the DPLVM equates to a CRF model if it has only one latent variable for each label.

For the sake of efficiency, the model is restricted to have disjoint sets of latent variables associated with each class label. Each h_j is a member in a set $\mathbf{H}_{y_j}$ of possible latent variables for the class label y_j. We define $\mathbf{H}$ as the union of all $\mathbf{H}_{y_j}$ sets, so sequences which have any $h_j \notin \mathbf{H}_{y_j}$ will by definition have $P(\mathbf{y}|\mathbf{x}, \Theta) = 0$, so that the model can be rewritten as in (2):

$$P(\mathbf{y}|\mathbf{x}, \Theta) = \sum_{\mathbf{h} \in \mathbf{H}_{y_1} \times \ldots \mathbf{H}_{y_m}} P(\mathbf{h}|\mathbf{x}, \Theta) \qquad (2)$$

where $P(\mathbf{h}|\mathbf{x}, \Theta)$ is defined by the usual conditional random field formulation, as in (3):

$$P(\mathbf{h}|\mathbf{x}, \Theta) = \frac{\exp\Theta \cdot \mathbf{f}(\mathbf{h}, \mathbf{x})}{\sum_{\forall \mathbf{h}} \exp\Theta \cdot \mathbf{f}(\mathbf{h}, \mathbf{x})} \qquad (3)$$

in which $\mathbf{f}(\mathbf{h}, \mathbf{x})$ is a feature vector. Given a training set consisting of n labeled sequences (x_i, y_i), for $i = 1 \ldots n$, parameter estimation is performed by optimizing the objective function in (4):

$$L(\Theta) = \sum_{i=1}^{n} \log P(y_i|x_i, \Theta) - R(\Theta) \qquad (4)$$

The first term of this equation is the conditional log-likelihood of the training data. The second term is a regularizer that is used for reducing over-fitting in parameter estimation.

For decoding in the test stage, given a test sequence $\mathbf{x}$, we want to find the most probable label sequence y^*, as in (5):

$$\mathbf{y}^* = \arg\max_{y} P(\mathbf{y}|\mathbf{x}, \Theta^*) \qquad (5)$$

Sun and Tsujii (2009) argued that for latent conditional models like DPLVMs, the best label path $\mathbf{y}^*$ cannot directly be generated by the Viterbi algorithm because of the incorporation of hidden states. They proposed a latent-dynamic inference (LDI) method based on A^* search and dynamic programming to efficiently decode the optimal label sequence $\mathbf{y}^*$. For more details of the LDI algorithm, refer to [11].

Our translation error detection is a binary classification task that annotates a word e of the translation hypothesis e_1^I as "correct" if it is translated correctly, or "incorrect" if it is a wrong translation. Therefore, the label set for the classification task can be denoted as $\boldsymbol{y} = \{c, i\}$, where $\boldsymbol{y}$ indicates the label set, c stands for class "correct" and i represents class "incorrect".

4   Features and Vector Representation

4.1   WPP Feature

WPP is served as a major and effective confidence estimation feature both in speech recognition and SMT post-processing. As to SMT, WPP refers to the probability of a word occurring in the hypothesis given a source input. Generally speaking, the underlying idea is that if the posterior probability of a word occurring in a hypothesis is high, then the chance that it is believed to be correct is big correspondingly. Thus, it is reasonable that the more useful information considered in the WPP algorithm, the better the performance would achieve.

The general mathematical description of WPP is as:

For an SMT system S, given the input sentence f_1^J, and the exported N-best list $e_{n,1}^{n,I_n}$, where $n = 1, \ldots, N$, e_n refers to the nth hypothesis with the probability $p(f_1^J, e_{n,1}^{n,I_n})$, then the WPP in the error detection task can be represented as calculating the probability $p_i(e|f_1^J, e_1^I)$ of the word e at position i in the 1-best hypothesis of the N-best list as in (6),

$$p_i(e|f_1^J, e_1^I) = \frac{\sum_{n=1}^{N} f(a, e_{n,i}, e) \cdot p(f_1^J, e_{n,1}^{n,I_n})}{\sum_{n=1}^{N} p(f_1^J, e_{n,1}^{n,I_n})} \qquad (6)$$

where a is a hidden variable which indicates an alignment measure; $f(a, e_{n,i}, e)$ is a binary sign function as in (7),

$$f(a, e_{n,i}, e) = \begin{cases} 1 & e_{n,i} = e \\ 0 & otherwise \end{cases} \qquad (7)$$

It can be seen from the description of N-best based WPP algorithm that the posterior probability of a word in a hypothesis can be worked out according to the sentence-level posterior probabilities of hypotheses in the N-best list. The vital information to be considered is the position of the word e which is determined by the alignment measure between the 1-best hypothesis and the rest of the N-best list.

Here we introduces three typical WPP methods to illustrate their different influence on the error detection performance over different kinds of classifiers.

4.1.1   Fixed Position Based WPP

The fixed position based WPP is also called "direct WPP". The basic idea is that given an input f_1^J, the posterior probability of a word e at position i in the hypothesis e_1^I can be calculated by summing the posterior probabilities of all sentences in the N-best list containing target word e at target position i, which is as in (8),

$$p_i(e|f_1^J, e_1^I) = \frac{\sum_{n=1}^{N} \delta(e_{n,i}, e) \cdot p(f_1^J, e_{n,1}^{n,I_n})}{\sum_{e'} \sum_{n=1}^{N} \delta(e_{n,i}, e') \cdot p(f_1^J, e_{n,1}^{n,I_n})} \qquad (8)$$

where $\delta(x, y)$ is the Kronecker function as in (9),

$$\delta(x, y) = \begin{cases} 1 & x = y \\ 0 & otherwise \end{cases} \tag{9}$$

This method only uses the original position information of each word without any extra alignment measure between the 1-best and any other hypotheses.

4.1.2   Flexible Position Based WPP

The potential problem of fixed position based WPP is that generally the hypotheses in the N-best list have different length that will make the same word occur at different positions so that the WPP would have a large error compared to the real probability distribution. Naturally the intuition to improve this method is to make the position flexible, e.g. using a sliding window.

The basic idea of sliding window is to consider the words around the position i, i.e., the context. Let the window size be t, then the sliding window at position i can be denoted as $i \pm t$. If the target word e appears inside the window, then we regard it occurring at position i and sum up the probability of the current hypothesis, which is formulated as in (10),

$$p_{i,t}(e|f_1^J, e_1^I) = \sum_{k=i-t}^{i+t} p_k(e|f_1^J, e_1^I) \tag{10}$$

where $p_k(e|f_1^J, e_1^I)$ is as illustrated in Eq. (8).

4.1.3   Word Alignment Based WPP

The sliding window based method needs to choose a proper window size which can only be determined by experiments. Thus, another straightforward way to improve the fixed position method is to perform the word alignment between the 1-best hypothesis and the rest of hypotheses in the N-best list, i.e., align the rest of hypotheses against the 1-best hypothesis.

Specifically, let $L(e_1^I, e_{n,1}^{n,I_n})$ be the Levenshtein alignment between e_1^n and other hypotheses, then the WPP of the word e at position i is as in (11):

$$p_{lev}(e|f_1^J, e_1^I) = \frac{p_{lev}(e, f_1^J, e_1^I)}{\sum_{e'} p_{lev}(e', f_1^J, e_1^I)} \tag{11}$$

where

$$p_{lev}(e, f_1^J, e_1^I) = \sum_{n=1}^{N} \delta(e, L_i(e_1^I, e_{n,1}^{n,I_n})) \cdot p(f_1^J, e_{n,1}^{n,I_n}) \tag{12}$$

$p(f_1^J, e_{n,1}^{n,I_n})$ is the posterior probability of each hypothesis in the N-best list, which is given by the SMT system. $\delta(x, y)$ is the Kronecker function as in Eq. (9).

4.2   Linguistic Features

4.2.1   Syntactic Features

Xiong et al. extracted syntactical feature by checking whether a word is connected with other words from the output of the LG parser. When the parser fails to parse the entire sentence, it ignores one word each time until it finds linkages for remaining words. After parsing, those ignored words which are not connected to any other words to be called *null*-linked words. These *null*-linked words are prone to be syntactically incorrect and the linked words are prone to be syntactically correct, then a binary syntactic feature for a word according to its links can be defined as in (13),

$$link(e) = \begin{cases} yes & \text{e has links with other words} \\ no & \text{otherwise} \end{cases} \tag{13}$$

Refer to detailed description in [4].

4.3   Lexical Features

Lexical features such as the word itself and the POS are common features used in NLP tasks. In this paper, we also utilize the word/pos with its context (e.g. the previous two words/pos and next two words/pos) to form a feature vector as follows,

- *word*: $(w_{-2}, w_{-1}, w, w_1, w_2)$
- *pos*: $(pos_{-2}, pos_{-1}, pos, pos_1, pos_2)$

4.4   Feature Vector Representation

Generally in the NLP classification task, context information is usually to be considered in the process of feature extraction. In our task, we have four kinds of features: *wpp*, *pos*, *word* and *link* (c.f. Section 4). To build a feature vector for a word e, we look at 2 words before and 2 words after the current word position as well. Thus, the feature vector $\mathbf{x}$ that includes four kinds of features can be denoted as,

$$\mathbf{x} = <wpp_{-2}, wpp_{-1}, wpp, wpp_1, wpp_2, pos_{-2}, pos_{-1},$$
$$pos, pos_1, pos_2, word_{-2}, word_{-1}, word, word_1,$$
$$word_2, link_{-2}, link_{-1}, link, link_1, link_2 >$$

As to the individual classifiers, we use the MaxEnt toolkit[1] as our MaxEnt classifier, use LibSVM[2] as our SVM classifier, and use Sun's open source toolkit [11] as the proposed DPLVM-based classifier respectively. Refer to [9] for more details about Maxent and SVM classifiers.

---

[1] http://homepages.inf.ed.ac.uk/s0450736/maxenttoolkit.html.
[2] Software available at http://www.csie.ntu.edu.tw/~cjlin/libsvm

5   Experiments and Analysis

5.1   Chinese-English SMT

We utilize Moses [15] to provide 10,000-best list with translation direction from Chinese to English. The training data consists of 3,397,538 pairs of sentences (including Hong Kong news, FBIS, ISI Chinese-English Network Data and Xin-Hua news etc.). The language model is five-gram built on the English part of the bilingual corpus and Xinhua part of the English Gigaword.

The development set for SMT training is the current set of NIST MT 2006 (1,664 source sentences) and the test sets are NIST MT-05 (1,082 sentences) and NIST MT-08 (1,357 sentences). Each source sentence has four references. During the decoding process, the SMT system exports 10,000-best hypotheses for each source sentence, i.e., $N = 10,000$.

Performance of SMT systems on two test sets is shown in Table 1 in terms of BLEU4, TER scoresand ratio of correct words (RCW) scores.

Table 1. SMT performance and the ratio of correct words (RCW)

dataset	BLEU4(%)	WER(%)	TER(%)	RCW(%)
NIST MT 2008	25.97	69.79	63.56	37.99
NIST MT 2005	33.17	69.50	61.40	41.59

5.2   Experimental Settings for Translation Error Detection Task

Development and test sets: In the error detection task, we use NIST MT-08 as the development set to tune the classifiers, and NIST MT-05 as the test set to evaluate the classification performance.

Data annotation: We use the WER metric in TER toolkit [16] to determine the true labels for words in the development and the test sets. Firstly, we perform the minimum edit distance alignment between the hypothesis and the four references, and then select the one with minimum WER score as the final reference to tag the hypothesis. That is, a word e in the hypothesis is tagged as c if it is the same as that in the reference, otherwise tag it as i.

There are 14,658 correct words and 23,929 incorrect words in the 1-best hypothesis of MT-08 set (37.99% ratio of correct words, RCW), 15,179 correct words and 21,318 incorrect words in the 1-best hypothesis of MT-05 set (41.59% RCW). See RCW in Table 1.

Evaluation Metrics: The commonly-used evaluation metrics for the classification task includes CER (classification error rate), precision, recall and F measure. In our translation error detection task, we use CER as the main evaluation metric to evaluate the system performance that is defined as in (14),

$$\text{CER} = \frac{\#\text{of wrongly tagged words}}{\#\text{of total words}} \tag{14}$$

Since the RCW is less than 50% (41.59%), i.e., the number of incorrect words is more than correct words, it is reasonable to use the RCW as the baseline of CER to examine the classification performance of classifiers.

We also use F measure as the auxiliary evaluation metrics to evaluate some performance of features and classifiers. See definitions in [4].

5.3 Error Detection Experiments

5.3.1 Classification Experiments Based on Individual Features

Results of three typical WPP features and three linguistic features on MaxEnt, SVM and the proposed DPLVM classifiers are shown in Table 2.

Table 2. Results of individual features over three classifiers

Feature	MaxEnt CER(%)	F(%)	SVM CER(%)	F(%)	DPLVM CER(%)	F(%)
Baseline	*41.59*	–	*41.59*	–	*41.59*	–
WPP_Dir	40.48	67.65	*37.64*	75.11	**37.16**	74.13
WPP_Win	39.70	68.51	*37.47*	75.18	**36.87**	74.90
WPP_Lev	40.12	72.83	*37.37*	75.25	**36.99**	73.84
word	39.11	69.04	*37.68*	71.48	**36.93**	73.11
pos	39.50	71.89	*39.12*	73.68	**37.39**	72.68
link	40.89	72.77	*37.70*	74.78	**37.38**	74.61

WPP_Dir represents the fixed position-based WPP, *WPP_Win* represents the flexible position-based WPP with the window size 2, and *WPP_Lev* represents word alignment-based WPP.

We can see that 1) three WPP features over three classifiers significantly reduce the CER compared to the baseline; 2) the *WPP_Win* and *WPP_Lev* perform better than *WPP_Dir* which shows that position information is helpful; 3) Regarding the linguistic features, they are helpful to significantly reduce the error rate compared to the baseline over three classifiers; 4) the proposed DPLVM performs best compared to the SVM and MaxEnt classifiers in terms of the CER, which verifies that the proposed classifier is effective.

5.3.2 Classification Experiment on Combined Features

The results of the feature combination experiment which combines three typical WPP and three linguistic features over three individual classifiers respectively are shown in Table 3.

In Table 3, *com*1 represents the feature combination of *WPP_Dir + Word + Pos + Link*, *com*2 stands for the feature combination of *WPP_Win + Word + Pos + Link*, and *com*3 indicates the feature combination of *WPP_Lev + Word + Pos + Link*. All these feature combinations are linearly combined without any weights in the model.

We can see from the results that compared to the MaxEnt and SVM classifiers over three feature combinations, namely *com*1, *com*2 and *com*3, the proposed

Table 3. Results of combined features over three classifiers

	MaxEnt		SVM		DPLVM	
Feature	CER(%)	F(%)	CER(%)	F(%)	CER(%)	F(%)
Baseline	*41.59*	–	*41.59*	–	*41.59*	–
com1	35.93	74.17	*35.36*	74.95	**35.30**	74.61
com2	35.55	73.83	*35.27*	74.86	**34.95**	74.69
com3	35.62	73.15	*35.44*	74.75	**34.69**	74.04

DPLVM classifier method achieved significant improvement respectively by relative 1.75%, 1.69%, 2.61%, and 0.17%, 0.91%, 2.12% in terms of CER.

From the systematic comparison of the results, we can conclude:

- generally speaking, *WPP_Win* performs the best and robust both in the three individual WPP features and the three combined features. The reason we consider is that the sliding window makes the alignment more flexible and considers more context information.
- linguistic features are helpful to the error detection.
- SVM classifier outperforms the MaxEnt classifier in all sets of experiments in terms of CER and F measures, and the proposed DPLVM-based classifier performs best in terms of the CER that shows its effectiveness in translation error detection task. It is analyzed that the latent variables can carry additional information and capture more relations between translation errors and features so that the classification performance can be significantly improved.

5.3.3   Observations

We carried out a deep analysis on the results classified, and based on the observations, we found that,

- the name entities (person name, location name, organization name etc.) are prone to be wrongly classified;
- the prepositions, conjunctions, auxiliary verbs and articles are easier to be wrongly classified due to the factors that they often have an impact on the word orders or lead to empty alignment links;
- the proportion of the notional words that are wrongly classified is relatively small.

6   Conclusions and Future Work

This paper presents a new classifier – DPLVM-based classifier – for translation error detection. Firstly a discriminative probabilistic latent variable model based classifier is proposed which takes advantage of hidden information to predict the label for each word in a hypothesis. Then three different kinds of WPP features, three linguistic features are introduced, and finally a systematic comparison among the MaxEnt classifier, SVM classifier and our DPLVM classifier using different individual and combined features is carried out. Experimental results on Chinese-to-English NIST MT data sets show that the proposed classifier performs best compared to two other individual classifiers in terms of CER.

In future work, we intend to carry out further study on the error detection task in the respects of 1) introducing paraphrases to annotate the hypotheses so that it can truly reflect the *correct* or *incorrect* at the semantic level; 2) introducing new useful features to further improve the detection capability; 3) performing experiments on more language pairs to verify our proposed method.

Acknowledgments. This work is supported by NSF project (61100085), SRF for ROCS, State Education Ministry, and Research Foundation of Education Department of Shaanxi Provincial Government (11JK1029). Thanks the reviewers for their insightful comments and suggestions.

References

1. Ueffing, N., Klaus, M., Hermann, N.: Confidence Measures for Statistical Machine Translation. In: Proceedings of the MT Summit IX, pp. 169–176 (2003)
2. Blatz, J., Fitzgerald, E., Foster, G., Gandrabur, S., Goutte, C., Kuesza, A., Sanchis, A., Ueffing, N.: Confidence Estimation for Machine Translation. In: Proceedings of the 20th International Conference on Computational Linguistics, pp. 315–321 (2004)
3. Ueffing, N., Ney, H.: Word-Level Confidence Estimation for Machine Translation. Computational Linguistics 33(1), 9–40 (2007)
4. Xiong, D., Zhang, M., Li, H.: Error detection for statistical machine translation using linguistic features. In: Proceedings of the 48th Annual Meeting of the Association for Computational Linguistics, pp. 604–611 (2010)
5. Nguyen, B., Huang, F., AI-Onaizan, Y.: Goodness: A Method for Measuring Machine Translation Confidence. In: Proceedings of the 49th Annual Meeting of the Association for Computational Linguistics, pp. 211–219 (2011)
6. Specia, L., Hajlaoui, N., Hallett, C., Aziz, W.: Predicting machine translation adequacy. In: MT Summit XIII: Proceedings of the Thirteenth Machine Translation Summit, pp. 513–520 (2011)
7. Mariano, F., Specia, L.: Linguistic features for quality estimation. In: WMT 2012: Proceedings of the 7th Workshop on Statistical Machine Translation, pp. 96–103 (2012)
8. Hardmeier, C., Nivre, J., Tiedemann, J.: Tree kernels for machine translation quality estimation. In: Proceedings of the 7th Workshop on Statistical Machine Translation, pp. 109–113 (2012)
9. Du, J., Wang, S.: A Systematic Comparison of SVM and Maximum Entropy Classifiers for Translation Error Detection. In: Proceedings of the International Conference on Asian Language Processing, IALP (2012)
10. Morency, L.P., Quattoni, A., Darrell, T.: Latent-dynamic Discriminative Models for Continuous Gesture Recognition. In: Proceedings of the CVPR 2007, pp. 1–8 (2007)
11. Sun, X., Tsujii, J.: Sequential Labeling with Latent Variables: An Exact Inference Algorithm and An Ecient Approximation. In: Proceedings of the European Chapter of the Association for Computational Linguistics (EACL 2009), pp. 772–780 (2009)

12. Du, J., Way, A.: A discriminative latent variable-based classifier for Chinese-English SMT. In: Proceedings of the 23rd International Conference on Computational Linguistics, pp. 286–294 (2010)
13. Specia, L., Cancedda, N., Dymetman, M., Turchi, M., Cristianini, N.: Estimating the sentence-level quality of machine translation systems. In: Proceedings of the 13th Annual Conference of the European Association for Machine Translation, pp. 28–35 (2009)
14. Specia, L., Saunders, C., Turchi, M., Wang, Z., Shawe-Taylor, J.: Improving the confidence of machine translation quality estimates. In: Proceedings of the Twelfth Machine Translation Summit, pp. 136–143 (2009)
15. Koehn, P., Hoang, H., Callison-Burch, C., Federico, M., Bertoldi, N., Cowan, B., Shen, W., Moran, C., Zens, R., Dyer, C., Bojar, O., Constantin, A., Herbst, E.: Moses: Open Source Toolkit for Statistical Machine Translation. In: Proceedings of the Demo and Poster Sessions, ACL 2007, pp. 177–180 (2007)
16. Snover, M., Dorr, B., Schwartz, R., Micciulla, L., Makhoul, J.: A study of translation edit rate with targeted human annotation. In: Proceedings of the 7th Conference of the Association for Machine Translation in the Americas, pp. 223–231 (2006)

Incorporating Entities in News Topic Modeling

Linmei Hu[1], Juanzi Li[1], Zhihui Li[2], Chao Shao[1], and Zhixing Li[1]

[1] Dept. of Computer Sci. and Tech., Tsinghua University, China
{hulinmei,ljz,shaochao,zhxli}@keg.cs.tsinghua.edu.cn
[2] Dept. of Computer Sci. and Tech., Beijing Information Science and Technology
University, China
wisdomlee0606@126.com

Abstract. News articles express information by concentrating on named entities like who, when, and where in news. Whereas, extracting the relationships among entities, words and topics through a large amount of news articles is nontrivial. Topic modeling like Latent Dirichlet Allocation has been applied a lot to mine hidden topics in text analysis, which have achieved considerable performance. However, it cannot explicitly show relationship between words and entities. In this paper, we propose a generative model, Entity-Centered Topic Model(ECTM) to summarize the correlation among entities, words and topics by taking entity topic as a mixture of word topics. Experiments on real news data sets show our model of a lower perplexity and better in clustering of entities than state-of-the-art entity topic model(CorrLDA2). We also present analysis for results of ECTM and further compare it with CorrLDA2.

Keywords: news, named entity, generative entity topic models.

1 Introduction

With the popularization of the Internet, reading online news has become an elementary activity in people's daily life. Named entities which refer to names, locations, time, and organizations play critical roles in conveying news semantics like who, where and what etc. In today's fast-paced life, capturing the semantic relationships between news and entities can help people to understand and explore news. It has abroad applications such as news summarization, multiple dimensional news search and news event extraction.

Recently, there is growing interest and lots of valuable researches in finding and analyzing entities mentioned in news using topic models. In [1], a generative entity-topic model is proposed to combine context information and topics for entity linking given global knowledge. [2] use nonparametric topic models and hierarchial topic models for entity disambiguation respectively. [3] presents a named entity topic model for named entity query, specifically finding related topics given a set of related entities. Though entity topic models have been widely used in many applications, in this paper, we focus on extracting relationships between entities and news article, which can be applied in the applications mentioned above.

G. Zhou et al. (Eds.): NLPCC 2013, CCIS 400, pp. 139–150, 2013.
© Springer-Verlag Berlin Heidelberg 2013

Figure 1 (a)-(c) illustrates different dependencies between entities and topics of previous topic models. As shown in Figure 1(a), LDA [4] can also be extended to detect interaction between entities and topics, but it cannot model the relationship between words and entities. Figure 1(b) illustrates ETM [5] modeling the generative process of a word given its topic and entity information, but it does not cover relationship among entities. As we can see from Figure 1(c), David Newman et al. propose entity topic model, called CorrLDA2, modeling word topic as a distribution over entity topics [6]. The model can cluster entities and explicitly show word topic related entity topics, while experimental results show unreasonable clustering of entities. In this paper, we propose an entity-centered topic model, ECTM shown in Figure 1(d) to model entity topics as mixtures of word topics. ECTM clusters entities better and obviously mines correlation among entities, words and topic, specifically entities-related word topics. The intuition underlying the idea is when writing a news article, usually person, time and location are determined first, then topics are generated by expanding around these entities.

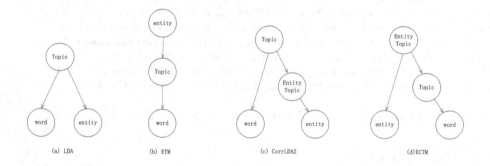

Fig. 1. Different Dependencies in News Modeling

In this paper, with the intuition that entities play a critical role in news articles and the content is usually generated around entities, we propose an entity-centered topic model, ECTM to model entities and topics from a large news articles set. Entity groups and entities-related word topics are demonstrated explicitly.

The main contributions of this paper can be summarized as follows:

- We propose an entity-centered topic model, ECTM to model generation of news articles by sampling entities first, then words.
- We give evidence that ECTM is better in clustering entities than CorrLDA2 by evaluation of average entropy and sKL.
- We apply ECTM on real news articles sets to analyze entity groups, also named entity topics and entities-related word topics. We also present analysis and further compare with entity topic model(CorrLDA2).

The rest of the paper is organized as follows. We review related work in section 2. In section 3, we will define problem and describe ECTM in detail. Experiments and analysis will be given in section 4. Finally, we conclude the paper in section 5.

2   Related Work

In early days, documents are represented as a vector of TF-IDF vlues[7]. In 1990, latent semantic indexing(LSI) [8] was presented to avoid missing related articles but with no keywords occurrence. With further probabilistic theory considered, Hofmann comes up with probabilistic LSI(pLSI)[9] for document modeling. The key idea underlying LDA [4] is that a document is a bag of words, which can be considered as a mixture of latent topics with each topic a distribution over words. Documents are represented as a distribution over K topics, having features reduced compared with TF-IDF representation. In comparison with pLSI, LDA has its merits in parameter estimation and inference.

A lot of topic models have been derived from LDA to meet various scenarios. Author Topic (AT) model [10] incorporates authors in LDA to model authors in different communities, where authors in same community have common interest. In academic searching and analysis, Author Conference Topic (ACT) model is proposed to simultaneously model topical aspects of papers, authors, and publication venues [11]. David Andrzejewski et al. incorporate domain knowledge into LDA to maximize the utilization of domain knowledge [12]. [6] presents a statistical entity topic model, CorrLDA2, modeling entities and topics, where word topics are mixtures of entity topics. However, it cannot meet certain scenarios, for example, presenting entity topic's distribution over word topics directly. Some improvements aim at modeling correlation among topics, such as correlated topic model (CTM) [13], Pachinko allocation model(PAM)[14] and even hierarchical Pachinko allocation model (HPAM)[15], hierarchical LDA (hLDA)[16] for learning hierarchical topic relationships. Gibbs sampling [17] is a widely-used alternative to variational method for topic model's inference.

Named entity has become a catch eye word currently. Various aspects of named entities including named entity recognition, entity linking, entity resolution have been researched. [18] recognizes and finds relationships between named entities in web pages. We address entity-centered summarization of the news articles set by utilizing ICTCLAS [1] for entity recognition. In terms of entity linking, [19] links named entities with knowledge base via semantic knowledge. As our model can enrich semantic information related with the given entity, it definitely can be applied in entity linking.

3   Models

In this section, we describe three graphical entity topic models for news modeling. We begin with existing topic models, LDA and CorrLDA2. Then we discuss

---

[1] http://www.nlpir.org/

about our proposed model, ECTM. All models discussed in this paper treat documents as bag of words. We first introduce some basic notations used in graphical models.

Table 1. Notation Definition

notation	defination
$K,\tilde{K}$	number of word topics, number of entity topics
θ	topic distribution of document
Ψ	super topic distribution over topic distribution
$\beta,\tilde{\beta}$	word distribution, entity distribution
$\alpha,\eta,\tilde{\eta},\mu$	prior of θ, $\beta,\tilde{\beta},\Psi$
M	number of documents in news articles collection
N_d	number of words and entities in document d
$N,\tilde{N}$	number of words, entities in a document

3.1 Previous Models

We illustrate LDA in Figure 2(a) where entities are identical to words. After post-processing, we can extract relationships between entities and topics. LDA models documents mixtures of topics which are mixtures of words. For each word, the model generates a topic according to multinomial distribution. Specifically, it generates a document in the following process:

1. For each $d \in D$
   - sample topic distribution $\theta \sim Dir(\alpha)$
   - for all topics $t = 1, 2, ...K$,sample word distribution $\beta \sim Dir(\eta)$
2. For each word $w \in d$
   - sample a topic $z \sim Multi(\theta)$
   - sample a word $w \sim Multi(\beta)$

Figure 2(b) presents statistical entity topic model, CorrLDA2, where words are sampled before entities. For each entity, it samples a super word topic first, then sample an entity topic. Therefore, the modelling results reveal word topic related different groups of entities. Another difference is that CorrLDA2 allows different topic numbers for word topic and entity topic. The generative process of it is as follows:

1. For all $d \in D$ sample $\theta_d \sim Dir(\alpha)$
2. For all $t = 1, 2, ..., K$ word topics sample $\beta_t \sim Dir(\eta)$ and $\psi_t \sim Dir(\mu)$
3. For all $t = 1, 2, ...\tilde{K}$ entity topics sample $\tilde{\beta}_t \sim Dir(\tilde{\eta})$
4. For each word $w \in d$
   - sample a topic $z \sim Mult(\theta_d)$
   - sample an word $w \sim Mult(\beta_d)$
5. For each entity $e \in d$
   - sample a super word topic $x \sim Mult(z_1, z_2, ..., z_K)$
   - sample an entity topic $\tilde{z} \sim Mult(\psi_x)$
   - sample an entity $e \sim Mult(be\tilde{t}az)$

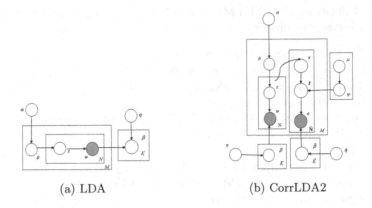

(a) LDA   (b) CorrLDA2

Fig. 2. Graph Representation of Previous Models

3.2 Entity-Centered Topic Model

With the intuition that entity play a pivotal role in news articles, we propose a new entity topic model, entity-centered topic model, ECTM. ECTM is similar with CorrLDA2 but differs from it mainly in sampling order of entity and word. With our model, entity topic contains a mixture of groups of words, for example, an entity topic of earthquake places may include word topics of earthquake disaster situation, personnel recovery, reconstruction of city and tsunami. However, previous models cannot produce such modelling results.

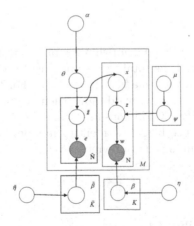

Fig. 3. Graph Representation of ECTM

Figure 3 illustrates our ECTM. In detail, ECTM models a news article following the generative process:

1. For all $d \in D$ sample $\theta_d \sim Dir(\alpha)$
2. For all entity topics $\tilde{t} = 1, 2, ...\tilde{K}$, sample $\tilde{\beta}_t \sim Dir(\tilde{\eta})$ and $\psi \sim Dir(\mu)$
3. For all word topics $t = 1, 2, ...K$, sample $\beta \sim Dir(\eta)$
4. For each entity $e \in d$
   - sample an entity topic $z \sim Multi(\tilde{\theta})$ according to Equation 1
   - sample an entity $e \sim Multi(\tilde{\beta})$
5. For each word $w \in d$
   - sample a super entity topic $x \sim Multi(\tilde{z}_1, \tilde{z}_2, ..., \tilde{z}_{\tilde{K}})$
   - sample a topic $z \sim Multi(\psi)$ according to Equation 2
   - sample a word $w \sim Multi(\beta)$

According to the graphical model of ECTM, we infer the equations of full conditional probabilities used in gibbs sampling as follows.

$$p(\tilde{z}_i = \tilde{k}|e_i = e, \tilde{z}_{\neg i}, e_{\neg i}, \alpha, \tilde{\beta}) \propto$$

$$\frac{N_{\tilde{m}_{\neg i}}^{\tilde{k}} + \alpha}{\sum_{k'=1}^{\tilde{k}'=\tilde{K}} N_{\tilde{m}_{\neg i}}^{\tilde{k}'} + \tilde{K}\alpha} \cdot \frac{N_{\tilde{k}_{\neg i}}^{e} + \tilde{\beta}}{\sum_{e'=1}^{e'=\tilde{V}} N_{\tilde{k}_{\neg i}}^{e'} + \tilde{V}\tilde{\beta}} \cdot \tag{1}$$

$$p(z_i = k, x = \tilde{k}|w_i = w, z_{\neg i}, \tilde{z}, w_{\neg i}, \beta) \propto$$

$$\frac{N_{\tilde{m}}^{\tilde{k}} + 1}{N + \tilde{K}} \cdot \frac{N_{\tilde{k}_{\neg i}}^{k} + \mu}{\sum_{k'} N_{\tilde{k}_{\neg i}}^{k'} + K\mu} \cdot \frac{N_{k_{\neg i}}^{w} + \beta}{\sum_{w'=1}^{w'=V} N_{k_{\neg i}}^{w'} + V\beta} \cdot \tag{2}$$

3.3 Time Complexity

Gibbs Sampling is a widely used algorithm for probabilistic models. We assume the iteration times is t and the total words and entities in the document set are N and $\tilde{N}$, then for LDA, the time is $O(t(N + \tilde{N}))$. For CorrLDA2, as for each entity, we will first sample a super word topic, then an entity topic, thus the time is $O(tN + 2t\tilde{N})$. Similarly, ECTM consumes time $O(t\tilde{N} + 2tN)$, where number of words, N is usually much bigger than entity number $\tilde{N}$. Therefore, ECTM is usually more time-consuming than previous models.

4 Experiments

4.1 Experiment Setup

To cover various kinds of news articles set, we collect three data sets from News-Miner[2]. One is an event about Chile Earthquake called Dataset1, in which all articles are about Chile Earthquake happened in February, 2010. Another is

---

[2] http://newminer.net

about various kinds of intranational news, Dataset2 containing various news in our country. The last data set is a collection about three events including Qinghai Earthquake, Two Sessions in 2013 and Tsinghua University, named Dataset3. Dataset1 and Dataset2 have 632 and 700 news articles respectively, Dataset3 has 1800 articles. We preprocess the data by 1) word segmentation and entity recognition with ICTCLAS which has been mentioned in section 2, 2) removing stop words. Afterwards, there are 5482 words, 1657 entities in Dataset1, 15862 words, 5357 entities in Dataset2 and 19597 words, 10981 entities in Dataset3.

CorrLDA2 has been proven more effective in entity prediction [6]. Therefore, we evaluate ECTM's performance by perplexity taking LDA and CorrLDA2 as baselines [4]. To further analyze the entity topics generated using different models, we measure with average entropy of entity topics computed as Equation 3 and average sKL between each pair of entity topics according to Equation 4. Finally, we analyze and compare overall results of different models.

4.2   Perplexity

Perplexity is usually used to evaluate a topic model's ability to fit data. All topic models presented in this paper use gibbs sampling for estimation and inference. The prior α is set to be $50/K$, so is μ, $50/\tilde{K}$, β is set to be 0.1, empirically [20]. In terms of topic number K, we empirically determine by choosing the value where the perplexity is lowest. Here, we conduct 10-fold cross validation and take the average perplexity of ten times as final performance. Each time, we choose 90% as training data and the remaining 10% as test data for which we calculate the perplexity. We choose different number of topics to get the perplexity curves of LDA as shown in Figure 4.

We can see from Figure 4, the best topic numbers for three data sets are 10, 35 and 45 respectively. Applying the topic number in CorrLDA2 and ECTM, we determine the number of entity topics where the perplexity is lowest. The best entity topic numbers are 10, 30, 35 for Dataset1, Dataset2, Dataset3 separately. In Table 2, we list corresponding perplexity with three models in different data sets.

Table 2. Perplexity

	LDA	CorrLDA2	ECTM
Dataset1	2991.9535	1508.8008	1412.5654
Dataset2	19805.3647	11593.1167	10415.7223
Dataset3	26230.7089	14891.4707	13544.4122

It can be apparently seen that our proposed model has lowest perplexity, which shows ECTM performs well. The reason behind that may be it is more reasonable for news article writing with entities going first. When one is going to write a news article, he should determine the person, organization, time, location that he's going to write about first, then what happened with the named entities.

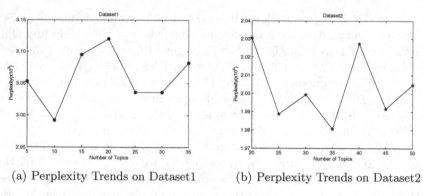

(a) Perplexity Trends on Dataset1   (b) Perplexity Trends on Dataset2

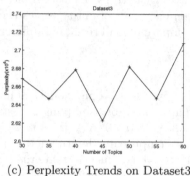

(c) Perplexity Trends on Dataset3

Fig. 4. Perplexity of LDA on Topic Trends

4.3   Evaluation of Entity Topic

As both CorrLDA2 and ECTM have entity topic which is a distribution of
entities. We set a probabilistic threshold and for each entity topic, we consider
entities whose probability is larger than threshold belonging to the entity topic.
Then we calculate the average entropy of all entity topics and average sKL for
each topic pair to evaluate the entity clustering performance of different models.
The results computed according to Equation 3 and Equation 4 are shown in
Table 3. The equations of entropy and sKL are shown as below:

$$Entropy of (Topic) = - \sum_z p(z) \sum_e p_z(e) \log_2[p_z(e)] . \tag{3}$$

$$sKL(i,j) = \sum_{e=1}^{\tilde{N}} [\tilde{\beta}_{ie} \log_2 \frac{\tilde{\beta}_{ie}}{\tilde{\beta}_{je}} + \tilde{\beta}_{je} \log_2 \frac{\tilde{\beta}_{je}}{\tilde{\beta}_{ie}}] . \tag{4}$$

As we all know, lower entropy and higher sKL means better clustering of
entities with small distance within entity topic and large distance between topics. From Table 3, we find that ECTM performs better than CorrLDA2 except
Dataset1 with threshold 0.001 and 0.01 and Dataset 2 with threshold 0.0001. For

Table 3. Entropy and sKL

| | Entropy | | | | | | sKL | |
| | 0.0001 | | 0.001 | | 0.01 | | | |
	CorrLDA2	ECTM	CorrLDA2	ECTM	CorrLDA2	ECTM	CorrLDA2	ECTM
Dataset1	0.9540	0.3340	0.0784	0.3244	0.0553	0.2841	7.6710	7.8022
Dataset2	2.4365	3.1221	0.0457	0.0251	0.0710	0.0171	3.2836	4.3278
Dataset3	0.0444	0.0331	0.0427	0.0369	0.0295	0.0219	2.7085	4.2780

(a) Results on Dataset1

智利地震华人情况

智利	0.2979
中国	0.2243
外交部	0.0201
汶川	0.0174
新浪	0.0127
袁子瞩	0.0121
孙士	0.0094
四川	0.0094
中国驻智利大使馆	0.0087
郭欣	0.0087
智利总统府文化中心	0.0074
香港	0.0074
普西	0.0067
国务院	0.0061
中国外交部	0.0054

0.7384 / 0.1647

华人伤亡

地震	0.0617
情况	0.0248
华人	0.0169
联系	0.0163
了解	0.0122
公民	0.0118
物资	0.0106
伤亡	0.0103
安全	0.0102
相关	0.0101
电话	0.0098
消息	0.0090
通讯	0.0087
华侨	0.0087
全球	0.0087

地震情况

工作	0.0179
记者	0.0130
进行	0.0089
表示	0.0075
部门	0.0074
人员	0.0066
政府	0.0060
情况	0.0059
发生	0.0058
全国	0.0057
要求	0.0050
可以	0.0049
地区	0.0048
群众	0.0047
出现	0.0045

(b) Results on Dataset2

外访

习近平	0.0529
拉美	0.0378
俄罗斯	0.0331
联合国	0.0255
印度	0.0255
南非	0.0180
巴西	0.0180
非洲	0.0171
李克强	0.0142
彭丽媛	0.0104
三亚	0.0076
普京	0.0067
拉丁美洲	0.0067
安理会	0.0057
程国平	0.0057

深圳

深圳	0.2309
高永侠	0.0161
邓小平	0.0125
小平	0.0099
肖幼美	0.0081
城中村	0.0072
深圳研究生院	0.0072
深圳特区	0.0063
比亚	0.0063
新加坡	0.0054
彭文乐	0.0054
关志成	0.0054
于明山	0.0045
深南大道	0.0045
深圳经济特区	0.0036

0.9493

0.5647 / 0.2850

国际合作

合作	0.0244
国家	0.0166
关系	0.0146
问题	0.0130
国际	0.0119
提案	0.0114
发展	0.0112
重要	0.0108
加强	0.0104
政协	0.0091
举行	0.0089
双方	0.0079
支持	0.0077
领域	0.0075
领导人	0.0061

体制改革

改革	0.0136
城市	0.0125
中小企业	0.0102
体制	0.0081
特区	0.0076
开放	0.0072
银行	0.0060
融资	0.0060
试点	0.0055
全球	0.0053
梦想	0.0048
证明	0.0044
口岸	0.0044
基地	0.0044
致敬	0.0039

经济发展

发展	0.0265
经济	0.0216
国家	0.0174
人民	0.0160
社会	0.0132
问题	0.0122
改革	0.0106
世界	0.0092
建设	0.0085
实现	0.0075
全国	0.0074
推进	0.0071
重要	0.0066
需要	0.0059
政府	0.0058

Fig. 5. Results of ECTM

Dataset1, the reason may be entity topics are very similar in an event collection. While for Dataset2, the reason is that the threshold is too low to be reasonable. In terms of sKL, we find for all data sets, even Dataset1, ECTM gets larger sKL between topics.

4.4   Analysis and Comparison of Results

In this section, we will display and analyze the results of topic modeling applied in three different data sets. To show the ability of ECTM to organize news articles as distributions over entity topics, where entity topic is a distribution over word topics, we show part of modeling results on Dataset1 and Dataset2 in Figure 5.

海啸预警		海啸预警		盗墓		盗墓	
海啸	0.1328	海啸	0.1148	食品	0.0214	盗墓	0.0119
预警	0.0376	地区	0.0301	馒头	0.0181	文物	0.0089
发布	0.0333	预警	0.0278	企业	0.0136	考古	0.0069
国家	0.0261	引发	0.0203	产品	0.0103	发掘	0.0053
影响	0.0174	居民	0.0201	生产	0.0098	水源	0.0053
地区	0.0131	警报	0.0194	监现	0.0091	就坏	0.0046
居民	0.0131	可能	0.0166	发现	0.0086	商业	0.0046
海浪	0.0131	抵达	0.0159	监管	0.0073	说法	0.0043
监测	0.0117	发出	0.0133	安全	0.0071	出土	0.0043
小时	0.0102	时间	0.0132	没有	0.0063	证据	0.0040
警报	0.0102	海浪	0.0128	考古	0.0055	被盗	0.0030
时间	0.0088	当地	0.0124	部门	0.0053	证明	0.0026
引发	0.0088	海岸	0.0116	整个	0.0053	墓	0.0026
沿海地区	0.0088	发布	0.0112	专家	0.0051	辛苦	0.0023
抵达	0.0088	报道	0.0096	可能	0.0045	确认	0.0023
太平洋	0.1052	日本	0.2320	曹操	0.0479	曹操	0.0649
日本	0.0901	太平洋	0.1644	贵州	0.0270	河南	0.0173
夏威夷	0.0651	日本气象厅	0.0523	北京	0.0225	安阳	0.0112
北京	0.0331	岩手县	0.0286	湖南	0.0158	刘备	0.0102
太平洋海啸预警中心	0.0296	北海道	0.0272	广西	0.0143	高陵	0.0092
新西兰	0.0294	青森县	0.0161	伊春	0.0128	孙权	0.0082
中国	0.0291	宫城县	0.0140	台湾	0.0120	魏武	0.0072
澳大利亚	0.0242	日本政府	0.0133	上海	0.0105	国家文物局	0.0062
俄罗斯	0.0239	法新社	0.0126	天津	0.0083	宋新潮	0.0062
菲律宾	0.0227	鸠山由纪夫	0.0112	成都	0.0075	央视	0.0062
日本气象厅	0.0220	小笠原群岛	0.0105	新华社	0.0075	华佗	0.0062
秘鲁	0.0203	冲绳	0.0091	刘备	0.0075	梅花山	0.0062
台湾	0.0170	岩手	0.0070	郑本禹	0.0075	成都	0.0052
美国	0.0152	日本共同社	0.0070	孙权	0.0061	李东东	0.0052
岩手县	0.0121	千叶县	0.0070	高陵	0.0060	丘中郎	0.0052

Dataset1   Dataset2

Fig. 6. Comparison of CorrLDA2 and ECTM

In Figure 5(a), we can see "智利", "中国", "外交部" these entities in the entity topic. We can judge the entity topic is about both China and Chile Earthquake. As expected, the entity topic is 73 percent talking about Chinese people situation in earthquake and 16 percent talking about Chile earthquake, which is shown on the edges. The top 15 words in a topic is listed below the topic label. It is unsurprising that we see "华人" in the word topic under the entity topic with many entities such as "中国", "外交部", "中国驻智利使馆" implying China.

In Figure 5(b), "外访" includes entities like "习近平", "拉美" and is almost only related to the word topic "国际合作"。However, the entity topic " 深圳" is almost 60% about "体制改革" and 30% about "经济发展" as shown in the figure. From those results, ECTM shows its ability to cluster entities and mine entities-related word topics.

We briefly compare ECTM's experimental results on Dataset1 and Dataset2 with CorrLDA2. The left is result of CorrLDA2 and the right is result of ECTM where result is presented with word topics above of most related group of entities. We choose almost the same word topic and pick up corresponding closely related entity topic representing by top 15 entities. As mentioned previously, ECTM is more powerful than CorrLDA2 in clustering entities and extracting entities-related word topics. We will illustrate this in following Figure 6.

We can see that ECTM clusters entities which are closely related to "日本", while corrLDA2 clusters all countries related with "海啸预警" on Dataset1. For Dataset2, the results of CorrLDA2 are worse. For one side, as "曹操" should be related with "河南安阳" where he was buried, the entities under the entity topic are not as relevant as those generated by ECTM. For another side, the words included in the word topic, "盗墓" are also not accurate by the reason of some unrelated words such as "食品", "安全" and so on.

4.5 Experimental Observations

In summary, our model, ECTM has three advantages. Firstly, it has lower perplexity than LDA and CorrLDA2. Secondly, ECTM mines hidden entity topic with better performance, specifically lower entropy and higher sKL than CorrLDA2. Lastly, ECTM extracts entities-related word topics as described in previous subsection, presenting correlation among entities, words and topics. Nevertheless, previous models cannot show entities related words and word topics directly.

5 Conclusions

In this paper, we address the problem of extracting correlation among entities, words and topics. We develop a new entity-centered topic model, ECTM which samples entity first and then samples words according to already-sampled super entity topics. Therefore, ECTM models news collection entity topics which are mixtures of word topics. Through experiments, we find ECTM better in clustering entities and mining entities-related word topics than state-of-the-art entity topic model CorrLDA2.

Entity has become an eye-catching word now. Various aspects about entity has been researched. Incorporating entities into news topic modeling is a challenging problem. There are still many potential future work. For example, we can develop hierarchial entity topic models to mine correlation between entities and topics. We can also research about different models fitting different news collections, specifically, what model fits a news event collection and what model fits collection with various topics.

Acknowledgement. The work is supported NSFC (No. 61035004), NSFC-ANR(No. 61261130588), 863 High Technology Program (2011AA01A207), FP7-288342, THU-NUS NExT Co-Lab, Doctoral Program of Higher Schools(No. 20110002110013), Natural Science Foundation of Inner Mongolia(2011ms0914), Chongqing Science and Technology Research Institute(cstc2011ggB40028).

References

1. Han, X., Sun, L.: An entity-topic model for entity linking. In: EMNLP-CoNLL, pp. 105–115 (2012)
2. Sen, P.: Collective context-aware topic models for entity disambiguation. In: Proceedings of the 21st International Conference on World Wide Web, WWW 2012, pp. 729–738 (2012)
3. Xue, X., Yin, X.: Topic modeling for named entity queries. In: Proceedings of the 20th ACM International Conference on Information and Knowledge Management, CIKM 2011, pp. 2009–2012 (2011)

4. Blei, D.M., Ng, A.Y., Jordan, M.I.: Latent dirichlet allocation. Journal of Machine Learning Research 3, 993–1022 (2003)
5. Kim, H., Sun, Y., Hockenmaier, J., Han, J.: Etm: Entity topic models for mining documents associated with entities. In: ICDM 2012, pp. 349–358 (2012)
6. Newman, D., Chemudugunta, C., Smyth, P.: Statistical entity-topic models. In: KDD, pp. 680–686 (2006)
7. Salton, G., McGill, M.: Introduction to Modern Information Retrieval. McGraw-Hill Book Company (1984)
8. Deerwester, S.C., Dumais, S.T., Landauer, T.K., Furnas, G.W., Harshman, R.A.: Indexing by latent semantic analysis. JASIS 41(6), 391–407 (1990)
9. Hofmann, T.: Probabilistic latent semantic indexing. In: SIGIR, pp. 50–57 (1999)
10. Rosen-Zvi, M., Griffiths, T.L., Steyvers, M., Smyth, P.: The author-topic model for authors and documents. In: UAI, pp. 487–494 (2004)
11. Tang, J., Zhang, J., Yao, L., Li, J., Zhang, L., Su, Z.: Arnetminer: extraction and mining of academic social networks. In: Proceedings of the 14th ACM SIGKDD International Conference on Knowledge Discovery and Data Mining, KDD 2008 (2008)
12. Andrzejewski, D., Zhu, X., Craven, M.: Incorporating domain knowledge into topic modeling via dirichlet forest priors. In: Proceedings of the 26th Annual International Conference on Machine Learning, ICML 2009, pp. 25–32 (2009)
13. Blei, D.M., Lafferty, J.D.: Correlated topic models. In: NIPS (2005)
14. Li, W., McCallum, A.: Pachinko allocation: Dag-structured mixture models of topic correlations. In: Proceedings of the 23rd International Conference on Machine Learning, ICML 2006, pp. 577–584 (2006)
15. Mimno, D.M., Li, W., McCallum, A.: Mixtures of hierarchical topics with pachinko allocation. In: ICML, pp. 633–640 (2007)
16. Blei, D.M., Griffiths, T.L., Jordan, M.I., Tenenbaum, J.B.: Hierarchical topic models and the nested chinese restaurant process. In: NIPS (2003)
17. Griffiths, T.L., Steyvers, M.: Finding scientific topics. Proceedings of the National Academy of Sciences of the United States of America 101(suppl. 1), 5228–5235 (2004)
18. Zhu, J., Uren, V., Motta, E.: ESpotter: Adaptive named entity recognition for web browsing. In: Althoff, K.-D., Dengel, A.R., Bergmann, R., Nick, M., Roth-Berghofer, T.R. (eds.) WM 2005. LNCS (LNAI), vol. 3782, pp. 518–529. Springer, Heidelberg (2005)
19. Shen, W., Wang, J., Luo, P., Wang, M.: Linden: linking named entities with knowledge base via semantic knowledge. In: Proceedings of the 21st International Conference on World Wide Web, WWW 2012, pp. 449–458 (2012)
20. Griffiths, T.L., Steyvers, M.: Finding scientific topics. Proceedings of the National Academy of Sciences of the United States of America 101(suppl. 1), 5228–5235 (2004)

An Efficient Framework to Extract Parallel Units from Comparable Data

Lu Xiang, Yu Zhou, and Chengqing Zong

NLPR, Institute of Automation Chinese Academy of Sciences, Beijing, China
{lu.xiang,yzhou,cqzong}@nlpr.ia.ac.cn

Abstract. Since the quality of statistical machine translation (SMT) is heavily dependent upon the size and quality of training data, many approaches have been proposed for automatically mining bilingual text from comparable corpora. However, the existing solutions are restricted to extract either bilingual sentences or sub-sentential fragments. Instead, we present an efficient framework to extract both sentential and sub-sentential units. At sentential level, we consider the parallel sentence identification as a classification problem and extract more representative and effective features. At sub-sentential level, we refer to the idea of phrase table's acquisition in SMT to extract parallel fragments. A novel word alignment model is specially designed for comparable sentence pairs and parallel fragments can be extracted based on such word alignment. We integrate the two levels' extraction task into a united framework. Experimental results on SMT show that the baseline SMT system can achieve significant improvement by adding those extra-mined knowledge.

Keywords: statistical machine translation, comparable corpora, two-level parallel units extraction, parallel sentences, parallel sub-sentential fragments.

1 Introduction

Parallel corpus is an important resource in many natural language processing tasks, such as statistical machine translation (SMT) and cross-lingual information retrieval. Especially for SMT system, the size and quality of the training data has a vital impact on its performance. However, parallel corpora are always very limited in size, domain, and language pairs. Moreover, it is impractical to build such parallel corpora manually for it will take enormous human material and financial resources. Hence, we have to shift our attention to the large amount of available resources from the Internet and try to extract useful information automatically.

While parallel data are very scarce, comparable corpora are much more available and diverse. To alleviate the lack of parallel data, many methods have been proposed to extract parallel text from comparable resources. These works include identifying parallel sentences[3,8,15,18,19,20] and finding parallel fragments[9,12,13].

For the task of identifying parallel sentences, most of the previous work adopts the classification method. However, the performance of various features has not been investigated in-depth, which cannot achieve a good balance on classification accuracy

G. Zhou et al. (Eds.): NLPCC 2013, CCIS 400, pp. 151–163, 2013.
© Springer-Verlag Berlin Heidelberg 2013

and speed. For the extraction of parallel fragments, most of the previous work has not found an appropriate method to build an alignment model for the comparable corpus. However, this alignment model is essential for the performance of the subsequent parallel fragments extraction. Furthermore, the previous solutions are restricted to extract either sentential or sub-sentential fragments. In reality, it's very common that both of them do coexist. In this case, existing approaches fail to extract both sentences and fragments at the same time, which will lead lots of useful resources unexploited.

Therefore, in this paper, we propose a two-level parallel text extraction framework which can extract both parallel sentential and sub-sentential fragments at the same time. At sentence level, a classifier is used to identify whether the bilingual sentence pair is parallel or not. We investigate the impact of different groups of features on the performance of classification and choose one set of features that can give us better performance. Moreover, at sub-sentential level, a novel word alignment model for comparable sentence pairs is presented, and a new approach is proposed to extract sub-sentential fragments from comparable sentences using our word alignment model. We applied our framework to the extraction of Chinese-English parallel units from Wikipedia. Experiments show that our framework can extract all parallel units at both sentential and sub-sentential level which can help to improve the translation quality significantly when adding the extracted data to large-scale Chinese-English training data.

The remainder of this paper is organized as follows: Section 2 introduces the related work. Section 3 gives our two-level parallel text extraction framework. Section 4 presents the experiments on data extraction and SMT results. Finally, we conclude the paper in Section 5.

2   Related Work

Much research work has been done on the task of mining parallel units from comparable corpus. Comparable corpora may contain parallel documents, parallel sentences, or parallel sub-sentential fragments. In existing approaches, the parallel sentence extraction process is often divided into two steps: (1) identify document level alignment, and (2) detect parallel sentences within the identified document pairs. [8] uses cross-lingual information retrieval methods to get more precious article pairs and a maximum entropy classifier is used to extract parallel sentences from the article pairs. [15] exploits "inter-wiki" links in Wikipedia to align documents. [18] implements hash-based algorithms to find cross-lingual article pairs efficiently. [19] extends parallel sentence alignment algorithm to align comparable news corpora. [3] calculates pair-wise cosine similarities to identify parallel sentence pairs. [17] extends the classification approach and adopts a beam-search algorithm to abandon target sentences early during classification.

Furthermore, not all comparable documents contain parallel sentence pairs but they could still have plenty of parallel sub-sentential fragments. Typical phrase extraction method used in SMT only works on parallel sentences and it only collects phrase pairs that are consistent with the word alignment [4, 10]. However, this typical method is not suitable for comparable sentence pairs since it will produce lots of non-parallel phrases due to the un-aligned parts. [9] firstly attempts to detect parallel sub-sentential fragments in comparable sentences and they use a word-based signal filter method to extract sub-sentential fragments. Since the source and target signals are filtered separately, there is no guarantee that the extracted sub-sentential fragments are translations of each other. [12] proposes two generative models for segment extraction from comparable sentences, but they don't show any improvements when applied to in-domain test data for MT. [13] uses a hierarchical alignment model and its derivation trees to detect parallel fragments. The experiments show their method can obtain good fragments but their method need some extra data like gold-standard alignments and parse trees for source and target sentences to train the alignment model.

3   Two-Level Parallel Units Extraction Framework

Our two-level parallel text extraction framework is shown as Fig. 1. Since our work mainly focuses on parallel sentences identifying and parallel sub-sentential fragments detecting, we suppose the given documents have been already aligned before.

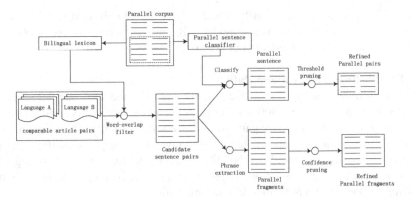

Fig. 1. Two-level parallel unit extraction framework

The resource our framework needed is only a small amount of parallel data used to train the classifier. The bilingual dictionary used for the word-overlap filter process is automatically learned from the small amount of data. First, we obtain a GIZA-lexicon by running GIZA++[1] from two directions on the corpus. Considering the GIZA-lexicon contains too much noise, we adopt log-likelihood-ratios[2,6,7] (LLR) statistic in two directions to get LLR-lexicon. This statistic can estimate the correlation of word pairs and can be calculated using the formula below:

$$2\log\left[\frac{P(y\,|\,x)^{C(x,y)} \cdot P(y\,|\,\neg x)^{C(\neg x,y)} \cdot P(\neg y\,|\,x)^{C(x,\neg y)} \cdot P(\neg y\,|\,\neg x)^{C(\neg x,\neg y)}}{P(y)^{C(y)} \cdot P(\neg y)^{C(\neg y)}}\right] \tag{1}$$

---

[1] http://www.statmt.org/moses/giza/GIZA++.html

In the formula, x and y represent two words for which we wish to estimate the strength of association. $C(y)$ and $C(\neg y)$ are the observed frequencies of y occurring or not occurring in the corpus; $C(x, y), \ldots, C(\neg x, \neg y)$ are the joint frequencies of the different possible combinations of x and y occurring and not occurring; and $p(y)$, $p(\neg y)$, $p(y|x), \ldots, p(\neg y|\neg x)$ are the maximum likelihood estimates of the corresponding marginal and conditional probabilities[7].

3.1   Candidate Sentence Pairs' Selection

We use a method based on word-overlap to filter the candidate sentence pairs. For each article pairs, we take all possible sentence pairs and pass them through the word-overlap filter. It checks that the percentage of words that have a translation in the other sentence must be above a threshold according to LLR-lexicon. Any sentence pairs that don't meet the condition will be discarded. This step can help to remove most unrelated sentence pairs and the remaining sentences will be passed on to the parallel sentences identifying and parallel fragments detecting stage.

3.2   Parallel Sentences' Identification

We use a binary classifier to identify whether a sentence-pair is parallel or not. Considering that the maximum entropy model (ME) proves to be effective in [8], we adopt the maximum entropy model in our classifier.

3.2.1   Establishment of Training Data

As Fig. 1 shows, the training data of the classifier is from the seed parallel sentence corpus. We randomly choose 5,800 parallel sentence pairs[2] as positive instances and then generate non-parallel sentence pairs from those sentence pairs. This will generate $(5800^2\text{-}5800)$ non-parallel sentence pairs. Since we only apply classifier on the sentence pairs passing the word-overlap filter, we randomly select 5,800 negative instances under the same condition. After training data is prepared, we use the features we proposed to train parallel sentence classifier.

3.2.2   Selection of Features

Features are quite important to the performance of classifier. Besides the features used in [8], we believe that there must be some other useful features. After comparing parallel and non-parallel sentence pairs, we find the following three features should be useful: strong translation sentinels[20] , log probability of word alignment and pair-wise sentences cosine similarity.

Log probability is word alignment score and pair-wise sentences cosine similarity can tell us the similarity between two sentences. Intuitively, if two sentences are translations of each other, the translated words should distribute in the whole sentence. Strong translation sentinels come from that intuition. In order to extract this feature conveniently, we only take the content words near the beginning and end

---

[2] We choose 5800 parallel sentence pairs in our experiment. This can be adjusted.

of the sentences into consideration (the first and last two content words) and count the number of these four words that have a translation on the other side. These three features are light-weight features and can be computed efficiently.

To sum up, we will use the following features[3] to train our classifier:

- The features in [8]:
  1) General features: Length feature; Translation coverage feature;
  2) Features derived from IBM Model-1 alignments.
- Our new features: 1) Log probability of the alignment; 2) Pair-wise sentences cosine similarity; 3) Strong translation sentinels.

We will investigate the impact of all above features to the classification performance in our experiment. By analyzing the impact, we can choose a group of features that can best meet our needs and train a better classifier for the parallel sentence extraction task.

After passing the candidate sentence pairs through the classifier, we extract those pairs that are classified as positive and finally we only keep the ones with classification confidence higher than a predefined threshold.

3.3   Parallel Sub-sentential Fragments' Extraction

3.3.1   Alignment Model

Since the comparable data is huge, we need a simple but efficient word alignment model to get the word alignment. IBM Model-1[1] is one such model. But it has some shortcomings like it often produces vast false word correspondences in high frequency words. Inspired by YAWA[16], we propose a modified IBM Model-1 that uses bilingual translation lexicons in two stages to obtain a better alignment.

Fig. 2. An example of our modified IBM Model-1. The solid lines in the left are the links of content words obtained in the first step. The dotted lines are the new added links of function words in the second step.

---

[3] We use all the features with numerical value in ME classifier.

Phase 1: Content Words Alignment. Content words can represent the skeleton of one sentence and the links between content words are much more reliable than those between function words[4]. First, we compute the content words alignment by greedily linking each content word in source sentence with its best translation candidate which has the highest log-likelihood (LL) association score from target sentence according to LLR-lexicon. If a pair of words doesn't exist in the LLR-lexicon or some words appear more than once in the target sentence, we just leave such words and align them in the second stage since the existing links in the first stage can give contextual information for the unaligned words. If the end punctuations are translations, we also link them. The left in Fig. 2 exemplifies the links created in end of the first phase.

Phase 2: Function Words Alignment. The existing links in stage 1 can be treated as phrase boundaries. In this stage, we will heuristically match the blocks and add links to the unaligned words. The algorithm is given as follows: align two blocks if the surrounding words are already aligned and then align words in the two blocks. We illustrate this situation in Fig. 2. For example, we have (了(le), 各(ge), 个(ge)) unaligned in the Chinese side after phase 1. Its surrounding words are "形成 (xingcheng)" and "国家(guojia)" which are aligned with "formed" and "country" respectively. Thus, the chunk (了, 各, 个) is aligned with block (the, culture, circle, of, each) and then we can align words in these two blocks. We can align the rest unaligned words in the same way. The new links are shown in the right side of Fig. 2 by the dotted lines.

3.3.2   Parallel Sub-sentential Fragments' Detection

Fig. 3 gives an example of a comparable sentence pair that contains two parallel sub-sentential fragments. In this part, we are concerned about finding such fragments.

以"一国 两 制"的 办法 解决 台湾 问题 ， 才 能 最大 限度 地 寻求 两 岸 利益 的 公分母 。
we have hoped for many years to use the formula of "one country, two systems" to peacefully resolve the taiwan issue .

Fig. 3. An example of comparable sentences containing parallel sub-sentential fragments

To detect the sub-sentential fragments, we generate word alignments using our modified IBM Model-1 from bi-directions for each comparable sentence pair and then use intersection [4] method to obtain better alignments. After that, we traverse the word alignment and extract phrases that satisfy the following constraints:

(a) The length of the source and target phrase is no less than 3;
(b) Words inside the source phrase can only be aligned with words inside the target phrase and the same for the words outside the phrase boundaries;
(c) The phrase span can contain a small percentage of content words without any connection;
(d) The unaligned boundary word of the phrase can only be function words.

---

[4] We count words appearing in the text we will experiment with and take the 100 most frequent words on each side as function words. The remaining words are treated as content words.

When traversing the word alignment, it will often produce short fragments which are not really parallel. And the fragment is more confident when it is longer. Constraint (a) helps us to exclude phrases with less than 3 words and extract long fragments. Constraints (b) and (c) are the content constraints. Constraint (b) limits us from extracting phrases that contain words aligned outside the phrases. Because of the coverage of the LLR-lexicon, not every word can find its translation in the other side. Constraint (c) allows us to extract fragments with a small percentage of words unaligned and such constraint can help us obtain some new lexicon entries. Constraint (d) decides whether a phrase can be extended or not. This makes some function words like "the" and "of" in English and "的(de)" and "了(le)" in Chinese can be included in the phrases.

After sub-sentential fragments extraction, we also need to do some pruning to get better fragments. We filter those low-frequent fragment pairs.

4   Experiments

We evaluate our two-level extraction framework following the steps blow: (1) investigating the impact of different features used in our classifier on the extraction of parallel sentence pairs, (2) describing the extraction of sub-sentential fragments, and (3) evaluating the impact of the extracted data on SMT performance.

4.1   Experiments Setup

We perform our two-level extraction method on Chinese and English Wikipedia articles. We download the dump files from Wikimedia dump[5]. For the seed corpora, we use a large bilingual training data from LDC corpus[6]. Since Wikipedia is a different domain from our seed corpora, we extract article titles from Wikipedia documents as the additional baseline training data. Thus, the initial parallel data consists of large bilingual data from LDC corpus and Wikipedia article title pairs and we denote it as LDC&WikiTitle. Table 1 shows the relevant statistics of LDC&WikiTitle.

Table 1. Statistics of our initial parallel corpus

	Parallel initial corpus	sentences	tokens
Corpus from LDC	Chinese	2,085,331	27,640,151
	English	2,085,331	31,826,668
Wikipedia title pairs	Chinese	236,565	639,813
	English	236,565	642,743
LDC&WikiTitle	Chinese	2,321,896	28,279,964
	English	2,321,896	32,469,411

---

[5] http://dumps.wikimedia.org/backup-index.html
[6] LDC category number: LDC2000T50, LDC2002E18, LDC2003E07, LDC2004T07, LDC2005T06, LDC2002L27, LDC2005T10 and LDC2005T34.

To obtain LLR-lexicon, we run GIZA++ with default setting on LDC&WikiTitle from two directions, use "grow-dial-final-and" strategy to combine the alignments and then keep lexicon with LLR score above 10. Finally, we obtain 4,631,477 GIZA-lexicon and 325,001 LLR positive lexicons.

4.2   Experimental Results on Parallel Sentences Extraction

We create training data from the large bilingual data of LDC as description in Subsection 3.2.1. A maximum entropy binary classifier using the Maximum Entropy Modeling Toolkit[7] is used as the classifier model.

4.2.1   Evaluation of Various of Features

In order to investigate the influence of features on the performance of ME classifier, we use the same method to build a test set of 1,000 positive instances and 1,000 negative instances from CWMT'2011 data[8]. We first test the features in [8] by incrementally adding features from F1 to F8. Table 2 reports the performance evaluation.

Table 2. Evaluation on different features. F2-F5 use only bidirectional alignments. F6-F8 add three combinations (intersection, union, refined) of the bi-directional alignments respectively.

Features	Precision	Recall	F-score
F1:General features	0.7021	0.608	0.6516
F2: +no connection	0.7414	0.889	0.8085
F3: +fertility	0.7395	0.9	0.8119
F4: +contiguous connected span	0.7300	0.933	0.8191
F5: +unconnected substring	0.7288	0.941	0.8214
F6: +intersection	0.7344	0.91	0.8128
F7: +union	0.7435	0.928	0.8256
F8: +refined	0.7606	0.896	0.8227

From Table 2, the classifier evaluation results show that the most useful features are F1 and F2. The other features are relatively difficult to calculate and don't help to improve the performance a lot. Due to the large amount of comparable data, we give up these features. Instead, we use three other features which are very easy to compute and the evaluation scores are given in Table 3. In order to compare the real performance of our features with those features in [8], we give the detailed scores both on speed and accuracy presented in Table 4.

---

[7] http://homepages.inf.ed.ac.uk/lzhang10/maxent_toolkit.html
[8] The 7th China Workshop on Machine Translation Evaluation.

Table 3. Evaluation on our added features

Features	Precision	Recall	F-score
F1:General features	0.7021	0.608	0.6516
F2:+no connection	0.7414	0.889	0.8085
F9:+log probability	0.7429	0.893	0.8110
F10:+cosine similarity	0.7439	0.895	0.8125
F11:+sentinels	0.7466	0.899	0.8157

Table 4. Performance comparison under different features

Features	F-score	Time (s)
F1-F5	0.8214	2259.26
F1-F8	0.8227	4097.63
F1+F2+F9+F10+F11	0.8157	403.45

Table 4 presents the time it costs to extract different set of features from 100,000 sentence pairs. Using F1-F8 cost nearly twice the time of using F1-F5, but the F-score improvements are slight. Our features have achieved the comparable performance to the features in [8], and it is much faster to extract these features. Thus we finally use the features in Table 3 to train a ME classifier and we can affirm that our classifier will be much efficient than Munteanu and Marcu's.

4.2.2   Parallel Sentences' Extraction

We use "inter-wiki" links to align Wikipedia article pairs and finally obtain 199,984 article pairs. Then we use word-overlap filter process to obtain the candidate sentence pairs based on LLR-lexicon. Here sentence pairs with translation coverage above 0.3 are maintained. Then we apply our ME classifier to the candidate sentence pairs and extract sentence pairs with confidence higher than 0.75. The amount of candidate sentence pairs and extracted parallel sentence pairs are shown in Table 5.

Table 5. Size of extracted parallel text

	Chinese-English
Candidate sentence pairs	2,101,770
Parallel sentence pairs	201,588
Parallel fragments	7,708,424

4.3   Experimental Results on Parallel Sub-sentential Fragments Extraction

We employ the method described in Sub-Section 3.3 to extract parallel sub-sentential fragments. We use the sentence pair shown in Fig. 3 to illustrate the extraction procedure. The word alignment result is shown in Fig. 4 and part of the extracted fragments is presented in Table 6.

From Table 6, we can see that our method can find the parallel sub-sentential fragments in comparable sentence pairs. Our method is quite simple and easy to be implemented. We apply this method to the candidate sentence pairs and the results are shown in Table 5. The number of the extracted sentence pairs is 201,588 and it makes up about 10% of the candidate sentence pairs. The amount of the fragments is 7,708,424 and it is nearly 40 times larger than the parallel sentences. This also shows the importance of the exploration of the parallel fragment resource.

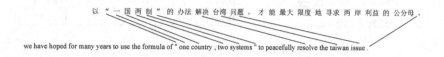

Fig. 4. Word alignment result using intersection strategy to combine bi-directional alignment

Table 6. Examples of the extracted fragments

Chinese	English
一 国 两 制	one country , two systems
一 国 两 制 "	one country , two systems "
一 国 两 制 " 的 办法 解决 台湾 问题	one country , two systems " to peacefully resolve the taiwan issue
两 制 " 的 办法 解决 台湾 问题	two systems " to peacefully resolve the taiwan issue
制 " 的 办法 解决 台湾 问题	systems " to peacefully resolve the taiwan issue
解决 台湾 问题	resolve the taiwan issue

4.4   Experimental Results on SMT Performance

We use LDC&WikiTitle as our baseline SMT training data. We adopt GIZA++ and grow-diag-final-and for word alignment, Moses toolkit[5] with default settings to train the SMT systems. Language model is trained on the English part of LDC&WikiTitle plus Wikipedia data with SRILM[14]. We have two development and testing sets: one is the 790 parallel sentence pairs manually selected from Wikipedia and half of them as development set (Dev A) and the rest as test set (Test A); the other is NIST MT 2003 evaluation data as the development set (Dev B) and NIST MT05 as test set (Test B). Translation performance is evaluated using BLEU metric[11].

In order to show the advantage of our two-level parallel text extraction method, we conduct the following evaluation respectively: (1) only adding the extracted parallel sentences, (2) only adding the extracted parallel sub-sentential fragments, and (3) adding both the extracted parallel sentences and sub-sentential fragments to the original corpora and then evaluate the impact to an end-to-end SMT system.

As Table 7 shows, the translation performance on Test A is much lower than that on MT05 under the baseline system. This is because the LDC&WikiTitle corpus is mainly consisted of news data and it can only learn less knowledge about Wikipedia. When adding the extracted parallel text, the SMT performance on Test A has been improved significantly (+16 BLEU points for extracted sentences and +20 points for extracted fragments). It is due to the extra data can provide much translation knowledge about Wikipedia. This means that our parallel sentences and fragments extraction method is useful for machine translation.

Table 7. SMT evaluation results

	Test A	Test B
baseline	24.49	29.96
baseline +extracted sentence (201,588 sentence pairs)	41.31	30.84
baseline+ extracted fragment (7,708,424 fragments)	45.20	30.21
baseline + sentence + fragment	50.52	30.23

However, the extracted fragments don't seem to be much too useful for MT05 by only slightly improvement for MT05. Intuitively, this could come down to the following reasons: (1) MT05 is in news domain, which is a different domain from Wikipedia. However, domain adaptation is a very difficult research task. (2) The fragments are much more than the baseline corpus which may be drowned by the new added data. We also conduct the evaluation on MT06. The evaluation results show 0.24 improvements when adding the extracted sentences and 0.27 improvements when adding both extracted sentences and fragments compared to the baseline.

In order to find why the effect is not so obvious on Test B, we give the statistical information of LLR positive lexicon size with different training corpus in Table 8. From Table 8 we can see that the new lexicon entries don't increase too much by the extracted sentences (19,067, 5.87%) but increase dramatically by the extracted fragments (364,613, 112.2%). This illustrates that the extracted sentences are very close to the baseline training data LDC&WikiTitle, thus the translation result is improved relatively significantly by 0.88 BLEU score. However, for the extracted fragments, it has two times of lexicon entries compared to the LDC&WikiTitle, so those two corpora have much difference in domain and the original data may be drowned by the new added fragments. Consequently the SMT performance did not meet our expectations on MT05 and MT06. In this respect, it is not wise to add all fragments directly to the LDC&WikiTitle to train translation model. We have to do further experiments to inspect and verify how to add our resource appropriately to the baseline SMT model as a beneficial supplement. However, this can also show our new framework is able to help mine much more useful information for SMT from another aspect.

Table 8. LLR positive lexicon size

	LLR positive lexicon size
LDC&WikiTitle corpus	325,001
LDC&WikiTitle corpus + extracted sentence	344,068
LDC&WikiTitle corpus+ extracted fragment	678,652
LDC&WikiTitle corpus + sentence + fragment	689,614

5   Conclusion

In this paper, we propose a simple and effective two-level parallel unit extraction method for extracting both sentential and sub-sentential parallel text from comparable corpora. At sentential level, we treat the task of identifying parallel sentences as a classification problem and investigate the impact of different features in detail to find the best group of features. For sub-sentential fragment, we developed a novel word alignment model for comparable sentence pairs and describe how to extract parallel sub-sentential fragments based on such word alignment. Our new framework can help us extract much more useful information with a good trade-off performance at accuracy and speed. We applied our framework to the extraction of Chinese-English parallel units from Wikipedia used for Chinese-to-English SMT. Experimental results show that it can improve the translation quality significantly by adding the extracted data to large-scale Chinese-English training data.

In the next step, we will study on the method of how to evaluate the confidence of the extracted sentences and fragments and how to use those mined parallel fragments appropriately for a SMT system with a given domain.

Acknowledgement. The research work has been partially funded by the Natural Science Foundation of China under Grant No. 61003160 and Hi-Tech Research and Development Program ("863" Program) of China under Grant No. 2011AA01A207, and also supported by the Key Project of Knowledge Innovation Program of Chinese Academy of Sciences under Grant No. KGZD-EW-501.

References

1. Brown Peter, F., Della Pietra, S.A., Della Pietra, V.J., Mercer, R.L.: The mathematics of machine translation: Parameter estimation. Computational Linguistics 19(2), 263–311 (1993)
2. Dunning, T.: Accurate methods for the statistics of surprise and coincidence. Computational Linguistics 19(1), 61–74 (1993)
3. Fung, P., Cheung, P.: Mining very non-parallel corpora: Parallel sentence and lexicon extraction vie bootstrapping and EM. In: EMNLP 2004, pp. 57–63 (2004a)
4. Koehn, P., Och, F.J., Marcu, D.: Statistical phrase based translation. In: Proceedings of the Joint Conference on Human Language Technologies and the Annual Meeting of the North American Chapter of the Association of Computational Linguistics, HLT-NAACL (2003)
5. Koehn, P., Hoang, H., Birch, A., Callison-Burch, C., Federico, M., Bertoldi, N., Cowan, B., Shen, W., Moran, C., Zens, R.-C., Dyer, C., Bojar, O.: Moses: Open source toolkit for Statistical Machine Translation. In: Proceedings of the ACL 2007 Demo and Poster Sessions, pp. 177–180 (2007)
6. Moore, R.C.: Improving IBM word alignment model 1. In: ACL 2004, pp. 519–526 (2004a)
7. Moore, R.C.: On log-likelihood-ratios and the significance of rare events. In: EMNLP 2004, pp. 333–340 (2004b)
8. Munteanu, D.S., Marcu, D.: Improving machine translation performance by exploiting non-parallel corpora. Computational Linguistics 31(4), 477–504 (2005)
9. Munteanu, D.S., Marcu, D.: Extracting parallel sub-sentential fragments from nonparallel corpora. In: Proceedings of the 21st International Conference on Computational Linguistics and the 44th Annual Meeting of the Association for Computational Linguistics, Sydney, Australia, pp. 81–88 (2006)

10. Och, F.J., Tillmann, C., Ney, H.: Improved alignment models for statistical machine translation. In: Proceedings of the Joint Conference of Empirical Methods in Natural Language Processing and Very Large Corpora, pp. 20–28 (1999)
11. Papineni, K., Roukos, S., Ward, T., Zhu, W.-J.: Bleu: a method for automatic evaluation of machine translation. In: Proceedings of ACL, Philadelpha, Pennsylvania, USA, pp. 311–318 (2002)
12. Quirk, C., Udupa, R.U., Menezes, A.: Generative models of noisy translations with applications to parallel fragment extraction. In: Proceedings of the Machine Translation Summit XI, Copenhagen, Denmark, pp. 377–384 (2007)
13. Riesa, J., Marcu, D.: Automatic parallel fragment extraction from noisy data. In: Proceedings of the 2012 Conference of the North American Chapter of the Association for Computational Linguistics: Human Language Technologies, pp. 538–542. Association for Computational Linguistics (2012)
14. Stolcke, A.: SRILM - An Extensible Language Modeling Toolkit. In: Proceedings of ICSLP, vol. 2, pp. 901–904 (2002)
15. Smith, J.R., Quirk, C., Toutanova, K.: Extracting parallel sentences from comparable corpora using document level alignment. In: Proceedings of the Human Language Technologies/North American Association for Computational Linguistics, pp. 403–411 (2010)
16. Tufiş, D., Ion, R., Ceauşu, A., Ştefănescu, D.: Improved Lexical Alignment by Combining Multiple Reified Alignments. In: Proceedings of EACL 2006, Trento, Italy, pp. 153–160 (2006)
17. Tillmann, C.: A Beam-Search extraction algorithm for comparable data. In: Proceedings of ACL, pp. 225–228 (2009)
18. Ture, F., Lin, J.: Why not grab a free lunch? Mining large corpora for parallel sentences to improve translation modeling. In: HLT-NAACL, pp. 626–630 (2012)
19. Zhao, B., Vogel, S.: Adaptive parallel sentences mining from web bilingual news collection. In: IEEE International Conference on Data Mining, Maebashi City, Japan, pp. 745–748 (2002)
20. Ştefănescu, D., Ion, R., Hunsicker, S.: Hybrid parallel sentence mining from comparable corpora. In: Proceedings of the 16th Conference of the European Association for Machine Translation (EAMT 2012), Trento, Italy (2012)

A Method to Construct Chinese-Japanese Named Entity Translation Equivalents Using Monolingual Corpora

Kuang Ru, Jinan Xu, Yujie Zhang, and Peihao Wu

School of Computer and Information Technology, Beijing Jiaotong University, Beijing, China
{11120471,jaxu,yjzhang,12120465}@bjtu.edu.cn

Abstract. The traditional method of Named Entity Translation Equivalents extraction is often based on large-scale parallel or comparable corpora. But the practicability of the research results is constrained by the relatively scarce of the bilingual corpus resources. We combined the features of Chinese and Japanese, and proposed a method to automatically extract the Chinese-Japanese NE translation equivalents based on inductive learning from monolingual corpus. This method uses the Chinese Hanzi and Japanese Kanji comparison table to calculate NE instances similarity between Japanese and Chinese. Then, we use inductive learning method to obtain partial translation rules of NEs through extracting the differences between Chinese and Japanese high similarity NE instances. In the end, the feedback process refreshes the Chinese and Japanese NE similarity and translation rule sets. Experimental results show that the proposed method is simple and efficient, which overcome the shortcoming that the traditional methods have a dependency on bilingual resource.

Keywords: named entity translation equivalents, Chinese Hanzi and Japanese Kanji comparison table, inductive learning method.

1 Introduction

Named entity generally refers to proper names and the meaningful quantifier appeared in the text. Named entity was divided into seven categories in the MUC-6[1], including: Person, Location, Organization, Date, Time, Percentage and Monetary value. Person, Location and Organization is the hardest and most important categories. Named entity described in this paper is a collection of these three types of named entities.

Named Entity research is a basic task of natural language processing. Mainstream extraction methods of named entity include rule-based approach, statistical approach and the combination of rule and statistics methods and etc.. With the development of named entity extraction technology, the main task of named entity extraction has changed to automatically construct the NE translation equivalents. The technology of Constructing NE translation equivalents have important significance for multilingual information processing, such as automatic summarization, machine translation, cross-language information retrieval and automatic question answering system.

In recent years, some of the cross-language automatic named entity extraction methods have been proposed, such as looking up the dictionary [2], transliteration

G. Zhou et al. (Eds.): NLPCC 2013, CCIS 400, pp. 164–175, 2013.
© Springer-Verlag Berlin Heidelberg 2013

model [2-4] and etc.. On the one hand, since the word-based transliteration models often cannot be as accurate as dictionary translation. And the bilingual dictionary translation method exist the problem that the dictionary has a limited coverage to NE translation equivalents. On the other hand, early studies on NE translation equivalents mainly focus on the named entities acquisition from the parallel corpus [5-7]. By this method the accuracy of NE extraction result is very high, but the parallel corpus acquisition is not a simple task. Especially when the relevant language resources are rare, acquisition of large-scale parallel corpora has become more difficult.

In order to avoid the huge cost to obtain parallel corpus, many researchers have turned to use the comparable corpus to obtain bilingual resources. Comparable bilingual corpus is a bilingual text set that is not parallel, but related to the same topic. For example, the Boston terrorist bilingual news could be considered comparable. Compared with the parallel corpus, comparable corpus is easier acquisition, resources are more abundant, therefore it's more suitable for large-scale NE translation equivalents extraction task.

One of the earliest researches in this field is based on word co-occurrence and proposed by Rapp [8]. This method assumes that if the joint probability of co-occurrence of two words larger than the occurrence probability of the respective word, these two words are more likely to appear in a similar context. In his paper, he used the similarity matrix and the joint probability to estimate the lexical mapping. Most of the existing methods are based on this assumption and put forward different similarity calculation method, according to the feature of different similarity matrix content, They can be classified as shown in table 1.

Table 1. Taxonomy of cross-language similarity metrics

	Entity	Relationship
Using entity names	E	R
Using textual context	EC	RC

1. E: Entity names in the two corpora can be compared based on their phonetic similarity, *e.g.*, high phonetic similarity between Obama and the Chinese translation of Obama, 奥巴马 (pronounced 'Aobama'), is evidence that they are a translation pair.
2. EC: Entity Context, i.e., common text surrounding the named entity translation pair in the two corpora, can be compared. For example, Obama and 奥巴马, surrounded by words with the same meanings, such as 'president' and '总统', support the inference that they are translation pairs.
3. R: Relationships between an NE pair in one corpus and an NE pair in other corpus, quantified by monolingual NE co-occurrence, can be used as relational evidence that they are translation pair. For example, Barack and Michelle (巴拉克 and 米歇尔) frequently co-occur in both corpora, and high translation similarity of (Obama, 奥巴马) supports the inference that Michelle and 米歇尔 are translation pair.

4. RC: Relationship Context, i.e., the surrounding text that explains the relationship of the NE pair in each corpus, is evidence for whether the two NE relationships are comparable. For example, Barack and Michelle described as a couple in both corpora is evidence that they have strong relationship, and, therefore, it can enhance the relationship similarity R.

Only use one feature as the similarity matrix is difficult to obtain satisfactory results [9-11]. Most recent approach is to integrate various features. Shao and Ng [12] integrate the E and EC. Lee and Aw [13] come together E, EC and R. You [14, 15] did not only merge all the features together, also joined the additional latent features into system such as time.

In summary, traditional methods require large-scale parallel corpus or other bilingual resources. Compared with monolingual corpora, large-scale bilingual resources are relatively scarce and high building costs. However the large-scale monolingual corpus construction technique is simple, low cost and easy to implement.

At present, the Chinese and Japanese bilingual resources are very few. While construct Japanese Chinese bilingual NE translation dictionary, in order to solve the above problem, we propose a method based on inductive learning Chinese and Japanese monolingual corpus for automatic extraction method of NE translation. This method uses the Chinese Hanzi and Japanese Kanji table calculate Chinese and Japanese named entity similarity between instances. Then use inductive learning method to extract the common part and different part in high similarity Chinese and Japanese NE pairs. And obtain partial translation rules from these two parts. In the end, through the feedback process updates on the Chinese and Japanese named entity similarity and partial translation rule set. Experimental results show that, the method proposed in this paper is simple and efficient, which can effectively use monolingual corpora building large-scale Chinese Japanese named entity translation dictionary.

In the following part of this paper, our research and resources are introduced in the 2nd section, mainly including inductive learning method and the Japanese Chinese characters table; The 3rd section describes the extraction method of named entity translation Equivalents; Section 4 discusses and analyses the experimental results; Finally make summarizes and give the future works.

2   The Related Research and Resources

Current mainstream machine learning methods include supervised, semi-supervised and unsupervised three categories. The proposed method uses example-based inductive learning method and use Chinese Hanzi and Japanese kanji table as existing knowledge.

2.1   Inductive Learning Method

The example-based inductive learning method is proposed by Professor Kenji Araki and etc. [16]. The basic idea mainly includes two aspects. One is the recursive extraction the common part and different part from two examples to obtain rules; the other, through the feedback processing screen and optimize rules. This paper acquires the inherent rules in the instance using inductive learning approach. Firstly we determine the corresponding relationship between the strings, secondly, to extract correspondence rules from unknown strings, as shown in Table 2.

Table 2. Extraction instance from Unknown string pairs

Input 1	αθσψδλν	
Input 2	ΞΣψδΥΦΘ	
Segment 1	αθσ	ΞΣ
Segment 2	ψδ	ψδ
Segment 3	λν	ΥΦΘ

The input 1 and input 2 in Table 2 exist corresponding relationship with an underline (ψδ). Subsequently, align the different parts according to the order of segments. The results are shown in Table 2, segment 1, segment 2 and segment 3 constitute corresponding relationship respectively. Except correspond to the sequence shown in Table 2, there may be the reverse mapping relation. As to the position order or reverse, will depend on the specific research goals and use the empirical method to resolve.

According to the same method we extract the common part from segment and reduce the segment to primitives. The example of extracting primitives from the segment is shown in Table 3. We extract the common part marked with an underline (θσ, ΦΘ) from segment 1, 2 as the primitive 2. Then we extract the different parts of both sides ((α,Υ), (γμ, Σ)) as primitive 1 and primitive 3. Thus, by separating the common part and different part, we can get three primitives.

Table 3. Extraction primitive from segments

Segment 1	αθσ	ΥΦΘ
Segment 2	θσγμ	ΦΘΣ
primitive 1	α	Υ
primitive 2	θσ	ΦΘ
primitive 3	γμ	Σ

Because the primitives can be merge to the segments, so these three primitives became the perfect substitutes of two segments. This extraction method usually needs the help of empirical rules which determine the correspondence between strings. This example-based method extracts the common part and different part by stages so as to obtain knowledge, which is a kind of inductive learning methods.

2.2   Chinese Hanzi and Japanese Kanji Comparison Table

Chinese characters are in widespread use [17]. Japanese Kanji comes from ancient Chinese. Therefore Japanese Kanji and Chinese Hanzi (including Simplified Chinese and Traditional Chinese) in many cases are the same. However, as shown in Table 4, the corresponding relationship between Japanese Kanji and Chinese Hanzi are very complicated. Goh, etc. [18] using the Japanese-Chinese dictionary, change the Japanese Kanji to Chinese Hanzi through direct matching method. Chu et al [17] use open source resources to build Japanese kanji, Traditional Chinese, Simplified Chinese Hanzi table.

Table 4. Extraction primitive from segment

Japanese Kanji	愛	国	書	氷
Traditional Chinese Hanzi	愛	國	書	冰
Simplified Chinese Hanzi	爱	国	书	冰

Chinese clients of Chinese-Japanese bilingual translation system typically contain only simplified Chinese Hanzi, so this paper construct Japanese Kanji and Simplified Chinese Hanzi table. In the process, this paper uses a total of three types of dictionary information:

1. Variants Dictionary. A Hanzi in a Chinese-Japanese dictionary may exist in a variety of different shape, while building the dictionary, we enumerate the circumstances of each Variant. Unihan Database is the CJK trilingual knowledge databases of Unicode Consortium. [1] The database contains variants feature information which recorded the relationships in Japanese kanji and Chinese Hanzi. In this paper, we use variants to change Japanese kanji shape. If there is a link between variants, then two characters can be transformed into each other.
2. Chinese and Japanese Kanji Dictionary. We use the Chinese-Japanese kanji dictionary of Kanconvit[2], which contains a total of 1159 vocabulary variants.
3. Traditional-Simplified Chinese Dictionary. As shown in Table 5, Traditional-Simplified Chinese Hanzi is not the simple one-to-one relationship. We use the Traditional-Simplified Chinese Dictionary in Chinese Encoding Converter[3] which contains a total of 6740 pairs of traditional Hanzi to simplified Hanzi.

Table 5. Hanzi converter standard conversion table

Traditional Hanzi	萹, 稨	變	並, 併	佈
Simplified Hanzi	扁	变	并	布

---

[1] http://unicode.org/charts/unihan.html
[2] http://kanconvit.ta2o.net
[3] http://www.mandarintools.com/zhcode.html

3   Our Method

The existing method for NE translation equivalents acquisition from bilingual corpus required that the bilingual corpora have a strong correlation. Even the methods using comparable corpus also require the correlation [19, 20]. The proposed method use large monolingual corpora, and reduce the difficulty of obtaining the corpus.

First we get two monolingual collection of NE through the monolingual named entity recognition tools. Secondly, we use the named entity translation rules and Chinese Hanzi and Japanese Kanji comparison table as additional knowledge and calculate the similarity between bilingual NEs to obtain the similarity list. Then we have an inductive learning process for high similarity NEs. For example in "BBC ウェールズ" (BBC Wales) and "BBC 威尔士", we get the different part is "ウェールズ" and "威尔士" when we take the word as the smallest semantics unit. We count up the different parts in NE list. Then we select the entries whose co-occurrence rate are higher than giving threshold and add them into partial translation rules. We use partial translation rules to calculate the similarity iteratively, until we cannot generate new NE translation equivalents. Procedure of the method is shown as Fig 1.

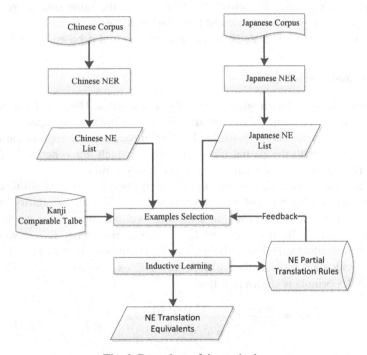

Fig. 1. Procedure of the method

3.1   Monolingual Named Entity Recognition

Monolingual named entity recognition technology has developed rapidly, the main method include rule-based, dictionary-based and statistical methods.

Generally, when the extracted rules can reflect the language phenomenon accurately, rule-based approach is superior to the performance of statistical methods. However, these rules are often dependent on the specific language and style of the text. Its compilation process is time-consuming. And the system is difficult to cover the entire language phenomenon. It is particularly prone to error, bad system portability, and it requires linguistic experts to rewrite new rules for different system.

Statistical methods use artificial annotated corpus for training which does not require extensive linguistics knowledge, and can be finished in short time. In CoNLL-2003 Conference, the all 16 participating systems based on statistical methods. The methods become the mainstream of current research. Such systems migrate to new areas cannot make big changes, just use new corpus for training. Statistical machine learning methods mainly include: Hidden Markov Model (HMM), Maximum Entropy (ME), Support Vector Machine (SVM), Conditional Random Fields (CRF) and etc..

In these four kinds of learning methods, maximum entropy model is compact with good versatility. The main drawback is that the training complexity is very high, and sometimes even lead to unbearable training costs. It needs the clear normalized calculation, resulting in large overhead. The CRF provides a flexible feature and global optimal annotation framework for NER. But at the same time, there are some problem such as slow convergence and long training time.

In this paper, monolingual named entity recognition tool is based on CRF.

3.2   Examples Selection

In the initial phase of this module, we mainly use Chinese Hanzi and Japanese Kanji comparison table, calculating NE similarity between Chinese and Japanese instances, and then obtain examples for inductive learning through given appropriate threshold values. Together with the partial translation rules, which are generate by inductive learning module, we further improve the named entity similarity.

There are many ways to calculate the similarity between named entities, such as edit distance, Hamming distance, cosine vector, Jaccard similarity and etc.. Considering the word frequency information, we use the cosine vector as the similarity Formula. The basic idea is: If the two named entity to use words more similar, their content should be more similar. Therefore, we can start from word frequency, calculate their similarity. Japanese NE express as A, and Chinese NE express as B. Formula is shown as follows:

$$S = \frac{A \cdot B}{|A| \times |B|} = \frac{\sum_{i=1}^{n}(A_i \times B_i)}{\sqrt{\sum_{i=1}^{n}(A_i)^2} \times \sqrt{\sum_{i=1}^{n}(B_i)^2}} \tag{1}$$

Cosine values closer to 1, it shows that the angle is close to 0 degrees, which means the two vectors are more similar.

Taking Japanese named entity "大原綜合病院附属大原医療センター" (Ohara subsidiary medical center of Ohara General Hospital) and Chinese named entity "大原综合医院附属大原医疗中心" for example, the processing steps are as follows:

1. Have monolingual word segmentation for Japanese and Chinese.
   Japanese Segmentation Results: 大原 綜合 病院 附属 大原 医療 センター
   Chinese Segmentation Results: 大原 综合 医院 附属 大原 医疗 中心

2. We use the NE Partial Translation Rules to translation the NEs. In the initial state of the rule base is empty, after a few iterations, in this case, "病院"(hospital) -> "医院", "綜合"(general) -> "综合" has been extracted as a partial rule, which can improve the similarity.
   Japanese partial translation results: 大原 综合 医院 附属 大原 医療 センター
   Chinese: 大原 综合 医院 附属 大原 医疗 中心

3. Convert the Japanese Kanji to Simplified Chinese Hanzi by Chinese Hanzi and Japanese Kanji comparison table. In this example, '療'-> '疗'
   Japanese kanji conversion results: 大原 综合 医院 附属 大原 医疗 センター
   Chinese: 大原 综合 医院 附属 大原 医疗 中心

4. We unified segmentation granularity and looked the Japanese word segmentation results as the standard. If unable to confirm the boundary, the unknown part keeps the initial state of Chinese word segmentation.
   Japanese: 大原 综合 医院 附属 大原 医疗 センター
   Chinese unified segmentation granularity results:
   大原 综合 医院 附属 大原 医疗 中心

5. List all the word bilingual named entity contains, forming a vector.
   [大原 综合 医院 附属 医疗 センター 中心]

6. Get the word frequency vector.
   Japanese word frequency vector:
   [大原/2 综合/1 医院/1 附属/1 医疗/1 センター/1 中心/0]
   Chinese word frequency vector:
   [大原/2 综合/1 医院/1 附属/1 医疗/1 センター/0 中心/1]

7. Calculate the similarity. We can think of them as two lines in space, are from the origin ([0, 0, ...]) starting, pointing in different directions. An included angle is formed between the two lines, if the angle is 0 degrees, mean line overlap and point the same direction; If the angle of 90 degrees, which means a right angle, the direction is completely dissimilar; If the angle is 180 degrees, which means the opposite direction. Therefore, we can judge the similarity through the included angle. The smaller the angle, the more similar it represents.

3.3   Inductive Learning

Inductive learning process is recursive extraction of the common part and the different part between the two NE instances. The pseudo code as follows:

```
Algorithm: Inductive Learning
INPUT: J_C_dict, Simlarity, Part_Trans_Rules
INITIALIZATION: Diff_count
For entity in Simlarity:
  If entity.value > Threshold.diff:
      #Get the same and different part in NEs.
      content = GetDiff(entity.ja, entity.ch)
      Diff_count[content]++
For content in Diff_count:
#If rule frequency higher than threshold, add it into partial
translation rules.
  If Diff_count[content] > Threshold.rules:

      Part_Trans_Rules += content
```

Like the example in section 3.1.

1. Select the high similarity instance, statistics on the frequency of occurrence of different parts.
2. Such as "センター"(center) and "中心" are the different part. The frequency of appearance above the threshold. Add the part into "Partial Translation rules".
   The new rules can be used to further improve the similarity calculation results. Iterative generalize rule, until no new rules.

4   Experiment and Result Analysis

4.1   Data and Evaluation Criteria

The source monolingual corpora used in the experiments come from the Wikipedia database. The corpora have a total of 69,874 Japanese monolingual texts and 84,055 Chinese monolingual texts. The monolingual NER tools used in the experiments are the CRF-based NER tools of our lab. Recognition results shown in Table 6, the results of the experiment were randomly selected 8000 entries from all the entries and manually aligned and use this part as an experimental golden answer.

Table 6. The result of NER

	Chinese	Japanese
PER	88203	73322
LOC	183677	152688
ORG	49442	41101

We use Precision, Recall and F-measure as the evaluation criteria of the results.

Table 7. Condition as determined by Gold standard

		True	False
Test outcome	Positive	True positive	False positive
	Negative	False negative	True negative

As shown in Table 7.

$$P = \frac{number\ of\ true\ positves}{number\ of\ true\ positives + false\ positives} \tag{2}$$

$$R = \frac{number\ of\ true\ positives}{number\ of\ true\ positives + true\ negatives} \tag{3}$$

$$F_\beta = \frac{(\beta^2+1)\cdot P\cdot R}{\beta^2\cdot P + R} \tag{4}$$

When the parameter $\beta = 1$, that is, the precision and recall rate have the same weight, it is generally called F1 values.

4.2   The Experimental Results

The results in Table 8.

Table 8. The experimental results

No. of iterations	P	R	F1
1	70.14	40.28	51.17
2	85.33	70.66	77.31
3	87.13	74.26	80.18
4	89.90	79.80	84.55
5	91.89	84.05	87.80
6	92.58	85.17	88.72

From the table 8, its effect is satisfactory that extracting NE translation equivalents from unrelated monolingual corpora use this method. With the increase in the number of iterations, the difference list of translations become larger and larger which makes similarity calculation results in ascending order. Experiments test and verify the proposed method is simple and effective. After careful analysis of the experimental results, we can find this kind of method is better if named entities contained kanji, but when the Japanese named entities all are kana and have no association with existing partial translation rules, this method does not recognize anything. Such as "コーネリアス(小山田圭吾)" (Keigo Oyamada), due to there is no correlation and internal rules. We are completely unable to identify this NE, whose similarity calculation result is 0. Different categories named entity extraction final results shown in Table 8 below:

Table 9. The different type of NE

	P	R	F1
PER	89.77	81.45	85.41
LOC	93.27	89.21	91.19
ORG	93.16	86.27	89.58

Among them, the number of iterations and the length of named entity have some relationship. The length of PER are lower than average length of NE, so we cannot get new rules after 2 iterations. But the ORG and LOC will give more iteration. In addition, in an iterative process, rule extraction threshold value should be gradually relax, otherwise we cannot extract the new rules after 2 iterations. But we cannot select the low threshold at the beginning neither, so that the rules will greatly improve redundancy. The threshold seems to exponentially decrease is a good choice.

5   Conclusions and Prospects

Compared with other methods, this paper combines the language features of Chinese and Japanese. We propose a method based on inductive learning for automatically extracting NE translation equivalents from Chinese and Japanese monolingual corpus. It effectively reduce the cost to build the corpus and the need for additional knowledge when we use a weak correlation bilingual text sets and minimal additional knowledge to extract named entity translation equivalents.

Using this method is facing the problem that pure Kana named entity may be unable to extract partial translation rules. Our future work will mainly focus on the pure kana named entity extraction.

References

1. Grishman, R., Sundheim, B.: Message understanding conference-6: A brief history. In: Proceedings of COLING, vol. 96, pp. 466–471 (1996)
2. Al-Onaizan, Y., Knight, K.: Translating named entities using monolingual and bilingual resources. In: Proceedings of the 40th Annual Meeting on Association for Computational Linguistics, pp. 400–408. Association for Computational Linguistics (2002)
3. AbdulJaleel, N., Larkey, L.S.: Statistical transliteration for English-Arabic cross language information retrieval. In: Proceedings of the Twelfth International Conference on Information and Knowledge Management, pp. 139–146. ACM (2003)
4. Virga, P., Khudanpur, S.: Transliteration of proper names in cross-lingual information retrieval. In: Proceedings of the ACL 2003 Workshop on Multilingual and Mixed-Language Named Entity Recognition, vol. 15, pp. 57–64. Association for Computational Linguistics (2003)
5. Kupiec, J.: An algorithm for finding noun phrase correspondences in bilingual corpora. In: Proceedings of the 31st Annual Meeting on Association for Computational Linguistics, pp. 17–22. Association for Computational Linguistics (1993)

6. Huang, F., Vogel, S., Waibel, A.: Automatic extraction of named entity translingual equivalence based on multi-feature cost minimization. In: Proceedings of the ACL, Workshop on Multilingual and Mixed-Language Named Entity Recognition, vol. 15, pp. 9–16. Association for Computational Linguistics (2003)
7. Feng, D., Lv, Y., Zhou, M.: A new approach for English-Chinese named entity alignment. In: Proc. of EMNLP, pp. 372–379 (2004)
8. Rapp, R.: Identifying word translations in non-parallel texts. In: Proceedings of the 33rd Annual Meeting on Association for Computational Linguistics, pp. 320–322. Association for Computational Linguistics (1995)
9. Wan, S., Verspoor, C.M.: Automatic English-Chinese name transliteration for development of multilingual resources. In: Proceedings of the 36th Annual Meeting of the Association for Computational Linguistics and 17th International Conference on Computational Linguistics, vol. 2, pp. 1352–1356. Association for Computational Linguistics (1998)
10. Rapp, R.: Automatic identification of word translations from unrelated English and German corpora. In: Proceedings of the 37th Annual Meeting of the Association for Computational Linguistics on Computational Linguistics, pp. 519–526. Association for Computational Linguistics (1999)
11. Fung, P., Yee, L.Y.: An IR approach for translating new words from nonparallel, comparable texts. In: Proceedings of the 17th International Conference on Computational Linguistics, vol. 1, pp. 414–420. Association for Computational Linguistics (1998)
12. Shao, L., Ng, H.T.: Mining new word translations from comparable corpora. In: Proceedings of the 20th International Conference on Computational Linguistics, p. 618. Association for Computational Linguistics (2004)
13. Lee, L., Aw, A., Zhang, M., et al.: Em-based hybrid model for bilingual terminology extraction from comparable corpora. In: Proceedings of the 23rd International Conference on Computational Linguistics: Posters, pp. 639–646. Association for Computational Linguistics (2010)
14. You, G., Hwang, S., Song, Y.I., et al.: Mining name translations from entity graph mapping. In: Proceedings of the 2010 Conference on Empirical Methods in Natural Language Processing, pp. 430–439. Association for Computational Linguistics (2010)
15. Kim, J., Hwang, S., Jiang, L., et al.: Entity Translation Mining from Comparable Corpora: Combining Graph Mapping with Corpus Latent Features (2012)
16. Araki, K., Takahashi, Y., Momouchi, Y., Tochinai, K.: Non-Segmented Kana-Kanji Translation Using Inductive Learning. In: The Transactions of the Institute of Electronics, Information and Communication Engineers, vol. J79-D-II(3), pp. 391–402 (1996)
17. Chu, C., Nakazawa, T., Kurohashi, S.: Chinese Characters Mapping Table of Japanese, Traditional Chinese and Simplified Chinese. In: Proceedings of the Eighth Conference on International Language Resources and Evaluation, LREC 2012 (2012)
18. Goh, C.L., Asahara, M., Matsumoto, Y.: Chinese word segmentation by classification of characters. Computational Linguistics and Chinese Language Processing 10(3), 381–396 (2005)
19. Udupa, R., Saravanan, K., Kumaran, A., et al.: Mint: A method for effective and scalable mining of named entity transliterations from large comparable corpora. In: Proceedings of the 12th Conference of the European Chapter of the Association for Computational Linguistics, pp. 799–807. Association for Computational Linguistics (2009)
20. Tao, T., Zhai, C.X.: Mining comparable bilingual text corpora for cross-language information integration. In: Proceedings of the Eleventh ACM SIGKDD International Conference on Knowledge Discovery in Data Mining, pp. 691–696. ACM (2005)

Collective Corpus Weighting and Phrase Scoring for SMT Using Graph-Based Random Walk

Lei Cui[1,*], Dongdong Zhang[2], Shujie Liu[2], Mu Li[2], and Ming Zhou[2]

[1] School of Computer Science and Technology
Harbin Institute of Technology, Harbin, China
leicui@hit.edu.cn
[2] Microsoft Research Asia, Beijing, China
{dozhang,shujliu,muli,mingzhou}@microsoft.com

Abstract. Data quality is one of the key factors in Statistical Machine Translation (SMT). Previous research addressed the data quality problem in SMT by corpus weighting or phrase scoring, but these two types of methods were often investigated independently. To leverage the dependencies between them, we propose an intuitive approach to improve translation modeling by collective corpus weighting and phrase scoring. The method uses the mutual reinforcement between the sentence pairs and the extracted phrase pairs, based on the observation that better sentence pairs often lead to better phrase extraction and vice versa. An effective graph-based random walk is designed to estimate the quality of sentence pairs and phrase pairs simultaneously. Extensive experimental results show that our method improves performance significantly and consistently in several Chinese-to-English translation tasks.

Keywords: data quality, corpus weighting, phrase scoring, graph-based random walk.

1 Introduction

Statistical Machine Translation (SMT) depends largely on the performance of translation modeling. The training of a translation model usually starts from automatically word-aligned bilingual corpus, followed by the extraction and scoring of phrase pairs. In real-world SMT systems, bilingual data is often mined from the web, meaning the low-quality data is inevitable. The low-quality bilingual data degrades the quality of word alignment and leads to incorrect phrase pairs and defective phrase scoring, which hurts the translation performance of phrase-based SMT systems. Therefore, it is crucial to exploit data quality information to improve the translation modeling.

Previous research has addressed the data quality problem by corpus weighting or phrase scoring, but these two kinds of methods are often investigated independently. On the one hand, conventional corpus weighting methods estimate the quality of each sentence pair in the bilingual corpus individually, but

---

* This work has been done while the first author was visiting Microsoft Research Asia.

G. Zhou et al. (Eds.): NLPCC 2013, CCIS 400, pp. 176–187, 2013.
© Springer-Verlag Berlin Heidelberg 2013

neglect that similar sentence pairs are usually in similar quality. On the other hand, the translation probability of phrase pairs are often estimated based on the assumption that the sentence pairs are equally well. In real-world SMT, these assumptions may not hold due to the varying quality of the bilingual corpus. Therefore, the mutual reinforcement should be leveraged for translation modeling, which means the quality of the sentence pairs depend on the extracted phrase pairs and vice versa.

To this end, we propose an intuitive and effective approach to address this problem. Obviously, high-quality parallel data tends to produce better phrase pairs than low-quality data. Meanwhile, it is also observed that the phrase pairs that appear frequently in the bilingual corpus are more reliable than less frequent ones because they are more reusable, hence most good sentence pairs are prone to contain more frequent phrase pairs [1, 2]. This kind of mutual reinforcement fits well into the framework of graph-based random walk. When a phrase pair p is extracted from a sentence pair s, s is considered casting a vote for p. The higher the number of votes a phrase pair has, the more reliable of the phrase pair. Similarly, the quality of the sentence pair s is also determined by the number of votes casted by all the extracted phrase pairs from s.

In this paper, we have developed a PageRank-style random walk algorithm [3, 4, 5] to iteratively compute the importance score of each sentence pair and each phrase pair that indicates its quality: the higher the better. In SMT, these scores are integrated into the log-linear model to help translation generation in decoding. The importance scores of sentence pairs are used as fractional counts to re-calculate the phrase translation probabilities based on Maximum Likelihood Estimation (MLE). In addition, the important scores of phrase pairs are directly used as new features. We evaluate our method on the colloquial text (IWSLT test sets) and the formal text (NIST test sets). Extensive experiments show that our method improves the performance significantly and consistently in several Chinese-to-English translation tasks, with up to 1.9 BLEU points.

The rest of the paper is organized as follows: The proposed approach is explained in Section 2. Experimental results are presented in Section 3. Section 4 introduces some related work. Section 5 concludes the paper and suggests future research directions.

2   The Proposed Approach

2.1   Graph-Based Random Walk

Graph-based random walk is a general algorithm for approximating the importance of a vertex within the graph in a global view. In our method, the vertices denote the sentence pairs and phrase pairs. The importance of each vertex is propagated to other vertices along the edges. Depending on different scenarios, the graph can take directed or undirected, weighted or un-weighted forms. Starting from the initial scores assigned in the graph, the algorithm is applied to recursively compute the importance scores of vertices until it converges, or the difference between two consecutive iterations falls below a pre-defined threshold.

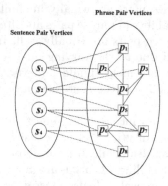

Fig. 1. The circular nodes stand for S and the square nodes stand for P. The dotted and solid lines capture the sentence-phrase and phrase-phrase recommendations.

2.2   Graph Construction

In this paper, we exploit the graph-based random walk to convert the translation modeling in SMT to a mutual recommendation problem. An undirected graph is constructed over the entire bilingual corpus. In the graph, we partition the vertices into two groups: sentence pair vertices and phrase pair vertices. The edges characterize the mutual recommendation relationships between vertices.

Formally, an undirected graph is defined as follows:

$$G = (V, E) \tag{1}$$

where $V = S \cup P$ is the vertex set, $E = E_{SP} \cup E_{PP}$ is the edge set. $S = \{s_i | 1 \leq i \leq n\}$ is the set of all sentence pairs. $P = \{p_j | 1 \leq j \leq m\}$ is the set of all phrase pairs that are extracted from S based on the word alignment. E_{SP} is a subset in which the edges are between S and P, thereby $E_{SP} = \{\langle s_i, p_j \rangle | s_i \in S, p_j \in P, \phi(s_i, p_j) = 1\}$.

$$\phi(s_i, p_j) = \begin{cases} 1 & \text{if } p_j \text{ can be extracted from } s_i \\ 0 & \text{otherwise} \end{cases} \tag{2}$$

$E_{PP} = \{\langle p_j, p_k \rangle | p_j, p_k \in P, j \neq k, \psi(p_j, p_k) = 1\}$ denotes a subset of edges between vertices in P.

$$\psi(p_j, p_k) = \begin{cases} 1 & \exists i, \phi(s_i, p_j) = 1 \wedge \phi(s_i, p_k) = 1 \wedge A_j \bigcap A_k \neq \emptyset \\ 0 & \text{otherwise} \end{cases} \tag{3}$$

where A_j and A_k are the sets of word alignment links contained in phrase pairs p_j and p_k.

Figure 1 illustrates the graph structure. The circular nodes stand for S and the square nodes stand for P. The edges represent the mutual recommendation relationships among vertices. There are two types of recommendation relationships. The dotted lines capture the *Sentence-Phrase Recommendation* (SPR) denoted by E_{SP} and the solid lines capture the *Phrase-Phrase Recommendation* (PPR) denoted by E_{PP}. If s_i is in high quality, it will recommend that p_j is a good phrase pair when $\phi(s_i, p_j) = 1$, and vice visa. Similarly, if p_j is a good phrase pair, it will recommend that the quality of p_k is good when $\psi(p_j, p_k) = 1$. The motivation behind this approach is that high quality sentence pairs can produce good phrase pairs. At the same time, a good phrase pair can recommend other phrase pairs that have good quality if they overlap within the same sentence pair. We do not consider the recommendation between sentence pairs because the dependency information between them is always missing during translation modeling in most SMT systems.

2.3   Graph Parameters

In general, graph parameters include importance scores for the vertices and weights for the edges. In our work, each edge is associated with a weight representing a recommendation score between two vertices. At the same time, each vertex is associated with a importance score representing the importance of the vertex within the graph.

The recommendation scores for SPR and PPR are computed in different ways. For SPR, a nonnegative recommendation score $h(s_i, p_j)$ is defined using the standard TF-IDF formula, which is similarly used in (Wan et al., 2007):

$$h(s_i, p_j) = \begin{cases} \dfrac{PF(s_i, p_j) \times IPF(p_j)}{\sum_{p' \in \{p | \phi(s_i, p) = 1\}} PF(s_i, p') \times IPF(p')} & \text{if } \phi(s_i, p_j) = 1 \\ 0 & \text{otherwise} \end{cases} \quad (4)$$

where $PF(s_i, p_j)$ is the phrase frequency in a sentence pair and $IPF(p_j)$ is the inverse sentence frequency of p_j in the whole parallel corpus, $h(s_i, p_j)$ can be abbreviated as h_{ij} if there is no ambiguity.

For PPR, its recommendation score is defined based on the statistics of word alignment links. Given an edge $\langle p_j, p_k \rangle \in E_{PP}$, let A_m be the set of word alignment links contained in a phrase pair p_m, the recommendation score of $\langle p_j, p_k \rangle$ is computed by the Dice's coefficient:

$$g(p_j, p_k) = \frac{2|A_j \cap A_k|}{|A_j| + |A_k|} \quad (5)$$

The larger $g(p_j, p_k)$ is, the more contexts between p_j and p_k are shared and thereby the stronger the recommendation between them. $g(p_j, p_k)$ is abbreviated as g_{jk}. Figure 2 illustrates an example of PPR based on the word alignment generated by GIZA++. p_1 and p_2 have strong mutual recommendation as well as p_3 and p_4, because they share many word alignment links, while p_2 and p_3 have less mutual recommendation. This kind of mutual recommendation is propagated among the vertices along the edges in the graph. Furthermore, through human checking, we find that p_3 is not a good phrase pair due to the word alignment error. Naturally, this strongly suggests that p_4 is a poor phrase pair but weakly suggests that p_2 is poor. Finally, the quality of each phrase pair is determined by the net effect of the positive and negative recommendations.

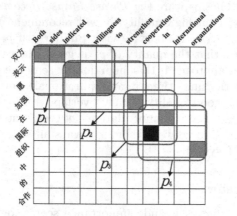

Fig. 2. A PPR example, $\langle guoji, cooperation \rangle$ is an incorrect link shared by p_3 and p_4

2.4 Weighted Mutual Recommendation Algorithm

In this section, we develop an algorithm to estimate the importance scores of the vertices using the weights of the edges in the graph. The importance score of a vertex is influenced by either the neighboring sentence pair vertices or the neighboring phrase pair vertices. Extending the PageRank algorithm [3], Mihalcea and Tarau [4] proposed a graph-based random walk algorithm for weighted graphs to calculate the importance of a vertex, which is determined by the importance of all its neighboring vertices:

$$I(V_i) = (1-d) + d \times \sum_{j \in E(V_i)} \frac{w_{ij}}{\sum_{k \in E(V_j)} w_{jk}} I(V_j) \qquad (6)$$

where V_i denotes vertex i, $I(V_i)$ is the importance of V_i, $E(V_i)$ is the set of vertices that are connected to V_i, w_{ij} is the weight of the edge between vertex i and j, d is the damping factor inherited from the PageRank algorithm.

Our graph contains two types of vertices: sentence pair vertices and phrase pair vertices. The importance scores of sentence pair vertices and phrase pair vertices are computed iteratively. Meanwhile, the weight w_{ij} is extended to h_{ij} and g_{ij} as well to reflect the relationships between two types of vertices.

Let $u(s_i)$ and $v(p_j)$ denote the importance scores of a sentence pair vertex s_i and a phrase pair vertex p_j. They are computed by Equations 7 and 8:

$$u(s_i) = (1-d) + d \times \sum_{j \in E_{SP}(s_i)} \frac{h_{ij}}{\sum_{k \in E_{SP}(p_j)} h_{kj}} v(p_j) \qquad (7)$$

$$v(p_j) = \alpha \times v_{SP}(p_j) + (1 - \alpha) \times v_{PP}(p_j) \qquad (8)$$

where $v_{SP}(p_j)$ and $v_{PP}(p_j)$ are the relative confidence contribution from neighboring sentence pair vertices and neighboring phrase pair vertices, which are computed by Equation 9 and 10:

$$v_{SP}(p_j) = (1 - d) + d \times \sum_{i \in E_{SP}(p_j)} \frac{h_{ij}}{\sum_{k \in E_{SP}(s_i)} h_{ik}} u(s_i) \qquad (9)$$

$$v_{PP}(p_j) = (1 - d) + d \times \sum_{i \in E_{PP}(p_j)} \frac{g_{ij}}{\sum_{k \in E_{PP}(p_i)} g_{ik}} v(p_i) \qquad (10)$$

where $\alpha \in [0, 1]$ is the interpolation factor that can be optimized on the development data; d is set to 0.85, which is the default value in the original PageRank algorithm, $E_{SP}(s_i) = \{j | \langle s_i, p_j \rangle \in E_{SP}\}$, $E_{SP}(p_j) = \{i | \langle s_i, p_j \rangle \in E_{SP}\}$ and $E_{PP}(p_i) = \{j | \langle p_i, p_j \rangle \in E_{PP}\}$.

Based on Equations 7-10, we devise a *Weighted Mutual Recommendation Algorithm* (WMRA) to iteratively compute the importance scores of all the vertices. Let $\mathbf{U} = [u(s_i)]_{n \times 1}$ and $\mathbf{V} = [v(p_j)]_{m \times 1}$ be two vectors denoting the importance scores of all sentence pair vertices and phrase pair vertices, $\mathbf{H} = [h_{ij}]_{n \times m}$ and $\mathbf{G} = [g_{ij}]_{m \times m}$ be the matrixes of the recommendation scores from SPR and PPR, $\hat{\mathbf{H}}$ and $\hat{\mathbf{G}}$ be the corresponding normalized matrixes in which the sum of each row equals to one, and $\tilde{\mathbf{H}}$ be the normalized version of $\mathbf{H}^T$. $\mathbf{I}_n$ is a column vector with n rows and all the elements are one, $\mathbf{V}_{SP} = [v_{SP}(p_j)]_{m \times 1}$ and $\mathbf{V}_{PP} = [v_{PP}(p_j)]_{m \times 1}$.

WMRA is illustrated in Algorithm 1, where $\mathbf{U}$ and $\mathbf{V}$ are initialized to $\mathbf{I}_n$ and $\mathbf{I}_m$ (Lines 1-2). They are iteratively computed and normalized (Lines 7-12), $\mathbf{U}^{(n)}$ and $\mathbf{Q}^{(n)}$ are the results of nth iteration. At the end of each iteration (Lines 13-15), the maximum difference δ of the importance scores between two consecutive iterations is calculated.[1] The above procedure will terminate when δ is lower than a pre-defined threshold (10^{-12} in this study). As shown in Algorithm 1, WMRA is a natural extension of the weighted graph-based random walk in [4]. The difference is that the computation for importance scores of sentence pair vertices and phrase pair vertices is performed individually. In addition, normalization is also conducted separately to guarantee the sum of the importance scores for each type of vertices is equal to one.

2.5   Integration into SMT Log-Linear Model

The importance scores of phrase pairs $\mathbf{V} = [v(t_j)]_{m \times 1}$ produced by WMRA can be directly integrated into the log-linear model as additional new features, which are called the *Phrase Scoring* (PS) features.

---

[1] For a n dimensional vector $\mathbf{x}$: 1-norm $\|\mathbf{x}\|_1$ equals to $\sum_{i=1}^{n} |x_i|$, while maximum-norm $\|\mathbf{x}\|_\infty$ equals to $\max(|x_1|, |x_2|, \cdots, |x_n|)$.

Algorithm 1. Weighted Mutual Recommendation Algorithm

Require: $\tilde{\mathbf{H}}, \hat{\mathbf{H}}, \hat{\mathbf{G}}$

1: $\mathbf{U}^{(0)} \leftarrow \mathbf{I}_n$
2: $\mathbf{V}^{(0)} \leftarrow \mathbf{I}_m$
3: $\delta \leftarrow$ Infinity
4: $\epsilon \leftarrow$ threshold
5: $n \leftarrow 1$
6: **while** $\delta > \epsilon$ **do**
7:     $\mathbf{U}^{(n)} \leftarrow (1-d) \times \mathbf{I}_n + d \times \tilde{\mathbf{H}}^T \times \mathbf{V}^{(n-1)}$
8:     $\mathbf{V}_{SP}^{(n)} \leftarrow (1-d) \times \mathbf{I}_m + d \times \hat{\mathbf{H}}^T \times \mathbf{U}^{(n-1)}$
9:     $\mathbf{V}_{PP}^{(n)} \leftarrow (1-d) \times \mathbf{I}_m + d \times \hat{\mathbf{G}}^T \times \mathbf{V}^{(n-1)}$
10:    $\mathbf{V}^{(n)} \leftarrow \alpha \times \mathbf{V}_{SP}^{(n-1)} + (1-\alpha) \times \mathbf{V}_{PP}^{(n-1)}$
11:    $\mathbf{U}^{(n)} \leftarrow \frac{\mathbf{U}^{(n)}}{\|\mathbf{U}^{(n)}\|_1}$
12:    $\mathbf{V}^{(n)} \leftarrow \frac{\mathbf{V}^{(n)}}{\|\mathbf{V}^{(n)}\|_1}$
13:    $\delta_{\mathbf{U}} \leftarrow \mathbf{U}^{(n)} - \mathbf{U}^{(n-1)}$
14:    $\delta_{\mathbf{V}} \leftarrow \mathbf{V}^{(n)} - \mathbf{V}^{(n-1)}$
15:    $\delta \leftarrow \max(\|\delta_{\mathbf{U}}\|_\infty, \|\delta_{\mathbf{V}}\|_\infty)$
16:    $n \leftarrow n+1$
17: **end while**
18: **return** $\mathbf{U}^{(n)}, \mathbf{V}^{(n)}$

The importance scores of sentence pair vertices $U = [u(s_i)]_{n \times 1}$ are used as the weights of sentence pairs to re-estimate the probabilities of phrase pairs by MLE method. Followed by the corpus weight estimation approach [6], given a phrase pair $p = \langle \bar{f}, \bar{e} \rangle$, $A(\bar{f})$ and $B(\bar{e})$ indicate the sets of sentences that $\bar{f}$ and $\bar{e}$ occur in. Then the translation probability is defined as:

$$P_{\text{CW}}(\bar{f}|\bar{e}) = \frac{\sum_{i \in A(\bar{f}) \cap B(\bar{e})} u(s_i) \times c_i(\bar{f}, \bar{e})}{\sum_{j \in B(\bar{e})} u(s_j) \times c_j(\bar{e})} \tag{11}$$

where $c_i(\cdot)$ denotes the count of the phrase or phrase pair in s_i. $P_{\text{CW}}(\bar{f}|\bar{e})$ and $P_{\text{CW}}(\bar{e}|\bar{f})$ are called Corpus Weighting (CW) based translation probability, which are also integrated into the log-linear model in addition to the conventional phrase translation probabilities [7].

3 Experiments

3.1 Setup

We evaluated our method on Chinese-to-English machine translation tasks over three experimental settings with different bilingual corpus for domains and sizes.

SLDB+BTEC Setting: A corpus in colloquial style from the DIALOG task of IWSLT 2010 was used, consisting of the Spoken Language Databases (SLDB) corpus and parts of the Basic Travel Expression Corpus (BTEC) corpus. The Chinese portion contained 655,906 words and the English portion contained 806,833 words. The language model was trained over the English portion of the training corpus. The development dataset was devset8 plus the Chinese DIALOG data set and the test data was devset9.

FBIS Setting: A news domain corpus (FBIS dataset, LDC2003E14) was used in this experiment. The Chinese portion contained 2.99 million words and the English portion contained 3.94 million words. The development dataset was the NIST 2003 evaluation dataset and the test datasets were the NIST 2006 and NIST 2008 evaluation datasets. The language model was trained over the English portion of FBIS plus the Xinhua portion of the Gigaword V4 corpus.

Mixed Domain Setting: This experiment used a mixed-domain bilingual corpus containing around 30 million sentence pairs. The bilingual data was mainly mined from the web, as well as the United Nations parallel corpus released by LDC and the parallel corpus released by China Workshop on Machine Translation (CWMT). The development and test datasets were the same as in the FBIS setting. The language model was trained over the English portion of the bilingual corpus plus the Xinhua portion of the Gigaword V4 corpus.

A phrase-based decoder was implemented based on chart-based CKY parsing with inversion transduction grammar [8]. We used the following feature functions in the log-linear model for the baseline system:

- phrase translation probabilities and lexical weights in both directions (4 features);
- 5-gram language model (1 feature);
- lexicalized reordering model (1 feature);
- phrase count and word count (2 features).

The translation model was trained over the word-aligned bilingual corpus conducted by GIZA++ [9] in both directions, and the diag-grow-final heuristic was used to refine the symmetric word alignment. A 5-gram language model was trained using the modified Kneser-Ney smoothing [10]. The lexicalized reordering model [11] was trained over the parallel data. Case-insensitive BLEU4 [12] was used as the evaluation metric. The parameters of the log-linear model were tuned by optimizing BLEU on the development data using MERT [13]. Statistical significance test was performed using the bootstrap re-sampling method [14].

3.2   Implementation Details

In the baseline system, the phrase pairs that appear only once in the bilingual corpus were simply discarded because most of them were noisy. In addition, the fix-discount method in [1] for phrase table smoothing was also used. This implementation made the baseline system perform much better and the model size was much smaller. In fact, the basic idea of our "one count" cutoff is very similar to the idea of "leaving-one-out" in [2]. The results in Table 1 show that the "leaving-one-out" method performs almost the same as our baseline, thereby cannot bring other benefits to the system.

When the random walk ran on the mixed-domain bilingual corpora, even filtering phrase pairs that appear only once would still require dozens of days of CPU time for a number of iterations. To overcome this problem, we used a distributed algorithm based on the iterative computation in the Section 2.4. Before the iterative computation starts, the sum of the outlink weights for each vertex was computed first. The edges were randomly partitioned into sets of roughly equal size. Each edge could generate key-value pairs, where the same key were summed locally and accumulated across different machines. Then, in each iteration, the score of each vertex was updated according to the sum of the normalized inlink weights. The algorithm fits well into the MapReduce programming model [15] and we used it as our implementation.

3.3   SMT Performance Evaluation

As mentioned in Section 2.5, we have integrated the new features of PS and CW into the SMT log-linear model as well as the baseline features. This section reports the evaluation results of different settings. The experimental results are shown in Table 1. The results show that WMRA leads to significant performance improvements compared to the baseline, which demonstrates that the recommendation scores propagated among the vertices are quite useful for SMT systems. It seems the integration of PS or CW leads to similar performance improvements, while integrating both of them achieves the best performance.

Table 1. BLEU(%) of Chinese-English translation tasks on three settings ($p < 0.05$)

	SLDB+BTEC	FBIS		Mixed Domain	
	test	nist2006	nist2008	nist2006	nist2008
Baseline	45.60	31.30	23.29	35.20	29.38
Leaving-one-out	-	-	-	35.30	29.33
+WMRA PS	46.77	32.01	24.13	-	-
+WMRA CW	47.08	32.03	24.10	-	-
+WMRA PS+CW	47.50	32.42	24.77	36.10	30.22

In general, our method improves the BLEU scores significantly over the bilingual corpus of different sizes. The largest improvement comes from the setting of SLDB+BTEC, which improves by 1.9 BLEU points over the baseline. The reason might be that the sentence pairs in SLDB+BTEC are quite similar, so that the graph-based random walk can effectively distinguish the good phrase pairs from the poor ones.

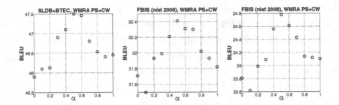

Fig. 3. SMT Performance as the relative contribution ratio α varies. From left to right, the three figures shows the SMT experiments on the *SLDB+BTEC* setting, the FBIS setting with Nist 2006 test set and Nist 2008 test set.

3.4   Interpolation Factor

The interpolation factor α in Equation 8 controls the relative contribution ratio from neighboring sentence pair vertices and neighboring phrase pair vertices. In principle, this ratio should be estimated automatically using machine learning techniques. In order to avoid the overhead of end-to-end training, we empirically tune it in the range of 0 to 1 with an interval of 0.1. Figure 3 shows the tuning results under three different settings when applying WMRA. As shown, the SMT performance arrives at the maximum when α is around 0.5. Therefore, without loss of generality, α is set to 0.5 for all the experiments in Section 3.3.

4   Related Work

4.1   Phrase Scoring and Corpus Weighting

A great deal of work has been done to get high quality translation knowledge and filter out the noise. There are two main categories of approaches addressing these problems. The first category was based on phrase scoring. Some non-parametric Bayesian techniques [16] were used to estimate the weights of phrase pairs. In addition to the generative models, discriminative training for phrase alignment and scoring [17] was also proposed. In this method, the objective function for phrase alignment was optimized jointly with SMT decoding to achieve end-to-end performance improvements. The second category was based on corpus weighting. They tried to handle the problem by corpus weight estimation according to the quality of sentence pairs. A discriminative corpus weighting method [6] was proposed to assign smaller weights to the low quality bilingual sentence pairs. In contrast to previous research, in which corpus weighting and phrase scoring are investigated separately, our method optimizes them collectively and gains more improvements in SMT performance.

4.2   Graph-Based Random Walk

Graph-based random walk was extensively used in web analysis and search. The most famous algorithms were Google's PageRank [3]. Beyond that, graph-based random walk was also successfully applied to other tasks, such as document summarization, keywords extraction [4] and tags recommendation [18], etc. Moreover, document summarization and keywords extraction were accomplished simultaneously [19, 5], with the graph being built using the relationships between sentences and words homogenously and heterogeneously. Recently, graph-based random walk has been used for SMT to clean the noisy bilingual data [20], which can be considered as an unsupervised approach for corpus weighting. Inspired by previous work, our method uses the graph-based random walk to distinguish high quality translation knowledge from noise, which is better than the traditional MLE approach for the parameter estimation.

5   Conclusion and Future Work

In this paper, we have developed an effective approach to optimize phrase scoring and corpus weighting jointly using graph-based random walk. The proposed approach automatically estimates the quality of parallel sentence pairs and phrase pairs by performing mutual recommendation. We convert the importance scores into new features and integrate them into the log-linear model of the SMT system. Significant improvements are achieved in our experiments.

In the future, we will extend our method to other SMT models such as the hierarchical phrase-based model and syntax-based models in which non-terminals are contained in syntactic translation rules. These extensions have higher complexity because more translation rules will be extracted from the bilingual corpus. To this end, we will further optimize our algorithm based on the divide-and-conquer strategy when the graph size is extremely large.

References

[1] Foster, G., Kuhn, R., Johnson, H.: Phrasetable smoothing for statistical machine translation. In: Proceedings of the 2006 Conference on Empirical Methods in Natural Language Processing, pp. 53–61. Association for Computational Linguistics, Sydney (2006)

[2] Wuebker, J., Mauser, A., Ney, H.: Training phrase translation models with leaving-one-out. In: Proceedings of the 48th Annual Meeting of the Association for Computational Linguistics, pp. 475–484. Association for Computational Linguistics, Uppsala (2010)

[3] Brin, S., Page, L.: The anatomy of a large-scale hypertextual web search engine. Computer Networks and ISDN Systems 30(1), 107–117 (1998)

[4] Mihalcea, R., Tarau, P.: Textrank: Bringing order into texts. In: Lin, D., Wu, D. (eds.) Proceedings of EMNLP 2004, pp. 404–411. Association for Computational Linguistics, Barcelona (2004)

[5] Wan, X., Yang, J., Xiao, J.: Towards an iterative reinforcement approach for simultaneous document summarization and keyword extraction. In: Proceedings of the 45th Annual Meeting of the Association of Computational Linguistics, pp. 552–559. Association for Computational Linguistics, Prague (2007)

[6] Matsoukas, S., Rosti, A.V.I., Zhang, B.: Discriminative corpus weight estimation for machine translation. In: Proceedings of the 2009 Conference on Empirical Methods in Natural Language Processing, pp. 708–717. Association for Computational Linguistics, Singapore (2009)

[7] Koehn, P., Och, F.J., Marcu, D.: Statistical phrase-based translation. In: Proceedings of HLT-NAACL 2003 Main Papers, pp. 48–54. Association for Computational Linguistics, Edmonton (2003)

[8] Wu, D.: Stochastic inversion transduction grammars and bilingual parsing of parallel corpora. Computational Linguistics 23(3), 377–403 (1997)

[9] Och, F.J., Ney, H.: A systematic comparison of various statistical alignment models. Computational Linguistics 29(1), 19–51 (2003)

[10] Kneser, R., Ney, H.: Improved backing-off for m-gram language modeling. In: 1995 International Conference on Acoustics, Speech, and Signal Processing, ICASSP 1995, vol. 1, pp. 181–184. IEEE (1995)

[11] Xiong, D., Liu, Q., Lin, S.: Maximum entropy based phrase reordering model for statistical machine translation. In: Proceedings of the 21st International Conference on Computational Linguistics and 44th Annual Meeting of the Association for Computational Linguistics, pp. 521–528. Association for Computational Linguistics, Sydney (2006)

[12] Papineni, K., Roukos, S., Ward, T., Zhu, W.-J.: Bleu: a method for automatic evaluation of machine translation. In: Proceedings of 40th Annual Meeting of the Association for Computational Linguistics, pp. 311–318. Association for Computational Linguistics, Philadelphia (2002)

[13] Och, F.J.: Minimum error rate training in statistical machine translation. In: Proceedings of the 41st Annual Meeting of the Association for Computational Linguistics, pp. 160–167. Association for Computational Linguistics, Sapporo (2003)

[14] Koehn, P.: Statistical significance tests for machine translation evaluation. In: Lin, D., Wu, D. (eds.) Proceedings of EMNLP 2004, pp. 388–395. Association for Computational Linguistics, Barcelona (2004)

[15] Dean, J., Ghemawat, S.: Mapreduce: simplified data processing on large clusters. Communications of the ACM 51(1), 107–113 (2008)

[16] DeNero, J., Bouchard-Côté, A., Klein, D.: Sampling alignment structure under a Bayesian translation model. In: Proceedings of the 2008 Conference on Empirical Methods in Natural Language Processing, pp. 314–323. Association for Computational Linguistics, Honolulu (2008)

[17] Deng, Y., Xu, J., Gao, Y.: Phrase table training for precision and recall: What makes a good phrase and a good phrase pair? In: Proceedings of ACL 2008: HLT, pp. 81–88. Association for Computational Linguistics, Columbus (2008)

[18] Guan, Z., Bu, J., Mei, Q., Chen, C., Wang, C.: Personalized tag recommendation using graph-based ranking on multi-type interrelated objects. In: Proceedings of the 32nd International ACM SIGIR Conference on Research and Development in Information Retrieval, SIGIR 2009, pp. 540–547. ACM, New York (2009)

[19] Zha, H.: Generic summarization and keyphrase extraction using mutual reinforcement principle and sentence clustering. In: Proceedings of the 25th Annual International ACM SIGIR Conference on Research and Development in Information Retrieval, SIGIR 2002, pp. 113–120. ACM, New York (2002)

[20] Cui, L., Zhang, D., Liu, S., Li, M., Zhou, M.: Bilingual data cleaning for smt using graph-based random walk. In: Proceedings of the 51st Annual Meeting of the Association for Computational Linguistics. Short Papers, vol. 2, pp. 340–345. Association for Computational Linguistics, Sofia (2013)

A Simple, Fast Strategy for Weighted Alignment Hypergraph

Zhaopeng Tu[1,2,*], Jun Xie[2], Yajuan Lv[2], and Qun Liu[2,3]

[1] Department of Computer Science,
University of California, Davis, USA
zptu@ucdavis.edu
[2] Key Laboratory of Intelligent Information Processing,
Institute of Computing Technology, CAS, Beijing, China
{tuzhaopeng,xiejun,lvyajuan,liuqun}@ict.ac.cn
[3] Centre for Next Generation Locolisation
Dublin City University, Ireland
qliu@computing.dcu.ie

Abstract. Weighted alignment hypergraph [4] is potentially useful for statistical machine translation, because it is the first study to simultaneously exploit the compact representation and fertility model of word alignment. Since estimating the probabilities of rules extracted from hypergraphs is an NP-complete problem, they propose a divide-and-conquer strategy by decomposing a hypergraph into a set of independent subhypergraphs. However, they employ a Bull's algorithm to enumerate all consistent alignments for each rule in each subhypergraph, which is very time-consuming especially for the rules that contain non-terminals. This limits the applicability of this method to the syntax translation models, the rules of which contain many non-terminals (e.g. SCFG rules). In response to this problem, we propose an inside-outside algorithm to efficiently enumerate the consistent alignments. Experimental results show that our method is twice as fast as the Bull's algorithm. In addition, the efficient dynamic programming algorithm makes our approach applicable to syntax-based translation models.

Keywords: statistical machine translation, weighted alignment hypergraph, optimization.

1 Introduction

Word alignment is the task of identifying translational relations (alignment links) between words in parallel corpora, in which a word at one language is usually translated into several words at the other language [1]. Following Moore [6], we divide alignment links into four categories: "one-to-one" (1-1), "one-to-many" (1-n), "many-to-one" (m-1) and "many-to-many" (m-n). Table 1 shows the distribution of links in a word-aligned corpus that contains 1.5 million sentence

---

* Corresponding author.

G. Zhou et al. (Eds.): NLPCC 2013, CCIS 400, pp. 188–199, 2013.
© Springer-Verlag Berlin Heidelberg 2013

pairs. From this table, we can see that nearly half of the links are not 1-1 links in both 1-best alignments and 10-best lists. This analysis suggests that the links are not irrelevant to each other and it is necessary to pay attention to the relations among them.

Table 1. The distribution of alignment links in a word-aligned corpus that contains 1.5 million sentence pairs

Alignments	1-1	1-n	m-1	m-n
1-best	56.5%	17.4%	12.9%	13.2%
10-best	56.4%	17.3%	12.8%	13.5%

To model this phenomenon, Liu et al., [4] propose a novel graph-based compact representation of word alignment, which takes into account the joint distribution of alignment links. They first transform each alignment to a bipartite graph (*bigraph* in short), in which the nodes are the words in the source and target sentences, and the edges are word-by-word links. Each bigraph can be decomposed into a set of disjoint minimal subgraphs, each of which is connected and corresponds to a set of interrelated links. These subgraphs work as fundamental units in the proposed approach to exploit the relations among the links. Then they employ a weighted alignment hypergraph to encode multiple bigraphs, in which each hyperedges corresponds to a subgraph in the bigraphs (§ 2.1).

Since estimating the probabilities of rules extracted from hypergraphs is an NP-complete problem, they propose a divide-and-conquer strategy by decomposing a hypergraph into a set of independent subhypergraphs. Indeed, the reduced number of hyperedges in the subhypergraphs make the strategy computationally tractable (§ 2.2). However, they employ a Bull's algorithm to enumerate all consistent alignments for each rule in each subhypergraph, which is very time-consuming especially for the rules that contain non-terminals (§ 2.3). This limits the applicability of this method to the syntax translation models, the rules of which contain many non-terminals (e.g. SCFG rules).

To alleviate this problem, we propose an inside-outside algorithm to further divide the subhypergraph into two independent parts (§ 3). With the inside-outside algorithm, we can employ shared structures for efficient dynamic programming. This is very important when calculating the probabilities of rules with non-terminals. Experimental results show that our approach is twice as fast as the conventional Bull's algorithm (§ 4.2). Specifically, the fact that we spend much less time in the rules with non-terminals makes our approach applicable to syntax-based translation models, whose rules contain many non-terminals (e.g. SCFG rules) (§ 4.2).

2 Background

2.1 Weighted Alignment Hypergraph

Each alignment of a sentence pair can be transformed to a bigraph, in which the two disjoint vertex sets S and T are the source and target words respectively, and the

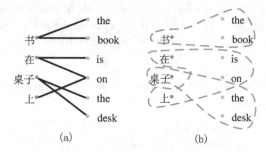

Fig. 1. (a) An example of bigraph constructed from an alignment between a pair of Chinese and English sentences, (b) the disjoint subgraphs of the bigraph in (a)

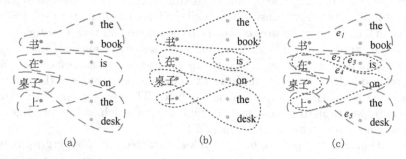

Fig. 2. (a) One alignment of a sentence pair; (b) another alignment of the same sentence pair; (c) the resulting hypergraph that takes the two alignments as samples

edges are word-by-word links. For example, Figure 1(a) shows the corresponding bigraph of an alignment. Since the bigraph usually is not connected, it can be decomposed into a unique set of *minimum connected subgraphs* (MCSs), where each subgraph is connected and does not contain any other MCSs. For example, the bigraph in Figure 1(a) can be decomposed into the MCSs in Figure 1(b). We can see that each MCS corresponds to a many-to-many link. Hereinafter, we use a bigraph to denote an alignment of a sentence pair.

A *weighted alignment hypergraph* [4] is a hypergraph that compactly encodes multiple bigraphs. For example, Figures 2(a) and 2(b) show two bigraphs of the same sentence pair. Then, a weighted alignment hypergraph can be constructed by encoding the union set of MCSs in each bipartite hypergraph, in which each MCS serves as a hyperedge, as in Figure 2(c). Accordingly, each hyperedge is associated with a weight to indicate how well it is, which is the probability sum of bigraphs in which the corresponding MCS occurs divided by the probability sum of all possible bigraphs.

Formally, a *weighted bipartite hypergraph* H is a triple $\langle S, T, E \rangle$ where S and T are two sets of vertices on the source and target sides, and E are hyperedges associated with weights. Liu et al., [4] estimate the weights of hyperedges from an n-best list by calculating relative frequencies:

$$w(e_i) = \frac{\sum_{BG \in \mathcal{N}} p(BG) \times \delta(BG, g_i)}{\sum_{BG \in \mathcal{N}} p(BG)}$$

where

$$\delta(BG, g_i) = \begin{cases} 1 & g_i \in BG \\ 0 & \text{otherwise} \end{cases} \tag{1}$$

Here $\mathcal{N}$ is an n-best bigraph (i.e., alignment) list, $p(BG)$ is the probability of a bigraph BG in the n-best list, g_i is the MCS that corresponds to e_i, and $\delta(BG, g_i)$ indicates that whether a subgraph g_i occurs in the bigraph BG or not.

2.2 Calculating Rule Probabilities

Liu et al., [4] calculate the fractional count of a phrase pair extracted from the hypergraph as the probability sum of the alignments with which the phrase pair is consistent, divided by the probability sum of all alignments encoded in a hypergraph. Therefore, they need to calculate two probability sums:

1. How to calculate the probability sum of all alignments encoded in a hypergraph?
2. How to efficiently calculate the probability sum of all consistent alignments for each phrase pair?

Enumerating All Alignments

Liu et al., [4] show that enumerating all possible alignments in a hypergraph can be reformulated as finding all possible *complete hypergraph matchings* in this

---

Algorithm 1. Algorithm for enumerating all possible complete hyperedge matchings in a bipartite hyperedge $H = \langle S, T, E \rangle$.

1: **procedure** ENUMERATION($\langle S, T, E \rangle$)
2:     $completes \leftarrow \emptyset$
3:     $paths \leftarrow \{\emptyset\}$
4:     **for** e in E **do**
5:         $new\_paths \leftarrow \emptyset$
6:         **for** $path$ in $paths$ **do**
7:             **if** $e \cap path == \emptyset$ **then**
8:                 $new\_path \leftarrow path \cup \{e\}$
9:                 **if** new_path connects all vertices **then**
10:                     add new_path to $completes$
11:                 **else**
12:                     add new_path to new_paths
13:         add new_paths to $paths$
14:     **return** $completes$

---

hypergraph, an NP-complete problem. Therefore, they propose a divide-and-conquer strategy by decomposing a hypergraph into a set of independent sub-hypergraphs. For example, Figure 3(b) shows the independent subhypergraphs of the hypergraph in Figure 3(a). The reduced number of hyperedges in the subhypergraphs makes the strategy computationally tractable. For each subhy-pergraph, they employ a Bull's algorithm for enumerating all possible complete hyperedge matchings in each subhypergraph, as shown in Algorithm 1. The complexity of this algorithm is $O(|E|)$, where $|E|$ is the number of hyperedges in the hypergraph.

Enumerating Consistent Alignments

To efficiently calculate the probability sum of all consistent alignments for each phrase pair, they only concern the *overlap subhypergraphs* which may generate the alignments that are not consistent with the phrase pair. As an example, consider the phrase pair in the grey shadow in Figure 3(a), it is consistent with all sub-alignments from both h_1 and h_2 because they are outside and inside the phrase pair respectively, while not consistent with the sub-alignment that contains hyperedge e_2 from $h3$ because it contains an alignment link that crosses the phrase pair. Liu et al., [4] show that nearly 90% of the phrase pairs only need to concern less than 20% of all subhypergraphs, suggesting that the enumeration of all consistent alignments for each rule is practically feasible.

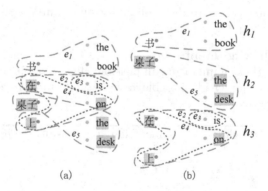

(a)   (b)

Fig. 3. (a) An example of a hypergraph in which the nodes in the grey shadow are the candidate phrase, (b) the independent subhypergraphs of the hypergraph in (a).

2.3   Drawbacks

For each overlap subhypergraph, Liu et al., [4] first enumerate all possible alignments using Algorithm 1, then check whether the translation rule is consistent with each alignment. This method has two drawbacks:

1. It is memory-intensive. As the number of alignments is exponential (although enumerable) in each hypergraph, it will consume a lot of memory to store all possible alignments, especially for the hypergraphs that have relatively many hyperedges.
2. It is time-consuming. To check consistence between an alignment and a rule that contains non-terminals (sub-phrase pairs in a phrase pair are replaced with non-terminals), they should check the consistency between the alignment and all phrase pairs (including the sub-phrase pairs). It will be time-consuming and not applicable to the rules that contain many non-terminals (e.g., SCFG rules in syntax-based translation models).

Given the great number of translation rules extracted from the hypergraphs, it will take most of the time to enumerate all consistent alignments for each rule. Therefore, we propose a simple and fast strategy to speed up the process, and make the weighted alignment hypergraph applicable to the syntax-based translation models.

3 Optimization

We borrow ideas from the inside-outside algorithm that successfully works in compact representations [5,9,10,7,8], and apply it to the weighted alignment hypergraph.

Given a phrase pair and a overlap subhypergraph, we divide the hyperedges in the subhypergraph into three categories: (1) *inside hyperedges* that only cover the vertices inside the phrase pair, (2) *outside hyperedges* that only cover the vertices that outside the phrase pair, and (3) *crossed hyperedges* that cover the vertices both inside and outside the phrase pair. Take the overlap subhypergraph h_2 in Figure 3(b) as example, e_4 is an inside hyperedge, e_3 is an outside hyperedge, and e_2 is a crossed hyperedge.

If we remove the crossed hyperedges from a overlap subhypergraph, we will obtain two independent partial hypergraphs: *inside partial hypergraph* whose vertices are connected by the inside hyperedges, and *outside partial hypergraph* whose vertices are connected by the outside hyperedges. Given a phrase pair P, the probability sum of all consistent sub-alignments encoded in the overlap subhypergraph h is:

$$p(A|h, P) = \sum_{a \in A} p(a|h, P)$$
$$= \sum_{a \in A_I} p(a|IPH) \times \sum_{a \in A_O} p(a|OPH) \tag{2}$$

Here IPH and OPH denote the inside and outside partial hypergraphs respectively, and A_I and A_O denote the sub-alignments generated from them individually. Let OS denotes the set of overlap subhypergraphs for the phrase pair, then

$$p(A|H, P) = \prod_{h_i \in OS} p(A|h_i, P) \times$$

$$\prod_{h_i \in H-OS} p(A|h_i) \tag{3}$$

Here the set of non-overlap subhypergraphs $(H-OS)$ are irrelevant to the phrase pair, and we have $p(A|h, P) = p(A|h)$ for each $h \in H - OS$. Then the fractional count of the phrase pair is:

$$count(P|H) = \frac{p(A|H, P)}{p(A|H)}$$

$$= \frac{\prod_{h_i \in OS} p(A|h_i, P)}{\prod_{h_i \in OS} p(A|h_i)} \tag{4}$$

We can easily extend this process to variable rules that contain non-terminals. For example, we have two sets of overlap subhypergraphs for a variable rule that contains one non-terminal (i.e., the phrase pair and the sub-phrase pair). Note that the subhypergraphs intersection set overlaps both the phrase and the sub-phrase. Therefore, we divide the hyperedges in the intersection set into four categories: (1) inside the sub-phrase pair, (2) outside the sub-phrase pair but inside the phrase pair, (3) outside the phrase pair, and (4) crossed hyperedges. Then we replace the two factors in Eq. 2 with the first three categories above. We use Eq. 2 for the other overlap subhypergraphs for the phrase and sub-phrase pairs respectively.

The advantage of inside-outside algorithm is we can employ shared structures for efficient dynamic programming. For example, when enumerating consistent alignments for a rule containing one non-terminal in Bull's algorithm, we should repeatedly check the consistency between the alignments and the phrases (sub-phrases). With inside-outside algorithm, we only need to concern the varied part of the structure (i.e. the intersection between the phrase and the sub-phrase), and re-used the previous calculated probabilities of the shared structures (i.e. the inside probability of the sub-phrase and the outside probability of the phrase). This greatly speeds up calculating probabilities of rules that contains non-terminals (§ 4.2).

4   Experiments

4.1   Setup

We carry out our experiments using a reimplementation of the hierarchical phrase-based system [2]. Each translation rule is limited to have at most two non-terminals. Our training data is FBIS corpus from LDC dataset that contains 239K sentence pairs.[1] We first follow Venugopal et al. [11] to produce n-best

---

[1] The FBIS corpus shares similar subhypergraph distribution with a larger corpus that contains 1.5 million sentence pairs. We believe that our results also suits large-scale corpora.

lists via GIZA++. We produce 20-best lists in two translation directions, and use "grow-diag-final-and" strategy [3] to generate the final 100-best lists by selecting the top 100 alignments. Finally we construct weighted alignment hypergraphs from these 100-best lists. For computational tractability, we follow Liu et al. [4] to only allow a subhypergraph has at most 10 hyperedges.

4.2   Results

Figure 4 shows the comparison results between the conventional Bull's algorithm (Bull) and our optimized approach (Optimization). We find that the optimization spends half of the time compared with Bull's algorithm, indicating that our approach speeds up the rule extraction.

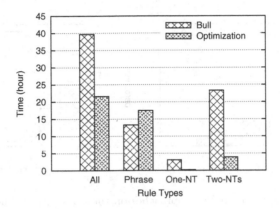

Fig. 4. The comparison results of two approaches

For both approaches, phrase extraction (rules without non-terminals) consumes a high portion of time. This is in accord with intuition, because we extract all possible candidate phrases from the hypergraphs. To maintain a reasonable rule table size, we only remain more promising candidates that have a fractional count higher than a threshold, which are used to generate rules with non-terminals. It should be emphasized that our approach consumes more time on phrase extraction, because we need to calculate the alignments probability sums for both inside and outside hyperedges, which can be reused in the calculation of rules with non-terminals.

Concerning translation rules with non-terminals (i.e. One-NT and Two-NT), we see that Bull's algorithm spends much more time than our approach. In Bull's algorithm, each alignment is repeatedly checked even they share many sub-alignments. To make things worse, for a rule with n non-terminals, each alignment is checked $(n+1)$ times (the phrase and the n sub-phrases). In contrast, our approach only need to concern the intersection of the phrase and the non-terminals. This proves that our approach is applicable to SCFG rules that contain many non-terminals.

4.3 Analyses

Why Our Approach Is Faster?. From Figure 4 we can see that our approach outperforms Bull's algorithm mainly due to we spend much less time on the rules with two non-terminals. In this section, we will investigate that why our approach is faster on the rules with two non-terminals. For the intersecting overlap subhypergraphs of the two sub-phrases (the two phrase that are replaced with non-terminals), Bull's algorithm should check whether the alignments generated from these subhypergraphs are consistent with the the phrase and the two sub-phrases. Figure 5(Bull) shows the comparison of two approaches on the rules with two non-terminals. We find that nearly half of the subhypergraphs have no less than 5 alignments, which makes the Bull's algorithm very time-consuming.

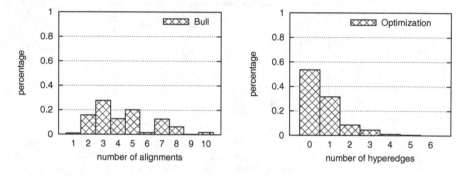

Fig. 5. The comparison of two approaches on the rules with two non-terminals

In contrast, our approach only focuses on the crossed hyperedges that may generate alignments that are not consistent with the rule. For example, given an overlap subhypergraph that overlaps both two sub-phrases, its vertices can be divided into three parts: (1) inside the first sub-phrase, (2) inside the second sub-phrase, (3) outside the two sub-phrases. Therefore, we divide the hyperedges in the subhypergraph into four categories: (1) inside the first sub-phrase, (2) inside the second sub-phrase, (3) outside the two sub-phrases, and (4) crossed hyperedges. The first two sets are previously calculated and we only need to concern (3): the hyperedges outside the two sub-phrases. Figure 5(Optimization) shows the distribution of the hyperedges outside the two sub-phrases. It should be noted that if there is no hyperedges outside the two sub-phrases, no sub-alignments can be constructed to cover the vertices outside the two sub-phrases. Then all the alignments generated from this subhypergraph are not consistent with the rule, and we can directly filter this rule without any calculation. Figure 5 shows that half of the overlap subhypergraphs have no hyperedges outside the two sub-phrases, which will greatly avoid the time-consuming calculation. Even in the rest subhypergraphs, most of them have no more than 3 hyperedges, which will spend few time for the calculation.

In conclusion, our approach avoids a great number of unnecessary and repeated calculation, and speeds up the process.

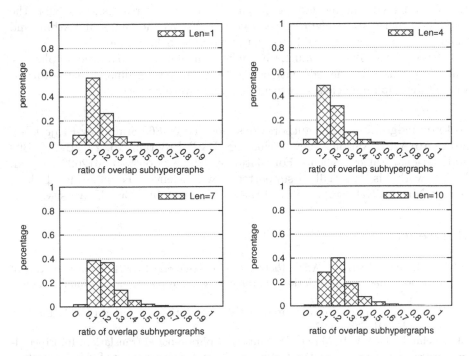

Fig. 6. The influence of phrase length on the ratio of overlap subhypergraphs to all subhypergraphs

The Influence of Phrase Length. As aforementioned, the percentage of overlap subhypergraphs in all subhypergraphs determines the efficiency of rule extraction. As one would expect, there are more overlap subhypergraphs for longer phrases, because a subhypergraph is more likely to cross the phrase and becomes an overlap subhypergraph for the phrase. Figure 6 shows the influence of phrase length on the proportion of overlap subhypergraphs, where xtics denotes the ratio of overlap subhypergraphs to all subhypergraphs and higher value means more overlap subhypergraphs need to be processed. We can see that the ratio of overlap subhypergraphs goes up with the increase of phrase length. For example, when the phrase length is 1 (the top left figure), nearly 90% of the phrase pairs only need to concern less than 30% of all subhypergraphs. When the phrase length increases to 10 (the bottom right figure), more than 30% of the phrase pairs need to process more than 30% of all subhypergraphs. The results indicate that the limit on the phrase length will speed up the rule extraction.

5   Conclusion and Future Work

In this paper, we propose a inside-outside algorithm to speed up the rule extraction in weighted alignment hypergraphs. Experimental results shows that the dynamic programming algorithm is twice as fast as the Bull's algorithm, and makes our approach applicable to syntax-based translation models.

Currently, we still spend much time on the calculating probabilities of phrases, which are reused in the calculation of rules with non-terminals. In the future, we will develop an efficient algorithm to speed up this process.

Acknowledgement. The authors are supported by 863 State Key Project No. 2011AA01A207, National Key Technology R&D Program No. 2012BAH39B03 and National Natural Science Foundation of China (Contracts 61202216). Qun Liu's work is partially supported by Science Foundation Ireland (Grant No.07/CE/I1142) as part of the CNGL at Dublin City University.

References

1. Brown, P.E., Pietra, S.A.D., Pietra, V.J.D., Mercer, R.L.: The mathematics of statistical machine translation: Parameter estimation. Computational Linguistics 19(2), 263–311 (1993)
2. Chiang, D.: Hierarchical phrase-based translation. Computational Linguistics 33(2), 201–228 (2007)
3. Koehn, P., Och, F.J., Marcu, D.: Statistical phrase-based translation. In: Proceedings of the 2003 Conference of the North American Chapter of the Association for Computational Linguistics on Human Language Technology, vol. 1, pp. 48–54. Association for Computational Linguistics (2003)
4. Liu, Q., Tu, Z., Lin, S.: A Novel Graph-based Compact Representation of Word Alignment. In: Proceedings of the 51th Annual Meeting of the Association for Computational Linguistics (2013)
5. Liu, Y., Xia, T., Xiao, X., Liu, Q.: Weighted alignment matrices for statistical machine translation. In: Proceedings of the 2009 Conference on Empirical Methods in Natural Language Processing, pp. 1017–1026. Association for Computational Linguistics, Singapore (2009)
6. Moore, R.C.: A discriminative framework for bilingual word alignment. In: Proceedings of Human Language Technology Conference and Conference on Empirical Methods in Natural Language Processing, pp. 81–88. Association for Computational Linguistics, Vancouver (2005)
7. Tu, Z., Jiang, W., Liu, Q., Lin, S.: Dependency Forest for Sentiment Analysis. In: Zhou, M., Zhou, G., Zhao, D., Liu, Q., Zou, L. (eds.) NLPCC 2012. CCIS, vol. 333, pp. 69–77. Springer, Heidelberg (2012)
8. Tu, Z., Liu, Y., He, Y., van Genabith, J., Liu, Q., Lin, S.: Combining Multiple Alignments to Improve Machine Translation. In: Proceedings of the 24th International Conference on Computational Linguistics (2012)

9. Tu, Z., Liu, Y., Hwang, Y.-S., Liu, Q., Lin, S.: Dependency forest for statistical machine translation. In: Proceedings of the 23rd International Conference on Computational Linguistics (Coling 2010), pp. 1092–1100. International Committee on Computational Linguistics, Beijing (2010)
10. Tu, Z., Liu, Y., Liu, Q., Lin, S.: Extracting Hierarchical Rules from a Weighted Alignment Matrix. In: Proceedings of 5th International Joint Conference on Natural Language Processing, pp. 1294–1303. Asian Federation of Natural Language Processing, Chiang Mai (2011)
11. Venugopal, A., Zollmann, A., Smith, N.A., Vogel, S.: Wider pipelines: n-best alignments and parses in mt training. In: Proceedings of AMTA, Honolulu, Hawaii (2008)

Research on Building Family Networks
Based on Bootstrapping and Coreference Resolution

Jinghang Gu, Ya'nan Hu, Longhua Qian, and Qiaoming Zhu

Natural Language Processing Lab, Soochow University, Suzhou, Jiangsu, 215006
School of Computer Science & Technology, Soochow University, Suzhou, Jiangsu, 215006
gujinghang59420@sina.com,
{20114227025,qianlonghua,qmzhu}@suda.edu.cn

Abstract. Personal Family Network is an important component of social networks, therefore, it is of great importance of how to extract personal family relationships. We propose a novel method to construct personal families based on bootstrapping and coreference resolution on top of a search engine. It begins with seeds of personal relations to discover relational patterns in a bootstrapping fashion, then personal relations are further extracted via these learned patterns, finally family networks are fused using cross-document coreference resolution. The experimental results on a large-scale corpus of Gigaword show that, our method can build accurate family networks, thereby laying the foundation for social network analysis.

Keywords: Family Network, Social Network, Bootstrapping, Cross-Document Coreference Resolution.

1   Introduction

In recent years, social network becomes more and more important in people's daily life with the rapid development of social digitalization, and its analysis and application could help improve the living quality and efficiency. As is known to all, a family is the basic unit of human society, thus family network should be the core of social network. Traditional Social Network Analysis (SNA) focuses on independent individuals and their functions, ignoring the influence of the whole family which is indispensible in social network. This paper starts with extracting family relationships, and then builds rich personal family networks in turn, laying the foundation for the research of constructing large-scale social networks.

Social Network Analysis is an active topic in the field of computer science and social science, and the construction of social network is the basis of SNA. Early research in building social networks mainly exploited the co-occurrence of personal names, such as Referral Web/Flink [1, 2]. Recently, machine learning methods come into fashion in order to excavate social networks in some specific fields, such as ArnetMiner [3], a kind of social network in academics; in literature works [4, 5], or in character biographies [6]. Traditional social network construction takes independent

G. Zhou et al. (Eds.): NLPCC 2013, CCIS 400, pp. 200–211, 2013.
© Springer-Verlag Berlin Heidelberg 2013

individuals of interest as the central subject and mines mutual relationships between them, without acknowledging families as the core of the social network. In addition, it does not perform well due to the over-simplicity of dealing with the name ambiguity issue.

In this paper, we extract personal relationships via bootstrapping with the notion of families as the core of social networks in mind. Then we aggregate these family relationships into family networks by addressing the problems of name variation and name ambiguity, i.e. Cross-Document Coreference Resolution (CDCR), using simple and effective methods. The performance of our work shows that it can construct family networks successfully from a large-scale Chinese text corpus.

This paper is structured as follows. After a brief survey of related work in Section 2, we describe our method of constructing personal family networks in Section 3. In Section 4 we present our evaluation measurement. The results of the experiments are reported in Section 5. We discuss our findings, draw conclusions, and identify future work in Section 6.

2   Related Work

The primary task of constructing social networks is to extract social relationships between persons, which is a specific branch of semantic relation extraction. Semantic relation extraction is an important part of Nature Language Processing (NLP) and Information Extraction (IE), whose objective is to extract the semantic relations between named entities. When named entities are limited to persons, semantic relation extraction is reduced to personal relation extraction. Most research of relation extraction adopts machine learning approaches. In terms of the scale of annotated labor it needs, we can divide relation extraction methods into supervised learning [7], weakly supervised learning [8], and unsupervised learning [9]. Usually both the quantity and quality of the annotated corpus determine the performance of relation extraction.

As a kind of the weakly supervised learning methods, bootstrapping comes into fashion because of its less demand of manual annotations, and can mine a great majority of instances using only a small scale of seeds at the beginning. Hearst [10] took the lead in using bootstrapping to extract the hyponym relation (is-a). It starts with several seeds and discovers more patterns and then more instances in turn in an iterative manner. Pantel et al. [11] proposed a bootstrapping system—Espresso, which is based on the framework in (Hearst [10]). Espresso effectively resolves the problem of the confidence calculation of patterns and instances when extracting relations from a large scale corpus like the Web. Yao et al. [12] and Gan et al. [13] took the advantage of the redundant information in Web pages to discover personal relations by employing a simulated annealing algorithm on top of bootstrapping. Peng et al. [14] explored the tree kernel-based method for personal relation extraction, expanding personal relations to static (family relations and business relations) and dynamic (personal interactive relations) ones.

In the field of social network construction, early research leverages the statistics of name co-occurrence in web pages to extract the personal relationships. Kautz et al. [1] propose a system named as Referral Web, which is based on personal name co-occurrence in order to automatically mine social networks. Mika et al. [2] adopted the same strategy as Referral Web with the exception of using personal emails as additional source data besides Web pages. Recent research turns to machine learning methods, with the purpose to extract more types of social relations. Tang et al. [3] proposed the ArnetMiner system to build social networks among academic scholars using SVM and CRF classifiers to classify the relations. Elson et al. [4] and Agarwal et al. [5] discuss social networks in literature works. They propose the notion of implicit social relations among different characters participating in the same event, such as Interaction and Observation. Camp and Bosch et al. [6] extract personal relations that entail emotional polarity, and build social networks with SVM classifiers.

It is worth noting that the StatSnowball system (Zhu et al. [15]) extracts social relations by bootstrapping in conjunction with Probability Models and Markov Logic Networks. StatSnowball achieves a promising performance on constructing social networks from the large scale Web corpus.

Although our paper chooses the same method of bootstrapping as before to mine social networks, we take a different perspective from previous works. We extract personal social relations in a family unit from a large scale text corpus, further, we investigate the issue of person coreference resolution in constructing family networks, laying the foundation for building large scale social networks.

3   Personal Family Network Construction

There are three phases in the procedure of constructing family networks from a large scale corpus, including Personal Family Relation Extraction (PFRE), Cross-Document Coreference Resolution (CDCR) and Family Network Aggregation (FNA). Family relations are the ones between persons in the same family, including husband-wife, father-son, mother-son, father-daughter, mother-daughter, brotherhood and sisterhood etc. Cross-Document Coreference Resolution attempts to group personal names from different documents into equivalence classes referred to as "coreference chains" with each chain representing the same person. The task of aggregating personal family networks is to cluster persons having family relationships into the same family network. After the first two phases of relation extraction and coreference resolution, family network construction would become easy and direct.

3.1   Personal Family Relation Extraction

In this phase, we adopt a minimally supervised learning method, i.e. bootstrapping, for the sake of reducing the amount of training set. Taking several seed instances of a particular relation type as input, our algorithm iteratively learns surface patterns to extract more instances and vice versa. When extracting patterns and instances, we calculate their reliability scores and retain the ones with high reliability.

In terms of the importance of family relations, we define two major types of family relationships, i.e. "Parent-Child" and "Husband-Wife". We further divide "Parent-Child" into four subtypes, such as "Father-Son", "Father-Daughter", "Mother-Son" and "Mother-Daughter" to facilitate the bootstrapping procedure. Totally, there are five types of family relations available for bootstrapping. However, the four subtypes should be combined into one just before the phase of Family Network Aggregation. We take Espresso as our prototype system, which include four steps as follows:

Pattern Induction
In order to quickly search the whole corpus for patterns and instances, we preprocess the corpus and load it into the Solr[1] search engine. As to a person pair {x, y} of a certain type of relation R_i, we submit both x and y as keywords to Solr and obtain text from the corresponding pages, then we extract the patterns co-occurring with {x, y}. For instance, given a seed of "Husband-Wife" relation type as "江泽民, 王冶坪" (*Jiang Zemin, Wang Yeping*), we can acquire the text "中国国家主席江泽民的夫人王冶坪今天下午……" (*This afternoon Chinese President Jiang Zemin's wife Wang Yeping…*). We select the string between the two person names as the candidate pattern, and here we can obtain the pattern "<Husband> 的夫人 <Wife>" (*<Husband>'s wife<Wife>*) for the "Husband-Wife" relation.

Pattern Ranking/Selection
We use Pointwise Mutual Information (PMI) [16] to measure the strength of association between the pattern p and the instance. The higher the PMI value is, the stronger the association is. Here, we adopt the PMI method suggested in (Pantel [11]).

A well-known issue is that PMI is usually biased towards infrequent events, therefore we multiply the PMI value with the discounting factor suggested in (Pantel and Ravichandran) [17].

We define the reliability score of a pattern p, $r_\pi(p)$, as the average strength of association across all instances, with each instance weighted by the product of its reliability score and the PMI value between the instance and the pattern:

$$r_\pi(p) = \frac{\sum_{i \in I} \left(\frac{pmi(i, p)}{\max_{pmi}} \times r_l(i) \right)}{|I|} \qquad (1)$$

Where $r_l(i)$ is the reliability score of an instance. The reliability score for each seed instance is 1.0 and for instance discovered in the subsequent iterations it is calculated as described in Formula (4).

After calculating all patterns' reliability scores, we choose the top 10% patterns carried over to the next iteration.

---

[1] http://lucene.apache.org/solr/

Instance Induction

In this phase, we retrieve from the corpus the set of instances that match any of the patterns acquired in the previous iteration. We submit the patterns as keywords to Solr and extract text from the corresponding pages. As to the sentences containing the pattern, we utilize ICTCLAS[2] to perform Chinese word segmentation and named entity recognition. If two personal names surround the pattern, we take them as an instance. For example, given the pattern "*<Husband>的夫人<Wife>*" (*<Husband>'s wife<Wife>*), we submit "*的夫人*" (*'s wife*) as keywords to Solr and get a sentence like "*中国国务院总理李鹏的夫人朱琳上午来到......*" (*On the morning, Chinese Premier Li Peng's wife Zhu Lin came to...*). After word segmentation and named entity recognition, a new instance "*李鹏, 朱琳*" (*Li Peng, Zhu Ling*) arises.

Instance Ranking/Selection

We define the reliability score of an instance i, $r_l(i)$, as its average strength of association across all patterns, with each pattern weighted by the product of its reliability score and the PMI value between the pattern and the instance:

$$r_l(i) = \frac{\sum_{p \in P} \left(\frac{pmi(i, p)}{\max_{pmi}} \times r_\pi(p) \right)}{|p|} \tag{2}$$

After calculating all instances' reliability scores, we choose the top 15% instances fed to the next iteration.

After we obtained all the patterns of the above five types of family relations by bootstrapping, we merged "Father-Son", "Father-Daughter", "Mother-Son" and "Mother-Daughter" relations into the "Parent-Child" relation and we could integrate their subtype patterns if possible. For example, the pattern "*<Son>的父亲<Father>*" (*<Son>'s father<Father>*) can be discovered by the relationship of "Father-Son" and the pattern "*<Daughter>的父亲<Father>*" (*<Daughter>'s father<Father>*) can also be discovered by "Father-Daughter". These two patterns are the same and can be combined into one pattern "*<Child>的父亲<Parent>*" (*<Child>'s father<Parent>*). Finally, we search the corpus again to acquire all the instances that satisfy the patterns corresponding to the two types of relations "Parent-Child" and "Husband-Wife", and take the instances as input to Family Network Aggregation. The reason in so doing is that, on one hand, the patterns are highly reliable so that the instances induced by them are highly reliable as well; on the other hand, this can help improve the system recall.

3.2 Personal Family Network Aggregation Based on Coreference Resolution

After finishing Personal Family Relation Extraction, we can start on aggregating our family networks, which is meant to assemble persons into families while merging

---

[2] http://www.ictclas.org/

their redundant relations. A family under consideration in this paper should contain no less than three valid persons and two valid relationships. When assembling family networks, an inevitable issue is the complexity of cross-document coreference. Here are several example sentences:

(a)"卡恩的妻子西蒙娜却站出来维护自己的丈夫，说……"(*But **Kahn's** **wife** **Simone** stood up for her husband and said...*)

(b)"巴博的妻子西蒙娜当日早些时候在执政党明确表示,法国并没有在……" (*Earlier the day, as a representative of the ruling party, **Gbagbo's** wife **Simone** expressed clearly that French did not ...*)

(c)"尼日利亚国家元首阿巴查的夫人玛丽亚姆·阿巴查26日在接受本社记者采访……" (*The wife of the head of Nigeria **Abacha**, **Mariam Abacha** received our interview on the 26th...*)

(d)"尼日利亚国家元首阿巴查和夫人玛利亚姆·阿巴查、外交部长……"(*The Head of Nigeria **Abacha** and his wife **Mariam Abacha** and the Foreign Minister...*)

(e)"这些人员中主要包括阿巴查的儿子穆罕默德·阿巴查和商人……"(*These individuals included **Abacha's** son **Mohammed Abacha** and merchant...*)

These five Chinese example sentences are from five respective documents. Among them, the person with the name of "西蒙娜" (*Simone*) in (a) is different from that in (b), so that the "Husband-Wife" relationships in (a) and (b) are different; the person whose name is "玛丽亚姆·阿巴查" (*Mariam Abacha*) mentioned in (c) is obviously the same person as "玛利亚姆·阿巴查" (*Mariam Abacha*) mentioned in (d), so that the relations in both (c) and (d) should be the same. Thus, the persons in (a) and (b) cannot constitute a family while (c), (d) and (e) can.

Through the above examples can we find that it is critical to address the problems of name ambiguity and name variation in Family Network Aggregation. The former means the same name can point to multiple persons in different documents. The latter means the same person can be referred to by different names in different documents. Therefore, during the phase of Family Network Aggregation, it is necessary to put the same name that refers to different persons into their respective coreference chains, i.e. name disambiguation, as well to put the various mentions of a person into one equivalence coreference chain, i.e. name variation clustering.

Cross-Document Coreference Resolution

General techniques of CDCR include unsupervised clustering [18] and supervised classification [19] etc. The features they adopt contain local context word features, global word features, global named entity features, entity semantic features and so on. Particularly, the relationship between persons often demonstrates to be a more powerful feature than the others, thus it should be taken into full consideration for CDCR. We follow the principle that if there are two instances (each instance contains a pair of persons) discovered from different documents with the same names and the same relationship, they should be regarded as the same instance and thus merged.

In this paper, we follow a simple, yet effective method of name string matching to aggregate multiple persons into the same family. The processing steps are as follows:

1. Exact Name Matching (ENM): compare person names involved in all instances regard those with the exactly same names as one person. These persons are taken as the linking point for families, through which initial families are formed. It is worth noting that different persons may have the same name, and in this step they are merged into the same family.

2. Name Disambiguation (ND): remove the namesake, i.e. the different person with the same name, from the initial family. We adopt global document entity features to compute the cosine similarity between the same names from different documents, and discard the names whose similarity score is below the empirical threshold.

3. Name Variation Aggregation (NVA): Inside a family, we adopt minimum Levenshtein distance to calculate the similarity score between two names. If the similarity score between two names is above a threshold (how to fix it), then these two names are merged into the same coreference chain. As such, family networks are generated.

Name Disambiguation and Name Variation Aggregation
For Name Disambiguation, the similarity score between two names is computed as the cosine between their corresponding feature vectors. We take names of entities that co-occur with the target name as its features. Only if the similarity score is above the empirical threshold can we regard the names as referring to the same person. The score is calculated as follows:

$$\cos\left(name_1, name_2\right) = \frac{\sum w_{1i} \cdot w_{2i}}{\sqrt{\sum w_{1i}^2} \cdot \sqrt{\sum w_{2i}^2}} \tag{3}$$

Where w_{1i} and w_{2i} are the weights of the feature t_i which is shared by both $name_1$ and $name_2$. The frequency of an entity occurring in the document is taken as its weight. Named entities are recognized using ICTCLAS, including person names tagged as "-nr", geographic names tagged as "-ns", organization names tagged as "-nt" etc.

For Name Variation Aggregation inside a family, we use the minimum Levenshtein distance to merge name variations. Minimum Levenshtein distance (a.k.a. edit distance) measures the similarity between two names by the number of edit operations needed to transform one string to another. Usually there are three operations, i.e. insertion, deletion and replacement. Each of them is given a value as its operation cost. The costs for three operations are 0.5, 1.5 and 2.0 for insertion, deletion and replacement.

It should be pointed out that, there are a very few instances that belong to the same family, yet they cannot be fused into a family due to diverse name expressions by our method. For example, in "Parent-Child" relation type, between the instances "苏哈多,

哈迪扬蒂" (*Suharto, Hardiyanti*) and "苏哈托, 鲁克马纳" (*Suharto, Rukmana*), the names of "苏哈多" (*Suharto*) and "苏哈托" (*Suharto*) actually refer to the same person, i.e. the former Indonesian president "苏哈托" (*Suharto*); and the names of "哈迪扬蒂" (*Hardiyanti*) and "鲁克马纳" (*Rukmana*) also refer to the same person, i.e. the daughter of "苏哈托" (*Suharto*), whose full name is "西蒂·哈迪扬蒂·鲁克马纳" (*Siti Hardiyanti Rukmana*). Nevertheless, due to the diversity in their name expressions, the two instances cannot be linked as one by Exact Name Matching, let alone the construction of the family thereafter.

4   System Performance Evaluation

There are three phases in constructing family networks, thus, for the sake of evaluating our work comprehensively, we devise three metrics for them.

4.1   Evaluation for Personal Family Relation Extraction

It is obvious that the performance of relation extraction phase determines the performance in the following phases. Because of lacking effective approaches to compute the recall from a large scale of corpus, instead we pay more attention to the precision in this phase. The precision score is defined as follows:

$$Precision = \frac{C}{T} \tag{4}$$

Where C is the number of correct instances extracted by our system, and T is the total number of instances we extracted.

Since it is difficult to check the validity of all extracted instances owing to its relatively large number, we select n ($n=40$) instances randomly and judge their validity manually. This process is repeated four times. Finally, the precision is calculated as the average of four times.

4.2   Evaluation for Cross-Document Coreference Resolution

We used the standard B-CUBE [21] scoring algorithm to evaluate the co-reference chain inside a family. The algorithm adopts object-oriented method to compute the score of each coreference chains created by our system. Then the Precision, Recall and F1 scores are calculated by comparing the ground-truth chains with the chains formed by the system.

It should be pointed out that when computing the scores for isolated mentions, which cannot be fused with any family, the below principle is followed: if the mention is linked to a coreference chain by mistake, we will calculate the loss of performance it causes; otherwise it is ignored.

4.3   Evaluation for Family Network Aggregation

As for family networks, there is not any existing measure available. Since the number of constructed families is not quite large, we annotate the families generated by our system manually. A family is regarded as correct only if it matches an annotated one exactly, then the corresponding precision, recall and F1 scored are normally calculated.

5   Experimental Results and Analysis

5.1   Corpus and Preprocessing

In this paper, we choose the Chinese corpus of Gigaword, which is gathered from various types of newspapers, as the experimental dataset, owing to its uniform in language expression. The dataset contains 1,033,679 articles of news, including *Xinhua News Agency* and *Lianhe Zaobao*. After transformed into XML format, the dataset was loaded into Solr for local retrieval.

When constructing family networks, the baseline is built with the exact matching of person names. Manual annotations are then performed on the baseline. We manually go through each family to rectify errors in coreference chains and families, i.e. separate ambiguous names for distinctive persons and merge various names for the same people, and then finalize the golden set. During annotation we follow the principle that the names that cannot be linked to a family are ignored. This will help us avoid the problem of prohibitive amount of manual annotation, though at the loss of a very few families (cf. Section 3.2). The statistics of the golden set is shown in Table1.

Table 1. Statistics on manual tagging results

# of coreference chains	# of families	# of persons in families
867	149	510

5.2   The Performance of Relation Extraction

Table 2 shows patterns and instances extracted in relation extraction phase. Note that each pattern can reliably describe the corresponding relationship between persons. From the table, we can see a sufficient number of patterns obtained by the bootstrapping procedure.

Table 2. Patterns learned from bootstrapping

Relation types	# of patterns	Examples
Parent-Child	26	<Parent>的儿子<Child>、< Parent >的次子< Child >、< Parent >同志的女儿< Child >…
Husband-Wife	33	<Husband>的夫人<Wife>、< Husband >的遗孀< Wife >、<Husband>的妻子<Wife>…

Table 3. Person pairs learned from bootstrapping

# of pairs discovered	Precision (%)
2167	94.0

Table 3 gives the total number of instances and its precision score. It shows that the precision score reaches 94.0%. Through error analysis, we find that the major error is caused by word segmentation. A person name would be segmented into various forms because of its high frequency of occurrence in documents. For instance, in the sentence "下午三点半，当李鹏总理和夫人朱琳来到厂区时......" (*When Chinese Premier Li Peng and his wife Zhu Lin came to the plant at 3:30pm...*), the name of "朱琳" (*Zhu Lin*) is segmented as "朱琳来" (*Zhu Linlai*) by mistake.

5.3   The Performance of Coreference Resolution

Table 4 compares the results, i.e. the performance of coreference chains discovered in families, from the different methods (i.e. Exact Name Matching, Exact Name Matching plus Name Variation Aggregation, Name Disambiguation and Name Disambiguation plus Name Variation Aggregation) for Cross-Document Coreference Resolution in family networks. From the table we can see:

(i)   Using the Exact Name Matching method the precision can reach as high as 97.3%, nevertheless the recall is only 77.3%. It means that the phenomenon of name variation is far more serious than that of name ambiguity.

(ii) After Name Variation Aggregation, the performance improves significantly, particularly when it is performed on top of Exact Name Matching.

(iii) Compared with Exact Name Matching, Name Disambiguation decreases recall significantly, though it can help to increase the precision moderately. This means that name disambiguation will split the correct person names as well as the wrong ones.

Table 4. Performance of CDCR with different methods

Methods	# of chains	# of correct chains	P (%)	R (%)	F1 (%)
ENM	1041	593	97.3	77.3	86.2
ENM+NVA	753	564	96.1	**90.9**	**93.4**
ND	896	479	**99.1**	73.7	84.5
ND+NVA	609	447	98.2	88.3	93.0

5.4   The Performance of Family Networks

Table 5 reports the total number of families discovered, precision, recall and F1 for various CDCR methods on the corpus. The table shows that Name Variation aggregation has significant effect on Family Network Fusion, increasing both precision and recall. There is an interesting phenomenon that though using name

Table 5. Performance of family networks with different CDCR methods

Methods	# of families	# of correct families	P (%)	R (%)	F1 (%)
ENM	264	93	35.2	62.4	45.0
ENM+NVA	211	107	50.7	**71.8**	59.4
ND	232	85	36.6	57.0	44.6
ND+NVA	176	98	**55.7**	65.8	**60.3**

disambiguation alone will decrease the performance for both CDCR and family networks, it can indeed improve the performance of family networks when used in conjunction with name variation aggregation. This suggests that Name Disambiguation can promote the precision, therefore it has a positive effect on family network fusion. Taking the sentences (a) and (b) in Section 3.2 as examples, accurate name matching will merge "卡恩" (*Kahn*) and "巴博" (*Gbagbo*) into one family with the linking point "西蒙娜" (*Simone*), and thus generate a spurious family containing two "Husband-Wife" relations. However name disambiguation will distinguish the mentions of the same name "西蒙娜" (*Simone*) in (a) and (b), thus it can remove the noise to improve family networks.

6   Conclusion and Future Work

In this paper, we present a method to use bootstrapping and coreference resolution techniques for constructing personal family networks. By adopting a bootstrapping architecture, we first learn patterns of different relations, and then discover pairs of persons as instances of patterns iteratively. After bootstrapping, we fuse pairs of persons into family networks by Cross-Document Coreference Resolution techniques. Experiments on the Chinese large-scale corpus of Gigaword show that our method can construct personal family networks accurately and efficiently.

However, the family networks we generated still have several shortcomings. For example, the types of family relations are not sufficient enough; we don't take the association between different families into consideration; the recall of performance is not good enough. For future work, we intend to import more types of family relations and the relations between different families to further expand the scale of families so as to enrich our family networks.

Acknowledgement. This work is funded by China Jiangsu NSF Grants BK2010219 and 11KJA520003.

References

1. Kautz, H., Selman, B., Shah, M.: Referral Web: combining social networks and collaborative filtering. Communications of the ACM 40(3), 63–65 (1997)
2. Flink, M.P.: Semantic web technology for the extraction and analysis of social networks. Web Semantics: Science, Services and Agents on the World Wide Web 3(2), 211–223 (2005)

3. Tang, J., Zhang, J., Yao, L., et al.: ArnetMiner: extraction and mining of academic social networks. In: Proceedings of the 14th ACM SIGKDD International Conference on Knowledge Discovery and Data Mining, pp. 990–998. ACM (2008)
4. Elson, D.K., Dames, N., McKeown, K.R.: Extracting social networks from literary fiction. In: Proceedings of the 48th Annual Meeting of the Association for Computational Linguistics, pp. 138–147. Association for Computational Linguistics (2010)
5. Agarwal, A., Corvalan, A., Jensen, J., et al.: Social Network Analysis of Alice in Wonderland. NAACL-HLT 2012, 88 (2012)
6. van de Camp, M., van den Bosch, A.: A link to the past: constructing historical social networks. In: Proceedings of the 2nd Workshop on Computational Approaches to Subjectivity and Sentiment Analysis, pp. 61–69. Association for Computational Linguistics (2011)
7. Zhou, G.D., Zhang, M.: Extracting relation information from text documents by exploring various types of knowledge. Information Processing & Management 43(4), 969–982 (2007)
8. Oh, J.H., Uchimoto, K., Torisawa, K.: Bilingual co-training for monolingual hyponymy-relation acquisition. In: Proceedings of the Joint Conference of the 47th Annual Meeting of the ACL and The 4th International Joint Conference on Natural Language Processing of the AFNLP, vol. 1, pp. 432–440. Association for Computational Linguistics (2009)
9. Zhang, M., Su, J., Wang, D., Zhou, G., Tan, C.-L.: Discovering relations between named entities from a large raw corpus using tree similarity-based clustering. In: Dale, R., Wong, K.-F., Su, J., Kwong, O.Y. (eds.) IJCNLP 2005. LNCS (LNAI), vol. 3651, pp. 378–389. Springer, Heidelberg (2005)
10. Hearst, M.A.: Automatic acquisition of hyponyms from large text corpora. In: Proceedings of the 14th Conference on Computational linguistics, vol. 2, pp. 539–545. Association for Computational Linguistics (1992)
11. Pantel, P., Pennacchiotti, M.: Espresso: Leveraging generic patterns for automatically harvesting semantic relations. In: Proceedings of the 21st International Conference on Computational Linguistics and the 44th Annual Meeting of the Association for Computational Linguistics, pp. 113–120. Association for Computational Linguistics (2006)
12. Conglei, Y., Nan, D.: An Extraction Method on Web. Pattern Recognition and Artificial Intelligence 2(6) (2007) (in Chinese)
13. Tian, G., Qian, M., Huaping, Z.: A Research on Social Network Extraction Based on Web Search Engine. Chinese Product Reviews Filtering (2009) (in Chinese)
14. Peng, C., Gu, J., Qian, L.: Research on Tree Kernel-Based Personal Relation Extraction. In: Zhou, M., Zhou, G., Zhao, D., Liu, Q., Zou, L. (eds.) NLPCC 2012. CCIS, vol. 333, pp. 225–236. Springer, Heidelberg (2012)
15. Zhu, J., Nie, Z., Liu, X., et al.: StatSnowball: a statistical approach to extracting entity relationships. In: Proceedings of the 18th International Conference on World Wide Web, pp. 101–110. ACM (2009)
16. Cover, T., Thomas, J., Proakis, J.G., et al.: Elements of information theory. telecommunications. Wiley series (1991)
17. Pantel, P., Ravichandran, D.: Automatically labeling semantic classes. In: Proceedings of HLT/NAACL, vol. 4, pp. 321–328 (2004)
18. Gooi, C.H., Allan, J.: Cross-document coreference on a large scale corpus. In: HLT-NAACL, pp. 9–16 (2004)
19. Mayfield, J., Alexander, D., Dorr, B., et al.: Cross-document coreference resolution: A key technology for learning by reading. In: AAAI Spring Symposium on Learning by Reading and Learning to Read (2009)
20. Malin, B.: Unsupervised name disambiguation via social network similarity. In: Workshop on Link Analysis, Counterterrorism, and Security, vol. 1401, pp. 93–102 (2005)
21. Bagga, A.: Evaluation of coreferences and coreference resolution systems. In: Proceedings of the First Language Resource and Evaluation Conference, pp. 563–566 (1998)

Learning Sentence Representation for Emotion Classification on Microblogs

Duyu Tang, Bing Qin*, Ting Liu, and Zhenghua Li

Research Center for Social Computing and Information Retrieval,
Harbin Institute of Technology, Harbin, China
{dytang,qinb,tliu,lzh}@ir.hit.edu.cn

Abstract. This paper studies the emotion classification task on microblogs. Given a message, we classify its emotion as happy, sad, angry or surprise. Existing methods mostly use the bag-of-word representation or manually designed features to train supervised or distant supervision models. However, manufacturing feature engines is time-consuming and not enough to capture the complex linguistic phenomena on microblogs. In this study, to overcome the above problems, we utilize pseudo-labeled data, which is extensively explored for distant supervision learning and training language model in Twitter sentiment analysis, to learn the sentence representation through Deep Belief Network algorithm. Experimental results in the supervised learning framework show that using the pseudo-labeled data, the representation learned by Deep Belief Network outperforms the Principal Components Analysis based and Latent Dirichlet Allocation based representations. By incorporating the Deep Belief Network based representation into basic features, the performance is further improved.

Keywords: Emotion Classification, Deep Belief Network, Representation Learning, Microblogs.

1 Introduction

Users of social media such as Twitter and Weibo often express freely their opinions and emotions with others. Social media are valuable sources to mine the opinions of users. Sentiment analysis (Opinion mining) [1, 2] is a fundamental research area in natural language processing. Recently, a large number of studies have investigated the problem of sentiment analysis on social media, in particular, microblogs [3, 4]. Generally, sentiment analysis on microblogs are divided into two perspectives, target-independent [3, 5] and target-dependent sentiment analysis [4]. The difference between the two tasks is that target-dependent sentiment analysis aims to analyze the opinion of a piece of text towards an aspect. This paper studies the task of emotion classification from the perspective of target-independent sentiment analysis. Namely, given a text, we classify its emotion as happy, sad, angry or surprise.

Although previous studies [6–8] have tested a large number of learning and classification methods for opinion and emotion mining such as SVM, CRF and so on, these

---

* Corresponding author.

G. Zhou et al. (Eds.): NLPCC 2013, CCIS 400, pp. 212–223, 2013.
© Springer-Verlag Berlin Heidelberg 2013

methods are mostly based on shallow representation structure, such as bag-of-word (BOW) representation [9]. The recent progress in machine learning suggests that deep learning that tries to build a deep representation structure can be more appropriate for many challenging tasks [10, 11]. In order to explore an abstract representation instead of BOW and deal with the curse of dimensionality, this paper studies the use of deep belief network (DBN) for representation learning on emotion classification. The sentence representation learned from corpus can be used as individual features or supplements to traditional features for emotion classification.

In microblogs, emoticons such as :-) :-(😀 😄 😡 😄 are widely explored as strong indicators to reflect users' opinions and emotions [12, 8, 13]. Our statistics of 10 millions random messages on Weibo [1] shows that 12% of them contain at least one emoticon. Users frequently use emoticons to express their emotion, such as the examples shown in Table 1. In these examples, the emoticons can be used to label the emotion of their corresponding plain texts [12]. For example, the emoticon 😀 in Table 1 shows a clear indicator of a happy emotion, so that the corresponding plain text *The movie is wonderful, I love it!* will be collected as a happy message. In this paper, the messages gathered via emoticons is called pseudo-labeled corpus. Although previous studies have tested the effectiveness of pseudo-labeled corpus by training distant supervision model [8] and emoticon-based language model [13] on sentiment classification task. Our preliminary experimental results with the distant supervision method on emotion classification show that the cross-validation accuracy is dissatisfied, which is just around 50%.

Table 1. Sampled Emoticon Messages from Weibo (translated examples)

Emotion type	Content of messages
Happy	The movie is wonderful! 😀 I love it!
Sad	My heart is broken 😢
Angry	😡 He pissed me off!
Surprise	OMG!! 😮 I'm shocked!!

In this paper, we take advantage of the pseudo-labeled corpus to learn the sentence representation in a DBN based framework. We have tested the approach on manually labeled corpus and experimental results in supervised learning framework show that the representation learned by DBN achieves comparable results with basic features, outperforms Principal Components Analysis and Latent Dirichlet Allocation based features, improves the basic features through feature incorporation.

This study shows that:

1. Using the pseudo-labeled data, Deep Belief Network can learn a better representation than Principal Components Analysis and Latent Dirichlet Allocation, and this can yield better results in the emotion classification task.
2. Compared with labeled data and randomly selected unlabeled data, the pseudo-labeled corpus shows positive impacts on sentence representation in the emotion classification task.

---

[1] http://www.weibo.com/

The reminder of this paper is organized as follows: Our method about representation learning for emotion classification is described in Section 2. Experimental results and analysis are reported in Section 3. Section 4 summarizes the existing work on emotion classification, Twitter sentiment analysis and deep learning for NLP. Section 5 concludes our work and presents the future work.

2   Methodology

Some steps are necessary to learn representation from pseudo-labeled corpus. In order to obtain pseudo-labeled corpus, emoticons for each category needs to be selected beforehand. For the purpose of reducing the manual work and meanwhile filtering the ambiguous emoticons, we propose to select representative emoticons based on their quality and quantity (in subsection 2.1). Subsequently, preprocessing and normalization are implemented to ensure the quality of the pseudo-labeled corpus (in subsection 2.2). Afterwards, basic features are proposed to map each message into the same dimensional feature space (in subsection 2.3) for further representation learning. Finally, deep belief network is explored to learn sentence representation by a unsupervised, greedy layer-wise algorithm (in subsection 2.4).

2.1   Emoticon Selection

Emoticons are frequently used in microblogs. In Weibo, there are 425 official emoticons[2], such as ⊙ ⊙ ⊛ ⊙. In addition to these official emoticons, some printable characters, such as :-) and :(, are also commonly used to indicate users' emotions. However, we observe that the emotions of some emoticons are ambiguous. For example, some users use ⊛ to show their happiness, however others use it as a sad indicator. These ambiguous emoticons make the automatic annotation difficult. To guarantee the quality of the automatic annotation, not all the emoticons can be retained, and the ambiguous ones should be filtered out. Therefore, an automatic ranking strategy based on the quality and quantity of the emoticons is essential. Inspired by the work of [14], the importance of each emoticon in each emotion category is calculated as the Equation 1 shows.

$$S_i(e_j) = Acc_i(e_j) \times log_{10}(freq(e_j)) \qquad (1)$$

$$Acc_i(e_j) = \frac{\sum_k co\_freq(e_j, sw_{ik})}{\sum_k \sum_I co\_freq(e_j, sw_{Ik})} \qquad (2)$$

In Equation 1, the first multiplier corresponds to the quality factor and the second multiplier indicates the quantity factor. $freq(e_j)$ in the second multiplier stands for the frequency of the emoticon e_j in the corpus. In Equation 2, $co\_freq(e_j, sw_{ik})$ refers to the frequency that the emoticon e_j and the k-th emotional word sw_{ik} in the i-th emotion category co-occur within a message in the corpus. Here, Peking Emotion Lexicon (EL)[3] is used as the external lexicon resource. EL contains approximate 90 tokens with high confidence for each kind of emotions. Finally, according to the calculation results, the top ranked emoticons are selected for each emotion, as shown in Table 2.

---

[2] Until 2011, there are totally 425 official emoticons.
[3] EL is available at http://icl.pku.edu.cn/icl_res/

Table 2. Emoticons for Each Category of Emotions

Emotion type	Selected emoticons
Happy	😊 😄 😊 😄 😊 :) :-) :D
Sad	😢 💔 😢 😢 😢 😢 :(:-(
Angry	😠 😠 😠
Surprise	😮 😮 😮 😮

2.2 Pseudo Labelled Corpus Collection

Manually annotating training examples is time consuming and expensive, in this subsection, the pseudo-labeled corpus are extracted without manually labeling. As described in Section 1, pseudo labeled corpus refers to the messages with emoticons in them. In order to generate high-quality data, a lot of preprocessing and basic natural language processing work need to be done beforehand, such as word segmentation and text normalization. The implementation details of preprocessing are described as follows:

1. remove the repost part of a message to keep the pure source content edited by the users.
2. replace the official metadata to the corresponding normalization form. Specifically, replace *@username* with *REF*, *#hashtag#* with *TAG*, *http://...* with *URL*. For example, the message "*#Taylow Swift# @David I love her so much!!! http://j.mp/d5Dupr*" will be unified to "*TAG REF I love her so much!!! URL*".
3. remove duplicated messages based on the Longest Common Subsequence (LCS) algorithm. If the rate of LCS between two messages is higher than a threshold, they will be recognized as duplicated and the shorter one will be ignored.
4. remove the messages whose length are less than 10.

After preprocessing, the messages containing only one kind of emoticons will be collected as pseudo-labeled messages. That is to say, the messages containing emoticons from different emotion categories are not collected. For example, the message containing 😊 and 😢 simultaneously is ignored. Subsequently, word segmentation is implemented by the Language Technology Platform (LTP) [4].

2.3 Basic Features

Previous work [9, 15–17] has discovered some effective features for sentiment analysis on movie reviews and tweets. The commonly used features include word unigram, POS tags, polarity of a word in the sentiment lexicon, etc. Before learning the deep representation, some basic features are needed to map the messages into the same dimensional feature space. Inspired by previous studies, the basic features used in this paper are described as follows:

1. Word unigram features. To control the dimension of the feature space, only the 2000 most frequent words in the pseudo training data are considered, as done by [18].

---

[4] http://ir.hit.edu.cn/demo/ltp/

2. Punctuation features. Some punctuation sequences which can reflect emotion are muanually selected, such as "!!!", "..." and "???". These punctuation features are utilized as binary features according to whether a predifined punctuation occurs in a message.

3. Emotion lexicon features. In order to map the emotional words in a message into predefined emotion category, the external lexicon ML is introduced. Given a message, the lexicon is used to judge whether the words of each emotion exist in the message, and the corresponding feature is used as a binary feature. For example, given a message "*I am very happy today*", the word happy occurs in the lexicon's happy category, and no word exists in the lexicon's other emotion categories (sad, angry and surprise). Thus, the feature is that: *happy(1), sad(0), angry(0) and surprise(0)*. Besides, the occurrences of emotional words in the message are treated as binary features too.

4. Onomatopoeia features. In microblogs, onomatopoeia words are frequently used to express sentiment, such as "aha", "hey" etc. Therefore, an Onomatopoeia Lexicon (OL) is built manually. The onomatopoeia feature is a binary one according to whether there exists any onomatopoeia word in the given message. Similar with Emotion lexicon features, the occurrences of onomatopoeia words in the message are treated as binary features.

5. Function word features. Function words are mostly verbs that can induce a subjection expression, such as *feel, think, consider*. A Function Word Lexicon (FWL) is manually collected. The usage of FWL is similar with emotion lexicon and onomatopoeia lexicon.

After extracting the basic features, each message will be mapped into the same dimensional feature space, which will be used as the input of the visible nodes to learn the sentence representation in the following subsection.

2.4 Representation Learning for Emotion Classification

In this paper, we assume that compared with randomly selected data, the pseudo-labeled corpus is closer to the emotional dataset. Thus, the learned representation on pseudo-label corpus has much potential to improve the performance of the emotion classification model. In this subsection, we explore deep belief network (DBN) [19] for representation learning in emotion classification. The illustration of the DBN model is given in Figure 1, which is composed of three layers, and each one of the three layers stands for the Restricted Boltzmann Machine (RBM). The training procedure of DBN is greedy layerwised, whose intuition is "re-construction" [19, 20]. The idea is to train one layer at a time, starting from lower layers, so that its training objective for the currently added layer is to reconstruct the previous layer. With unsupervised layer-wise training, each layer is trained to model the abstract distribution of the previous layer.

Restricted Boltzmann Machine [21] is proposed to model an ensemble of binary vectors as a two-layer network. Take the bottom layer in Figure 1 as an example, the observed basic features of a message correspond to the "visible" units in the layer $\mathbf{v}$ and the latent features correspond to the hidden units in the layer $\mathbf{h}^1$. A joint configuration $(\mathbf{v}, \mathbf{h})$ of the visible and the hidden units has an energy given by

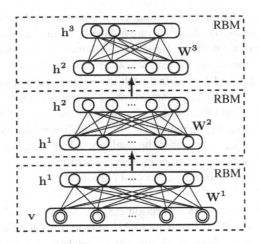

Fig. 1. The Deep Belief Network for Representation Learning

$$E(\mathbf{v}, \mathbf{h}) = - \sum_{i \in \text{inputs}} \mathbf{b_i v_i} - \sum_{j \in \text{features}} \mathbf{b_j h_j} - \sum_{i,j} \mathbf{v_i h_j w_{ij}} \qquad (3)$$

where v_i and h_j are the binary states of the i-th node in the visible layer and the j-th node in the hidden layer, b_i and b_j are their biases respectively, and w_{ij} is the weight between them.

In the training process, each RBM performs a nonlinear transformation on its input vectors and the output vectors will be used as the input for the next layer. The sigmoid function is used to calculate the probability of each node is on. After activating the hidden units stochastically, a confabulated vector is produced. The states of the hidden units are then updated by the confabulation vector in the same way. The parameters are updated by

$$\triangle w_{ij} = \epsilon(< v_i h_j >_{data} - < v_i h_j >_{recon}) \qquad (4)$$

where ϵ is the learning rate, $< v_i h_j >_{data}$ is the probability of the i-th node in $\mathbf{v}$ and the j-th node in h are on together when the hidden features are driven by the real data, and $< v_i h_j >_{recon}$ is the corresponding probability in the reconstruction stage.

3   Experiment

3.1   Experiment Setup

Dataset We collect 1.2 million Chinese messages from September 2009 to September 2010 using the Weibo API[5]. One million messages are randomly selected to get the pseudo-labeled corpus. After removing the duplicate messages, 20,000 emoticon data are obtained as the pseudo labeled data with 5,000 messages for each kind of emotions.

---

[5] http://open.weibo.com/

And the same number of messages without emoticons are randomly selected as unlabelled data. In consideration of that there are no available annotated corpus for emotion classification in Weibo, we manually annotate 5,000 messages without emoticons from the rest of 0.2 million messages. Two annotators are required to conduct the annotation, and each annotator is asked to annotate each message as happy, sad, angry, surprise or others. The inter-agreement of the annotators is 87.54%. Finally, after removing the inconsistent annotations and the messages labeled as "others", 2,875 instances are collected as the gold standard for emotion classification. There are 548 happy, 837 sad, 905 angry and 567 surprise messages in the final labeled dataset. The accuracy of cross-validation on the gold dataset is used as evaluation metric. For each type of feature, we utilize LibLinear [6] to train models for emotion classification.

Details of Lexicon Resources. In subsection 2.3, we utilize several lexicon resources, such as Emotion Lexicon (EL), Onomatopoeia Lexicon (OL) and Function Word Lexicon (FWL), to extract basic features. Figure 3 gives the detailed information about these lexicons.

Table 3. Details of Lexicon Resources

Lexicon	EL				OL	FWL
	Happy	Sad	Angry	Surprise		
Size	83	89	101	91	166	188

Architecture of the Network. In this study, different architectures are designed to check the usefulness of representation learned by DBN. For example, there are three layers in the architecture of 2,729-2,000-1,000-500, each of which corresponds to RBM with $2,729 \times 2,000$, $2,000 \times 1,000$, $1,000 \times 500$ individually. In the bottom layer, 2,729 visible units corresponds to the basic features described in subsection 2.3 and the number of hidden units is 2,000. In the training stage, each layer is trained for 50 times greedily. Using this network, a 2,729-dimension binary vector will be represented by a 500-dimension distributed vector. In the preliminary experiment, we conduct two architectures, 2,729-2,000-1,000-500 and 2,729-1,500-750-500, to discover the influence of the architecture. Due to their close performance, we will just report the results achieved from the former architecture.

3.2   Results and Analysis

Below we first present the finding of comparing DBN based representation with the classical text-based feature and PCA or LDA based feature. Then, we compare the effectiveness of the pseudo-labeled corpus with the unlabeled data and small-scale labeled data on representation learning for emotion classification.

Comparison between Representations. In the first set of experiments, we compare the learned representation by DBN with the following methods:

---

[6] http://www.csie.ntu.edu.tw/~cjlin/liblinear/

- BOW: Bag-Of-Word representation [8] is widely used feature for opinion and emotion classification.
- BF: Basic Feature (in subsection 2.3) is re-used as a sentence representation.
- PCA: Principal Components Analysis [22] is adopted to find the directions of the greatest K variances in the dataset and represent each data by these directions.
- LDA: Latent Dirichlet Allocation [23] is utilized to map each sentence into the topic space, whose dimension is K.

In this set of experiments, pseudo-labeled corpus is used for representation learning in the PCA and DBN algorithm. To make fair comparison with DBN, K is set to 500 in the PCA algorithm. Experimental results are listed in Table 4. Each line corresponds to a kind of feature for emotion classification. For example, the first line (BOW) means that bag-of-words are used as features and the last line (BF + DBN) indicates that we use the composition of basic feature and representation learned by DBN.

Table 4. Experimental Results for Emotion Classification on Weibo

Method		Accuracy(%)
Text Feature	BOW	69.97
	BF	72.03
Learned Feature	PCA	70.54
	LDA	67.72
	DBN	**73.28**
Combined Feature	BF + PCA	72.46
	BF + LDA	70.19
	BF + DBN	**75.60**

By comparing the results of different methods, we draw the following observations:

(1) Using the pseudo-labeled data, the sentence representation learned by DBN based method achieves better than PCA and LDA based method for the task of emotion classification. In the setting of using the learned representation as feature individually, DBN-based method (73.28% in Line 4) outperforms PCA (70.54% in Line 3) by 2.74 points in accuracy. In the setting of combining basic feature with learned representation, DBN (75.60% in Line 6) outperforms PCA (72.46% in Line 5) by 3.14 points in accuracy. The same trend is observed when DBN is compared with LDA method.

(2) By concatenating the DBN based representation with basic features, the performance is further improved. The incorporation of DBN based representation (75.60%) improves the basic feature (72.03% in Line 2) by 3.57% points in accuracy. The introduce of DBN has positive impacts on the emotion classification task.

Sensitivity to Corpus. In order to further investigate the sensitivity of the DBN based method to the corpus for representation learning, in Table 5, we show the emotion classification accuracy using the learned representation as individual feature. Each line corresponds to one type of corpus used for representation learning. For example, the first line means that the small-scale labeled data is used to learn representation by DBN algorithm.

Table 5. Sensitivity of DBN to Corpus for Representation Learning

Corpus	Accuracy(%)
Labeled Data	67.31
Unlabeled Data	71.55
Pseudo-Labeled Data	**73.28**

By comparing the results of different corpus, we draw the following observations:

(1) Compared with pseudo-labeled corpus, small-scale labeled data is not sufficient for represent learning based on DBN algorithm. In Table 5, compared with using pseudo-labeled corpus (73.28% in Line 3), the accuracy achieved using the labeled
data(67.31% in Line 1) decreases by 5.97 points in accuracy, which is worse that the
basic feature (72.03%) by 4.72 points. The experimental results demonstrate that DBN
algorithm is sensitive to the training corpus.

(2) Compared with unlabeled data, representation learned from the same number
of pseudo-labeled corpus achieves better performance for emotion classification. The
representation learned from pseudo-labeled corpus (73.28% in Line 3) outperforms the
one learned from unlabeled data (71.55% in Line 2). The introduce of pseudo-labeled
corpus has positive impacts on representation learning for emotion classification.

4 Previous Work

With the popularity of blogs and social media, sentiment analysis has become a hot
point in natural language processing research community. Overall, sentiment analysis on microblogs could be viewed from two perspectives, target-independent [3, 5]
and target-dependent [4] sentiment analysis. This paper studies the task of target-
independent emotion classification.

4.1 Emotion Classification and Twitter Sentiment Analysis

The original attempt of sentiment analysis [9, 24] aims to classify whether a whole
document expresses a positive or negative sentiment. [9] treat the sentiment classification of reviews as a special case of text categorization problem and first investigate
machine learning methods. In their experiments, the best performance is achieved by
SVMs with bag-of-words representation. Apart from positive and negative evaluations,
some researchers aim to identify the emotion of text, such as happy, sad, angry, etc. [7]
uses emoticons labelled by the blogger to collect corpus in LiveJournal. And similar
with [9], SVMs is utilized to train a emotion classifier with a variety of features over
100 emotions. Mishne and [25] use a similar method to identify words and phrases
in order to estimate aggregate emotion levels across a large number of blog posts. [6]
combine SVMs and CRF for emotion classification at the document level. As social
media become popular, Twitter sentiment analysis attracts much researcher's attention.
[8] collect positive and negative data automatically with emoticons such as :-) and :-(.
[12, 26] go further and use both hashtags and smileys to collect corpus. In addition,
they use a KNN-like classifier for multiple emotion classification. [15] leverage three

sources with noisy labels as training data and use a SVM classifier with a set of features. From a different perspective, [13] train a language model based on the manually labelled data, and then use the noisy emoticon data for smoothing. However, the majority of existing methods use the bag-of-word representation, which cannot capture the complex linguistic phenomena.

4.2 Deep Learning for NLP

The recent revival of interest deep learning, or representation learning [27], has a strong impact in the area of Natural Language Processing, such as multi-task learning [28], domain adaptation [29], parsing [30], entity disambiguation [31], etc. Majority of the existing work are based on word embedding, which means learning a distributed representation for each word [32]. In sentiment analysis, [33, 34] propose the Semi-Supervised Recursive Autoencoders for sentiment distribution prediction. [35] learn word vectors capturing semantic term-document information for document-level sentiment classification. [36] propose a deep learning approach based on Stacked Denoising Autoencoders to study the problem of domain adaptation for sentiment classification. Glorot et al verified the effectiveness of unlabelled data for domain adaptation. However, these methods mostly need labeled data or crowd intelligence. In this work, we use pseudo-labeled corpus, which is extracted automatically from microblogs, to learn the sentence representation for emotion classification on microblogs, in particular, Weibo.

5   Conclusion and Future Work

In this paper, we propose a deep learning approach that automatically learns sentence representation for emotion classification on microblogs. The sentence representation is learned leveraging pseudo labeled corpus, without any manual effort of annotating messages. Experiment reveals the importance of DBN algorithm and the usefulness of pseudo-labeled corpus in this field. By incorporating the DBN based representation into basic features, performance is further improved.

As to future work, the first plan is to learn word representation (word embedding) for emotion classification. The sentence is potential to have positive impacts on emotion classification based on a more meaningful word representation. In addition, as we observed that when pseudo-labeled data, whose size is larger than labeled data, was used, better performance was achieved. So a natural question is whether the performance will continue to increase with even more pseudo-labeled corpus.

Acknowledgments. This work was supported by National Natural Science Foundation of China (NSFC) via grant 61133012, NSFC via grant 61073126 and NSFC via grant 61273321.

We thank Jianyun Nie greatly for valuable comments and helpful suggestions, and thank Yaming Sun for refining the language of this paper, and thank Qiuhui Shi for preparing dataset. We would also thank the anonymous reviewers for their comments and suggestions.

References

1. Pang, B., Lee, L.: Opinion mining and sentiment analysis. Foundations and Trends in Information Retrieval 2(1-2), 1–135 (2008)
2. Liu, B.: Sentiment analysis and opinion mining. Synthesis Lectures on Human Language Technologies 5(1), 1–167 (2012)
3. Hu, X., Tang, L., Tang, J., Liu, H.: Exploiting social relations for sentiment analysis in microblogging. In: Proceedings of the Sixth WSDM, pp. 537–546. ACM (2013)
4. Jiang, L., Yu, M., Zhou, M., Liu, X., Zhao, T.: Target-dependent twitter sentiment classification. In: Proc. 49th ACL: HLT, vol. 1, pp. 151–160 (2011)
5. Kouloumpis, E., Wilson, T., Moore, J.: Twitter sentiment analysis: The good the bad and the omg! In: Fifth International AAAI Conference on Weblogs and Social Media (2011)
6. Yang, C., Lin, K., Chen, H.: Emotion classification using web blog corpora. In: IEEE/WIC/ACM International Conference on Web Intelligence, pp. 275–278. IEEE (2007)
7. Mishne, G.: Experiments with mood classification in blog posts. In: Proceedings of ACM SIGIR 2005 Workshop on Stylistic Analysis of Text for Information Access, p. 19 (2005)
8. Go, A., Bhayani, R., Huang, L.: Twitter sentiment classification using distant supervision. CS224N Project Report, Stanford, 1–12 (2009)
9. Pang, B., Lee, L., Vaithyanathan, S.: Thumbs up?: sentiment classification using machine learning techniques. In: Proceedings of the Conference on EMNLP, pp. 79–86. ACL (2002)
10. Dahl, G.E., Yu, D., Deng, L., Acero, A.: Context-dependent pre-trained deep neural networks for large-vocabulary speech recognition. IEEE Transactions on Audio, Speech, and Language Processing 20(1), 30–42 (2012)
11. Krizhevsky, A., Sutskever, I., Hinton, G.: Imagenet classification with deep convolutional neural networks. In: NIPS, pp. 1106–1114 (2012)
12. Read, J.: Using emoticons to reduce dependency in machine learning techniques for sentiment classification. In: Proceedings of the ACL Student Research Workshop, pp. 43–48 (2005)
13. Liu, K., Li, W., Guo, M.: Emoticon smoothed language models for twitter sentiment analysis. In: Twenty-Sixth AAAI Conference on Artificial Intelligence (2012)
14. Li, F., Pan, S.J., Jin, O., Yang, Q., Zhu, X.: Cross-domain co-extraction of sentiment and topic lexicons. In: Proceedings of the 50th ACL, pp. 410–419. ACL (July 2012)
15. Barbosa, L., Feng, J.: Robust sentiment detection on twitter from biased and noisy data. In: Proceedings of the 23rd COLING Posters, pp. 36–44. ACL (2010)
16. Johansson, R., Moschitti, A.: Extracting opinion expressions and their polarities–exploration of pipelines and joint models. In: Proceedings of ACL, vol. 11 (2011)
17. Wiebe, J., Wilson, T., Cardie, C.: Annotating expressions of opinions and emotions in language. Language Resources and Evaluation 39(2-3), 165–210 (2005)
18. Salakhutdinov, R., Hinton, G.: Semantic hashing. International Journal of Approximate Reasoning 50(7), 969–978 (2009)
19. Hinton, G., Salakhutdinov, R.: Reducing the dimensionality of data with neural networks. Science 313(5786), 504–507 (2006)
20. Bengio, Y., Lamblin, P., Popovici, D., Larochelle, H.: Greedy layer-wise training of deep networks. Advances in Neural Information Processing Systems 19, 153 (2007)
21. Hinton, G.: Training products of experts by minimizing contrastive divergence. Neural Computation 14(8), 1771–1800 (2002)
22. Hotelling, H.: Analysis of a complex of statistical variables into principal components. Journal of Educational Psychology 24(6), 417 (1933)
23. Blei, D.M., Ng, A.Y., Jordan, M.I.: Latent dirichlet allocation. The Journal of Machine Learning Research 3, 993–1022 (2003)

24. Turney, P.: Thumbs up or thumbs down?: semantic orientation applied to unsupervised classification of reviews. In: Proceedings of the 40th ACL, pp. 417–424. ACL (2002)
25. Mishne, G., De Rijke, M.: Capturing global mood levels using blog posts. In: AAAI 2006 Spring Symposium on Computational Approaches to Analysing Weblogs, pp. 145–152 (2006)
26. Davidov, D., Tsur, O., Rappoport, A.: Enhanced sentiment learning using twitter hashtags and smileys. In: Proceedings of the 23rd COLING: Posters, pp. 241–249. ACL (2010)
27. Bengio, Y., Courville, A., Vincent, P.: Representation learning: A review and new perspectives. arXiv preprint arXiv:1206.5538 (2012)
28. Collobert, R., Weston, J., Bottou, L., Karlen, M., Kavukcuoglu, K., Kuksa, P.: Natural language processing (almost) from scratch. JMLR 12, 2493–2537 (2011)
29. Chen, M., Xu, Z., Weinberger, K., Sha, F.: Marginalized denoising autoencoders for domain adaptation. In: ICML (2012)
30. Socher, R., Bauer, J., Manning, C.D., Ng, A.Y.: Parsing with compositional vector grammars. In: ACL (2013)
31. He, Z., Liu, S., Li, M., Zhou, M., Zhang, L., Wang, H.: Learning entity representation for entity disambiguation. In: ACL (2013)
32. Turian, J., Ratinov, L., Bengio, Y.: Word representations: a simple and general method for semi-supervised learning. Urbana 51, 61801 (2010)
33. Socher, R., Pennington, J., Huang, E., Ng, A., Manning, C.: Semi-supervised recursive autoencoders for predicting sentiment distributions. In: EMNLP, pp. 151–161 (2011)
34. Socher, R., Huval, B., Manning, C.D., Ng, A.Y.: Semantic Compositionality Through Recursive Matrix-Vector Spaces. In: Proceedings of the 2012 Conference on EMNLP (2012)
35. Maas, A.L., Daly, R., Pham, P., Huang, D., Ng, A., Potts, C.: Learning word vectors for sentiment analysis. In: Proceedings of the 49th ACL, ACL 2011 (2011)
36. Glorot, X., Bordes, A., Bengio, Y.: Domain adaptation for large-scale sentiment classification: A deep learning approach. In: Proceedings of ICML (2011)

Every Term Has Sentiment:
Learning from Emoticon Evidences
for Chinese Microblog Sentiment Analysis*

Fei Jiang, Anqi Cui, Yiqun Liu, Min Zhang, and Shaoping Ma

State Key Laboratory of Intelligent Technology and Systems,
Tsinghua National Laboratory for Information Science and Technology,
Department of Computer Science and Technology,
Tsinghua University, Beijing 100084, China
{f91.jiang,cuianqi}@gmail.com, {yiqunliu,z-m,msp}@tsinghua.edu.cn

Abstract. Chinese microblog is a popular Internet social medium where users express their sentiments and opinions. But sentiment analysis on Chinese microblogs is difficult: The lack of labeling on the sentiment polarities restricts many supervised algorithms; out-of-vocabulary words and emoticons enlarge the sentiment expressions, which are beyond traditional sentiment lexicons. In this paper, emoticons in Chinese microblog messages are used as annotations to automatically label noisy corpora and construct sentiment lexicons. Features including microblog-specific and sentiment-related ones are introduced for sentiment classification. These sentiment signals are useful for Chinese microblog sentiment analysis. Evaluations on a balanced dataset are conducted, showing an accuracy of 63.9% in a three-class sentiment classification of positive, negative and neutral. The features mined from the Chinese microblogs also increase the performances.

Keywords: Microblog, Sentiment Analysis, Sentiment Lexicon Construction, Support Vector Machine.

1   Introduction

Microblog is a new form of social networking service where millions of people express their feelings and the posts are colloquial and irregular. A high percentage of messages have positive or negative sentiment.Sentiments of people in social events draw wide attentions of the public and sentiment analysis on microblog messages has become a popular research topic.

Sentiment analysis can be applied to many topics in microblogs. On business topics, we can obtain word-of-mouth reputation of brands or products from a large number of users, thus helping companies to improve their products [6]. On stock markets, people's sentiment polarities towards a hot topic may affect the

---

* This work was supported by Natural Science Foundation (61073071), National High Technology Research and Development (863) Program (2011AA01A207). Part of this work has been done at the NUSTsinghua EXtreme search centre (NExT).

G. Zhou et al. (Eds.): NLPCC 2013, CCIS 400, pp. 224–235, 2013.
© Springer-Verlag Berlin Heidelberg 2013

stock prices [2]. On political events, the sentiments of citizens reflect election situations [13]. Generally speaking, most of these studies are in English microblogs (such as Twitter), but similarly they are also important in Chinese microblogs.

The objective of sentiment classification is to classify the sentiment of a piece of text into three classes: Positive, negative and neutral. Traditional sentiment analysis methods mainly concentrate on a specific target in reviews, such as product reviews or movie reviews. In these domains, users post their comments as well as the ratings (in scores or stars) for a certain product or movie. Based on the texts and ratings, supervised machine learning models can be utilized to learn semantic information of the products such as feature-opinion pairs, which are then applied to texts in the same domain. However, for microblog messages, they have all types of topics which do not belong to a certain domain. What is more, they do not have labels or ratings like product reviews; it costs much time and efforts to label many messages manually. The above difficulties for microblog sentiment analysis are of main concerns in the research area.

In Chinese microblogs, there are even more challenges on sentiment analysis, including word segmentation with out-of-vocabulary (OOV) words recognition, syntactical analysis on informal sentences. Hence, we propose the following contributions to reduce these difficulties:

First, we propose a new method for automatic sentiment lexicon construction with emoticon evidences, meanwhile dealing with out-of-vocabulary words and commonly used phrases. More over, in our lexicon, every word has a potential sentiment, which is reflected by continuous positive score and negative score. It is more flexible to extract features other than discrete-valued scores. Further more, in sentiment classification, we use different types of features, which represent different views of chacteristics of microblog messages. And finally, unlike many three-class classification methods, our method does not necessarily need large amounts of neutral corpora, which are really difficult to obtain.

The rest of this paper is organized as follows: Section 2 briefly describes some related work. In section 3, we introduce emoticons and present our methods of sentiment lexicon construction. Section 4 presents our methods in feature extraction and classification strategies. We conduct experiments in section 5 and conclude the paper in section 6.

2   Related Work

Sentiment analysis is usually considered as a classification problem: Classify the sentiments of microblog messages into positive, negative or neutral. Traditionally, machine learning methods have been applied to sentiment classification [11]. More specifically, in Twitter sentiment analysis, the noisy tweets can be used as training data to train a classification model [1]. Part of the noisy data is obtained by some rules (e.g. tweets containing specific sentiment words), hence the features of the classifier are restricted to some limited ones generated from the formal words. Different from them, emoticons are used as approximate labels of tweets to obtain a large amount of noisy data [10]. In these methods, the quality and bias of the noisy data limit the performance of classification. More over, when perform three-class classification, assumptions about neutral corpora in twitter such as [10] do not hold in Chinese microblog.

To ensure the quality of training corpus, the best method is manually labeling [8]. However, the scale of labeled data is limited – then the features extracted have to be more general, while the dimension of features is also reduced. Sentiment lexicons make it possible to map a high dimension of word vector to a low dimension of several sentiment strengths.

Lexicons can be constructed manually [16,18]. The advantage is of higher accuracy, but they are limited for the cost and coverage [9,12]. Meanwhile, large numbers of spoken words, buzz words and dialects (e.g. Cantonese) make the coverage of manually constructed lexicons even more limited.

Lexicons can also be constructed automatically from the corpus. Starting with a few sentiment words and making use of the relationship of words in the corpus, the sentiment polarities of more words can be discovered [5,7,14]. Some emoticons can serve as seeds, However, the interrelation of words must be reliable. Hence discovering a proper relationship of words is important when building a lexicon from the corpus, especially when the corpus is noisy.

3   Sentiment Lexicon Construction

3.1   Emoticons in Chinese Microblogs

Emoticon is one of the main characteristics of Chinese microblogs. Instead of typing characters to compose emoticons (e.g. ":-)") in English microblogs, in Chinese microblogs users "type" emoticons by clicking on some icons on the web interface. The icons are mapped to characters surrounded with brackets to store and transfer as texts; these texts are displayed as emoticon images when rendering the web page. The emoticons are usually animated, making microblog messages more vivid, and more accurate to show users' emotions.

In previous work, emoticons such as :-) or :-(are used to collect positive or negative tweets from noisy data. However, there are much more emoticons in Chinese microblogs who indicate strong emotions. Hence we examine ten commonly used emoticons, including five positive ones: [笑哈哈] (laughing), [太 开心] (very happy), [哈哈] (Haha), [给力] (*Geili*, awesome), [good]; and five negative ones: [泪] (tears), [悲伤] (sad), [弱] (weak), [鄙视] (despise), [怒] (angry). For each of these emoticons, we randomly labeled 100 microblog messages containing it. The proportions of positive, neutral and negative messages are shown in Fig. 1.

It shows that messages containing or , are mostly neutral instead of positive. These two emoticons do have positive sentiments as shown in their appearances, but many users are used to posting them in any messages. Compared with them, the other three: , and have stronger positive sentiments, thus are more suitable for collecting positive messages from the corpus.

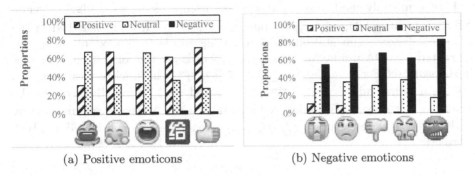

(a) Positive emoticons   (b) Negative emoticons

Fig. 1. Proportions of sentiment polarities of microblog messages with emoticons

Similarly, for the negative emoticons, 😊 and 😊 have more noises than 🖕,
😊 and 😊 – the former two have less negative but more positive messages. This
may because they are ambiguous; people use them not only when they are sad,
but also when they are moved. Therefore, the latter three emoticons are more
suitable for collecting negative messages from the corpus.

3.2 Phrase Extraction and Out-Of-Vocabulary Word Recognition

Because of the irregular expressions, traditional segmenters do not work well on
microblog messages. And Out-Of-Vocabulary (OOV) words are also commonly
used. Besides, many phrases (n-grams) occur very often and have less ambiguity
compared to treating them as separate words, such as "太次"(too bad). These
phrases are also put in the lexicon which benefits sentiment analysis.

In a large set of segmented sentences(with NLPIR2013[17]), we concatenate
adjacent words to get every phrase (n-grams, n is not limited to two) with less
than M characters. Then we compute two metrics of each phrase t:

1. Frequency $freq(t)$: the number of its occurrences in the corpus.
2. Tightness $T(t)$: Denote the words in the phrase t as $\{w_i\}$, the tightness of
t is defined as:

$$T(t) = \frac{freq(t)}{\sqrt[n]{\prod freq(w_i)}} \tag{1}$$

With some proper thresholds, phrases of at least one large enough metric are
selected, which cover OOVs. In this paper about 60,000 phrases and OOVs are
extracted (without POS tags). In the following part of this paper, all the basic
words, OOVs and phrases are referred to as *words*. They make a *word set*.

3.3 Modified-by-Degree-Adverbs Words Recognition

Modified by Degree Adverbs (MDA) words are the words that can be modified by
degree adverbs. These words often have obvious opinions, such as "喜欢" (favor),
"讨厌" (disgusting) and "好" (good). Therefore, recognition of MDA words are
helpful to sentiment analysis.

Five commonly used degree adverbs are used: "很" (very), "非常" (very), "比较" (a little bit), "太" (too) and "十分" (very). They are matched in the sentences before segmentation; their following words (just next to them) are extracted as MDA words. Note these MDA words are the longest possible ones in the *word set*. For example, in "这位叔叔很友好" (This uncle is very friendly), "很" is a degree adverb; both "友" (friend) and "友好" (friendly) exist in the *word set*, but only "友好" is kept as an MDA word. Moreover, words starting with degree adverbs (such as "太棒",, very great) are also considered as MDA words.

3.4 Negation Words

Negation is a common phenomenon in Chinese, which may inverse the sentiment of a word or a sentence. Some sentiment words are often modified by negations, such as "靠谱" (reliable). Negation has a significant influence on the sentiment words, so it is an important part of lexicon construction and sentiment analysis.

We complement some negations to the list [15] to generate a list of 53 negations, which are then added into the *word set*. The first adjectives, verbs or words without POS tag (i.e. phrases, OOV words or emoticons) in the *word set* modified by each negation are extracted. But if there is no such word within N words after the negation, the negation is ignored. In the experiments $N = 3$.

For example, the segmentation result of the sentence "这位先生,您真是站着说话不腰疼😿" (Sir, what you think is really easier said than done): "这/rzv 位/q 先生/noun /wd 您/rr 真/d 是/vshi 站/n 着/uzhe 说/v 话/n 不/d 腰/n 疼/v 😿" Assume we have {真, 是, 站, 着, 说, 话, 不, 腰, 疼, 您, 真是, 站着 说 话, 腰疼, 这位, 先生, 😿} in the *word set*, this sentence is transformed to the following *intermediate result*: "这位, 先生, 您, 真是, 站着, 说话, 腰疼(−1), 😿", where words labeled by −1 are modified by negations.

After converting the messages to *intermediate results*, the sentiment lexicon can be constructed. Depending on whether or not we have sufficient corpus containing the specified emoticons (in Section 3.1), we introduce two methods to compute the positive and negative scores of all the words in our *word set*.

3.5 Frequency Statistics Algorithm for Sufficient Corpus

Messages containing some specified emoticons (😊, 给 or 👍 for positive, and 👎, 😿 or ⊖ for negative) can be extracted as noisy labeled data for training in supervised learning algorithms. We call the corpus *sufficient* if it contains enough messages of these emoticons. Messages in the positive and negative sets are then transformed to the *intermediate result*.

Considering all the words in the above results. Define a positive word set A: Words not modified by negations in the positive message set and words modified by negations in the negative message set, and a negative word set B: Words modified by negations in the positive message set and words not modified by negations in the negative message set. Compute the positive and negative score of each word by their occurrences, as shown in the following equations:

$$score_+(w) = \frac{freq_A(w) + SMOOTH_A}{size(A) + N \cdot SMOOTH_A}, score_-(w) = \frac{freq_B(w) + SMOOTH_B}{size(B) + N \cdot SMOOTH_B} \tag{2}$$

where w is the word, $freq$ is the number of its occurrence in the word set, and $size$ is the sum of occurrences of all the words in each set. $SMOOTH$ is a parameter for smoothing, which should satisfy $\frac{size(A)}{size(B)} = \frac{SMOOTH_A}{SMOOTH_B}$.

The two scores are then normalized to one. We have no absolute sentiment words or non-sentiment words, but the sentiment polarity and strength of one word are reflected by the difference between positive and negative score.

3.6   Label Propagation Algorithm for Insufficient Corpus

If the corpus is *not sufficient* enough of messages containing the specified emoticons, we have to learn the polarities of words regarding the certain amount of the messages. Similarly as in [4], we construct a co-occurrence graph whose nodes are the words in the *intermediate result*, edges are their co-occurrences and apply the unsupervised label propagation algorithm on it. The three positive emoticons and three negative emoticons are used as positive seeds and negative seeds, respectively. Compared to the original algorithm, we also need to:

1. Dealing with negations: The weights of edges between every two node are initialized to zero. If two words in an *intermediate result* are both or neither modified by negations, the weight of their edge is increased by one. If there is only one word modified by negations, the weight is decreased by one.

2. Refine the iteration equation into:

$$s_{n+1} = \alpha \cdot W \cdot s_n + (1 - \alpha) \cdot \mathbf{b} \tag{3}$$

where $\mathbf{b}$ is the normalized static score vector, the dimension of $\mathbf{b}$ is the number of words (nodes) in the graph. For the positive (or negative) seed words, the corresponding elements in $\mathbf{b}$ are $1/m$ (m is the number of seeds). For other words, the corresponding elements are zero. W is the normalized symmetric matrix of the undirected co-occurrence graph. In [4], every element in W is non-negative, but after we introduce in negations, element in W can be negative, then the sum of the *absolute* value of elements in each row is 1. The vector s_n is the positive (or negative) score of each word after the n-th iteration, and the initial value s_0 is set to $\mathbf{b}$. α is a parameter between $[0,1]$ to control the impact of seeds. Hence, n (before convergence) and α are the only variables in a determinated seed set and co-occurrence graph.

The positive and negative scores are propagated from positive and negative seeds, respectively. Finally they are normalized as well.

4   Sentiment Classification Based on Sentiment Lexicon

Based on the constructed sentiment lexicon, we extract features from microblog messages, and use Support Vector Machine (SVM) to perform sentiment classification with different strategies.

4.1   Feature Extraction

In this subsection, we will extract different types of features from microblog messages. Each type of features has their specific relationship with the sentiment of messages.

Microblog Structure Features. *Microblog structure features* include mentioning labels (@), URLs, etc. are relavant to the sentiment. For example, URLs in one message indicate that it may be an advertisement, the geo-location statement ("我在:" + URL, I'm at) indicates the message is more likely to be posted by individuals instead of organizations. Hence the following microblog structure features are extracted:

(1) Existence of geo-location statement (boolean).
(2) Number of URLs.
(3) Number of mentioning labels (@).
(4) Number of hashtags (texts quoted by a pair of hash symbols "#").
(5) Number of reply labels ("回复@" + username).

Sentence Structure Features. Sentences in microblog messages have typical features (*sentence structure features*), including:

(6) Number of semicolons (;).
(7) Number of ideographic comma (、).
(8) Number of percent sign (%).
(9) Existence of continuous serial numbers (numbers in a sequence) (boolean).
(10) Number of decimal points.

These features are related to an objective message. For example, messages with many semicolons usually have parallelism sentences, which are less likely to be subjective. Similarly, numbers in a sequence are used to list items formally. The percent sign and decimal points usually appear in news texts that present data.

Sentiment Lexicon Features. Features from the sentiment lexicon are helpful to learn the sentiment of messages. First, from the *intermediate result* we get the words and their sentiment scores (positive and negative). For words modified by negations, their positive and negative scores are swapped. Then, compute the product and maximum of positive (negative) scores of words. The product reflects an accumulative influence of all the words in a message, while the maximum considers the word with the strongest sentiment strength. The *basic lexicon features* are listed below:

(11) Product of positive scores of all the words.
(12) Product of negative scores of all the words.
(13) The maximum of positive scores of all the words.
(14) The maximum of negative scores of all the words.

In addition, single-character words are more ambiguous than multi-character words; the differences between their positive and negative scores are less significant. So the features from single-character words are treated separately:

(15) Product of positive scores of single-character words.
(16) Product of negative scores of single-character words.

(17) The maximum of positive scores of single-character words.

(18) The maximum of negative scores of single-character words.

MDA words are more likely to have sentiments than ordinary words, thus we have the following *MDA features* to reflect their impacts:

(19) Product of positive scores of MDA words.

(20) Product of negative scores of MDA words.

(21) The maximum of positive scores of MDA words.

(22) The maximum of negative scores of MDA words.

Emoticon Features. During the construction process of the sentiment lexicon, emoticons and ordinary words are treated equally. However, emoticons are the special characteristics of microblog messages which are commonly used and have strong sentiments, so we extract *emoticon features* listed as follows:

(23) Product of positive scores of emoticons.

(24) Product of negative scores of emoticons.

(25) The maximum of positive scores of emoticons.

(26) The maximum of negative scores of emoticons.

4.2   Sentiment Classification Based on SVM

The sentiment polarities of microblog messages are classified into three classes: positive, negative and neutral. An SVM classifier is set up with the linear kernel and other default settings in the LibSVM library [3]. Three strategies of classification are introduced:

1. One-stage three-class classification: The sentiment of a message is directly classified into three classes.
2. Two-stage two-class classification (hierarchical): In the first stage, the sentiment is classified into neutral or non-neutral. In the second stage, the non-neutral messages are classified into positive or negative.
3. Two-stage two-class classification (parallel): In the first stage, the sentiment is classified into positive or non-positive. In the second stage, the same message is classified into negative or non-negative. The final sentiment class of the message is determined by:

$$\text{sentiment} = \begin{cases} positive & \text{first stage: } positive, \text{ second stage: } non\text{-}negative \\ negative & \text{first stage: } non\text{-}positive, \text{ second stage: } negative \\ neutral & \text{otherwise} \end{cases}$$

$$(4)$$

5   Experiments and Discussions

5.1   Dataset and Metrics for Sentiment Lexicons Evaluation

We first evaluate the performance of the sentiment lexicon. The golden standard is 467 positive words and 469 negative words from [18]. The error rate of a sentiment lexicon is defined as:

$$E = \frac{\sum\limits_{w \in POS\_E} freq(w) \cdot bias(w, NEG)) + \sum\limits_{w \in NEG\_E} freq(w) \cdot bias(w, POS)}{|NEG| \cdot \sum\limits_{w \in POS} freq(w) + |POS| \cdot \sum\limits_{w \in NEG} freq(w)}$$

(5)

Where $freq(w)$ is the frequency of word w in the corpus. POS and NEG are sets of labeled positive and negative words (golden standard). POS_E is the set of words who are in POS but have higher negative scores than their positive scores, and NEG_E similarly. $bias(w, NEG)$ means: For word $w \in POS\_E$, the number of words in NEG whose quotient of positive and negative score is larger than that of w. And $bias(w, POS)$ similarly. Obviously, $E \in [0, 1]$.

The sizes of POS_E and NEG_E are the number of misclassified words (a word is correctly classified if the difference between its positive and negative score is in accordance with its label). $freq(w)$ is the frequency of w; the larger it is, the more important w is to influence the sentiment. The $bias$ reflects the degree of errors for misclassified words. In all, this definition takes these three main factors into consideration. In addition, the scores of a labeled word who is not in the sentiment lexicon are both 0.5, and it is put into POS_E or NEG_E.

5.2   Sentiment Lexicons Evaluation

For the *sufficient corpus*, we separately collect one million and six million messages that contain the six emoticons mentioned before. The error rates are 0.0342 and 0.0158, respectively, both less than 5%.

For the *insufficient corpus*, we randomly collect one million messages, and fit them into the label propagation algorithm. With different iteration times and different α's, different lexicons are constructed. Their error rates are shown in Fig. 2. When the iteration times are two, the error rates of the lexicon are relatively low. One iteration only is not enough to propagate accurate scores, but excessive iterations make more noise. The figure also shows the lowest error rate is achieved when α is around 0.9. We can also see that after the number of iterations reaches 5, the error rate is very sensitive to α.

To examine the relationship between the accuracy of sentiment classification (the details of classification are introduced later) and the error rate, six points are chosen from Fig. 2: (1-5) Iteration times = 5 and $\alpha = 0.5, 0.8, 0.9, 0.95, 1$, where the error rate varies in a wide range, and (6) the point with the minimal error rate, iteration times = 2 and $\alpha = 0.9$. Besides, (7-8) points in the sufficient corpus with one million and six million messages. We perform sentiment classification based on the corresponding lexicons. The relationship between the accuracy of classification and the error rate of lexicons is shown in Fig. 3. As we can see from the figure, the accuracy and E have a significant negative correlation.

5.3   Dataset and Metrics for Sentiment Classification

The sampled data from the Conference on Natural Language Processing & Chinese Computing (NLP&CC) 2013 evaluation task two is used to evaluate

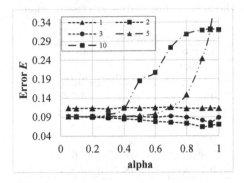

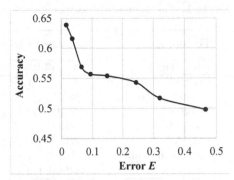

Fig. 2. Error rate of label propagation algorithm to the # of iterations and α

Fig. 3. The accuracy of classification to the error rate E of sentiment lexicons

the sentiment classification results. This task is a moods classification including anger, disgust, fear, happiness, like, sadness and surprise. To turn it into a three-class classification problem, messages of happiness or like are selected as the positive dataset, of disgust, anger or sadness as the negative set, and those with no labels as the neutral set. We sample the same number of messages in these three classes, and eventually get 968 messages in each class as the evaluation data. We use accuracy as the evaluation metric. That is, the number of correctly classified messages divided by the number of all messages.

5.4 Experiments on Sentiment Classification

To evaluate the effects of different groups of features, we divided all the 26 features into seven groups: *microblog structure features* (1–5), *sentence structure features* (6–10), *basic lexicon features* (11–18), *MDA features* (19–22), and *emoticon features* (23–26), and some overlapped groups: *maximum value features* (13, 14, 17, 18, 21, 22, 25, 26) and *product features* (11, 12, 15, 16, 19, 20, 23, 24). Table 1 shows the accuracy of the three-class classification with all features, as well as features with each group removed, in a 5-fold cross-validation.

Table 1 shows that among the three classification strategies, the direct one-stage three-class has the best performance. At the level of features, except for the *microblog structure features* in the third strategy that has a lower accuracy by 0.2%, all other feature groups contribute to the accuracy improvement in all the three strategies. Meanwhile, the *basic lexicon features* have the strongest influence on the performances; the *maximum value features* contribute much more than the *product features*, which indicates words with the highest sentiment strength affect the sentiment of messages more.

We also compared our method with two other methods. Method I had the same features, but the lexicon was replaced with human constructed one in [16]. Method II was that proposed in [10]. For method II, as the assumption about neutral corpora did not hold in Chinese microblog, we only computed the

Table 1. The influence of feature groups on the accuracy of sentiment classification

Feature group	One-stage three-class	Two-stage two-class	
		hierarchical	parallel
All features	**63.9%**	**60.1%**	61.0%
−microblog structure	62.3% (-1.6%)	58.2% (-1.9%)	**61.2% (+0.2%)**
−sentence structure	60.8% (-3.1%)	54.3% (-5.8%)	57.3% (-3.7%)
−emoticon	61.4% (-2.5%)	58.0% (-2.1%)	60.5% (-0.5%)
−basic lexicon	59.1% (-4.8%)	54.1% (-6.0%)	48.7% (-12.3%)
−MDA	63.7% (-0.2%)	59.7% (-0.4%)	60.7% (-0.3%)
−maximum value	61.3% (-2.6%)	57.8% (-2.3%)	57.4% (-3.6%)
−product	63.6% (-0.3%)	59.1% (-1.0%)	58.2% (-2.8%)

likelihood of positive and negative class, s and t, then classified the messages into neutral class when $\alpha < s - t < \beta$. We adjusted α and β to get the best accuracy in the evaluation data mentioned above. The accuracies of these methods are shown in table 2. We can see that both our lexicon and features performed very well in the evaluation.

Table 2. Comparison among the methods

Our method	Method I	Method II
63.9%	54.5%	56.1%

6 Conclusions and Future Work

In this paper, we present new methods for sentiment analysis on unlabeled Chinese microblog messages. We make use of the emoticons in Chinese microblogs and construct sentiment lexicons with the frequency statistics algorithm and the label propagation algorithm. Within different corpus, OOV words, commonly used phrases and negation words are handled at the same time. Based on the lexicons from sufficient or insufficient corpora, we extract lexicon features from microblog messages, along with structural features. These features are microblog-specific and are different from other domains. Then we perform sentiment classifications with an SVM classifier. Experimental results show that the lexicon features and other features are effective.

The main contributions of us are: First, we propose sentiment information labeling with selected emoticon evidence for sentiment lexicon construction without manual annotation, and many commonly used OOV words and phrases can be discovered and introduced into our lexicon. Second, every word has a potential sentiment, which is reflected by its positive and negative scores in the lexicon, and it is finer-grained than those only contain strong-sentiment words and those discretized to few levels. Third, we introduce different types of features which represent multi-views of microblog's characteristics.

Although our method does not necessarily need large amounts of neutral corpora, they may do help in improving the performance. In the future, we will take some effort to get neutral corpora for lexicon construction, thus adding a neutral score to each word. Some methods, such as taking the neutral outputs of current classifer can be attempted.

References

1. Barbosa, L., Feng, J.: Robust sentiment detection on twitter from biased and noisy data. In: Coling 2010: Posters, Beijing, China, pp. 36–44 (2010)
2. Bollen, J., Mao, H., Zeng, X.: Twitter mood predicts the stock market. Arxiv preprint arXiv:1010.3003 (2010)
3. Chang, C.C., Lin, C.J.: Libsvm: A library for support vector machines. ACM Trans. Intell. Syst. Technol. 2(3), 27:1–27:27 (2011)
4. Cui, A., Zhang, M., Liu, Y., Ma, S.: Emotion tokens: bridging the gap among multilingual twitter sentiment analysis. In: Proceedings of the 7th Asia Conference on Information Retrieval Technology, AIRS 2011, pp. 238–249 (2011)
5. Hu, M., Liu, B.: Mining and summarizing customer reviews. In: Proceedings of the 10th ACM SIGKDD Conference, pp. 168–177. ACM (2004)
6. Jansen, B.J., Zhang, M., Sobel, K., Chowdury, A.: Micro-blogging as online word of mouth branding. In: CHI 2009, pp. 3859–3864 (2009)
7. Kim, S.M., Hovy, E.: Determining the sentiment of opinions. In: Proceedings of the 20th COLING Conference, p. 1367. ACL (2004)
8. Liu, K.L., Li, W.J., Guo, M.: Emoticon smoothed language models for twitter sentiment analysis. In: 26th AAAI Conference on Artificial Intelligence (2012)
9. Neviarouskaya, A., Prendinger, H., Ishizuka, M.: Sentiful: A lexicon for sentiment analysis. IEEE Transactions on Affective Computing 2(1), 22–36 (2011)
10. Pak, A., Paroubek, P.: Twitter as a corpus for sentiment analysis and opinion mining. In: Proceedings of LREC, vol. 2010 (2010)
11. Pang, B., Lee, L.: Opinion mining and sentiment analysis. Foundations and Trends in Information Retrieval 2(1-2), 1–135 (2008)
12. Strapparava, C., Mihalcea, R.: Learning to identify emotions in text. In: Proceedings of the 2008 ACM Symposium on Applied Computing, pp. 1556–1560 (2008)
13. Tumasjan, A., Sprenger, T.O., Sandner, P.G., Welpe, I.M.: Predicting elections with twitter: What 140 characters reveal about political sentiment. In: Proceedings of the 4th AAAI Conference on Weblogs and Social Media, pp. 178–185 (2010)
14. Turney, P.D.: Thumbs up or thumbs down?: semantic orientation applied to unsupervised classification of reviews. In: ACL 2002, pp. 417–424 (2002)
15. Wang, H., Liu, C., Zheng, Y., Liu, J., Qu, P., Zou, C., Xu, R., Cheung, R.: Sentiment analysis of negative sentences and comparative sentences. In: The Fourth Chinese Opinion Analysis Evaluation, pp. 52–67 (2012)
16. Xu, L., Lin, H., Pan, Y., Ren, H., Chen, J.: Constructing the affective lexicon ontology. Journal of the China Society for Scientific and Technical Information 27(2), 180–185 (2008)
17. Zhang, H.: Nlpir chinese word segmentation system, http://ictclas.nlpir.org/
18. Zhang, W., Liu, J., Guo, X.: Positive and Negative Words Dictionary for Students. Encyclopedia of China Publishing House (2004)

Active Learning for Cross-Lingual Sentiment Classification

Shoushan Li[1,2], Rong Wang[1], Huanhuan Liu[1], and Chu-Ren Huang[2]

[1] Natural Language Processing Lab,
School of Computer Science and Technology, Soochow University, China
[2] CBS, The Hong Kong Polytechnic University, Hong Kong
{shoushan.li,wangrong2022,huanhuanliu.suda,
churenhuang}@gmail.com

Abstract. Cross-lingual sentiment classification aims to predict the sentiment orientation of a text in a language (named as the target language) with the help of the resources from another language (named as the source language). However, current cross-lingual performance is normally far away from satisfaction due to the huge difference in linguistic expression and social culture. In this paper, we suggest to perform active learning for cross-lingual sentiment classification, where only a small scale of samples are actively selected and manually annotated to achieve reasonable performance in a short time for the target language. The challenge therein is that there are normally much more labeled samples in the source language than those in the target language. This makes the small amount of labeled samples from the target language flooded in the aboundance of labeled samples from the source language, which largely reduces their impact on cross-lingual sentiment classification. To address this issue, we propose a data quality controlling approach in the source language to select high-quality samples from the source language. Specifically, we propose two kinds of data quality measurements, intra- and extra-quality measurements, from the certainty and similarity perspectives. Empirical studies verify the appropriateness of our active learning approach to cross-lingual sentiment classification.

1 Introduction

Sentiment classification is a task of predicting the sentimental orientation (e.g., positive or negative) for a certain text (Pang et al., 2002; Turney, 2002). This task has drawn much attention in the natural language processing (NLP) community due to its wide applications (Pang and Lee 2008; Liu, 2012). Up to now, extensive studies have been conducted on this task and various kinds of resources are available, such as polarity lexicons and labeled corpora. However, these resources are rather imbalanced across different languages. For example, due to dominant studies on English sentiment classification, the labeled data in English is often in a large scale while the labeled data in some other languages is much limited. This motives the research on cross-lingual sentiment classification, which aims to perform sentiment classification

G. Zhou et al. (Eds.): NLPCC 2013, CCIS 400, pp. 236–246, 2013.
© Springer-Verlag Berlin Heidelberg 2013

in a resource-scarce language (named as the target language) with the help of labeled data from another resource-rich language (named as the source language). Representative studies include Wan (2008, 2009), Wei and Pal (2010), Lu et al. (2011), and Meng et al. (2012).

Although existing studies have yielded certain progress in cross-lingual sentiment classification, the classification performance of only using the labeled data in the source language remains far away from satisfaction due to the huge difference in linguistic expression and social culture. For example, in Wan (2009) where English is considered as the source language and Chinese is considered as the target language, only using the labeled data from English yields the performance of around 0.75 in accuracy which is much lower than 0.92 that achieved by using 1000 labeled samples from the target language (Chinese). Even when the unlabeled data from the target language is employed via co-training, the obtained performance can be only improved to around 0.82 in accuracy (Wan, 2009).

One possible solution to handle this dilemma is to deploy active learning, where a small scale of samples (called newly-added data) are actively selected and manually annotated to quickly improve the classification performance for the target language. However, one challenge in active learning-based cross-lingual sentiment classification lies in the much imbalanced labeled data from the source and target languages. For example, in Wan (2009), the labeled samples in the source language can be around 8000 while the labeled samples in the target language are generally as less as 200, a reasonable number one can expected to be manually annotated in a fast deploying application. Such huge imbalance in the labeled data easily floods the small amount of the labeled target data in the abundance of labeled source data and largely reduces the contribution of the labeled data in the target language.

In this paper, we address above challenge by proposing a data quality controlling approach to select high-quality samples in the source language instead of using all the samples. Consequently, the data imbalance can be much reduced when only a small partition of labeled samples in the source language is employed. We believe that using a partition of them could be as useful as (or even possibly better than) using all of them for cross-lingual sentiment classification. For example, consider following three reviews from the product-review corpora, introduced in Blitzer et al. (2007):

E1: *This book is not worth wasting your money on. To the novice, this book may appear to represent the art of cabales serrada escrima, but it does not. More than half of the book is unrelated to the system of serrada. ......*

E2: *This fourth installment of becky's trying tribulations is the worst. I don't understand how kinsella's editor didn't draw the line (and the red pencil) at the litany of shopping expeditions. I am not making this up. ......*

E3: *This is one of the worst books ever, it is not worth wasting your money on. Don't buy it.*

While **E1** has a strong sentimental expression of *"not worth wasting"* and **E2** has another strong sentimental expression of *"the worst"*, **E3** has both of them. Therefore, once **E3** is selected, we can safely throw away **E1** and **E2**.

Accordingly, we propose a certainty-based quality measurement, together with cross-validation to select high-quality samples in the source language. Besides, we propose a similarity measurement to select the samples in the source language that are similar to those in the target language. In this paper, we call the former the intra-quality measurement because it only employs the data in the source language to measure the quality of the samples in the source language, and the latter the extra-quality measurement due to the consideration of the samples in the target language. For a particular data in the target language, these two kinds of measurements are integrated to select high-quality samples in the source language. After obtaining the high-quality samples in the source language, we employ standard uncertainty sampling for active learning-based cross-lingual sentiment classification.

The remainder of this paper is organized as follows. Section 2 overviews the related work on cross-lingual sentiment classification. Section 3 presents our approach to data quality controlling. Section 4 applies the data quality controlling to active learning-based cross-lingual sentiment classification. Section 5 evaluates the proposed approaches. Finally, Section 6 gives the conclusion and future work.

2   Related Work

Although sentiment classification have been extensively studied in the last decade (Pang et al., 2002; Turney, 2002), cross-lingual sentiment classification only merges in recent years (Wan, 2008; Wan 2009; Pan et al., 2011; Prettenhofer and Stein, 2011; Lu et al., 2011; Meng et al., 2012).

Wan (2008) proposes an ensemble method to combine one classifier trained with labeled data from the source language and another classifier trained with their translated data. Subsequently, Wan (2009) incorporates the unlabeled data in the target language with co-training to improve the classification performance.

Wei and Pal (2010) regard cross-lingual sentiment classification as a domain adaptation task and apply a structural correspondence learning approach (SCL) to tackle this problem. Their approach is shown to more effective than the co-training algorithm.

More recently, Lu et al. (2011) perform cross-lingual sentiment classification from a different perspective. Instead of using machine translation engines, they use a parallel corpus to help perform semi-supervised learning in both English and Chinese sentence-level sentiment classification.

Unlike all of them, this study suggests to use only those high-quality samples instead of all of them to perform cross-lingual sentiment classification. As a result, the data imbalance between the labeled data in the source and target languages can be largely reduced. This largely eliminates obstacles towards active learning to cross-lingual sentiment classification. To the best of our knowledge, this is the first attempt to consider data quality, active learning and integrate them in cross-lingual sentiment classification.

3   Data Quality Controlling in the Source Language

Let X_S be the set of the labeled samples in the source language and X_T the set of the unlabeled samples (testing data) in the target language. The objective of cross-lingual sentiment classification is to estimate a hypothesis h: $X_S \rightarrow C$ which classifies the samples in X_T into C, the predefined set of class labels, i.e., *negative* and *positive*.

In contrast to traditional sentiment classification, where the training and testing data are from the same language, it is not possible to directly train a hypothesis h: $X_S \rightarrow C$ to classify X_T because the training and test samples have different feature spaces due to the language difference. Therefore, the feature spaces for the training and test data need to be unified. One common way to achieve this is to translate the samples in the source (or target) language into the target (or source) language. Let X_S^t be the set of the translated samples in the source language and X_T^t the set of the translated samples in the target language. Then, the objective of cross-lingual sentiment classification is changed into estimating the hypothesis h: $X_S^t \rightarrow C$ which classifies the samples in X_T or the hypothesis h: $X_S \rightarrow C$ which classifies the samples in X_T^t. For simplicity, in the following, we only focus on the solution of translating the labeled data in the source language into the target language. Note that our research is certainly suitable for the case of translating the test data in the target language into the source language.

As stated in Introduction, the task of data quality controlling in cross-lingual sentiment classification is first to measure the quality of the samples in X_S^t and then select a subset of X_S^t (i.e. those high-quality samples, denoted as X_{S-sub}^t) to train a classifier rather than using all the labeled samples in the source language. In the following, we describe two measurements to evaluate the quality of a translated sample in the source language.

3.1   Intra-quality Measurement with Certainty and Cross-validation

The quality measurement that measured only through the resource from the source language is called intra-quality measurement.

To obtain a high-quality sample that representing some other samples, we first split the labeled data from the source language into two different parts. One is severed as the training data and the other is severed as the validation data. Then, we use the training data to train a classifier which is used to predict the samples in the validation data. After the prediction process, all posterior possibilities of the validation samples are provided and we assume that the samples with high posterior possibilities are capable of representing the classification knowledge in the training data. Formally, the certainty measurement is employed to rank the validation samples, which is defined as follows:

$$Cer(x) = \max_{y \in \{pos, neg\}} P(y \mid x) \tag{1}$$

Where x is a sample in the validation data and $P(y \mid x)$ is its posterior possibility estimated by the classifier trained with the training data.

To represent all the data in the source language, the cross-validation strategy is applied (Kohavi, 1995). In k-fold cross-validation, X_S^t is randomly partitioned into k equal size subsamples. Of the k subsamples, a single subsample is used as the validation data, and the remaining $k - 1$ subsamples are used as the training data. The cross-validation process is then repeated k times (the *folds*). In this way, each of the k subsamples used exactly once as the validation data to find the high quality samples.

3.2   Extra-Quality Measurement with Similarity

Instinctively, the quality of the samples in the source language is also related to the testing samples in the target language. We name the quality measurement measured with the resource from the target language as the extra-quality measurement. In this study, the samples with higher similarity to the target language are thought to be of higher quality.

Suppose the labeled data in the source language contains n samples, i.e., $X_S^t = (x_{S1}, x_{S2}, ..., x_{Sn})$ and the testing data in the target language contains m samples, i.e., $X_T = (x_{T1}, x_{T2}, ..., x_{Tm})$. The similarity between one sample x_{Si} in the source language and the target language is defined as following:

$$SIM(x_{Si}, X_T) = \frac{1}{m} \sum_{j=1}^{m} sim(x_{Si}, x_{Tj}) \tag{2}$$

Where $sim(x_{Si}, x_{Tj})$ is the similarity between the sample x_{Si} and x_{Tj}. In this study, the standard cosine method is applied to compute the similarity between two samples.

3.3   Integrating   Intra- and Extra-Quality Measurements

One straightforward way to integrate the two quality measurements is to linearly combine the certainty and similarity scores. However, in fact, the similarity measurement, as the extra-quality measurement in this study, is not a good way to select high-quality samples. In contrast, it performs even worse than the random selection strategy. This is mainly because the similarity measurement does not take the sentimental information into account and thus the selected samples are not useful for sentiment classification.

Input:

 Translated training data from the source language X_S^t

 Testing data from the target language X_T

Output:

 The selected data set X_{S-sub}^t

Procedure:

(1) Initialize the selected data set: $X_{S-sub}^t = \varnothing$

(2) Compute the similarity between each sample in X_S^t and X_T with formula (2)

(3) Repeat until the predefined stop criterion is met

 a) Perform k-fold cross-validation in X_S^t

 b) Rank the samples in each validation data sets according to their certainty values computed with formula (1).

 c) Select top-N certainty samples that take the higher similarities to X_T than σ in each validation data, which is denoted as $X_l^{Cer}\,(l = 1, 2, ..., k)$

 d) $X_{S-sub}^t = X_{S-sub}^t + \sum_{l=1}^{k} X_l^{Cer}$

 e) $X_S^t = X_S^t - \sum_{l=1}^{k} X_l^{Cer}$

Fig. 1. Algorithm of data quality controlling in the source language

Therefore, we consider the certainty measurement as the main ranking factor and leave the similarity measurement as a supplementary one when designing the way to integrate them. Specifically, we select high-certainty samples that take the similarities to the target language higher than a threshold σ. In this way, only the samples that are similar to the source language are possibly be selected as the high-quality candidates.

Our algorithm of data quality controlling in the source language is shown in Figure 1. This algorithm integrates the intra- and extra-quality measurements in the steps of b) and c) respectively.

4 Active Learning-Based Cross-Lingual Sentiment Classification

As mentioned in Introduction, the performance of cross-lingual sentiment classification usually remains very limited and unsatisfactory. To quickly improve the performance, a small amount of informative samples in the target language are encouraged to be annotated and leveraged. This is a typical active learning task.

Input:
>   Translated training data from the source language X_S^t
>   Unlabeled data U_T
>   Testing data from the target language X_T

Output:
>   The classifier for cross-lingual sentiment classification

Procedure:

(1) Obtain the high-quality data set X_{S-sub}^t from X_S^t

(2) Initialize the labeled data $L_T = X_{S-sub}^t$

(3) Loop for M iterations

  a) Learn a classifier using L_T

  b) Use the current classifier to label all samples in U_T

  c) Use the uncertainty measurement to select n most uncertainty samples for manual annotation

  d) Move the newly-annotated sample from U_T to L_T

(4) Learn the classifier with L_T for cross-lingual sentiment classification

---

Fig. 2. Algorithm of active learning for cross-lingual sentiment classification

However, different from traditional active learning-based sentiment classification, the initial labeled data in active learning-based cross-lingual sentiment classification is from a different language and in a large amount. This makes the small amount of informative samples in the target language submersed and thus difficult to well affect the classification decision.

Our solution to the above challenge is to use only those high-quality samples from the source language as the initial labeled data instead of using all the data. Then, the standard uncertainty sampling method is employed to add the informative samples from the target language for manual annotation, with the uncertainty measurement defined as follows:

$$Uncer(x) = \min_{y \in \{pos, neg\}} P(y \mid x) \tag{3}$$

Figure 2 illustrates the detailed algorithm.

5   Experimentation

5.1   Experimental Settings

Labeled Data in the Source Language: The labeled data from the source language contains English reviews from four domains: Book (B), DVD (D), Electronics (E) and

Kitchen (K)[1] (Blitzer et al., 2007). Each domain contains 1000 positive and 1000 negative reviews. All together, 8000 labeled samples are available in the source language. All these labeled samples are translated into Chinese ones with *Google Translate*[2].

Testing Data in the Target Language: The testing data from the target language contains Chinese reviews from two domains. they are from the data collection by Wan (2011): Chinese reviews from IT168 (451 positive and 435 negative reviews) and Chinese reviews from 360BUY (560 positive and 370 negative reviews)[3], together with 2000 unlabeled reviews.

Unlabeled Data in the Target Language: We manually annotate the unlabeled reviews collected by Wan (2011) and select 500 positive and 500 negative as the unlabeled samples for active learning.

Feature Space: Each review text is treated as a bag-of-words and transformed into binary vectors encoding the presence or absence of word unigrams.

Classification Algorithm: The maximum entropy (ME) classifier implemented with the public tool, Mallet Toolkits[4] is employed in all our experiments. The posterior probabilities belonging to the categories are also provided in this tool.

5.2   Experimental Results on Active Learning-Based Cross-Lingual Sentiment Classification

In this section, we compare following approaches to active learning in cross-lingual sentiment classification.

Random+No_source: Perform active learning in the target language by randomly selecting samples in the target language and no samples in the source language are used. We perform 5 runs of such approaches and report the average results.

Uncertainty+No_source: Perform active learning in the target language with the uncertainty selection strategy and no samples in the source language are used. 20 samples are randomly selected as the initial labeled data.

Uncertainty+All_source: Perform active learning in the target language with the uncertainty selection strategy. All the translated samples in the source language are served as the initial labeled data.

Uncertainty+Selected_source: Perform active learning in the target language with the uncertainty selection strategy. 500 high-quality translated samples selected by our quality controlling approach in the source language are served as the initial labeled data. In the implementation of sample selecting in the source domain, the fold number is set to 10 ($k=10$) and top 10 certainty samples are selected in each validation data ($N=10$). As for the parameter of σ, we set it to 0.27, 0.14 in the domains of IT168 and 360BUY respectively. These values are referred to the average similarity between each sample and all the other samples in the target language.

---

[1] http://www.seas.upenn.edu/~mdredze/datasets/sentiment/
[2] http://translate.google.com/translate_t
[3] http:// google.com/site/wanxiaojun1979/
[4] http://mallet.cs.umass.edu/

Table 1. The classification performance by using all 8000 samples in the source domain

Domain	IT168	360BUY
Accuracy	0.756	0.754

Table 1 shows the classification performance by using all the samples in the source domain. From the results, we can see that only using the labeled samples (even the scale of data is big) from the target domain, the obtained performances are very limited (less than 0.8 in both domains).

Figure 3 shows the performances of different active learning approaches for cross-lingual sentiment classification. From this figure, we can see that:

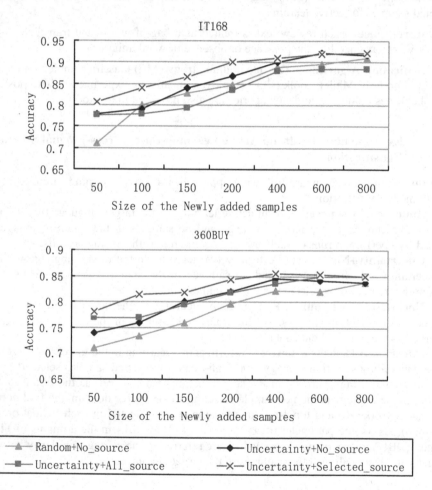

Fig. 3. Performances of different approaches to active learning-based cross-lingual sentiment classification

Employing labeled samples from the target language is indeed effective for sentiment classification in the target language. For example, as shown in Table 1, using all 8000 samples from the source language yields the accuracy of 0.756 in IT168. In contrast, as shown in Figure 4, using only 100 randomly-selected samples from the target language could yield a higher accuracy, i.e., 0.8.

Uncertainty+No_source generally performs better than **Uncertainty+All_source** when the labeled samples in the target language are more than 100. This result demonstrates that the labeled samples in the source language become unhelpful when a certainty number of labeled data in the target language is available.

Uncertainty+Selected_source performs best. The high quality samples, together with only 100-200 samples, achieve a comparable performance to that of using more than 800 samples in the target language. This result verifies the necessity of data quality controlling in the source language when performing active learning in cross-lingual sentiment classification.

6   Conclusion

In this paper, we propose an active learning approach for cross-lingual sentiment classification and address the huge challenge of the data imbalance by controlling data quality in the source language. Specifically, we design a certainty measurement, together with a similarity measurement, to select high quality samples in the source language. Experimentation verifies the appropriateness of active learning for cross-lingual sentiment classification. Specifically, the results show that with the selected samples in the source language, manually annotating only 100-200 samples in the target language can achieve a comparable performance to that of using more than 800 samples only in the target language.

Acknowledgments. This research work has been partially supported by two NSFC grants, No.61003155, and No.61273320, one National High-tech Research and Development Program of China No.2012AA011102, one General Research Fund (GRF) sponsored by the Research Grants Council of Hong Kong No.543810.

References

1. Balahur, A., Turchi, M.: Multilingual Sentiment Analysis using Machine Translation? In: Proceedings of the 3rd Workshop on Computational Approaches to Subjectivity and Sentiment Analysis, pp. 52–60 (2012)
2. Blitzer, J., Dredze, M., Pereira, F.: Biographies, Bollywood, Boom-boxes and Blenders: Domain Adaptation for Sentiment Classification. In: Proceedings of ACL 2007, pp. 440–447 (2007)
3. Boyd-Graber, J., Resnik, P.: Holistic Sentiment Analysis across Languages Multilingual Supervised Latent Dirichlet Allocation. In: Proceedings of ACL 2010, pp. 45–55 (2010)
4. Kohavi, R.: A Study of Cross-validation and Bootstrp for Accuracy Estimation and Model Selection. In: Proceedings of IJCAI, pp. 1137–1143 (1995)

5. Liu, B.: Sentiment Analysis and Opinion Mining (Introduction and Survey). Morgan & Claypool Publishers (May 2012)
6. Lu, B., Tan, C., Cardie, C., Tsou, B.: Joint Bilingual Sentiment Classification with Unlabeled Parallel Corpora. In: Proceedings of ACL 2011, pp. 320–330 (2011)
7. Pang, B., Lee, L.: Opinion Mining and Sentiment Analysis: Foundations and Trends. Information Retrieval 2(12), 1–135 (2008)
8. Pang, B., Lee, L., Vaithyanathan, S.: Thumbs up? Sentiment Classification using Machine Learning Techniques. In: Proceedings of EMNLP 2002, pp. 79–86 (2002)
9. Prettenhofer, P., Stein, B.: Cross Language Text Classification Using Structural Correspondence Learning. In: Proceedings of ACL 2010, pp. 1118–1127 (2010)
10. Turney, P.: Thumbs up or Thumbs down? Semantic Orientation Applied to Unsupervised Classification of reviews. In: Proceedings of ACL 2002, pp. 417–424 (2002)
11. Wan, X.: Using Bilingual Knowledge and Ensemble Techniques for Unsupervised Chinese Sentiment Analysis. In: Proceedings of ACL 2008, pp. 553–561 (2008)
12. Wan, X.: Co-Training for Cross-Lingual Sentiment Classification. In: Proceedings of ACL 2009, pp. 235–243 (2009)
13. Wan, X.: Bilingual Co-Training for Sentiment Classification of Chinese Product Reviews. Computational Linguistics 37, 587–616 (2011)
14. Wei, B., Pal, C.: Cross Lingual Adaptation An Experiment on Sentiment Classifications. In: Proceedings of ACL 2010, pp. 258–262 (2010)

Expanding User Features with Social Relationships in Social Recommender Systems

Chengjie Sun, Lei Lin, Yuan Chen, and Bingquan Liu

School of Computer Science and Technology, Harbin Institute of Technology, Harbin, China
{cjsun,linl,ychen,liubq}@insun.hit.edu.cn

Abstract. Although recommender system has been studied for many years, the research of social recommender system is just beginning. Plenty of information can be used in social networks to improve the performance of recommender system. However, some information is very sparse when used as features. We call this feature sparsity problem. In this paper, we aimed at solving feature sparsity problem. A new strategy was proposed to expand user features by social relationships. Experiments on two real world datasets demonstrated that our method can significantly improve the recommendation performance.

Keywords: social recommender system, feature expanding, social relationships, feature sparsity.

1   Introduction

With the rapid development of the Internet, social networking services such as Twitter, Facebook, Last.fm and Tencent Weibo become more and more popular, even become an important part of many people's daily life. There are thousands of new users joining in these social networks and huge amount of information being generated from there. For example, there are more than 200 million registered users currently and 40 million messages being generated each day on Tencent Weibo [1]. People make friends, get information, and express their views on social network day and night. While benefiting us a lot, it also wastes us too much time to search useful information from massive information. So how to choose good information sources is very important for users in social networks. In different social networks, information sources are different, such as users in microblog, artists in music online system and sellers in e-commerce website. There are many ways to choose information sources, like getting from friend's recommendation or using search engine. But getting from friend's recommendation is inefficient and sometimes it is hard to express the requirements by a few keywords for many users when using search engine in social networks. Therefore, to deal with the problem of choosing information sources efficiently, it is important to develop effective social recommender system to help users easily find the potential items they want to follow.

Social recommender system is the kind of recommender system whose target domain is social media. Although all kinds of recommender systems' common goal is modeling the relation between users and items, social recommender system has much

G. Zhou et al. (Eds.): NLPCC 2013, CCIS 400, pp. 247–254, 2013.
© Springer-Verlag Berlin Heidelberg 2013

more social information to use than traditional recommender system such as e-commerce recommender system and music recommender system. Social information includes social relationships, user's profile, user's social action and so on. How to take advantage of these information to improve the performance of social recommender system is both a good way and a big challenge. In this paper, we concentrate on exploring the methods of combining social relationships into recommendation algorithm to improve the performance of social recommender system.

The rest of this paper is organized as follows. Section 2 will introduce the background and related works of our research. Section 3 will discuss the methods of modeling social relationships with recommendation algorithm. In section 4, we will present our experiments and results on two real world datasets. Then we will make our conclusion in section 5.

2   Related Work

We will review the related works of social recommender system from two aspects: the popular methods of recommender system and the research of social recommendation.

The goal of recommender system is suggesting users with items which may fit the users' tastes. Recommendation methods can be classified into the following three categories: content-based, collaborative filtering (CF), and hybrid recommendation approaches [2]. Recently, as one of the most successful methods, CF has been widely used in business and deeply studied in academia. CF is a kind of algorithm whose fundamental assumption is that if user A and user B rate k items similarly, they share similar tastes, and hence will rate other items similarly. Approaches differ in how they define a "rating", how they define k, and how they define "similarly" [3]. One of the major factors which limit the performance of CF is data sparsity. In real commercial recommender system, the data density is often lower than 1% [4]. To deal with the data sparsity challenge, many algorithms of CF have been proposed by recent years, such as Singular Value Decomposition (SVD) [5] and SVD++ [6]. SVD is a method of matrix factorization which can reduce the dimension of rating matrix. As a result, it represents the original rating matrix information by several latent factors with lower dimension and higher data density. However, this is at the cost of information loss. SVD++ is an extension of SVD, which can handle external information of rating matrix to improve the performance.

Social recommendation aims at forming a recommender system by using recommendation methods with information from social networks such as user profile, user action, and social relationships [7]. User recommendation in social networks has become one of the hottest topics [8]. The task of KDD Cup 2012 Track1 is to develop such a system aiming at recommending items (celebrities) which could be persons, organizations, or groups in Tencent Weibo. In [9-11], researchers have tried to improve the recommender system's performance by sufficiently making use of social information, such as the items user followed in the past, user age and gender, user's click rate and so on. For another task, artist recommendation in Last.fm online music system, [12] proposes a novel hierarchical Bayesian model which jointly incorporates topic modeling and probabilistic matrix factorization of social networks. However, in the above situations, researchers have not taken full use of one important kind of information in social networks, the social relationships among users. In our paper, we will present how to utilize social relationships to expand user features to improve the performance of social recommender system.

3   Methods

3.1   Latent Factor Model

Recently, latent factor models have been widely used in rating prediction problem. The main idea of latent factor model is to predict a rating $\tilde{r}_{u,i}$ by the dot product of a user latent factor p_u and an item latent factor q_i which can be learned from history rating matrix. Singular Value Decomposition (SVD) is one of the most popular latent factor models. The basic SVD model with user bias, item bias and global bias can be described in the following equation:

$$\tilde{r}_{u,i} = p_u^T \cdot q_i + b_u + b_i + b_g \tag{1}$$

Here b_g is the global bias, b_u is the user bias, b_i is the item bias, p_u is the user latent factor and q_i is the item latent factor. Instead of L2 loss function, we choose pairwise loss function in this work. So the above parameters can be trained by minimizing the following cost function:

$$\min \sum_{\substack{<u,k,h> \\ \in D}} \ln(1+e^{-(\tilde{y}_{u,k}-\tilde{y}_{u,h})}) + \lambda_1 \parallel p_u \parallel^2 + \lambda_2 \parallel q_i \parallel^2 + \lambda_3 \parallel b_u \parallel^2 + \lambda_4 \parallel b_i \parallel^2 + \lambda_5 \parallel b_g \parallel^2 \tag{2}$$

Here D is the set all $\langle u,k,h \rangle$ pairs in training set, k is item u gives positive review and h is item u gives negative review. In the equation, the first term is used to learn the best parameters, the other terms are regularizations with constants to avoid overfitting.

Stochastic Gradient Descent algorithm (SGD) [5] is an efficient and popular strategy to solve the above optimization problem. The main idea of SGD is to minimize the error by taking a small step on parameters along the direction of gradient descent in each loop. SGD uses the following update rules to learn the model parameters:

$$p_u \leftarrow p_u + \eta(e_{ui}p_u - \lambda_1 p_u) \tag{3}$$

$$q_i \leftarrow q_i + \eta(e_{ui}q_i - \lambda_2 q_i) \tag{4}$$

$$b_u \leftarrow b_u + \eta(e_{ui}b_u - \lambda_3 b_u) \tag{5}$$

$$b_i \leftarrow b_i + \eta(e_{ui}b_i - \lambda_4 b_i) \tag{6}$$

$$b_g \leftarrow b_g + \eta(e_{ui}b_g - \lambda_5 b_g) \tag{7}$$

Here e_{ui} is the prediction error and η is the learning rate.

3.2   Incorporate Implicit Feedback Information as Features

The basic SVD model is good at handling simple dataset which only includes rating matrix information. However, the datasets are usually much more complicated for building recommender system in the real world. For example, in a movie recommender system, except for the rating matrix information, there are many other kinds of information which may include movie tags, movie category, user profile, user social network and so on. These information can be called implicit feedback information [5]. How to utilize these diverse implicit feedback information is beyond the ability of SVD, while SVD++ can do it well by modeling them as latent features. The only thing has to be done is extending the SVD equation to the following form:

$$\tilde{r}_{u,i} = (p_u^T + \sum_{j \in N(u)} \alpha_j y_j) \cdot q_i + b_u + b_i + b_g \tag{8}$$

The adding sum term represents the perspective of implicit feedback. $N(u)$ can be user's neighbors, tags or other implicit feedbacks. y_j is the latent factor and α_j is its weight.

3.3   Expand Features with Social Relationships

Social relationships are not usually used in the same way as other information such as tags and profiles which are used via a factorization process, while social relationships are used via a regularization process [13]. Using social relationships as factorization has been proved to be effective, but to my best knowledge this has just been used in the basic SVD model and the social network is not sufficient enough. This is probably because in SVD++ model or in big social network there are too many latent factor parameters to learn with social regularization. So how to use social relationships of big social network in SVD++ model is a still a big challenge.

    We find that it is easy to add features in SVD++ model, while it is hard to model social relationships as features directly. Therefore we need to find a compromise way. The main idea is that we can expand some user features by using social relationships. From the social network, we can get user u 's friends set $F(u)$. For each friend i in $F(u)$, we can get the same kind of feature z_i as u 's feature and β_i is its weight. We call the friends' features as expanding features. The equation of user latent factor in SVD++ with the expanding features can be described as following:

$$p_u \leftarrow p_u^T + \sum_{j \in N(u)} \alpha_j y_j + \sum_{i \in F(u)} \beta_i z_i \tag{9}$$

    For example, in the friend recommendation problem of social media, some user information such as user's tags, keywords and history following records are very sparse which will lead to the features being ineffective. Using social relationships can deal with the feature sparsity problem to some extent. We can use friends' tags, keywords and history following records as a kind of expanding features.

4   Experiments

4.1   Data Description

We conducted our experiments on two real world datasets. The first one is a subset of dataset of Track 1 in KDD Cup 2012 [1] provided by Tecent Weibo which is one of the two biggest microblog platforms in China. The dataset is a snapshot of Tencent Weibo of five days. We used the first three days records as training set and next two days records as testing set. Except training set and testing set, there are lots of other information including user profile, keywords, item categories, social action and social graph. This is a friend recommendation problem. The items in the dataset are a small group of specific users which can be celebrities, famous organizations or some well-known groups. Another dataset is hetrec2011-lastfm-2k [14] obtained from Last.fm online music system. There are listening histories, tagging histories and friend relationships in the dataset. The items in the dataset are artists. So this is an artist recommendation problem. We prepared training set and testing set by dividing listening histories into 9 to 1. Because there are only positive records, we produced 20 negative records by randomly selecting 20 artists whom have not been listened to for each positive record. Table 1 shows the statistical properties of the datasets.

Table 1. Statistical properties of the datasets

Element	Size (Tencent Weibo)	Size (Last.fm)
Training set	7,105,220	1,554,819
Testing set	4,265,397	392,910
Users	266,615	1892
Items	6,095	17,632
Edges of social group	50,655,143	25,434

4.2   Evaluation Metrics

We used the MAP@n (Mean Average Precision of Top N) and recall@n for two datasets respectively as our evaluation metrics which are the same as the metric used in the competition and other researchers. The metric is defined as:

$$ap @ n = \sum_{k=1}^{n} P(k) / m \tag{10}$$

$$MAP @ n = \sum_{i=1}^{N} ap @ n_i / N \tag{11}$$

$$recall @ n = \frac{number\ of\ items\ the\ user\ likes\ in\ Top\ n\ recommendations}{total\ number\ of\ items\ the\ user\ likes} \tag{12}$$

where $P(k)$ is the precision at cut-off k in the recommender item list, m is the number of items clicked by the user and N is the number of users.

4.3   Experiment Description

For Tencent Weibo dataset, we conducted our experiments on four user features: follow histories, tags, keywords and actions. Follow histories refer to items one user has followed. Tags are a few keywords from user's profile added by himself or herself. The number of tags is less than ten and usually three to eight. Keywords are selected from user's tweets whose number is more than that of tags and usually twenty to fifty. Actions mean the number of comments, at, retweets from a user to another user.

The definition of friends is different with environments. In Tencent Weibo dataset, the social network is directed. There are three kinds of relationships between two users: follow, be followed, and follow each other. We just used the follow relationship because it is the result of active action which is more representative of one user's interests. So friends in our experiments on Tencent Weibo dataset mean other users followed by the user.

For Last.fm dataset, we conducted our experiments on the feature of tags. There is a little different from tag feature in Tencent Weibo dataset. Tag features in Last.fm dataset are tags a user has made for artists. It is also a kind of implicit feedback information representing user's tastes.

There are many friends for some users and each friend has several features, so this will lead to too many expanding features for a user. For example, a user has 100 friends and each friend has 5 tags. The total number of the user's friends' tags is 500, which is too large to use. Therefore, we need a selection strategy. In our experiments, we chose k most common ones of user's friends' features. The weight of each feature is its count in friends' features after normalization. We tried both k=30 and k=20 and different weight strategies, but experiment results indicated that there were not much differences. So k is set to 30 in the following reported results. The SVDFeature toolkit [15] was used in our experiments.

4.4   Results and Analysis

Table 2 and Table 3 showed the results of our experiments on Tencent Weibo dataset and Last.fm dataset. We can see that all of the expanding features can achieve improvement when used independently or in combination. Except follow history in Tencent Weibo dataset, other expanding features in both datasets were even more useful than the original features. This is because the original features of tags, keywords, actions are every sparse while the expanding features are denser.

Table 2. Improvement on MAP@3 in Tencent Weibo Dataset

Feature	Model	MAP@3
	SVD	0.3595
follow history	SVD + follow history	0.3714
	SVD + friends' follow history	0.3677
	SVD + follow history + friends' follow history	0.3743
tags	SVD + user tags	0.3609
	SVD + friends' tags	0.3629
	SVD + user tags + friends' tags	0.3669
keywords	SVD + user keywords	0.3653
	SVD + friends' keywords	0.3705
	SVD + user keywords + friends' keywords	0.3770
action	SVD + user action	0.3644
	SVD + friends' retweet	0.3676
	SVD + user action + friends' retweet	0.3712
follow history + tags + keywords + action	SVD + follow history + user tags + user keywords + user action	0.3823
	SVD + friends' follow history + friends' tags + friends' keywords + friends' retweet	0.3754
	SVD + follow history + friends' follow history + user tags + friends' tags + user keywords + friends' keywords + user action + friends' retweet	0.3853

Table 3. Improvement on recall@n in Last.fm Dataset

Model + Feature	recall@50	recall@100	recall@150	recall@200	recall@250
SVD	14.91%	22.45%	27.99%	34.31%	38.65%
SVD + user tags	15.93%	25.87%	31.87%	40.46%	44.43%
SVD + friends' tags	17.23%	25.97%	33.11%	43.14%	47.84%
SVD + user tags + friends' tags	21.22%	29.67%	36.03%	43.23%	48.25%

5   Conclusion

In this paper, we explored a new way of using social relationships by expanding user features in social recommender systems. We trained SVD++ model on Tencent Weibo and Last.fm datasets. Experiment results showed that expanding features by social relationships can improve the performance of recommender system efficiently which indicated that it can help to solve features' sparsity problem.

Acknowledgments. We thank three anonymous reviewers for their helpful comments on an earlier version of this work. This work is supported by the National Natural Science Foundation of China (61100094, 61300114) and Research Fund for the Doctoral Program of Higher Education of China (20102302120053).

References

1. Niu, Y., Wang, Y., Sun, G., Yue, A., Dalessandro, B., Perlich, C., Hamner, B.: The tencent dataset and kdd-cup'12. In: KDD-Cup Workshop 2012 (2012)
2. Adomavicius, G., Tuzhilin, A.: Toward the next generation of recommender systems: A survey of the state-of-the-art and possible extensions. IEEE Transactions on Knowledge and Data Engineering 17(6), 734–749 (2005)
3. Goldberg, K., Roeder, T., Gupta, D., Perkins, C.: Eigentaste: A Constant-Time Collaborative Filtering Algorithm. Information Retrieval 4(2), 133–151 (2001)
4. Sarwar, B., Karypis, G., Konstan, J.A., Riedl, J.: Item-Based Collaborative Filtering Recommendation Algorithms. In: Proceedings of the 10th International Conference on World Wide Web, Hong Kong, pp. 285–295. ACM Press, New York (2001)
5. Koren, Y., Bell, R.M., Volinsky, C.: Matrix factorization techniques for recommender systems. IEEE Computer 42(8), 30–37 (2009)
6. Koren, Y.: Factorization meets the neighborhood: a multifaceted collaborative filtering model. In: KDD 2008: Proceeding of the 14th ACM SIGKDD Int. Conf. on Knowledge Discovery and Data Mining, pp. 426–434. ACM, New York (2008)
7. King, I., Lyu, M.R., Ma, H.: Introduction to social recommendation. In: Proceedings of the 19th International Conference on World Wide Web, pp. 1355–1356. ACM, New York (2010)
8. Ma, T.L., Yang, Y.J., Wang, L.W., Yuan, B.: Recommending People to Follow Using Asymmetric Factor Models with Social Graphs. In: Proceedings of the 17th Online World Conference on Soft Computing in Industrial Applications. AISC, Springer (2012)
9. Chen, T., Tang, L., Liu, Q., Yang, D., Xie, S., Cao, X., Wu, C., Yao, E., Liu, Z., Jiang, Z., Chen, C., Kong, W., Yu, Y.: Combining factorization model and additive forest for collaborative followee recommendation. In: KDD-Cup Workshop 2012 (2012)
10. Rendle, S.: Network and Click-through Prediction with Factorization Machines. In: Workshop 2012 (2012)
11. Zhao, X.: Scorecard with Latent Factor Models for User Follow Prediction Problem. In: KDD-Cup Workshop 2012 (2012)
12. Purushotham, S., Liu, Y., Kuo, C.C.J.: Collaborative topic regression with social matrix factorization for recommendation systems. In: Proceedings of the 29th International Conference on Machinelearning. ACM, New York (2012)
13. Ma, H., Zhou, D., Liu, C., Lyu, M.R., King, I.: Recommender systems with social regularization. In: Proceedings of the Fourth ACM International Conference on Web Search and Data Mining (WSDM 2011), pp. 287–296 (2011)
14. Cantador, I., Brusilovsky, P., Kuflik, T.: Second workshop on information heterogeneity and fusion in recommender systems (HetRec2011). In: Proc. of 5th ACM Conf. on Recommender Systems, RecSys 2011, pp. 387–388 (2011)
15. Chen, T., Zhang, W., Lu, Q., Chen, K., Zheng, Z., Yu, Y.: SVDFeature: A Toolkit for Feature-based Collaborative Filtering. Journal of Machine Learning Research 13, 3619–3622 (2012)

A Hybrid Approach for Extending Ontology from Text[*]

Wei He[1], Shuang Li[1], and Xiaoping Yang[2]

[1] Department of Applied Mathematic, Huaihua College, Huaihua, Hunan, China
[2] School of Information, Renmin University of China, Haidian, Beijing, China
{whe,yang}@ruc.edu.cn

Abstract. Ontology is applied to various fields of computer as a conceptual modeling tool, and is used to organize information and manage knowledge. Ontology extension is used to add the new concepts and relationship into the existing ontology, which is a more complex task. In this paper, we propose a hybrid approach for ontology extension from text using semantic relatedness between words, which exploit co-occurrence analysis, word filter and semantic relatedness between words to find the potential concepts from text, denoted as the extended concepts. And we take advantage of extension rules and subsumption analysis to find the relationship between concepts, which is used to add the extended concepts into the existing ontology. The improved recall, precision and F1-Measure have been presented and used to evaluate our method proposed in this paper. Experimental results show that the proposed method is more reasonable and promising. It has a stronger competitiveness and application ability.

Keywords: Ontology, Ontology extension, Co-occurrence analysis, Semantic relatedness.

1 Introduction

Ontology is seen as a model of conceptualization, which is used to effective semantically describe the information system. It supports shared understanding for users in interested areas by eliminating the conceptual and terminological confusion. Since ontology was carried out, it was drawn an attention by many domestic and foreign researchers, and applied to the various fields of computer. In the opening environment, the importance of the ontology has been widely perceived, but for the most people, such as domain experts, ontology engineer, it is still a complex physical labor to creating ontology.

Once the ontology constructed, it is a time-consuming and laborious to manually add a new concept into an existing ontology, and is still a great challenge to extend an existing ontology automatically. To solve this problem, we propose a hybrid approach for semi-auto extending ontology from text using semantic relatedness between words in this paper. The method requires the users manually choose a seed ontology from

---

[*] This research was partly supported by the Project Foundation of The Education Department of Hunan Province under Grant No.13C716.

G. Zhou et al. (Eds.): NLPCC 2013, CCIS 400, pp. 255–265, 2013.
© Springer-Verlag Berlin Heidelberg 2013

external knowledge bases, such as WordNet, HowNet, and then can semi-automatic extend the seed ontology to generate a large ontology with saving a large number of manpower, material resource and time. Firstly, we use search engine to get a document set for each concept of the seed ontology, and exploit co-occurrence analysis and word filter to obtain the candidate concepts closely related to the concept of the seed ontology from the documents. Secondly, we find the extended concepts from the candidate concepts using semantic relatedness between words. Finally, the extended concepts are added into the appropriate position of the seed ontology to implement the ontology extension process.

The remainder of the paper is organized as follows. Related work for Extending ontology is described in detail in section 2. We give a detailed description of our proposed method in section 3. The experiment and evaluation are presented in section 4. We conclude the paper in section 5.

2   Related Work

The automatic and semi-automatic ontology extension has been studied for two decade years. There are three kinds of approaches of ontology extension, which include natural language processing (NLP) based approach [1,2], network based approach[3,4], and user interaction approach[5,6,7].

Sabrina et al.[2] have proposed a method for extending ontology tree using NLP technology, which exploit NLP to extract new concepts from Web and link the new concepts with the concepts in Yahoo based on a clearly defined relationship. Liu et al.[3] have presented a semi-automatic ontology extension using spreading activation. They exploited spreading activation to identify the terms form a network generated via directed weight links between terms. However, Witbrock et al.[5] have proposed a semi-automatic approach for Cyc Knowledge Base (Cyc KB) extension based on the user-interactive dialogue system for knowledge acquisition, where, the user is engaged in a natural-language mixed-initiative dialogue.

In this paper, we proposed a semi-automatic method for extending ontology from text, which used semantic relatedness between terms to discover the new concepts, and positioned them into seed ontology through various kinds of rules.

3   Our Proposed Method

In this section, we present our proposed method for ontology extension in detail. The co-occurrence analysis and word filter are exploited to acquire the candidate concepts for each concept of the seed ontology from documents in this method. To improve the speed of ontology extension, we use semantic relatedness between words to compress the extended concept space. The extension rules and subsumption analysis are exploited to add the extended concepts into the seed ontology with generating the extended ontology.

3.1   Identifying the Candidate Concepts Using Co-occurrence Analysis and Word Filter

In natural document, words are directly or indirectly related. The words in same domain are more closely related than those in different area. Word co-occurrence is a direct representation of relationship between words in document and reflects the related strength between words. Co-occurrence analysis is a better method, which is used to identify whether two words is closely related or not. It is based on this hypothesis: for two semantically related words, they may co-occur in the same text segment. Meanwhile, word filter is used to filter the words which are less informative and unimportant. So the combination of the two methods can better find more important related words from documents. First of all, for each concept C of the seed ontology, we exploit search engine to acquire the domain documents related to the concept C. And then, co-occurrence analysis is used to identify the co-occurrence words related to C from the documents. Finally, we exploit the word filter to discard the noisy, less informative and unimportant words, and the remainder are regarding as the candidate concepts of the concept C.

Definition 1. Given a word W, we define its *co-occurrence word* as these words which distance from it to W is not more than δ word. Where δ is a windows threshold, generally $\delta=2,3,4,5$. Denoted by CoWord(W).

CoWord(W)=$\{W_i|Distance(W,W_i)\leq\delta\}$, where $Distance(W,W_i)$ is the path length from W_i to W in the same sentence.

Definition 2. *word co-occurrence frequency* is the number that the co-occurrence word w_i of W occur in the document segment where W appears. It is the most important basis to judge whether two word is related or not, denoted by CoFreq(w_i). The more the word co-occurrence frequency is, the more related two words hold.

Definition 3. *absolute frequency* is the total number of the occurrence of the word W in all documents. It reflects the extent that the word W is applied. If the absolute frequency of a word is higher, it shows that the word is common and is not served as a flag to identify the domain knowledge. At the same time, if the absolute frequency of a word is too lower, the words are infrequently applied to this area. Denoted by Afreq(W).

Definition 4. Given a word W, we define its *relative importance* as an important degree of word W that W is used to describe and differentiate the document. It is represented by TF-IDF of word W and calculated by formula (1), denoted by RI(W).

$$RI(W) = TF - IDF(W) = tf(W) * log(\frac{N}{df(W)}) \tag{1}$$

Where tf(W) is the frequency that W occur in the documents, df(W) is the document frequency of W, N is the total number of the documents.

Definition 5. Given a word W, we define its *entropy* as the total sum of information content of W in the documents. It is used to measure information content of a word, which is contained in a document set. It is denoted by Entropy(W) and computed by formula (2).

$$Entropy(W) = \sum_{i=1}^{n} IC(W) = -\sum_{i=1}^{n} p_i(W)log(p_i(W)) \tag{2}$$

Where $p_i(W)$ is the probability that word W occur in the document D_i, n represents the total number of all documents. $p_i(W)$ can be estimated by formula (3).

$$p_i(W) = \frac{Freq(W)}{\sum_{W_i \in D_i} Freq(W_i)} \tag{3}$$

Where Freq(W) is the frequency that W occur in document D_i.

We present our method for identifying and acquiring the candidate concepts using the definition described above in the following. The co-occurrence analysis and word filter are contained in this method. It mainly includes the following several steps:

For each concept C of the seed ontology, we do the following operator:

1) exploiting search engine to get a domain document set related to C, named as D, and looking for the CoWord(C) from D to generate the co-occurrence word set, denoted as CoWordSet(C), CoWordSet(C)={$w_i|w_i \in$ CoWord(C)}; then counting the CoFreq(w_i) and AFreq(w_i) for each w_i in CoWordSet(C) in document set D, and discarding the words which hold the AFreq(w_i) >> CoFreq(w_i) and CoFreq(W_i)<5; finally ranking the remaining the co-occurrence words in CoWordSet(C) according to theirs CoFreq(W) on descending order;

2) In the document set D, using formula (1) to calculate the relative importance of each w_i in CoWordSet(C), RI(w_i);

3) In the document set D, exploiting formula (2) to compute the entropy of each w_i in CoWordSet(C), Entropy(w_i);

4) Selecting the overlap words, which hold a higher RI and Entropy scores from CoWordSet(C) and generating the candidate concept set of concept C, denoted by CandCpt(C).

3.2   Obtaining the Extended Concepts Using Semantic Relatedness between Words

In this subsection, we present the method that uses semantic relatedness between words to compress the extended concept space and obtain the extended concepts. Although we exploit the method described in section 4.1 to generate the candidate concept set, CandCpt(C), and remove some noisy co-occurrence words. There still is a difficult task to add the remaining concepts in CandCpt(C) into the seed ontology because of time and space complexity. In order to improve this problem, we use semantic relatedness between words to compress the extended concept space. We only select a portion of the concepts in CandCpt(C) as the extended concepts. The process of selection is followed: for each concept C_i in CandCpt(C), we measure semantic relatedness between C_i and C, and select the concepts which have a highly score of semantic relatedness as the extended concepts. In this paper, we only use the top 3 concepts.

Definition 6. Give two words W_1, W_2, we define *semantic relatedness* between them as the Jaccard indicator, which is used to describe co-occurrence between them in the document set D. It is calculated by formula (4).

$$DomainRel(W_1,W_2) = Jaccard(W_1,W_2) = \frac{CoFreq(W_1,W_2)}{AFreq(W_1) + AFreq(W_2) - CoFreq(W_1,W_2)} \quad (4)$$

Where W_1W_2 is not necessarily in this form, but they can be as W_1*W_2, * representing less than 5 characters. Similarly, W_2W_1 also has the same form.

We suppose that a concept C holds a candidate concept set CandCpt(C) = $\{C_1,C_2,....,C_n\}$, and then use formula (4) to calculate semantic relatedness for each $C_i(1\leq i\leq n)$, DomainRel(C_i,C). We select the top 3 concepts which have a highly score of semantic relatedness as the extended concepts of C and generate the extended concept set, denoted by ExtendedCpt(C).

After doing this described above, we compress the extended concept space and reduce the number of the extended concepts. Thus the time and space complexity are dropped at the same extent.

3.3   Extending Ontology Using Extension Rules and Subsumption Analysis

It is one of an important problem of ontology extension how to add the extended concepts into the seed ontology. In order to solve this problem, we carefully analyze the distributed situation of the scores of semantic relatedness between the extended concepts and the concepts of the seed ontology, and develop a set of extension rules based on semantic relatedness, with combing the improved subsumption analysis to complete the ontology extension.

Using the methods described in previous, for each concept C of the seed ontology, we construct an extended concept set ExtendedCpt(C). We exploit the score of semantic relatedness and subsumption analysis to add the concept C_i in ExtendedCpt(C) into the seed ontology.

Extension Rule 1. if the score of semantic relatedness between the concept C_i and C is equals to 1 or approximately 1, it means that they are consistent in semantic and hold the synonym relationship. We add the concept C_i into the synonym attribute of concept C. It is shown as Fig. 1.

Extension Rule 2. if the score of semantic relatedness between the concept C_i and C is the maximum, but it does not satisfy the extension rule 1, we use subsumption analysis to identify the semantic relationship between C_i and C.

Subsumption analysis assumes that if two concepts co-occur, general concept should co-occur more frequently than specific concept. It means that the documents containing specialized concepts are a subset of the documents containing general terms. Given two concepts C_i and C, the concept C is said to more general than concept C_i if the following condition holds:

$$P(C \mid C_i) \geq 0.8, \quad P(C_i \mid C) < 1 \qquad (5)$$

We think there hold a hyponym/hypernym relationship between C_i and C and add the concept C_i into the hyponym attribute of concept C. Where 0.8 is chosen through informal analysis of hyponym/hypernym pairs identified through subsumption analysis. It is shown as Fig.2.

Extension Rule 3. if the score of semantic relatedness between the concept C_i and C is the maximum and does not satisfy the extension rule 1,2, we think there hold a related relationship between C_i and C. We add the concept C_i into the related attribute of concept C. It is shown as Fig.3.

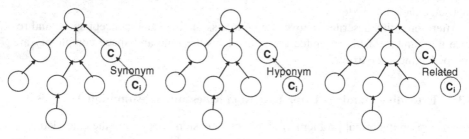

Fig. 1. Add synonym attribute   **Fig. 2.** Add hyponym attribute   **Fig. 3.** Add related attribute

Through the above extension rules, the extended concepts are automatically placed into the seed ontology, increasing the number of the concepts of the seed ontology. We complete the first round of ontology extension.

4   Experiment and Evaluation

4.1   Experiment

We select some terms related to education field that is a sub-field of E-government and constructed seed ontology in our experiment. The seed ontology is consist of 10 concepts and includes three kinds of relationship between this concepts, such as synonym, hyponym/hypernym (is-a) and related relationship. The depth of the seed ontology is three. It is shown as Fig.4.

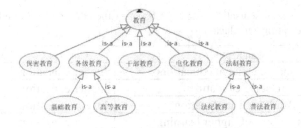

Fig. 4. The "education" seed ontology

We download about 4,000 pages related to education from the website[1] of Education Ministry of China, and then exploit htmlparser[2] to acquire the content of these pages and generate the domain document set D. For each document D_i in D, we use ICTCLAS[3], a Chinese word segmentation system developed by The Chinese Academy of Sciences, and E-government thesaurus to preprocess it, e.g. word segmentation, POS-tagging.

We illustrate the extension process of the "education" seed ontology using the method proposed in this paper in the following.

For each concept C of the "education" seed ontology, the concept "higher education (高等教育)" as an example in the follows.

1) First of all, we exploit the co-occurrence analysis and word filter to identify and acquire the candidate concept set CandCpt(C) from D. CandCpt(higher education)= { "Higher vocational education(高等职业教育)","Degree education (学位教育)","Adult higher education (成人高等教育)","Institutions of higher learning (高等院校)","teaching (教学)","The assessment of undergraduate teaching (本科教学评估)", …}.

2) Secondly, in order to compress the extended concept space and reduce the time and space complexity in ontology extension process, we use formula (4) to calculate semantic relatedness between C_i in the CandCpt(C) and C and choose the top 3 concepts as the extended concept, which have a highly score of semantic relatedness. The scores of semantic relatedness between the concept "higher education" and the concepts in CandCpt(higher education) are shown in table 1.

As can be seen from table 1, the top 3 concepts with closely related to the concept "higher education(高等教育)" include "Adult higher education(成人高等教育)", "Institutions of higher learning(高等院校)", "Higher vocational education(高等职业教育)" that their scores of semantic relatedness rank in top 3. So, we choose them as the extended concepts of the concept "higher education" and generate the extended concept set. ExtendedCpt(higher education)={"Adult higher education", "Institutions of higher learning", "Higher vocational education"}.

---

[1] http://www.moe.edu.cn/publicfiles/business/htmlfiles/
moe/info_category_query/index.html
[2] http://sourceforge.net/projects/htmlparser/files/
[3] http://ictclas.org/ictclas_download_more.aspx

Table 1. The scores of semantic relatedness between the concept "higher education" and the concepts in CandCpt(higher education)

CandCpt(C)	Concept C	DomainRel
Higher vocational education	higher education	**0.4405**
Degree education	higher education	0.2538
Adult higher education	higher education	**0.8964**
Institutions of higher learning	higher education	**0.6965**
teaching	higher education	0.3122
The assessment of undergraduate teaching	higher education	0.2158
...	...	...

3) We use extension rules 1, 2, 3 to identify the relationship between C and the concepts in ExtendedCpt(C) and position the concepts of ExtendedCpt(C) into the seed ontology. The semantic relationship between the concept "higher education (高等教育)" and the concepts in ExtendedCpt(higher education) are shown in table 2.

Table 2. The semantic relationship between the concept "higher education" and the concepts in ExtendedCpt(higher education)

ExtendedCpt(C)	Concept C	Extension rule 1	Extension rule 2		Extension rule 3	Semantic relationship
			$P(C|C_i)$	$P(C_i|C)$		
Adult higher education	higher education	—	1	0.135	—	Is-a
Institutions of higher learning	higher education	—	0.289	0.239	√	related
Higher vocational education	higher education	—	0.817	0.117	—	Is-a

After the fifth iteration of ontology extension, we generate the extended "education" domain ontology. A part of it has been shown as Fig.5. It has over 4,000 concepts.

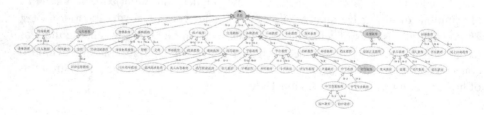

Fig. 5. The extended "education"ontology

Fig.5 is acquired by protégé[4]. Because the protégé can not display the synonym and related relationship, it only display the hyponym/hypernym (is -a) for user.

4.2   Evaluation

We choose a part of a gold standard E-government domain ontology constructed by E-government thesaurus[11] as our reference ontology, which is concerned to education. It has about 4,500 terms and three kinds of relationship between terms, such as synonym, hyponym/hypernym (is-a) and related relationship. The improved recall, precision and F1-Measure have been used to evaluate our proposed method. Because ontology is consisting of the concepts and relationship between concepts, we define the improved recall, precision and F1-Measure as following formula (6), (7) and (8).

$$Recall = \sqrt{Recall_{Concept} * Recall_{Relationship}}$$

$$= \sqrt{\frac{|Cpt_{Extended} \cap Cpt_{Standard}|}{|Cpt_{Standard}|} * \frac{|Rel_{Extended} \cap Rel_{Standard}|}{|Rel_{Standard}|}} \quad (6)$$

$$Precision = \sqrt{Precision_{Concept} * Precision_{Concept}}$$

$$= \sqrt{\frac{|Cpt_{Extended} \cap Cpt_{Standard}|}{|Cpt_{Extended}|} * \frac{|Rel_{Extended} \cap Rel_{Standard}|}{|Rel_{Extended}|}} \quad (7)$$

Where $Cpt_{Extended}$, $Rel_{Extended}$ represent the set of the concepts and the relationship of the Extended Ontology respectively, and $Cpt_{Standard}$, $Rel_{Standard}$ represent the set of the concepts and the relationship of the Reference Ontology respectively.

$$F1\text{-}Measure = \frac{2}{\frac{1}{Recall} + \frac{1}{Precision}} \quad (8)$$

The results have been shown in Table 3, the first column represents the number of iteration of ontology extension used our proposed method.

Table 3. The Evaluation Results Obtained from Our Proposed Methods

Number of iteration	Number of the concepts	Recall of the concepts	Precision of the concepts	Recall	Precision	F1-Measure
1	40	0.0089	1.000	0.0098	0.9899	0.0194
2	160	0.0338	0.9500	0.0427	0.9560	0.0817
3	624	0.1251	0.9022	0.1779	0.8627	0.2950
4	2253	0.4138	0.8265	0.3981	0.7873	0.5281
5	4480	0.7568	0.7567	0.6428	0.7278	0.6827

---

[4] http://protege.stanford.edu/download/download.html

From Table 3 can be seen, F1-Measure has been raised with the increment of the number of iteration of ontology extension. It reaches 0.6827 after the fifth iteration achievement, which is a promising value. It indicates that the proposed method is valuable. And the precision has been maintained at a higher level. It ranges from 0.7278 to 0.9899. Meanwhile, the growth rate of the concepts slows down because the condition used to identify the new concepts is too stronger. However, we have an observation that we obtain the largest number of related relationship during the course of ontology extension. It maybe generated because we define the related relationship is too lax. This is our next research work too.

5 Conclusion

With the massive new web information, the existing ontology serious lags in the emergence of the new concepts and has not suitable to organize and manage the new information. To solve this problem, we propose a hybrid approach for extending ontology from text using semantic relatedness between words in this paper, and add the new concepts discovered in documents into the existing ontology. Through extending "education" domain ontology, the proposed method has shown a stronger competitiveness, and the extended ontology is reasonable. Evaluation results on the improved recall, precision and F1-Measure demonstrate that our proposed method in this paper is promising and logically. But there is a little drawback because of relationship definition during the course of ontology extension. Therefore, in next work, we will explore others methods to make up this weakness and improve the efficiency of the proposed method.

Reference

1. Burkhardt, F., Gulla, J.A., Liu, J., Weiss, C., Zhou, J.: Semi Automatic Ontology Engineering in Business Applications. GI Jahrestagung 2, 688–693 (2008)
2. Sabrina, T., Rosni, A., Enyakong, T.: Extending Ontology Tree Using NLP Technique. In: Proceedings of National Conference on Research & Development in Computer Science REDECS 2001 (2001)
3. Liu, W., Weichselbraun, A., Scharl, A., Chang, E.: Semi-Automatic Ontology Extension Using Spreading Activation. Journal of Universal Knowledge Management (1), 50–58 (2005)
4. McDonald, J., Plate, T., Schvaneveldt, R.: Using pathfinder to extract semantic information from text. In: Schvaneveldt, R.W. (ed.) Pathfinder Associtive Networks: Studies in Knowledge Organisation, pp. 149–164 (1990)
5. Witbrock, M., Baxter, D., Curtis, J., Schneider, D., Kahlert, R., Miraglia, P., Wagner, P., Panton, K., Matthews, G., Vizedom, A.: An Interactive Dialogue System for Knowledge Acquisition in Cyc. In: Proceedings of the Eighteenth International Joint Conference on Artificial Intelligence, pp. 138–145 (2003)
6. Cimiano, P., Völker, J.: Text2Onto A Framework for Ontology Learning and Data-driven Change Discovery. In: Montoyo, A., Muñoz, R., Métais, E. (eds.) NLDB 2005. LNCS, vol. 3513, pp. 227–238. Springer, Heidelberg (2005)

7. Novalija, I., Mladenić, D.: Ontology Extension towards Analysis of Business News. Informatica 34(3), 517–522 (2010)
8. Li, Y., Bontcheva, K.: Hierarchical Perception-like Learning for Ontology Based Information Extraction. In: Williamson, C., Zurko, M.E. (eds.) WWW 2007 Proceedings of the 16th International Conference on World Wide Web, pp. 777–786. ACM, New York (2007)
9. Schutz, A., Buitelaar, P.: RelExt: a tool for relation extraction from text in ontology extension. In: Gil, Y., Motta, E., Benjamins, V.R., Musen, M.A. (eds.) ISWC 2005. LNCS, vol. 3729, pp. 593–606. Springer, Heidelberg (2005)
10. Qian, G., Chong, G.: Concept Extraction in Automatic Ontology Construction Using Words Co-occurrence. New Technology of Library and Information Service (2), 43–49 (2006)
11. The Complication Group of E-government Thesaurus, Integrated e-government Thesaurus. Scientific and Technical Document Publishing House, Beijing (2005)

Linking Entities in Short Texts
Based on a Chinese Semantic Knowledge Base

Yi Zeng, Dongsheng Wang, Tielin Zhang, Hao Wang, and Hongwei Hao

Institute of Automation, Chinese Academy of Sciences, Beijing, China
{yi.zeng,dongsheng.wang,hongwei.hao}@ia.ac.cn

Abstract. Populating existing knowledge base with new facts is important to keep the knowledge base fresh and most updated. Before importing new knowledge into the knowledge base, entity linking is required so that the entities in the new knowledge can be linked to the entities in the knowledge base. During this process, entity disambiguation is the most challenging task. There have been many studies on leveraging name ambiguity problem via a variety of algorithms. In this paper, we propose an entity linking method based on Chinese Semantic Knowledge where entity disambiguation can be addressed by retrieving a variety of semantic relations and analyzing the corresponding documents with similarity measurement. Based on the proposed method, we developed CASIA_EL, a system for linking entities with knowledge bases. We validate the proposed method by linking 1232 entities mined from Sina Weibo to a Chinese Semantic knowledge base, resulting in an accuracy of 88.5%. The results show that the CASIA_EL system and the proposed algorithm are potentially effective.

Keywords: Entity linking, Chinese Semantic Knowledge, Semantic similarity, Entity disambiguation.

1   Introduction

This paper introduces our results on the competition of entity linking task organized by the second conference on Natural Language Processing and Chinese Computing (NLP&CC 2013). The task of entity linking is to link the entity name from Sina Weibo microblog posts to Baidu Encyclopedia knowledge base. The organizer provides a part of Baidu Encyclopedia knowledge base and a number of Sina Weibo microblog posts within which entities are tagged. If the entities in the microblog posts can be linked to the entities in the knowledge base, we are supposed to output the identity of the entity in the knowledge base (denoted as "*KB_ID*"). If the knowledge base does not contain the given entity, we should output a "*NIL*". We build up an entity linking system called CASIA_EL according to the task requirement and produce one group of result. Finally, we ranked the second place among 10 teams with an overall linking accuracy of 88.5%.

This competition focuses on linking entities from short texts (e.g. microblog posts) to knowledge bases. The motivation of this work is to enable and evaluate possible

G. Zhou et al. (Eds.): NLPCC 2013, CCIS 400, pp. 266–276, 2013.
© Springer-Verlag Berlin Heidelberg 2013

techniques to enrich existing knowledge base with dynamic and new knowledge from short texts based social media such as microblog. One of the most important step is linking possible entities from microblog posts with entities in the existing knowledge base, so that relevant entities within and outside the knowledge base can be linked together and organized as interconnected Web of knowledge. Some key issues need to be considered for the entity linking task. On the one hand, a specific entity may have various names while they actually refer to the same entity. In this case, we need processing techniques (such as creating and maintaining a synonym set) to link possible entity names together. On the other hand, different entities may share the same name. In this case, entity disambiguation algorithms are needed to link the entity from short texts with appropriate candidate entity in the knowledge base.

This competition is challenging in several perspectives. Firstly, microblog posts are very short (only 140 characters are allowed), and traditional entity linking algorithm may not perform well since they may be short of enough meaningful contents. Secondly, the representation of entity names and language style in microblog posts are extremely free, which brings many potential difficulties for linking the entity names to appropriate entities in the knowledge base.

In this paper, we propose an entity linking method and implement an entity linking system, named CASIA_EL, by utilizing various semantic relations among entities in a Chinese semantic knowledge base with knowledge from various sources. First of all, we construct the Chinese semantic knowledge base from scratch by using semantic techniques including RDF, N3, triple store, etc. In order to support the linking process, we automatically construct a synonym set from multiple Web-based wiki-encyclopedias. Secondly, in order to make a balance between the contents of a microblog post and the wiki page contents in the knowledge base, we attempt to make an understanding of microblog posts by adding relevant contents from the knowledge base. For example, the post *"My Company is bad, I like Apple"* is one single sentence with just two nouns while the description of *"Apple Inc."* in the knowledge base may contain several hundred sentences. Therefore, when it is hard to find appropriate entities in the knowledge base, we extend the post by adding other documents of associated entities within the same context. For this example, we add the wiki page contents of *"Company"* from the knowledge base to this short post. This method is formalized as the stepwise bag-of-words entity disambiguation algorithm. With the experimental results on the competition, we conclude that the proposed entity linking method and the system is potentially effective.

The rest of the paper is organized as follows: Section 2 introduces related works of this paper. Section 3 introduces the constructed Chinese semantic knowledge base and the entity linking method. Section 4 provides evaluation results and detailed analysis on the performance of our system.

2   Related Works

Here we define the entity name from the microblog post as the target entity, and the possibly identical entities from the knowledge base as the candidate entity. The task of entity linking generally focuses on the problem of entity disambiguation that has been discussed extensively in different areas. There have been many studies addressing this issue, and one of the most widely used method is the Bag-of-Words (BOW) model [2, 3], which utilizes a bag of words to express the entity's document and calculate the similarity via vector cosine similarity. Some researchers extend the work by adding social network relations to obtain background knowledge. For instance, Bekkerman and McCallum utilized the inter-link and out-link structures of web pages as well as the similarity between two persons' page documents for disambiguation [4]. A graph-based framework was adopted by Jiang et al. to disambiguate person entity appeared on the Web by capturing personal information [5]. However, both the BOW method and the social-graph based method suffer the insufficiency of corpus or information.

Recently, because of the public availability of Wiki Encyclopedias and knowledge bases such as Wikipedia, DBpedia, and YAGO [1], some researchers take advantages of these sources, which contain large and abundant knowledge, to leverage entity disambiguation. For example, Han and Zhao constructed the semantic knowledge from Wikipedia, based on which the semantic similarity measurement is proposed [6]. Shen et al. utilized the taxonomy information in YAGO, a semantic knowledge base which is built based on Wikipedia and WordNet, to obtain agreement on the categories associated with candidate entities [7]. Compared to the efforts in English, Chinese entity linking has not been well studied and needs further investigations. Some recent progresses include Zhishi.me (a multi-source Chinese Web of Data platform based on infobox knowledge from Baidu Encyclopedia, Hudong Encyclopedia and Wikipedia Chinese sources) [8] and cross-lingual knowledge linking among different Chinese Knowledge Bases [9].

3   Chinese Semantic Knowledge Based Entity Linking

In this paper, we propose to investigate on the Chinese entity linking task through analysis and utilization of various semantic relations among entities from the Chinese Semantic Knowledge Base. In this section, we firstly introduce the fundamental work on how the Chinese Semantic Knowledge base is constructed from scratch in Section 3.1. Then we discuss techniques for linking unambiguous entities in Section 3.2. We detail our proposal on stepwise entity disambiguation based on the Chinese semantic knowledge base in Section 3.3.

3.1   Semantic Knowledge Base Construction

The competition organizer provides a portion of Baidu Encyclopedia contents in the form of XML, which are composed of entities, corresponding infobox knowledge, and unstructured wiki-page contents. We extract the infobox knowledge from the XML file and represent them in *N3* format. An example is provided in Table 1.

Table 1. An Example on Representing Infobox Knowledge in N3 Format

Infobox Knowledge	苹果公司, 外文名称, Apple Inc.
N3 format	http://www.ia.cas.cn/baidu_baike/resource/KBBD010956, http://www.ia.cas.cn/baidu_baike/resource/外文名称, "Apple Inc."^^xsd:string. http://www.ia.cas.cn/baidu_baike/resource/KBBD000001, http://www.w3.org/2000/01/rdf-schema#label "苹果公司"^^xsd:string.

For knowledge represented in N3 format, every entity is identified by an URL containing a unique knowledge base ID (denoted as "*KB_ID*"). The corresponding properties are expressed via a variety of relations such as the URI containing "外文名称" in the upper example.

Instead of traditional storage methodology which is generally based on relational databases, we employ semantic storage methodology based on Jena TDB[1] and the data are represented in RDF N3 format. Since the RDF data can be explained as a graph, consisting of interconnected nodes and relations, it is flexible to add new schema and new data (i.e. nodes and relations) without modification of the original database design.

In this Chinese knowledge base, every entity resource is with a variety of relations. The most significant relation is the "*rdfs:label*," by which a bag of possible input keywords is created for a given entity resource. The labels are generated from entity *name*, *English name*, *Chinese name* from the infobox knowledge. In addition, we extend the labels by synset, *nick names* and *redirect titles* crawled from Baidu Encyclopedia, Hudong Encyclopedia and Wikipedia Chinese pages (476,086 pair of synonyms are added). Also, we split the western people's name by "." into smaller keywords, for example, "*Michael·Jordan*" is split into "*Michael*" and "*Jordan*" and both of them are added as possible labels for "*Michael Jordan*". In this way, we enlarge the coverage of keywords for a given entity resource to support various entity names written by different user with different preference. Consequently, it is common phenomenon that several entity resources can share the same label. For example, as shown in Fig. 1, the Company "苹果公司(Apple Inc.)" and the fruit "苹果(Apple)" share the same label "苹果". In other words, given the entity name "苹果" in a microblog post, our system firstly returns two or more candidate entity resources from the knowledge base and they are delivered to entity disambiguation processing. The entity disambiguation process will be discussed in Section 3.3.

---

[1] http://jena.apache.org/documentation/tdb/

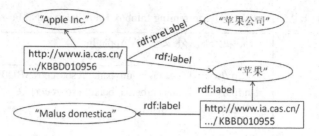

Fig. 1. An Example of Connected Semantic Data

Since the number of labels of an entity resource can be very large, we create a sub-relation "*CAS:preLabel*" (preferred label) of "*rdfs:label*" to express the representative keywords for an entity resource. Namely, we entitle higher priority to the relation "*CAS:preLabel*" than "*rdfs:label*". If the entity name is consistent with both "*preLabel*" and "*rdfs:label*" values, our system would performs linking to the corresponding "*preLabel*" entity resource first.

3.2 Linking Unambiguous Entities

As discussed in section 3.1, given an entity name appeared in a piece of short text, the retrieval of "*rdfs:label*" can result in one, several, or even no candidate entity resources returned from existing knowledge base.

For the case that only one single candidate entity resource was returned, we link the entity name with the corresponding entity resource in the knowledge base directly (In this case, the entity is unambiguous), and outputs the *KB_ID* of the entity.

For the case that there are no candidate entity returns, it is not clear whether there is no corresponding entity in the knowledge base or there might be typos for the entity name. Hence, we automatically deliver the entity name to Google's "*Did you mean * ?*" function to check whether it's a wrong spelling keyword (In the upper sentence, * is a possible correct alternative for the original entity name). If it returns possible new keywords, we change the entity name to the proposed new literal and process the new keyword again for the entity linking process. Otherwise, we assume there is no corresponding candidate entity in the knowledge base, and we produce the output result as "*NIL*".

In addition, considering the characteristics of Chinese entities, we made some extra processing if the original entity name cannot be directly found in the knowledge base. For example, in Chinese, many entities are with punctuation marks around them, such as book names, film, TV program names, etc. Hence, before a keyword is delivered to process, we check if it contains characters in the following set: {<, >, 《, 》, ",",",", …}. If it contains, we process it as it is since the synonym set might be able to handle it, and if it returns "*NIL*", we delete them and re-process the keywords again. For example, " 《霸王别姬》 " is delivered to process as it is and if it outputs a "*NIL*," we split it into "霸王别姬" and process it again. For person names, when writing microblog posts, the character "·" in the middle of the given name and the family name is always replaced with a space or "-".

For example, "勒布朗·詹姆斯" is the entity name in the knowledge base, but in microblog posts, it is referred to as "勒布朗-詹姆斯" or "勒布朗 詹姆斯". In our system, we firstly process the entity as it is, and if there are no relevant *KB_ID*, the space or "-" are replaced by "·" and the entity name is reprocessed again on the knowledge base.

3.3   Stepwise Entity Disambiguation Based on a Chinese Knowledge Base

If there are several candidate entity resources in the knowledge base that may be relevant to the target entity in the piece of short text, then we need the entity disambiguation process to decide which candidate should be linked to. Since every entity in Baidu encyclopedia corresponds to a wiki page (or a part of a wiki page) that is used to describe this entity, we can use these contents for the entity disambiguation process. Our general design is describing the target entity and the candidate entity with their contexts respectively, and then we compare the similarity of these two contexts to obtain the similarity between the target entity and the candidate entity. Based on these considerations, we propose the Stepwise Bag-of-Words (S-BOW) based Entity Disambiguation Algorithm, as shown in the following.

Algorithm 1: The Stepwise Bag-of-Words based Entity Disambiguation Algorithm

Input: target entity name (e_{st}) and the short text (d_{st}), semantic knowledge base (KB)

Output: *KB_ID* from the KB, which corresponds to e_{st}

1   Begin
2   Generate bags of word terms (denoted as *bag[d_{st}]* and *bag[d_{kb}]*, only noun and entity type word terms are selected to put in the bags) which are used to describe d_{st} and several d_{kb}.
3   Get the intersection of *bag[d_{st}]* and *bag[d_{kb}]*, which contains word terms that *bag[d_{st}]* and *bag[d_{kb}]* share, and obtain $sim(d_{st}, d_{kb})$ for each d_{kb}.
4   Get the biggest $sim(d_{st}, d_{kb})$ and output the corresponding *KB_ID*.
5   If more than one $sim(d_{st}, d_{kb})$ share the same value, extend *bag[d_{st}]* to *bag'[d_{st}]* and calculate $sim'(d_{st}, d_{kb})$, else go to Step 7.
6   Get the biggest $sim'(d_{st}, d_{kb})$ and output the corresponding *KB_ID*.
7   End

Here we briefly explain the general steps in this algorithm. Firstly, we get a piece of short text (denoted as d_{st}) which contains the target entity name (In this paper, a piece of short text refers to a microblog post from Sina Weibo.) and the contents that describe possible candidate entity resources from knowledge base (denoted as d_{kb}. In this paper, the document corresponding to a candidate entity resource in the knowledge base is a (or part of) the wiki page from Baidu Encyclopedia). Then, we measure the similarity values between d_{st} and each d_{kb} based on the bag of words used to describe d_{st} and d_{kb}. The similarity value between d_{st} and each d_{kb}, is characterized as the number of shared word terms in both *bag[d_{st}]* and *bag[d_{kb}]*, namely:

$$sim(d_{st,} d_{kb})=|\ bag[d_{st}]\ \cap bag[d_{kb}]|. \tag{1}$$

The d_{kb} with the highest similarity value is selected and the target entity is linked to the corresponding entity resource in the knowledge base. However, in some cases, two or more d_{kb} still share the same similarity value with the d_{st}, and it is hard to select out only one of them. This often happens due to the short length of d_{st}, which leads to a relatively smaller number of word terms in $bag[d_{st}]$. On the contrary, the d_{kb} is generally very long and the amount of word terms in $bag[d_{kb}]$ is almost always big. In order to make a balance among the size of $bag[d_{st}]$ and $bag[d_{kb}]$, we enrich $bag[d_{st}]$ by adding bags of word terms that are used to describe each word terms in $bag[d_{st}]$.

$$bag'[d_{st}]= bag[d_{st}]\cup bag[t_1]\ \cup bag[t_2]\ \cup...\cup bag[t_n]. \tag{2}$$

where $bag'[d_{st}]$ denotes the extended bag of word terms. $\{\ t_1, t_2,...,t_n\}$ is a set of terms obtained from the short text d_{st}. $bag[t_n]$ denotes the bag of word terms obtained from the wiki page which uses the term t_n as its title in the semantic knowledge base.

After extending the bag of word terms for d_{st} from $bag[d_{st}]$ to $bag'[d_{st}]$, the similarity among d_{st} and d_{kb} is recalculated according to the intersection of $bag'[d_{st}]$ and $bag[d_{kb}]$, as shown in the following formula:

$$sim'(d_{st,} d_{kb})=|\ bag'[d_{st}]\ \cap bag[d_{kb}]|$$
$$=|\ (bag[d_{st}]\cup bag[t_1]\ \cup bag[t_2]\ \cup...\cup bag[t_n])\ \cap bag[d_{kb}]\ |. \tag{3}$$

The selection criteria for candidate entity is the same, and the *KB_ID* with the largest $sim'(d_{st,} d_{kb})$ value is produced as the output.

This algorithm uses the idea of bag-of-words model in a stepwise manner. Nevertheless, the extension of the original short text only happens when there are more than one $sim(d_{st,} d_{kb})$ which share the same value. The next section will experimentally verify the proposed algorithm by using the competition data.

4   Experimental Results and Analysis

The NLP&CC 2013 Entity Linking contest provides 779 microblog posts within which 1232 entities are tagged, and these entities are required to be linked to the entities in the knowledge base. Therefore, it is not necessary to detect entity names automatically from the microblog posts, and the focus is on the linking process. According to the results produced by the organizer, the total amount of accurate output is 731, and the overall precision is 0.885. Detailed results are listed in Table 2.

Table 2. Evaluation Result Produced by the Competition Organizer

Accurate Output	precision	In-KB precision	In-KB recall	In-KB F1	NIL precision	NIL recall	NIL F1
731	0.885	0.8662	0.8456	0.8558	0.9036	0.9260	0.9146

The whole process of our entity linking system is based on the method discussed in Section 3. Here we extend our discussion based on the experimental results.

A key step for the S-BOW entity disambiguation algorithm is the generation of the bags of word terms that are used to describe the contexts of the target entity and the candidate entity. We use NLPIR[2], a refined version of ICTCLAS[3] for word segmentation and lexical category tagging. Table 3 provides practical reasons why noun and literal string are selected as basic elements to generate bag of word terms.

Table 3. The Effects of Lexical Categories on the Correctness of Entity Disambiguation

Lexical Category	Labels in ICTCLAS	Entity Disambiguation Correctness
noun	n, nr, nr1, nr2, nrj, nrf, ns, nt, nz, nl	0.75
verb	v, vd, vn, vf, vx, vi, vl, vg	0.685
adjective	a, ad, an, ag, al	0.48
literal string	x, xx, xu	0.714

We make additional test on the entity disambiguation correctness when only the specified lexical category is selected as the source to generate the bag of word terms. Here we can find that noun and literal string (usually entity type word terms, such as "GDP", "CEO", "KFC", "DVD", etc.) are better sources for generating the bag of word terms. Hence, these two lexical categories are selected for creating the contexts of target entity and candidate entity in the semantic knowledge base. In addition, we examined the effect of word term length on the correctness of entity disambiguation, and the result is listed in Table 4.

Table 4. The Effects of Word Term Length on the Correctness of Entity Disambiguation

Length	Entity Disambiguation Correctness
All lengths	0.655
Equal to or longer than 2 Chinese characters	0.776

According to Table 4, we can conclude that it can lead to negative effect when we involve the word terms that only contain one Chinese character. As a consequence, only the noun and literal string type of word terms whose length is greater than 1 are selected to represent the contexts of the target entity and the candidate entity.

During the design of the S-BOW entity disambiguation algorithm, we assume that extending the number of word terms can make a balance between the contexts of target entity and candidate entity. Fig. 2 provides an experimental evidence on the assumption, which reflects a general positive relevance between the number of entities in the context and the correctness of entity disambiguation.

---

[2] The NLPIR Chinese Word Segmentation System: http://ictclas.nlpir.org/
[3] The ICTCLAS Chinese Word Segmentation System: http://ictclas.org

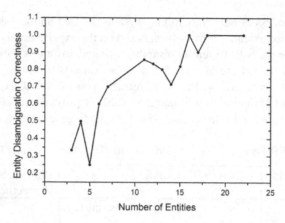

Fig. 2. The Relation Between the Number of Entities and the Entity Disambiguation Correctness

Although it seems that the number of candidate entities may not have any clear correlation with the entity disambiguation correctness, our system produce even better results when the number of candidate entities goes larger, as shown in Fig. 3.

Due to the reason that we add many synonyms to the original entity resource in the knowledge base (e.g. the family name and the given name of a person are added as synonyms for this person). There are many cases that the amount of candidate entities reaches more than 10, or even 50, as shown in Table 5 (with 56 candidate entities) and Fig. 4. Even in this case, the entity disambiguation process performs very well. It is noted that when the number is greater than 9, there are no incorrect disambiguations.

Table 5. An Example of Multiple Candidate Entities in the Knowledge Base

Target Entity and the Microblog Post	Candidate Entities	Name	Produced KB_ID
weibo id = aonierqiuyituiyi914 name id = 詹姆斯 content = "奥尼尔球衣退役了，突然联想到如果詹姆斯以后退役了，克里夫兰会退役他的球衣吗??????"	KBBD000035	詹姆斯·普雷斯科特·焦耳	KBBD000092
	KBBD000092	勒布朗·詹姆斯	
	KBBD000609	詹姆斯·西蒙斯	
	KBBD000707	詹姆斯·克拉克·麦克斯韦	
	KBBD000875	詹姆斯·弗兰克	
	KBBD000876	詹姆斯·弗兰克	
	...	...	
	KBBD018850	詹姆斯·瓦特	

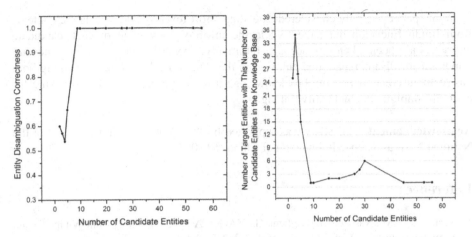

Fig. 3. The Relation Between the Number of Candidate Entities and the Entity Disambiguation Correctness in CASIA_EL

Fig. 4. Ambiguous Entity Number Distribution in the Test Data

Our system detected 161 entity disambiguation tasks in the test data. When we only try to disambiguate entities by using the original microblog posts, 123 entities were disambiguated, and the correctness is 82.1% (101 out of 123 entities were correctly disambiguated). When we extend the original microblog posts by adding the Baidu Encyclopedia contents (Following Step 5 and 6 in Algorithm 1), another 38 entities were disambiguated. For the second phase, the correctness is 63.2% (24 out of 38 entities were correctly disambiguated). Hence, the overall entity disambiguation correctness based on the proposed algorithm is 77.6% (125 out of 161 entities are correctly disambiguated).

5   Conclusion

Updating existing knowledge base with new facts is important to maintain the knowledge base and keep it fresh and updated, and the importing of new facts from the real-world requires entity linking in advance with existing knowledge base, challenging us with the named entity disambiguation.

There have been many studies on addressing entity disambiguation problem via a variety of algorithms. They are insufficient with information and some methods that adopt knowledge bases are less well-structured. In this paper, we proposed an entity linking method based on Chinese Semantic Knowledge where the named entity disambiguation can be addressed by retrieving a variety of semantic relations and analyzing the corresponding documents with similarity measurement. What's more, for the short texts (e.g. microblog posts) which are unfeasible for the similarity measurement, we extend the content by adding other documents of entities those that are within the same context. The proposed method was validated by linking 1232 entities, mined from Weibo, to Chinese Semantic knowledge base, resulting in an accuracy of 88.5%, demonstrating a satisfactory linking efficiency.

In this paper, we only considered extending short texts by adding relative contents from Baidu Encyclopedia pages, while the infobox knowledge of each candidate entity has not been taken into account. Intuitively, properties and property values are important for disambiguate one entity from the others. In the future, combining both unstructured contents and infobox knowledge in the wiki-pages seems promising for entity disambiguation and entity linking.

Acknowledgement. This study was supported by "the Young Scientists Fund" of the National Natural Science Foundation of China (61100128).

References

1. Suchanek, F.M., Kasneci, G., Weikum, G.: YAGO: A Large Ontology from Wikipedia and WordNet. Journal of Web Semantics 6(3), 203–217 (2008)
2. Bagga, A., Baldwin, B.: Entity-based Cross-document Coreferencing Using the Vector Space Model. In: Proceedings of the 17th International Conference on Computational Linguistics (COLING 1998), pp. 79–85. ACL, Montreal (1998)
3. Mann, G.S., Yarowsky, D.: Unsupervised personal name disambiguation. In: Proceedings of the 7th Conference on Natural Language Learning (CONLL 2003), pp. 33–40. ACL, Edmonton (2003)
4. Bekkerman, R., McCallum, A.: Disambiguating Web appearances of people in a social network. In: Proceedings of the 14th International Conference on the World Wide Web (WWW 2005), pp. 463–470. ACM Press, Chiba (2005)
5. Jiang, L., Wang, J., An, N., Wang, S., Zhan, J., Li, L.: GRAPE: A Graph-Based Framework for Disambiguating People Appearances in Web Search. In: Proceedings of the 9th IEEE International Conference on Data Mining (ICDM 2009), pp. 199–208. IEEE Press (2009)
6. Han, X., Zhao, J.: Named entity disambiguation by leveraging Wikipedia semantic knowledge. In: Proceedings of the 18th ACM Conference on Information and Knowledge Management (CIKM 2009), pp. 215–224. ACM Press, Hong Kong (2009)
7. Shen, W., Wang, J., Luo, P., Wang, M.: LINDEN: linking named entities with knowledge base via semantic knowledge. In: Proceedings of the 21st International Conference on the World Wide Web (WWW 2012), pp. 449–458. ACM Press, Lyon (2012)
8. Niu, X., Sun, X., Wang, H., Rong, S., Qi, G., Yu, Y.: Zhishi.me - Weaving Chinese Linking Open Data. In: Aroyo, L., Welty, C., Alani, H., Taylor, J., Bernstein, A., Kagal, L., Noy, N., Blomqvist, E. (eds.) ISWC 2011, Part II. LNCS, vol. 7032, pp. 205–220. Springer, Heidelberg (2011)
9. Wang, Z., Li, J., Wang, Z., Tang, J.: Cross-lingual Knowledge Linking across Wiki Knowledge Bases. In: Proceedings of the 21st World Wide Web Conference (WWW 2012), pp. 459–468. ACM Press, Lyon (2012)

Entity Linking from Microblogs to Knowledge Base Using ListNet Algorithm

Yan Wang*, Cheng Luo, Xin Li, Yiqun Liu, Min Zhang, and Shaoping Ma

State Key Laboratory of Intelligent Technology and Systems
Tsinghua National Laboratory for Information Science and Technology
Department of Computer Science and Technology, Tsinghua University
Beijing 100084, China
{yan-wang10,c-luo12,xli12}@mails.thu.edu.cn,
{yiqunliu,z-m,msp}@mail.thu.edu.cn

Abstract. Entity Linking (EL) is a fundamental technology in Natural Language Processing and Knowledge Engineering. Previous works mainly focus on linking mentioned names recognized in news or articles to knowledge base. However, in social network, user-generated content is quite different from typical news text. Users sometimes use words more informally, even create new words. One entity may have different aliases mentioned by web users, so identifying these aliases calls for more attention than before. Several methods are proposed to mine aliases and a learning-to-rank framework is applied to combine different types of feature together. A binary classifier based on SVM is trained to judge whether the top one candidate given by ranking algorithm is accepted. The evaluation results of NLP&CC 2013[1] Entity Linking Track shows the effectiveness of this framework.

Keywords: Entity Linking, Microblog, Learning to Rank.

1 Introduction

Recent years have witnessed a big bloom in social network system (SNS), such as Facebook, Twitter, and Microblog in China. According to Sina.com, the number of active users on Sina Weibo is about 46.2 million in December, 2012[2]. Users create and share microblogs in large scale. A microblog is a short paragraph with limited number of characters, or even just a sentence. It is similar with a web page to the extent of carrying and transmitting message. The difference between a microblog and a news article is that a microblog is much more easier to produce and spread via the social network. Every user on SNS could be both information receiver and provider. Besides the spreading efficiency, some contents or opinions that are not allowed for public media could appear in users' personal pages, because individuals publish microblogs on behalf

---

* This work was supported by Natural Science Foundation (60903107, 61073071) and National High Technology Research and Development (863) Program (2011AA01A205) of China.
[1] NLP&CC (CCF Conference on Natural Language Processing and Chinese Computing) http://tcci.ccf.org.cn/conference/2013/
[2] http://news.xinhuanet.com/newmedia/2013-02/21/c_124369896.htm

G. Zhou et al. (Eds.): NLPCC 2013, CCIS 400, pp. 277–287, 2013.
© Springer-Verlag Berlin Heidelberg 2013

of themselves. In this way, microblogs contribute to the variety of information on the Internet.

It is valuable to understand what microblogs are talking about. The topic trends often indicate social events, such as natural disasters, scandals and other hot spots. [1] detects earthquake through analyzing Twitter contents. [2] identifies emerging topics on Twitter by monitoring keywords whose frequencies of appearance suddenly rise up, many of which are named entities such as names of people, organizations or geographical locations. In addition, microblogs are helpful in personalized applications because the contents of microblogs shared and commented by a user suggest the user's preferences and interests. Such information is worth of mining to improve the personalized advertising and content recommendation.

Discovering what the named entities stand for is important for understanding microblogs. For example, a microblog reviews the performance of someone in a game. If the mentioned person is an NBA player, there is a great possibility that the microblog is about a certain basketball game. If we find the person in a knowledge base, we could find the team he plays in and recommend this microblog to other fans of this team. On the other hand, sharing and commenting microblogs with names of NBA players suggests the user is a fan of NBA and basketball, we can recommend related news and business items to him. From this point of view, linking entities to encyclopedia helps to understand the topic of microblogs and is useful to other applications.

Judging the real indication of an entity in microblog could be challenging. The language of a microblog is more like spoken language than written language. Word usage in microblogs is much more irregular than traditional Web articles. There are three typical ways of using words. The first one is the vast usage of abbreviations. "国移动通信集团公司", or China Mobile Communications Corporation(CMCC) could be abbreviated to "中国移动" or "中移动". Obviously the latter two abbreviations are more popular on SNS for briefness. The second one is usage of nicknames or different ways of translation. For example, "禅师", or *The Zen Master*, refers to the NBA star *Philip Douglas Jackson*. Users who are familiar with these starts tend to use nicknames. The third one is typo, such as "阿里爸爸" instead of the correct name "阿里巴巴". "巴" and "爸" share the same input sequence of *ba* in Pinyin input method, so it is possible to make a mistake. On the other hand, some users may type a typo on purpose for many reasons,for instance, the original word is forbidden to appear in a microblog.

All these three types of word usage are obstacles to finding out what the entities stand for. But luckily, we could conclude some assumptions lying behind. The common essence of all the three cases before is that an entity could have multiple aliases. And the set of aliases remains stable in a relatively short period of time. The first two kinds of aliases are generally accepted, because they are formed by convention. Even kinds of typos could be stable because the reason could derive from the fact that different Chinese characters share the same Pinyin code. Based on these two assumptions, we could design methods to find aliases for each entity. Given a mentioned name that is informal or less frequently used, we can find its more formal or more frequently used names. That will help a lot in an entity linking task.

The rest of the paper is organized as follows. Section 2 reviews some related works. Section 3 describes the entity linking task and gives a formal definition. Section 4

introduces the algorithm framework we use with discussions about the alias list generation. Section 5 presents the experiment and analyzes some typical cases. Conclusion
is drawn in Section 6.

2 Related Work

Named entity recognition is the foundation of entity linking. [3] applied Conditional
Random Fields to discover the named entities. Our work is based on the assumption that
entities have been pointed out from microblogs and the boundaries are correct. Other
works focus on the disambiguation of named entities. [4] used bag-of-words model to
compute similarities between documents and built a cross-document coreference system to disambiguate person names. [5] worked on named entity disambiguation with the
help of encyclopedia. The disambiguating process is very similar with entity linking.
[6] proposed a listwise learning-to-rank algorithm, ListNet, and illustrated its promising performance over other ranking algorithms in entity linking task. [7] introduces a
framework of system to link the entities in articles to Wikipedia. This framework is
reformed by [8] and SVM [9]is used to execute top 1 result validation.

3 Task Description and Problem Formulation

In this section, we are going to give a formal description of Entity Linking Task and review some existing methods. Learning-to-rank algorithms are applied and have shown
promising performance in this task mainly in the environment of online news and articles.

3.1 NLP&CC 2013 Entity Linking Evaluation Task

The NLP&CC 2013 Entity Linking Task requires linking the entities appeared in microblogs to the knowledge base entries, which is similar with Entity Linking Track in
TAC-KBP task. The Entity Linking Track in TAC-KBP task contributes to constructing
and expanding the knowledge base mainly with online news corpora.

3.2 Problem Formulation

In the entity linking task, there is a set of documents $DS = \{D_1, D_2, ..., D_M\}$. Each
document D_i has a list of entities $EL = \{E_1, E_2, ..., E_n\}$ to be linked. The knowledge
base is a set of entries $KB = \{K_1, K_2, ..., K_m\}$. Each entry K_j has multiple fields,
including $Name, ID, AnchorText, Doc$ and other fields which depend on what the
entry represents. The task is to link each entity in a document to the corresponding entry
in knowledge base. If there is no entry matching the entity, NIL should be returned.

4   Algorithms

The outline of our algorithm framework is as follows.

1. For each entity, find a list of possible aliases.
2. Search for potential candidate in the knowledge base and return a list of entries.
3. Use learning-to-rank algorithm to find the entry with the highest rank score.
4. Use binary classifier to validate the top 1 entry. If the entry is accepted by classifier, return its ID. Otherwise return NIL.

In Step 1, we design several methods to find a list of aliases for each entity. It helps to find potential candidate, and provide features to train learning-to-rank algorithm and binary classifier. The details of related methods would be described further in Section 4.1. In Step 2, we search for all entries in which the entity or one of its aliases occurs. If no candidate knowledge entry is found, our system just skips the rest two steps and return NIL for this entity. In Step 3, we apply ListNet as ranking algorithm and return the knowledge entry with the highest score. We will discuss this algorithm in detail in Section 4.2. In Step 4, we build a binary classifier to judge whether to accept the entity.

4.1   Alias List Generation

In Microblog environment, one specific entity might be mentioned by users in many different ways. For example, when people talk about something related to Kobe Byrant, who is a very famous star in National Basketball Association (NBA), they may mention him as 'Black Mamba' or 'KB24', which are his popular nicknames or aliases. In the knowledge base, for some entities, we have some attributes about their aliases, for example, nicknames, used names and so on. However, it is difficult to maintain a complete alias list for every entity. This is because aliases of an entity always change over time, language and geographic area. To solve this problem, we tried to utilize different features extracted from search engine click-through data, from search engine result page and from a local search engine built on knowledge base.

In the following subsections, we will introduce the methods to mining possible aliases for an entity.

Random Walk on Click-through Bipartite Graph. When people use search engines, the interaction process between users and the search engine will be record as many kinds of logs. One of them is the Click-through log which records two kinds of user behavior: **submitting query** and **clicking search result**.

The click-through log C can be represented as a set of triples $\langle q, u, f_{qu} \rangle$, where q is a query, u is a URL, and f_{qu} is the times URL u is clicked when query q is issued. Define $Q = \{q | q\ appears\ in\ C\}$, and $U = \{u | u\ appears\ in\ C\}$. Click-through data C can be presented as another equivalent form – a click-through bipartite graph $G = (Q, U, E)$. There are two types of nodes in the graph, queries and URLs. A sample portion of a bipartite graph constructed with search engine log, as shown in Figure 1.

A widely accepted assumption is that queries leading to same URLs usually reflect similar user intent. Therefore, the aggregation of a large number of user clicks is likely

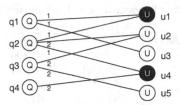

Fig. 1. An example of query-URL bipartite graph

to provide valuable 'soft' evidence of whether different queries are similar or not. The click-through graph can be constructed either at the page level or at the site level. In this study, we choose the URL itself to construct graph because the content of a Web site might be very comprehensive.

On the Query-URL bipartite graph, we can define a 2-step random walk process on the graph as follows:

$$s(q_i, q_j) = \sum_{k \in U} p_{i,k} \cdot p_{k,j} \tag{1}$$

where

$$p_{i,j} - \frac{f_{i,j}}{\sum_{(i,k) \in E} f_{i,k}} \tag{2}$$

$p_{i,j}$ can be interpreted as the transition probability from Node i to Node j and $s(q_i, q_j)$ can be interpreted as the similarity between query i and query j. Therefore, for each query which is going to be linked to knowledge base, we can generate similar queries as a alias list ranked by similarity in descending order. It is very possible that the alias contains the name which is the entity name in knowledge base.

For example, for query "禅师" and query "禅师菲尔", the alias list is shown in Table 1. Both of these two queries refer to the NBA player *Philip Douglas Jackson*, who is also called *Phil Jackson* for short. Alias lists for both queries contain the alias of "杰克逊", the Chinese name for *Jackson*. For query "皇马", we can find the full name "皇家马德里" in its alias list, which is translated from *Real Madrid*.

However, this method may fail for some long-tail queries, because it is probably that the query does not exist on the graph or is not connected with other query nodes. The more data we use to build the graph, the more likely we can find some similar queries for most of the queries.

N-gram Model on Search Engine Result Page. In modern search engines, when a user submits a query, the search engine will return a list of ranked results. All the results are closely related to the query, which provide a good resource to extract aliases of the query. We submit each of the entities to a popular Chinese search engine and extract the title and summary of each search result. To find the possible aliases of the entities, we propose the n-gram model. We change k from 2 to 10 and extract all the k-grams (continuous k characters) of the titles and summaries of the results. We retain the most

Table 1. Aliases from Random Walk on Click-through Bipartite Graph

Query	Aliases	Probability
禅师	禅师	0.0890
	杰克逊	0.0494
	禅师杰克	0.0398
	禅师杰克逊	0.0398
	hanshi	0.0151
	chanshi	0.0151
禅师菲尔	**杰克逊**	0.2222
	克逊	0.2222
	菲尔杰克逊	0.1277
	菲尔杰克	0.1277
	教过NBA全	0.0500
	过NBA全明星	0.0500
皇马	皇马	0.8214
	马德里	0.2997
	家马德里	0.2990
	皇家马德里	0.2984
	皇马球迷俱乐	0.1351
	皇马球迷俱乐部	0.1351

Table 2. Aliases from N-gram Model on Search Engine Result Page

Length	Results of titles	Results of summaries
2	TV	TV
3	BTV	BTV
4	北京电视	北京卫视
5	北京电视台	北京电视台
6	视台BTV在	201305
7	视台BTV在线	BTV北京卫视
8	电视台BTV在线	北京电视台养生堂
9	京电视台BTV在线	V北京电视台养生堂
10	北京电视台BTV在线	BTV北京电视台养生

frequent k-gram as the alias of length-k of the entity. We apply the n-gram model on the titles and summaries separately and get 2 lists of possible aliases. For example, when we apply the model on the entity *'BTV'*, which stands for the Beijing TV station, the results of titles and summaries with length from 2 to 10 are shown in Table 2.

From the results, the aliases "北京卫视" and "北京电视台" are two Chinese names of *'BTV'* and they are exactly what we want.

Local Search on Knowledge Base. It is very possible that an entity which is going to be linked to knowledge base does not appear in the target entity's name, but appears in its Infobox or body text. To solve this problem, we tried to build a local search engine which index the knowledge base including entity name, Infobox and full body text. In the search engine, each entity in the knowledge base is organized as a document while each entity going to be linked is regarded as a query. When a query is issued, top 30 entities returned by search engine are selected as a entities candidate list. It is ranked by relevance given by search engine in descending order.

Moreover, when indexing the knowledge base, different domains of entities have different weights. An entity's name has the greatest weight, and its Infobox data follows, and its body text has the smallest weight. The relevance is calculated based on Vector Space Model (VSM). A simple example for entity "北航" is presented as following. In the Infobox of knowledge entry "北京航空航天大学", the university's abbreviations are provided as "北航" and *BUAA*. When searching the entity in our local search engine, this entry is returned at the top of all results.

```
<entity>
<entity_id>KBBD043253</entity_id>
<category>科学\数理化\航空航天\北京航空航天大学.html</category>
<name>北京航空航天大学</name>
<fact>
<中文名>北京航空航天大学</中文名>
<外文名>Beihang University</外文名>
<简称>北航（BUAA）</简称>
<校训>德才兼备，知行合一</校训>
<创办时间>1952年10月25日</创办时间>
<类别>公立大学</类别>
...
</fact>
</entity>
```

4.2 ListNet

ListNet is a supervised learning-to-rank algorithm proposed by [6]. It uses a probabilistic method and a listwise loss function to rank a list of objects. In Step 3, we apply ListNet to rank the candidate knowledge entries for each entity. Given entity e_i and a set of candidates $\{K_1^{(i)}, K_2^{(i)}, ..., K_{n_i}^{(i)}\}$, if each $K_j^{(i)}$ is assigned with a score s_j, then we can get a permutation π according to the score, and the probability would be

$$P_s(\pi) = \prod_{t=1}^{n_i} \frac{\exp(s_t)}{\sum_{l=t}^{n_i} \exp(s_l)} \tag{3}$$

If the permutation of the top k candidates is $G_k = (K_{j_1}^{(i)}, K_{j_2}^{(i)}, ..., K_{j_k}^{(i)})$, the probability would be

$$P_s(G_k) = \prod_{t=1}^{k} \frac{\exp(s_{j_t})}{\sum_{l=t}^{n_i} \exp(s_{j_l})}$$

Then we assign each $K_j^{(i)}$ with a score $y_j^{(i)}$, and define a ranking function f_ω that can calculate a score $z_j^{(i)}$ for each candidate

$$z_j^{(i)} = f_\omega(x_j^{(i)}) \tag{4}$$

where $x_j^{(i)}$ is the feature vector of entry $K_j^{(i)}$ given e_i. The probability for permutation G_k to be the top k candidates would be $P_{y^{(i)}}(G_k)$ and $P_{z^{(i)}}(G_k)$ with the two scoring strategy. ListNet algorithm uses cross entropy as loss function

$$L(y^{(i)}, z^{(i)}) = - \sum_{\forall g \in G_k} P_{y^{(i)}}(g) \log(P_{z^{(i)}}(g)) \tag{5}$$

The gradient of cross entropy could be calculated by

$$\Delta\omega = \frac{\partial L(y^{(i)}, z^{(i)})}{\partial \omega} = - \sum_{\forall g \in G_k} \frac{\partial P_{z^{(i)}}(g)}{\partial \omega} \frac{P_{y^{(i)}}(g)}{P_{z^{(i)}}(g)} \tag{6}$$

In stochastic gradient descent, ω is updated with $-\eta\Delta\omega$ in each iteration. Here η is the learning rate.

5 Experiments

5.1 Dataset

We use data set from NLP&CC 2013 Entity Linking Evaluation Track. The data set is divided into two parts, the training set and the testing set. The training set is annotated. The annotating set is a subset of testing set, annotated to compute the precision, recall, and F1 measure. The scale of each set is shown in Table 3.

Table 3. Comparison results of accuracies

Data Set	# of microblogs	# of entities	Linkable	Unlinkable
Training Set	176	248	141	107
Testing Set	787	1249	–	–
Annotating Set	560	826	421	405

The knowledge base we use is a subset of Baidu Baike, a Chinese online encyclopedia just like Wikipedia. In this dump provided by NLP&CC, nearly 45, 000 knowledge entries are included. Each entry has a name, id, anchor text, infobox and an article.

5.2 Experiment Setup

We find the alias list for each entity in advance, using method described in Section 4.1. We build the local search engine with Lucene.

In entity linking task, we only care about whether the entry with highest score is correct. So we use top 1 permutation in ListNet. During training process, we manually assign score 1 to the correct knowledge entry, and 0 to others.

As for top 1 validation, we use SVM as the binary classifier. To balance the number of negative and positive samples, we select the correct entry for each entity as positive sample and other 2 entries with the highest score as negative samples. We append the rank score returned by ListNet to the feature vector input into ListNet, and generate the input feature vector for SVM.

5.3 Feature Selection

Considering the relationships among context, knowledge base, entity and aliases, we use three sets of features described below.

1. The compatibility of an entity and a knowledge entry.
   - Whether entity is substring of entry's name or anchor text, 1 for true and 0 for false.
   - The edit distance between the entity and the entry's name.
   - The minimum edit distance between the entity and each field of the entry's infobox.
   - Number of times the entity occurs in entry's article.
   - Whether this entry is in the top 30 results when searching the entity in local search engine.

2. The compatibility of aliases and a knowledge entry.
   - Whether one of aliases is substring of entry's name or anchor text, 1 for true and 0 for false.
   - The length of the longest common sequence of each field of entry's infobox and each alias.
   - The minimum edit distance between the the entry's name and each one of alias.
   - The sum of times each alias occurs in entry's article.

3. The compatibility of other entities co-occurs in the same microblog and the entries in knowledge base.
   - The sum of times each other entity in the same microblog occurs in the entry's article.

5.4 Experiment Result

The result on annotating set is shown in Table 4. The result of 'THUAI-RUN1' is given by this framework. We achieve an overall precision of 87.89% with a rank of 6th position. Considering the in-KB Results, we achieve a precision of 87.59% with a rank of 3rd position. This fact again illustrates that as a learning-to-rank algorithm, ListNet is suitable for entity linking. One limit of the performance is the inadequate size of training set. What's more, we tie the first place on recall of 93.83% among NIL Results. That means our binary classifier used for top 1 validation tends to refuse the result. If we had found better features for input of SVM, the performance might have been better.

Table 4. NLP&CC Evaluation Result

ID	Overall Results		in-KB Results			NIL Results		
	Correct	Precision	Precision	Recall	F1	Precision	Recall	F1
1	628	0.7603	0.7576	0.6532	0.7015	0.7624	0.8716	0.8134
2	638	0.7724	0.7819	0.6556	0.7132	0.7653	0.8938	0.8246
3	664	0.8039	0.7360	0.7482	0.7420	0.8769	0.8617	0.8692
4	731	0.8850	0.8662	0.8456	0.8558	0.9036	0.9260	0.9146
5	589	0.7131	0.7339	0.6583	0.6940	0.7694	0.8516	0.8084
6	622	0.7530	0.7452	0.7864	0.7652	0.8536	0.8047	0.8284
7	751	0.9092	0.8983	0.8812	0.8897	0.9201	0.9383	0.9291
8	743	0.8995	0.8859	0.8670	0.8764	0.9130	0.9333	0.9231
9	698	0.8450	0.8342	0.7767	0.8044	0.8548	0.9160	0.8844
10	697	0.8438	0.8142	0.7910	0.8024	0.8729	0.8988	0.8856
11	730	0.8838	0.8602	0.8480	0.8541	0.9075	0.9210	0.9142
12	730	0.8838	0.8602	0.8480	0.8541	0.9075	0.9210	0.9142
13	702	0.8499	0.8523	0.7815	0.8154	0.8477	0.9210	0.8828
14	701	0.8487	0.8497	0.7791	0.8129	0.8477	0.9210	0.8828
THUAI-RUN1	**726**	**0.8789**	**0.8759**	**0.8219**	**0.8480**	**0.8817**	**0.9383**	**0.9091**
THUAI-RUN2	**536**	**0.6489**	**0.6726**	**0.5416**	**0.6000**	**0.6324**	**0.7605**	**0.6906**
16	536	0.6489	0.6726	0.5416	0.6000	0.6324	0.7605	0.6906
17	673	0.8148	0.8407	0.8070	0.8235	0.8775	0.9141	0.8954
18	675	0.8172	0.8504	0.8120	0.8308	0.8731	0.9141	0.8931

6   Conclusion and Future Work

While data mining on microblogs has attracted more and more attention, entity linking on microblogs is an important foundation of many other applications. We propose a novel framework combining different possible aliases mining together to help linking entities from microblogs to knowledge base. This method utilizes external information such as query logs created by Web users. The effectiveness of this method is illustrated by the result of NLP&CC Evaluation Entity Linking Track. In our future work, we could use more features such as similarity on knowledge graphs to improve the performance.

References

1. Sakaki, T., Okazaki, M., Matsuo, Y.: Earthquake shakes Twitter users: real-time event detection by social sensors. In: Proceedings of the 19th International Conference on World Wide Web. ACM (2010)
2. Mathioudakis, M., Koudas, N.: Twittermonitor: trend detection over the twitter stream. In: Proceedings of the 2010 ACM SIGMOD International Conference on Management of Data. ACM (2010)
3. McCallum, A., Li, W.: Early results for named entity recognition with conditional random fields, feature induction and web-enhanced lexicons. In: Proceedings of the Seventh Conference on Natural Language Learning at HLT-NAACL 2003, vol. 4, Association for Computational Linguistics (2003)

4. Bagga, A., Baldwin, B.: Entity-based cross-document coreferencing using the vector space model. In: Proceedings of the 17th International Conference on Computational Linguistics, vol. 1. Association for Computational Linguistics (1998)
5. Bunescu, R.C., Pasca, M.: Using Encyclopedic Knowledge for Named entity Disambiguation. In: EACL, vol. 6 (2006)
6. Cao, Z., et al.: Learning to rank: from pairwise approach to listwise approach. In: Proceedings of the 24th International Conference on Machine Learning. ACM (2007)
7. Mihalcea, R., Csomai, A.: Wikify!: linking documents to encyclopedic knowledge. In: Proceedings of the Sixteenth ACM Conference on Conference on Information and Knowledge Management. ACM (2007)
8. Zheng, Z., et al.: Learning to link entities with knowledge base. In: Human Language Technologies: The 2010 Annual Conference of the North American Chapter of the Association for Computational Linguistics. Association for Computational Linguistics (2010)
9. Boser, B.E., Guyon, I.M., Vapnik, V.N.: A training algorithm for optimal margin classifiers. In: Proceedings of the Fifth Annual Workshop on Computational Learning Theory. ACM (1992)
10. Salton, G., Wong, A., Yang, C.-S.: A vector space model for automatic indexing. Communications of the ACM 18(11), 613–620 (1975)
11. Craswell, N., Szummer, M.: Random walks on the click graph. In: Proceedings of the 30th Annual International ACM SIGIR Conference on Research and Development in Information Retrieval. ACM (2007)

Automatic Assessment of Information Disclosure Quality in Chinese Annual Reports

Xin Ying Qiu[1], Shengyi Jiang[1], and Kebin Deng[2]

[1] CISCO School of Informatics
Guangdong University of Foreign Studies, Guangzhou, China
[2] School of Finance
Guangdong University of Foreign Studies, Guangzhou, China

Abstract. Information disclosure in annual reports is a mandatory requirement for publicly traded companies in China. The quality of information disclosure will reduce information asymmetry and therefore support market efficiency. Currently, the evaluation of the information disclosure quality in Chinese reports is conducted manually. It remains an untapped field for NLP and text mining community. The goal of this paper is to develop automatic assessment system for information disclosure quality in Chinese annual reports. Our assessment system framework incorporates different technologies including Chinese document modeling, Chinese readability index construction, and multi-class classification. Our explorative and systematic experiment results show that: 1) our automatic assessment system can produce solid predictive accuracy for disclosure quality, especially in "excellent" and "fail" categories; 2) our system for Chinese annual reports assessment achieves better predictive accuracy in certain perspective than the counterparts of the English annual reports prediction; 3) our readability index for Chinese documents, as well as other findings from system performance, may provide enlightenment for a better understanding about the quality features of Chinese company annual reports.

Keywords: Text classification, Natural language processing, Information disclosure quality, Application.

1 Introduction

Publicly traded companies in China are required to disclose important information about their companies annually to its investors on the market. Mandatory information disclosure includes company's financial performance, changes in strategies, explanations for such changes, and projections for future performance. The clarity and completeness in information disclosure have an important impact on reducing information asymmetry and therefore improving market efficiency. Historically, Chinese annual reports are mainly studied by researchers in finance, economics, and accounting fields in China. Their study have been focusing on how the quality of annual reports have caused economic consequences or impact corporate governance [1,2]. The quality of information disclosure has

G. Zhou et al. (Eds.): NLPCC 2013, CCIS 400, pp. 288–298, 2013.
© Springer-Verlag Berlin Heidelberg 2013

been deemed as an important factor in both economic practices as well as academic research. However, the assessment of the quality of information disclosure remains a manual and time consuming process in China. Analysts manually evaluate the quality of Chinese reports each year to assign a grade category for each report. The study of the quality of information disclosure, especially pertaining to Chinese reports, remains an untapped area to the text mining and natural language processing communities.

The application of computer science research in the area of disclosure quality was first proposed by Core (2001) [3]. He suggested that computing the measure of disclosure quality could greatly benefit from the techniques of other research areas such as computer science, computational linguistics, and artificial intelligence. Some relevant works in this direction are those of Davis, Piger, and Seor (2006)[4], Li (2008, 2010)[5,6], Kogan, Levin, Routledge, Sagi, and Smith (2009)[7], Feldman, Govindaraj, Livnat, and Segal (2010)[8], and Lehavy, Li, and Merkley (2011)[9]. Davis et al.(2006)[4] showed that the positive or negative tone in earnings press releases is associated with firms future performance, and captured in market returns. Kogan et al.[7] apply regression techniques to annual reports to construct models for the financial risk level for the period following the reports. Their model results outperform past volatility and are more accurate for annual reports after the Sarbanes-Oxley Act. In F. Li (2010)[6], naive Bayesian machine learning algorithm was applied to study how the information contained in the forward-looking statements in annual reports are related to different financial indicators. Feldman et al. (2010)[8] used regression analysis to show that tone changes in annual reports are associated with immediate market reactions and can be used to predict future stock prices. In general, these studies have focused on specific features of company reports, such as readability, positive and negative tone, and risk level, in stead of the overall quality assessment and its impact.

The SEC (Securities and Exchange Commission) used to conduct manual quality assessment by analysts for annual reports in the US. Researchers in accounting and finance domains have explored this data to study how the quality of mandatory disclosure is related to the forecast of company performance in the US. For example, Gelb and Zarowin [10] empirically confirmed that high disclosure firms provided greater stock price informativeness to the investors. However, these studies relied on the ratings from analysts' manual evaluation, which are no longer available after 1996. Otherwise, such quality index study relies on data of a smaller sample size from labor-intensive document analysis process. In China, analysts' evaluation of annual reports disclosure quality are available for all companies traded at the Shenzhen Stock Exchange. Researchers in the accounting and finance field have explored the disclosure quality ratings to study how disclosure quality is related to cost of equity capital (Wang and Jiang 2004 [1]), corporate governance (Wang and Shen) [11], and stock liquidity (Chen 2007 [12]). These studies mainly focus on the association of quality measure with other economic, managerial, or financial indicators. The methods these studies employ are generally semi-automatic, including content analysis, manual annotation and categorization, linear discriminant analysis, logit model and other statistical analysis.

We observe from the above literature analysis that automatic assessment of the disclosure quality in Chinese annual reports remains an open research question untapped by the text mining and NLP community. Our overall research goal is to explore the feasibility of applying text categorization methods in constructing automatic models for evaluating Chinese annual reports quality. We believe the significance of such study is three-fold: 1) the development of automatic methods for disclosure quality assessment can supplement the expensive and labor intensive manual evaluation process currently in place; 2) the assessment system can discover the important language and document-level features related to disclosure quality, instead of predefining ex ante limited textual features for further analysis; 3) our results could be compared with those of the more mature study of English annual reports to shed lights on the better understanding of how disclosure quality may be perceived and utilized in different country and economy.

We propose to address our research goals with the following approaches: 1) We use a multi-class text categorization approach and the quality rating data from Shenzhen Stock Exchange to build quality assessment model. Model performance is evaluated with accuracy, and analyzed according to different term weighting schemes, and per-class evaluation. Performance is further compared with the relevant counterpart of English annual reports. 2) Since annual report readability is one of the most popular features in English annual reports[5,9], we implement a Chinese document readability index and evaluate the association between readability measurement and analysts effort. Overall, our paper contributes a foundation of both methodology and results on automatic assessment and analysis of Chinese annual reports quality. The rest of the paper is organized as follows. First, we present our methodologies and experiment design. Next, we analyze our results addressing from our approaches. Our conclusions and directions for future research are then presented at the end.

2   Methodology and Design

Our hypothesis is that we could construct automatic system to assess Chinese annual reports' quality, as a supplement to analysts' manual evaluation. We formulate our design to build automatic assessment system with a multi-class classifier approach. We use the analysts manual quality ratings for annual reports at Shenzhen Stock Exchange as our gold standard. To validate the system's feasibility and evaluate the model's performance, we conduct a series of stratified cross-validation experiments. The details of this approach is presented as follows. We pick readability as a special feature to consider as it has been studied in depth in English annual reports analysis [5,9]. We implemented a Chinese readability index and report results from a regression model to evaluate its association with analysts effort. Our study of how readability and its component features are associated with disclosure quality is currently under way.

2.1   Data Collection and Class Definitions

We automatically retrieved all the Chinese annual reports with disclosure quality ratings for companies traded at the Shenzhen Stock Exchange from 2001 to 2009. After filtering out reports with errors, we obtain a sample set of a total of 4753 company annual reports with manual quality rating data spanning from 2001 to 2009. The distribution of the reports along with quality ratings is indicated in Table 1.

Table 1. Distribution of Annual Reports with Quality Assessment

Year	Number of Docs	Excellent	Good	Pass	Fail
2001	420	28	169	198	25
2002	434	32	204	166	32
2003	461	39	245	155	22
2004	452	28	281	126	17
2005	332	25	176	106	25
2006	538	53	289	170	26
2007	637	62	336	215	24
2008	715	77	432	191	15
2009	764	93	521	134	16
Total	4753	437	2653	1461	202

2.2   Readability Index

Readability is one of the interesting index in the study of English annual reports. Researchers have found out that reports with firms with low readability (i.e. hard to read) have lower earnings [5], and higher number of analysts following [9]. Our goal is to discover how Chinese report readability is associated with disclosure quality, and whether the association between Chinese reports readability and analysts efforts is the same as with English reports. We adopt a readability index as proposed by Yang [13] which has been applied to Chinese documents in other studies. We use the 7-factor and the 3-factor calculations as follow:

$$7 - factor\ readability: \quad Y = 13.90963 + 1.54461 \times FULLSEN +$$
$$39.01497 \times WORDLIST - 2.52206 \times STROKES -$$
$$0.29809 \times COUNT5 + 0.36192 \times COUNT12 +$$
$$0.99363 \times COUNT22 - 1.64671 \times COUNT25$$

$$(1)$$

$$3 - factor\ readability: \quad Y = 14.95961 + 39.07746 \times WORDLIST +$$
$$1.11506 \times FULLSEN - 2.48491 \times STROKES$$

$$(2)$$

where $STROKES$ is the average number of strokes of the Chinese characters in each document; $WORDLIST$ is the proportion of words in the basic word list for each document; $FULLSEN$ is the proportion of full sentences in all sentences in each document; $COUNT5$ is the proportion of 5 strokes characters in all characters for each document; $COUNT12$, $COUNT22$ and $COUNT23$ are calculated similarly as $COUNT5$ but for 12 strokes, 22 strokes and 23 strokes characters respectively.

As a note to our calculation of $WORDLIST$ factor, in absence of a "basic word list" from the original readability paper by Yang, we construct our own basic word list using the vocabulary lists of HSK (Hanyu Shuiping Kaoshi). There are 4 levels of vocabulary for HSK. We use the first three levels to construct a basic word list of 5081 terms (including both single word and multi-word Chinese terms), the size of which is closest to that of the original basic word list.

2.3 Document Models

In information retrieval, documents are typically modeled as vectors of terms with weighting for each term to indicate the importance of term in contributing to the documents' main content. Our research goal is to explore potential indicating textual features that may characterize the different qualities in Chinese annual reports. Besides analyzing certain popular disclosure features such as readability as in Section 2.2, we intend for this baseline system an approach to adopt the typical Bag-Of-Word representation model with TF*IDF weighting scheme. This model is the most successful and widely used where the positions of terms are ignored and the term weighting scheme measures the descriptive information contained in terms.

In Chinese language, terms may compose of single words as well as multi-word phrases. In our pilot study, we experimented with two approaches. One is to use Lucene system and Lucene's ICTCLAS dictionary to segment and index documents. Second is to first use ICTCLAS tool to first segment the documents and then index them with Lucene. We do not observe significant difference in the indexing results and therefore adopt the first approach using Lucene alone. Our indexing experiment originally extracted 54701 terms (including single word and multi-word terms). We observe that some features extracted were meaningless symbols and alphabet combinations. We did a coarse automatic filtering to preserve a feature set of 37809 Chinese terms.

For the TF*IDF weighting schemes, we experimented with 4 variations, namely "atn", "atc", "ltn", and "ltc". The "ltn" and "atn" weights are calculated as follows:

$$ltn: \quad w_i = (\ln(tf) + 1.0) \times \ln(\frac{N}{n}) \tag{3}$$

$$atn: \quad w_i = (0.5 + 0.5 \times \frac{tf}{maxtf}) \times \ln(\frac{N}{n}) \tag{4}$$

where tf is raw term frequency; $maxtf$ the highest term frequency in the document; N is the total number of documents in the collection; n is the number of documents containing term i; w_i is the weight of term i. The difference between "atc" and "atn", and between "ltc" and "ltn" weights are in the normalization factor only such that $weight(term_i) = \frac{w_i}{\sqrt{\sum_i w_i^2}}$, where w_i is either the "ltn" or the "atn" weight as stated above.

2.4   Classifier, Regression, and Experiment Design

Our quality assessment model is based on SVM classifiers. Since we have a four-class categorization problem, we need to consider different options. First, we could perform a one-against-rest classification for each class and combine the results to make a final decision. Second, we could perform a one-against-one classification for n(n - 1)/2 pairs of classes, and combine the results to make a final decision. Third, we could use algorithms designed specifically for multi-class classification. Currently, this article reports results for the first option, as the experiments for options two and three are under way.

For Option one, we use linear SVM to produce three one against-rest models. There are two variants of this in terms of how we combine the results of the three models. First, since we use three binary classifiers to predict the three classes of outperforming, average, and underperforming, each firm will have three scores assigned to it by each of the three classifiers. Our first strategy for combining is to use the highest score to assign a class label. We denote this model as SVM-score. Second, we use LinPlatts method (Platt, 1999)[14] to transform each of the three scores into a probability that the firm belongs to one of the three classes. Then, we use the highest probability to assign a class label to the firm. We denote this model as SVM-prob. We split all the 4753 documents into 10 sets with stratification, so that each the class distribution of each set is equivalent. We perform 10-fold cross validation with these 10 sets of data. Average accuracies are computed for all folds as well as for each binary classification for each of the four classes.

Our regression analysis of how Chinese readability is associated with analysts effort emanates from the study by Lehavy [9] on the English reports. Our hypothesis is that disclosure readability is positively related to number of analysts following, as in the following model:

$$Analysts = \beta_0 + \beta_1 Readability_{i,t} + \beta_2 Logsize_{i,t-1} + \beta_4 Lsegments_{i,t}$$
$$+\beta_5 Std_r ed_{i,t} + \beta_6 Growth_{i,t} + \beta_7 ADV_{i,t} + \beta_8 Mfcount_{i,t}$$
$$+\eta_i + g_t + v_{i,t}$$

$$(5)$$

where $Analysts$ is the number of analysts following a firm; $Logsize_{i,t-1}$ is the size of a firm; $Lsegments_{i,t}$ is number of reported business segments prior fiscal year; $Std_r ed_{i,t}$ is the stock return difference; $Growth_{i,t}$ is the earnings growth rate; $ADV_{i,t}$ is the advertisement expense; $Mfcount_{i,t}$ is the total forecasts times by analysts; η_i, g_t, and $v_{i,t}$ are dummy variables.

3   Results and Analysis

In this section, we present the performance of our automatic model for disclosure quality assessment, and the regression analysis of Chinese report readability.

Table 2 presents the average predictive accuracy from 10-fold cross validation of our automatic assessment model, using different term-weighting schemes and classifier constructions.

Table 2. Average Accuracy of Four-Class Classification Models

Weighting Schemes	Classifier Models	
	SVM-score	SVM-prob
atn	0.61542	0.61605
ltn	0.62192	0.61793
atc	0.61751	0.61603
ltc	0.62192	0.61604

As we observe from the Table 2, the choice of different multi-class label assignments methods do not perform significantly differently from each other. Nor does the different weighting schemes. We remind our readers that this classification is based on analysts manual ratings as gold standard. When compared with other research[15,16,17], *the best accuracy achieved at 62.19% for Chinese reports in fact is about 10% improvement over the performance of other classification research on English reports using financial indicators for class definitions.* We pick SVM-score model with ltn weighting scheme to look into the binary classification performance for each of the four quality ratings, namely "Excellent", "Good", "Pass", and "Fail". Results are shown in Table 3.

Table 3 shows *higher classification accuracy for each class than for overall 4-class classification.* In particular, *the prediction for the "Fail" class reports and "Excellent" achieves the highest two accuracies.* We look into the details of the prediction with a contingency table analysis of SVM-score model with ltn weight. As shown in Table 4, the true number percentage of "Excellent" and "Fail" reports is 13.45% of the total sample set. Although the predictions for the "Excellent" and "Fail" categories of annual reports achieve the highest accuracy up to 95%, the percentage of these two prediction is only 5% of the model's total predictions. This implies that the multi-class model is able to *identify "Excellent" or "Fail" quality reports with good precision,* but inefficient in identifying the majority of the "Excellent" or "Fail" quality reports. Another observation is that the two incorrect classification errors with the largest percentage occur for predicting "Pass" reports as "Good report" (18.22%) and predicting "Good" reports as "Pass" (6.94%). This indicates that *it is more difficult for our multi-class model to distinguish between "Good" and "Pass" reports. On the contrary, our model did not make*

Table 3. Accuracy of SVM-score Binary Classifier with ltn Weights for Predicting Each Class

SVM-score Binary Classifier Models with ltn Weight			
Folds	Excellent	Good	Pass	Fail
Fold 1	92.00%	68.21%	69.68%	96.00%
Fold 2	90.95%	67.79%	70.95%	95.79%
Fold 3	92.21%	65.47%	70.32%	95.79%
Fold 4	92.65%	61.34%	69.75%	95.80%
Fold 5	91.79%	66.11%	70.74%	95.79%
Fold 6	91.77%	70.04%	71.31%	95.99%
Fold 7	92.03%	68.34%	71.91%	96.44%
Fold 8	91.37%	66.53%	70.95%	95.79%
Fold 9	91.39%	65.97%	68.49%	95.59%
Fold 10	91.37%	66.53%	68.42%	95.79%
Average	91.75%	66.63%	70.25%	95.88%

Table 4. Contingency Table of SVM-score Multi-class Models with ltn Weights

SVM-score Multi-class Model with ltn Weight					
	True Excellent	True Good	True Pass	True Fail	Total
Predicted Excellent	2.69%	1.24%	0.27%	0.00%	4.21%
Predicted Good	6.29%	47.53%	18.22%	1.07%	73.11%
Predicted Pass	0.21%	6.94%	11.74%	2.95%	21.84%
Predicted Fail	0.00%	0.11%	0.51%	0.23%	0.84%
Total	9.20%	55.82%	30.74%	4.25%	100.00%

any mistakes in predicting "Excellent" as "Fail" (0%) or predicting "Fail" as "Excellent" (0%).

About our regression analysis on the association of Chinese report readability and analysts effort, we present our results in Figure 1. Models 1 and 4 are fixed effect models without controlled variables. Models 2 and 5 are fixed effect models with controlled variables. The significantly negative coefficient values indicate the negative association between the readability measure (which indicates the level of difficulty in reading) and the number of analysts following the reports. Models 3 and 6 are fixed effect models with controlled variables and dummy variable. The coefficient values are still negative, although the association is not significant. These results indicate that *analysts effort in following annual reports is negatively associated with the level of difficulty in reading the reports. In other words, easier to read annual reports attract more attention from analysts in their evaluation.*

Independent Variables	Dependent Variable: *ANALYST*					
	(1)	(2)	(3)	(4)	(5)	(6)
Readability (The first index)	-.0764401***	-.0751219***	-.0022596			
	-8.86	-10.3	-0.11			
Readability (The second index)				-.0813372***	-0.0798391***	-.0024844
				-8.87	-10.29	-0.11
Logsize		0.0215916	-0.1725738		0.0214627	-0.1725269
		0.37	-1.48		0.37	-1.48
Pinst		0.02735339***	0.0598901**		0.027352***	0.059891***
		4.96	5.09		4.96	5.09
Lsegments		0.0429698	-0.462776*		0.0424126	-0.46279*
		0.16	-2.01		0.16	-2.01
Std_red		3.446439***	1.041596**		3.445953****	1.041664**
		4.85	3.90		4.85	3.9
Growth		0.0072067	-0.1158578*		.0072127	-0.1158493*
		0.09	-2.38		0.09	-2.38
ADV		2.178051	3.156798		2.186037	3.158065
		0.7	1.41		0.7	1.41
Mfcount		0.2687364***	0.2343682***		0.268734***	0.2343686***
		42.32	10.61		42.32	10.61
Prob > chi2	0	0	0	0	0	0
Within R²	0.0419	0.3908	0.4599	0.0419	0.3908	0.4599
obs	4847	4847	4847	4847	4847	4847
Model	F	F	F, T	F	F	F, T
Methods	OLS	OLS	OLS	OLS	OLS	OLS

Fig. 1. Regression Analysis of Report Readability. Readability one is the 3-factor readability index. Readability 2 is the 7-factor readability index. Models 1 and 4 are fixed effect models without controlled variables. Models 2 and 5 are fixed effect models with controlled variables. Models 3 and 6 are fixed effect models with controlled variables and dummy variable.

4   Conclusion

We presented a series of experiments designed to explore the feasibility of constructing automatic assessment system for evaluating the information disclosure quality in annual reports. In contrast to the evaluation of English annual reports using financial performance indicators as surrogates, we exploit the manual ratings from analysts to train our learning classifiers. Our model for overall four-class classification achieves better performance to the extent of classification accuracy than the counterpart research on English reports. We speculate that the use of manual ratings could serve as better guidelines for automatic assessment of disclosure quality than financial or accounting measure.

Further analysis of the classifiers performance shows that distinguishing between "Excellent" versus "Fail" quality reports is much more efficient than between "Good" and "Pass" quality reports. Our current methods could supplement analysts manual process in identifying "Excellent" and "Fail" reports. Future research may be directed towards performance improvement of evaluating "Good" and "Pass" reports.

We further calculates the readability measure (i.e. level of reading difficulty) for Chinese annual reports. We studied the association of readability with analysts following effort. Our findings suggest that easier to read report may attract more analysts attention in following and analyzing the reports. Our study on how readability index and its component factor are related to disclosure quality is ongoing. Results will be presented in our future study.

From this study, we conclude that exploiting the manual ratings to develop automatic assessment model for disclosure quality not only is highly feasible, but also can supplement manual evaluation process. Our findings have give us a better understanding of the opportunities and challenges in automatic assessment of disclosure quality and prepare us for future work in this direction.

Acknowledgments. We thank the workshop participants at CISCO School of Informatics and the School of Finance at Guangdong University of Foreign Studies for their helpful comments and support. This work was partially supported by Grant 12YJAH103 from the Ministry of Education of China Project, and Grant 2011J5100004 from Guangzhou Science and Technology Program Project.

References

1. Wei, W., Gaofeng, J.: Information Disclosure, Transparency and the Cost of Capital. Economic Research Journal 7 (2004)
2. Ying, Z., Zhengfei, L.: The Relationship between Disclosure Quality and Cost of Equity Capital of Listed Companies in China. Economic Research Journal 2 (2006)
3. Core, J.E.: A Review of the Empirical Disclosure Literature: Discussion. Journal of Accounting and Economics 31(13), 441–456 (2001)
4. Davis, A., Piger, J., Seor, L.: Beyond the Numbers: An analysis of optimistic and pessimistic language in earnings releases. Working paper, Washington University in St. Louis (2006)
5. Li, F.: Annual report readability, current earnings, and earnings persistence. Journal of Accounting and Economics 45(2-3), 221–247 (2008)
6. Li, F.: The information content of forward-looking statements in corporate filings A nave Bayesian machine learning approach. Journal of Accounting Research 48(5), 1049–1102 (2010)
7. Kogan, S., Levin, D., Routledge, B.R., Sagi, J.S., Smith, N.A.: Predicting risk from financial reports with regression. In: NAACL 2009 Proceedings of Human Language Technologies, pp. 272–280 (2009)
8. Feldman, R., Govindaraj, S., Livnat, J., Segal, B.: Managements tone change, post earnings announcement drift and accruals. Review of Accounting Studies 15(4), 915–953 (2010)

9. Lehavy, R., Li, F., Merkley, K.: The effect of annual report readability on analyst following and the properties of their earnings forecasts. The Accounting Review 86(3), 1087–1115 (2011)
10. Gelb, D.S., Zarowin, P.: Corporate disclosure policy and the informativeness of stock prices. Review of Accounting Studies 7, 33–52 (2002)
11. Wang, X., Shen, W.: The Empirical Research on the Relationship between Control Structure and the Quality of Information Disclosure. Securities Market Herald 4 (2008)
12. Chen, Q.: Disclosure Quality and Market Liquidity. South China Journal of Economics 10 (2007)
13. Yang, S.-J.: A Readability Formula For Chinese Langauge. Ph.D. thesis. The University of Wisconsin (1971)
14. Platt, J.C.: Probabilistic outputs for support vector machines and comparison to regularized likelihood methods. In: Advances in Large Margin Classifiers, pp. 61–74. MIT Press, Cambridge (1999)
15. Balakrishnan, R., Qiu, X.Y., Srinivasan, P.: On the predictive ability of narrative disclosures in annual reports. European Journal of Operational Research 202, 789–801 (2010)
16. Qiu, X.Y.: Towards building ranking models with annual reports. Journal of Digital Information Management 8(5), 338–343 (2010)
17. Qiu, X.Y., Srinivasan, P., Hu, Y.: Supervised Learning Models to Predict Firm Performance with Annual Reports. Journal of the American Society for Information Science and Technology (forthcoming)

A Fast Matching Method Based on Semantic Similarity for Short Texts

Jiaming Xu[*], Pengcheng Liu, Gaowei Wu, Zhengya Sun,
Bo Xu, and Hongwei Hao

Institute of Automation, Chinese Academy of Sciences, 100190, Beijing, P.R. China
{jiaming.xu,pengcheng.liu,gaowei.wu,zhengya.sun,boxu,
hongwei.hao}@ia.ac.cn

Abstract. As the emergence of various social media, short texts, such as weibos and instant messages, are very prevalent on today's websites. In order to mine semantically similar information from massive data, a fast and efficient matching method for short texts has become an urgent task. However, the conventional matching methods suffer from the data sparsity in short documents. In this paper, we propose a novel matching method, referred as semantically similar hashing (SSHash). The basic idea of SSHash is to directly train a topic model from corpus rather than documents, then project texts into hash codes by using latent features. The major advantages of SSHash are that 1) SSHash alleviates the sparse problem in short texts, because we obtain the latent features from whole corpus regardless of document level; and 2) SSHash can accomplish similar matching in an interactive real time by introducing hash method. We carry out extensive experiments on real-world short texts. The results demonstrate that our method significantly outperforms baseline methods on several evaluation metrics.

Keywords: Short Text, Semantically Similar Matching, Topic Model, Hash.

1 Introduction

Short texts are prevalent on the Web, no matter in traditional Web sites, e.g. Web page titles, text advertisements and image captions, or in emerging social media, e.g. weibos, instant messages, and questions in Q&A websites [1]. Facing the massive short texts, a fast matching method for short texts has become an urgent task to mine semantically similar information for many NLP (Natural Language Processing) applications such as Machine Translation, Text Coherence Detection, etc [2]. Similarity matching can also improve the traditional search engines and user experience [3].

The approaches which improve matching performance between the query and documents can be mainly divided into two categories. The approaches in the first category attempt to do query refinement, such as spelling error correction, word splitting, phrase segmentation, acronym expansion and so on. For example, Li et al. [4] conducted spelling error correction for web search by using a Maximum Entropy

G. Zhou et al. (Eds.): NLPCC 2013, CCIS 400, pp. 299–309, 2013.
© Springer-Verlag Berlin Heidelberg 2013

model as well as the Source Channel model. Peng et al. [5] performed automatic word stemming for web search by means of a Statistical Language model. Guo et al. [6] described a unified and discriminative model by using Conditional Random Field model for query refinement tasks. However, those works are not beyond sentence level.

In recent years, more researchers focus attention on the second category of methods, latent semantic approaches. NMF (Nonnegative Matrix Factorization) [12], PLSI (Probabilistic Latent Semantic Indexing) [14] and LDA (Latent Dirichlet Allocation) [7] are the most popular latent semantic approaches, and many extensions of those approaches have proposed. However, those approaches are rough clustering methods and time-consuming for online matching.

On the other hand, hashing methods can perform highly efficient but approximate similarity search, and have gained great success in many applications such as Content-Based Image Retrieval [8], near-duplicate document detection [9], etc. Hashing methods project high-dimensional objects to compact binary codes called fingerprints and make similar fingerprints for similar objects [10]. Nevertheless, the previous works, including topic models and hashing methods, suffer from the sever data sparsely in short texts. One popular method for short texts is to extend the short text by knowledge database, such as WordNet[1] or HowNet[2]. However, the social media data are often event-driven, temporal information. For example, typically a short text containing the word "jobs" is likely to be about employment, but right after October 5, 2011, a short text containing "job" is more likely to be related to Steve Jobs' death [11]. A knowledge database with sufficiently good performance must to be updated timely that result in high labor and material resources for maintaining the database.

To tackle the problems above, this paper attempts to introduce latent semantic approaches and hash methods to our matching method, referred as semantically similar hashing (SSHash). SSHash is based on the following two main ideas. 1). Since hashing methods have bad performance due to the few observed words, we extend the observed features using latent features by latent semantic approaches, rather than knowledge database. 2). Since the conventional methods suffer from the sparsity problem due to the less discriminative observed features in short texts, we directly modeling the generation of features in the whole corpus, rather than the document level. Compared with conventional similar matching method, SSHash combines the merits of topic model and hashing method.

The remainder of this paper is organized as follows. Section 2 reviews the relevant research for each of our components. Section 3 describes our method SSHash and gives implementation details. Experimental results are presented in Section 4. Finally, conclusions are made in the last section.

---

[1] http://wordnet.princeton.edu: a lexical database for English.
[2] http://www.keenage.com: Chinese message structure base.

2   Related Works

In this section, we first introduce the two building blocks of our method: latent semantic approaches and hashing methods. Using the topic models allow us to achieve semantic similarity, while using hashing methods give our SSHash method interactive similarity matching time.

2.1   Latent Semantic Approaches

Latent semantic approaches, also known as topic models, have two approaches, non-probabilistic approach and probabilistic approach. The typical non-probabilistic approaches, such as NMF [12], and LSA [13], are all based on vector space model. Maximum likelihood estimation can be used for learning probabilistic general models such as PLSI [14] and LDA [7]. The non-probabilistic models can be reformulated as probabilistic models.

In recent years, topic models for short texts have been extensively studied. However, the early studies mainly focused on exploiting external knowledge to solve the sparsity problem of short text. For example, Phan et al. [15] learned hidden topics from large external resources to enrich the representation of short texts. These methods are overdependence on the performance of knowledge base. Researchers propose several other approaches to improve the topic models on short texts. For example, Rosen-Zvi et al. [16] expanded topic distributions from document-level to user-level, aggregate the short texts by each user into longer texts, and then train a conventional topic model. Zhao et al. [17] simply supposed that each short text only contains a single topic. Diao et al. [11] further assumed short texts published around the same time have a higher probability to belong to the same topic. However, such heuristic methods are high data-dependent, not be suitable for other datasets, like short questions or news titles, because of too many strict assumptions and sparse constraints be imposed in those approaches.

Yan et al. [1] proposed such idea that learning the latent semantic association by directly modeling the generation of word co-occurrence patterns in the whole corpus, rather than document level. With such idea, we develop our matching method SSHash based on semantic similarity for short texts to alleviate the sparse problem and improve the semantic correlation matching.

2.2   Hashing Methods

As hashing methods can perform highly efficient but similarity matching, approximate nearest neighbor search in Hamming space is widely applied in image retrieval [8], image classification [18], information retrieval [9], and so on. A notable method is Locality Sensitive Hashing (LSH), proposed by Indyk et al. [19]. LSH scheme is that hash codes of similar objects collide with high probability and the hash codes of dissimilar objects collide with low probability, such that for objects A and B:

$$\Pr[h(A) = h(B)] = sim(A, B), \tag{1}$$

Where $sim(A, B) \in [0,1]$ is some similarity function. Broder, et al. [21] provided an elegant construction of LSH with Jaccard similarity coefficient:

$$sim(A,B) = J(A,B) = \frac{|A \cap B|}{|A \cup B|} \qquad (2)$$

Charikar [20] explored constructions of LSH functions for various other interesting similarity measures, referred as simhash. Those hash codes possesses two conflicting properties: 1). the fingerprint of a document is a "hash" of its features; 2). similar documents have similar hash values.

Manku, et al. [9] represented a detailed algorithm for simhash for similar documents matching. Manku's algorithm process is as follows: we first convert a document into a set of features, each feature tagged with its weight. Features are computed using standard IR techniques like tokenization, case folding, stop-word removal, and stemming and phrase detection. Then, we transform the features into an f -bit fingerprint where f is small, say 64.

However, Manku's algorithm for similarity matching encounters the sparsity problem in short texts. Because of the few observed features, some non-overlapping features lead to a very low similarity score despite the high semantic relatedness. One solution is to enlarge the Hamming distance to increase the recall rate. However, the larger Hamming distance, the lower precision. Fig. 1 shows an example to reveal the correspondence between similarity and Hamming distance, and Fig. 2 describes the problem that the larger Hamming distance lead to the lower precision. We can see that it is not a wise choice by enlarging Hamming distance to solve short text problem.

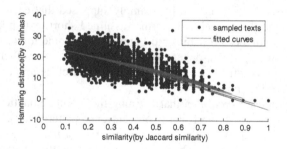

Fig. 1. The correspondence between similarity and Hamming distance (one probe query and 8359 sampled texts)

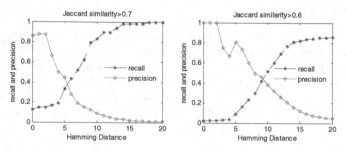

Fig. 2. Larger Hamming distance leads to the lower precision. (Respectively define the lower matching limit by Jaccard similarity as 0.7, 0.6 and 0.5)

Another approach is to refine the hash function to increase the collision probability within a same cluster. He, et al. [22] presented a k-means hashing method (KMH) to learn hashing code whose Hamming distance approximates the data similarity. In order to preserve the similarity between Euclidean and Hamming distances of k-means clusters, KMH simultaneously minimize the quantization error and the affinity error among sample x, k-means center $c_{i(x)}$ and Hamming code $h_{i(x)}$ by Expectation Maximization (EM) algorithm. However, KMH lead to a high computation complexity due to EM method.

In our works, SSHash solves the two problems of matching efficiency and semantic similarity simultaneously by combining the merits of latent semantic approaches and hashing methods.

3   Semantically Similar Hashing

In order to increase the recall of similar matching, we should increase the collision probability of hash codes between the similar short texts, and avoid enlarging Hamming distance. In this paper, we implement this idea by introducing biterm topic model to hash method. Fig.3 illustrates our matching method named SSHash.

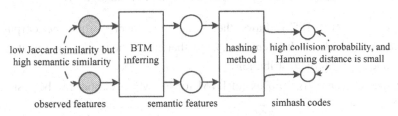

Fig. 3. Schematic representation of SSHash

3.1   Biterm Extraction

Since conventional topic models, such as PLSI and LDA, implicitly count the frequency of word co-occurrence by modeling word generation form the document level, in this paper, we follow Yan's biterm topic model (BTM) to directly model the words co-occurrence patterns based on biterms. Here, we give an example to explain what a biterm is. In a short text "A forum for the NLP researchers", we first preprocess the raw texts, such as filtering the stop words, lower case and stemming the words, and then extract the biterms with its frequency as shown in table 1. Then, we put the all biterms into corpus to train BTM.

Table 1. Biterms extracted from the example short text

Biterms	Frequency
forum, nlp	1
forum, research	1
nlp, research	1

3.2   Biterm Topic Model

BTM supposes that both words in the biterm are drawn from the same topic, and considers that the whole corpus as a mixture of topics. That is different from conventional generative models such as LDA. The difference in graphical representation is described as shown in Fig.4.

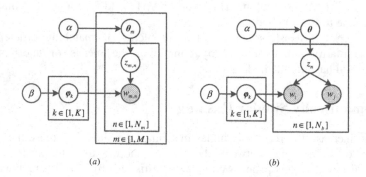

(a)   (b)

Fig. 4. Graphical representation of (a) LDA and (b) BTM

We can see that BTM draws the topic assignment z_n from the corpus-level distribution θ, which are different from LDA that draws the topic assignment $z_{m,n}$ from the document-level topic distribution θ_m.

The specific generative process of BTM for the whole corpus can be assumed as follows:

1. Draw a topic distribution θ ~Dirichlet(α) for the whole collection
2. For each topic z_n
    (a) Draw a topic-specific word distribution φ_k ~Dirichlet(β)
3. For each biterm b
    (a) Draw a topic assignment z_n ~Multinomial(θ)
    (b) Draw two words: w_i , w_j ~Multinomial(φ_k)

And the joint probability of a biterm $b = (w_i, w_j)$ can be written as:

$$P(b) = \sum_z P(z)P(w_i \mid z)P(w_j \mid z) = \sum_z \theta_z \varphi_{i|z} \varphi_{j|z} \tag{3}$$

The parameters, θ and φ, can be inferred by Gibbs sampling. More details can be found in [1].

3.3   Features Representation

In order to represent the observed features in short texts by using the latent topic distribution in a document, we should infer the topic distribution in a document level.

Although BTM has no regard for document concept, the inferring process is similar with training process just considering the word distribution φ_k is constant. However, Gibbs sampling is time-consuming and not suit for online text matching because of many iterations until convergence. Here is a compromise approach to solve the dilemma problem that parameters can be estimated based on the observed frequency. BTM assumes that latent topic distribution in a document is that:

$$P(z \mid d) = \sum_b P(z \mid b) P(b \mid d) \tag{4}$$

Where $P(z \mid b)$ can be derived by the parameters estimated during the training process:

$$P(z \mid b) = \frac{P(z) P(w_i \mid z) P(w_j \mid z)}{\sum_z P(z) P(w_i \mid z) P(w_j \mid z)} \tag{5}$$

In this equation, $P(z) = \theta_z$, and $P(w_i \mid z) = \varphi_{iz}$, and $P(b \mid d)$ can be calculated simply by the observed frequency:

$$P(b \mid d) = \frac{n_d(b)}{\sum_b n_d(b)} \tag{6}$$

Now, the semantic features in a document can be represented by the latent topic distribution $P(z \mid d)$, and each topic is a distribution over words $P(w_i \mid z)$. In order to reduce the feature dimension, we select the most likely words for each topic such as top 20. We call the selected words tokens, denoted as t to distinguish word concept w in the corpus. Note that the weights of tokens should be normalized as follow:

$$P(t_i \mid d) = \sum_z P(t_i \mid z) P(z \mid d) = \sum_z \frac{P(w_i \mid z)}{\sum_{top 20} P(w \mid z)} P(z \mid d) \tag{7}$$

3.4   Fingerprinting with Hash Method

Since we have taken the tokens selected from each topic to represent the semantic features, short text are fingerprinted with hash method by using tokens with their weights. The fingerprinting process incorporated semantic information for each short text can be described as follows:

1. Initialize two arrays W and B with f zeros
2. For each token t_i
   (a) Compute a f-bit hash code h_i
   (b) Iterate through each bit h_{ij}, where $j \in [1, f]$
       (i) If $h_{ij} = 1$, $W[j] = W[j] + P(t_i \mid d)$, where $P(t_i \mid d)$ is calculated in Eq.(7)
       (ii) If $h_{ij} = 0$, $W[j] = W[j] - P(t_i \mid d)$

3. Revisit the all bits of array W, where $j \in [1, f]$
   (a) If $W[j] \geq 0$, then set the bit to 1, $B[j] \leftarrow 1$
   (b) If $W[j] < 0$, then set the bit to 0, $B[j] \leftarrow 0$
4. Return the array B, this is a hash code fingerprinted for short text.

3.5   Similarity Matching for Online Query

When a short text is inputted by user for online matching, we should preprocess the text, as section 3.3 and 3.4, to get the fingerprint and then do approximate nearest neighbor search in Hamming space. All pairs of fingerprints found within a certain Hamming distance of each other are semantic similar texts, as shown in Fig. 5,

Fig. 5. Similarity matching for query

In our method, we apply block-permuted Hamming search (BPHS) and column-oriented database management system HBase[3] to speed up the online matching for large collections, the more implement details of BPHS can be found in [9].

4   Experimental Design, Comparison and Analysis

4.1   Data Set

In our experiments, we made use of real-world short text collections which are random selected from Weibo[4] between September 1st and December 13rd, 2012. Thanks for some weibos labeled by authors with hashtags to denote a specific topic, we organize those weibos with the same hashtag into a semantic similar cluster. Here, we select 20 specific topics and process the raw texts via the following steps: 1). removing hashtags and non-Chinese characters; 2). word splitting and filtering stop words; 3). removing words with documents frequency less than 5; 4). filtering out weibos with length less than 5. At last, we left 151,629 valid weibos, 34,099 words and the average document length is 14.9.   The texts are randomly split into a training set containing 137,929 texts and a test set containing 13,700 texts.

4.2   Evaluation Metrics

In order to evaluate our method's performance, we measure the recall and precision of our method. Intuitively, we want to maximize the number of correct positives and

---

[3] http://hbase.apache.org: a Hadoop database, a distributed, scalable, big data store.
[4] http://weibo.com: a popular Chinese microblog website.

minimize the number of false positives. A correct positive is defined as a semantically similar match between a probe query and one of short text collections. To decide whether a semantically similar match, we simply test if the two weibos have the same hashtag. Recall and precision are defined as:

$$recall = \frac{number\ of\ matched\ semantic\ similar\ texts}{total\ number\ of\ all\ semantic\ similar\ texts} \tag{8}$$

$$precision = \frac{number\ of\ matched\ semantic\ similar\ texts}{total\ number\ of\ matched\ texts} \tag{9}$$

4.3   Results and Analysis

Using 64-bit hash codes, we compute a query's fingerprint and match all of the texts stored in a Hamming ball of radius from 0 to 20. Fig.6 shows the matching performance comparison by using simhash, LDA+hash and SSHash.

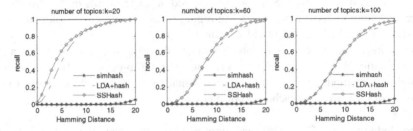

Fig. 6. Matching performance comparison with different Hamming distance (topic number: K=20, 60,100)

We can see SSHash and LDA+hash has a high recall in a little Hamming distance, and SSHash achieves higher recall rate than LDA+hash.

In Fig.7, the precision-recall curves reveal that SSHash and LDA+hash always dominate simhash, and SSHash is better than LDA+hash.

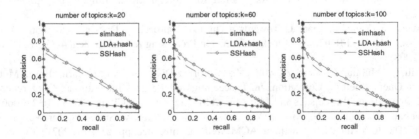

Fig. 7. Precision-Recall curves for Weibo datasets (topic number: K=20, 60,100)

From the results, we can further see that the recall is more notable when the topic number is 20. That is because that the semantic features discovered are very general when the number of topics is small. In such case, the collision probability of hash codes between the similar texts or dissimilar texts will be increased. This interpretation is verified in Fig.7. Although the recall rate is higher, the precision is lower when the number of topics is small and within a little Hamming distance. In contrast, when the number of topics is large, the semantic features discovered are very specific.

5   Conclusion

In this paper, we describe a novel method based on semantic similarity for short texts, namely semantically similar hashing (SSHash). SSHash can project the shorts text into binary hash codes with semantic information but alleviate the sparse problem due to regardless the document concept. We can find semantically similar texts in an interactive real time by using SSHash. We carried on experiments on Weibo datasets. The results demonstrated that we achieve higher recall and precision than simhash or LDA+hash applied to the real-world short texts.

For future work, there are still lots of work to do. First, we will do more analysis on computational cost. Second, the off-line training process is time-consuming, although our method can speed up the online matching. We would like to introduce online latent semantic approaches to our method.

Acknowledgements. This work is supported by the National Natural Science Foundation of China under Grant No. 61175050 and No. 61203281.

References

1. Yan, X., Guo, J., Lan, Y., Cheng, X.: A Biterm Topic Model for Short Texts. In: Proc. 22th International Conference on World Wide Web, pp. 1445–1455 (2013)
2. Weiwei, G., Diab, M.: Modeling Sentences in the Latent Space. In: Proceedings of the 50th Annual Meeting of the Association for Computational Linguistics, pp. 864–872 (2012)
3. Wan, X., Yang, J., Xiao, J.: Towards a Unified Approach to Document Similarity Search Using Manifold-Ranking of Block. Information Processing & Management 44(3), 1032–1048 (2008)
4. Mu, L., Muhua, Z., Yang, Z., Ming, Z.: Exploring Distributional Similarity Based Models for Query Spelling Correction. In: Proceedings of the 21st International Conference on Computational Linguistics and 44th Annual Meeting of the ACL, pp. 1025–1032 (2006)
5. Fuchun, P., Ahmed, N., Xin, L., Yumao, L.: Context Sensitive Stemming for Web Search. In: The 30th Annual International ACM SIGIR Conference, pp. 23–27 (2007)
6. Jiafeng, G., Gu, X., Hang, L., Xueqi, C.: A Unified and Discriminative Model for Query Refinement. In: The 31st Annual International ACM SIGIR Conference, pp. 379–386 (2008)

7. Blei, D.M., Ng, A.Y., Jordan, M.I.: Latent dirichlet allocation. The Journal of Machine Learning Research 3, 993–1022 (2003)
8. Yan, K., Sukthankar, R., Huston, L.: Efficient Near-duplicate Detection and Sub-image Retrieval. In: Proceedings of the 12th ACM International Conference on Multimedia, pp. 869–876 (2004)
9. Manku, G.S., Jain, A., Sarma, A.D.: Detecting near-duplicates for web crawling. In: Proceedings of the 16th International Conference on World Wide Web, pp. 141–150 (2007)
10. Qixia, J., Maosong, S.: Semi-Supervised SimHash for Efficient Document Similarity Search. In: The 49th Annual Meeting of the Association for Computational Linguistics, pp. 93–101 (2011)
11. Qiming, D., Jing, J., Feida, Z., Lim, E.-P.: Finding Bursty Topics from Microblogs. In: The 50th Annual Meeting of the Association for Computational Linguistics, pp. 536–544 (2012)
12. Lee, D.D., Seung, H.S.: Learning the parts of objects by non-negative matrix factorization. Nature 401, 788–791 (1999)
13. Deerwester, S., Dumais, S.T., Furnas, G.W., Landauer, T.K., Harshman, R.: Indexing by Latent Semantic Analysis. Journal of the American Society for Information Science 41(6), 391–407 (1990)
14. Hofmann, T.: Probailistic Latent Semantic Indexing. In: Proceedings of the 22nd Annual International ACM SIGIR Conference on Research and Development in Information Retrieval, pp. 50–57 (1999)
15. Phan, X.H., Nguyen, M.L., Horiguchi, S.: Learning to Classify Short and Sparse Text & Web with Hidden Topics from Large-Scale Data Collections. In: Proceedings of the 17th International Conference on World Wide Web, pp. 91–100 (2008)
16. Rosen-Zvi, M., Griffiths, T., Steyvers, M., Smyth, P.: The Author-Topic Model for Authors and Documents. In: Proceedings of the 20th Conference on Uncertainty in Artificial Intelligence, pp. 487–494 (2004)
17. Zhao, W.X., Jiang, J., Weng, J., He, J., Lim, E.-P., Yan, H., Li, X.: Comparing Twitter and Traditional Media Using Topic Models. In: Clough, P., Foley, C., Gurrin, C., Jones, G.J.F., Kraaij, W., Lee, H., Mudoch, V. (eds.) ECIR 2011. LNCS, vol. 6611, pp. 338–349. Springer, Heidelberg (2011)
18. Boiman, O., Shechtman, E., Irani, M.: In Defense of Nearest-Neighbor Based Image Classification. In: IEEE Computer Society Conference on Computer Vision and Pattern Recognition (2008)
19. PiotrIndyk, R.M.: Approximate Nearest Neighbors: Towards Removing the Curse of Dimensionality. In: Proceedings of the Thirtieth Annual ACM Symposium on the Theory of Computing, pp. 604–613 (1998)
20. Charikar, M.: Similarity Estimation Techniques from Rounding Algorithms. In: Proceedings on 34th Annual ACM Symposium on Theory of Computing, pp. 380–388 (2002)
21. Broder, A.Z., Charikar, M., Frieze, A.M., Mitzenmacher, M.: Min-Wise Independent Permutations. In: Proceedings of the Thirtieth Annual ACM Symposium on the Theory of Computing, pp. 327–336 (1998)
22. Kaiming, H., Fang, W., Jian, S.: K-means Hashing: an Affinity-Preserving Quantization Method for Learning Binary Compact Codes. In: The 24th IEEE Conference on Computer Vision and Pattern Recognition (2013)

Query Generation Techniques for Patent Prior-Art Search in Multiple Languages

Dong Zhou, Jianxun Liu, and Sanrong Zhang

Key Laboratory of Knowledge Processing and Networked Manufacturing &
School of Computer Science and Engineering,
Hunan University of Science and Technology,
Xiangtan, Hunan 411201, China
{dongzhou1979,wuyunzsr}@hotmail.com, ljx529@gmail.com

Abstract. Patent prior-art search is an necessary step to ensure that no previous similar disclosures were made before granting an patent. The task is to identify all relevant information which may invalidate the originality of a claim of a patent application. Using the whole patent or extracting high indicative terms to form a query reduces the search burden on the user. To date, There are no large-scale experiments conducted specifically for evaluating query generation techniques used in patent prior-art search in multiple languages. In the following paper, we firstly introduced seven methods for generating patent queries for ranking. Then a large-scale experimental evaluation was carried out on the CLEF-IP 2009 multilingual dataset in English, French and German. A detail comparison of the different methods in terms of performance and efficiency has been performed in addition to the use of full-length documents as queries in the patent search. The results show that some methods, work well in information retrieval in general, fail to achieve the same effectiveness in the patent search. Different methods demonstrated distinct performance w.r.t query and document languages.

Keywords: Patent Prior-Art Search, Multilingual Information Access, Query Generation.

1 Introduction

Patent information retrieval is an active sub-domain of information retrieval that aims to support patent experts to retrieve patents that satisfy their information needs and search criteria [1]. A common scenario in patent information retrieval is prior-art search, which is performed by patent experts to ensure that no previous similar disclosures were made before granting a patent. They will normally need to use some sort of information retrieval systems and tools to automate this process. To improve the usefulness of such systems and tools, researchers from around the world gathered in CLEF[1] and NTCIR[2] for automating this specific

---

[1] http://www.clef-initiative.eu/
[2] http://research.nii.ac.jp/ntcir/index-en.html

G. Zhou et al. (Eds.): NLPCC 2013, CCIS 400, pp. 310–321, 2013.
© Springer-Verlag Berlin Heidelberg 2013

task. Many state-of-art patent search systems have been developed. A general trend is to use the full patent document as an input, after preprocessing, search over previous filed patents with the aim of retrieving relevant documents, which may invalidate or at least describe prior art work in a patent application [2–4]. This is of high commercial value to many companies and organizations.

The aim and challenges of patent prior-art search are different from those of standard ad-hoc information retrieval and/or web search. One challenge would be the vocabulary mismatch between existing filed patents and the query patent. This is often caused by the patent writing style. Long patent queries comprising of several hundreds of terms fail to represent a focused information need required for high precision retrieval. On the other hand, the primary focus of the patent prior-art search is to retrieve all relevant documents at early ranks. Carefully balance of precision and recall would be necessary.

Recent work in both CLEF and NTCIR favor to use either full patent documents as queries or key terms extracted from a patent application to produce a more focus information need. For example, all participants in CLEF 2010 [5] and CLEF 2011 [3] adopted the same way. TF-IDF scheme, language model-based weighting scheme, text summarization or phrases extraction techniques were frequently used [6–9]. Multilingual aspect has been addressed in recent CLEF campaigns, specifically for English, French and German [5, 3]. The tasks organized in those workshops did not restrict the language used for retrieving the documents, but participants were encouraged to use the multilingual characteristic of the collection. This is because the claims in granted patent documents may be provided in all three languages. Researchers attempted different search tasks on the provided data. However, there is lack of direct comparison between the performance in different languages.

In this paper, we firstly introduce seven methods for generating query representations. These include a method for removal of unit frequency terms, the TF method, the TFIDF method, the BM25 method, the language model-based approach, the relevance feedback-based method, and the method based on IPC classification. Large-scale experimental evaluation was then carried out on the CLEF-IP 2009 dataset investigating retrieval effectiveness across different languages used. This includes English, French and German. A detail comparison of the different methods in terms of performance and efficiency has been performed in addition to the use of full-length documents as queries in the patent search. Note that the scenario investigated in this paper can not be treated as cross-lingual or multilingual patent search [10, 11], as it only deals with monolingual retrieval in three different languages.

The remainder of this paper is organized as follows. In §2, we summarise related work from the fields of patent information retrieval. In §3, we describe seven methods for generating patent queries. §4 documents the experiments we used to evaluate the methods in three different languages. §5 presents our results. §6 concludes the paper and proposes future work.

2   Related Work

Our work relates to patent information retrieval in general. It is an active research field [3, 5]. To date, a significant amount of development is driven by the Intellectual Property task within the CLEF initiative and NTCIR workshops. The systems developed early days at these evaluation campaigns replicated the work performed by patent examiners, who consider high term frequency in the document to be strong indicator of a good query term [12, 13]. A recent line of work advocates the use of full patent application or automatically extracted terms as the query to reduce the burden on patent examiners. Xue and Croft [4] firstly conducted a series of experiments in order to examine the effect of different patent fields in a patent document. Their work on the USPTO corpus concluded that the best Mean Average Precision is achieved using the query generated from description section of the query patent with raw term frequencies. However, the relevance judgements in their system were not annotated by real patent experts but rather automatically extracted from the citation fields.

Terms extracted from description field have been proved to produce highest retrieval performance by many other research teams. For example, Magdy et al. [14] showed that the second best performing run of CLEF-IP 2010 uses a list of citations extracted from the patent numbers within the description field of some patent queries. Mahdabi et al. also confirmed in a series of experiments that under a language model framework, terms extracted from the description field shown to be effective [2, 15]. They also showed that automatically disambiguated query terms could be informative by extraction of noun phrases from the global analysis of the patent collection. However, the use of phrases is of some controversial. Becks et al. [7] demonstrated that with a different patent corpus (CLEF 2011 rather than CLEF 2010) phrase queries reported negative results.

Another important feature of the patent retrieval w.r.t to the ordinary ad-hoc search and web search is that the pseudo-relevance feedback technique performs poorly in this particular context [16, 2]. This may be due to the reasons that the precision at top ranks is usually low, the information focus is not clear and added terms are noisy. Ganguly et al. [16] tackled this problem from a different angle. They decomposed a patent application into constituent text segments and computed the language similarities by calculating the probability of generating each segment from the top ranked documents. However, their method could be viewed as a very slight modification to use the query with a full set of terms in a document.

Due to the increase and distribution of inventions across the world, the necessity of research and commercial tools that support patent search in different languages has increased. Despite the popularity of query generation techniques described above, to our knowledge, there is no comparison between using these techniques in multiple languages.

3   Query Generation Techniques

The reference model presented in our paper uses the full length document as input after stopwords removal, stemming and number removal. Unlike many previous experiments conducted by different CLEF participants [7, 17], we did not use patent-specific stopwords, phrases or sophisticated summarization methods. This model is denoted as $FULL$ subsequently.

Clearly the $FULL$ method fails to represent a focused information need required for high precision retrieval. We now introduce seven different query generation techniques that use many state-of-art methods to reduce the full-length query. The following three models extract key terms according to the usual TF-IDF, BM25 and simple term frequency schemes. Defined as follows:

$$P(t|q_{TFIDF}) = \frac{n(t,d)}{\max_{t'} n(t',d)} \cdot \log \frac{N}{df_t}$$

$$P(t|q_{TF}) = \frac{n(t,d)}{\max_{t'} n(t',d)}$$

$$P(t|q_{BM25}) = \sum_t w_t \frac{(k_1+1)n(t,d)}{K+n(t,d)} \frac{(K_3+1)n(t,d)}{k_3+n(t,d)}$$

where $w_t = \log \frac{N-df_t+0.5}{df_t+0.5}$, $K = k_1 \cdot ((1-b) + b \cdot \frac{|d|}{avg|d|})$, and $n(t,d)$ is the term frequency, df is document frequency. These three query generation techniques were denoted as $TFIDF$, TF and $BM25$ respectively.

The next technique adopts the unigram model proposed by Mahdabi et al. [2], which could be regarded as a strong baseline because it produces comparable results to the second best runs in CLEF 2010. It is defined by estimating the importance of each term according to a weighted log-likelihood based approach as expressed below:

$$P(t|q_{LM}) = Z_t P(t|\Theta_q) \log \frac{P(t|\Theta_q)}{P(t|\Theta_C)}$$

where Θ_q and Θ_C are language model estimation for a term in the query patent and in a test collection, respectively. $P(t|\Theta_q)$ is defined as:

$$P(t|\Theta_q) = (1-\lambda) \cdot P_{ML}(t|d) + \lambda \cdot P_{ML}(t|C)$$

with $P_{ML}(t|d) = \frac{n(t,d)}{\sum_{t'} n(t',d)}$. $Z_t = 1/\sum_t P(t|q)$ is the normalization factor and defined as the Kullback-Leibler divergence between Θ_q and Θ_C. This model is named LM in the reminder of the paper.

The next technique moves one step further by considering International Patent Classifications (IPC[3]) in the patent documents as in [2]. IPC provides for a hierarchical system of language independent symbols for the classification of patents and utility models according to the different areas of technology to which

---

[3] http://www.wipo.int/classifications/ipc/en

they pertain. Thus the IPC classes resemble tags assigned to documents. We build a relevance model Θ_{IPC} by employing documents that have at least one tag in common with the query topic. The result model is defined as:

$$P(t|q_{IPC}) = (1 - \lambda) \cdot P(t|\Theta_{IPC}) + \lambda \cdot P(t|q_{LM})$$

where $P(t|\Theta_{IPC})$ is calculated by using:

$$P(t|\Theta_{IPC}) = \sum_{d \in IPC} P(t|d) \cdot P(d|\Theta_{IPC})$$

and

$$P(D|\Theta_{IPC}) = Z_d \sum_{t} P(t|\Theta_d) \log \frac{P(t|\Theta_{IPC})}{P(t|\Theta_C)}$$

where $Z_d = 1/\sum_{D \in IPC} P(D|\Theta_{IPC})$ is a document specific normalization factor. This query generation technique is denoted as $LMIPC$ subsequently.

The sixth technique we used is simply full-length query by removing unit frequency terms (i.e. terms which occur only once in the patent query), denoted as UFT henceforth.

The last technique, denoted as QR, is a method using Pseduo Relevance Feedback for reducing patent queries [16]. The technique decomposes a patent application document into s constituent text segments (sentences) and computes the language modeling similarities by calculating the probability of generating each segment from r top ranked document. Finally, the method selects τ fraction of sentences to retain in the query. The language similarity equation is shown below:

$$logP(q_s|d) = \sum_{t \in q_s} n(t)log(1 + \frac{\lambda P(t|d)}{(1 - \lambda)} P(t))$$

The final score of each segment is the sum of all r documents. This completes our description of the query generation techniques used in our experiments. In the next section we will detail a large-scale experiment involving read-world patent data in three different languages.

4 Evaluation

In the following section, we describe a series of experiments designed to answer the following questions:

1. How effective are the state-of-art query generation techniques when used in patent prior-art search
2. Does the query produced by the seven query generation techniques perform better than using the full-length document as the query?
3. How effective are the various techniques in different languages?
4. What is the optimal number of keywords for selective-based query generation techniques (i.e. $BM25, TF, TFIDF, LM$ and $LMIPC$)?

4.1 Experimental Data

To make a fair comparison, the text corpus used in our evaluation was built using components of the CLEF-IP 2009 test collections. This collection contains patents, physically stored as a collection of XML files encoding patent document. A patent document maybe an application document, a search report, or a granted patent document. The data is extracted from the MAREC [4] data corpus and contains a number of approximately 1,958,955 million patent documents, referring to approximately 1,022,388 million patents. We also used the CLEF-IP 2009 query set, which contains 311 English topics, 164 German topics and 25 French topics. Each topic is a patent application composed of several fields (e.g. *Title, Abstract, Description, Claims* etc.). We used the *Description* field for building the query as it previously showed the best performance. We used relevance judgements produced by the CLEF workshops. Note that we did not use the citation information of the patent applications in our experiments. Prior to indexing and retrieval, a suffix stemmer [18] and a stopword list[5] were applied to all documents and queries for English texts. We did not apply any linguistic processes on German and French texts.

4.2 Evaluation Metrics

We used the following evaluation metrics in this experiment:

- The precision of the top 10, top 50 and top 100 documents (P@10, P@50 and P@100)
- Normalized Discounted Cumulative Gain (NDCG) [19]
- The recall of the top 10, top 50 and top 100 documents (R@10, R@50 and R@100)
- Mean average precision (MAP).

Unless otherwise stated, the results given indicate *average performance* across all test topics. Statistically-significant differences in performance were determined using a paired t-test at a confidence level of 95%.

4.3 Retrieval Systems

All information retrieval functions in our experiments were handled by the Terrier open source platform[6] [20]. As described in §3, the results are obtained by seven models: *TFIDF, TF, BM*25, *LM, LMIPC, UFT* and *QR*. For comparison purposed we also used *FULL* as our reference model.

---

[4] It is a collection of over 19 million patent documents, available from information retrieval facility (http://www.ir-facility.org/)

[5] ftp://ftp.cs.cornell.edu/pub/smart/

[6] http://terrier.org/

4.4   Parameter Settings

The parameters in the baseline systems are set according to the tuning procedures in their original papers if detailed. k_1, b, k_3 used in the $BM25$ model were set to 1.2, 0.75 and 7 respectively. The number of pseduo-relevant documents (i.e. r) used in QR were set to 20, s and τ were set to 20 and 90% respectively.

5   Results

5.1   Precision-Oriented Performance

In our first evaluation, we compare the precision-oriented performance across all methods described. Statistical significant results are obtained when using $FULL$ as the baseline. The number of key terms selected for $BM25$, TF, $TFIDF$,

Table 1. Precision-oriented performance across three languages, statistically significant results are marked with ∗

	MAP	NDCG	P@10	P@50	P@100
French					
FULL	0.0435	0.1031	0.048	0.0128	0.008
BM25	0.0695*	0.1426*	0.064*	0.0152*	0.0084*
UFT	0.0389	0.0879	0.04	0.0112	0.006
TF	0.0465	0.098	0.048	0.0112	0.006
TFIDF	0.0559*	0.1195*	0.052	0.0128	0.008
LMIPC	0.044	0.111	0.044	0.012	0.008
LM	0.0547	0.1173	0.048	0.0136	0.0084
QR	0.0432	0.1013	0.052	0.0128	0.008
German					
FULL	0.0732	0.164	0.0524	0.0163	0.0103
BM25	0.1045*	0.2155*	0.0707*	0.023*	0.013*
UFT	0.0716	0.1565	0.0543	0.016	0.0098
TF	0.0745	0.1648	0.0524	0.0162	0.0099
TFIDF	0.0907*	0.1921*	0.0622*	0.0191*	0.0122*
LMIPC	0.0753	0.1687	0.0549	0.0183*	0.0113
LM	0.0864*	0.1875*	0.0598*	0.019*	0.012*
QR	0.0715	0.162	0.0506	0.0162	0.0098
English					
FULL	0.0825	0.2105	0.0717	0.0289	0.0178
BM25	0.0794	0.2109	0.0688	0.0282	0.0175
LMIPC	0.0893*	0.2312*	0.0746	0.0301	0.0196*
LM	0.0881	0.2306*	0.0768*	0.03	0.0188
QR	0.0808	0.2071	0.0736	0.0284	0.0175
TF	0.0826	0.2226*	0.0736	0.0292	0.0183
TFIDF	0.0903*	0.2319*	0.0781*	0.0306*	0.0196*
UFT	0.0822	0.206	0.0669	0.0257	0.015

LM and $LMIPC$ will be discussed in section 5.3. From Table 1, we note that $FULL$, UFT and QR methods consistently deliver lowest performance, only slightly better than $BM25$ in English. These three methods are quite similar as they keep most of terms in the query. Next, we observed that the TF method only increases the mean average precision by a modest amount. This shows significantly different behaviour when deployed in the USPTO corpus as in [4]. The $TFIDF$ method works well in English and the $BM25$ method works well in French and German. Amazingly, the $BM25$ method demonstrates opposite performance in English test collection, achieved lowest performance. The reason may be the language complexity of French and German comparing to English. Given the performance obtained by $BM25$ and $TFIDF$, we must be cautious in drawing conclusions from the experiments w.r.t to the best term weighting methods in a multilingual setting.

Mahdabi et al. [2] showed that using IPC information could increase the effectiveness of the retrieval system. It is confirmed from the results that using the IPC information could help improving the performance (in terms of $LMIPC$ works better than LM) in English. However, the improvements are only modest and not statistically significant. The same results could not be replicated in French and German. This shows the accuracy of IPC information attached to the French and German documents is low.

Overall, we notice that $TFIDF$ works the best in the English test collection, showing statistically significant improvements across all evaluation metrics. $BM25$ works the best in the French and German test collections, with statistically significant results observed in all metrics.

5.2   Recall-Oriented Performance

We now measure the performance of the methods using various recall-based metrics in three languages. Bare in mind that patent prior-art search is a recall oriented task where the primary focus is to retrieve all relevant documents at early ranks in contrast to ad hoc and web search. Same trend can be observed from Table 2 as in the precision-oriented evaluation. $TFIDF$ works better in English, while $BM25$ works better in French and German. The improvements over $FULL$

Table 2. Recall-oriented performance across three languages, statistically significant results are marked with *

	French			German			English		
	R@10	R@50	R@100	R@10	R@50	R@100	R@10	R@50	R@100
$FULL$	0.0789	0.1122	0.1424	0.1116	0.1729	0.2125	0.1151	0.2194	0.2622
$BM25$	0.1189*	0.1436*	0.1436	0.1554*	0.2346*	0.2621*	0.1093	0.211	0.2557
UFT	0.0556	0.08	0.088	0.1136	0.1636	0.1988	0.1109	0.2021	0.2344
TF	0.0778	0.0889	0.0933	0.1074	0.1672	0.2047	0.1139	0.22*	0.276*
$TFIDF$	0.0844*	0.1089	0.1391	0.132*	0.1987*	0.246*	0.1273*	0.2309*	0.2783*
$LMIPC$	0.0833	0.1091	0.1391	0.1135	0.1864	0.2274	0.1247*	0.2366*	0.2961*
LM	0.0778	0.1167	0.1469	0.1268	0.196*	0.2409*	0.1234	0.2295	0.2828
QR	0.0856	0.1122	0.1424	0.1077	0.1714	0.2039	0.117	0.2164	0.2573

were quite stable across all evaluation metrics. $LMIPC$ also frequently delivers statistically significant results. This performance of the IPC-based method has an intuitive explanation. Relevant documents are being 'found' by using the IPC information. The low performance of QR confirms that using PRF is not a wise choice for the patent search. In summary, the methods achieves good precision-oriented performance usually perform well in the recall-oriented evaluation.

5.3 Selection of the Number of Key Terms

Recall that in five of the methods, $BM25$, TF, $TFIDF$, LM and $LMIPC$, the top terms with higher weights must be picked and used to build the query. In this section we study the optimal number across three different languages. Results in Figure 1-3 show that 65-95 terms in English, 20-65 terms in French and 55-90 terms are sufficient to capture the most information in a long query.

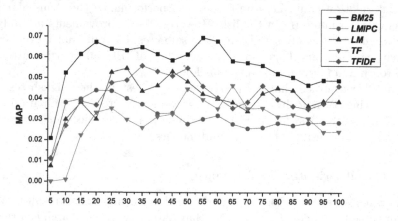

Fig. 1. Selection of the number of key terms in French

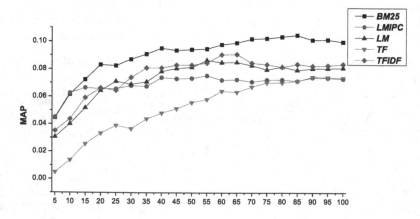

Fig. 2. Selection of the number of key terms in German

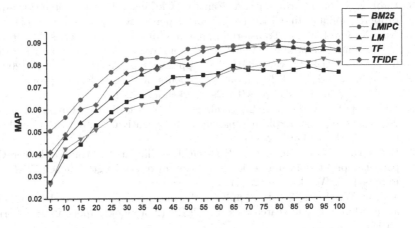

Fig. 3. Selection of the number of key terms in English

6   Conclusion and Further Work

In this paper, we introduce seven methods for generating queries from a full-length patent query. Large-scale experimental evaluation has been carried out on the CLEF-IP 2009 multilingual dataset in English, French and German. A detail comparison of the different methods in terms of performance and efficiency has been performed in addition to the use of full-length documents as queries in the patent search. The experimental results show that the TFIDF method achieved the highest performance in English, the BM25 method works the best in French and German. The methods achieve good precision-oriented performance usually perform well in the recall-oriented evaluation. The paper also found that in general less than 100 selected key terms can obtain good results for selective-based methods.

In future work, we plan to explore additional sources of intellectual property documents beyond CLEF-IP (NTCIR and USPTO) to investigate the differences. We also plan to explore more term weighting methods commonly used in the information retrieval field.

Acknowledgments. This research is supported by the National Natural Science Foundation of China under grant No. 61300129 and No. 61272063, Excellent Youth Foundation of Hunan Scientific Committee No. 11JJ1011.

References

1. Tait, J. (ed.): Proceedings of the 1st ACM workshop on Patent Information Retrieval, PaIR 2008, Napa Valley, California, USA, October 30. ACM (2008)
2. Mahdabi, P., Andersson, L., Keikha, M., Crestani, F.: Automatic refinement of patent queries using concept importance predictors. In: Proceedings of the 35th International ACM SIGIR Conference on Research and Development in Information Retrieval, SIGIR 2012, pp. 505–514. ACM, New York (2012)

3. Piroi, F., Lupu, M., Hanbury, A., Zenz, V.: Clef-ip 2011: Retrieval in the intellectual property domain. In: CLEF (Notebook Papers/Labs/Workshop) (2011)

4. Xue, X., Croft, W.B.: Transforming patents into prior-art queries. In: Proceedings of the 32nd International ACM SIGIR Conference on Research and Development in Information Retrieval, SIGIR 2009, pp. 808–809. ACM, New York (2009)

5. Piroi, F.: Clef-ip 2010: Retrieval experiments in the intellectual property domain. In: CLEF (Notebook Papers/LABs/Workshops) (2010)

6. Mahdabi, P., Andersson, L., Hanbury, A., Crestani, F.: Report on the clef-ip 2011 experiments: Exploring patent summarization. In: CLEF (Notebook Papers/Labs/Workshop) (2011)

7. Becks, D., Eibl, M., Jürgens, J., Kürsten, J., Wilhelm, T., Womser-Hacker, C.: Does patent ir profit from linguistics or maximum query length? In: CLEF (Notebook Papers/Labs/Workshop) (2011)

8. Magdy, W., Jones, G.J.F.: Applying the kiss principle for the clef- ip 2010 prior art candidate patent search task. In: CLEF (Notebook Papers/LABs/Workshops) (2010)

9. Lopez, P., Romary, L.: Experiments with citation mining and key-term extraction for prior art search. In: CLEF (Notebook Papers/LABs/Workshops) (2010)

10. Zhou, D., Truran, M., Brailsford, T., Wade, V., Ashman, H.: Translation techniques in cross-language information retrieval. ACM Computing Surveys 45(1), 1:1–1:44 (2012)

11. Zhou, D., Truran, M., Brailsford, T., Ashman, H.: A hybrid technique for english-chinese cross language information retrieval. ACM Transactions on Asian Language Information Processing 7(2), 5:1–5:35 (2008)

12. Iwayama, M., Fujii, A., Kando, N., Takano, A.: Overview of patent retrieval task at ntcir-3. In: Proceedings of the ACL-2003 Workshop on Patent Corpus Processing, PATENT 2003, vol. 20, pp. 24–32. Association for Computational Linguistics, Stroudsburg (2003)

13. Itoh, H., Mano, H., Ogawa, Y.: Term distillation in patent retrieval. In: Proceedings of the ACL-2003 Workshop on Patent Corpus Processing, PATENT 2003, vol. 20, pp. 41–45. Association for Computational Linguistics, Stroudsburg (2003)

14. Magdy, W., Lopez, P., Jones, G.J.F.: Simple vs. Sophisticated approaches for patent prior-art search. In: Clough, P., Foley, C., Gurrin, C., Jones, G.J.F., Kraaij, W., Lee, H., Mudoch, V. (eds.) ECIR 2011. LNCS, vol. 6611, pp. 725–728. Springer, Heidelberg (2011)

15. Mahdabi, P., Keikha, M., Gerani, S., Landoni, M., Crestani, F.: Building queries for prior-art search. In: Hanbury, A., Rauber, A., de Vries, A.P. (eds.) IRFC 2011. LNCS, vol. 6653, pp. 3–15. Springer, Heidelberg (2011)

16. Ganguly, D., Leveling, J., Magdy, W., Jones, G.J.: Patent query reduction using pseudo relevance feedback. In: Proceedings of the 20th ACM International Conference on Information and Knowledge Management, CIKM 2011, pp. 1953–1956. ACM, New York (2011)

17. Mahdabi, P., Andersson, L., Hanbury, A., Crestani, F.: Report on the clef-ip 2011 experiments: Exploring patent summarization. In: CLEF (Notebook Papers/Labs/Workshop) (2011)

18. Porter, M.F.: Readings in information retrieval, pp. 313–316. Morgan Kaufmann Publishers Inc., San Francisco (1997)
19. Järvelin, K., Kekäläinen, J.: Ir evaluation methods for retrieving highly relevant documents. In: Proceedings of the 23rd Annual International ACM SIGIR Conference on Research and Development in Information Retrieval, SIGIR 2000, pp. 41–48. ACM, New York (2000)
20. Ounis, I., Amati, G., Plachouras, V., He, B., Macdonald, C., Lioma, C.: Terrier: A High Performance and Scalable Information Retrieval Platform. In: Proceedings of ACM SIGIR 2006 Workshop on Open Source Information Retrieval, OSIR 2006 (August 2006)

Improve Web Search Diversification
with Intent Subtopic Mining[*]

Aymeric Damien, Min Zhang, Yiqun Liu, and Shaoping Ma

State Key Laboratory of Intelligent Technology and Systems,
Tsinghua National Laboratory for Information Science and Technology,
Department of Computer Science and Technology, Tsinghua University, Beijing 100084, China
aymeric.damien@gmail.com, {z-m,yiqunliu,msp}@tsinghua.edu.cn

Abstract. A number of search user behavior studies show that queries with unclear intents are commonly submitted to search engines. Result diversification
is usually adopted to deal with those queries, in which search engine tries to
trade-off some relevancy for some diversity to improve user experience. In this
work, we aim to improve the performance of search results diversification by
generating an intent subtopics list with fusion of multiple resources. We based
our approach by thinking that to collect a large panel of intent subtopics, we
should consider as well a wide range of resources from which to extract. The
resources adopted cover a large panel of sources, such as external resources
(Wikipedia, Google Keywords Generator, Google Insights, Search Engines
query suggestion and completion), anchor texts, page snippets and more. We
selected resources to cover both information seeker (What a user is searching
for) and information provider (The websites) aspects. We also proposed an efficient Bayesian optimization approach to maximize resources selection performances, and a new technique to cluster subtopics based on the top results snippet information and Jaccard Similarity coefficient. Experiments based on TREC
2012 web track and NTCIR-10 intent task show that our framework can greatly
improve diversity while keeping a good precision. The system developed
with the proposed techniques also achieved the best English subtopic mining
performance in NTCIR-10 intent task.

1 Introduction

Nowadays, most people are using Web search to look for information they need. Even
if many of them will use targeted keywords, a great part will provide queries that can
be interpreted in many different ways. So without further information about the user
intent to disambiguate, search-engines have to focus on web search results diversification to produce a set of diversified results. There are two major kinds of query that
needs to be diversified: ambiguous queries (e.g. "Jaguar"; that can be interpreted as

---

[*] This work was supported by Natural Science Foundation (60903107, 61073071) and National
High Technology Research and Development (863) Program (2011AA01A205) of China.

G. Zhou et al. (Eds.): NLPCC 2013, CCIS 400, pp. 322–333, 2013.
© Springer-Verlag Berlin Heidelberg 2013

the car brands, the animal, the Mac OS ...) and broad queries (e.g. "Star Wars"; the user intent can be the movies, the video games, the books ...). So for such queries, it is important that search-engines not only consider the relevancy of documents, but also provide a diversified set of documents that are covering different subtopics.

Other works proposed to solve this problem using different solutions, but most of these methods only rely on one or a few resources. As far as we know, this is the first time that resources fusion is explored to improve web search diversification and that a study is made about the different resources used to mine subtopics.

In this work, we first introduce the different resources used to extract subtopics and their processing methods. We applied two different process for candidates coming from external resources (such as Wikipedia, Google Keywords Generator, Search-Engines Suggestion ...) and candidates coming from web pages (Retrieved through top results snippet information, anchor texts and page h tags of commercial search-engines or our own built search engine based on ClueWeb). For the first one, we introduce a new and efficient way to cluster the subtopics, based on the top results snippet information and Jaccard Similarity Coefficient. For the other one, we use the popular BM25 and Partition Around Medoid algorithms to cluster the subtopics.

We then propose a fusion of these resources in order to improve web search diversification. Furthermore we propose an interesting optimization to combine resources in order to maximize the performances of our framework.

Later, we give a complete analysis of our system performance using the Average Precision and D#-nDCG metrics, as well as a study of the good performances of the snippet based clustering method and a comparative review of the different resources used and their effectiveness by comparing different statistics.

Our work provide some new and original ways to improve web search results diversification:

- Fusion strategy of diverse and complementary resources are investigated to improve the results diversity while keeping an optimal relevancy.
- An optimization of the framework regarding the query type when selecting the resources to combine.
- A new subtopics clustering technique based on the top-results snippet information and Jaccard similarity coefficient is proposed and is evaluated to show its very good precision.
- Resources performance are comparatively studied to analyze each different resource effectiveness regarding the resource range of subtopic retrieved and relevancy, providing information about the best external resources to use in web search results diversification.
- Google Keywords Generator is used thought our work to generate a large list of subtopic candidates and get their popularity, and can be regarded as a really effective alternative source for finding query logs.

2   Related Work

Web search results diversification naturally appeared after the firsts page ranking algorithms in order to improve the search results ranking. Indeed, Zhai et al. [1] demonstrated that the relevancy could not only hold in a simple set of relevant results because of the correlations between these results, and that diversification were needed. Carbonell et al. [2] first introduced a model called re-ranking maximal marginal relevance (MMR) that not only focus on the relevance of the documents but also maximize the non-similarity between the results, in order to minimize the redundancy. As this algorithm does not imply classification of either the result or the query, diversification is leaded by the choice of similarity functions.

A later great concept was introduced by Ziegler et al. [3] about the diversification problem as a "recommendation" system. For each potential product result, the algorithm calculates the disparity between the item and all the other potential product result. Then it fusions this disparity to the original relevance order and then return the recommended products. Moreover they demonstrate experimentally that users were more likely to prefer more diversified results. This concept was then improved by Yu et al. [4] that proposed another recommendation system for results diversification by optimizing the balance between diversity and relevance. Indeed, the algorithm minimizes the correlation between documents by considering the constraint of relevance.

Agrawal et al. [5] introduced an approach of minimizing the risk of dissatisfaction of users, using taxonomy for classifying queries and documents, and creates a diverse set of results in accordance to it. The idea is that users only care about the top k returned result, and not the whole set.

Hu et al. [6] presented a method to understand the intent behind a user's query using Wikipedia. This system can help search engines to automatically route the query to some specific vertical search engines and obtain very relevant information. Their system is working by mapping the query into the Wikipedia intents representation space. They restricted their study to three different applications: travel, job, and person name.

Recently, Jiafeng et al. [7] also proposed an interesting method to measure query similarity with the awareness of potential search intents using a regularized topic model based on words from search result snippets and regularization from query co-clicks.

A part of our work uses similar techniques used by Han et al. [8] for subtopic mining from search-engines top results, using the BM25 and a partitioning around medoid clustering algorithm based on the cosine similarity. In this study, we adapted this method to fit our needs in the process of top-results pages subtopic extraction.

3   External Resources Based Subtopic Mining

Over the internet, there are many interesting services that we can use to help us to disambiguate a query. Indeed, from these resources, we can extract sub-intents of an ambiguous query as well as, for some, interesting information about the sub-intents popularity. In this part, we propose a new and efficient way to collect, filter and cluster all these sub-intents.

3.1   Resources Used

We decided to use a wide range of external resources, coming from commercial search-engines, such as query completion and suggestion, as well as specialized service providing popular query logs, such as Google Insights and Google Keywords Generator. At last, we also used Wikipedia encyclopedia for its disambiguation feature.

3.2   Subtopic Candidates Extraction and Filtering

Subtopics candidates had been extracted from different external resources: Query Suggestion and Completion from Google, Yahoo and Bing, Google Insights, Google Keywords Generator, and Wikipedia. For all, we can easily extract the candidates "as it". For example, Google Insights or Google Keywords Generator works like query logs, by giving the most popular keywords related to a query. So we submitted all our test queries to these resources and combine all the results data gathered using a linear combination.

Many data collected from these external resources are irrelevant or duplicated, that's why we applied a filter in order to keep only the valid ones. We applied a filter that remove all subtopics that do not contain all the query words, in any order. The original query stop words are discarded, so stop words does not need to be found in the candidates.

3.3   Snippet Based Clustering

Clustering has always been an important aspect in query diversification. The snippet information provided by each web page, bring us very relevant information that usually summarize the page, and list some important keywords. So we propose here a solution using this feature to cluster our subtopics. For each subtopic candidates, we first submit each one to the search engines (Google, Bing, Yahoo) and crawl the 50 top results snippet information. Then we set a table with every words found from these snippet and get their frequencies. After, in order to know if two subtopics are similar or not, we calculate the Jaccard similarity coefficient:

$$J(A, B) = \frac{|A \cap B|}{|A \cup B|} \tag{1}$$

Where A and B are the two different term frequencies vectors of the two subtopics to compare. We extended this coefficient by considering both the words and their frequencies. (So even if many words retrieve for the two subtopics are the same, but their frequencies is really different, then their similarity will be reduced). We implemented this feature because we think that both words retrieved and their frequencies are important feature to know if two subtopics have similar intent or not. So when we calculate the intersection or the union of A and B, we added the average score of their frequencies:

$$J_{ext}(A, B) = \frac{\sum_{i \in A \cap B} \frac{f_{A_i} + f_{B_i}}{2}}{\sum_{i \in A \setminus B} f_{A_i} + \sum_{i \in B \setminus A} f_{B_i} + \sum_{i \in A \cap B} \frac{f_{A_i} + f_{B_i}}{2}} \tag{2}$$

With A and B the two frequencies vectors for every word and   the frequency of i-th term of the vector. We then created a clustering algorithm using this extended Jaccard Similarity. The Jaccard similarity for a cluster is computed as the average similarity between all its subtopic candidates and all the other cluster subtopic candidates.

---

1. Select k (define experimentally)
2. Create for every subtopic candidate a cluster
3. For each cluster
   1. For each remaining cluster
      1. If Jext similarity of the the two clusters > k Then combine clusters
4. Repeat 3 while the similarity between two clusters is above k.

Alg 1. Bottom-up hierarchical clustering algorithm with extended Jaccard similarity coefficient

3.4   Resources Features Based Cluster Ranking

To rank our clusters, we based our approach on a multi criteria ranking. We used the different scores provided by the external resources; for example, in Google Insights or Google Keywords Generator, a score is associated with each term: the popularity for Google Insights and the amount of searches for Google Keywords Generator. So we applied a ranking based on the following features with their weight:

— Jaccard Similarity between the subtopic and the original query: 5%
— Google Insights score: 15%
— Google Keywords Generator score: 75%
— Belongs to the query suggestion/completion: 5%

We also considered that, if a subtopic belongs to the Wikipedia disambiguation feature, then the subtopic is important, and grants him a better score. In order to normalize all the scores to be able to compare them together, we convert each score into a percentage of the maximum score. So for example, the top search in Google insights or Google keywords generator will have a score of 1. Thanks to this normalization, even if the data come from different resources, we are still able to use them together.

4   Top Results Based Subtopic Mining

In this second approach, we propose to find the subtopics directly from the web pages. To get web pages related to the query to disambiguate, we used different search-engines: the commercial ones: Google, Bing and Yahoo, and the one built by THUIR (TMiner) that is based on the Clueweb data. In this way, we are sure to only extract pages that are very relevant to the query. We based our approach using a slightly similar method to the one proposed by Han et al. [8].

4.1 Subtopics Candidates Extraction

We first submitted the query to the search-engines, and get the page results. For TMiner run, we extracted the candidate subtopics from different fragments coming from page snippet, page h1 tags and in-link Anchors Text. For the commercial search-engines run, we only extracted the candidate subtopics from page snippet (page title and description). We adopted a vector space model to represent each fragment.

$$f = \left(w_{1,f}, w_{2,f}, \dots, w_{n,f} \right) \tag{3}$$

Where $w_{i,f}$ is the weight of a unique word i contained in f. We removed stop words and query words from the fragments, because they do not help us to distinguish the different fragments. We then used the BM25 [13] algorithm to evaluate the weight:

$$w_{i,f} = \frac{(k_1 + 1)tf_i}{k_1 \left((1 - b) + b \frac{dl}{avdl} \right) + tf_i} \log \frac{N - df_i + 0.5}{df_i + 0.5} \tag{4}$$

Where tf_i is the occurrence of word i in fragment f, and df_i is the number of documents that contains i in the corpus. dl is the length of the fragment f. $avdl$ is the average fragment length for the query. N is the total number of documents in the entire corpus. We set k_1=1.1 and b=0.7.

4.2 Subtopic Candidates Clustering

We apply a modified Partitioning Around Medoids (PAM) clustering algorithm to group similar fragments together. Here is the algorithm:

1. Initialize: randomly select k of the n data points as the medoids
2. Associate each data point to the closest medoid. ("closest" here is defined using cosine similarity)
3. For each medoid m
4. For each non-medoid data point o
   1. Swap m and o and compute the total cost of the configuration
      1. Select the configuration with the lowest cost.
5. Repeat steps 2 to 4 until there is no change in the medoid.

Alg 2. Modified paritioning around medoid algorithm

The similarity between two fragments is determined using the cosine similarity between their corresponding weight vectors calculated as above using the BM25 algorithm. The PAM algorithm first computes k representative objects, called medoids. A medoid can be defined as that object of a cluster, whose average dissimilarity to all the objects in the cluster is minimal. After finding the set of medoids, each object of the data set is assigned to the nearest medoid. k is the number of clusters we want to generate and traditionally it is fixed as an input of PAM. However, in our task, it is not suitable as we do not know the number of cluster (intent) a query has; indeed the number is not predictable. Those we had to modify the PAM algorithm to make it able to decide an appropriate k. We first randomly choose k points as initial cluster medoids. We then assign each other points to the closest medoid. If the closest of the medoid is over a value we set experimentally, then we set this point as a new medoid, and recalculate from the beginning.

4.3   Clusters Ranking

We rank the clusters according to their popularity; using the fragment rank inside the commercial search-engine or TMiner and the URLs diversity from the different fragments from a cluster. So we give a greater score to the clusters that contains fragments from higher ranked pages and clusters that contains fragments from many different URLs. Here is the formula used to calculate the score for each cluster:

$$Score(c) = \sum_{f \epsilon Frag(c)} 1 - \frac{w(f)}{N} \qquad (5)$$

Where $w(f)$ is the weight of the fragment, calculated by the fragments average position in the search results. Learning to rank techniques can also be adopted with sufficient training examples and we would like to add this to our future work.

4.4   Clusters Name Generation

From the different fragments, we need to generate a readable name for the cluster. We first select the most frequent word and then extend it to an n-gram based on the frequency of the other words. We also set that frequency limit experimentally. We kept stop words because they can be interesting to name the intent. Then we check if we need to add or not the keyword (that we removed from every fragment). So we compare if any original fragment contains or not the keyword, and if more than 50% contains it, we add it, using its position between the most frequent words, in order to place it correctly.

5   Resources Fusion

In order to improve the diversity, we combined the sub-intents we extracted from both external-resources and top-results pages mining. Indeed, both data are coming from two different aspect of the internet: one, from the external resources represents the queries that people are looking for on internet. And another one, the subtopic mining from the top-results pages, that shows the information provided by the website owners or participants.

A fusion is necessary over a unified model because the two sources of information are treated in two different ways; the external resources represent query logs key-words that we then cluster and rank, while in the top results mining, we do not direct-ly cluster the subtopics, but we cluster sentence fragments, extracted from snippets, h1 tags or anchor texts. And then, we judge if a cluster is valid or not and generate a name to the intent. So the two approach are quite different and, in order to maximize the performances, a fusion approach is better than a unified model.

To combine our data, we used a linear combination of the sub-intents obtained from the external resources based mining and the top results based mining. After that combination, we expected that many sub-intents were actually duplicated, so we had to choose a way to recluster and rerank the sub-intents. We applied again our snippet-based clustering algorithm and experimentally define a similarity value to decide whether or not two candidates should be clustered together. At last, to rerank the data, we first normalized them by assigning them a percentage of the maximum sub-intent score for each query, so we could then compare the score of all sub-intents.

6   Fusion Optimization

Combining resources may not only result in performances increase, but may provoke a loss of relevancy or diversity. So we optimized the fusion process in order to get the best resources combination. So we ran some experiments to verify each resource per-formances compared to the fusion performance and we found out that the query type (navigational: Queries that aim to access a specific website or informational: Queries that aim to get general information about a topic) could impact the fusion. Indeed, we can see from figure 1 that navigational queries got worst performances after the fusion. So we optimized our system to take consider the query type and not apply the fusion, but only keep the candidate subtopics coming from the top results based mining method.

Fig. 1. Fusion Performances for Navigational Queries

Indeed, navigational queries aim to directly access a specific website, so subtopic extracted through the query logs like resources (like Google Key. Gen.) may not be that accurate and diverse. On the other hand, a webpage provide us a lot of possible intent subtopics, independently of the query type. So in the case of navigational queries, the mining from top results pages will outperform the one from external resources and the fusion.

7   Experiments and Discussions

7.1   Experiments Setup

Our experiment is based on a set of 50 queries, used for the TREC Web Track 2012. We tested our framework for each one of this queries and evaluated the system. To evaluate our work, we used several metrics and statistics, such as Average Precision metrics and D#-nDCG. Using these features, we aim to analyses three main part of our work: The efficiency of the snippet-based clustering, the different resources analysis, comparisons and performances and the entire method efficiency analysis for the web search results diversification.

D#-nDCG is a linear combination of intent recall (or "I-rec", which measures diversity) and D-nDCG (which measures overall relevance across intents). The advantages of D#-nDCG over other diversity metrics such as α-nDCG [11] and Intent-Aware metrics [5] are discussed elsewhere [12]. We used the NTCIREVAL toolkit T. Sakai [10] to compute the above three metrics: thus, D#-nDCG is a simple average of I-rec and D-nDCG. We use the document cutoff of l = 10 throughout this paper, as a post hoc analysis of the runs showed that significance test results based on l = 20 and l = 30 are not so reliable.

7.2   Methods and Fusion Effectiveness

To test the fusion efficiency, we calculated the D#-nDCG of the fusion run, as well as the D#-nDCG for every one of its component (External Resources Mining and Top Results Mining). From the table 1, we can see that the I-rec value is higher for the fusion, meaning that the diversity is better. And on the other hand, the D-nDCG stay the same, implying that the subtopic relevancy has not been impacted by the fusion of the subtopics. Furthermore, the optimization run got even better performances, especially in term of relevancy, contributing to increase the framework efficiency in improving web search diversification.

The run with the Baseline and Wikipedia did not have much better performances due to the fact that few queries out of the 50 query set had a disambiguation topic in Wikipedia. Furthermore, the fusion did not get much better results than the Fusion because our 50 query set only contained 12% of navigational queries. But if we only analyze our system through these navigational queries, we can notice a raise of 23.40% in terms of D#-nDCG, with a raise of 40.14% in relevancy (D-nDCG). So we can conclude that this optimization really improve our system efficiency for navigational queries.

Table 1. Multi-resources fusion performances

Runs	D#-nDCG	I-rec	D-nDCG
Baseline (Query suggestion & completion)	0.23	0.2398	0.2203
Baseline + Wikipedia Disambiguation	0.2627	0.2735	0.2519
Baseline + Google Insights	0.3294	0.3116	0.3472
Baseline + Google Keywords Generator	0.367	0.3811	0.3529
Baseline + Google Keywords Generator + Google Insights + Wikipedia	0.3707	0.3908	0.3506
Baseline + TMiner Snippets, Anchor Texts and h1 Tags	0.3732	0.3971	0.3492
Baseline + Search-Engines & TMiner Snippets	0.3685	0.3809	0.3561
Baseline + Search Engines Snippets + TMiner Snippets, Anchor Texts and h1 tags	0.3787	0.4021	0.3553
Fusion (Baseline + Ext. Res. + SE & TMiner Snippets + TMiner h1 & Anchors)	0.4023	0.4542	0.3504
Fusion Optimization	0.4106	0.4587	0.3625

7.3   Resources Analysis and Comparisons

We can see from the table 2 that number of unique sub-intent coming from Google keywords generator is really higher than any other else resource. Then come the sub-intents extracted from the top-results pages titles, h1 tag and anchors. Finally, the other external resources like the query suggestion and completion, Google Insights and Wikipedia, brought relatively few unique queries. Indeed, these resources only brings the popular sub-intents, and not a large range of sub-intents. And we found that the percentage of unique sub-intents were quite similar for Google Key. Gen. and the

Table 2. Subtopic mining uniqueness performance of different resources of information

Resources	Unique Sub-intents	% of Unique Sub-intents
Google Key. Gen.	41.43	47.37%
TMiner Titles	13.00	43.07%
TMiner Anchors	12.50	46.23%
SE Titles	12.22	41.99%
TMiner H1	8.68	36.50%
Query Completion	3.12	5.57%
Query Suggestion	3.07	4.50%
Google Insights	2.75	3.17%
Wikipedia Disamb.	0.23	0.26%

subtopic extracted from top-results mining. Implying that combining data from both information seeker and information provider side has a great complementarity, and as a conclusion, improves the search result diversity. Moreover, even if some external resources could not provide some new intents, such as query suggestion or completion, we can still use them to evaluate the popularity of the sub-intent. So, these resources are still important to rank the subtopics.

7.4   Snippet-Based Clustering Performances

We found interesting to give some performance about the new clustering way we presented, based on the Jaccard Similarity of top results page snippets. We evaluated our technique by giving the average precision of the average percentage of clusters that first does not contains any subtopic incompatible with the other subtopics of that cluster. And then the percentage of clusters that does not have a duplicated intent with another cluster. At last, we deducted the percentage of clusters that are valid.

Table 3. Snippet based clustering precisions

	Average Precision
% clusters without wrongly added subtopics	0.953
% clusters with no duplicated intent	0.941
Total % of valid clusters	0.894

From our analysis, we can see that the precision for the two specific features of wrongly added subtopics and duplicated clusters are around the same and good, implying that the clustering performs well for both. As a result, the average precision of the clustering technique is very good by reaching 89.4%.

8   Conclusion and Future Work

To conclude, we can say that multi-resource fusion can greatly improve the web search result diversification. Indeed, considering both sub-intent mining from external services and web pages, enable us to have a wild range of different sub-intent sources. Indeed, we could explain it by the fact that, the external resources such as query suggestion or Google keywords generator, represent the information that the user is seeking, like query logs. While the web page, provide us another complementary range of topics, because they are information provided by websites that are expecting to fit the users information seeking needs. Furthermore, considering the query type to adapt the resources fusion let us improve our system and get even better results.

Then, we can observe that using query suggestion or completion and Google keywords generator external resources could be a good alternative for people seeking for query logs information. Indeed, no recent public query logs has been released by any commercial search-engine. So they could use these data instead. Moreover that the data has already been processed and some interesting features, like the amount of searches by month is provided.

We think that learning to rank techniques can also be adopted for our subtopics ranking in both method, and we would like to test different in order to improve the framework. At last, in this paper, we only focused on sub-intent extraction, clustering and ranking. In a future work, we would like to combine these data with document ranking and compare the results with some commercial search-engines results.

References

1. Zhai, C.X., Cohen, W.W., Lafferty, J.D.: Beyond independent relevance: methods and evaluation metrics for subtopic retrieval. In: SIGIR, pp. 10–17 (2003)
2. Carbonell, J., Goldstein, J.: The use of MMR, diversity-based reranking for reordering documents and producing summaries. In: SIGIR 1998: Proceedings of the 21st Annual International ACM SIGIR Conference on Research and Development in Information Retrieval, New York, NY, USA, pp. 335–336 (1998)
3. Ziegler, C.-N., McNee, S.M., Konstan, J.A., Lausen, G.: Improving recommendation lists through topic diversification. In: WWW 2005: Proceedings of the 14th International Conference on World Wide Web, pp. 22–32. ACM, New York (2005)
4. Yu, C., Lakshmanan, L., Amer-Yahia, S.: It takes variety to make a world: diversification in recommender systems. In: EDBT 2009: Proceedings of the 12th International Conference on Extending Database Technology, pp. 368–378. ACM, New York (2009)
5. Agrawal, R., Gollapudi, S., Halverson, A., Ieong, S.: Diversifying search results. In: WSDM 2009: Proceedings of the Second ACM International Conference on Web Search and Data Mining, pp. 5–14. ACM, New York (2009)
6. Hu, J., Wang, G., Lochovsky, F., Tao Sun, J., Chen, Z.: Understanding user's query intent with Wikipedia. In: Proceedings of WWW 2009, pp. 471–480 (2009)
7. Guo, J., Cheng, X., Xu, G., Zhu, X.: Intent-aware query similarity. In: CIKM 2011, pp. 259–268 (2011)
8. Han, J., Wang, Q., Orii, N., Dou, Z., Sakai, T., Song, R.: Microsoft Research Asia at the NTCIR-9 Intent Task. In: NTCIR-9 Proceedings, pp. 116–122 (December 2011)
9. Varelas, G., Voutsakis, E., Raftopoulou, P., Petrakis, E., Milios, E.: Semantic similarity methods in wordNet and their application to information retrieval on the web. In: Proceedings of the 7th Annual ACM International Workshop on Web Information and Data Management, pp. 10–16 (2005)
10. Sakai, T.: NTCIREVAL: A generic toolkit for information access evaluation. In: Proceedings of FIT 2011, vol. 2, pp. 23–30 (2011)
11. Clarke, C.L.A., Craswell, N., Soboroff, I., Ashkan, A.: A comparative analysis of cascade measures for novelty and diversity. In: Proceedings of ACM WSDM 2011, vol. (2011)
12. Sakai, T., Song, R.: Evaluating Diversified Search ResultsUsing Per-Intent Graded Relevance. In: Proceedings of ACM SIGIR 2011, pp. 1043–1052 (2011)
13. Robertson, S.E., Walker, S., Hancock-Beaulieu, M., Gatford, M., Payne, A.: Okapi at TREC-4. In: NIST Special Publication 500-236: The Fourth Text Retrieval Conference (TREC-4), pp. 73–96 (1995)

Understanding Temporal Intent of User Query Based on Time-Based Query Classification

Pengjie Ren, Zhumin Chen*, Xiaomeng Song, Bin Li,
Haopeng Yang, and Jun Ma

School of Computer Science and Technology,
Shandong University, Jinan, 250101, China
chenzhumin@sdu.edu.cn

Abstract. Web queries are time sensitive which implies that user's intent for information changes over time. How to recognize temporal intents behind user queries is crucial towards improving the performance of search engines. However, to the best of our knowledge, this problem has not been studied in existing work. In this paper, we propose a time-based query classification approach to understand user's temporal intent automatically. We first analyzed the shared features of queries' temporal intent distributions. Then, we present a query taxonomy which group queries according to their temporal intents. Finally, for a new given query, we propose a machine learning method to decide its class in terms of its search frequency over time recorded in Web query logs. Experiments demonstrate that our approach can understand users' temporal intents effectively.

Keywords: Temporal Intent, Query Classification, Machine Learning.

1 Introduction

World Wide Web is a dynamic information space in which the number and content of pages continuously change over time. And, many queries could only be answered accurately under a specific temporal pattern. That is, queries are dynamic. When a user submits a query to a search engine, *Query's Temporal Intent* is the time of the target information which satisfies the user's needs. The temporal intent may include one/several time points or periods of time. And, it is dynamic and varies with time. A direct application of query's temporal intent is to provide search result pages for users more accurately by limiting these pages' publishing time belonging to the intent. In addition, search results can be grouped according to the multiple temporal intents. This can ensure the diversity of the search results. For example, a user specifying a query 'presidents cup' may need information related to one of many possible subtopics: the Presidents Cup in golf, chess, tennis, football etc., and they are belong to different temporal periods. Obviously, detecting all these subtopics by semantics is difficult. However, it

---

* Corresponding author.

G. Zhou et al. (Eds.): NLPCC 2013, CCIS 400, pp. 334–345, 2013.
© Springer-Verlag Berlin Heidelberg 2013

is relatively easy to identify the query's temporal intents. Then, they can be utilized to improve or diversify the search results. Therefore, it is necessary to study a query temporal intent detection algorithm which can be used to discover a query's temporal intent automatically. However, due to queries submitted by users are usually short and ambiguous, as well as temporal intent is dynamics and its statistical properties of the target variable change over time in unforeseen ways, this problem is non-trivial.

In this paper, we propose a time-based query classification approach to try to detect user query's temporal intent automatically. We first analyze the shared features of queries' temporal intents distributions, such as full-time intent, most recent time intent, or burst time intent. And, these features can help to obtain some time-related latent semantics under queries. Based on this intuitional observation, we present a query taxonomy which group queries according to their temporal intents. Then, we observed that query's temporal intent can be detected from its search frequency distributions over time. Thus, for a new given query, we propose an algorithm to decide its class in terms of its search frequency curve recorded in Web query logs. The class of a query implicitly represents the user's temporal intent of her information need which can help to understand the query better. We have collected a large amount of queries from TREC (Text REtrievl Conference) and manually annotated their categories. Experimental results indicate that our time-based query classification algorithm can group queries effectively.

The rest of this paper is organized as follows. We introduce related work in Section 2. In Section 3, we present a query taxonomy which group queries according to their temporal intents. Section 4 gives our method of temporal intent based query classification. In section 5 we discuss the corresponding experiments. We make some conclusions and our future work in Section 6.

2   Related Work

There is a large amount of previous work on exploring temporal characteristics of Web queries. Zhou et al. [1] defined temporal intent variability as popularity changes between the subtopics of a single topic (query) over time. For a given query, they first calculated the probability of interest of each subtopic over its all subtopics. Then they used the mean of the standard deviation of each subtopic as the temporal intent variability of the query. Shokouhi [2] investigated seasonal query type which represent seasonal events repeat every year and initiate several temporal information needs. He focused on detecting seasonal queries using time-series analysis. He first decomposed a query's sequence into three components: level, trend and season. Then, if the decomposed season component and raw sequence have similar distributions, he classified the query as seasonal. [3] presented an approach for understanding the time-varying search query relationships which express commonality in user intent among multiple search queries at a given time. The time-varying query interactions reflect the changing user needs over some time period.

Zhang et al. took the temporal features of queries into consideration in query substitution for ad search [4]. They extracted temporal features from query frequency curves and proposed a novel temporal similarity measurement by integrating these new features with the query frequency distribution. Jones and Diaz in [5] pointed out that temporal properties of queries can be used to diagnose the quality of the retrieval. They presented three temporal classes of queries: atemporal query, temporally unambiguous query and temporally ambiguous query. Metzler et al. [6] investigated implicitly year qualified queries which is a query that does not actually contain a year, but yet the user may have implicitly formulated the query with a specific year in mind. Asuar et al. [7] studied temporal signatures of three different types of queries - Navigational, Adult and News queries, and proposed a method to classify a query into these three types by computing trends in query-clicks over time.

Chien and Immorlica utilized temporal correlation to identify sets of similar queries, suggesting that queries with similar frequency patterns are likely to be related [8]. They defined a formal metric for temporal similarity between queries and used it to mine sets of related queries from a search log. Nunes et al. [9] investigated the use of temporal expressions in Web queries. They found that temporal expressions are scarcely used in the queries. They also found that these expressions are more frequently used in certain topics such as Autos, Sports, News and Holidays. Dakka et al. in [10] proposed a framework for handling time-sensitive queries and automatically identify the important time intervals that are likely to be of interest for a query. Then, they built scoring techniques integrating the temporal aspect into the overall ranking mechanism.

Kira et al. [11] proposed a method to compute word relatedness using temporal semantics analysis. For a given word, they first represented it as a weighted vector of concepts extracted from concept repository such as Wikipedia or Flickr image tags and denoted by a time series. Then, they got two words semantic relatedness by computing the similarity of all possible concept pairs. Giuseppe et al. in [12] examined the correlation between relevance and time. Then, they proposed an approach exploiting the detection of publication time peaks for the query expansion in the Blog search domain. Kira et al. explored how to use time series technique to model and predict user behavior over time including trends, periodicities and surprises[13]. Jaewon and Jure explored temporal dynamics of online content[14]. They treated mentions or interactions with a particular piece of contents as a time series. Then, they proposed a k-means like algorithm which uses a special distance measure to cluster time series by their shape.

Although there is a growth in research investigating temporal characteristics of queries recently, to the best of our knowledge until now few work has been done to understand user query's temporal intent. The most similar work is that Anagha et al. analyzed the distribution of query popularity along four dimensions: the number of spikes, the shape of the spikes, the periodicity of the queries, and the overall trend in popularity [15]. However, most of them either focused on only one query type, or did not did not propose an approach to understand a query's temporal dynamics automatically.

3   Temporal Intent Based Query Taxonomy

Understanding queries temporal intent is fundamental to understanding the retrieval experience. In order to obtain some latent semantics from the distribution of queries' temporal intents, we first observe that queries' temporal intents include full-time intent, most recent time intent, burst time intent or periodic intent. Then, we discover that a query's temporal intent can be reflected by its search frequencies over time which can be seen as a time series. Finally, we group queries to the corresponding temporal intent classes according to their temporal characteristics reflected by their time series, as shown in Figure 1.

Bellow we present definitions of these query classes and corresponding search time series shapes in terms of their temporal intents.

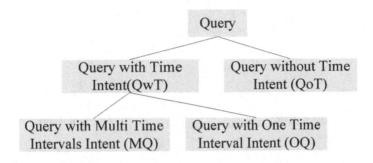

Fig. 1. Temporal Intent based Query Taxonomy

Query without Time Intent QoT denotes queries whose target information does not belong to any specific time. That is, there is no temporal constraint for their results. On the other hand, the temporal intent of QoT is full time. QoT denotes users' common, frequent and constant information needs. Consequently, their search frequency curves share a stable trend, for instance "Java JDK" as shown in Figure 2(a) derived from Google Trends [16].

Query with Time Intent QwT denotes queries which contain implicit time intents.

Query with One Time Interval Intent OQ are these queries whose target information belongs to one specific time period. These queries are often triggered by one time unexpected event. As a result, their search curves all contain a single spike which occurs when there is a sudden increase followed by a corresponding decrease in query frequency. For example, Octopus Paul and Haiti Earthquake are OQ, as depicted in Figure 6(d) and 2(c) respectively.

Query with Multi Time Intervals Intent MQ are these queries whose target information belongs to multi time periods. These queries are often triggered by an event which repeated multi-times.

Query with Aperiodic Time Intervals Intent AMQ describes MQ whose
multi time intervals are aperiodic. These queries are often triggered by an unexpected event or user requests, issued aperiodically. Search curves of AMQ
share a common shape with multi aperiodic peaks. For example, "Earthquake" is a AMQ, as illustrated in Figure 2(d).

Query with Periodic Time Intervals Intent PMQ denotes MQ whose
multi time intervals are periodic. These queries are often triggered by an
expected event which follows identical or almost identical patterns during
corresponding months of successive years. Search curves of PMQ share a
common shape with multi periodic peaks. For example, "Christmas Present"
gets hot in an annual cycle since it is time for people to select card for their
friends in every Christmas, as shown in Figure 2(e). And, "World Cup" has
the longer period of four years, as shown in Figure 2(f).

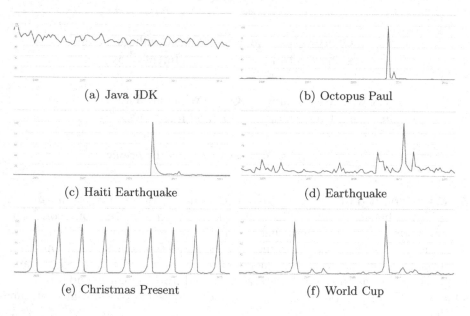

(a) Java JDK

(b) Octopus Paul

(c) Haiti Earthquake

(d) Earthquake

(e) Christmas Present

(f) World Cup

Fig. 2. Query Examples from Google Trends

4   Temporal Intent Based Query Classification

As mentioned above, we can see that the search frequency curves of these queries
with the same temporal intent exhibit a common shape. And, queries with different temporal intents have different shapes. Therefore, we can understand queries'
temporal intents by classifying queries into corresponding groups shown in Figure 1 according to their search frequency curve shapes.

Thus, the remaining problem is that for a new query, we propose a machine leaning algorithm to justify its category. To achieve this goal, the primary task is to compare the query data located at different positions of the time axis from Web query logs in order to detect pattern of the query. We use the conventional time series to represent temporal query data [17]. Let f_t denotes the frequency of query q issued by all users during the tth time interval, that 'month' is used here. $t = 1...N$ in which N is the number of time intervals. The frequency function F of a query q over N time intervals is a random f_t sequence, denoted as:

$$F = f_{t\ (t=1...N)} = \{f_1, f_2, ..., f_N\} \tag{1}$$

Preprocessing. F can be decomposed into three components [17], as shown in:

$$F = m_t + s_t + Y_t \tag{2}$$

Where m_t is a slowly changing function known as a trend component, s_t is a function with known period referred to as a seasonal component, and Y_t is a random, burst and irregular component. We first need to separate QoT and QwT, so we estimate and extract the s_t and Y_t. In other words, we remove m_t from F. Here we use Polynomial Fitting to get m_t [17],

$$m_t = \sum_{i=0}^{k} w_i x^i \tag{3}$$

In which k is set to 4 in this paper according the experiments. We choose the parameter w_i by minimizing the following target function:

$$L(W) = \sum_{t=1}^{N} (f_t - m_t)^2 + \frac{\lambda}{2}||W||^2 \tag{4}$$

Where $W = (w_0, w_1, w_2, w_3, w_4)$. After removing m_t, we get $F^q = s_t + Y_t$. An example is shown in Figure 3.

Features. We use 11 features for the machine learning model in this paper.

Feature1-2 QoT is stable while QwT is burst, so in order to distinguish QwT from QoT, Mean and Standard Deviation of F^q are two obvious features.

Feature3 However, it is difficult to separate OQ and MQ because all their Standard Deviations are larger. Hence we define a new feature as follows:

$$SR = \frac{f_M - \text{Max}(\{f_1, f_2, ..., f_N\} - \{f_{M-m}, ..., f_{M-1}, f_M, f_{M+1}, ..., f_{M+m}\})}{\sum\limits_{t=1}^{N} f_t} \tag{5}$$

In which, $f_M = \text{Max}(\{f_1, f_2, ..., f_N\})$ is the frequency of the highest spike. $\{f_1, f_2, ..., f_N\}$ - $\{f_{M-m}, ..., f_{M-1}, f_M, f_{M+1}, ..., f_{M+m}\}$ denotes remove these points $\{f_{M-m}, ..., f_{M+m}\}$ from the set $\{f_1, f_2, ..., f_N\}$. m is a predefined parameter and $2m$ represents the duration of a spike. We determine m by analyzing these

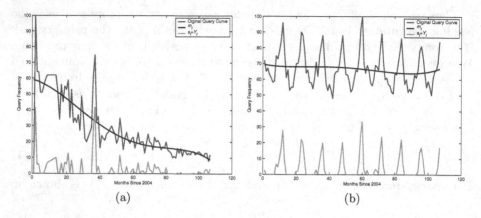

Fig. 3. Examples of Removing Trend Component

maximum spikes of all QwT in the query dataset [18]. First we define a threshold ratio r. If i and j satisfy all $\{f_{M-i}, ..., f_{M-1}, f_M, f_{M+1}, ..., f_{M+j}\} > r * f_M$, then $2m = i + j$. The analyzing result is shown in Figure 4. We can see that if $2m=4$, it can cover at least 74.6% queries regardless of the value of r. Thus, without loss of generality, in this paper we set $m = 2$.

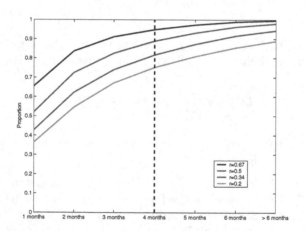

Fig. 4. Analyzing of Spike Duration

Feature4 Another feature is defined as:

$$MR = \frac{\text{Max}(\{f_1, f_2, ..., f_N\})}{\sum\limits_{t=1}^{N} f_t} \tag{6}$$

Which represents the proportion of the maximum frequency and the sum of all frequencies.

Feature5-8 We adopt a distance measure that is invariant to scaling and translation of the time series [14]. Given two query curves $F1$ and $F2$, the distance $Distance(F_1, F_2)$ is defined as follows:

$$Distance(F1, F2) = \min_{\alpha, q} \frac{||F1 - \alpha F2_{(q)}||}{||x||} \qquad (7)$$

where $F2_{(q)}$ is the result of shifting time series $F2$ by q time units, and $|| \cdot ||$ is the l_2 norm. This measure finds the optimal alignment (translation q) and the scaling coefficient α for matching the shapes of the two time series. With q fixed, $\frac{||x - \alpha y_{(q)}||}{||x||}$ is a convex function of α, and therefore we can find the optimal α by setting the gradient to zero: $\alpha = \frac{x^T y_{(q)}}{||y_{(q)}||^2}$. It is difficult to find the optimal q. In practice, we traverses all possible values of q to find out the minimum distance.

For a given query curve F, we compute its similarity to all cures of the other query categories in the training set. We use the mean similarity of the same query class as one feature. Then, we get four features, represented as D_{QoT}, D_{OQ}, D_{AMQ} and D_{PMQ}, corresponding to the query groups QoT, OQ, AMQ and PMQ respectively.

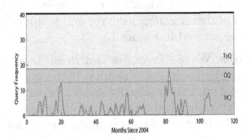

Fig. 5. Approximate *cutoff* of Training Data

Feature9-11 First we define the 9th feature *cutoff* as:

$$cutoff(X) : R^n -> R \qquad (8)$$

Where R^n is the feature space. We need to learn *cutoff* from the training data. However, there are no annotated *cutoff* on ptraining data. So we have to get an approximate value of *cutoff* with Function 9 as shown in Figure 5.

$$cutoff = \begin{cases} \text{value of the median line of "yellow(first)" area} & if\ query = QoT \\ \text{value of the median line of "blue(second)" area} & if\ query = OT \\ \text{value of the median line of "pink(third)" area} & if\ query = MT \end{cases} \qquad (9)$$

Then, we use the former 8 features *Feature 1-8* as the input of SVR (Support Vector Regression) [19] to get the *cutoff* of the testing data. In SVR, we use gaussian kernel function with model parameter $C = 22$.

The *cutoff* is used to detect spikes, and we define the number of these spikes as the 10th Feature. A spike is defined as some continuous points whose values are larger than *cutoff*.

In order to identify PMQ well, we define a new feature *PD*. According to *Feature10*, if there exist multi spikes, we use y_i to represent the time interval between two neighboring spikes as shown in Figure 3(b). We get a sequence $\{y_1, y_2, ..., y_w\}$. Then, *PD* is computed as the Standard Deviation of the sequence. Else if there is no or one spike, we set *PD* with extreme values.

5   Experiments

Corpora. For the lack of standard corpora for evaluating temporal intent based query classification algorithm, we have to construct data sets. We first extracted 5,000 queries from Web Track of TREC [18] and submit every query to Google Trends [16] and download its query frequency file. The numbers on the file reflect how many searches have been done for the particular query, relative to the total number of searches done on Google over time. We have to use the file as the corresponding query's frequency data to demonstrate our query classification algorithm because it is very difficult to get real and large-scale query logs from commercial search engines. Finally, we manually annotated categories of these queries in terms of their frequency curves and temporal intent based query taxonomy definitions described in Figure 1.

Evaluation Measures. We use *Precision* and *Recall* in evaluation of the temporal intent based query classification results. If the query category classified by the algorithm agrees with the manually annotated category, we view it as a correct classification. *Precision* is the fraction of classified query categories that are correct. *Recall* is the fraction of correct query categories that are classified. *F1-score* is calculated using following function: $F1 = 2 * (P * R)/(P + R)$.

Classifier and Parameter. With respect to the machine learning model, Support Vector Machine (SVM) [19] is used in this paper. The input are the eleven features and the output are the four categories. We used the C-Support Vector Classification in LIBSVM with the gaussian kernel function and set $C = 22$.

Table 1. Classification Performance Comparison for Different Query Categories

Query Class	QoT	OQ	AMQ	PMQ	average
P	0.952	0.928	0.846	0.914	0.910
R	0.973	0.915	0.831	0.924	0.911
F1	0.962	0.922	0.838	0.919	0.910

Results and Discussion. Table 1 shows the results. Because none of the previous approaches has provided an efficient method to group queries based on temporal intents, to the best of our knowledge, we have to only analyze our own approach. Obviously, our approach achieves high performance for all four query classes. We can see that the classification performance of AMQ is the worst. This is because queries tends to fluctuate caused by many factors and AMQ has more than one spike. If the fluctuation of the spike is not large enough, it is difficult to detect it. As a result, the query will be mistakenly classified as QoT. It is obvious the performance for QoT is the best among these four query classes for the reason that the Mean and Standard Deviations of all QoT's frequency curves are very low and our algorithm can identify it effectively. To our surprise, the performance of PMQ is also very high. This may because the feature SR and MR can distinguish it from the other query classes well.

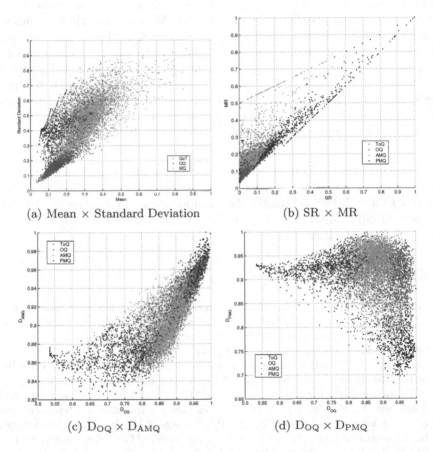

(a) Mean × Standard Deviation   (b) SR × MR

(c) $D_{OQ} \times D_{AMQ}$ (d) $D_{OQ} \times D_{PMQ}$

Fig. 6. Feature Effect Analysis. Query Classes Distribution in Pair of Features Space

Feature Effect Analysis. We further analyze some typical features' effects by compute the query class distribution on feature space, as shown in Figure 6. It is obvious that the feature Mean and Stand-Deviation can distinguish QoT from QwT effectively as illustrated in Figure 6(a). The main reason for this is that

QoT's curves Means and especially Stand-Deviations are low. From the Figure 6(b), we can see that the feature combination of MR and SR can classify OQ and MQ well. MR is used to evaluate the proportion of the second spike frequency and the sum of all frequencies. As described in the figure, SRs of all MQ are high. As illustrated in Figure 6(c) and 6(d), the distance between queries of the same classes are small. This can be used to distinguish queries well.

6   Conclusion

In this paper, we study the problem of how to understand the implicit temporal intents of user queries. We propose a query classification method to solve this problem. We first analyze the temporal intents of Web queries. Then, we propose a query taxonomy based on queries' frequency over time. Finally, we introduce a machine learning method based on four features to classify queries into four categories. Experimental results demonstrate that our approach is effective.

In future work, we will explore more features for temporal intent based query classification. We also plan to explore the application of temporal intent. Especially, we will study how the temporal intent can be used to construct a page ranking model to improve information retrieval performance.

Acknowledgement. This work is supported by the Natural Science Foundation of China (61272240,61103151), the Doctoral Fund of Ministry of Education of China (20110131110028), the Natural Science foundation of Shandong province (ZR2012FM037) and the Excellent Middle-Aged and Youth Scientists of Shandong Province(BS2012DX017).

References

1. Zhou, K., Whiting, S., Jose, J.M., Lalmas, M.: The impact of temporal intent variability on diversity evaluation. In: Serdyukov, P., Braslavski, P., Kuznetsov, S.O., Kamps, J., Rüger, S., Agichtein, E., Segalovich, I., Yilmaz, E. (eds.) ECIR 2013. LNCS, vol. 7814, pp. 820–823. Springer, Heidelberg (2013)
2. Shokouhi, M.: Detecting seasonal queries by time-series analysis. In: Proceedings of the 34th International ACM SIGIR Conference on Research and Development in Information Retrieval, SIGIR 2011, pp. 1171–1172. ACM. R, New York (2011)
3. Johansson, F., Färdig, T., Jethava, V., Marinov, S.: Intent-aware temporal query modeling for keyword suggestion. In: Proceedings of the 5th Ph.D. Workshop on Information and Knowledge, PIKM 2012, pp. 83–86. ACM, New York (2012)
4. Zhang, W., Yan, J., Yan, S., Liu, N., Chen, Z.: Temporal query substitution for ad search. In: SIGIR 2009, pp. 798–799 (2009)
5. Jones, R., Diaz, F.: Temporal profiles of queries. ACM Transactions on Information Systems 25(3), 14 (2007)
6. Metzler, D., Jones, R., Peng, F., Zhang, R.: Improving search relevance for implicitly temporal queries. In: SIGIR 2009, pp. 700–701 (2009)
7. Asur, S., Buehrer, G.: Temporal analysis of web search query-click data. In: SNA-KDD 2009, pp. 1–8. ACM (2009)

8. Chien, S., Immorlica, N.: Semantic similarity between search engine queries using temporal correlation. In: WWW 2005, pp. 2–11. ACM (2005)

9. Nunes, S., Ribeiro, C., David, G.: Use of Temporal Expressions in Web Search. In: Macdonald, C., Ounis, I., Plachouras, V., Ruthven, I., White, R.W. (eds.) ECIR 2008. LNCS, vol. 4956, pp. 580–584. Springer, Heidelberg (2008)

10. Dakka, W., Gravano, L., Ipeirotis, P.G.: Answering general time sensitive queries. In: CIKM 2008, pp. 1437–1438. ACM (2008)

11. Radinsky, K., Agichtein, E., Gabrilovich, E., Markovitch, S.: A word at a time: computing word relatedness using temporal semantic analysis. In: Proceedings of the 20th International Conference on World Wide Web, WWW 2011, pp. 337–346. ACM, New York (2011)

12. Amodeo, G., Amati, G., Gambosi, G.: On relevance, time and query expansion. In: Proceedings of the 20th ACM International Conference on Information and Knowledge Management, CIKM 2011, pp. 1973–1976. ACM, New York (2011)

13. Radinsky, K., Svore, K., Dumais, S., Teevan, J., Bocharov, A., Horvitz, E.: Modeling and predicting behavioral dynamics on the web. In: Proceedings of the 21st International Conference on World Wide Web, WWW 2012, pp. 599–608. ACM, New York (2012)

14. Yang, J., Leskovec, J.: Patterns of temporal variation in online media. In: Proceedings of the Fourth ACM International Conference on Web Search and Data Mining, WSDM 2011, pp. 177–186. ACM, New York (2011)

15. Kulkarni, A., Teevan, J., Svore, K.M., Dumais, S.T.: Understanding temporal query dynamics. In: Proceedings of the Fourth ACM International Conference on Web Search and Data Mining, WSDM 2011, pp. 167–176. ACM, New York (2011)

16. Google trend, http://www.google.com/trends?hl=en

17. Brockwell, P.J., Davis, R.A.: Introduction to time series and forecasting. Springer (2002)

18. TREC. Million query track, http://trec.nist.gov/data/million.query.html

19. Chang, C.-C., Lin, C.-J.: Libsvm: a library for support vector machines. ACM Transactions on Intelligent Systems and Technology (TIST) 2(3), 27 (2011)

Research on Semantic-Based Passive Transformation in Chinese-English Machine Translation

Wenfei Chang, Zhiying Liu, and Yaohong Jin

Institute of Chinese Information Processing, Beijing Normal University, Beijing, China
changwenfei07@126.com, {liuzhy,jinyaohong}@bnu.edu.cn

Abstract. Passive voice is widely used in English while it is less used in Chinese, which is more prevalent in patent documents. The difference requires us to transform the voice in Chinese-English machine translation in order to make the result more smooth and natural. Previous studies in this field are based on statistics, but the effect is not very good. In this paper we propose a strategy to deal with the Chinese-English passive voice transformation from the perspective of semantic. Through analyzing the sentences, a series of transformation rules are summarized. Then we test them in our system. Experiment results show that the transformation rules can achieve an accuracy of 89.1% overall.

Keywords: passive voice, patent documents, Machine translation, Transformation rules.

1   Introduction

Voice refers to the expression of the relationship between a verb and a noun phrase in a language [1]. It includes two types: active voice and passive voice. Active voice indicates that the subject is the agent of the action; passive voice means that the subject is the patient of the action. There are passive sentences both in Chinese and English, but they have a lot of differences in grammar grammatical concept, form of structure, typical usages and semantic roles. In English, passive voice will be used when the agent is uncertain or inconvenience to implicit or can be seen from the context. In addition, when the sentence emphasizes on the event or action itself rather than the agent, the passive voice is adopted, too. However, in Chinese we use active voice in most cases except the sentence is used to express the feeling of unhappy or unsatisfied. As a result, passive voice is widely used in English while it is less used in Chinese. These differences require us to transform the voice in order to make the translation result more smooth and natural.

With the rapid development of the world economy, the update velocity of the technical knowledge becomes faster than ever. According to The World Intellectual Property Organization (WIPO), patent applications increased year by year and reached 1.8 million in 2010. Most applications are from China or Europe and effective in these areas. In order to better protect the benefit of the applicants, several major Intellectual Property Office actively exploring how to improve the effect of machine translation.

G. Zhou et al. (Eds.): NLPCC 2013, CCIS 400, pp. 346–354, 2013.
© Springer-Verlag Berlin Heidelberg 2013

Patent documents as official and juridical documents, they tend to have some fixed formats and they are suitable for machine translation (MT). However, the present MT systems don't have a good strategy to deal with the problem of passive transformation, thus greatly degrades the whole quality of MT.

The writing Center of University of Delaware has done a statistics, result shows that the passive form accounts for 65% of all predicate verbs in science and technology [2]. According to [3], passive voice is one of the most important characteristics in English. There is 1/3, even more than 1/2 verbs appear in passive voice in the field of science and technology. 500 Chinese-English bilingual abstracts of patent documents has been analyzed in [4], and found that the passive voice is not appeared only in 22 English abstracts. That means more than 95% English patent abstracts use passive voice. So it is essential to explore the passive translation methods in Chinese-English patent machine translation.

The remainder of this paper is organized as follows. We discuss the related work in Section 2. Semantic analysis of the passive voice is performed in Section 3. Next is the transformation process in Section 4. The experiments and discussion are presented in section 5. Finally, a conclusion is given and the further work is expected in Section 6.

2   Related Work

There mainly two fields research on the passive transformation. One field is traditional linguistic and the other is information processing field.

In traditional linguistic field, many papers have realized that passive voice is widely used in English, especially in the field of science and technology. Some researchers [5][6] has discovered that only transitive verbs can be used in the passive voice. Besides the verb must be used to express a kind of act and followed by an object. The difference between English and Chinese has been analyzed in [2], they proposed that we should follow the language habit and translate the voice as much as possible. Meanwhile, they present six methods about how to transform voice. But they mainly pay attention to the transformation from English into Chinese. The similarities and differences of the constituent components in Chinese and English passive sentences have been discussed in [7].They described the situation which should transform voice by analyzing the features of the subject, object, predicate or the passive preposition in the sentence.

Though they have an in-depth study on the passive transformation, most of the present studies are from the perspective of human rather than the machine, so it doesn't apply to machine translation.

In information processing field, some researchers has put forward some translation methods from the perspective of lexical semantic and syntactic structure [8][9].And [10] present a method to dispose the passive transformation based on the Case Grammar. However, the related study is still limited in this field.

Besides in present MT systems, most of them are based on statistics. Among them, Google Translator (name it Google for short) is the best. So we select some sentences from the patent documents and put them in Google to check the effect.

Example 1 根据各齿轮的旋转，*夹持*光盘，并*装载*托盘12。

Reference[1]: In accordance with the revolutions of the combined gears, an optical disk [is chucked], and a tray [is loaded].

Google: According to the rotation of the gears, the [clamping] disc, and the [loading] tray 12.

Example 2 这个字通过在光学领域内执行逐个比特的布尔"与"运算来*识别*。

Reference: The word [is recognized] by carrying out in the optical domain a bit-wise Boolean "AND" operation.

Google: The word through the implementation of the bit by bit in the optical field within the Boolean "and" operation to [identify].

Example 1 has omitted the subject, and the object has omitted in Example 2. In these cases, the words showed by italics should be transformed into passive voice according to the usage of English. But the result show that Google failed to transform it. After test some kinds of sentences, we find the accuracy of passive transformation is low. As we can see though statistical method is the mainstream, it doesn't have a good strategy to treat the passive transformation at the moment. The results reflect that it is difficult to achieve a good effect without using syntactic and semantic analysis when translating long patent sentences.

Hence, in this paper, from the perspective of semantic, we propose a systematic processing strategy which composed by a series of rules according to the features of the patent documents, which has greatly improved the effect of MT.

3   Semantic Analysis of the Passive Voice

In English, the structure of "be+V-ed" is used to indicate the sentence is a passive sentence, that is to say, it is the mark of the passive sentence. However, in Chinese, many passive meaning are expressed by the active form, thus judging whether a sentence should be translated into passive sentence in Chinese-English MT system should not only rely on the passive mark but also have to observe the sentence semantic. Sentences with passive mark are only one kind of the sentences which should be transformed, there are many kinds of sentences without passive mark should transformed when translating, too. They all should use passive voice when translated into English. Different transform methods are adopted in the process of transformation according to whether can find a passive mark in the sentence or not.

3.1   Sentences with Passive Mark in Chinese

In Chinese, the preposition BEI or SUO are used to mark the passive voice. But there are some differences in usage.

---

[1] The bilingual corpus is provided by China Patent Information Center.

- **Passive Mark BEI**

BEI is an unconditional transformation mark whenever we find BEI before a verb in the sentence. Regardless of whether BEI is closely adjacent to the verb, the passive voice will be used when translated into English.

1)Patient+ BEI+ Verb: In this kind of sentences, BEI is immediately before the verb, there is no other part between them, the order of the language blocks in the sentence would keep unchanged when translated into English.

Example 3因此提交订单的交易者将被通知成交。(Thereby the trader that sent in the order will be informed about the deal.)

2)Patient + BEI +...+Verb: It is allowed to have an agent or adverb or other components between BEI and the verb in this kind of sentences. And the order of the language blocks would keep unchanged, too.

Example 4 如图中可见的，排列单元被匹配单元分离并连接到输入机构3。 (As can be seen in the figure the ranking unit is separated by the matching unit and connected to the input mechanism 3.)

- **Passive Mark SUO**

SUO is also a mark of the passive voice. Unlike BEI, there isn't allow any part between SUO and the verb, therefore if we find the word SUO located immediately before a verb in Chinese, then we should transform the verb into passive form when translated into English.

Example 5 因此，它不需要处理在第一排列单元所接收的并且不是最优排列的订单。(Hence, it does not need to handle the order that was received at the first ranking unit and which was not top ranked.)

3.2   Sentences without Passive Mark in Chinese

Through the statistical analysis of 1000 sentences, we find that sentences should be transformed into passive voice when translating and without passive mark can achieve the proportion as high as 61%. The data can be seen in Table 1.

Table 1. Classification of Passive Sentence

Type	Sentence number	Proportion
Sentences with passive mark	390	39%
Sentences without passive mark	610	61%

From the table we can see that most of the passive sentences are without passive mark in Chinese. So it is difficult for the MT systems to recognize the passive meaning and transform the verb into passive voice when translating. Though they are difficult to distinguish, they have an important role in enhancing the transformation accuracy rate. Consequently, they are the emphasis of our research.

Our research are performed based on the Hierarchical Network of Concepts theory (HNC theory)[11], which is a natural language understanding theory from the perspective of semantic. HNC views the language processing as a mapping process from the natural language space to the language concept space. The language concepts can be divided into two categories: action concept (presenting GX) and effect concept (presenting GY) (The action is cause and the effect is result.)[12]. According to the concept category of the main verb in the sentence, two sentence categories have been classified: global action sentence and global effect sentence. And in this section, our work is done based on the division of the two sentence categories.

- **Action Sentence**

The verb in global action sentence mainly expresses the meaning of one participant exerts a power to the other. Generally speaking, this category of sentences needn't transform into passive voice if the components are complete. But when there is a component ellipsis or there is a preposition immediately next to the main verb in the sentence, then the sentence should be transformed into passive voice.

Component ellipsis in sentence. The complete sentence structure is SVO both in Chinese and English. However, the sentence without subject or object can be frequently found in Chinese. Then the structure of the sentence will become the form of "V+NP" or "NP+V". In these structures, NP acts the patient of the action. So the sentences should be transformed into passive voice when translated into English.

"Verb+Prep" structure in sentence. The compound structure composed by the main verb and an immediately adjacent preposition is used to describe an objective phenomenon. The subject in this kind of sentences no longer acts the agent, but the patient of the action. So we should transform the sentence into passive voice when translating.

- **Effect Sentence**

Unlike the action sentences, there is no agent or patient in the sentence, the effect sentences are used to describe a kind of objective phenomenon. But when the verb expresses a strong result meaning, the word itself implies an agent, so it should be translated into passive voice, too. In view of this situation, we have chosen to add related property "ALL_PASS" in the knowledge base in order to provide information for the MT system. As long as the main verb has the property of "ALL_PASS[Y]", it would be transformed into passive voice in the translation process.

4   Transformation Rules and Algorithm

According to several situations we have mentioned above, a series of rules are drawn up to transform the passive voice in MT system.

4.1   Transformation Rules

- **Transformation with Passive Mark in Chinese**

There are mainly two rules in this part according to [13].

Rule 1:

(b)^2{(-1)CHN[被
]}+(0)LC_CHK[E,EG,EP]=>DEL_NODE(-1)+COPY[-1,0]+(0){VOI=P}$

Rule 2:

(-1)CHN[所]&LC_CHK[QE]+(0)LC_CHK[E,EG,EP]=>DEL_NODE(-1)+(0){
VOI=P}$

Rule 1 means that if we can find the preposition BEI(被) before E,EG,EP[3] regardless of whether they are immediately adjacent to node 0, then preposition BEI(被) will be deleted, components between preposition BEI(被) and node 0 will be copied as well as node 0 will be transformed into passive voice.

Example 6　一条指定水平线的像素数据的扫描级被有次序地存储在一个地址存储器中。(A scanning level of pixel data for a given horizontal line is regularly stored in an address memory.)

Rule 2 means that if SUO(所) act QE[4] and immediately adjacent to node 0, then delete SUO(所) and transform node 0 into passive voice.

Example 7　图像传感器装置所测定的色彩范围取决于光源的色彩。(The range of colors measured by an image sensor device depends on the color of the illuminant.)

- **Transformation without Passive Mark in Chinese**

In action sentences, we give different transform rules according to the different situations. Several examples are given below.

Rule 3:

(-1){BEGIN%}+(b){!LC_CHK[GBK]}+(0){LC_CHK[E,EG,EP]&LC_SC_KEY[
GX]&!CHN[使,具有,使得]}+(1)LC_CHK[GBK]=>(-1)+COPY[-1,0]+(1)+(0){VOI
=P}$

Rule 3 means that if the verb belongs to [GX][5] except the words "使", "具有", "使得", and we can't find GBK[6] before it, then node (1) will be put forward before the verb and the verb will be transformed into passive voice in the process of translation.

Example 8　在外壳118中在叶片120的径向向内的位置处形成环形凹槽122。(An annular recess 122 is formed in housing 118 radially inward of blade 120.)

Rule 4:

(b){(-1)BEGIN%}+(b){!LC_CHK[L0]}+(0)LC_CHK[E,EG,EP]&LC_SC_KEY[
GX]+(1){END%}=>(-1)+COPY[-1,0]+(0){VOI=P}+(1)$

Rule 4 means that if the verb belongs to [GX] and we can't find L0[7] before it as well as it locates at the end of the sentence, then the verb will be transformed into passive voice.

---

[2] (b) means looking for something forward.

[3] E, EG, EP are terminologies in HNC which mean the verb in sentence.

[4] QE is a terminology in HNC which means the modifier of E.

[5] GX means action concept.

[6] GBK is short for general object chunk.

[7] L0 is a terminology in HNC which means the mark of main semantic chunk.

Rule 5:

(0)LC_CHK[E]+(1)CHN[至,到,给,于,成]&LC_CHK[HV]=>(0){VOI=P}+
DEL_NODE(1)+ADD_NODE(ENG=[to])$

Rule 5 means that if there is a preposition immediately behind E and act HV[8], then we will transform the verb into passive voice and HV will be substituted by the English word "to" when translating.

Example 9 在步骤505中，已标准化的像素数据子集投射到色空间子集中。 (In step 505, the normalized pixel data subset is projected into the color space subset.)

In effect sentence, we will take advantage of the information which in the knowledge base to determine whether to transform the voice or not. One rule is used to invoke the information.

Rule 6:

(0)LC_CHK[E,EG,EP]&LC_SC_KEY[ALL_PASSIVE]=>(0){VOI=P}$

Example 10 具有预定形状的反光板形成于一下壳体中。(A reflection plate with a predetermined shape is formed inside a lower casing.)

Rule 6 means that if the verb has been labeled the tag of "ALL_PASSIVE" in knowledge base, it will be transformed into passive voice.

4.2   Algorithm

According to the features of the transformation rules, we design the procedure of transforming the passive voice in MT system semantically as below:

Step 1: To determine if there is a passive mark in Chinese sentence. If yes, go to step 6; if no, go to step 2.

Step 2: To determine the concept category of the predicative verb. If GX, go to step 3; if GY, go to step 5.

Step 3: To determine if there is a component ellipsis in the sentence. If yes, go to step 6; if no, go to step 4.

Step 4: To determine if it is the "Verb + Prep" structure in the sentence. If yes, go to step 6; if no, go to end.

Step 5: To determine if the main verb has the property of ALL_PASS[Y]. If yes, go to step 6; if no, go to end.

Step 6: To transform the verb into passive voice.

5   Experiments and Result Analysis

5.1   Experiments

In this experiment, we have selected 1000 sentences randomly and put them into our rule-based system (name it RB for short) to test the transformation effect. Meanwhile, we test them in Google, too. Three types of data are counted and the definite data can be seen in Table2.

---

[8] HV is a terminology in HNC which means the verb suffix.

Table 2. Types of data

Type	Total number	Should be transformed	Transformed	Right transformed
RB	1000	632	540	481
Google	1000	632	515	430

Then, the Precision (P) and Recall(R) are calculated, and the results are shown in Table 3:

Table 3. Result of transformation

System	Precision	Recall
RB	89.1%	76.1%
Google	83.4%	68.1%

From table 3 we can see that our system has achieved the higher Precision and Recall than Google, and the accuracy can reach as high as 89% overall. The result indicates that our method can efficiently improve the translation performance in Chinese-English machine translation system.

5.2   Result Analysis

Although our system has achieved good results, there are still areas for improvement. By analyzing errors in the result, we find there are mainly have four reasons: a) Rules have not covered all the kinds of linguistic phenomenon. b) In effect sentence, the passive voice transformation mainly relies on the information in knowledge base, so if the verb has been wrongly given the information of "ALL_PASS[Y]", it will be wrongly transformed. c) Our work is performed based on the verb; if the verb is wrongly recognized in the sentence, then it will not match the right transformation rule. That is the main reason that leading to the low Recall. d) The system may be left some sentences unanalyzed, thus leading to the transformation work can't be proceeded.

6   Conclusions and Future Work

Passive voice is widely used in English patent documents while it is less used in Chinese. So it is an important problem in Chinese-English machine translation. In this paper, with the guidance of HNC, we first classify the sentences into two types: sentences with passive mark in Chinese and sentences without passive mark in Chinese. And then analyze them in detail. Wherein sentence without passive mark in Chinese is our emphasis, in this part, we further analyze the sentences which should be transformed when translating in action sentence and effect sentence respectively. Through analyzing amount of bilingual sentences, we have concluded the transformation rules then tested them in our system. Results show that the precision of our system has achieved 89.1%.

In the future, in view of the reasons for the error, we will investigate more sentences in order to supplement and refine the existing rules. On the other hand, we will further improve the related information in the knowledge base.

Acknowledgements. This work was supported by the Hi-Tech Research and Development Program of China (2012AA011104), and the Fundamental Research Funds for the Central Universities.

References

1. Richards, J.C., Schmidt, R.W.: Longman Dictionary of Language Teaching and Applied Linguistics, 3rd edn. Foreign Language Teaching and Research Press, Beijing (2005)
2. Man, B., Zijuan, S., Shengtao, Z.: A method of translating English passive voice into Chinese. Journal of Guangdong Mechanical Institute 14(2) (June 1996)
3. Bin, L.: The comparative approach to the translation of English typical patterns in MT software. Southwest Jiaotong University, 5 (2004)
4. Zhiying, L., Yaohong, J.: Passive sentence transformation in Chinese-English patent machine translation. The Journal of China Universities of Posts and Telecommunications 19(suppl. 2), 135–139 (2012)
5. Baoyu, B.: A discussion on English voice transformation. Journal of Daqing College 16(3) (August 1996)
6. Yongxin, Z.: Comparison of Chinese and English passive structure. Foreign Language Teaching (February 1983)
7. Wenhua, X.: Comparison of passive sentences in Chinese and English. Language Teaching and Linguistic Studies (April 1983)
8. Yaohong, J.I.N., Zhiying, L.I.U.: Improving Chinese-English patent machine translation using sentence segmentation. In: IEEE 7th International Conference on Natural Language Processing and Knowledge Engineering (NLP-KE 2011), Tokushima, Japan, pp. 620–625 (2011)
9. Nunberg, G.: The Linguistics of Punctuation. CSLI Lecture Notes, No. 18, Stanford CA (1990) (July 2012); Bai, X., Zhan, W.: Constraints of BEI and process of English passive in machine translation, New expansion of Chinese passive expression, 1–17 (2006)
10. Jian, L., Bingxi, W., Yonghui, G.: Rule-Based Converter and Generation in English-Chinese MT System. In: The 2nd National Conference on Computational Linguistics for Students, pp. 390–393 (2004)
11. Zengyang, H.: Hierarchical Network of Concepts (HNC) Theory. Tsinghua University Press (1998)
12. Chuanjiang, M.: HNC (hierarchical network of concepts) theory introduction. Tsinghua University Press, Beijing (2005)
13. Yun, Z., Yaohong, J.: A Chinese-English patent machine translation system based on the theory of hierarchical network of concepts. The Journal of China Universities of Posts and Telecommunications 19(suppl. 2), 140–146 (2012)

Research of an Improved Algorithm
for Chinese Word Segmentation Dictionary
Based on Double-Array Trie Tree

Wenchuan Yang, Jian Liu, and Miao Yu

Beijing University of Posts and Telecommunication, Beijing, 100876, China
yangwenchuan@bupt.edu.cn

Abstract. Chinese word segmentation dictionary based on the Double-Array Trie Tree has higher efficiency of search, but the dynamic insertion will consume a lot of time. This paper presents an improved algorithm-iDAT, which is based on Double-Array Trie Tree for Chinese Word Segmentation Dictionary. After initialization the original dictionary. We implement a Hash process to the empty sequence index values for base array. The final Hash table stores the sum of the empty sequence before the current empty sequence. This algorithm adopt Sunday jumps algorithm of Single Pattern Matching. With slightly and reasonable space cost increasing, iDAT reduces the average time complexity of the dynamic insertion process in Trie Tree. Practical results shows it has a good operation performance.

Keywords: Double-Array, Trie Tree, Time Complexity, Word Segmentation Dictionary.

1 Introduction

Presently the matching algorithms based on dictionary is still the method used by the dominant search engine company. The foundation of Chinese word automatic segmentation is dictionary, and its structure is directly related to the speed and efficiency for word segmentation. Automatic word segmentation is basis for Chinese information processing system, which leads to further syntax and semantic analysis of Chinese text[1]. Lexicon will directly influence the segmentation speed. The data structure of dictionary is mainly through the indexed methods, which include index table, inverted lists, hash tables and search tree[2].

A maximum matching algorithm is presented in paper[3]. The nearest neighbor matching algorithm document is put forward in paper[4] based on the first word Hash algorithm. In paper[5], it presents the dictionary organization method and algorithm to combine first word Hash and entire word binary search, and this further improve the segmentation speed. Since there are so many Chinese words, it's hard to use the Hash table to control the data distribution, and reduce the conflict. There are 6768 commonly used Chinese characters in GB-2312, each Chinese characters can be mapped uniquely to 1-6768[6]. So we can use Double-Array Trie Tree as the data

G. Zhou et al. (Eds.): NLPCC 2013, CCIS 400, pp. 355–362, 2013.
© Springer-Verlag Berlin Heidelberg 2013

structure of the Chinese word segmentation dictionary. A linear table based Trie Tree is presented in paper[7], and the double array Trie Tree is an improved version.

The searching efficiency of Double-Array Trie Tree is $O(n)$, n for matching character length. It has a good search performance, and weak insert performance. Its insert performance is still $O(cm^2)$ even after tuning. Here m is the character set size, constant C. For the study of Chinese dictionary based on Double-Array Trie Tree, method for processing node with more branch first to improve space utilization in paper[8].

As we mentioned before in paper[2], there's a method to arrange the conflict nodes into the Hash table without redistribute node to improve the efficiency of the insertion process. Yet the Hash conflict is inevitable, and the use of Hash will increase the number of search. A optimization method based on genetic algorithm and Sherwood double array Trie Tree is purposed in paper[8]. It improves the space utilization rate, and it also avoid the local optimal solution for the algorithm.

In this paper, we will propose an improved algorithm-iDAT, which is based on Double-Array Trie Tree for Chinese Word Segmentation Dictionary. iDAT optimize the efficiency of inserting together with the ability of search performance as for Double-Array Trie Tree.

2   Double-Array Trie Tree

2.1   Double Array Trie Tree

Trie Tree is essentially a deterministic finite state automata, each node represents a state. Its state transferred according to the different input variables.

Double array uses two arrays as base[] and check[] to implement Trie Tree. Assume the input character is c, and Double-Array Trie Tree changes from state s to state t, it fits for the following conditions.

$$base[s]+c=t \qquad (1)$$

$$check[t]=s \qquad (2)$$

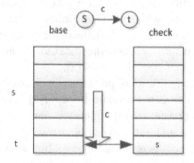

Fig. 1. Structure of Double array Trie Tree

For Double-Array Trie Tree shown in the Fig.1, s and t is the array index. With input c, the state s transfer to state t, so we have t=base[s]+c, and check[t]=s. So we can say that check array keeps record of the translated state for state t.

2.2   Insert Processing

Assuming that each state corresponds to an array index. For state s, if base[s] and check[s] are both 0, s stands for an empty place(Note: check can be when the node is idle). Assume t_1, $t_2...t_n$ is the suffix state begin with s , $c_1,c_2...c_n$ is respectively corresponding to the input state transition. base[s] is defined by the following process:

If there's a base[s], where $base[s]+c_1=0$, $base[s]+c_2=0$, ...$base[s]+c_n=0$, the base[s] can be accepted. The suffix state t_i can be stored in the $base[s]+c_i$.

If the new t_x suffix state appears, and the corresponding array for $base[s]+c_x$ is not empty, then we need to redo the above process, and recalculate value for base[s].

To determine the value of base[s], the entire array need to be traversed. The initial value of base[s] is determine by finding the empty node.

2.3   Insert Optimization

To avoid traversing arrays for an empty node from the very beginning, empty state can be used to construct the empty state sequence based on double linked table structure, as follows:

Assume $r_1,r_2...r_{cm}$ are the array index of the empty state for double array state

$$check[0] = - \; r_1 \tag{3}$$

$$check[\, r_i\,] = - \; r_i+1 \; ; \qquad (i \in [1, cm-1]) \tag{4}$$

$$check[\, r_{cm}\,] = 0 \tag{5}$$

$$base[0] = - \; r_{cm} \tag{6}$$

$$base[\, r_1\,] = 0 \tag{7}$$

$$base[\, r_i+1] = - \; r_i \; ; \qquad (i \in [1, cm-1]) \tag{8}$$

From the above definition, when the check value is negative, it indicates that the location is empty.

Under the array based double linked table structure, we can choose the value for initial state base[i] by directly traverse empty nodes.

This reduces the time compared with the traversal of the entire array. It also optimizes the node deletion operation with double linked table structure.

3   Improved Algorithm

The Double-Array Trie Tree saves the space compared with the traditional Trie Tree. When this insert processing encountered conflict, it need to determine the maximum sub-prefix base value, and this is time costly. To solve this problem, we propose a iDAT algorithm to optimize its insertion time complexity with the same search efficiency.

3.1   Definitions for iDAT

We have the following definitions for iDAT.

1. $N = \{n_1 n_2 ... n_l\}$ is the base(or check) array node set, n_i denotes the i node, i is corresponding the array index, l is the array size, and $l=N\_Length$;

2. $R = \{r_1 r_2 ... r_m\}$ is the all empty node set in N, r_j is the j-th empty node, m is empty node length; m=R_Length;

3. T is the maximum sub-prefix under insert state, $S = \{S_1 S_2 ... S_k ... S_{s\_length}\}$ is T's child nodes character set. Since $base[s]+c=t$, the character sequence in S set, which was created by traversal N, is in ascending order. So we have $S_k > S_{k-1}$ and its length is s_length;

4. Assume $S^* = \{S_1^* S_2^* ... S_k^* ... S^*_{s\_length}\}$ is all the inserted child nodes character set. $pos(S_1^*)$ is the index for the latest insert character S_1^*;

5.Assume START as the last character to be inserted position in Set S. Since $base[r_i+1] = - r_i$, we have $START = -base[pos(S_1^*)]$;

3.2   Hash Table

Assume the length of Hash table $D=N\_Length/10$, and mapping function as $Hash(t)=t\%D$. We use linked list to solve the node conflict.

step 1: For the empty node counting, we have a temporary variable $tem=0$ to initialize the Hash table $ht[D]$;

step 2: After double array dictionary is initialized, we traverse the empty node from the $check[0]$ position;

step 3: For the empty nodes corresponding array index, a Hash transform is done sequentially.

step 4: Let $ht[Hash(i)]=tem$; tem value increased by 1,here i is the current empty array index.

Here count is sum of all the empty node before the array position.

3.3   Skip Function

To improve and accelerate the algorithm, we design a skip function $isAccept(S,START)$ to determine whether to skip certain base.

The detail work flow is listed as,

step 1: Assume $\Delta s = s_{length} - s_1$, Δs stands for intervals between s_{length} and s_1. So the insertion position for s_1 should be $START - \Delta s$. Try to find whether $check[START - \Delta s]$ is less than 0. If it is less than 0, the location is empty and enter step2. Otherwise it jump out and returns false;

step 2: Calculate $\Delta count = hash(START) - hash(START - s\_length) - 1$, Here $Hash(START)$ is the empty position number before $START$. $\Delta count$ is the empty node numbers between the head node and tail node in Set S. IF $\Delta count < s\_length - 2$, jump out and returns false. Otherwise enter step3;

step 3: $base^0[T] = START - S_{s\_length}$, here $base^0[T]$ is the initial values of base[T]. Let's record the value and return true

3.4   Tree Construction

The construction steps are described as,

step1: initialization the dictionary according to the Double-Array Trie Tree optimization flow described before. For the initialized array, let's construct empty node linked table as formula (3)-(8). Then create Hash table.

step2: Assume insert word is Ts_x, $base[T] + s_x$ is not empty. Let's traverse the check table, and get the character set $S = \{S_1 S_2 ... S_k ... S_{s\_length}\}$, whose suffix is the maximum sub-prefix T.

step 3: Set S as input parameter for $isAccept(S,START)$. If the return value is true, it determines the initial value of base[T], and enter step4. Otherwise enter step5.

step 4: Process node inserting as described in iDAT algorithm. If the initial value for base is found, let's record the pos(S_1^*). Otherwise enter step5.

step 5: According to the formula $base[r_i+1] = -r_i$, change the value of $START$, and jump to step3.

step 6: If pos(S_1^*) is 0, let's update the Hash table as described in step1.

The skip function $isAccept(S,START)$ is a convergence algorithm. Its ordinary time complexity is $O(1)$, and its worst-case complexity is $O(cm^2)$(here c is constant,m is empty node number). Since the $isAccept$ function has the ability to skip and jump quickly. It avoids some unnecessary compare, and also reduces the average time complexity of the algorithm.

To improve the average time complexity, we create a Hash table. It does cost some space. In order to minimize the number of maintenance for Hash table. iDAT achieves inserting from back to front.

4   Evaluations

The experiment try to compare our improved double array Trie Tree(iDAT) solution with the optimized double array solution proposed in paper[8].

The experimental environment: CPU Core i7, Memory 16Gb, Operating system is window7, Programming language is Java over Eclipse. The dictionary to be tested is the open Chinese lexicon provided by sogou (http://www.sogou.com/), which in- cludes 157201 entries. After we load the test dictionary with Double-Array Trie Tree, the base (check) array size is 574464.

During the constructing of Double-Array based Chinese dictionary, we find through the actual simulation ,that there is a certain relationship among the success rate of insertion, double array empty node proportion, and insert node number.

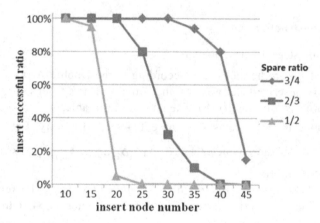

Fig. 2. Diagram of relation between insert successful ratio and insert node number

Fig. 2 shows relation between insert successful ratio and insert node number. Idle rate is the proportion of empty nodes in the array sizes. There are three array idle rate, which are 3/4, 2/3, and 1/2. The X-axis is the insert node number, and the Y-axis is the success rate. From Fig. 2, we can find that with constant idle rate, the success rate of insertion may have radical transition under certain insert values.

For the insertion algorithm, the word with a number of child nodes has the high priority. Based on the idle rate of array, it choose to allocate new space in the tail of word. This can help to skip the insertion position selection process for entire array, and can further improve the efficiency of the insertion algorithm.

From the simulation data, we find that the idle rate in array is about 2/3. So we use the red curve to mark them. When the node number exceeds 35, we allocate some new space in the end of the array.

The size of new space is determined by the mapping code range for the child nodes. The time cost comparison for iDAT and EDS is shown in table 2.

Table 1. Time cost comparison for iDAT and EDS

Insert entry \ Algorithm	EDS	iDAT
100	6.47	5.49
200	9.23	7.01
300	12.89	10.72
400	22.58	18.36
500	31.59	22.61
600	40.04	28.18

As can be seen from Table 1, the advantage of iDAT is not obvious for less inserting entry. Accompany the   increasing for entry, the optimized solution will skip more unnecessary compare. It seem more effective.

The Hash table used in iDAT need extra space cost. The simulation result shows that ,when the size of hash table is about 1/10 to the total double array size, the performance can meet the requirements. Table 2 shows the analysis of the space cost of two methods.

Table 2. Space cost comparison for EDS and iDAT

algorithm	space cost	
EDS	array size 574,464	
iDAT	Array size 583,632	Hash table size 57,449

5   Conclusions

In this paper, we introduce iDAT, which is an improved algorithm for Chinese word segmentation dictionary based on double array Trie Tree. iDAT can implement fast mechanical word segmentation, such as maximum matching or reverse matching. Time cost for search in iDAT is almost the same with the original solution. But it is more effective than other solutions in insertion operation. In iDAT also can solve the space cost problem for traditional Trie Tree during Chinese word segmentation. Anyway, the idle rate for array is about 60% in the actual simulation process. Further research on the algorithm to optimize the space cost need to be done.

Acknowledgment. This paper is supported by the Opening Project of State Key Laboratory of Digital Publishing Technology.

References

1. Huang, C.N.: A review of ten years of Chinese word segmentation. Journal of Chinese Information 147, 195–199 (2007)
2. Zhao, H.Y.: A study on Chinese word segmentation based on Double-Array Trie Tree. Journal of Hunan University 22, 322–329 (2009)
3. Zhao, C.Y.: A word segmentation method based on the word. Journal of Soochow University 18, 44–48 (2002)
4. Chen, G.L.: An improved fast segmentation algorithm. Journal of Computer Research and Development 37, 418–424 (2009)
5. Li, Z., Xu, Z., Tang, W.: A full two points maximum matching in Computer Engineering and application of fast segmentation algorithm. Journal of Computer Science 38, 102–108 (2005)
6. Li, J.: A fast algorithm for query Chinese dictionary. Journal of Chinese Information 137, 97–101 (2006)
7. Wang, S.: Research on Double-Array Trie Tree algorithm optimization and its application. Journal of Chinese Information 138, 131–137 (2006)
8. Wang, S., Li, Z., Ke, X.: Based on improved genetic algorithm and Sherwood thought the Double-Array Trie Tree. Journal of Computer Engineering 78, 231–236 (2009)

Study on Tibetan Word Segmentation as Syllable Tagging

Yachao Li and Hongzhi Yu

Key Lab of Chinese National Linguistic Information Technology,
Northwest University for Nationalities, Lanzhou, China 730030
harry_lyc@foxmail.com

Abstract. Tibetan word segmentation (TWS) is the basic problem for Tibetan natural language processing. The paper reformulates the segmentation as a syllable tagging problem, and studies the performance of TWS with different sequence labeling models. Experimental results show that, the TWS system with conditional random field achieves the best performance in the condition of current 4-tag set, at the same time, the other models achieve good results too. All the above show that, the segmentation as a syllable tagging problem that is an efficient approach to deal with TWS.

Keywords: Tibetan, word segmentation, sequence label.

1 Introduction

Tibetan is alphabetic writing that contains 30 vowels and 4 consonants and spoken by about 6 million people in China. There is no space delimiter between adjacent Tibetan words, therefore, tokenization itself, is challenging task in Tibetan information processing.

Tibetan word segmentation dates back to the work by Zhaxiciren in 1999 [1], and has many important researches. Chen [2] proposed a TWS scheme based on case auxiliary words and continuous features, which could detect and eliminate segmentation ambiguities and deal with unknown words. The scheme has much more practical and achieves better performance. Qi [3] proposed a three level method to segment Tibetan text, this approach is based on the research of Tibetan form logic case, semantic logic case, phonological tendency studies. Caizhijie [4] introduced a TWS system using reinstallation rules to identify abbreviated words (AW) for the first time. Liu [5-6] proposed a method to identify Tibetan numbers based on classification of number components, and presented a novel approach for TWS using the conditional random fields. The approach combines the TWS and abbreviated word recognition in a unified tag set, is one of the most major results of TWS.

Most of the methods above are based on dictionary matching (maximum matching) or linguistic rules, and use some simple statistical information as auxiliary method, such as word frequency, entropy and so on. The TWS with machine learning has received less attention, because of there is lack of human-annotated corpus in Tibetan. Liu reformulates the segmentation as a syllable tagging problem, one of the latest research results, this approach uses statistical machine learning model and achieves the best performance [6].

G. Zhou et al. (Eds.): NLPCC 2013, CCIS 400, pp. 363–369, 2013.
© Springer-Verlag Berlin Heidelberg 2013

TWS as a syllable tagging problem dates back to the fundamental work by Xue [7], published in the first SIGHAN in 2002, this approach reformulates word segmentation as a sequence tagging problem, namely identify the position information of a character. In recent years, many experimental results show that, the method with character tagging effetely, becoming the mainstream, and implement in the TWS successfully.

The paper studies the TWS as syllable tagging, and implements experiment with maximum margin markov networks (M^3N), maximum entropy (ME), conditional random fields (CRF) respectively. The plan of the paper is as follows. In Section 2 we introduce the Tibetan syllable tagging problem, and compare the performance of different sequence labeling models. Section 3 introduces the sequence labeling models used in the paper. Section 4 gives the experimental results, and Section 5 concludes the paper.

2   The TWS as Syllable Tagging

TWS based on syllable tagging dates back to the work by Xue [7], which reformulates the segmentation problem as a character tagging problem. The approach has become the mainstream in Chinese word segmentation.

Tibetan is alphabetic writing and Tibetan word constituted by syllables. Many Tibetan syllables can occur in different position within different words. We can get segmentation results according to the position of syllable. Therefore, it is an effective method that, reformulates the segmentation as a syllable tagging problem, and then use machine learning model to label syllables automatically.

Table 1. The Tibetan syllable can occur in many word-internal positions

Position	Example	Meaning	Tag
Single	ཡོན་	Reword	S
Begin	ཡོན་ཏན་	Knowledge	B
Middle	ཤེས་ཡོན་ཅན་	Intellectual	M
End	འདོད་ཡོན་	Desire	E

We can use "BMES" to denote the four tag-set of Tibetan syllables. It is tagged B if it occurs at the begin of a word. It is tagged M if it occurs in the middle of a word. It is tagged E if it occurs at the end of a word. It is tagged S if it forms a word by itself. In the light of the 4-tag set of Tibetan syllables, Liu introduced a method, it add two tag SS and ES besides "BMES", SS denotes a monosyllabic word contains abbreviated word, ES denotes a multi-syllable word contains abbreviated word. Li [8] proposed an approach called TagSet-2 in the next section, which is the prophase study of this paper. Experiments show that the TWS system adopted TagSet-2 achieved a better performance. So in this paper, we adopt the TagSet-2 as our syllable tag set. The different between Liu and TagSet-2 showed in table 2.

Table 2. Examples of TagSets

type of word	Example	TagSet-2	Liu
1 syllable+AW	ངས་ (ngs)	S-S	SS
2 syllable+AW	གནས་པའི་(bnas pvi)	B-E-S	B-ES
3 syllable+AW	མ་བྱས་པའམ་(ma byas pavm)	B-M-E-S	B-M-ES

Syllables segmented by "·" (tsheg) in the ancient Tibetan, however, there are no "tsheg" between some case auxiliary words and its prior syllable, these words called abbreviated words. For example "འདས་པ་ལི་ལོ་ལྔ་།" (In the past five years, vdas pai lo lnga), there is no "tsheg" between in the third segmentation unit and the second segmentation unit. In Tibetan word segmentation, we should properly handle six abbreviated words, namely "ས་" (sa), "ར་" (ra), "འི་" (vi), "ༀ་" (vo), "འང་" (vang), "འམ་" (vam). Abbreviated words recognition has great influence on Tibetan syllable recognition, which is an important problem that we must face in the Tibetan word segmentation.

In the light of abbreviated words recognition problem, Li [8] proposed an AW recognition method with sequence labeling, which reformulates segmentation problem as a binary classification problem, and then adopts sequence labeling model to recognition syllables. Tibetan word segmentation system, using AW recognition method listed above, need two steps, first recognizes the syllable sequence; second syllable labeling. The system is time consuming. To solve the problem, we consider the six abbreviated words as a unit, in order to alleviate the balance between of the precision of abbreviated words recognition and the system efficiency. The approach is the results of this paper's preliminary study, and has a best performance [8].

Example1:"ཚོང་ཟོག་རྫུན་མ་བཟོ་འཚོང་བྱེད།" (Manufacturing and selling inferior products, tsong sog rdzun ma bso vtsong byed). Example1 is listed to illustrate the Tibetan word segmentation based on syllables tagging. First, sequence labeling model was used to label syllables, the result is "ཚོ/Bཟོག/Eརྫུན/Bམ/Eབཟོ/Sའཚོང/Sབྱེད/S།/S"; on the basis of labeling result, we can reduction preliminary segmentation result "ཚོང་ཟོག/རྫུན་མ/བཟོ/འཚོང/བྱེད/།"; in the next, the processing of digital, time and date; finally, output the segmentation result.

3   Sequence Labeling Model

Statistical machine learning models are widely used in word segmentation tasks, these models can be classified into two categories: one is based on maximum margin learning, such as support vector machine (SVM) [9], which is widely used in classification; the other is based on the criterion of maximum likelihood estimation, such as maximum entropy (ME) [10], conditional random field (CRF) [11], these models are successfully used in Chinese word segmentation.

Maximum entropy and conditional random field are widely used in Chinese word segmentation. Maximum entropy was used in the early study of Chinese word segmentation; conditional random field has been proved to be an excellent sequence tagging model; at the same time, maximum margin markov networks (M^3N) was used in segmentation also. Conditional random field is successfully used in Tibetan word segmentation too, but no references have given about the effect of others model. We hope in this article that, implement these three models in the Tibetan word segmentation and compare these models in the same condition. The feature templates used in this paper showed in table 3.

Table 3. Feature templates

Features	Meaning
$C_n(n = -2,-1,0,1,2)$	The *ith* syllable to the left/right of the current syllable
$C_nC_{n+1}(n = -2,-1,0,1)$	Adjacent two syllables
$C_{-1}C_1$	Two syllables before and after the current

3.1   Maximum Entropy

Maximum entropy was proposed by E.T.Jaynes in 1950s [10], and was used in natural language processing by Della Pietra. The basic principle of ME is that using the given samples, and select a probability distribution conform to the training sample, it must be satisfy all the facts that known. Without additional assumptions and constraints conditions, for those uncertain samples, ME will give a uniform probability distribution. Entropy is measure of the uncertain, the greater the uncertain, the greater the entropy, and the more uniform distribution. Maximum entropy model:

$$P^* = \arg\max_{p \in C} H(P) \qquad (1)$$

$H(P)$ is the entropy of model P,C is the collection of model that satisfy constraints, the following need to seek P^*, P^* represented as follows:

$$P^*(y|x) = \frac{1}{Z(x)} \exp\left(\sum_i \lambda_i f_i(x,y)\right) \qquad (2)$$

$Z(x)$ is the normalization constant, represented as follows:

$$Z(x) = \sum_y \exp\left(\sum_i \lambda_i f_i(x,y)\right) \qquad (3)$$

λ_i is the weight parameters of features.

3.2   Conditional Random Field

Conditional random field, proposed by Lafferty [11], is a statistically sequence labeling model, for more information in the reference 12.

We reformulate the segmentation problem as a syllable tagging problem, and generates a linear-chain CRF based on a undirected graph G = (V,E). V is a set of random variables Y, Y = {Yi|1 ≤ i ≤ n}, for the n units needed to label in the input sentence, E = {(Yi-1, Yi) |1 ≤ i ≤ n} is the linear-chain composed of n-1 edges. For each sentence x, define two non-negative factors:

$$\text{For each edge: } \exp\left(\sum_{k=1}^{k} \lambda_k f_k(y_{i-1}, y_i, x)\right) \tag{4}$$

$$\text{For each node: } \exp\left(\sum_{k=1}^{\acute{K}} \acute{\lambda}_k \acute{f}_k(y_i, x)\right) \tag{5}$$

f_k is a binary feature function, K and K' is the number of features defined in each edges and each nodes respectively.

Given a sequence x need to label, conditional probability corresponding tag sequence y is:

$$P(y|x) = \frac{1}{Z(x)} \exp\left(\sum_{(i,k)} \lambda_k f_k(y_{i-1}, y_i, x) + \sum_{(i,k)} \acute{\lambda}_k \acute{f}_k(y_i, x)\right) \tag{6}$$

$Z(x)$ is normalized function, given the sequence x, the corresponding tag sequence y is given by $Argmax_y P(y'|x)$.

3.3   Maximum Margin Markov Networks

M³N is the extension of multi-class support vector machine (SVM) in the condition of structure prediction [12], the goal of M³N is constructing a mapping function $h: X \rightarrow Y$ from observation example set $S = \{(x^i, y^i = t(x^i))\}(i = 1, ..., m)$. $h: X \rightarrow Y$ is defined by weight coefficient vectors $w_i(i=1,...,n)$, each weight coefficient vector corresponds a feature function $f(x, y_i, y_j)$, the function denoted by $f(x, y)$, the goal of classifier is the solution of function h_w:

$$h_w(x) = \arg\max \sum_{i=1}^{n} w_i f_i(x, y) = \arg\max w^T f(x, y) \tag{7}$$

4   Experiments

In our experiments, the training set and the test set are come from CWMT2011. Total corpora divided into two parts according to the ratio of 3:7. The training set contains 856647 words, and the test set contains 300000 words, and out of vocabulary rate is 1.7%.

We can evaluate the approach by Precision (P), Recall (R) and F-score (F). P, R and F calculated as follows:

$$P = \frac{the\ number\ of\ correctly\ segmented\ words}{the\ total\ number\ of\ words\ in\ the\ segmented\ corpus} \times 100\% \tag{8}$$

$$R = \frac{the\ number\ of\ correctly\ segmented\ words}{the\ total\ number\ of\ words\ in\ the\ gold\ standard} \times 100\% \tag{9}$$

$$P = \frac{2 \times R \times P}{R+P} \times 100\% \tag{10}$$

We implemented three Tibetan word segmentation systems based on CRF, ME, M³N respectively. CRF model, ME model and M³N mode are implemented by

CRF++[1], maximum entropy toolkit[2] and pocket_m3n[3] respectively. There are illegal tags in ME and M3N, but is rarely in M3N. Therefore, we add feature tags and use dynamic programming to post-processing in the system with ME, called ME+D below. Experimental results showed in Table 4.

Table 4. Experimental results

TWS	R(%)	P(%)	F(%)
ME	94.11	93.02	93.56
ME+D	95.05	93.89	94.47
M^{3}N	94.38	94.34	94.36
CRF	95.35	95.32	95.33

Table 4 shows that, F-score of all the system reach 93%. This suggested that, reformulates the segmentation as a syllable tagging problem gets a good treatment of Tibetan word segmentation problem.

In the four TWS systems, F-score of the system based on CRF achieves 95%, gets the best result, which shows that, at the condition of four-tag set, CRF model gets a better treatment of Tibetan word segmentation problem compared to the other models.

5   Conclusion

This paper adopts the method based on syllable tagging, and compares the performance of different sequence labeling models. Experiments on our training set and test set show that the TWS system based on CRF outperforms all the system and achieves the best F-score. According to the experimental results Tibetan word segmentation based on syllable tagging can achieves a good performance.

Acknowledgments. The research work has been funded by the Natural Science Foundation of China under Grant No.61032008 and 61262054.

References

1. Bai, G.: Research on the Segmentation Unit of Tibetan Word for Information Processing. Journal of Chinese Information Processing 24(3), 124–128 (2009)
2. Chen, Y., Li, B., Yu, S.: A Tibetan Segmentation Scheme Based on Case-auxiliary Word and Continuous Features. Journal of Chinese Information Processing 17(3), 15–20 (2003)
3. Kun-Yu, Q.: On Tibetan Automatic Participate Research with the Aid of Information Treatment. Journal of Northwest University for Nationalities (Philosophy and Social Science) (4), 92–97 (2006)

---

[1] http://crfpp.googlecode.com/svn/trunk/doc/index.html
[2] http://homepages.inf.ed.ac.uk/lzhang10/maxent_toolkit.html
[3] http://sourceforge.net/projects/pocket-crf-1/

4. Zhi-Jie, C.: Identification of Abbreviated Word in Tibetan Word Segmentation. Journal of Chinese Information Processing 23(1), 35–37 (2009)
5. Liu, H., Zhao, W., Nuo, M., Jiang, L., Wu, J., He, Y.: Tibetan Number Identification Based on Classification of Number Components in Tibetan Word Segmentation. In: Proceedings of the 23rd International Conference on Computational Linguistics (Posters Volume) (Coling 2010), pp. 719–724 (2010)
6. Liu, H., Nuo, M., Ma, L., Wu, J., He, Y.: Tibetan Word Segmentation as Syllable Tagging Using Conditional Random Fields. In: Proceedings of the 25th Pacific Asia Conference on Language, Information and Computation (PACLIC 2011), pp. 168–177 (2011)
7. Xue, N., Converse, S.P.: Combining classifiers for Chinese word segmentation. In: Proceedings of the First SIGHAN Workshop on Chinese Language Processing, Taipei, Taiwan, pp. 63–70 (2002)
8. Yachao, L., Yangkyi, J., Chengqing, Z., Hongzhi, Y.: Research and Implementation of Tibetan Automatic Word Segmentation with Conditional Random Field. Journal of Chinese Information Processing 4(27), 52–58 (2013)
9. Cortes, C., Vapnik, V.: Support- vector networks. Machine Learning 20(3), 273–297 (1995)
10. Berger, A.L., Pietra, S.A.D., Pietra, V.J.D.: A Maximum Entropy Approach to Natural Language Processing. Computational Linguistics (22), 39–71 (1996)
11. Lafferty, J., McCallum, A., Pereira, F.: Conditional Random Fields: Probabilistic Models for Segmenting and Labeling Sequence Data. In: Proceedings of ICML 2001, pp. 282–289 (2001)
12. Taskar, B., Guestrin, C., Koller, D.: Max-margin Markov networks. In: Processing Syst., Vancouver (2003)

The Spoken/Written Language Classification of English Sentences with Bilingual Information

Kuan Li[1,*], Zhongyang Xiong[1], Yufang Zhang[1], Xiaohua Liu[2], Ming Zhou[2], and Guanghua Zhang[1]

[1] College of Computer Science, Chongqing University, Chongqing, China
sloweater@163.com, {zyxiong,zhangyf}@cqu.edu.cn,
Guanghua0420@gmail.com
[2] Microsoft Research Asia, Beijing, China
{xiaoliu,mingzhou}@microsoft.com

Abstract. To alleviate the problem with Chinese being poor at telling the difference between spoken and written English which is important for learning and using the language, we propose to classify English sentences with bilingual information into the two categories automatically. Based on the text categorization technology, we explore a variety of features, including words, statistics and their combinations, and find that a classification accuracy nearly 95% can be achieved in the open test through Chinese characters + sentence length + average syllable number, or other similar combinations.

Keywords: Text categorization, Sentence classification, Spoken and written language, Bilingual sentences.

1 Introduction

Back in the early twentieth century, foreign academics began the studies on spoken and written English. Spoken English (or Colloquialism) refers to the expressions employed in conversational or informal language but not in formal speech or formal writing [1]. Colloquialisms include words (such as *gonna* and *wanna*), phrases (such as *old as the hills*, *raining cats and dogs* and *dead as a doornail*) and aphorisms (such as *There's more than one way to skin a cat*) [1].

Professor Chafe indicates that fragmentation and involvement are related to the spoken language, while integration and detachment are associated with the written [2]. Due to very little time for utterance planning and deep involvement of communicators in the conversational context, the spoken sentences are simple and short, one or a few of which express a fragmental idea unit. In contrast, writers tend to integrate more information into an idea unit and detach the language from specific conversational context by using a variety of devices such as clauses, the passive voice or nominalization. [2]

---

[*] This work had been done while the author was visiting Microsoft Research Asia.

G. Zhou et al. (Eds.): NLPCC 2013, CCIS 400, pp. 370–377, 2013.
© Springer-Verlag Berlin Heidelberg 2013

Statistics online show that in 2006 about 300 million Chinese people were learning English, over one third of which were students, and the number was growing quickly. Gui and Yang [3] point out that most learners of English as a Second Language (ESL) write as native English speakers talk. The English learners from Chinese universities show a strong colloquial tendency in their written, which isn't improved significantly by more time spent on learning [4].

Sample sentences are very useful for English learners. Today we can mine millions of English-Chinese bilingual sentence pairs from web to build a tremendous sample sentence corpus. If we can further label them with spoken or written English with a relatively high accuracy, learners may hopefully get the ability to tell between spoken and written through reading many labeled samples besides theories. It would be an excellent complement to the mainstream English teaching.

The idea above seems promising thanks to the fast development of the text categorization (TC) in the recent years. The research on TC has long focused on the document classification (DC), such as the spam detection in e-mails [5], the news classification [6][7], etc. Recently, some researchers have moved their focus onto the sentence classification (SC) and achieved some results, such as the Chinese question classification [8], the classification of sentences in e-mails [9], in legal documents [10], in the abstracts of medical literatures [11], with different class sets.

To alleviate the problem with Chinese being poor at telling the difference between spoken and written English which is important for learning and using the language, we propose to classify English-Chinese bilingual sentence pairs mined from web into the two categories, spoken and written English, automatically. We focus on exploring a variety of features to find a feature group performing adequately in our experimental environment and to help English learners in practice.

2   Problem Formulation and Method

2.1   Problem Description and Data Set

Our mission is to classify a sentence into spoken or written English. A sentence s refers to an English sentence with its bilingual counterpart, like "*Nice to meet you! / 很高兴见到你！*". The class set is $C=\{Spoken, Written\}$. We put the mission as a classical supervised machine learning problem. Given a few labeled sentences $S=\{(s_1, c_1), (s_2, c_2), ..., (s_n, c_n) \mid c_{1...n} \in C\}$ as a training set, a target function $f:S \rightarrow C$ [12] is learned on it, which is called the training phase. In the predicting phase, given an s as the argument, f outputs its label $c \in C$.

Due to the lack of standard data sets for our mission, we constructed the data set by our own. The training set contains about 20,000 bilingual sentence pairs in movie lines mined from web as the spoken part, and about 25,000 sample sentences (bilingual) from authorized English-Chinese dictionaries like "*A bond is a promissory note, usually issued for a specified amount. / 债券是一种期票，通常以一定数额发行。*" as the written part. We randomly sampled hundreds of bilingual pairs from another big set automatically mined from web, and manually labeled 800 ones (400 spoken + 400 written) for the open test.

2.2   Sentence Representation

We use Vector Space Model (VSM) to represent the sentence space. If only words are put as features, a sentence can be represented as an N-dimensional vector $<w_1, w_2, \ldots, w_N>$, where N represents the number of different words in the training set, and w_k is the weight of the kth word in the sentence. We follow Khoo to use 1/0 as the weight value [9] representing if the word appears in the sentence. Other features than words will be also introduced into sentence vectors, which will be discussed in Section 3.

2.3   Classification Algorithm

Support Vector Machines (SVM) solves some critical problems for machine learning, such as the small sample, nonlinear, high dimension and local minima, etc. [14] The SVM classifier does well in [9-12], and it is essentially a two-class classifier [13], suitable for our mission. Through survey, we chose LIBLINEAR [15] for our experiments. The performance of its linear SVM classifier meets our requirements.

2.4   Evaluation Metrics

We use the classification accuracy A to evaluate the overall performance of the two-class classification, as defined below:

$$A = \frac{TP_1 + TP_2}{TP_1 + FP_1 + TP_2 + FP_2} \tag{1}$$

Here TP_1, TP_2, FP_1, FP_2 represent the number of true positive on Class 1/2, false positive on Class 1/2 respectively.

For each class, we use precision P, recall R and $F1$ to evaluate the performance, as defined below (taking Class 1 as example):

$$P_1 = \frac{TP_1}{TP_1 + FP_1} \tag{2}$$

$$R_1 = \frac{TP_1}{TP_1 + FN_1} \tag{3}$$

$$F1_1 = \frac{2 \times P_1 \times R_1}{P_1 + R_1} \tag{4}$$

Here TP_1, FP_1 represent the same as above, and FN_1 represents the number of false negative on Class 1.

3 Sentence Features

3.1 English Words and Chinese Characters

Following the reported DC and SC experiments, we use English words (EW) and Chinese characters (CC) as features to encode the class information. For *"Nice to meet you! / 很高兴见到你! "*, the features are:

- EW (lowercased): *nice, to, meet, you;*
- CC: 很, 高, 兴, 见, 到, 你.

3.2 Statistic Information of Sentences

Sentence Length. According to [2], most spoken sentences are simpler and shorter than written ones, which inspires us to adopt sentence length (SL) as a feature. In practice, we put the number of the words in an English sentence as its SL.

Average Syllable Number. According to [1-2], the spoken language often occurs in a conversation, easy to speak and understand, so syllables of its most words could be less than those of big words in the written. Therefore we introduce average syllable numbers (ASN) as a feature, as defined below:

$$ASN = \frac{\sum_{k=1}^{M} sw_k}{M} \tag{5}$$

Here M represents the number of the words in an English sentence, and sw_k represents the number of the kth word syllables gotten from a syllable dictionary. If the jth word doesn't exist in the dictionary, we assign sw_j an approximate value, one third of the word letter number.

Flesch–Kincaid Grade Level [16]. The Flesch–Kincaid grade level (*F-K*) is designed to indicate the readability of a piece of English text. The lower its value is, the easier the text is to understand. As mentioned above, the spoken language is easier to understand than the written, which means that their *F-Ks* could be different. Therefore we introduce *F-K* as a feature. The formula to calculate *F-K* is defined below:

$$F - K = 0.39 \times \frac{Total\ Words}{Total\ Sentences} + 11.8 \times \frac{Total\ Syllables}{Total\ Words} - 15.59 \tag{6}$$

Here *Total Words, Total Sentences, Total Syllables* represent the numbers of all the words, sentences, syllables of the text respectively. For a single English sentence, *Total Words* is *SL* defined above, *Total Sentences* is 1, and *Total Syllables* divided by *Total Words* is *ASN* defined above. Therefore the formula can be transformed into the following one:

$$F - K = 0.39 \times SL + 11.8 \times ASN - 15.59 \tag{7}$$

So, *F-K* is a weighted sum of *SL* and *ASN* when used for a sentence.

4   Experiment Results and Analysis

To verify the features discussed above and to find feature combinations performing well, we conduct the following three experiments, in all of which there are close and open tests. In the close test, we adopt 10-fold cross-validation [17]. Meanwhile, for the practical application, we pay more attention to the open one, and use the evaluation metrics *P, R, F1* only in it.

4.1   Words as Features

Table 1 shows the experiment results of using English words (EW), Chinese characters (CC) and EW+CC as features. In the open test, CC performs best, while EW does far from expected. In the close test, the three kinds of features do better than in the open one, especially EW.

The results indicate that data is more consistent with each other inside the training set than with that from the testing set, which is not surprising due to the lack of manual labeling for the training set. There must be spoken sentences in the samples from dictionaries. Many spoken words were introduced into the written part when we constructed the training set. The classifier trained on it labels the spoken with the written in the open test. That is why the spoken recall is much less than the precision, and the written is in reverse.

From the perspective of Chinese characters, the training data is more consistent with the testing data, because the Chinese part of a sample in dictionaries is relatively formal no matter its English counterpart is the written or not. Therefore the classifier trained with CC performs better.

Table 1. The experiment results of words as features (%)

(C: close test, O: open test, S: spoken, W: written)

Feature(s)	A(C)	A(O)	F1(S)	R(S)	P(S)	F1(W)	R(W)	P(W)
CC	93.11	**90.75**	**90.19**	**85.00**	**96.05**	91.25	**96.50**	**86.55**
EW	94.39	81.25	79.67	73.50	86.98	82.60	89.00	77.06
CC+EW	**95.57**	87.38	86.37	80.00	93.84	88.24	94.75	82.57

4.2   Statistics as Features

Table 2 shows the experiment results of using sentence length (SL), average syllable number (ASN), Flesch–Kincaid Grade Level (F-K) and their combinations as features. We can see that SL or ASN doesn't perform well alone. SL can't distinguish some short written sentences from the spoken, while ASN can't distinguish long written ones if their simple words are so many to lower their ASN too much. However, they are complements to each other, so we need their combinations as features. There are two ways to combine them:

- A weighted sum of SL and ASN: F-K alone
- Vector: 2 or 3- dimension feature vector consisting of SL, ASN or F-K.

The combinations improve the performance significantly as the last five lines show in Table 2. Interestingly, the open test results of the last four lines are exactly the same, and their A(O) is the highest in this experiment, which means SL+ASN and the other three similar combinations are almost the same good in performance in our data sets.

Table 2. The experiment results of statistics as features (%)

(C: close test, O: open test, S: spoken, W: written)

Feature(s)	A(C)	A(O)	F1(S)	R(S)	P(S)	F1(W)	R(W)	P(W)
SL	82.17	78.00	80.31	89.75	72.67	75.07	66.25	86.60
ASN	67.97	81.75	79.50	70.75	90.71	83.56	92.75	76.02
F-K	79.07	88.88	88.30	84.00	**93.07**	89.39	**93.75**	85.42
SL+ASN	**86.89**	**89.88**	**89.96**	**90.75**	89.19	**89.79**	89.00	**90.59**
SL+ F-K	**86.89**	**89.88**	**89.96**	**90.75**	89.19	**89.79**	89.00	**90.59**
ASN+ F-K	86.88	**89.88**	**89.96**	**90.75**	89.19	**89.79**	89.00	**90.59**
SL+ASN+ F-K	**86.89**	**89.88**	**89.96**	**90.75**	89.19	**89.79**	89.00	**90.59**

4.3   Combinations of Words and Statistics

In this experiment, we combine CC performing best in 4.1 with the last four feature groups performing best in 4.2 to do the mission. The results in Table 3 show that their performances are the same in the open test, and more importantly, their A(O) is higher than the best results in 4.1 and 4.2 by 4~5%, which means a best classification accuracy (94.88%) in our data set can be achieved through CC+SL+ASN or other similar combinations.

Table 3. The experiment results of combinations of words and statistics (%)

(C: close test, O: open test, S: spoken, W: written)

Feature(s)	A(C)	A(O)	F1(S)	R(S)	P(S)	F1(W)	R(W)	P(W)
CC+SL+ASN	93.81	**94.88**	**94.65**	**90.75**	**98.91**	**95.08**	**99.00**	**91.45**
CC+SL+ F-K	93.82	**94.88**	**94.65**	**90.75**	**98.91**	**95.08**	**99.00**	**91.45**
CC+ASN+ F-K	93.81	**94.88**	**94.65**	**90.75**	**98.91**	**95.08**	**99.00**	**91.45**
CC+SL+ASN+ F-K	**93.83**	**94.88**	**94.65**	**90.75**	**98.91**	**95.08**	**99.00**	**91.45**

We randomly selected some sentences classified by CC+SL+ASN, manually checked them and found that most of the results are convincing and useful. For example, *"She has an elegant style. / 她具有优雅的风格。"* is labeled as the written even if it is short, which is believed reasonable due to its complete structure and no colloquialism word. Another sentence *"I'm up to my ears in work. / 我工作忙得不可开交。"* is labeled as the spoken, which is also convincing due to its *"I'm"* and *"up to my ears"*.

A kind of obvious error made by our system is to classify some titles and organization names into the spoken, like *"Study on Multifunctional Teaching DPTV Platform /* 多功能DPTV教学演示平台的研制*", "State Bureau of Machine Building Industry /* 国家机械工业局*", etc. We manually checked our training set and found that there are barely any titles or organization names in the written part. Meanwhile, their grammatical structures are not complete. Therefore it is difficult for the classifier to label them all correctly. However, since they are easy to recognize for English learners, this type of error doesn't affect the practical application of our research much.

5   Conclusions and Future Work

English learners in China suffer from being poor at telling the difference between spoken and written English. We propose to classify English sentences with bilingual information into the two categories automatically. The experiments show that the best classification accuracy nearly 95% can be achieved in the open test through Chinese characters + sentence length + average syllable number, or other similar combinations.

Since our training set is far from perfect, which is mentioned in 4.1, and several feature combinations achieve the same scores in 4.2 and 4.3, we are going to:

- Overcome the size and quality problems of the training set with semi-supervised learning technologies;
- Build a bigger testing set and design more experiments to find out which is the best feature combination.

Acknowledgements. We thank the anonymous reviewers for their valuable comments. We also thank Long Jiang, Shidou Jiao, Shiquan Yang and Wei Li from MSRA NLC group for their great support to our research.

References

1. Colloquialism, http://en.wikipedia.org/wiki/Colloquialism
2. Chafe, W.L.: Integration and Involvement in Speaking, Writing, and Oral Literature. In: Norwood, D.T. (ed.) Spoken and Written Language: Exploring Orality and Literacy, ABLEX Pub. Corp., New Jersey (1982)
3. Gui, S., Yang, H.: Chinese Learner English Corpus. Shanghai Foreign Language Education Press, Shanghai (2002)
4. Liu, X.: The Colloquial Tendency in the Written English of English Learners from Chinese Universities. Journal of Technology College Education 24(1) (2005)
5. Drucker, H., Wu, D., Vapnik, V.N.: Support Vector Machines for Spam Categorization. IEEE Transactions on Neural Network 10(5), 1048–1054 (1999)
6. Yang, Y., Pedersen, J.O.: A Comparative Study on Feature Selection in Text Categorization. In: Proceedings of ICML 1997: The 14th International Conference on Machine Learning, Nashville, US, pp. 412–420 (1997)

7. Joachims, T.: Text Categorization with Support Vector Machines: Learning with Many Relevant Features. In: Nédellec, C., Rouveirol, C. (eds.) ECML 1998. LNCS, vol. 1398, pp. 137–142. Springer, Heidelberg (1998)
8. Jia, K., Chen, K., Fan, X., Zhang, Y.: Chinese Question Classification Based on Ensemble Learning. In: Proceedings of SNPD 2007: The 8th ACIS International Conference on Software Engineering, Artificial Intelligence, Networking, and Parallel/Distributed Computing, Qingdao, China, vol. 3, pp. 342–347 (2007)
9. Khoo, A., Marom, Y., Albrecht, D.: Experiments with Sentence Classification. In: Proceedings of the 2006 Australasian Language Technology Workshop (ALTW 2006), pp. 18–25 (2006)
10. Hachey, B., Grover, C.: Sequence Modelling for Sentence Classification in a Legal Summarisation System. In: Proceedings of SAC 2005: The 2005 ACM Symposium on Applied Computing, New Mexico, US, pp. 292–296 (2005)
11. Yamamoto, Y., Takagi, T.: A Sentence Classification System for Multi Biomedical Literature Summarization. In: Proceedings of the 21st International Conference on Data Engineering, ICDE 2005 (2005)
12. Mitchell, T.M.: Machine Learning. McGraw-Hill, New York (1997)
13. Chen, X., Chen, Y., Wang, L., Li, R., Hu, Y.: Text Categorization Based on Classification Rules Tree by Frequent Patterns. Journal of Software 17(5), 1017–1025 (2006)
14. Ren, S., Fu, Y., Li, X., Zhuang, Z.: Feature Selection Based on Classes Margin. Journal of Software 19(4), 842–850 (2008)
15. Fan, R.-E., Chang, K.-W., Hsieh, C.-J., Wang, X.-R., Lin, C.-J.: LIBLINEAR: A Library for Large Linear Classification. Journal of Machine Learning Research 9, 1871–1874 (2008), Software available at http://www.csie.ntu.edu.tw/~cjlin/liblinear
16. Flesch-Kincaid Readability Test, http://en.wikipedia.org/wiki/Flesch-Kincaid_Readability_Test
17. Duda, R.O., Hart, P.E., Stork, D.G.: Pattern Classification. Wiley, New York (2001)

Design and Implementation of News-Oriented Automatic Summarization System Based on Chinese RSS

Jie Wang[1], Jie Ma[1,*], and Yingjun Li[2]

[1] College of Software, Nankai University, Tianjin, China
[2] Collage of Information Technology Science, Nankai University, Tianjin, China
majie1765@nankai.edu.cn, {nkwangjie,3handsome}@gmail.com

Abstract. Automatic summarization is an important research branch of natural language processing. The automatic summarization should provide information to users from different point of views for better understanding. Aiming at the characteristics of the news, an automatic summarization system is constructed from two aspects: keywords and key sentences. Then, the location factor is added to optimize the keywords extraction algorithm. Meanwhile, the key sentences extraction algorithm is improved through introducing keywords factors. On this basis, in allusion to the existing problems of RSS, this paper builds a user-interest model. Finally, after the verification in terms of the feasibility and the effectiveness, the result shows it is effective to improve the accuracy and the user experience of the RSS feeds

Keywords: Keywords extraction, Key sentences extraction, RSS feeds.

1 Introduction

As a way to share content among sites, RSS has been widely used [1].While huge RSS feeds bring us rich resources, they also produce difficulties to get effective information. How to locate the news that users are interested in and learn main content of them has become a crucial problem.

Under this background, we put forward an idea: we first extract key information from two aspects: keywords and key sentences, and use user-interest model to extract the abstracts which confirm to the user's interests. Meanwhile, we design and implement a personalized automatic summarization system to provide users high-quality services, which has the function of keywords and key sentences automatic extraction. Finally, we do some experiments in terms of the feasibility and effectiveness, and analyze the recall rate and accuracy of the results.

2 Related Work

RSS provides a quick and easy way for the Internet information sharing. RSS information aggregation and customization have obtained certain achievements.

---

* Corresponding author.

G. Zhou et al. (Eds.): NLPCC 2013, CCIS 400, pp. 378–385, 2013.
© Springer-Verlag Berlin Heidelberg 2013

Mu, L. [2] implements a personalized information service system of science and technology based on RSS. In this paper, specific user-interest model is established, which can effectively improve the accuracy.

Since 1958 Luhn proposed the concept of automatic summarization [3], many scholars have achieved fruitful work. Kruengkrai, C. et al.[4] used some key information to determine the weight of the sentences, but did not consider the effect of keywords. Meanwhile, the domestic has multiple experiment systems, Lanke system[1] includes an automatic summarization subsystem, which is based on the relevance of the words to calculate. This paper achieves better effect through optimizing the keywords and key sentences algorithm.

3   System Design

3.1   Principle of the Summarization System

The research shows that news writing has obvious features, known as the "5W1H": when, where, who, What, Why and How. Therefore, provided the abstract covers these aspects, it can be considered as meeting requirements.

3.2   Overall Architectural Design of the Summarization System

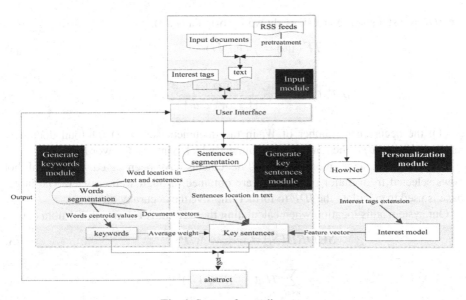

Fig. 1. System frame diagram

---

[1] http://www.languagetech.cn/class_demo.aspx

4   Core Algorithm

4.1   Optimized Keywords Extraction Algorithm

High frequency words often have a large ratio to become keywords [5,6].In order to improve the accuracy of extraction, we need to add the location of the keywords. Implement method is shown in figure 2:

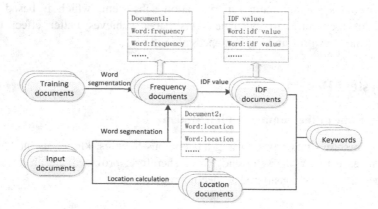

Fig. 2. Keywords extraction module

TF-IDF is a statistical method, as shown in formula (1)(2).

$$TF(w_i) = f(w_i, D) \tag{1}$$

$$IDF(w_i) = \log \frac{|D|}{|\{j : w_i \in d_j\}|} \tag{2}$$

(1): the occurrence number of W_i in the document set D.(2) $|D|$:total document numbers,$|\{j : w_i \in d_j\}|$:the number of document which contains the word W_i.

In the training stage, more than 1000 documents have been saved, they are all hot news selected from major portals, and are obtained through web crawler. The larger base is used to calculate the *IDF* to further improve the accuracy.

Our system adds location when calculating the weight. As shown in formula (5)

$$SCORE(S_i) = w_c C_i + w_p P_i \tag{3}$$

$$C_i = \sum_{w \subset S_i} TF(w) \times IDF(w) \tag{4}$$

$$P_i = \left(\sum_{\alpha \subset \beta} \lambda \alpha \right) \Big/ \beta \tag{5}$$

(4):the centroid value of words,(5):the location of word Si in article, $\beta$is the total occurrence numbers of word S_i, $\lambda a$is the weighted values, when the sentence is the title or summary, λa=2; when the sentence is the head or tail of the paragraph, λa=1.5;in other cases ,λa=1. w_c w_p are two constants ,w_c =w_p=1.

4.2   Optimized Key Sentences Extraction Algorithm

In this system, each document is divided into a collection of entries by using the *VSM* model. The implementation is shown in figure 3:

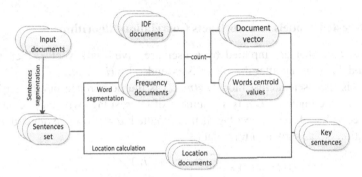

Fig. 3. Key sentences extraction module

The definition of centroid value of document is formula (6):

$$d_i = (Vw_0, Vw_1, \ldots, Vw_n) \tag{6}$$

$$Vw_i = TF(w_i) * IDF(w_i) \tag{7}$$

Assume S_i is the *i-th* sentence , and   the centroid value is formula (8):

$$C_i = \sum_{w \in Si} V_w \bullet f(w, S_i) \tag{8}$$

$f(w,S_i)$ is the frequency of W in the sentence S_i.

   Assume P_i is the location of the *i-th* sentence, λi is the weighted value, when the sentence is the title or summary, λi =2; when the sentence is the head or tail of the paragraph ,λi =1.5; in other cases ,λi=1.

$$P_i = \lambda_i * (n - i + 1) / n \tag{9}$$

Assume F_i is the overlap with the title, the inner product as shown in formula(10):

$$F_i = S_i \bullet S_1 = \sum_{w \in Si \cap S1} f(w, S_1) \bullet f(w, S_i) \tag{10}$$

Assume T_i is the average weight of the keywords in the *i-th* sentence:

$$T_i = \sum_{\lambda \in Si} f(\lambda, S_i) \Big/ Len \tag{11}$$

$f(\lambda, S_i)$ is the occurrences numbers of word λ in sentence S_i, Len is the number of keywords that S_i contains. Integrated score of a sentence as shown in formula(12):

$$SCORE\,(S_i) = (w_c C_i + w_f F_i + w_t T_i) * P_i \tag{12}$$

$w_c\,w_f\,w_t$ are three constants. $w_c = w_f = w_t = 1$

Experimental results show that the title and abstract are most important to understand the news, next are the head and tail of a paragraph, so it's necessary to improve the weights of these positions when calculating the score.

4.3   Interested Models and Abstracts Correlation Algorithm

The interest tags that are inputted by a user are saved as a vector, then the user-interest model is built up after the vector is extended by *HowNet*.

Assume m_j is the user-interest model, $g(m_j, L_i)$ is the occurrence numbers of the *j-th* interest tag in document L_i, Len is the number of interest tags which L_i contains, α is the weighted value of the interest tag, if it is inputted ,$\alpha = 1$; if it is extended ,$\alpha = 0.5$, so the correlation is   as shown in formula(13):

$$SCORE\quad(L_i) = \sum \alpha \cdot g\,(m_j, L_i)\Big/_{Len} \tag{13}$$

5   Realization

The system is mainly divided into four modules: input module, keywords generation module, key sentences generation module and personalization module. Keywords generation module is composed of the centroid value of words and the word position; Key sentences generation module is composed of the sentence centroid value, the sentence position, the weights of contained keywords and the overlap with title; Personalization module is composed of the user-interest model.

6   Experiments

6.1   Evaluation Criterion

In 1995, Jones divided the evaluation methods into two categories: internal evaluation method and external evaluation method [7].

Here we use the internal evaluation method. By comparing the key information between automatic generation and artificial extracting, we use the recall ratio, the accuracy ratio and the harmonic value(*F_measure*) as evaluation criteria.

6.2   Experimental Method

This paper from two angles verified the feasibility and validity. 160 articles are selected from the RSS feeds of *ifeng* ,*sina* and *sohu*, which are grouped into eight categories: national ,international, financial, military, education, science , history, and sport. Compression rates were divided into 20%, 25%, 30%, 35%, 40%.

Feasibility Verification
Firstly, according to the compression rate, we manually identified the corresponding number of key information, which was used as the evaluation corpus. Then we compared the key information generated by our system with the evaluation corpus, and calculated the average recall rate and accuracy rate. Meanwhile, the mainstream five-point scoring mechanism was used. Eight students were tested about the eight kinds of news, and were given a mark from three angles: the abstract sets accuracy, the abstract content coverage rate and whether easy to understand.

Effectiveness Verification
Our system was compared with the automatic summarization subsystem provided by Lanke, which did not use the key factors to optimize, and its compression ratio was 25%. In order to verify whether the abstract consist of keywords and key sentences can reach better effect, the evaluation mechanism of Q&A was used. A certain number of problem sets and the corresponding standard answers were provided, reviewers were asked to read three different contents: the full text, key sentences, keywords and key sentences. Then we compared their average response time and the accuracy of their answer.

6.3   Experimental Results and Analysis

Feasibility Verification

Table 1. The *F_measure* of different news under compression ration

M Category	20%	25%	30%	35%	40%
education	0.592	0.645	0.621	0.613	0.625
financial	0.473	0.515	0.541	0.537	0.565
international	0.532	0.646	0.666	0.699	0.707
national	0.496	0.553	0.596	0.611	0.646
sport	0.665	0.703	0.724	0.717	0.721
science	0.641	0.662	0.675	0.684	0.697
military	0.511	0.532	0.547	0.539	0.556
history	0.438	0.456	0.479	0.459	0.461

After using this system, the ratings of users' are as shown in figure 4:

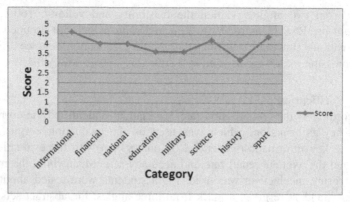

Fig. 4. The scores of all kinds of news

By researching the results in table 1 and finger 4, two groups of independent users gave the same conclusion: the results of international and sport news were better, while history and education news were worse. It is mainly because the extraction algorithm and user-interest model have better effect in international and sport news. Further analysis, we find that for the news emphasizes the timelines such as international news, the title and paragraphs positions are very important. On the contrary, for those timeliness requirements are not that strict or contents are relatively loose, these positions are sometimes not important, and the themes of these articles are often more than one, so when the compression ratio is restricted, it's easy to lose some useful information. Meanwhile, for news having multiple themes, the obtained set of abstracts according to the user-interest model is not often needed by the user. Also this reduces the abstract content coverage rate. So we should consider different strategies for different types of news.

Effectiveness Verification

The difference is given to highlight the results. Results as shown in table 2

Table 2. The comparative result between the two types of system

System / Category	Our system	Lanke system	D-value
Sport	0.703	0.558	0.145
International	0.646	0.412	0.234
History	0.456	0.365	0.091
Education	0.645	0.449	0.196
National	0.553	0.405	0.148
Financial	0.515	0.465	0.050
Science	0.662	0.549	0.113
Military	0.532	0.371	0.161

In table 2, the experimental results show our system has achieved better effect. Especially the international news, with a maximum gap 0.234. Analyzing the Lanke system, we find it just used the method of statistical frequency to extract abstract, which is the fundamental cause leading to different experimental results, in addition, compared with our system, it lacks of the supplementary of keywords.

Table 3. The Q&A evaluation results

Content	Average time(min)	Accuracy rate
Full text	1.5	93%
Key sentences	0.7	76%
Keywords+Key sentences	1	86%

According to table 3, the advantage and disadvantage of reading full text or key sentences are very obvious, in contrast, the accuracy of reading the keywords and key sentences declines by only 7%, but time reduces by one third. Relatively speaking, the abstract consists of the keywords and key sentences can better achieve the balance between time and accuracy.

7   Conclusion

In this paper, aiming at the existing problems of RSS feeds and the characteristics of the news, we put forward the idea that uses keywords and key sentences as abstract, and select the abstracts which are more relevant to the user-interest model. Experimental results show that our system can effectively improve the quality of automatic summarization in News field.

In the future, the accuracy of the algorithm will be further improved by expanding the data set to correct the weight of the parameters in the formulas.

References

1. Hu, J., Zhang, Z.: Research on personalized information service based on RSS. Computer Applications and Softwar 26(5), 40–42 (2009)
2. Mu, L.: Research on personalized scientific and technological information service system based on really simple syndication. Dalian University of Technology (2008)
3. Luhn, H.P.: The automatic creation of literature abstract. IBM Journal of Research and Development, 159–165 (1958)
4. Kruengkrai, C., Jaruskulchai, C.: Generic test summarization using local and global properties of sentences. In: Proceedings of the IEEE/WIC International Conference on Web Intelligence, pp. 201–206. IEEE, USA (2003)
5. Sebastiani, F.: Machine learning in automated text categorization. ACM Computing Surveys 34(1), 1–47 (2002)
6. Frasconi, P., Soda, G., Vullo, A.: Text categorization for multi-page documents: A hybrid naive Bayes HMM approach. In: ACM/IEEE Joint Conference on Digital Libraries, pp. 11–20. IEEE, USA (2001)
7. Zhang, J., Wang, X., Xu, H.: Survey of automatic summarization evaluation methods. Journal of Chinese Information Processing 22(3), 81–88 (2008)

Grey Relational Analysis for Query Expansion

Junjie Zou, Zhengtao Yu*, Huanyun Zong, Jianyi Guo, and Lei Su

School of Information Engineering and Automation,
Kunming University of Science and Technology, Kunming, 650051, China
Intelligent Information Processing Key Laboratory,
Kunming University of Science and Technology, Kunming, 650051, China
ztyu@hotmail.com

Abstract. For one-sidedness of the various qualitative expansion methods, we propose a query terms selection method based on Grey Relational Analysis (GRA).We called the fusion expansion technique with GRA (FET-GRA). It calculates weight of expansion term by varied qualitative expansions and comprehensive weight by FET-GRA and thus extracts expansion term in terms of the weight. The experiment result of TREC dataset shows the method (FET-GRA) is substantially superior to TF-IDF, Mutual Information , Local Context Analysis.

Keywords: query expansion, grey relational analysis, FET-GRA.

1 Introduction

Query expansion is the critical process to improve precision of retrieval. At present, there are many effective qualitative expansion methods[1,2,3], however, they all base on a single theory to calculate and select candidate expansion terms, such as TF-IDF, Mutual Information (MI), Local Context Analysis (LCA) which have certain one-sidedness. For example, TFIDF on the assumption of independent term is good to simple query regardless semantic problem but poor performance to query expansion which requires context, on the contrary of LCA. Grey Relational Analysis (GRA) is a part of Grey System Theory[4]. It can offer a new evaluation of estimate after integrating the relation of each qualitative method. Taking expansion of airlines that currently use Boeing 747 planes as example, candidate term Singapore gets low and common scores in TFIDF and MI but a good score in LCA. GRA can be used in the decision problem whether Singapore is a good expansion term. It integrates and calculates the evaluations of estimate according to the three differences and set-term topology and other information. The evaluations estimate the importance of Singapore. The thesis uses Relational Analysis method[5] to integrate and revalue query terms weights from different qualitative query expansion methods. It thus extracts and expands the optimal expansion term.

This paper is organized as follows: Section 2 describes related work. Section 3 presents the query expansion and grey relation theory; Section 4 combines the

---

* Corresponding author.

G. Zhou et al. (Eds.): NLPCC 2013, CCIS 400, pp. 386–393, 2013.
© Springer-Verlag Berlin Heidelberg 2013

Grey Relational Analysis with query expansion. In Section 5, we describe our experimental methodology and the results as well as analysis.

2 Related Work

Early scholars proposed the query expansion technology based on global analysis, it holds that there were correlations between words in a corpus, which reflected by the co-occurrence times they appeared in the corpus. Latent semantic analysis (LSA)[6] is an earlier proposed global method; its core idea is to map high-dimensional vector space into low-dimensional latent semantic space by singular value decomposition. It may be more appropriate for system with small corpus, but for larger or even web data, the feasibility of LSA method comes into a serious challenge, because the web data is too large to make global analysis. Previous work[7,8] is also a kind of global analysis technology based on document, which selects the words with higher word frequencies by statistics as expansion terms added to the original query. This method also has a great weakness in big computation cost.

Local analysis technology usually consists of two steps. First step, use the original query to obtain the original search results from retrieval system, and select the top N documents of original initial search results as local documents collection D. Second step, take out the top ranked candidate words analyzed in D, which added to the original query to reconstruct the query. Atter and Fraenkel first proposed the idea of local analysis in the literature[9], Xu and Croft in the literature[1] further refined local analysis technology and put forth the local context analysis method , rank concepts according to calculate the terms similarity between original query and local documents collection, the top ranked concepts are added to original query to expand query. On this basis, Sun et al in the literature[10,2] used Google for initial retrieve, later expanded query with local context analysis method and obtained certain effects. However, these methods also have the corresponding problems, for example, the top N documents retrieved by initial query is not quite constant with user requirements, whereas the query terms expanded from those methods far from improve retrieval accuracy ,it would weaken retrieval performance.

In terms of Language model, since Ponte and Croft first introduced it into the field of information retrieval[11], it has been widely used. Bai et al in the literature[12] made a further research on Language model, focused on how to take advantage of hyper-spatial analysis of Linguistics and co-occurrence frequency methods to calculate the probability of words to query model, used the high probability of words to expand query. In addition, Collins-Thompson et al used random walk model[13] to expand the query expansion, Cui et al conducted a personalized query expansion based on user log[14].

The above methods each possess its advantages and disadvantages, how to improve the accuracy of the query expansion with these different methods is the key to the study. This paper presented a fusion evaluation technique integrated the existing expansion methods by using grey relational analysis.

3   Query Expansion and Grey System Theory

In order to verify the effectiveness of the fusion expansion technique with GRA (FET-GRA), this paper chosen three basic expansion methods for fusion evaluation. What follows is a brief sketch of these three basic expansion methods, and describes the core theory of fusion expansion technique with GRA (FET-GRA).

3.1   Query Expansion Methods

The idea in Local context analysis[1] is that noun groups are used as concepts and concepts are selected based on co-occurrence with query terms. Calculate and rank the concepts according to the relevance between concepts and query, the top ranked concepts are chosen as expansion terms. The concepts of context are similar to local feedback, relevance calculation used the original top ranked N documents in traditional feedback technology, but the best passage are used instead of whole document in Local context analysis technology. Local context analysis technology is a practical technology, which combines global analysis and local feedback, often used in query expansion.

We adopt a similar method to literature [1,2] for expanding query Q in tourism domain. The first thing is to determine context of the paragraphs set SP, use Google to retrieve the top N information fragments collection $SP = \{s_i, i = 1, ..., n\}$ segment sentence for each s_i. Then, calculate the relevance $SIM(Q, c)$ between each concept and query Q using paragraphs collection SP, the calculation formula is as follows:

$$SIM(Q, c) = \frac{1}{Z} \cdot \prod_{t_i \in Q} \left\{ \delta + \frac{\log\left[\sum_{j=1}^{n} (tf_{ij} \cdot tf_{cj}) \right] \times \log(\frac{N}{N_c})}{\log(n)} \right\}^{\log(\frac{N}{N_i})} \tag{1}$$

Where Z is normalized factor, denotes smoothing factor for preventing the equation is zero, tf_{ij} and tfcj stand for word frequency of t_i and concept c in paragraph SP, N is the total number of paragraphs in paragraph collection, N_i and Nc are the number of t_i and concept c appeared in paragraph collection.

Next, rank the above results of calculation. Finally select the top-k concepts as candidate words added to the original query. For meaningful on words ranking, we use Indri query language of Indri retrieval platform to refectory the query, the refactor query expression is as #weight($w_0q_1...w_0q_mw_1c_1...w_kc_k$). Where q_i indicates the key words of the original query Q, c_i indicates the ith ranked concept, w_i denotes the weight of key words in refactor query. w_i calculation method is shown in Equation (2).

$$w_i = \begin{cases} 2.0, i = 0 \\ (k - 0.9 \times i)/k, \text{else} \end{cases} \tag{2}$$

For the query expansion method based on TF-IDF, its core TF-IDF[15]. Based on the original mutual information[16], we use an improved method to calculate the mutual information of candidate words w_i and query Q, the details are shown in Equation (5).Where m is the number of keywords, Z_m is normalized factor,δ is anti-zero factor, $\delta = 0.01$ in this paper.

$$I(w_i : Q) = \frac{1}{Z_m} \cdot \sum_{t=1}^{m} \left(\left[\log_2 \frac{P(w_i, q_t)}{P(w_i) \cdot P(q_t)} \right] + \delta \right) \tag{3}$$

3.2   Grey Relation Analyses

Grey relation analysis (GRA) was pioneered by Deng Julong in 1984.It used to solve these problems, having incomplete running mechanism, lacking of behavior data, devoid of experience in treatment, being naked to inherent connotation. We introduced relational definition about GRA in this section.

For the elements(factors) between two systems, the measurement of relevance changed over time or different objects called Grey Relational Grade. In the course of system development, if two elements have much consistency in developmental trends, namely high degree of synchronous changes, which can be described as a high-related degree of two factors, on the contrary, it is relatively low. Consequently, grey relational analysis method established on the similarity or diversity of developmental trends of these elements, namely Grey Relational Grade, as a measurement approach of related degree of these elements. Grey system theory proposed the concept of grey relational analysis for each subsystem with an intension to seek the numerical relations between every subsystems (or elements) by certain means. Therefore, gray relational analysis is a kind of quantitative description and comparison for the developmental trends of a system, its basic idea is to determine the similarity degree of geometric figures between reference sequence and several compare sequences to judge whether closely related, which reflected the correlation between curves.

This paper regarding different expansion methods as different systems, each system can score a certain candidate term, and takes data sequence formed by query terms as reference sequence, other data sequence formed by candidate terms as compare sequence. Hence, we can calculate the similarity of reference sequence and compare sequence by using gray relational analysis.

4   Fusion Expansion Technique with GRA

The modeling procedure of Fusion expansion technique GRA(FET-GRA) method. Firstly, we use several qualitative query expansion methods to generate feature matrix of candidate terms compare sequence. Secondly, GRA method requires the optimal collocation of feature value, so it requires to confirm a feature reference sequence. Thirdly, to calculate the grey relational coefficient between feature reference sequence and candidate terms compare sequence, thereafter solve the relational sequence of candidate terms and rank them. Lastly, we can then extract the candidate terms ranking higher as an expansion terms.

The detailed modeling process of GRA method in query expansion is as follows.

Step 1: Build model grade feature matrix $\Gamma(\mathcal{M})$. We use longitudinal vector $\mathcal{M} = \{m1, m2, m3\}$ of feature matrix from TFIDF, LCA and improved MI with weight factors, and choose the candidate terms from relative documents as horizontal vector to construct Equation (4).

$$\Gamma(\mathcal{M}) = [m_i(k)]_{n \times d}, \qquad where \; i = 1 \; to \; n; k = 1 \; to \; d \qquad (4)$$

Where $m_i(k)$ denotes the value of the ith candidate term from the kth qualitative method, $d = 3$ in our paper.

Step 2: Construct reference sequence. We design an auto-selected optimal reference sequence method. We assume the query input by users has a positive effect on the result while does not digress expansion topic. Suppose $\mathcal{Q} = \{q_1, q_2, \ldots, q_w\}$ be a partition of query keywords, the method for constructing reference sequence $\mathcal{V}$ by using query $\mathcal{Q}$ as shown in the formula(5).

$$\mathcal{V} = [\max_k \{m_i(k)\} \mid i \in \mathcal{Q}]_{1 \times d}, \qquad where \; k = 1 \; to \; d \qquad (5)$$

Step 3: Generate n×d relational matrix $\mathcal{Z}$. Firstly, calculate the grey relational coefficient (GRC) $\zeta_i(k)$ of each candidate term corresponding to comparison sequence and reference sequence respectively. Secondly, compose matrix $\mathcal{Z}$ using $\zeta_i(k)$, where the meaning of horizontal vector and longitudinal vector is similar to step 1 . The details are shown in Equation (6).

$$\mathcal{Z} = [\zeta_i(k)]_{n \times d}, \zeta_i(k) = \frac{\min\limits_i \min\limits_k CS_{ik} + \rho \times \max\limits_i \max\limits_k CS_{ik}}{CS_{ik} + \rho \times \max\limits_i \max\limits_k CS_{ik}}$$

$\zeta_i(k)$ is a GRC based with q_i and $\mathcal{V}(k)$.

CS_{ik} is a absolute values of $\mathcal{V}(k) - m_i(k)$.

$\mathcal{V}(k)$ is kth feature value of reference vector $\mathcal{V}$. $\qquad (6)$

$\quad i$ is a term suffix that it is a value of 1 to n.

$\quad \rho$ is a distinguishing coefficient.

$\quad k$ is a feature suffix that it is a value of 1 to d.

Step 4: Calculate the grey relational sequence γ_i of candidate terms. First, calculate γ_i using grey relational coefficient.Then, rank the candidate terms according to γ_i, and select the first n with maximal value γ_i of candidate terms as expansion terms. Equation (7) illustrates the calculation of γ_i.

$$\gamma_i = \frac{1}{d} \sum_{k=1}^{d} \mathcal{W}_k \cdot \zeta_i(k), \; \mathcal{W}_k \; is \; weight \; of \; feature \qquad (7)$$

5   Experiments

We conducted experiments to verify the effectiveness of query expansion using FET-GRA.In this section,we first introduce the data sets used in experiments. Then we demonstrate the effectiveness of our approach(FET-GRA) in query expansion.

5.1   Data Set

The purpose of the experiments is to evaluate the performance of query expansion by FET-GRA method. We conduct the experiments in TREC ClueWeb09 (category B set), and build the retrieval experiment platform with the help of Lemur toolkit (www.lemurproject.org). We construct a query set including 50 questions. It consists of two parts. Part 1 is TREC2009 Entity Track's query set. Only the entity name are used as queries. Part 2 is the queries that were the query log of a commercial web search engine. The top-100 snippets are extracted by Google retrieval and map with the retrieval result of Lemur toolkit.

5.2   FET-GRA Experiments

In our experiments,TF-IDF,LCA and MI with weight's factor make up the fusion expansion set.Then we use fusion expansion technique with GRA(FET-GRA) and distinguishing coefficient $\rho = 0.5$ of GRA query expansion method, relational sequence $\mathcal{W}_k = 1$,namely, without weighting. Table 1 illustrates the results of the experiments. The value outside of bracket indicates relevant precision and the one inside is the improved rate compared to the baseline methods.

Table 1. Precision of different expansion methods

%	TF-IDF	MI	LCA	FET-GRA
p@5	55.6	70.0(+25.9)	75.4(+35.6)	92.2(+62.2)
p@10	53.4	65.5(+22.7)	57.5(+7.7)	75.6(+41.6)
p@20	43.8	45.5(+3.9)	51.3(+17.1)	66.4(+51.6)
p@30	37.5	47.5(+26.7)	49.6(+32.3)	60.4(+61.1)
p@40	31.8	32.6(+2.5)	42.5(+33.6)	52.8(+66.0)
p@50	26.0	28.5(+9.6)	36.3(+39.6)	43.3(+66.5)
p@60	22.9	23.7(+3.4)	31.1(+35.8)	38.3(+67.2)
average	38.7	44.8(+26.1)	49.1(+26.9)	61.0(+57.6)

From the experimental results in Table 1, we can see the precision of MI, LCA and FET-GRA improves over TF-IDF method. The performance of MI and LCA improve 26.1% and 26.9% respectively while the one of FET-GRA improves obviously 57.6%. In order to validate the relevance of different expansion methods, we use Spearman's rank correlation test [17], take the precision of Table 1 as a test sample, four methods as random variables , and then test FET-GRA with other three methods respectively, In consequence, we obtain the following values: $P - value_{TFIDF} = 3.97 \times 10^{-4}$, $P - value_{MI} = 6.74 \times 10^{-3}$, $P - value_{LCA} = 3.97 \times 10^{-4}$. Each $P - value$ is less than $\alpha = 0.01$, so it indicates that the random variables have correlation, namely, FET-GRA method improves expansion capability under the premise of keeping to qualitative methods.

Figure 1 illustrates the analytical result of stable improved rate of MI, LCA and FET-GRA by using the improved rate data in Table 1.

As can be seen from Figure 1, FET-GRA has higher robustness as well as a better improved rate compared to the baseline methods than LCA's and MI's.

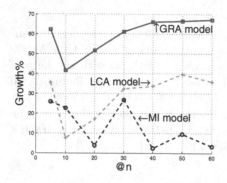

Fig. 1. Growth Curve of three method

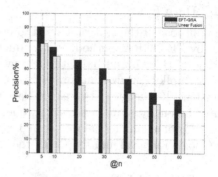

Fig. 2. FET-GRA v.s. Linear

6   Conclusions

We apply FET-GRA method to query expansion. It can effectively select the query relational terms and also improve the precision of query expansion as well as robustness. In the future work, we will study the inaccurate reference sequence caused by query drift problem.

Acknowledgments. This paper is supported by National Nature Science Foundation (No.61175068), and the Open Fund of Software Engineering Key Laboratory of Yunnan Province (No.2011SE14), and the Ministry of Education of Returned Overseas Students to Start Research and Fund Projects.

References

1. Xu, J., Croft, W.B.: Query expansion using local and global document analysis. In: 19th ACM SIGIR, pp. 4–11. ACM Press, Zurich (1996)
2. Sun, R., Ong, C.H., Chua, T.S.: Mining dependency relations for query expansion in passage retrieval. In: Proceedings of the 29th Annual International ACM SIGIR Conference on Research and Development in Information Retrieval, pp. 382–389. ACM Press, Washington (2006)
3. Nen-Townsend, S., Zhou, Y., Croft, W.B.: A framework for selective query expansion. In: Proceedings of the Thirteenth ACM International Conference on Information and Knowledge Management, pp. 236–237. ACM Press (2004)
4. Deng, J.L.: Control problems of grey systems. Systems & Control Letters 1(5), 288–294 (1989)
5. Deng, J.L.: Introduction to grey system theory. The Journal of Grey System 1(1), 1–24 (1989)
6. Deerwester, S.C., Dumais, S.T., Landauer, T.K., et al.: Indexing by latent semantic analysis. JASIS 41, 391–407 (1990)
7. Jing, Y., Croft, W.B.: An association thesaurus for information retrieval. In: Proceedings of RIAO, pp. 146–160 (1994)

8. Callan, J.P., Croft, W.B., Broglio, J.: TREC and TIPSTER experiments with INQUERY. Information Processing & Management 31(3), 327–343 (1995)
9. Attar, R., Fraenkel, A.S.: Local feedback in full-text retrieval systems. Journal of the ACM (JACM) 24(3), 397–417 (1997)
10. Cui, H., Sun, R., Li, K., et al.: Question answering passage retrieval using dependency relations. In: Proceedings of the 28th Annual International ACM SIGIR Conference on Research and Development in Information Retrieval, pp. 382–389. ACM Press, Salvador (2005)
11. Ponte, J.M., Croft, W.B.: A language modeling approach to information retrieval. In: Proceedings of the 21st Annual International ACM SIGIR Conference on Research and Development in Information Retrieval, pp. 275–281. ACM Press, Melbourne (1998)
12. Bai, J., Song, D., Bruza, P., et al.: Query expansion using term relationships in language models for information retrieval. In: Proceedings of the 14th ACM International Conference on Information and Knowledge Management, pp. 275–281. ACM Press, Bremen (2005)
13. Collins-Thompson, K., Callan, J.: Query expansion using term relationships in language models for information retrieval. In: Proceedings of the 14th ACM International Conference on Information and Knowledge Management, pp. 704–711. ACM Press, Bremen (2005)
14. Cui, H., Wen, J.R., Nie, J.Y., et al.: Probabilistic query expansion using query logs. In: Proceedings of the 11th International Conference on World Wide Web, pp. 325–332. ACM Press, Honolulu (2002)
15. Liu, Y., Ciliax, B.J., Borges, K., et al.: Comparison of two schemes for automatic keyword extraction from MEDLINE for functional gene clustering. In: Computational Systems Bioinformatics Conference 2004, pp. 394–404. ACM Press, Honolulu (2004)
16. Church, K.W., Hanks, P.: Word association norms, mutual information, and lexicography. Computational Linguistics 16(1), 22–29 (1990)
17. Gibbons, J.D., Chakraborti, S.: Nonparametric statistical inference. CRC press (2003)

A Comprehensive Method for Text Summarization Based on Latent Semantic Analysis

Yingjie Wang and Jun Ma

School of Computer Science and Technology, Shandong University, Jinan, China
yingj_wang@hotmail.com, majun@sdu.edu.cn

Abstract. Text summarization aims at getting the most important content in a condensed form from a given document while retains the semantic information of the text to a large extent. It is considered to be an effective way of tackling information overload. There exist lots of text summarization approaches which are based on Latent Semantic Analysis (LSA). However, none of the previous methods consider the term description of the topic. In this paper, we propose a comprehensive LSA-based text summarization algorithm that combines term description with sentence description for each topic. We also put forward a new way to create the term by sentence matrix. The effectiveness of our method is proved by experimental results. On the summarization performance, our approach obtains higher ROUGE scores than several well known methods.

Keywords: Text Summarization, Latent Semantic Analysis, Singular Value Decomposition.

1 Introduction

The widespread use of the Internet has dramatically increased the amount of accessible information and it becomes difficult for users to sift through the multitude of sources to find out the right document. With the help of search engine, the majority of irrelevant documents are filtered out, however, users still hesitate to determine which particular search result should navigate to. Automated summarizing system can be used as an instrument for deciding whether a document is related to their needs.

The summary of a document is defined as: a text that is produced from the document that conveys important information in the original text, and that is no longer than half of the original text and usually significantly less than that [1].

Automatically generating the summary of a document has long been studied since 1950s and it is still a research hotpot until now [2, 3, 4]. One of the most famous approaches is using LSA [5, 6, 7, 8, 9, 10] to get the ideal summary.

The foundational work that uses LSA for text summarization selects one sentence for each topic according to topic importance [6]. The work in [7] starts with calculation of the length of each sentence vector and then chooses the longest sentences as the summary. In the work [9], the length strategy proposed in [7] is improved and a cross method is proposed. In [8], for each topic, the number of sentences to be collected is determined by getting the percentage of the related singular values over the sum of all singular values.

G. Zhou et al. (Eds.): NLPCC 2013, CCIS 400, pp. 394–401, 2013.
© Springer-Verlag Berlin Heidelberg 2013

However, there are some disadvantages of the previous algorithms. The main drawback is that sentences that are closely related to the chosen topic somehow but do not have the highest index value will not be selected. Also, all chosen topics are composed of only one sentence [6], whereas the single sentence fails to fully express the topic. The length strategy [7, 9] requires a method of deciding how many LSA dimensions to include in the latent space. For the work in [8], if there is a wide gap between the current singular value and the next one, then there is little chance to include the topics whose corresponding singular values are less than the current one.

In our work, we propose a comprehensive method that combines term description with sentence description for each topic. We endeavor to select a set of sentences that not only have the best representation of the topic but also include the terms that can best represent this topic. Also, in order to utilize the mutual reinforcement between neighbor sentences, we put forward a new way to create the term by sentence matrix.

This paper is organized as follows: in Section 2, we introduce LSA briefly. Section 3 progresses to present our method in detail. In Section 4, the effectiveness of our method is confirmed by experimental results. Finally, we conclude this paper in Section 5.

2   Latent Semantic Analysis

LSA uses Singular Value Decomposition (SVD) to find out the semantic meaning of sentences. The SVD of a matrix A with the dimension of $m \times n$ $(m > n)$ can be defined as: $A = U \Sigma V^T$, where $U = [u_1, u_2, \cdots, u_n]$ is an $m \times n$ column-orthogonal matrix whose left singular vector u_i is an m-dimensional column vector, $V = [v_1, v_2, \cdots, v_n]$ is an $n \times n$ column-orthogonal matrix whose right singular vector v_j is an n-dimensional column vector. $\Sigma = diag \ (\sigma_1, \sigma_2, \cdots, \sigma_n)$ is an $n \times n$ diagonal matrix whose diagonal elements are non-negative singular values sorted in descending order.

From semantic perspective, we assume that SVD generates the concept dimension [11]. Each triplet (left singular vector and right singular vector) can be viewed as representing such a concept, the magnitude of its singular value represents the degree of importance of this concept.

3   Text Summarization Based on Latent Semantic Analysis

3.1   Document Analysis

This step contains two tasks: Document Representation and Singular Value Decomposition. First, each document needs to be represented by a matrix. The matrix is constructed by terms (words with stop words eliminated) that occurred in the document representing rows and sentences of the document representing columns, thus it is called term by sentence matrix. For a text with m terms and n sentences where without loss of generality $m > n$, it can be represented by $A = [a_{ij}]_{m \times n}$. The cell a_{ij} can be filled out with different approaches. We will elaborate on the weighting schemes in section 4.

Once the term by sentence matrix is constructed, SVD will be employed to break it into three parts: U, Σ and V^T. Based on the discussion in section 2, we take U as term by concept matrix, V^T as concept by sentence matrix while the magnitude of singular values in Σ suggests the degree of importance of the concepts.

3.2   Sentence Selection

As with [6], a concept can be represented by the sentence that has the largest index value in the corresponding right singular vector, we make another hypothesis: a concept can also be represented by a few of terms, and these terms should have the largest index values in the corresponding left singular vector. The two forms of description of a concept are called sentence description and term description. Here each concept is treated as an independent topic.

Since sentences are composed of terms, it is hoped that the most representative sentences of the current concept should include the terms that best represent this concept. Therefore, each topic in the summary can be reconstructed by selecting sentences according to the magnitude of the index values in the right singular vector until a few of most representative terms that have the largest index values in the left singular vector are fully included.

The process of selecting summary sentences can be illustrated as follows.

— **Formulation.** For a document D with m terms and n sentences, suppose $term_i$ ($1 \leq i \leq m$) denotes the i-th term, and $sent_j$ ($1 \leq j \leq n$) denotes the j-th sentence, then $D=\{sent_1, sent_2,..., sent_n\}$. M is the maximum number of sentences to be selected, k is the number of concepts that can be selected and N_k is the number of sentences for the k-th concept, k and N_k are initialized to 1 and 0 respectively. Let set S contain the summary sentences and initialize S to null.

— **Sentence Selection and Term Selection.** While $|S|<M$, for the k-th concept, select the sentence that has the largest index value from the k-th right singular vector v_k. Get l that l satisfies $v_{kl}=\text{Argmax}(v_{ki})$, include the l-th sentence $sent_l$ into S and delete the l-th element v_{il} for v_i ($1 \leq i \leq n$), update V^T and increase N_k. Then select three terms u_{kp}, u_{kq}, u_{ks} that are represented by the $Top3$ largest index values from the k-th left singular vector u_k, and let set $T=\{term_p, term_q, term_s\}$.

— **Combination.** Delete terms that appear both in T and $sent_l$ from T. While T is not null, if $N_k<3$ and $|S|<M$, continue to select sentences for this concept, update V^T and T, increase N_k, else set T to null. Then increase k and begin to select sentences for the next concept.

Based on the above discussion, we give the formal description of our Sentence Selection method in Algorithm 1.

Algorithm 1. Sentence Selection based on LSA
Input: Document D, Matrix U, Matrix V^T, M
Output: Set S
1 **Initialize** $S=\phi$, $k=1$
2   **while** $|S|<M$
3   get l in v_k, $S=S \cup \{$ $sent_l$ $\}$, update V^T, $N_k =1$
4   get p, q, s in u_k, $T=\{$ $term_p$, $term_q$, $term_s$ $\}$
5         $T_0=T \cap sent_l$, $T=T-T_0$
6   **while** $(T \neq \phi)$
7   **if** $(N_k<3$ and $|S|<M)$
8   get l in v_k, $S=S \cup \{$ $sent_l$ $\}$, update V^T, $N_k = N_k +1$
9                 $T_0=T \cap sent_l$, $T=T-T_0$
10   **else** $T=\phi$
11   **end while**
12         $k=k+1$
13   **end while**
14 **Return** S

---

4   Experiments and Evaluation

4.1   Weighting Schemes

In order to elaborate on the weighting schemes, we define:

$$a_{ij} = L(t_{ij}) * G(t_{ij}) + N(t_{ij}), \tag{1}$$

where $L(t_{ij})$ is the Local Weight for $term_i$ in $sent_j$, $G(t_{ij})$ is the Global Weight for $term_i$ in the whole document, $N(t_{ij})$ is the Neighbor Weight of $term_i$ in $sent_j$.

In the following, we use tf_{ij} denotes the number of times that $term_i$ occurs in $sent_j$, tf_{max} denotes the frequency of the most frequently occurring term in $sent_j$, n is the total number of sentences, n_i is the number of sentences that contain $term_i$, gf_i is the number of times that $term_i$ occurs in the whole document..

For Local Weight, we choose to use the following four alternative strategies:

- **Binary Representation** (BR): If $term_i$ appears in $sent_j$, $L(t_{ij}) = 1$, otherwise 0.
- **Term Frequency** (TF): $L(t_{ij}) = tf_{ij}$.
- **Augment weight** (AW): $L(t_{ij}) = 0.5 + 0.5 * (tf_{ij} / tf_{max})$.
- **Logarithm Weight** (LW): $L(t_{ij}) = \log(1 + tf_{ij})$.

For Global Weight, possible weighting schemes can be:
- **No Global Weight** (NG): $G(t_{ij}) = 1$.
- **Inverse Sentence Frequency** (ISF): $G(t_{ij}) = 1 + \log(n / n_i)$.

- **Entropy Frequency** (EF): $G(t_{ij}) = 1 + \sum_j \dfrac{p_{ij} \log p_{ij}}{\log n}$, where $p_{ij} = \dfrac{tf_{ij}}{gf_i}$.

In order to make use of terms that occur in the neighbor sentences, we put forward the concept of Neighbor Weight and define Neighbor Weight as $N(t_{ij}) = \lambda[L(t_{i,j-1}) * G(t_{i,j-1}) + L(t_{i,j+1}) * G(t_{i,j+1})]$, where λ is a parameter which we will explore in the following experiments. So in the weighting schemes, we may add Neighbor Weight (AN) or just let Neighbor weight equals to 0 (NN).

Neighbor Weight is added mainly by the following three notable considerations: (1) Neighbor sentences can be affected by each other thus form clusters to make the topics more convince. (2) It helps to resolve anaphora resolution, since most of the time a pronoun and what it demonstrates appear in the adjacent sentences. (3) With neighbor weight added, it helps to resolve the issue of data sparsity.

4.2   Datasets and Evaluation Methods

The datasets that are used for the evaluation of our LSA-based summarization approach are DUC2002 dataset and DUC2004 dataset[1]. DUC2002 dataset contains 567 documents, each document is provided with two 100-word human summaries. The dataset of DUC2004 includes 5 tasks, while in our work, we only use task 2. In this task, documents are clustered into 50 topics of 10 documents each.

Two kinds of   metrics that F score and ROUGE toolkit [12] are adopted.

$$P = \frac{S_{cand} \cap S_{ref}}{S_{cand}}, R = \frac{S_{cand} \cap S_{ref}}{S_{ref}}, F = \frac{(1+\beta^2)PR}{\beta^2 P + R}, \qquad (2)$$

$$ROUGE - N = \frac{\sum_{S \in S_{ref}} \sum_{gram_n \in S} Count_{match}(gram_n)}{\sum_{S \in S_{ref}} \sum_{gram_n \in S} Count(gram_n)}, \qquad (3)$$

where S_{cand} denotes the candidate summary and S_{ref} denotes the reference summary, n stands for the length of the n-gram, $Count(gram_n)$ is the number of n-grams in the reference summaries, $Count_{match}(gram_n)$ is the maximum number of n-grams co-occurring in a candidate summary and the reference summaries.

In our experiments, Longest Common Subsequence ROUGE-L together with ROUGE-SU4 [12] are also being used.

4.3   Experimental Results and Analysis

First, in order to compare the different weighting schemes we conduct experiments on DUC2002 dataset. We set λ in the Neighbor Weight to 0.5 initially.

---

[1] http://www-nlpir.nist.gov/projects/duc/data.html

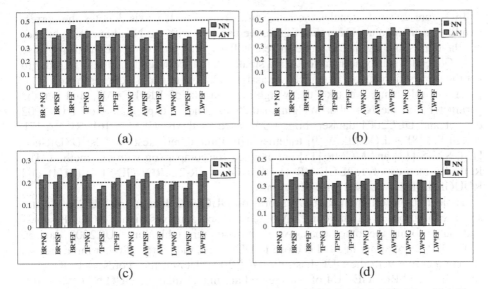

Fig. 1. Comparison of different weighting schemes (Local Weight*Global Weight +Neighbor Weight) for (a) F-1 score, (b) ROUGE-1, (c) ROUGE-2 and (d) ROUGE-L

From Figure 1 we can tell: the best combination of Local Weight and Global Weight is BR*EF, it performs better than other combinations at large. With Neighbor Weight added, nearly the results of all combinations acquire an improvement.

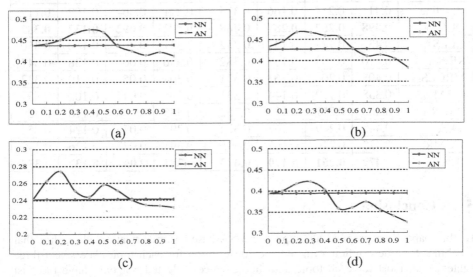

Fig. 2. Relationship between λ and (a) F-1 score, (b) ROUGE-1, (c) ROUGE-2 and (d) ROUGE-L

We apply the weighting scheme of BR*EF+AN in our experiments to show the impact that λ makes on the performance and get Figure 2.

In Figure 2, x-axis denotes the range of λ from 0 to 1, y-axis denotes the corresponding metrics value. From this figure, we can tell: with the Neighbor Weight added, the corresponding metric value increases firstly and then decreases with the raise of λ. Generally it is beneficial for λ in a small interval between 0 and 0.5. In order to get the most satisfying performance, we assign 0.25 to λ to make a compromise.

In the following, we take the weighting scheme of BR*EF+AN, and set the parameter λ in the Neighbor Weight to 0.25 to conduct experiments on DUC2002 dataset and DUC2004 dataset. Four LSA-based methods: GLLSA [6], SJLSA [7], MRCLSA [8] and OCALSA [9] together with three other latest models: DSDR-non [13], SATS [14] and MCMR [15] are adopted for comparison with our method. The ROUGE metrics of ROUGE-1(R-1), ROUGE-2 (R-2), ROUGE-SU4 (SU4) and ROUGE-L (R-L) are used for evaluation.

Table 1 shows different ROUGE scores on DUC2002 dataset and DUC2004 dataset. It can be observed that our LSA-based method achieves higher ROUGE scores and outperforms the other ones. As seen from this table, on DUC2002 dataset, ROUGE-1 score of our method is close to DUC-best, the scores of other three metrics are competitive with the DUC-best. On DUC2004 dataset, the scores of ROUGE-1, ROUGE-2 and ROUGE-SU4 of our method are higher than the DUC best. More importantly, our approach, nearly in terms of all ROUGE scores, outperforms the other methods that are based on LSA and is better than the three other latest modes.

Table 1. ROUGE results on datasets of DUC2002 and DUC2004

Algorithm	DUC2002 dataset				DUC2004 dataset			
	R-1	R-2	SU4	R-L	R-1	R-2	SU4	R-L
Baseline	0.411	0.211	0.166	0.375	0.221	0.064	0.102	0.117
DUC-best	**0.498**	**0.252**	**0.284**	**0.468**	**0.382**	**0.092**	**0.132**	**0.387**
GLLSA	0.432	0.174	0.137	0.352	0.341	0.065	0.120	0.350
SJLSA	0.410	0.207	0.158	0.382	0.356	0.064	0.138	0.347
MRCLSA	0.408	0.205	0.161	0.371	0.364	0.055	0.119	0.327
OCALSA	0.358	0.179	0.144	0.331	0.205	0.045	0.100	0.337
DSDR-non	0.466	0.267	0.138	0.352	0.385	0.098	0.118	0.329
SATS	0.448	0.209	0.164	0.374	0.295	0.076	0.124	0.354
MCMR	0.422	0.240	0.165	0.395	0.391	0.072	0.126	0.348
Ours	**0.472**	**0.261**	**0.170**	**0.423**	**0.384**	**0.097**	**0.137**	**0.355**

5   Conclusion

In this paper, we propose an improved LSA-based summarization algorithm that combines term description with sentence description for each topic. We select three sentences at most for each topic and the sentences selected not only have the best representation of the topic but also include the terms that can best represent this topic. We also put forward the concept of Neighbor Weight and propose a novel way that tries to utilize the mutual reinforcement between neighbor sentences to create the term by sentence matrix. Experimental results prove that our method achieve higher ROUGE scores than several well known methods.

<cyrillic>A Comprehensive Method for Text Summarization Based on LSA</cyrillic>

References

1. Radev, D.R., Hovy, E., McKeown, K.: Introduction to the special issue on summarization. Computational Linguistics-Summarization 28(4), 399–408 (2002)
2. Vodolazova, T.: The role of statistical and semantic features in single-document extractive summarization. Artificial Intelligence Research 2(3), 35–44 (2013)
3. Gupta, V., Lehal, G.S.: A survey of Text Summarization Extractive Techniques. Journal of Emerging Technologies in Web Intelligence 2(3) (2010)
4. Das, D., Martins, A.: A Survey on Automatic Text Summarization. In: Literature Survey for the Language and Statistics II Course at CMU (2007)
5. Deerwester, S.C., Dumais, S.T., Landauer, T.K., Furnas, G.W., Harshman, R.A.: Indexing by latent semantic analysis. Journal of the American Society for Information Science and Technology, 391–407 (1990)
6. Gong, Y.H., Liu, X.: Generic text summarization using relevance measure and latent semantic analysis. In: Proceedings of the 24th Annual International ACM SIGIR Conference on Research and Development in Information Retrieval, pp. 19–25. ACM, New York (2002)
7. Steinberger, J., Ježek, K.: Text Summarization and Singular Value Decomposition. In: Yakhno, T. (ed.) ADVIS 2004. LNCS, vol. 3261, pp. 245–254. Springer, Heidelberg (2004)
8. Murray, S.: Renals, and J. Carletta. Extractive Summarization of Meeting Recordings. In: Proceedings of the 9th European Conference on Speech Communication and Technology, pp. 593–596 (2005)
9. Ozsoy, M.G., Clicekli, I., Alpaslan, F.N.: Text summarization of Turkish Texts using Latent semantic analysis. In: Proceedings of the 23rd International Conference on Computational Linguistics (Coling 2010), Beijing, pp. 869–876 (2010)
10. Ai, D., Zheng, Y., Zhang, D.: Automatic text summarization based on latent semantic indexing. Artif. Life Robotics 15, 25–29 (2010)
11. Berry, M.W., Dumais, S.T., O'Brien, G.W.: Using linear algebra for intelligent information retrieval. SIAM Review 37(4), 575–595 (1995)
12. Lin, C.Y.: Rouge: a package for automatic evaluation of summaries. In: Proceedings of the ACL Text Summarization Workshop, pp. 74–81 (2004)
13. He, Z., Chen, C., Bu, J., Wang, C., Zhang, L.: Document Summarization Based on Data Reconstruction. In: Proceeding of the Twenty-Sixth AAAI Conference on Artificial Intelligence, pp. 620–626 (2012)
14. Chandra, M., Gupta, V., Paul, S.K.: A statistical approach for Automatic Text Summarization by Extraction. In: 2011 International Conference on Communication Systems and Network Technologies, pp. 268–271 (2011)
15. Alguliev, R.M., Aliguliyev, R.M., Hajirahimova, M.S., Mehdiyev, C.A.: MCMR: Maximum coverage and minimum redundant text summarization model. Expert Systems with Applications 38(12), 514–522 (2011)

A Time-Sensitive Model for Microblog Retrieval

Cunhui Shi, Bo Xu, Hongfei Lin, and Qing Guo

School of Computer Science and Technology,
Dalian University of Technology, Liaoning, Dalian, 116024
{smart,xubo2011,guoqing}@mail.dlut.edu.cn, hflin@dlut.edu.cn

Abstract. Microblog, as a way of online communication, can generate large amounts of information in a very short period. Therefore, how to retrieve the latest relevant information becomes a hot research area. Different from traditional information retrieval (IR), the microblog retrieval emphasizes fresh contents of the information. In order to solve this problem, we extend the traditional IR methods by taking into account the posting time. We propose a time-sensitive retrieval model, which takes the time factor as a prior probability. In the retrieval model, we introduce the pseudo relevance feedback technology as a query expansion approach to improve retrieval performance. Furthermore, we introduce a strategy to filter the initial retrieval results, which takes post quality factors into account including entropy and link features. Experiments on Twitter corpus show that our algorithm is effective to improve the retrieval performance, and the retrieval results can meet the real time retrieval need well.

Keywords: Microblog, Time-Sensitive, Retrieval Model, Entropy.

1   Introduction

In recent years, with the development of microblog, more and more users take part in it to share and obtain information. Statistics shows that until May of 2013, there are totally 288 million active users in Twitter, and they update more than 400 million tweets every day. Meanwhile, microblog becomes more and more popular in China, and many internet companies, such as Sina, Tencent and Sohu, start to provide microblog services. Another statistics shows there are 635 million registered users in Sina microblog until March of 2013, which includes 49.8 million active users and 76.5% of them use microblog on mobile terminals. Since users can update, review and forward microblog posts quickly and easily through mobile terminals, such as cellphones and tablet PCs, microblog generally becomes the first information source of some important issues. Therefore, it poses a challenge to meet the real time requirements for microblog retrieval, and obtaining the most fresh and relevant information becomes increasingly necessary.

In this paper, we propose a method to construct a time-sensitive retrieval model in microblog retrieval, which can retrieve the most relevant and fresh information for microblog users. This model combines the traditional IR methods with a time factor, which is taken as a prior probability. Besides, the pseudo relevance feedback

G. Zhou et al. (Eds.): NLPCC 2013, CCIS 400, pp. 402–409, 2013.
© Springer-Verlag Berlin Heidelberg 2013

technology is introduced to expand the queries for improving the retrieval performance. Furthermore, we introduce a strategy to filter the initial retrieval results, which takes quality factors into account including entropy and link features. Experimental results on the Twitter corpus show that our algorithm is effective to improve the microblog retrieval performance and meet the real time retrieval requirements well.

The contributions of this paper are as follows: 1) we propose a time-sensitive retrieval model aiming at meeting the real time requirements for microblog. 2) Pseudo relevance feedback technology is introduced to boost the retrieval performance in this process. 3) We take advantage of entropy and link features to get rid of noises in microblog messages in order to obtain more relevant information.

The rest of the paper is organized as follows: Section 2 reviews some related work. In Section 3, we illustrate our time-sensitive retrieval model and some details on our retrieval process. In Section 4, we introduce the experimental settings and present the comparison and analysis of different methods. Section 5 concludes this paper .

2   Related Work

Microblog provides an easier access for us to obtain abundant information and communicate with each other. Along with the data growing rapidly, retrieval in microblog become more and more necessary for users to find the exact information they prefer. There are many researches focusing on microblog retrieval in terms of various aspects. In order to study user behaviors in microblog, Miles Efron [1] gives a general view of microblog retrieval focusing on many important problems to be solved by analyzing semantic features and researching on authority and quality of abstract models and entity retrieval. Besides, the paper is also focusing on the temporal issue, i.e. the influence of the time factor on microblog retrieval, which includes continuous indexing problem and tolerance of information delay in microblog.

Since traditional information retrieval methods like key words matching cannot meet the requirements of massive data very well, some researchers are focusing on real time retrieval, which takes factors, such as timestamp and authority, into account during microblog retrieval to boost the performance [2-9]. For example, Teevan et al. [8] present that microbloggers tend to utilize short queries (always relate to some hot issues) and choose the latest results by analyzing the query logs and searching results. Chen et al. [10] propose an adaptive retrieval framework, which make use of the relationship between users and messages to classify the messages into different categories. They demonstrate that the framework can solve the problem of real time retrieval at the cost of results quality, i.e. it is a trade-off between real time requirements and retrieval performance. Arjumand Youns et al. [11] take twitter as the source of consulting to estimate the popularity of news. Kamran Massoudi [12] improves retrieval performance by using some unique characteristic in microblog, such as forwards and comments. Rinkesh Nagmoti et al. [13] rank the searching results by using information from social network and get good results. By analyzing the structure of social network, Meredith Ringel Morris et al. [14] estimate the reliability of messages on microblog.

Different from the researches referred above, our research explores the possibility of adding time information to traditional retrieval model, which aims at changing the prior probability between documents and the query. Meanwhile, we take some measures, such as pseudo relevance feedback and quality filters, to improve the retrieval performance further.

3   Microblog Oriented Time-Sensitive Retrieval Model

In this section, we will illustrate some details about our time-sensitive microblog retrieval model. Specifically, there are two steps in our retrieval process. Firstly, we introduce time factors to traditional retrieval models through query expansion techniques. Secondly, we use entropy and short links to filter the result documents. Next, we will show the two steps in details.

3.1   Time-Sensitive Language Model

To construct our retrieval model, we focus on the improvement of traditional language model. Traditionally, documents are ranked based on relevance with the query. According to Bayes rules, the relevance is represented as follows.

$$P(D|Q) = \frac{P(D)P(Q|D)}{P(Q)} \propto P(D)P(Q|D) \tag{1}$$

where D is the document. $P(Q)$ is the normalization factor, which can be omitted in calculation. $P(Q|D)$ is the likelihood function w.r.t the document D. $P(D|Q)$ is the probability that query Q is generated from D, which is used to measure the relevance between D and Q. Since $P(D)$, as the document prior probability, is uniform and invariable for documents, it is always omitted in calculation. However, our retrieval model is more focused on the latest microblog documents, i.e., our model is time-sensitive. So $P(D)$ here should reflect something related to the timestamp labeled on the document in order to adapt to microblog retrieval. Therefore, we present our basic retrieval model based on language model as the Eq. (2).

$$P(D|Q) = \frac{P(D)P(Q|D)}{P(Q)} \propto P_{real}(D)P(Q|D) \tag{2}$$

where $P_{real}(D)$ is the document prior probability with time information, which distinguish the documents in their timestamps. Specifically, the later the document is delivered, the higher the probability is. In other words, a user takes the time he submitted the query as the baseline. If the timestamp of a document is nearer to the baseline, the document has more probability to be ranked higher in the final ranking list and vice versa.

However, if a user wants to search for information related to a certain period (not the time the query submitted), the model in Eq. (2) may not work well. In order to deal with the problem, we present the concept of the key time point with large amounts of information delivered, which is denoted as $T_{realQuery}$. For example, a hot issue can cause the information explosion in microblog in the short period. We average the timestamp of the documents delivered in the period as the key time point to modify the time factor in Eq. (2) as shown in Eq. (3).

$$T_{realQuery} = \frac{1}{N} \sum_{i=1}^{N} t(FbDoc(i)) \tag{3}$$

where $t(FbDoc(i))$ is the timestamp of a document i. We introduce pseudo relevance feedback to choose the top-N documents from initial retrieval and average the timestamp to obtain the key time point of a query. Empirically, we set $N=10$ in our experiments.

$$P_{real}(D) = \frac{P'_{real}(D)}{\sum_{d \in C} P'_{real}(d)} \propto P'_{real}(D) \tag{4}$$

$$P'_{real}(D) = e^{-\frac{|T_D - T_{realQuery}|}{T_{max} - T_{realQuery}}} \tag{5}$$

Eq. (4) and Eq. (5) is the calculation of the prior probability with time factors, where T_D is the timestamp of a document, T_{max} is the timestamp with the max distance with the key time point in a period. We calculate the probability using Eq. (5) instead Eq. (4) in order to embody the time information in document prior more reasonably. The final retrieval model we construct could contribute to microblog retrieval in consideration of the time information.

3.2   Quality Based Results Filter

Since the messages in microblog are always short and limited to a certain length, it is difficult to extract text features as traditional information retrieval methods do. What's more, there are lots of noises in microblog messages including some advertisements and some useless comments. In order to solve the problems above, we introduce information entropy to measure and filter the instant messages.

$$Entropy = -\sum_{i=1}^{m} \frac{n_i}{n} \log \frac{n_i}{n} \tag{6}$$

where n is number of words appeared in a piece of message, in which m is the number of words appeared only once and n_i is the number of words appeared more than once. The entropy indicates the importance of a message. We filter the messages with the entropy below a certain threshold to decrease the noises.

Besides, there are always some hyperlinks in the messages, which enrich the contents of messages. So we take the link information as another way to measure the importance of the messages, i.e., if a message contains some hyperlinks, the score of the message will be multiplied by a constant as the following equation shows.

$$score_{new} = \alpha * score \tag{7}$$

In our experiments, we set $a = 1.2$ since relative good performance can be achieved under this setting. We remove the useless information using the two measures above to obtain the documents with abundant information in microblog retrieval.

3.3   The Overall Retrieval Process

In this section, we will give more details about our retrieval process. We examine our retrieval model on TREC datasets from Microblog Track in our experiments. Table 1 shows the overall retrieval process of our algorithms.

Table 1. The time-sensitive retrieval model of microblog

Algorithms	Time-Sensitive Retrieval Model
Input	An original query
Output	documents ranking list
Step 1	Original Query=constructQuery(words[]);
	PRFDocs[1,2,···,10]=Retrieval(Original Query);

Step 2	For i=1 to10
	    For each term in PRFDocs[i]
	        If(term !=stopper) Weight(term)= tf * idf ;
	    End for
	    TermsWeight[i]=Combine(Score(PRFDocs[i]),weight(PRFDocs[i]));
	End for

Step 4	RealQueryTime=avgTime($\sum_{i=1}^{10}$ Time(PRFDocs[i]))
Step 5	For each doc computeP(Q|D) $= \frac{P(D)P(Q\|D)}{P(Q)} \propto P_{real}(D)P(Q\|D))$ End for
Step 6	If(HasLink) $score_{new} = \alpha \cdot score$ Else $score_{new} = score$

Step 7	For each doc in the runs
	        If(Entropy>=EntropyThrethold&&$score_{new}$>=ScoreThrethold)
	            Resultdocs.add(doc)
	End for

Step 8	Return docs[1,2,···,N]

Initial Retrieval. A user submits a query and then our system conducts initial retrieval based on traditional language model and vector space model.

Query Expansion. We choose the top 10 documents in the initial ranking list as feedback documents. Then, we select expansion terms from these documents as follows. Firstly we stem the words in documents and remove stop words. Secondly, we use traditional TF-IDF model to score each term. Thirdly, we choose k terms with the highest scores as expansion terms for expanding the query.

Further Retrieval Using Time-Sensitive Model. We retrieve again using query expansion. Meanwhile, entropy and link information is utilized to filter documents and obtain the final ranking list.

4   Experiments

4.1   Experimental Settings

Corpus. We evaluate our method on TREC dataset from Microblog Track based on Twitter. The dataset contains 50 topics with relevance judgments, which is one of the standard dataset in Microblog research. Tweets in the dataset are stored in a standard format, i.e., <*tweetid, username, status, time, text*>, where *tweedid* is the identifier of each tweet, *username* is the name of user who delivers the tweet, *time* is a number indicating the timestamp and *text* is the content.

Evaluation Methods. We take Indri as our basic search environment, and MAP (Mean of Average Precision) is adopted as the evaluation measure. In evaluation, the higher the value of MAP is, the better the performance is.

Baselines. To measure the effectiveness of our method, we compare our method with some traditional and state-of-the-art methods on the dataset. Tfidf is the retrieval model using vector space models twice, where the terms are weighted using TFIDF. TfidfFb is the retrieval model using vector space model in initial retrieval and time-sensitive model in second retrieval. LM is the retrieval model using language models twice. LMFb is the retrieval model using language model in initial retrieval and time-sensitive model in second retrieval. MixSp is the linear interpolation of Tfidf and LM methods. MixFb is the linear interpolation of TfidfFb and LMFb methods.

4.2   Experimental Results and Analysis

Table 2 presents the evaluation results of the 6 retrieval models. From the table we can see that no matter what retrieval models is used in consideration of time factor, the performance can be improved. In comparison, language model performs better than Tfidf, indicating that language model is more suitable and stable for microblog documents in extracting key information. What's more, the performance of LMFb and MIXFb is increased over LM and MixSp by nearly 10%, while TfidfFb is increased over Tfidf by only 2%. This phenomenon also indicates that the time-sensitive retrieval model is more effective when used with language model.

We also conduct experiments under 50 topics in the dataset. Figure 1 shows the results of time-sensitive models with different initial retrieval methods. From the results we can see that the performance of two methods linear interpolation is better compared with other methods. Notably, we find that TfidfFb performs the best among all methods in some query topics, which indicates the time-sensitive Tfidf model is not stable on all the queries.

Table 2. Comparision of different retrieval methods

Methods	MAP	
Tfidf	0.2185	
TfidfFb	0.2219	1.56%
LM	0.2603	
LMFb	0.2851	9.53%
Mix	0.2674	
MixFb	0.2936	9.80%

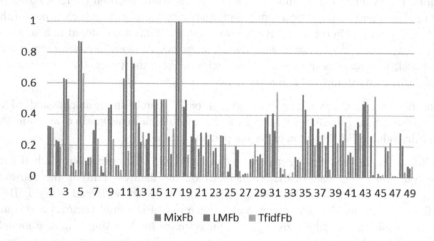

Fig. 1. MAP histogram of 50 topics

5   Conclusion

In this paper, we propose a microblog retrieval model by adding time factor to the traditional language model. Specifically, we use query expansion technique, pseudo relevance feedback, to boost retrieval performance and filter the result documents using entropy and link information. Experiments on TREC datasets show that our method outperforms traditional language model and vector space model. Our retrieval model can meet users' information need better.

Acknowledgements. This work is partially supported by grant from the Natural Science Foundation of China (No.60673039, 60973068, 61277370), the National High Tech Research and Development Plan of China (No.2006AA01Z151), Natural Science Foundation of Liaoning Province, China (No.201202031), State Education Ministry and The Research Fund for the Doctoral Program of Higher Education (No.20090041110002).

References

1. Efron, M.: Information search and retrieval in microblogs. Journal of the American Society for Information Science and Technology 62(6), 996–1008 (2011)
2. Cheong, M., Lee, V.: Integrating web-based intelligence retrieval and decision-making from the twitter trends knowledge base. In: Proceeding of the 2nd ACM Workshop on Social web Search and Mining, pp. 1–8 (2009)
3. Dong, A., Zhang, R., Kolari, P., et al.: Time is of the essence: improving recency ranking using Twitter data. In: Proceedings of the 19th International Conference on World Wide Web, pp. 331–340 (2010)
4. Efron, M.: Hashtag Retrieval in a microblogging environment. In: Proceeding of the 33rd International ACM SIGIR Conference on Research and Development in Information Retrieval, pp. 787–788 (2010)
5. Evans, M., Chi, E.H.: Towards a model of understanding social search. In: Proceedings of the 2008 ACM Conference on Computer Supported Cooperative Work, pp. 485–494 (2008)
6. Geer, D.: Is It Really Time for Real-Time Search? Computer 43(3), 16–19 (2010)
7. Horowitz, D., Kamvar, S.D.: The anatomy of a large-scale social search engine. In: Proceedings of the 19th International Conference on World Wide Web, pp. 431–440 (2010)
8. Teevan, J., Ramage, D., Morris, M.R.: TwitterSearch: A Comparison of Microblog Search and Web Search. In: Proceedings of the Fourth ACM International Conference on Web Search and Data Mining, pp. 35–44 (2011)
9. Weng, J., Lim, E., Jiang, J., et al.: TwitterRank: finding topic-sensitive influential twitterers. In: Proceedings of the Third ACM International Conference on Web Search and Data Mining, pp. 261–270 (2010)
10. Chen, C., Li, F., et al.: TI: An efficient indexing mechanism for real-time search on tweets. In: Proceedings of the 2011 International Conference on Management of Data, pp. 648–660 (2011)
11. Younus, A., Qureshi, M.A., Ghazi, A.N., et al.: Ins and Outs of News: Twitter as a Real-Time News Analysis Service. In: Proceedings of the Workshop on Visual Interfaces to the Social and Semantic Web (2011)
12. Massoudi, K., Tsagkias, M., Rijke, M.D., et al.: Incorporating Query Expansion and Quality Indicators in Searching Microblog Posts. In: The 33rd European Conference on Information Retrieval, pp. 362–367 (2011)
13. Nagmoti, R., Teredesai, A., Cock, M.D.: Ranking Approaches for Microblog Search. In: International Conference on Web Intelligence and Intelligent Agent Technology, pp. 153–157 (2010)
14. Meredith Ringel, M., Scott, C., Asta, R., Aaron, H., Julia, S.: Tweeting is Believing? Understanding Microblog Credibility Perceptions. In: The 12th Computer Supported Cooperative Work, pp. 441–450 (2012)

Feature Analysis in Microblog Retrieval
Based on Learning to Rank

Zhongyuan Han[1,2], Xuwei Li[1,*], Muyun Yang[1], Haoliang Qi[2], and Sheng Li[1]

[1] School of Computer Science and Technology,
Harbin Institute of Technology, Harbin, China
{zyhan,xwli,ymy}@mtlab.hit.edu.cn, lisheng@hit.edu.cn
[2] School of Computer Science and Technology,
Heilongjiang Institute of Technology, Harbin, China
haoliang.qi@gmail.com

Abstract. Learning to rank, which can fuse various of features, performs well in microblog retrieval. However, it is still unclear how the features function in microblog ranking. To address this issue, this paper examines the contribution of each single feature together with the contribution of the feature combinations via the ranking SVM for microblog retrieval modeling. The experimental results on the TREC microblog collection show that textual features, i.e. content relevance between a query and a microblog, contribute most to the retrieval performance. And the combination of certain non-textual features and textual features can further enhance the retrieval performance, though non-textual features alone produce rather weak results.

Keywords: microblog retrieval, learning to rank, feature combination.

1   Introduction

Current retrieval models are usually built on so-called learning-to-rank strategy, which typically involves multiple features from the queries and the documents. This strategy has also been applied to microblog retrieval [1]. In TREC microblog track, both the USC/ISI team (top 1 in TREC 2011) and the HIT team (top 1 in TREC 2012) used Learning to Rank algorithm [2,3]. Several other teams also adopted similar methods [4-8], differing only in the different features employed.

In the literature, however, the features for microblog ranking have not been well examined. Besides the classical textual features, microblog retrieval is further enriched by various non-text features, which has been proved to be more effective. Duan et al employed learning to rank algorithms to determine the best set of features, in which the textual features hardly contribute to the retrieval performance [1].

Following this thread, the feature contribution is reexamined in microblog retrieval in this paper, including the single feature and the feature combination via the Ranking SVM framework. Specifically, we focus on the textual features, i.e. the content relevance between the query and the microblog.

---

* Corresponding author.

G. Zhou et al. (Eds.): NLPCC 2013, CCIS 400, pp. 410–416, 2013.
© Springer-Verlag Berlin Heidelberg 2013

The rest of this paper is organized as follows: First, the features in Ranking SVM for microblog retrieval are introduced. Second, the experiment and evaluation are given. Last, we draw a conclusion for this paper and future direction in this field is discussed.

2   Features in Ranking SVM for Microblog Retrieval

Ranking SVM, one of the pair-wise ranking methods, is an application of support vector machine, which is used to solve certain ranking problems. In microblog retrieval, the training data is a set of $(x_{u,v}, y_{u,v})$. $x_{u,v}$ is a microblog pair(u,v). Here u and v indicate a microblog presented by a feature vector. If u<v, $y_{u,v}=1$; otherwise $y_{u,v}=-1$. It means that the train sample is positive if the microblog u has a higher relevant level than microblog v. Thus the ranking task is changed into a classification task. The retrieval model can be trained by SVM.

In learning to rank, the feature set is crucial to the model performance. To determine the contribution of each feature, a common practice is to re-build the model by each single feature as well as different feature combinations in addition to the whole feature set. The differences in the model performances are then deemed as a good proof for the feature influence in the retrieval modeling.

In this paper, we classify the features for microblog ranking into three groups: content relevance features, author features and microblog unique features, which arc detailed in the following section.

2.1   Content Relevance Features

Content relevance features, often referred as the textual features, specify the content relevance between queries and tweets. Under language model framework, here we use Kullback-Leibler Divergence to measure the content relevance between query model Q and microblog model M. The standard KL function is:

$$KL(Q \mid M) = \sum_w P(w \mid M) \log \frac{P(w \mid M)}{P(w \mid Q)} \tag{1}$$

Then four content relevance features can be obtained as shown in Table 1.

Table 1. Content relevance features

Features	Description
KL_OQ_OM	KL score of original query and original microblog
KL_EQ_OM	KL score of expanded query and original microblog
KL_OQ_EM	KL score of original query and expanded microblog
KL_EQ_QM	KL score of expanded query and expanded microblog

OQ is denoted as original query model and OM is denoted as original microblog model. For short queries and short microblogs in microblog retrieval, the query expansion and microblog expansion are used to estimate query model (denoted by EQ) and microblog model (denoted by EM).

OQ (Original Query) and OM (Original Microblog) are estimated by maximum likelihood estimation on original query and original microblog.

EQ (Expanded Query) is modeled by the relevance feedback model [9]. According to the relevance model, a query term is generated by a relevance model $p(w|\theta_R)$, which is derived by top-ranked feedback documents by assuming them to be samples from the relevance model as follows:

$$p(w|\theta_R) \propto \sum_{d \in F} p(w|d)p(d|\theta_R)$$ (2)

where F denotes the feedback documents, usually approximated by the top-ranked retrieved documents for the query; $p(w|d)$ is the probability that the term w appears in the document d, and $p(d|\theta_R)$ is the probability that d is generated by θ_R. θ_R is estimated by the original query, thus we can obtain:

$$p(w|\theta_R) \propto \sum_{d \in F} p(w|\theta_R)p(\theta_R)\prod_{i=1}^{m} p(q_i|\theta_R)$$ (3)

The above relevance model is used to enhance the original query model by the following interpolation:

$$p(w|\theta'_q) = (1-\alpha)p(w|\theta_q) + \alpha \, p(w|\theta_R)$$ (4)

where α is the interpolation weight. In our experiments, α=0.8 and the number of top-ranked retrieved documents is set 20.

EM (Expanded Microblog) is estimated by DELM (Document Expansion Language Model) [10] to improve the representation of short tweets. That is, for a document d (i.e. tweet), decide its k (set as 100 in our experiment) nearest neighbors $\{b_1,...,b_k\}$ by the cosine similarity score between b_k and d. Then it assigns a confidence value $r_d(b)$ to every document b to indicate our confidence about that b is sampled from d's hidden model. The confidence value is defined as below:

$$r_d(b) = \frac{sim(d,b)}{\sum_{b' \in C-\{d\}} sim(d,b')}$$ (5)

In fact, the confidence value $r_d(b)$ is set by normalizing the cosine similarity scores. Then a pseudo document d' is obtained with the following pseudo term count:

$$c(w,d') = \beta c(w,d) + (1-\beta) \sum_{b \in C-\{d\}} (\gamma_d(b) \times c(w,b))$$ (6)

where parameter β (set as 0.8 in our experiment) controls the degree of relying on neighborhood document. This technique is proved to be valid in improving search results in TREC texts by [6].

2.2   Author Features and Microblog Unique Features

Author features, listed in table 2, reflect the publisher of a tweet.

Table 2. Author features

Features	Description
FOLLOWERS_COUNT	How many people are following this author
FRIENDS_COUNT	How many people this author is following
LISTS_COUNT	How many groups is the author in
STATUS_COUNT	How many microblogs are posted by the author
FAVOURITE_COUNT	How many microblogs are the author's favorite
IS_VERIFIED	Is the author verified

Microblog unique features refer to the particular characteristics of a tweet, which are summarized in Table 3.

Table 3. Microblog unique features

Features	Description
HAS_URL	Whether the microblog contains a URL
IS_REPLY	Whether the microblog is a reply microblog
HAS_MENTION	Whether the microblog contains a mention("@")
HAS_HASHTAG	Whether the microblog contains a hashtag("#")
RETWEET_COUNT	How many is retweet count

2.3   Feature Sets

Several feature sets mentioned above are examined in the subsequent experiments. The performance of the model built by all features (RankSVM_all) is denoted as the baseline, and the varied feature settings consist of the following:

Leave_one_out_from_all, in which each single feature is removed respectively from the total 15 features, demonstrates the contribution of each feature in the feature set.

Single_feature, in which only one feature is involved to model the microblog retrieval, is used to reveal the importance of each feature in the model alone.

Feature_group is used to examine different kinds of features in three groups. This setting compares the different aspects of features existing in microblogs to some extent.

Best_feature is an optimized subset with the best retrieval performance. We generate several feature sets randomly and use the advanced greedy feature selection method proposed by Duan et al [1], to find the best feature combinational set with the best performance.

3   Experiment and Evaluation

3.1   Experimental Settings

The experiment data is TREC 2011 tweets corpus. The corpus, which is comprised of 2 weeks tweets sampled from Twitter, contains about ten million tweets[1]. We download 10,397,336 tweets by twitter crawler provided by track organizers, and there remain 3,754,077 tweets for the experiment after being filtered in accordance with TREC [11]. The statistics of dataset are shown in Table 4. Note that the index is built for each query with only tweets before its query time.

Table 4. Statistics of tweets in dataset

# of Total tweets	# of Null tweets	# of Retweets	# of Non-English tweets	# of Indexed Tweets
10,397,336	0	342,652	6,300,607	3,754,077

The 50 queries and the corresponding answer sets in TREC 2011 are used to train the retrieval model via SVMrank[2] by Thorsten Joachims. The 60 queries of TREC 2012 are the test set. Following TREC 2012 microblog tack, the performance is evaluated by standard metrics: P@30. Meanwhile, MAP and R-Prec are reported for reference.

3.2   All Features vs. Single

As is shown in table 5, the performance of RankSVM_all is better than that of any single feature. Although any feature from the author aspect and the tweet unique produce poor result, they can enhance the text relevance features as a whole to achieve a significantly better result.

We further examine the feature contribution by removing one from the all-set respectively, and the corresponding results are shown in Fig. 1. According to this figure, most features cause a performance drop if they are removed. The most significant drops occur with the removal of the HAS_URL feature and the KL_EQ_EM feature. The HAS_MENTION is harmful for ranking.

We then examine the features in three groups and compare them with the best feature set achieved. According to Table 5, it is revealed that the performance of each feature group is inferior to that of the all features. The best feature set can boost the retrieval performance from 0.2593 to 0.2621($p<0.05$) in P@30, with the following 9 features left in the core: 4 content relevance scores, FOLLOWERS_COUNT, LISTS_COUNT, HAS_URL, HAS_HASHTAG and RETWEET_COUNT.

A notable finding in the experiment is that the content relevance features are strong indicators for tweet retrieval performance. This fact indicates that the content relevance between query and tweet is still essential to tweet retrieval performance. In addition, the expansion techniques consistently exhibit positive effectiveness in performance improvement.

---

[1] https://ir.nist.gov/tweets2011/id-status.01-May-2012.gz
[2] http://www.cs.cornell.edu/people/tj/svm_light/svm_rank.html

Table 5. Performance comparisons of using all features vs. single feature

	P@30	MAP	R-Prec
RankSVM_all	0.2593	0.2475	0.2684
RankSVM_best	**0.2621**	**0.2479**	**0.2685**
KL_OQ_OM	0.2062	0.1855	0.2207
KL_EQ_OM	0.2345	0.2302	0.2471
KL_OQ_EM	0.226	0.2059	0.2345
KL_EQ_EM	0.2446	0.2356	0.2575
Group_content_relevance	0.2458	0.2371	0.2569
FAVOURITE_COUNT	0.0181	0.0225	0.0204
FRIENDS_COUNT	0.0418	0.0339	0.0407
FOLLOWERS_COUNT	0.0542	0.0511	0.0555
LISTS_COUNT	0.0435	0.0361	0.0392
STATUS_COUNT	0.0475	0.0533	0.0494
IS_VERIFIED	0.0542	0.042	0.0533
Group_Author	0.048	0.0413	0.0452
RETWEET_COUNT	0.0429	0.0356	0.0378
IS_REPLY	0.0469	0.0531	0.0494
HAS_MENTION	0.0486	0.0554	0.0524
HAS_URL	0.0706	0.0715	0.0758
HAS_HASHTAG	0.0345	0.0363	0.0399
Group_Unique	0.0695	0.0554	0.065

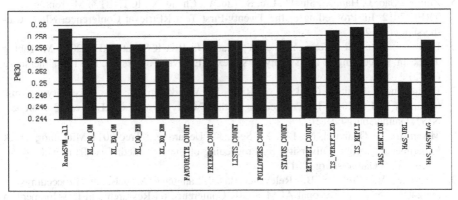

Fig. 1. Performance of leave_one_out_from_all

4   Conclusion and Future Work

This paper investigates the feature contribution in microblog retrieval modeling under learning-to-rank framework. 15 features, which can be classified into three groups: text relevance, author and tweet unique, are examined via Ranking SVM. Experiment results show that the most important features are content relevance features, which lie in the core for the model performance. Both query expansion and microblog expansion are the most important features in content features. Meanwhile, the non-textual features could enrich the text relevance scores, though they produce unsatisfactory results alone. Among non-textual features, the HAS_URL produces the most significant effect to the performance.

In future work, we would explore how to combine the content relevance scores with the non-textual features. In addition, certain factors which have not covered in this paper, such as time influence to microblog search, should also be addressed.

Acknowledgements. This work is supported by the NSF China (No. 61272384 & 61105072), and the National High Technology Research and Development Program of China (863 Program, No. 2011AA01A207).

References

1. Duan, Y., Jiang, L., Qin, T., Zhou, M., Shum, H.Y.: An Empirical Study on Learning to Rank of Tweets. In: Proceedings of the 23rd International Conference on Computational Linguistics, pp. 295–303. Association for Computational Linguistics, Beijing (2010)
2. Metzler, D., Cai, C.: USC/ISI at TREC 2011: Microblog Track. In: Proceeding of the Twentieth Text REtrieval Conference. NIST, Gaithersburg (2011)
3. Han, Z., Li, X., Yang, M., Qi, H., Li, S., Zhao, T.: HIT at TREC 2012 Microblog Track. In: Proceeding of the Twenty-First Text REtrieval Conference. NIST, Gaithersburg (2012)
4. Zhang, X., Lu, S., He, B., Xu, J., Luo, T.: UCAS at TREC-2012 Microblog Track. In: Proceeding of the Twenty-First Text REtrieval Conference. NIST, Gaithersburg (2012)
5. Zhu, B., Gao, J., Han, X., Shi, C., Liu, S., Liu, Y., Cheng, X.: ICTNET at Microblog Track TREC 2012. In: Proceeding of the Twenty-First Text REtrieval Conference. NIST, Gaithersburg (2012)
6. Liang, F., Qiang, R., Hong, Y., Fei, Y., Yang, J.: PKUICST at TREC 2012 Microblog Track. In: Proceeding of the Twenty-First Text REtrieval Conference. NIST, Gaithersburg (2012)
7. Berendsen, R., Meij, E., Odijk, D., de Rijke, M., Weerkamp, W.: The University of Amsterdam at TREC 2012. In: Proceeding of the Twenty-First Text REtrieval Conference. NIST, Gaithersburg (2012)
8. Miyanishi, T., Okamura, N., Liu, X., Seki, K., Uehara, K.: Trec 2011 Microblog Track Experiments at Kobe University. In: Proceeding of the Twentieth Text REtrieval Conference. NIST, Gaithersburg (2011)
9. Lavrenko, V., Croft, W.B.: Relevance-Based Language Models. In: Proceedings of the 24th Annual International ACM SIGIR Conference on Research and Development in Information Retrieval, pp. 120–127. ACM, New York (2001)
10. Tao, T., Wang, X., Mei, Q., Zhai, C.: Language Model Information Retrieval with Document Expansion. In: Proceedings of the Main Conference on Human Language Technology Conference of the North American Chapter of the Association of Computational Linguistics, pp. 407–414. Association for Computational Linguistics, New York (2006)
11. Ounis, I., Macdonald, C., Lin, J., Soboro, I.: Overview of the TREC-2011 Microblog Track. In: Proceeding of the Twentieth Text REtrieval Conference. NIST, Gaithersburg (2011)

Opinion Sentence Extraction and Sentiment Analysis for Chinese Microblogs

Hanxiao Shi, Wei Chen, and Xiaojun Li

School of Computer Science and Information Engineering, Zhejiang GongShong University,
Hangzhou 310018
hxshory@foxmail.com

Abstract. Sentiment analysis of Chinese microblogs is important for scientific research in public opinion supervision, personalized recommendation and social computing. By studying the evaluation task of NLP&CC'2012, we mainly implement two tasks, namely the extraction of opinion sentence and the determination of sentiment orientation for microblogs. First, we manually label the sample of microblog corpus supplied by the organization, and expand the sentiment lexicon by introducing the Internet sentiment words; second, we construct the different feature sets based on the analysis of the characteristic of Chinese microblogs. Finally, we use SVM classifier to generate a model based on training corpus, and implement the predication of test corpus. Evaluation results show our work has good performance on two tasks.

1 Introduction

In the context of Web 2.0, microblog, as an important way for people to communicate with each other, has the characteristics of large amount and fast update. It is a reliable source to explore people's view and sentiment orientation. And the research on the natural language processing technology for microblogs has currently become a new research hotspot, of which sentiment analysis is an important topic.

The aim of sentiment analysis or opinion mining is to know people's opinion and sentiment orientation. At present the main technology is divided into two categories: one is to classify emotions according to the number of positive sentimental words and negative sentimental words in the text, with the method of combining sentiment lexicon with rules; the other is to adopt machine learning by which features in text are discovered and classifiers like Naive Bayes, Max Entropy and Support Vector Machine are applied.

At present English microblog research has made progress in sentiment analysis, for example, sentiment classification research for emoticons and hashtag as the features, while sentiment analysis research for Chinese microblogs relatively lagged behind either in resources or in methods.

By studying the evaluation task of NLP&CC'2012, we mainly implement two tasks, namely the extraction of opinion sentence and the determination of sentiment orientation for Chinese microblogs supplied by the evaluation organization. Experiment results show our work has good performance on two tasks.

G. Zhou et al. (Eds.): NLPCC 2013, CCIS 400, pp. 417–423, 2013.
© Springer-Verlag Berlin Heidelberg 2013

2   Related Work

In the last decade, sentiment analysis attracted the attention of many researchers and has become a hot research topic in the field of information retrieval and natural language processing. As evaluation task is mainly about extraction of opinion sentence and determination of sentiment orientation, the following will introduce the related research from two aspects.

2.1   Subjective Text Recognition

Subjective text is the main object of text sentiment analysis. Therefore, it is very important to identify a large amount of subjective and objective web texts in advance to effectively narrow the analysis scope and reduce interference [1]. In order to effectively identify and extract factual information in an extraction task, Riloff et al. [2] designed a variety of filtering methods, using subjective classifiers to filter out subjective text, then extracted information, and tested in MUC-4 terrorism data sets; Toprak and Gurevych [3] finished a subjectivity classification experiment of English and French documents in DEFT'2009 Text Mining Challenge. In addition, Finn et al. [4] concluded that feature selection method based on POS tagging can get better effect than that on bag-of-words by studying subjective and objective sentence classification.

Above all, subjectivity text recognition is mainly based on sentiment words, using various methods of text feature expression and classifiers to classify. This method is clearly defined, and the essential problem is the selection of features.

2.2   Sentiment Orientation Analysis

In sentiment orientation analysis, a subjectivity text is generally divided into two or three types, namely positive, negative and neutral, to measure the preference of evaluated object. According to the different knowledge sources such as sentiment lexicon and corpus, and to different methods of classification, sentiment orientation analysis can be divided into the two kinds of methods.

The first method is based on sentiment lexicon and rules. It is to separately calculate the number of mixed sentimental words in text. If the number of positive word is greater than that of negative word, text is for positive sense, otherwise for negative sense, if equal for neutral. As the method relies on the quality of sentiment lexicon, the construction of sentiment lexicon should be focused on. Its main idea is: based on the collection of words with the known polarity as sentiment lexicon seed, new words with unknown sentiment polarity can be predicted by using some correlated method in the sentiment seed lexicon to find out similar words or similar semantic words, and then to calculate the new sentiment orientation through the polarity of these words. This method requires high coverage of the seed word. At present, the most commonly used lexicons are WordNet in English and HowNet in Chinese.

The second method is based on machine learning. With sentiment words and phrases, syntactic dependency and theme-related characteristics as classification features, a classification model is generated by classifier training. By using the constructed model, classification of test documents can be implemented in order to realize sentiment orientation discrimination of test documents. Pang et al. [5], by the bag-of-words technology, used Naive Bayes, Maximum Entropy and Support Vector Machines to do text sentiment polarity research, and made a comparative analysis of these three methods. Through experiments, the conclusion is that the performance of SVM is better, with the highest accuracy 80%.

The focus of the current Chinese sentiment analysis research is in the field of product reviews, news comments and film reviews. As for microblogs, it develops in recent years as a new type of social media while sentiment analysis research for microblogs is relatively less. A lot of people are working at Twitter sentiment analysis research in foreign countries. Go [6] and others used classifiers such as NB, ME and SVM to carry out the Twitter sentiment classification and the results show that the performance of SVM is better than other two classifiers. As to feature selection, features can be selected by the use of Unigram and Bigram models with the combination of parts-of–speech (POS). Barbosa and Feng [7], according to grammar characteristics of Twitter, observed its influence on the sentiment classification, considering forwarding messages, labels, links, punctuation, and exclamation marks, etc. Joshi [8] and others devised a sentiment analyzer to analyze and calculate microblog sentiment. Domestically, the study of microblog has emerged, but lack of further and advanced research. Basically it still adopts the traditional text analysis methods and it is short of depth analysis of features of micro blog, meanwhile, theory system is still not standard.

With the rapid development of microblog and the sharp increase of microblog users, the sentiment analysis for microblog should become a research hotspot with business, economic and cultural value.

3   Evaluation Task Analysis

Evaluation object is the micro blog provided by the organizers, including 20 topics and each topic has about 1000 items. Task 1 is to determine each sentence in micro blog is an opinion sentence or a non-opinion one. On the basis of task 1, task 2 is to judge sentiment orientation of the opinion sentence in task 1, including positive, negative and neutral. According to these two tasks, we first analyzed the sample text, and implemented the specific task decomposition.

3.1   Opinion Sentence Extraction

First we can consider extraction task of opinion sentences as a machine learning task, which is on how to make use of the existing micro blog sample to do manual label and feature extraction, construct model with the corresponding machine learning method, and then use the generated model to predict the test set.

According to the rules in NLP&CC '2012, opinion sentence does not include the sentences of sentiment self-expression, for example, "I am very happy.", defined by evaluation, this sentence is sentimental but not an opinion sentence. Opinion sentence defined by evaluation is confined to the evaluation of other objects, not including the inner self sentiment. So we have to design the corresponding rules to filter out this kind of sentence patterns. Based on the characteristics of micro blog corpus, we have carried out three steps to pre-process micro blog corpus. The first step is to remove the topic labels. The second step is to determine Chinese word segmentation. The last step is to filter self sentiment sentences by rules. Then as for the filtered sentences, we extract features, use the training set to train SVM model and predict the test set, and get the results of opinion sentences.

This article uses the word segmentation cloud services (research version) supplied by HYLANDA corp. Due to the input and output of results as XML format, it is very suitable for evaluating the processing of corpus. After word segmentation, we first filter subjective expressive sentence from its results in line with the requirements of opinion sentence identification.

Finally, we extract nine features as a feature set to judge opinion sentences, such as whether to contain an emoticon, a sentiment word, number of sentimental words, an exclamation point or a question mark, a consecutive exclamation mark or a question mark, inversion words, a degree adverb, a modal particle, and the network language, etc.

3.2   Sentiment Orientation Analysis

Task 2 is to determine sentiment orientation of micro blog, including positive, negative and neutral. Evaluation of this task is based on task 1.

We had a feature selection of sentiment classification mainly on the basis of the feature of sentiment words in combination with the characteristics of the micro blog. There are seven features mainly considered, such as the number of positive and negative emoticons, number of positive and negative sentiment words, the existence and non-exsistence of inversion word (the premise: the word should be in front of sentiment words), question mark and continuous question marks, etc.

First is manual labeling training. Sentiment polarities are divided into positive, negative and neutral. It is observed that the considered neutral micro blogs generally do not contain the sentiment words. Second, by using SVM classifier for training micro blog of three sentimental polarities, the corresponding model is generated. Finally, with the classification model, the public test set provided by the organization can be predicted.

4   Experimental Results

On the basis of some existing sentiment lexicons (such as the sentiment analysis words set in "Hownet", "Tongyici Cilin" provided by HIT IR-Lab), we extract a basic polarity vocabulary of 7926 words, 1993 words for positive sentiment and 5936 words for negative sentiment. In addition, we establish a degree adverb lexicon and a polarity shifting word lexicon. The adverb lexicon mainly collects 219 Chinese degree level words in the sentiment analysis words set in "Hownet". Due to the relatively limited number of polarity shifting words, the polarity shifting word lexicon is constructed mainly through manual collection and develops with the help of "Hownet" and "Tongyici Cilin ".

Based on this, we also extend the existing sentiment lexicons, such as increasing the cyberword: 51 for positive and 405 for negative, and increasing expression symbol lexicon: 84 for positive and 46 for negative, so as to solve the problem that the current word segmentation system can't distinguish some network language and emoticons. Moreover, there are modal particles and subjective word lexicons, the former is given that the tone of the users would affect the judgment of microblog opinion sentence; and the latter can help to filter out the sentences that self-sentiment expressing sentences do not belong to the opinion sentences, according to the evaluation sets.

4.1   Opinion Sentence Extraction Experiment

(1) Training set construction and training model generation

Training set is constructed by extracting the features from microblog corpus about 1219 microblogs labeled manually, and then converting them into SVM training format, including the following steps:

◆   Extraction of the features of network language emoticons

The part of the work is to extract network language and emoticons from the manual labeled corpus of microblogs. The present word segmentation technology is not able to identify the network language and emoticons, therefore it should be done before word segmentation. The way to extract is to do text matching consulting the content of the network language lexicon and network emoticons lexicon, recording the corresponding features whether being contained or not, and the number of occurrences.

◆   Word segmentation

Word segmentation includes the following steps:

1) to convert the corpus that needs to be segmented into XML format in accordance with HYLANDA corp.'s cloud segmentation rules, and to set the corresponding parameters;

2) to request HYLANDA corp.'s cloud segmentation word API to operate on segmentation;

3) to obtain word segmentation results and save them.

◆   Extraction of features from the segmentation results, and training set generation

This part of the work is to use the XML parsing technology to analyze segmentation results, extract features from segmentation results according to the existing sentiment lexicon, and convert them into the format that can be trained by SVM. We label 0 and 1 for the features whether being contained or not, here 0 for non-opinion sentences and 1for opinion sentences. At this point, we get a training set containing 1219 data.

◆   Training model generation

By using SVM classifier to train the acquired training set, the training model is generated.

(2)Test set construction and results

Test set construction is similar to the previous process. First of all, the predicted microblogs are preprocessed. In addition, to predict microblog corpus also needs word segmentation. It converts into the corresponding format, and then predicts it by using the previously generated training model. We respectively predict 20 themes of microblog and 20000 sentences, and the results obtained are shown in table 1.

Table 1. The evaluation results of task 1

Micro-average			Macro-average		
Precision	Recall	F-Measure	Precision	Recall	F-Measure
0.645	0.959	0.772	0.649	0.960	0.770

The evaluation results of the task in NLP&CC'2012 rank in top 3 in all evaluation teams, the performance on the Recall is particularly great. The reason of our good performance is that we carried out effective sentiment lexicon expansion as well as the relevant preprocessing, which make the results more comprehensive.

4.2   Sentiment Orientation Analysis Experiment on Microblogs

This task is to determine sentiment orientation of microblogs, including positive, negative and neutral. Evaluation of this task is based on a task 1, namely to analyze sentiment orientation of the opinion sentences. So before task 2, according to the result of task 1, we need to extract opinion sentences in microblogs as the test set in task 2.

(1) Training set construction and training model generation

In this part, extract 451 microblogs labeled opinion sentences from 1219 microblogs labeled manually as the training corpus. Specific process is familiar with the training set construction in task 1, also including extraction of network language emoticons, word segmentation, feature extraction, and training model generation. At this point, we get the training set containing 451 data, and its model after training.

(2) Test set construction and the results

The part of the work uses the microblogs predicted as opinion sentence in task 1, with reference to the previous method of training set construction to build the test set. We evaluate 20 themes of microblog for sentiment orientation and the results are shown in table 2.

Table 2. The evaluation results of task 2

Micro-average			Macro-average		
Precision	Recall	F-Measure	Precision	Recall	F-Measure
0.804	0.771	0.787	0.809	0.778	0.793

The evaluation results of the task in NLP&CC'2012 rank in top 2 in all evaluation teams. Compared with the results from other units, the Recall is still our advantage. We carried out rich features as well as sentiment sources, which make the results more comprehensive.

5   Conclusion

The social network represented by microblog in recent years made rapid development and sentiment analysis task in microblog attracted people's attention. In the evaluation task, our team makes full use of natural language processing technology and machine learning, as well as optimize feature design and process scheme. At last we obtained the ideal results in the evaluation task 1 and task 2 of NLP&CC'2012. In our future work, we will continue to study especially on social events in microblog discussion, on how to effectively analyze the orientation of events, emotional state recognition and degree of emotion recognition, etc. As time goes on, we can even study the changing process of netizen's sentiment orientation of a social event in the process of spread.

Acknowledgement. This paper was supported by the Zhejiang Provincial Natural Science Foundation of China (grant no. LY13F020007, LY13F020010, Z1110551), the Humanity and Social Science on Young Fund of the Ministry of Education (grant no. 12YJC630170), and the Science and Technology Department of Zhejiang Province of China (grant no. 2011C23075).

References

1. Yu, H., Hatzivassiloglou, V.: Towards Answering Opinion Questions: Separating Facts from Opinions and Identifying the Polarity of Opinion Sentences. In: Proceedings of EMNLP 2003, pp. 129–136 (2003)
2. Riloff, E., Wiebe, J., Phillips, W.: Exploiting Subjectivity Classification to Improve Information Extraction. In: Proceedings of AAAI 2005, pp. 1106–1111 (2005)
3. Toprak, C., Gurevych, I.: Document Level Subjectivity Classification Experiments in DEFT'09 Challenge. In: Proceedings of the DEFT 2009 Text Mining Challenge, pp. 89–97 (2009)
4. Finn, A., Kushmerick, N., Smyth, B.: Genre Classification and Domain Transfer for Information Filtering. In: Proceedings of the 24th BCS-IRSG European Colloquium on Information Retrieval Research: Advances in Information Retrieval, pp. 353–362 (2002)
5. Pang, B., Lee, L., Vaithyanathan, S.: Thumbs up?: Sentiment Classification using Machine Learning Techniques. In: Proceedings of EMNLP 2002, pp. 79–86 (2002)
6. Go, A., Bhayani, R., Huang, L.: Twitter sentiment classification using distant supervision. Technical report, Stanford (2009)
7. Barbosa, L., Feng, J.: Robust sentiment detection on twitter from biased and noisy data. In: Proceedings of the 23rd International Conference on Computational Linguistics, pp. 36–44 (2010)
8. Joshi, A., Balamurali, A.R., Bhattacharyya, P., Mohanty, R.: C-Feel-It: A Sentiment Analyzer for Micro-blogs. In: Proceedings of ACL 2011, pp. 127–132 (2011)

Research on the Opinion Mining System for Massive Social Media Data

Lijun Zhao, Yingjie Ren, Ju Wang, Lingsheng Meng, and Cunlu Zou

Technology Strategy & Development Department, Neusoft Corporation, China
{zhaolj,renyj,wang-ju,menglsh,zou.cl}@neusoft.com

Abstract. The authors are supposed to discover the valuable public opinions based on the massive social media data (the comments data, social relation data and location data collected from social website like twitter), so that it could help users to make better decisions during shopping. In order to solve this problem, the authors used micro-blog data collected from Sina as an example and proposed an opinion mining system based on the distributed computing system (Hadoop and related projects). This system was designed for a general purpose. It is not only for the restaurant area but also for the other fields like electronic products.

Keywords: big data, sentiment analysis of micro-blog, text classification, topic search, data deduplication.

1 Introduction

Large and complex data is being produced everyday in various areas such as electronic business, health care, geographic information and so on. The amount of social media data is increasing dramatically due to the growth of social network applications (e.g. Sina micro-blog). According to the data published by Sina, the number of users in Sina micro-blog exceeds 500 million (a 74% increase year-on-year) and the number of active users is about 50 million by the end of November 2013[1]. Social media data is semi-structured, non-relational and may not have a well defined schema. In order to process these data automatically and assist making market decisions, it typically requires statistician, mathematician and data mining expert to construct the data model by using nature language processing and semantic analysis techniques. This could be a tough task since the data is large, noisy and time-sensitive.

The opinion mining research and sentiment analysis are hot research topics. This paper analyzed the Sina Micro-blog data by using distributed computing techniques to capture, filter and classify the data in real-time. This solution could be applied on enterprise marketing management by assisting the marketing decision according to the public opinions related to specific brands. On the other side, it could also help individual consumers to make right shopping decisions by filtering out the paid posters.

G. Zhou et al. (Eds.): NLPCC 2013, CCIS 400, pp. 424–431, 2013.
© Springer-Verlag Berlin Heidelberg 2013

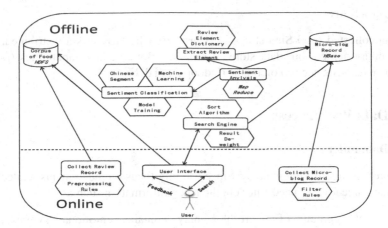

Fig. 1. System architecture

Fig.1 displays the architecture of the opinion mining system. The system collects data of reviews from the DianPing Web (The web site for sharing comments to restaurants in China http://www.dianping.com) as training data stored in a distributed file system (HDFS). The micro-blog data collected from Sina is stored in a NoSQL database (HBase). The algorithm of segmentation, text classification and distributed computing is used for sentiment analysis. The consumer could find the public opinions to any restaurants via the search engine. In addition, the idea of crowd sourcing is applied, the user could also correct the sentiment analysis results and this could improve the system performance and accuracy.

2   Social Media Data Capture

Currently, about 100 million micro-blogs are created in Sina everyday. It contains huge information about personal views.   The purpose of this paper is to dig out the public opinions hide in the micro-blog based on the sentiment analysis techniques.

2.1   Data Capture

The open API provided by Sina is used to collect the micro-blog. There are several tips for using these open APIs.

- The   OAuth2.0   used   for   authorize   that   requires   CLIENT_ID   and CLIENT_SECRET. These keys can be obtained by creating an application in Sina.
- A sleep interval has to be set after each request otherwise it will be blocked if the request frequency exceeds the limitation.
- The AccessToken, which is used for authorize, expired periodically. The Selenium toolbox is used to simulate the user operation for requesting a new AccessToken. The Hudson is also used to set the timed task based on the expiring information, so that the AcessToken is refreshed automatically without manual interruption.

2.2   Data Store

The data collected from Sina stores in HBase. Apache HBase is a distributed, scalable, column-oriented, big data store. It provides Bigtable-like capabilities (random, real time read/write access) on top of Hadoop and HDFS.

3   Data Pre-Process

3.1   Data Filter

The content of micro-blog is noisy. Since we only focus on the contents related to the emotional tendency, we need filter out the noisy information such as:

1. The whole content of micro-blog only contains emotional symbols, tags, @someone, url and so on, are removed from database.
2. The micro-blogs that have irrelevant words or symbols are filtered by regular-expression. For example,

    " #翠峰苑火锅#黄浦路的翠峰苑还不错哦 开心]@小王 我在http://t.cn/HJK2KD"

    " @小王 我在http://t.cn/HJK2KD" is removed since it is irrelevant to the sentiment analysis.

3.2   Data Transformation

Because of the complex coding background of Chinese character, conversions from traditional to simple, from Single byte to Double byte are applied before word segmentation process.

3.3   Word Segmentation

Word segmentation is the fundamental for Chinese process. There are two kinds of methods for word segmentation, one is based on the grammar rule and the other one is based on the statistics. The method based on the statistics requires a large corpus which is hard and expensive to collect. For this reason, this paper used grammar rule method for word segmentation. Three rules are used in order:

1. Maximum matching, apply greedy algorithm to choose the longest words.
2. Maximum average, choose the biggest average value of word length
3. Minimum variance, choose the smallest variance value of word length.

4   Sentiment Analysis

This paper describes how to find public opinions (positive, neutral and negative) related to a specific restaurant. The sentiment analysis method used in this paper is based on the supervised machine learning algorithm.

4.1 Naïve-Bayes Classification Model

Naïve-Bayes classification algorithm[2] estimates the probability distribution of words based on the assumption that every word is independent[3]. Although this assumption is incorrect, Naïve-bayes algorithm has been applied in many business scenarios[4][5] since it is easy to be modified and stable.

Supposed we have a feature set (or phrases) $W = \{w_1, w_2, \cdots, w_n\}$ and a document set $D = \{d_1, d_2, d_3, \cdots, d_k\}$. Each Document can be labeled as one of m classes $c = \{1, 2, \cdots, m\}$. Naïve-Bayes classification estimates the parameters $\vec{\theta} = \{\theta_{c1}, \theta_{c2}, \cdots, \theta_{cn}\}$ which θ_{ci} is the probability that feature i occurs in class c and satisfies $\sum_i \theta_{ci} = 1$. The probability of a document can be described as:

$$p(d|\vec{\theta}) = \frac{(\sum_i f_i)!}{\prod_i f_i!} \prod_i (\theta_{ci})^{f_i} \tag{1}$$

f_i is the occurrence frequency of feature i. The classification of document can be obtained by using minimum error method[6]:

$$l(d) = \text{argmax}_c \left[\log p(\vec{\theta}) + \sum_i f_i \log \theta_{ci} \right] \tag{2}$$

$$= \text{argmax}_c [b_c + \sum_i f_i w_{ci}] \tag{3}$$

b_c is the classification threshold, w_{ci} is the weight that feature i occurs in class c.

4.2 Feature Extraction

From the equation (3), Naïve-Bayes estimates the occurrence probability of features in a specific class and use this parameter to estimate the class probability of a document. Feature extraction is very important during the process of Naïve-bayes. If the whole vocabulary is used as features, it would cost more time for the model training and the accuracy would be affected if the over fitting problem occurs.

In this paper, the features are initially extracted from sentiment dictionaries, that one is HowNet and the other one is NTUSD from Taiwan University. The emotional symbols from Sina Micro-blog are also collected. In this step, 26902 unique sentiment words are collected. However, there is a limitation for these sentiment words since the rapid growing of the new sentiment vocabulary especially in the environment of internet. Therefore a method that could automatically collect, update and extend the sentiment features is required. The common method for automatically collecting sentiment words is based on the sentiment word seeds, massive corpus and iteratively computing the Pointwise Mutual Information (PMI) between candidate words and seed words. The problem for this kind of method is that the complexity of computing dramatically increases with the number of iteration, and the threshold of each iteration depends on the prior knowledge and is hard to be determined.

To solve this problem, this paper calculates the PMI between feature and class label instead, and the slope of PMI values is used to extract features. 400 thousands review data with rating labels was collected from DianPing website as corpus, i.e.

<4,瑞福园,朋友们对这家店的映像真的很好我也就来看看没想到 真的是好吃 好看呢客人那么多 服务还不错环境也不错非常喜欢>

The number 4 represents the rating levels (from 1 to 5, negative to positive), and the rest is the detailed comment description about the service, environment and so on. After segmentation, the PMI can be calculated by using following equation:

$$I(t, c) = \log \frac{p(t \wedge c)}{p(t) \times p(c)} \tag{4}$$

$p(t \wedge c)$ is the co-occurrence frequency of word t and class c, $p(t)$ is the occurrence frequency of word t, $p(c)$ is the occurrence frequency of class c. From the experiment, the rating levels of sentiment words are highly correlated with the PMI values calculated in equation (4), for example:

大骗子,3.360147741333341,2.207347516687106,0.4764436162124497,0.0,0.0,-1.44185209274292

拾金不
昧,0.0,0.0,0.20465547507840182,0.3010152255720754,1.3918172978557635,0.5935808420181274

The first 5 numbers after a sentiment word are the PMI values for different rating levels (1-5), and the sixth number is the slope of PMI values. From the results, one can easily find that the slopes of positive sentiment words are great than 0, and the slopes of negative sentiment words are smaller than 0. According to these results, features can be determined by using slope values (greater than 0.12 and smaller than minus 0.2 used in this paper). In addition, the frequency of word is also considered, the sentiment words that only occur in 2 classes or less are removed from candidates.

By using this method, 20982 sentiment words were obtained. After removed the words already occurred in sentiment dictionaries, the actual number of new sentiment words is 17081. The classification accuracy was compared with different feature set (based on sentiment dictionary and PMI extraction method).The experiment result shows that, by incorporating the features extracted from the PMI method, the strict accuracy (the predicated class label is exactly same as the actual label) increases from 48.64% to 54.75% (increased about 6%), and the loose accuracy (with fault tolerance 1) increases from 84.59% to 93.05% (increased about 10%).

4.3   Model Training

Since the training set is large (400 thousands comments collected in a week), the traditional model training method cannot be processed in a reasonable time. In this paper, distributed computing techniques are adopted. The Mahout toolbox[7][8], which is implemented on the top of Hadoop, is used for training the Bayes model. The method of training Bayes Model can be described as below:

Suppose vector $\vec{d} = (\vec{d_1}, \vec{d_2}, \cdots, \vec{d_n})$ is the document set, $\vec{d_n}$ is a document. d_{ij} is the frequency of feature i occurring in document j. suppose $\vec{y} = (y_1, y_2, \cdots, y_n)$ is class label set, then the feature weight can be calculated by following steps:

1. $TF_{ij} = \log(d_{ij} + 1)$ (calculate term frequency)
2. $TFIDF_{ij} = TF_{ij} \times \log \frac{\sum_k 1}{\sum_k \delta_{ik}}$ (calculate term frequency inverse document frequency)

3. $\text{Norm\_TFIDF}_{ij} = \frac{\text{TFIDF}_{ij}}{\sqrt{\sum_k(\text{TFIDF}_{ij})^2}}$ (normalize the TFIDF)

4. $\hat{\theta}_{ci} = \frac{\sum_{j:y_j=c} d_{ij} + \alpha_i}{\sum_{j:y_j=c} \sum_k d_{kj} + \alpha}$ (calculate the probability that feature i occurs in class c)

5. $w_{ci} = \log \hat{\theta}_{ci}$ (normalize the probability parameter with log operation)

6. $\text{Norm\_w}_{ci} = \frac{w_{ci}}{\sum_i w_{ci}}$ (normalize the weight)

7. $l(t) = \arg\max_c \sum_i (t_i \times \text{Norm\_w}_{ci})$ (calculate the class label)

The MapReduce architecture is applied in Mahout toolbox for distributed computing, and 5 iterations are required for training the model:

- First iteration: segment the context, filter the stop words and extract the feature words in the Map Step.
- Second iteration: calculate the TF and IDF values respectively
- Third iteration: calculate the TFIDF values for each feature.
- Forth iteration: calculate the sum of feature weight.
- fifth iteration: calculate the normalized feature weight

4.4   Sentiment Analysis

The trained Bayes model is implemented via distributed computing. The Sina micro-blog data stored in HBase can be directly adopted as data input in the distributed computing (data stored in HBase is divided into different regions, data in one region is processed in one Map job). In the Map step, the content for micro-blog is extracted. Segmentation, feature extraction, and Bayes classification processes are applied for data analysis then. In order to improve the performance, incremental calculation is applied for avoid repeated computing by using filter function provided by HBase.

5   Vertical Search

5.1   Review Elements Extraction

The micro-blog related to the restaurant review can be determined by the food description. The key words related to the restaurant review are collected, e.g. menu, the material of food. In addition, the words occurred in DianPing website frequently are also used, such as "delicious", "reasonable price". Each key word is assigned with a weight, and the weight of micro-blog is calculated as the sum of weights. The weight is a factor to determine the order of search results.

5.2   Removal of Duplication

The users in Sina commonly use copy and paste to propagate the messages they like, and it leads to a duplication problem. How to detect the duplication is a big problem since the computing complexity especially when the data set is large. In this paper, the simhash algorithm[9][10] is adopted. The main idea of simhash is to map a high dimensional feature space to a f-bit fingerprint, and then apply fingerprint comparisons between documents. The MapReduce architecture is also used for cluster computing, 36.67% micro-blogs are detected as redundant.

5.3   Ranking Algorithm

The ranking of the search result is mainly determined by 3 factors: the influence, the rating correlation and temporality. The influence of a micro-blog is calculated by using the number of reply, forward and the author's followers. The rating correlation is determined by the weight of review key words. For the temporality, the latest micro-blogs are preferred since the rating of a restaurant could be changed.

5.4   Search Engine

The open source Apache Solr search engine is adopted in this application. Solr provides REST API, so that the user can send a request via HTTP POST or GET protocol. Not only the contents of micro-blog are incorporated into the search engine for index, the related factors such as publish time, number of followers, replies, forwards are also used for ranking weight calculation.

6   The Opinion Mining System

The Fig. 2. shows the opinion mining System, user can search a restaurant name in the textbox. The search result displays the micro-blogs related to this restaurant and also the predicated rating values. By adopting the idea of crowd sourcing, the predicated rating values can be corrected by the users, so that the feedback from users can be applied on the model training for improving the accuracy. The left side shows the estimated restaurant score and statistical information for different rating levels.

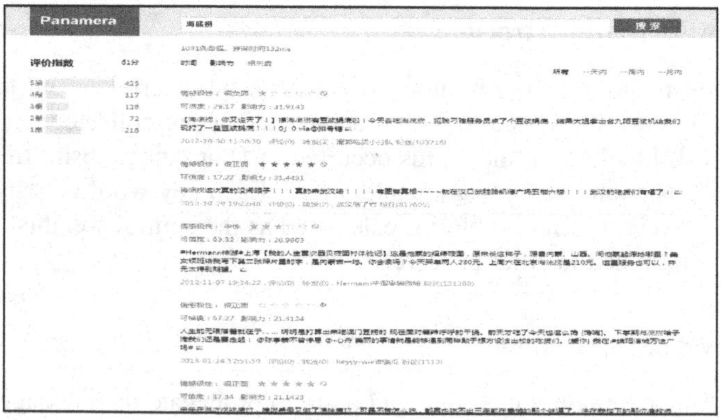

Fig. 2. The Opinion Mining System

7   Conclusion

This paper demonstrates that the opinion mining system can be implemented in the restaurant field based on the big data techniques (Hadoop and related projects). It could be easily adopted into other fields (i.e. electronic product) by changing the data source. By adopting the idea of crowd sourcing, the accuracy can be automatically improved with the growth of corpus provided by the feedback system, so that it would assist enterprise and consumer making better decisions according to the public views.

Acknowledgement. We thank the National Basic Research Program of China (973 Program) (2012CB724107) for the support of this research. Specially thank Chang-hong Liu for the consultation of this project.

References

1. Sina Data Statistical Information,
   http://www.199it.com/archives/95537.html
2. Klawonn, F., Angelov, P.: Evolving Extended Naive Bayes Classifiers. In: Data Mining Workshops, pp. 643–647 (2006)
3. Kim, S.-B., Han, K.-S., Rim, H.-C., Myaeng, S.H.: Some Effective Techniques for Naive Bayes Text Classification. Knowledge and Data Engineering 11(18), 1457–1466 (2006)
4. Huang, J., Wan, Y.: School of Remote Sensing and Information Engineering. Wuhan University, Wuhan 430079; China, P.R.: Using Bayesian Networks for Automobile Diagnosis. In: Proceedings of 6th International Symposium on Test and Measurement, vol. 7 (2005)
5. Pratap, A., Kanimozhiselvi, C.S.: Application of Naive Bayes dichotomizer supported with expected risk and discriminant functions in clinical decisions — Case study. In: Advanced Computing (ICoAC), pp. 1–4 (2012)
6. Chou, W., Li, L.: A minimum classification error (MCE) framework for generalized linear classifier in machine learning for text categorization/retrieval. Machine Learning and Applications, 26–33 (2004)
7. Ingersoll, G.: Introducing Apache Mahout (2011), http://ibm.com (last update) (retrieved September 13, 2011)
8. Slobojan, R.: Apache Mahout: Highly Scalable Machine Learning Algorithms (2011), http://infoq.com (last update) (retrieved September 13, 2011)
9. Sadowski, C., Levin, G.: Simhash: Hash-based similarity detection. Technical report, Google (2007)
10. Uddin, M.S., Roy, C.K., Schneider, K.A., Hindle, A.: On the Effectiveness of Simhash for Detecting Near-Miss Clones in Large Scale Software Systems. In: Reverse Engineering (WCRE), pp. 13–22 (2011)

Grammatical Phrase-Level Opinion Target Extraction on Chinese Microblog Messages

Haochen Zhang, Yiqun Liu, Min Zhang, and Shaoping Ma*

State Key Laboratory of Intelligent Technology and Systems,
Tsinghua National Laboratory for Information Science and Technology,
Department of Computer Science and Technology,
Tsinghua University, Beijing 100084, China
zhang-hc10@mails.tsinghua.edu.cn, {yiqunliu,z-m,msp}@tsinghua.edu.cn

Abstract. Microblog is one of the most widely used web applications. Weibo, which is a microblog service in China, produces plenty of opinionated messages every second. Sentiment analysis on Chinese Weibo impacts many aspects of business and politics. In this work, we attempt to address the opinion target extraction, which is one of the most important aspects of sentiment analysis. We propose a unified approach that concentrates on phrase-level target extraction. We assume that a target is represented as a subgraph of the sentence's dependency tree and define the grammatical relations that point to the target word as **TAR-RELs**. We conduct the extraction by classifying grammatical relations with a cost-sensitive classifier that enhances performance of unbalanced data and figuring out the target subgraph by connecting and recovering **TAR-REL**s. Then we prune the noisy targets by empirically summarized rules. The evaluation results indicate that our approach is effective to the phrase-level target extraction on Chinese microblog messages.

Keywords: sentiment analysis, opinion target, phrase-level target extraction, grammatical relation.

1 Introduction

Opinion targets are the entities and the properties that carry authors' opinion. In product review corpus, target is also known as aspect or feature of the product. Detecting and extracting these targets is one of the most important steps to analyze the authors' sentiment. It helps to figure out the entities that users are discussing.

Opinion targets often contain attributives or modifiers. For instance, 'screen' is a target but too ambiguous. Author often describes it with some modifiers like 'iPad screen' or 'computer screen'. These phrases are indeed the complete opinion targets.

---

* This work was supported by Natural Science Foundation (60903107, 61073071), National High Technology Research and Development (863) Program (2011AA01A207). This work has been done at the NUS–Tsinghua EXtreme search centre (NExT).

G. Zhou et al. (Eds.): NLPCC 2013, CCIS 400, pp. 432–439, 2013.
© Springer-Verlag Berlin Heidelberg 2013

However, some existing work ignores the completeness of target and only focuses on word-level target extraction [1–5]. Meanwhile, the other work addresses completing phrase-level targets by extending candidates, which is difficult to control the boundaries of the targets.

We proposed a extraction approach that unifies discovering candidates and extending them to the phrase-level target. It is based on the assumption that a phrase-level target is the subgraph of the sentence's dependency tree. We figure out the subgraph by classifying grammatical relations to **TAR-REL**s and **O-REL**s and connecting **TAR-REL**s.

By participating the evaluation task of the 2nd Conference on Natural Language Processing & Chinese Computing(NLP&CC 2013), our approach shows the capacity to extract phrase-level opinion targets from Chinese microblog messages.

2   Related Work

Opinion target extraction is one of the most important aspects of sentiment analysis, which has been investigated by many researchers. There are mainly several different types of approaches, which are summarized as follow:

1. Qin et al. [1] and Liu et al. [6] propose iterative extraction approaches that adopt targets and opinions to expand each other iteratively.
2. Sayeed et al. [3] investigates the structured information and proposes a word-level extraction approach that introduces syntactic features. Ku et al. [7] concentrates on morphological structures of Chinese content and adopts SVM and CRFs to classify words and identify targets.
3. Several work [6, 8] addresses the target extraction in multilingual corpus. They attempt to employ language characteristics to enhance performance on both language corpus.
4. Probabilistic models, especially topic models, are employed to extract targets [2, 4, 5]. These approaches performance well and are domain-independent. However, phrase-level target and informal corpus cannot be well solved.

In this work, we address this problem by a grammatical method since we want to discover phrase-level target directly from dependency tree of the sentence.

3   Problem Definition

In this work, we concentrate on the completeness of the target. The completeness of the target extraction requires more efforts on detecting the targets' boundary, which encloses all attributives and descriptive modifiers of the targets. By statistics on the annotated dataset, there are average 2.02 segmented words in a target and only 35% targets consist of only one word. Therefore completeness is quite significant to the target extraction.

As illustrated in Figure 1, nodes of the dependency tree correspond to words of the sentence, and directed edges correspond to grammatical relations. Each

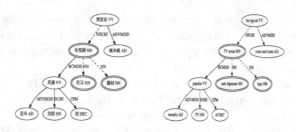

(a) 近来风靡荧屏的抗日题
材电视剧越来越类型化。

(b) The anti-Japanese type
TV series that are popular
on TV are more and more
typical.

Fig. 1. Illustration of dependency tree and subgraph-based target

relation has a grammatical relation type. The start word of directed edge is named as governor, while the end word is named as dependent.

We intuitively proposed an assumption that a target is the subgraph of the dependency tree, which is illustrated in Figure 1–(a). The double-circle nodes correspond to words inside the target. Therefore, phrase-level target extraction is then converted to figuring out the target subgraph from the dependency tree.

To figure out expected subgraphs, we classify the directed edges, i.e. the grammatical relations. All relations whose dependents belong to targets are defined as **TAR-REL**, while other relations are defined as **O-REL**. In Figure 1, all **TAR-REL**s are represented in dashed lines.

4   Approach

4.1   Word-Level Sentimental Signal

Before target extraction, we first estimate sentimental signal of each word. Cui *et al.* [9] proposed a graph-based approach that propagates the sentimental signal within the co-occurrence graph and assigns word a positive score and a negative score after the propagation is convergent. The sentimental signal then is estimated by the average of the positive score and the negative score.

4.2   Grammatical Relations Classification

In this section, we explain how to classify grammatical relations by a supervised cost-sensitive learning method.

We adopt nine features, which consist of three categories: general features, sentimental features and grammatical features. These features are extracted from the relation and its corresponding words, which are described in detail as follow:

1. **General Feature:** General features consist of dependent's location (indexed by segmented tokens and denoted as Loc_{dep}), signal of whether dependent

is a named-entity (denoted as NE_{dep}) and dependent and governor's word frequency (denoted as $Freq_{dep}$ and $Freq_{gov}$).

2. **Sentimental Feature:** Sentimental features are dependent and governor's sentimental signals estimated by graph-based propagation. We intuitively assume that targets carry more opinion than those functional or descriptive expressions. They are denoted as $Senti_{dep}$ and $Senti_{gov}$.

3. **Grammatical Feature:** We adopt the relation's dependency type, dependent's POS tag and governor's POS tag as the grammatical features (denoted as Rel, POS_{dep} and POS_{gov}). Grammatical information, especially POS tags, is widely adopted to extract opinion targets.

We employ the Naïve Bayes, one of the most widely adopted classifiers, as the base classifier taking all the above features to classify the relations.

Notice that the **TAR-REL**s and **O-REL**s are not balanced, where there are over 10 times more **O-REL**s. We need a proper boosting meta-algorithm to enhance the performance. MetaCost [10] is a state-of-the-art cost-sensitive algorithm that wraps an arbitrary base classifier. It relabels the result of a base classifier according to Bayes optimal prediction that reduces the conditional risk. By specifying different cost, we actually give a bias on a specific class. In this work, cost of false **TAR-REL**s is assigned to 10 empirically and cost of false **O-REL**s is assigned to 1. Greater cost of false **TAR-REL**s results in bias on the **TAR-REL** class and finally produces more target candidates.

4.3   Phrase-Level Target Candidates

We connect the tagged relations to generate phrase-level target subgraphs. As illustrated by Figure 1, adjacent **TAR-REL** relations are assembled to one target subgraph, and all dependents within this subgraph generate the target. Notice that target excludes the governor of the root relation.

Since these relations are classified independently, targets are probably partially misclassified. we summarize two types of misclassification and reclassify these relations to **TAR-REL**s. We distinguish the misclassification with the following criteria.

1. The **O-REL** that is surrounded by **TAR-REL**s. The governor and dependent of this relation both belong to other two **TAR-REL** relations. Figure 2–(a) illustrates this type of misclassification. E2 is surrounded by **TAR-REL**s and is reclassified as **TAR-REL**. Notice that E5 does not satisfy this criterion and remains **O-REL**.

2. The **O-REL** whose dependent is a leaf node and governor is within a no-less-than-3-word target graph. Figure 2–(b) illustrates this type of misclassification. N1, N2, N4 and N5 construct a 4-word target and N3 is a leaf node. Thus E2 is reclassified as **TAR-REL**.

Afterward, we achieve target subgraphs represented in tree structures. Dependents of relations inside a subgraph generate a target candidate.

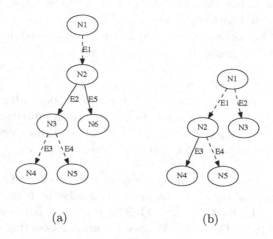

(a)   (b)

Fig. 2. Illustration of two different misclassification types. Solid and dashed lines represent original **O-REL** and **TAR-REL** respectively.

4.4   Rule-Based Pruning

We propose grammatical rules and textual rules to prune these noises after reviewing the dataset and empirical summarization.

The grammatical rules are based on our observation of microblog messages. Microblog messages are more informal and less objective. Therefore subjectives in opinionated microblog sentences are quite more probable to be opinion targets comparing to co-occurred objectives or predicatives, which helps us to establish the grammatical rule: Given a governor and all relations governed by it, if there exists subjective relation and the corresponding dependent is tagged as target, then all targets connected to the governor by objective/predicative relations are pruned.

Figure 3 illustrates one typical case adopting this rule. The double circle nodes are extracted by previous steps. Both subjective and objective are recognized as targets. By following our rule, the objective is pruned, illustrated as dashed border. In this work, we take {**NSUBJ, TOP**} as subjective relations and {**DOBJ, LOBJ, POBJ, ATTR**} as objective/predicative relations.

We also summarize several textual rules by conducting overview of the false targets. These textual rules are presented as follow.

1. If there is only one word in the target, the word must be noun or pronoun.
2. Target's length must be less than $0.8L_{clause}$, where L_{clause} is the length of the clause.
3. Target must be continuously written in the message. As we extract targets from dependency tree, the target may not sequentially adjacent.

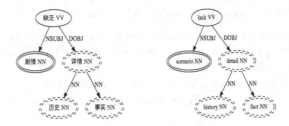

(a) 剧情缺乏详细历史事实。(b) The scenario lacks details of history fact.

Fig. 3. Illustration of typical case that follows grammatical rule

4.5 Target Polarity Classification

As we have estimated word-level sentimental signal in previous sections, we take the average score of all words' sentiment scores within the target as the target's lexicon sentimental score. Meanwhile, we take the sentimental signal of the adjacent adjective of the target as the target's modifier sentimental score.

Finally we take the signal with maximum absolute value between lexicon sentimental score and modifier sentimental score. If the signal is greater than upper threshold or less than lower threshold, the target is classified as positive or negative respectively. Otherwise, the target is classified as neutral (Other). In this work, upper and lower threshold are both assigned to 0.

5 Experiment

We conduct our grammatical phrase-level target extraction approach on the Chinese microblog sentiment analysis contest held by the 2nd Conference on Natural Language Processing & Chinese Computing(NLP&CC 2013).

5.1 Dataset

The dataset is provided by contest holder and are crawled from Tencent Weibo. It consists of two parts: one is pre-released smaller dataset with only 2 topics, 200 Weibo messages and 473 sentences, which is employed as training set; the other is contest dataset with 10 topics, 12382 Weibo messages, 27499 sentences and 1000 randomly sampled annotated messages.

In training dataset, all sentences are annotated whether they are opinionated and targets are extracted from the sentences. In contest dataset, randomly sampled messages are annotated whether they are opinionated and only these annotated sentences are required to be processed. Notice that only opinionated sentences contain opinion targets.

5.2   Ground Truth and Evaluation Metrics

The ground truth targets are provided by contest holder. A target is represented as a tuple including target's content, offset of the target within microblog message and target's polarity.

There are two types of evaluation metrics: Strict Evaluation and Lenient Evaluation. Precision, Recall and F_1-measure are employed to evaluate approach performance.

In strict evaluation, extracted targets are correct if and only if their offset, textual content, polarity exactly equal to annotations.

In lenient evaluation, extracted targets do not have to exactly equal to annotated targets. We adopt coverage to estimate the true positive of the precision and recall.

Given any extracted target r and any annotated target r', the coverage $C(r, r')$ between them is defined as:

$$C(r, r') = \begin{cases} \frac{|s \cap s'|}{|s'|} & s \cap s' \neq \emptyset \\ 0 & otherwise \end{cases} \tag{1}$$

where s and s' is the corresponding range to r and r' respectively. Afterward, the overall coverage between proposed target set and annotated target set is the summation of all extracted target and annotated target pairs' coverage. Taking this coverage as the true positive, we get the lenient precision and recall.

5.3   Evaluation Results

There are two ways to measure evaluation results. Micro-average result is calculated on overall contest dataset directly, while macro-average result is the average performance calculated topically. Notice that micro-average has the bias on performance of topics with more targets.

Table 1. Evaluation results of the grammatical phrase-level target extraction

| Evaluation | Micro-average | | | Macro-average | | |
	Precision	Recall	F_1-measure	Precision	Recall	F_1-measure
Strict	0.202	0.236	0.218	0.200	0.226	0.210
Lenient	0.288	0.340	0.312	0.283	0.323	0.299

Table 1 presents evaluation results on both strict and lenient criteria. The evaluation results are balanced between precision and recall. Furthermore, recall is better than precision in lenient evaluations. This is because we prefer more targets while extracting candidates. Notice that we do not consider pronouns and implicit targets, which hurt the performance on recall.

Our approach does not make significant improvement to lenient evaluation. It is mainly caused by the extraction strategy that we concentrate on the accurate boundaries of the targets, which prunes entirely error cases and partially correct cases equally.

6   Conclusion

We investigate the Chinese microblog messages and propose a grammatical phrase-level target extraction approach. The approach is based on the assumption that a target is the subgraph of the sentence's dependency tree. We figure out the target subgraphs directly by conducting classification of the **TAR-REL**s that connecting the targets. After recovering misclassified relations and pruning with some empirically summarized rules, we finally achieve targets from the microblog corpus.

The evaluation results indicate that our approach is feasible and effective on phrase-level extraction from Chinese microblog corpus. In future, we'd like to continue our research on investigating the extraction with structured information of sentences, attempting to involve contextual grammatical relations, adopting probabilistic model and more effective features for phrase-level target extraction.

Acknowledgments. The NExT Search Centre is supported by the Singapore National Research Foundation and Interactive Digital Media R&D Program Office, MDA under research grant (WBS: R-252-300-001-490).

References

1. Qiu, G., Liu, B., Bu, J., Chen, C.: Opinion Word Expansion and Target Extraction through Double Propagation. Computational Linguistics 37(1), 9–27 (2011)
2. Brody, S., Elhadad, N.: An Unsupervised Aspect-sentiment Model for Online Reviews. In: Brody, S., Elhadad, N. (eds.) HLT 2010, Stroudsburg, PA, USA, pp. 804–812 (2010)
3. Sayeed, A.B., Boyd-Graber, J., Rusk, B., Weinberg, A.: Grammatical Structures for Word-level Sentiment Detection. In: NAACL HLT 2012, Stroudsburg, PA, USA, pp. 667–676 (2012)
4. Mukherjee, A., Liu, B.: Aspect Extraction through Semi-supervised Modeling. In: ACL 2012, Stroudsburg, PA, USA, pp. 339–348 (2012)
5. Lin, C., He, Y.: Joint Sentiment/Topic Model for Sentiment Analysis. In: CIKM 2009, New York, NY, USA, pp. 375–384 (2009)
6. Liu, K., Xu, L., Zhao, J.: Opinion Target Extraction Using Word-based Translation Model. In: EMNLP-CoNLL 2012, Stroudsburg, PA, USA, pp. 1346–1356 (2012)
7. Ku, L.W., Huang, T.H., Chen, H.H.: Using Morphological and Syntactic Structures for Chinese Opinion Analysis. In: EMNLP 2009, Stroudsburg, PA, USA, pp. 1260–1269 (2009)
8. Zhou, X., Wan, X., Xiao, J.: Cross-language Opinion Target Extraction in Review Texts, pp. 1200–1205 (December 2012)
9. Cui, A., Zhang, H., Liu, Y., Zhang, M., Ma, S.: Lexicon-based Sentiment Analysis on Topical Chinese Microblog Messages. In: Semantic Web and Web Science, pp. 333–344. Springer Proceedings in Complexity (2013)
10. Domingos, P.: Metacost: A General Method for Making Classifiers Cost-sensitive. In: KDD 1999, New York, NY, USA, pp. 155–164 (1999)

Simple Yet Effective Method for Entity Linking in Microblog-Genre Text

Qingliang Miao, Huayu Lu, Shu Zhang, and Yao Meng

Fujitsu Research & Development Center CO., LTD,
No. 56 Dong Si Huan Zhong Rd, Chaoyang District, Beijing, China
{qingliang.miao,zhangshu,mengyao}@cn.fujitsu.com,
lvhuayu@gmail.com

Abstract. Semantic analysis microblog data is a challenging, emerging research area. Unlike news text, microblogs pose several new challenges, due to their short, noisy, contextualized and real-time nature. In this paper, we investigate how to link entities in microblog posts with knowledge base and adopt a cascade linking approach. In particular, we first use a mention expansion model to identify all possible entities in the knowledge base for a mention based on a variety of sources. Then we link the mentions with the corresponding entities in the knowledge base by collectively considering lexical matching, popularity probability and textual similarity.

1   Introduction

With the emergence of knowledge base population projects like DBPedia [9] and YAGO [14], more and more large-scale knowledge bases are available. These knowledge bases include rich semantic knowledge about entities, their properties and relationships. Ideally, automatically linking web data with knowledge bases can facilitate many applications such as entity retrieval, advertising and product recommendation. On the other hand, creating links between web data and knowledge bases could enrich the knowledge base as well.

A key technology to implement the above vision is entity linking, which aims to link the mentions in a document with corresponding entities in the knowledge base. Given a mention m, a document d and a knowledge base KB including a set of entities $\{e_1, e_2...e_n\}$, an entity linking system is a function $f: m \rightarrow e_i$ which links mention m with corresponding entity e_i in KB [15]. Figure 1 illustrates the entity linking task. The linking process includes two steps, first identify all the entity candidates that may link with mention "Apple", and then identify which entity should be linked with the mention. The entity linking task, however, can be no-trivial due to the mention ambiguity and variation issues [15].

Recently, microblogs have become an important web data due to its real-time nature. In this paper, we analyze the challenges of entity linking in microblog-genre text and adopt a cascade approach to create links between mentions and entities in knowledge base.

G. Zhou et al. (Eds.): NLPCC 2013, CCIS 400, pp. 440–447, 2013.
© Springer-Verlag Berlin Heidelberg 2013

The rest of the paper is structured as follows. In the following section we review the existing literature. We introduce the proposed approach in section 3. We conduct comparative experiments and present the experiment results in section 4. At last, we conclude the paper with a summary of our work and give our future working directions.

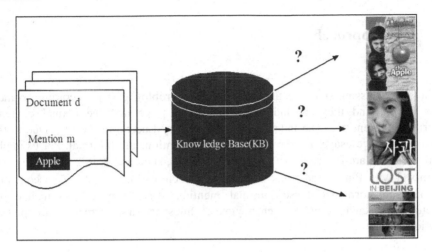

Fig. 1. An example of Entity Linking

2   Related Work

Generally speaking, entity linking is a kind of semantic annotation [6], which is characterized as the dynamic creation of interrelationships between entities in knowledge base and mentions in unstructured or semi-structured documents [5].

In particular, most existing semantic annotation approaches annotate documents with links to Wikipedia or DBPedia. For example, Mihalcea and Csomai [7] first propose Wikify system to use Wikipedia to annotate text. Milne and Witten [8] implement a similar system called Wikipedia Miner, which adopts supervised disambiguation approach using Wikipedia hyperlinks as training data. Han and Sun [15] propose a generative probabilistic model, called entity mention model, which can leverage entity popularity knowledge, name knowledge and context knowledge for the entity linking task. In practical applications, several entity linking systems have been developed [8] [9] [10] [11] [12]. DBpedia Spotlight [10] is a system for automatically annotating text documents with DBpedia URIs. TagMe [9] system adopts a collective disambiguation approach, which computes agreement score of all possible bindings, and uses heuristics to select best target. The disambiguation model of Illinois Wikifier [11] is based on weighted sum of features such as textual similarity and link structure. AIDA [12] is a robust system based on collective disambiguation exploiting the prominence of entities, context similarity between the mention and its candidates, and the coherence among candidate entities for all mentions.

Recently, more and more works have been focusing on entity linking in short informal texts (e.g. tweets) [1][3]. Stephen Guo et al. [2] propose a structural SVM algorithm for entity linking that jointly optimizes mention detection and entity disambiguation. Cassidy et al. [4] mainly test the effects of two tweet context expansion methods, based on tweet authorship and topic-based clustering.

3   The Approach

3.1   Preprocess

In the preprocessing step, we first group each microblog post p_i according to their topic $TP(p_i)$, and then we index the microblog posts and the textual contents describing the entities. The index is implemented by Lucene index API. Due to the creative language usage in microblog posts, the mentions are informal. For example, some mentions are in traditional Chinese characters, such as "鄭州", some mentions are mixed with Pinyin and Chinese characters, such as "fudan大學". Consequently, we have to normalize these informal mentions first. We also normalize the punctuations such as common, French quotes, whitespaces and correct the misspelling mentions if any.

3.2   Knowledge Repository

After preprocessing step, we build a knowledge repository of entities that contains vast amount of name variations of entities such as acronyms, confusable names, spelling variations, nick names etc. We use Wikipedia, BaiduBaike and the Web to build the knowledge repository. In particular, we utilize the following resources to build the knowledge repository.

Redirect Pages

Redirections in Wikipedia and other encyclopedias like BaiduBaike are good indicators for synonyms. For example, Wikipedia page "湖人" redirect to "洛杉矶湖人". In this paper, we use redirect pages to identify alternative names, synonyms, abbreviations, scientific or common terms and alternative spellings etc.

Bold Phrases

The bold phrases in the first paragraph usually summarize name variants of the entity [13], e.g. full names, nick names, alias names etc. For example, in Wikipedia page about "IBM", we could obtain variants such as "国际商业机器股份有限公司", "International Business Machines Corporation" and "万国商用机器公司".

Disambiguation Pages

Disambiguation pages are used for ambiguous entities, which consist of links to Wikipedia pages defining the different meanings of the same mention. They are useful in homonym resolution and help in extracting abbreviations etc. For example, disambiguation page "詹姆斯" contains more than 40 persons such as "詹姆斯·加菲尔德", the twenty-president of the United States and "勒布朗·詹姆斯", American professional basketball player.

Anchor-Entity Association

Anchor links could also be used to trace to which entity the mention links. In this work, we use anchor texts from inter WikiPedia links. In addition, we quantify the strengths of associations between entity and mention pairs using basic statistics. The score of strength is computed as the number of times that mention m links to entity e divided by the total number of anchors with mention m.

Besides the above four sources, we also extract alias from the attributes parts $A(e_i)$ of the given knowledge base. For example, we can obtain alias "京", "Peking" and "Municipality of Beijing" for mention "北京" from the attributes parts of the knowledge base.

3.3 Candidate Generation

In this module, we use heuristics to expand the mentions and obtain all possible variants of the mention from the knowledge repository. Besides the variants expanded by the knowledge repository, we also use contextual information and the Web to expand the mentions. The contextual content of mention usually contains rich information about its entity candidate, especially for abbreviation name mentions. For example, given the following microblog post "北京时间3月12日，2013亚冠联赛小组赛第二轮，广州恒大足球俱乐部客场挑战全北现代，广州恒大首发已经公布". We can identify the entity of all above abbreviations using simple rules, for example, "广州恒大" refers to "广州恒大足球俱乐部".

Even though we expand the mention with knowledge repository and contextual content, we still cannot exhaustively detect all the entity candidates of mention. Therefore, we try to exploit the whole web information for detecting the candidates through web search. Given a mention, we submit it with string "维基百科" or "百度百科" to the Google API and retrieve only the web pages within these encyclopedias. For example, given the mention "詹皇", we submit the queries like "詹皇 百度百科" and retrieve the search result "勒布朗·詹姆斯".

3.4 Microblog Post Expansion

As discussed above microblog-genre text has less disambiguation context, consequently, we have to expand the initial microblog posts. We use two methods to expand microblog posts, namely, keywords based and unambiguous entities based method. In particular, we first extract keywords or unambiguous entities around the mention from initial microblog posts, and then use these keywords or entities to retrieval topical related text from the given microblog post corpus or the web. In this paper, we use normalized Google distance to extract keywords.

$$NGD(x, y) = \frac{\max\{\log f(x), \log f(y)\} - \log f(x, y)}{\log M - \min\{\log f(x), \log f(y)\}} \tag{1}$$

3.5   Entity Resolution

In this section, we introduce the cascade approach for entity resolution. The main goal of the module is to link a mention with a knowledge base (K) entity or NIL. The flow chart of this module is shown in Figure 2.

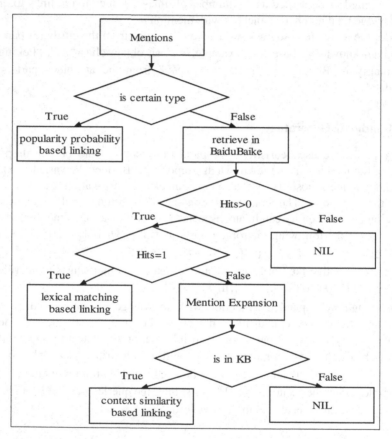

Fig. 2. Flow chart of entity resolution module

The entity resolution module contains four steps. In the first step, we adopt popularity probability to link some specific kind mentions. In microblog post, users usually talk about popular or common entities such as geographic name, teams and players names. For example, mention "北京" means the capital of China in most cases, and "热火" denotes "迈阿密热火队", the professional basketball team based in Miami. Although for some mentions it may be a dangerous bias to prefer popular or common entities, it seemed helpful for entity linking in microblog-genre text. In the second step, we feed mentions to Baidu Baike, and retrieve the results. If the search results do not contain the mention, we think the mention does not exist in the given knowledge base, because the knowledge base is a subset of Baidu Baike encyclopedia. If we find the unique result, we use a lexical matching based method to identify the entity. In the third step, we use the mention expansion module described in section 4.3 to expand a mention, and then we search these entity candidates in the knowledge base. If no candidate exists in the KB, we assign NIL to this mention, otherwise, we adopt a contextual similarity based method to identity the entity in step four. In step four, we use a threshold to determine whether the mention should be linked with an entity or NIL. In this work, we use validation data set to tune the threshold.

4   Experiments

In this section, we report a primary experiment aimed at evaluating the proposed system MSAS.

4.1   Experimental Setup

In this experiment, we use the Chinese microblog entity linking evaluation data sets provided by Natural Language Processing and Chinese Computing Conference[1].

Table 1. The statistics of the dataset

Data Set	Microblog posts	Mentions	Topics
Training data	177	249	12
Test data	787	1249	63

4.2   Experimental Results

In this experiment, we report the experiment results of two systems. The first system MSAS1 expands the initial microblog post by retrieving both the given microblog post corpus and the web, while the second system MSAS2 does not use the web data. The threshold is assigned 0.06 and 0.03 in MSAS1 and MSAS2, respectively. Table 2 and 3 shows the experiment result of two systems. From table 2, we can see that microblog post expansion is useful in contextual similarity based disambiguation. From table 3, we can see NIL detection methods achieve both high precision and recall. Generally speaking, contextual similarity can achieve promising results, but it fails in some cases when the entity candidates are in similar domain. For example, "霸王别姬" can refer to different entity in movie and literature domain. Another example is "凯恩斯", which could refer to the a famous economist "John Maynard Keynes" and a netizen with network name "凯恩斯" who usually publish economic content in his blogs. Some informal mentions are also hard to link, such as "CCAV", "毛总", "周同学".

---

[1] http://tcci.ccf.org.cn/conference/2013/pages/page04_eva.html

Table 2. The overall results on micro-averaged accuracy

System	micro-averaged accuracy
MSAS1	0.9092
MSAS2	0.8995

Table 3. The In-KB linking and NIL linking result on precision, recall and F-measure

System	In-KB results			NIL results		
	Precision	Recall	F1	Precision	Recall	F1
MSAS1	0.8983	0.8812	0.8897	0.9201	0.9383	0.9291
MSAS2	0.8859	0.8670	0.8764	0.9130	0.9333	0.9231

5   Conclusion

In this paper we investigate how to link mentions in microblog posts with knowledge base entities and present a microblog semantic annotation system (MSAS). This system can automatically create links between mentions and entities in knowledge base. In particular, we first build knowledge repository by mining entity knowledge from multiple sources. Second, we develop a mention expansion model to identify all possible entities in the knowledge base. Finally, we employ a divide and conquer strategy to identity the entity in knowledge base or NIL. In addition, we test the effects of microblog context expansion method, based on topic-based retrieval and web search. Experimental results on real world datasets show promising results and demonstrate the proposed system is effective. As a future research, we plan to use more sophisticated mention normalization methods to solve informal name variant issues. For entity disambiguation, we also plan to exploit reasoning with local and global evidence to reach a collective agreement.

References

1. Meij, E., Weerkamp, W., Rijke, M.D.: Adding Semantics to Microblog Posts. In: Proceedings of the Fifth ACM International Conference on Web Search and Data Mining, pp. 563–572 (2012)
2. Guo, S., Chang, M.W., Kıcıman, E.: To Link or Not to Link? A Study on End-to-End Tweet Entity Linking. In: Proceedings of the 2013 Conference of the North American Chapter of the Association for Computational Linguistics: Human Language Technologies (2013)
3. Derczynski, L., Maynard, D., Aswani, N., Bontcheva, K.: Microblog-Genre Noise and Impact on Semantic Annotation Accuracy. In: Proceedings of the 24th ACM Conference on Hypertext and Social Media, pp. 21–30 (2013)
4. Cassidy, T., Ji, H., Ratinov, L., Zubiaga, A., Huang, H.Z.: Analysis and Enhancement of Wikification for Microblogs with Context Expansion. In: Proceedings of 24th International Conference on Computational Linguistics, pp. 441–456 (2012)

5. Bontcheva, K., Rout, D.: Making Sense of Social Media Streams through Semantics: a Survey. Semantic Web Journal (2012)
6. Kiryakov, A., Popov, B., Ognyanoff, D., Manov, D., Kirilov, A., Goranov, M.: Semantic Annotation, Indexing and Retrieval. Journal of Web Semantics 1(2), 49–79 (2004)
7. Mihalcea, R., Csomai, A.: Wikify! Linking Documents to Encyclopedic Knowledge. In: Proceedings of the 17th ACM Conference on Information and Knowledge Management, pp. 233–242 (2007)
8. Milne, D., Witten, I.H.: Learning to Link with Wikipedia. In: Proceedings of the 17th ACM Conference on Information and Knowledge Management, pp. 509–518 (2008)
9. Ferragina, P., Scaiella, U.: TAGME: On-the-fly Annotation of Short Text Fragments. In: Proceedings of the 19th ACM International Conference on Information and Knowledge Management, pp. 1625–1628 (2010)
10. Mendes, P.N., Jakob, M., García-Silva, A., Bizer, C.: DBpedia Spotlight: Shedding Light on the Web of Documents. In: Proceedings of the 7th International Conference on Semantic Systems, pp. 1–8 (2011)
11. Ratinov, L., Roth, D.: Design Challenges and Misconceptions in Named Entity Recognition. In: Proceedings of the Thirteenth Conference on Computational Natural Language Learning, pp. 147–155 (2009)
12. Yosef, M.A., Hoffart, J., Bordino, I., Spaniol, M., Weikum, G.: AIDA: an Online Tool for Accurate Disambiguation of Named Entities in Text and Tables. In: Proceedings of the PVLDB 2011, pp. 1450–1453 (2011)
13. Varma, V., Bharat, V., Kovelamudi, S., Bysani, P.: GSK, S., Kumar, N. K., Reddy, K., Kumar, K., Maganti, N.: IIIT Hyderabad at TAC 2009. In: Proceedings of Text Analysis Conference, TAC (2009)
14. Suchanek, F.M., Kasneci, G., Weikum, G.: YAGO: A Core of Semantic Knowledge Unifying WordNet and Wikipedia. In: Proceedings of the International World Wide Web Conference, pp. 697–706 (2007)
15. Han, X.P., Sun, L.: A Generative Entity-Mention Model for Linking Entities with Knowledge Base. In: Proceedings of the 49th Annual Meeting of the Association for Computational Linguistics: Human Language Technologies, vol. 1, pp. 945–954 (2011)

Author Index

Printed in the United States
by Baker & Taylor Publisher Services

Printed in the United States
by Baker & Taylor Publisher Services